ASP.NET Website Programm

Problem – Design – Solution
Visual Basic .NET Edition

Marco Bellinaso

Kevin Hoffman

Visual Basic .NET Code Provided by
Demian Martinez and Norbert Martinez

Wrox Press Ltd. ®

ASP.NET Website Programming

Problem – Design – Solution (Visual Basic .NET Edition)

© 2002 Wrox Press

First Printed in December 2002

Published by Wrox Press Ltd,
Arden House, 1102 Warwick Road, Acocks Green,
Birmingham, B27 6BH, UK
Printed in the United States
ISBN 1-86100-816-3

Trademark Acknowledgments

Credits

Authors
Marco Bellinaso
Kevin Hoffman

Commissioning Editor
Dan Kent

Technical Editors
Dan Kent
Dianne Arrow
David Barnes

Index
Andrew Criddle

Project Manager
Charlotte Smith

Managing Editor
Louay Fatoohi

Visual Basic .NET Code
Demian Martinez
Norbert Martinez

Technical Reviewers
Mark Horner
Don Lee
Dan Maharry
Christophe Nasarre
Matthew Rabinowitz
Marc H Simkin

Cover
Natalie O'Donnell

Production Coordinator
Sarah Hall

Proofreader
Chris Smith

About the Authors

Marco Bellinaso

Marco Bellinaso lives in a small town close to Venice, Italy. He works as a software developer and trainer for Code Architects Srl (www.codearchitects.com), an Italian company that specializes in .NET. He has been working with VB, C/C++, ASP, and other Microsoft tools for several years, specializing in User Interface, API, and ActiveX/COM design and programming, but is now spending all his time on the .NET Framework, using C# and VB.NET.

He's been working with the .NET Framework since the Beta 1, and is now particularly interested in e-commerce design and implementation solutions with SQL Server, ASP.NET, and web services, with both C# and VB.NET. He is part of the VB-2-The-Max team (www.vb2themax.com), a popular website for VB and .NET developers, for which he writes articles and commercial software, such as add-ins for MS Visual Studio and other utilities for VB and .NET developers. In particular, he co-authored the award-winning VB Maximizer VB6 add-in.

Marco also loves writing and talking about technical stuff. He recently co-authored *ASP.NET Website Programming – C# edition*, *Fast Track ASP.NET* and *Visual C#: a Guide for VB6 developers*, all from Wrox Press, and is also a contributing editor for two leading Italian programming magazines: *Computer Programming* and *Visual Basic Journal* (Italian licensee for *Visual Studio Magazine*). Reach him at mbellinaso@vb2themax.com.

Acknowledgments

Writing this book has been a real pleasure to me. It gave me the opportunity to work with ASP.NET on a good project, and to improve my knowledge of the technology along the way. So it surely has been worth the effort! And of course, everyone likes to be published writing about what they like to do and how to do it. :-)

I owe many thanks to Wrox Press for giving me the opportunity to write the book: this is the most English I've ever written, so I guess the editors and reviewers had some extra work with me, although they were so kind as to never confess it. Some of these people are Daniel Kent, David Barnes, and Dianne Arrow.

Other people contributed to this project, in a way or another, now or in the past, and I'd like to mention at least a few names. First of all a really big thank you goes to Francesco Balena, famous speaker and author, and editor in chief of the Italian licensee of VBPJ (now Visual Studio Magazine). He reviewed and published an article about VB subclassing that I wrote some years ago, when I had no editorial experience at all. Since that moment he has continued to help me by advising how to improve my writing style, pushing me to start writing in English, suggesting the hottest technology to study, and giving the opportunity to work on some cool software projects as part of the VB-2-The-Max team. Francesco, all this is greatly appreciated!

Two other developers I work with for the Italian magazines, who helped me in different ways, are Dino Esposito and Alberto Falossi.

Giovanni – Gianni – Artico is the person who initiated me in the programming art, suggesting to start with VB and then to learn C/C++ as well. Thank you for answering my questions when I was at the beginning, and for still helping me in some situations.

A mention goes also to my closest friends. They still remember me after several "sorry, I can't come today" rebuttals, and have put up with me when I was under pressure and not the nicest person possible.

Last but not least I have to say thank you to my family, who bought my first computer and a lot of programming books when I was in high school and couldn't buy all that stuff by myself. They didn't offer much moral support during the work – mostly because they didn't have a clue of what I was doing! I kept it a secret to almost everybody – I hope it will be a nice surprise. :-)

Kevin Hoffman

Kevin has always loved computers and computer programming. He first got hooked when he received a Commodore VIC-20 from his grandfather, who had repaired it after finding it in the trash. He then started a prolific but unprofitable career writing shareware games and utilities for electronic bulletin board systems.

He started working as a programmer while still in college, writing computer interfaces to solar measurement devices and various other scientific instruments. Moving to Oregon, he did everything from technical support to tuning Unix kernels, and eventually working as an ASP programmer for 800.COM, a popular on-line electronics retailer. From there he moved on to working on large, enterprise ASP applications.

Then he finally found .NET, which he now spends 100% of his programming and learning efforts on. A big C# fan, who would use it to do everything including brush his teeth if only he could figure out how, Kevin has been writing on .NET for Wrox since the middle of Beta 1. He plans to continue until we get tired of him. He's currently in Houston, Texas sweating a lot and working on web services and other large-scale .NET applications.

Acknowledgments

I'd like to dedicate this book to the rest of my "family", without whom I could not have accomplished many of the things I am proud of today. I would like to thank Gerald for all his support – a best friend in every sense of the word – and his daughter Keely for making me laugh. I would also like to thank Jen, Jocelyn, and Emily for their support and being there for me. And as always I want to dedicate my work to my wife, Connie – without her support I would never have published a single word.

About the Code Converters

Usually, Wrox books include biographies and dedications for the authors only. In this case, it was decided that the contribution that the code converters had made to this edition was sufficient that they should be included in this section.

The authors of this book originally wrote all of the code in C#. Demian and Norbert did a great job of converting all of the code to Visual Basic .NET for this edition. The careful presentation and informative commenting in the code show the dedication that they had to creating a useful resource for ASP.NET developers who use VB.NET.

Demian Martinez & Norbert Martinez

Demian and Norbert have been messing with computers ever since their parents, also computer engineers, taught them to play games on their Apple II. In spite of being aeronautical engineers by degree, they have devoted most of their careers to computing. Their combined working experience in companies such as Gartner, PriceWaterhouseCoopers Consulting, British Airways, and Airbus has given them the opportunity to understand all phases of the software development lifecycle, from analysis to end-user training, through design, construction, and implementation.

Demian and Norbert are currently working in No Red Inc., a small technology consulting company they co-founded in Barcelona, Spain. They specialize in the development of web applications for small- to medium-sized companies using ASP.NET, VB.NET, and C#.

Acknowledgements

Demian would like to thank his wife Mary for her support, her understanding, and her amazing smile. Norbert would like to thank his partner Iratxe for her support, her love, and for not being too jealous when he spends some time with the computer. Both Demian and Norbert would also like to thank their parents for being so special (and letting them play with the Apple II).

Table of Contents

Introduction   **1**

    What Does This Book Cover?   **1**

    Who Is This Book For?   **3**

    What You Need to Use This Book   **3**

    Conventions   **3**

    Customer Support   **4**

        How to Download the Code for the Website   4
        Errata   4
        E-mail Support   5
        p2p.wrox.com   5
            Why This System Offers the Best Support   6

Chapter 1: Building an ASP.NET Website   **9**

    The Problem   **9**

    The Design   **10**

        Working from Different Locations   10
        A Maintainable, Extendable Site   11
        Community   11
        Interesting Content   12
        Advertising   12
        Frequent Visits   12

    The Solution   **13**

        Working from Different Locations   13
        Building a Maintainable, Extendable Site   13
        Providing Interesting Content   13
        Managing Adverts   14
        Encouraging Community   14
        Getting Repeat Visitors   14
        Deploying the Site   14

    Summary   **15**

Table of Contents

Chapter 2: Foundations   17

The Problem   18
The Problem Statement   19
     The Vision   19
     The Requirements   20

The Design   20
Naming and Coding Conventions   21
     Naming Guidelines   21
     Namespace Hierarchy   23
Programming Language   27
Folder Structure   27
Designing the Database   28
Building the Data-Services Tier   29
Building the Business-Services Tier   30
Error Handling and Fault Tolerance   32
Deployment Issues   32
User Interface Design   33

The Solution   33
The DbObject Class   34
The BizObject Class   38
The AppException Class   39
     Logging Events to a File   40

Summary   42

Chapter 3: Foundations for Style and Navigation   45

The Problem   46
The Problem Statement and Requirements   46

The Design   47
Cascading Stylesheets   48
XSLT   50
The Page Base Class   51
A Reusable Navigation Control   51
Headers and Footers   53
Error Handling   54

The Solution   54
Styles   54
The PhilePage Class   57
The Navigator Control   58
The SiteHeader Control   63
The SiteFooter Control   65
Error Handling   65
Home Page Draft   68

Summary   70

Chapter 4: Maintaining the Site   73

The Problem   **74**
FTP Versus Online File Management   74
Database Management   75

The Design   **75**
Implementation Design   76
Security Design   77

The Solution   **77**
Classes to Work with Files and Directories   78
Header and Footer Controls   79
The File Manager's Main Page   80
     Listing the Contents of a Folder   82
     Displaying Additional Attributes   87
     Downloading Files   99
     Uploading Files   102
     Creating Directories   105
     Creating Text Files   109
     Building the Text File Editor   111
     Editing Files   115
     Renaming Files and Directories   117
     Modifying the Attributes of Files and Directories   122
     Deleting Files   125
     Copying and Moving Files   129
Securing the File Manager Using Windows Security   133

Summary   **136**

Chapter 5: Users and Authentication   139

The Problem   **139**

The Design   **140**
Forms Authentication   141
Designing the Database   142
     Stored Procedures   144
The Data Tier   145
The Business Tier   147
     The User Class   147
     The Role Class   148
     Extending .NET Framework User Handling   149
Module Configuration   151
     The ModuleConfig Class   152
     The ModuleSettings Class   152
Administration   153

The Solution   **153**
The Database   154
     Stored Procedures   155

Table of Contents

The Data Tier   155
     User   156
     Role   163
     Permission   166
     PermissionCategory   169
     AccountsTool   170
The Business Tier   171
     SitePrincipal   171
     SiteIdentity   174
     User   176
     Role   179
     AccountsTool   182
Configuration Classes   183
     ModuleSettings   183
     ModuleConfig   183
Modifying the UI to Support Authentication   185
     Modifying the SiteHeader Control   185
     The Login Page   186
     Picking up the Authentication Cookie in Subsequent Requests   187
     Configuring Forms Authentication   188
     Modifying the PhilePage Class   188
     The User Details Page   189
Administering Roles and Accounts   191

Summary   **199**

Chapter 6: News Management   **201**

The Problem   **201**

The Design   **202**
Features to Implement   203
Database Design   203
     The News_Categories Table   204
     The News_News Table   205
     Stored Procedures   206
Designing the Data Layer   208
     The CategoryDetails Class   209
     The Categories Class   209
     The NewsDetails Class   210
     The News Class   210
Designing the Business Layer   211
     The Category Class   211
     The News Class   214
Storing and Retrieving Settings   215
Designing the Presentation Layer   216
     Plug-in Headlines   216
     The Headlines Web Service   216
The Need for Security   217

The Solution   **218**

Working on the Database   218
    Relationships Between the Tables   218
    A Trigger for the UserID Foreign Key   221
    Creating the Stored Procedures   221
Implementing the Data Access Assembly   226
    The News Class   226
The Configuration Assembly   232
    The ModuleSettings Class   232
    The ModuleConfig Class   233
    The Settings File   235
Implementing the Business Classes   235
    The News Class   235
    The Category Class   239
The User Interface   240
    Administration   240
Showing News to the User   267
    Showing the Categories   267
    Showing the Abstracts   269
    Showing the Whole News Item   270
User-Submitted News   271
The Headlines User Control   272
    Testing the Control   274
Securing the Module   275
The Headlines Web Service   277
    Testing the Web Service   278
    The News Ticker Application   280

Summary   **283**

Chapter 7: Advertising   **287**

The Problem   **287**

Impressions   287
Hits   288
Requirements   288

Design   **289**

Using the AdRotator   289
The Database   290
The Data Services Layer   292
The Business Layer   293
The Presentation Layer   293
    Advertising Administration   293
Configuration   293

The Solution   **294**

The Database Tables   294
    AdsManager_Advertisements Table   294
    AdsManager_Companies Table   294
    AdsManager_Impressions Table   295
    AdsManager_Clicks Table   295

Table of Contents

Stored Procedures 295
The Data Services Layer 297
The AdMaster Class 297
The Advertisement Class 298
The Business Layer 303
The AdMaster Class 303
The Advertisement Class 304
The Presentation Layer 307
The Pass-through Page 307
The New SiteFooter Control 308
Administering Advertisements 309
Module Configuration 315

Summary **316**

Chapter 8: Polls 319

The Problem 319

The Design 321
Features to Implement 321
Handling Multiple Votes 322
Designing the Database Tables 324
The Polls_Questions Table 324
The Polls_Options Table 325
The Polls_Votes Table 325
The Stored Procedures that Manage the Database 326
Designing the Data Layer 328
The QuestionDetails Class 328
The Questions Class 329
The OptionDetails Class 329
The Options Class 329
The VoteDetails Class 330
The Votes Class 330
Storing and Retrieving Settings 330
Designing the Business Layer 331
The Question Class 331
The Option Class 333
Designing the User Interface Services 334
The Poll User Control 334
The Poll Web Service 336
The Need for Security 337

The Solution 337
Working on the Database 337
Creating the Relationships 338
Creating the Stored Procedures 339
Implementing the Data-Access Assembly 344
The Configuration Assembly 344
The ModuleSettings Class 344
The ModuleConfig Class 345
The Settings File 345

The Business Assembly   346
   The Question Class   346
The Administration User Interface   351
   Creating the Header and Footer User Controls   352
   The Questions Manager Page   352
   The Questions.aspx Page   353
   The Code-behind for Questions.aspx   357
   Deleting a Question   360
   Creating a Question   360
Managing the Options   361
   The Options.aspx Page   362
   The Code-behind File for Options.aspx   363
Modifying the Settings Online   364
   The Settings.aspx Page   364
   The Code-behind for Settings.aspx   366
The Poll User Control   367
   The Code-behind for the Poll User Control   369
   Handling the Postback Event   372
   Optimizing the Poll User Control   373
   Testing the Control   377
The ShowArchive.aspx Page   381
   The Code-behind for ShowArchive.aspx   383
Securing the Module   384
The Poll Web Service   385
   Testing the Web Service   385
   The Windows Client Application   386

Summary   **389**

Chapter 9: Mailing Lists   **393**

The Problem   **393**
   The Problem Statement   395

The Design   **396**
Designing the Database Tables   396
   The MLists_Lists Table   396
   The MLists_Users Table   397
   The MLists_Subscriptions Table   398
   The MLists_History Table   399
The Stored Procedures that Manage the Database   399
Designing the Data Services   402
   The ListDetails Class   402
   The Lists Class   402
   The SubscriptionDetails Class   403
   The Subscriptions Class   403
   The NewsletterDetails Class   403
   The Newsletters Class   403
Storing and Retrieving Settings   404
Designing the Business Services   405
   The List Class   405
   The Subscription Class   407

Table of Contents

The Newsletter Class   408
The Helper Class   409
Designing the User Interface Services   410
The Need for Security   411

The Solution   **411**
Working on the Database   411
Creating the Stored Procedures and Triggers   411
Implementing the Data and Configuration Assemblies   415
Implementing the Business Layer   415
The Subscription Class   415
The Newsletter Class   419
The Helper Class   423
The Administration User Interface   425
Sending out Newsletters to Subscribers   429
Managing the Newsletters Archive   432
Modifying the Settings Online   433
Creating a Subscription Form for the User   434
Subscribing to a Mailing List   438
The Subscribe.aspx Page   440
The Code-behind for Subscribe.aspx   440
Securing the Module   441

Summary   **442**

Chapter 10: Forums and Online Communities   **445**

The Problem   **445**
Cross-Site Scripting   446

The Design   **446**
The Database   446
The Forums_Categories Table   448
The Forums_Forums Table   448
The Forums_Topics Table   449
The Forums_Replies Table   450
The Forums_Members Table   451
Database Views   451
Stored Procedures   452
Designing the Data Services   454
Configuration   454
The Business Layer   455
The Forum Class   455
The Helper Class   456
Designing the User Interface Layer   456

The Solution   **457**
Creating the Database Tables   458
Creating the Views   458
Creating the Stored Procedures   461
Implementing the Data Layer   463
Implementing the Configuration Layer   463

Implementing the Business Layer   464
    The Forum Class   464
    The Helper Class   468
The Presentation Layer   471
    The Categories and Forums Page   471
    The Header Control   481
    The Forum.aspx Page   483
    The Topic.aspx Page   489
    The PostMessage.aspx Page   496
    The MyProfile.aspx Page   503

Summary   **505**

Chapter 11: Deploying the Site   **509**

The Problem   **510**

The Design   **510**
Deploying the Data Store   510
Preparing the Site for Deployment   511
Manual (XCopy) Deployment   513
    Configuring IIS for your Application   513
Deploying to a Hosting Service   514
Automated Deployment (Building Installers)   515

The Solution   **515**

Summary   **519**

Chapter 12: The End   **521**

Get Building   **521**

Join Our Community   **521**

Read More   **522**
Web Services   522
Security   522
ADO.NET   522
Server Controls   522

Index   **525**

Introduction

Welcome to ASP.NET Website Programming. In this book we will build an interactive, content-based website using expandable, interchangeable modules. By the end of the book you will have developed your ASP.NET skills for producing effective, well-engineered, extendable websites.

ASP.NET is a great tool for building websites. It contains many built-in features that would take thousands of lines of code in classic ASP, and it does not require admin rights in order to deploy compiled components – your whole site can be deployed in one folder.

This book will guide you through the bewildering features available to ASP.NET developers, highlighting the most useful and exciting.

The book concentrates on websites that focus on content. It does not show how to produce an e-commerce system, although a lot of the advice will apply to e-commerce sites. We could add a shopping basket module using the same foundations, for example.

This book is different from most Wrox books, because we build a single working website throughout the book. However, each chapter stands alone and shows how to develop individual modules, which you can adapt for your own websites. We also suggest a framework that allows us to create modules and slot them in to the website quickly and easily.

What Does This Book Cover?

The chapters in this book follow a problem-design-solution pattern. First we identify what we need to achieve, then we sketch out how we will achieve it, and finally we build the software in Visual Studio .NET.

Most chapters involve building a 3-tier system, with data, business, and presentation layers. We will also see how to build separate modules so that they integrate well into the whole site.

Chapter 1 looks at the website as a whole. We identify the problem that it is trying to solve, and discuss how we will go about solving it. We then come up with a solution – which involves building and integrating the modules detailed in the other chapters.

Chapter 2 builds the foundations of our site. We set coding standards and design our folder and namespace structure. We create our initial database – although at this stage we have no data to put in it. We also build site-wide error handling code and base classes for our data and business layer objects.

Chapter 3 extends our foundations to the presentation layer. We build base classes for the ASP.NET pages in the site, a custom error page, and site-wide navigation, header, and footer controls.

Chapter 4 presents a file management module, which we can use to download and upload source code for the site, and make changes online. We will also look at Microsoft's Data Manager, which enables us to manage SQL Server databases through our website.

Chapter 5 covers user accounts. We look at how to create a powerful role-based security system, and integrate it with ASP.NET's built-in authentication features.

Chapter 6 shows how to provide regularly changing news content through a website. We also build a web service to expose news headlines to other sites and applications, and a Windows news ticker that uses this web service.

Chapter 7 looks at advertising. We create our advertising system by extending the ASP.NET `AdRotator` control to provide the power we need. We look at logging *hits* and *impressions*, and providing reports to advertisers.

Chapter 8 covers opinion polls and voting. We look at how to administer questions, log votes, and collate them into useful reports.

Chapter 9 provides the tools to create e-mail newsletters. We will look at how to create messages in plain text and HTML, and how to administer lists and set up new ones.

Chapter 10 looks at forums. We create everything you need to post and read messages, and give administrators special permissions. Along the way, there is some powerful use of the `DataList` and `DataGrid` controls. We also look at how to use regular expressions to provide limited HTML support, without opening our forum to the risk of cross-site scripting.

Chapter 11 shows how to deploy the site. We will look at the ways Visual Studio .NET allows us to provide source-free distributable versions of our software, and how to deploy our sites onto hosting services.

Chapter 12 looks to the future. We've only just begun our lives as ASP.NET website developers and here we will look at ways in which Wrox can support your continued development. In particular this includes the book's P2P list, where you can work together with fellow readers and benefit from each other's ideas and experience.

Who Is This Book For?

The book is for developers who have a reasonable knowledge of ASP.NET, and want to apply that knowledge to building websites. You will get the most from this book if you have read a decent amount of Wrox's *Beginning ASP.NET using Visual Basic .NET*, or *Professional ASP.NET* and a VB.NET book.

You should be comfortable using Visual Studio .NET to create ASP.NET projects, and that you know VB.NET.

What You Need to Use This Book

To run the code samples in this book you need to have the following:

❑   Windows 2000 or Windows XP.

❑   Visual Studio .NET 1.0. We have tested the code for version 1.0, although most of the code should work in late pre-release versions. Nearly everything will also work in Visual Basic .NET Standard.

❑   SQL Server 2000 – although most of the techniques we use could apply to any database system, including Access.

To get the site working you may also need an ASP.NET web host. We will give some guidance on choosing one towards the end of the book.

Conventions

We've used a number of different styles of text and layout in this book to help differentiate between the different kinds of information. Here are examples of the styles we used and an explanation of what they mean.

Code has several styles. If it's a word that we're talking about in the text – for example, when discussing a For...Next loop, it's in this font. If it's a block of code that can be typed as a program and run, then it's also in a gray box:

```
<?xml version 1.0?>
```

Sometimes we'll see code in a mixture of styles, like this:

```
<?xml version 1.0?>
<Invoice>
   <part>
      <name>Widget</name>
      <price>$10.00</price>
   </part>
</invoice>
```

In cases like this, the code with a white background is code we are already familiar with; the line highlighted in gray is a new addition to the code since we last looked at it.

Advice, hints, and background information comes in this type of font.

> **Important pieces of information come in boxes like this.**

Bullets appear indented, with each new bullet marked as follows:

❑ **Important Words** are in a bold type font.

❑ Words that appear on the screen, or in menus like File or Window, are in a similar font to the one you would see on a Windows desktop.

❑ Keys that you press on the keyboard, such as *Ctrl* and *Enter*, are in italics.

Customer Support

We want to hear from you! We want to know what you think about this book: what you liked, what you didn't like, and what you think we can do better next time. Please send us your comments, either by returning the reply card in the back of the book, or by e-mailing feedback@wrox.com. Please mention the book title in your message.

We do listen to these comments, and we do take them into account on future books.

How to Download the Code for the Website

It is well worth getting the website working on your own machine before reading too much of this book. It will help you follow the descriptions, because you will be able to see how code snippets relate to the whole application, and experience the modular approach first hand.

To get the code, visit www.wrox.com and navigate to *ASP.NET Website Programming Visual Basic .NET Edition*. Click on Download in the Code column, or on Download Code on the book's detail page.

The files are in ZIP format. Windows XP recognizes these automatically, but Windows 2000 requires a de-compression program such as WinZip or PKUnzip. The archive contains the whole site, plus a readme describing how to get it up and running.

Errata

We've made every effort to make sure that there are no errors in the text or in the code. If you do find an error, such as a spelling mistake, faulty piece of code, or any inaccuracy, we would appreciate feedback. By sending in errata you may save another reader hours of frustration, and help us provide even higher quality information.

E-mail your comments to support@wrox.com. Your information will be checked and if correct, posted to the errata page for that title, and used in subsequent editions of the book.

To find errata for this title, go to www.wrox.com and locate *ASP.NET Website Programming Visual Basic .NET Edition*. Click on the Book Errata link, which is below the cover graphic on the book's detail page.

E-mail Support

If you wish to directly query a problem in the book with an expert who knows the book in detail then e-mail support@wrox.com, with the title of the book and the last four numbers of the ISBN in the subject field of the e-mail. Please include the following things in your e-mail:

- ❑ The **title of the book**, **last four digits of the ISBN** (8163), and **page number** of the problem in the Subject field.

- ❑ Your **name**, **contact information**, and the **problem** in the body of the message.

We *won't* send you junk mail. We need the details to save your time and ours. When you send an e-mail message, it will go through the following chain of support:

- ❑ Customer Support – Your message is delivered to our customer support staff, who are the first people to read it. They have files on most frequently asked questions and will answer anything general about the book or the website immediately.

- ❑ Editorial – Deeper queries are forwarded to the technical editor responsible for that book. They have experience with the programming language or particular product, and are able to answer detailed technical questions on the subject.

- ❑ The Authors – If even the editor cannot answer your problem, they will forward the request to the author. We do try to protect the author from any distractions to their writing, but we are happy to forward specific requests to them. All Wrox authors help with the support on their books. They will e-mail the customer and the editor with their response, and again all readers should benefit.

The Wrox Support process can only offer support to issues that directly relate to the content of the book. Support for questions that fall outside the scope of normal book support is provided via the community lists of our http://p2p.wrox.com/ forum.

p2p.wrox.com

For author and peer discussion join the P2P mailing lists. Our unique system provides **programmer to programmer**™ contact on mailing lists, forums, and newsgroups, all in addition to our one-to-one e-mail support system. If you post a query to P2P, you can be confident that the many Wrox authors and industry experts who use our mailing lists will examine it. At p2p.wrox.com you will find a number of different lists that will help you, not only while you read this book, but also as you develop your own applications.

This book has its own list called `aspdotnet_website_programming`. Using this, you can talk to other people who are developing websites using the methods and framework presented here. You can share ideas and code for new and improved modules, get help with programming headaches, and show off the sites you've written!

To subscribe to a mailing list just follow these steps:

1. Go to http://p2p.wrox.com/.

2. Choose the appropriate category from the left menu bar.

3. Click on the mailing list you wish to join.

4. Follow the instructions to subscribe and fill in your e-mail address and password.

5. Reply to the confirmation e-mail you receive.

6. Use the subscription manager to join more lists and set your e-mail preferences.

Why This System Offers the Best Support

You can choose to join the mailing lists or you can receive them as a weekly digest. If you don't have the time, or facility, to receive the mailing list, then you can search our online archives. Junk and spam mails are deleted, and the unique Lyris system protects your e-mail address. Queries about joining or leaving lists, and any other general queries about lists, should be sent to listsupport@p2p.wrox.com.

Building an ASP.NET Website

In this book we are going to build a content-based ASP.NET website. This website will consist of a number of modules, which will all fit together to produce the finished product.

We will build each module in a standard order:

❑ Identify the **problem** – What do we want to do? What restrictions or other factors do we need to take into account?

❑ Produce a **design** – Decide what features we need to solve the problem. Get a broad idea of how the solution will work.

❑ Build the **solution** – Produce the code, and any other material, that will realize the design.

This book focuses on programming. When we talk about design, we generally mean designing the software – we will not be looking at graphic or user interface design.

Your website will not be solving all of the same problems as ours, but many of the modules we build – and the programming techniques we use – are very transferable.

In this chapter we will take a high-level look at the whole site – what it needs to do, and how it will do it.

The Problem

We will be building a website for DVD and book enthusiasts. In outlining the site's problem, we need to consider the purpose and audience. In real life this stage would be business oriented – taking into account things like advertising demographics, competition, and availability of funding. These processes need to be analyzed rigorously, but we will leave all that to the managers.

Our site will cater for lovers of books and DVDs. It will provide useful content and try to build community. Our visitors will want to read about these things, and contribute their opinions, but each visit will be fairly short – this will not be a huge database in the style of the Internet Movie Database (www.imdb.com). It will be funded by advertising, and will rely on repeated (but fairly short) visits from its readers.

We also need to consider constraints. These are more practical. One of the major constraints that this site faced was the development team – the members would never meet, because they were on opposite sides of the world. This meant that the design must allow one developer to work on sections of the site without interfering with other developers working on different sections. But all of the sections needed to eventually work together smoothly. In most cases the separation between developers will be less extreme, but giving each developer the ability to work independently is very useful. We need to design and build methods to enable this.

Site development never really finishes – sites tend to be tweaked frequently. Another key to successful websites is to design them in a way that makes modification easy. We will need to find ways to do this.

> We will call our site ThePhile.com, because it is a site for lovers of books (bibliophiles) and DVDs (DVD-philes). It's also a play on the word 'file', because our website will be a definitive source of information.

The Design

We have outlined what our site needs – now let's look at how we can provide it. The main points raised in the problem section were:

- ❏ Enable developers to work from many different locations
- ❏ Build a maintainable, extendable site
- ❏ Build community
- ❏ Provide interesting content
- ❏ Provide revenue through advertising
- ❏ Encourage frequent visits

Let's discuss each of these in turn.

Working from Different Locations

Our developers need to work on sections of the site with relatively little communication. Our developers are in different countries so face-to-face meetings are impossible. Telephone conversations can be expensive, and different time zones cause problems.

We need to design the system so that developers can work on their own section of the site, knowing that they will not damage the work of others.

A good way to solve this is to develop the site as a series of **modules**, with each module being fairly independent. Of course there will be shared components, but changes to these will be rare and can be done in a controlled way. In this book, we work in modules. We also make frequent use of **controls**. This means that components for a page can be developed independently, and easily 'dropped in' as needed – changes to the actual pages of the site are kept to a minimum.

A Maintainable, Extendable Site

Most websites have new features added quite frequently. This means that from the start the site needs to be designed to make that easy.

Working in modules and using controls already goes some way towards this. Particularly, using controls means that non-programmers can edit the pages of our site more easily – nearly all they see is HTML code. A control just looks like another HTML tag.

Working in modules means that new modules can be added to the site at any time, with minimum disruption. All modules are fairly independent, so new ones can be added – and changes made – pretty easily.

Each individual module needs to be easy to change. A good way to do this is to work in layers, or 'tiers'. We will be using a three-layer design for most modules. We have a data layer, a business layer, and a presentation layer. Data passes from **data layer** to **business layer**, and from business layer to **presentation layer**, and back again. Each layer has a job to do. Underneath the data layer is a data source, which it is the data layer's job to access.

The data layer obtains fairly raw data from the database (for example, "-10"). The business layer turns that data into information that makes sense from the perspective of business rules (for example, "-10 degrees centigrade"). The presentation layer turns this into something that makes sense to users (for example, "Strewth! It's freezing!").

It's useful to do this, because each layer can be modified independently. We can modify the business layer, and provided we continue to accept the same data from the data layer, and provide the same data to the presentation layer, we don't need to worry about wider implications. We can modify the presentation layer to change the look of the site, without changing the underlying business logic.

This means we can provide versions of the site for different audiences. We just need new presentation layers that call the same business objects. For example, providing different languages: "Zut alors! Comme il fait froid!", "Allora, è freddo!", and so on.

We need methods to get changes we make onto the live site. This could be through FTP uploads, but in many circumstances it is better to work through a web interface.

We will also need tools to administer the other sections – ban problem users, add news articles, and so on. This is all part of providing a maintainable site.

Community

Sites generally benefit from allowing readers to contribute. Because our site is not intended for users to spend hours looking at, our community features must not require a lot of users' time.

There are two ways that we will build our community: through polls and forums. Polls give users the opportunity to give their opinion in a single click – so they require very little time from the user, but can make a site seem far more alive.

Forums enable users to discuss topics with other users. Messages remain in the system, and replies are posted. Readers can leave a post, and then come back later to see if there are replies. This is more appropriate for our purposes than a chat room, which requires the reader to concentrate on the site for the whole duration of the chat.

Community can really give a site a life of its own. Over time, strong characters, heroes, and villains emerge. Many sites depend entirely on community, and become extremely popular – for example www.plastic.com.

For any of this to work, we need to identify users and provide them with unique logons. So our system will need some form of user accounts system.

Interesting Content

The content most relevant to our users will be movie- and-book-related news and reviews. This content tends to be highly relevant for a short period of time: after a story has broken, or immediately after a release. Our site will need tools to manage news in this way.

Another way to provide interesting content is to get somebody else to provide it! This is part of what we're doing with our community section. Part of the purpose of building community is to get people contributing content.

Advertising

Advertising generates revenue (or in some cases it is used to exchange banners with other sites). We need to display adverts, and record data about how often each advert has been displayed and clicked on.

We also need to gather information about what the users of the site like, so we can target our advertising content. Polls and forums can provide us with useful information when finding products to advertise.

The biggest sites target individual users based on their demographic and any other information gathered about them (for example, Yahoo! and Amazon.com target advertising and product recommendations to the demographic and buying habits of each user). Our site already has a fairly narrow target demographic, and is not particularly big, so we don't need to do this.

Frequent Visits

A good site will make people want to return. If the content is compelling, and there's plenty of discussion going on, then people visit again and again.

It's still a good idea to remind users from time to time. We want to draw attention back to the site, even when the user isn't viewing it. One way we'll be doing this is through an e-mail newsletter, which gives users useful information and subtly reminds them to visit the site.

We will also build a Windows application that acts as a news ticker, with automatically updating news headlines. Users can click a headline to view the full story on the site.

The Solution

We've seen what we want the site to do, and sketched out some rough ideas of how we might provide it. Now we'll look at how to build our solution. This really encompasses the whole of the book. Here we'll look at how each chapter relates to our initial problem and design.

Working from Different Locations

In the next two chapters, we will provide a framework for development. This will lay down coding standards, and a framework for organizing the modules into folders and Visual Studio .NET projects.

We will decide what namespaces we will use for each module, and all the other things that will make team working as hassle free as possible. We will also develop some initial UI features to use across the site, promoting a unified feel. These include a header, footer, and navigation control, and stylesheets.

Building a Maintainable, Extendable Site

Chapters 2 and 3 will also set us on the road to a maintainable site. We will develop base classes, giving each new module a solid foundation to build on.

We will develop a web-based file manager in Chapter 4. Through this we can download and upload files, create new ones, move them, change their attributes, and even edit files online with a built in, web-based text editor. If you've ever wanted to provide file upload facilities, offer source code for download, or provide online editing tools then this is the place to look!

Most of the modules we develop will have administration features. For these to be useful, we need to identify administrators. In Chapter 5 we will develop a user accounts system. Using this, we can collect user information and give different users different privileges. Our final site will support full role-based security, with login details stored in a SQL Server database.

Providing Interesting Content

In Chapter 6 we create a news management system. This will enable our administrators to add and edit news articles, receive and approve suggested articles from readers, and place new articles in categories, and of course, it lets users read the news. We will create a control so that we can easily display headlines on any page that we like.

The news system will be flexible enough to also cover reviews, which will eventually form the core of our site.

Managing Adverts

Advertising will be covered in Chapter 7. We will develop a system to display adverts, and log impressions (when an ad is displayed) and hits (when an ad is clicked). This will allow us to create reports from this data to give to advertisers.

There will be admin facilities to create adverts, select how frequently they should be displayed, and start and end campaigns.

Encouraging Community

Chapter 8 will cover our voting system, and forums will be covered in Chapter 10. The voting system will allow administrators to create new questions to vote on. Answers will be recorded and displayed, and an archive of old results maintained – accessible from a standalone Windows application. We guard against multiple votes from the same user by using cookies and IP number.

The forums system will let each user choose an avatar image to represent them, and start posting. Discussion will be organized into categories, and within them there will be various topics. Users can post new topics, and reply to existing topics. We use regular expressions to allow formatting tags in messages, but prevent images or JavaScript.

Getting Repeat Visitors

As well as providing all this great content, we will include two features specifically for getting visitors back to the site.

The first is covered in Chapter 6 where we look at news. We will develop a web service that exposes our news headlines. We will then build a Windows client that displays the headlines, updating itself regularly. Clicking a headline will open a browser on the correct page for the full story.

The second is covered in Chapter 9. We will create the facility for visitors to subscribe to receive e-mail updates from us. Once they are subscribed, we send a mail out regularly to encourage repeat visits. This mail will include highlighted news and features, and links back to the site. We will develop a system that enables administrators to create plain text and HTML messages. We then develop a mailing list admin module for creating subscription forms for new mailing lists, administering list members, adding newsletters, and managing subscriptions. Messages can include custom tags so that each list member receives an e-mail tailored to their own details.

Deploying the Site

Although we haven't mentioned it before, we will eventually need to move the site from our production machine to the live server. This can be a complex task, because we need to separate the files needed for the site to run from the source code files that we only need for development. We will look at this in Chapter 11, and see how Visual Studio .NET gives us tools to make the process easy.

Summary

We're now ready to look at the site in detail. Before reading the following chapters, it's worth getting hold of the code download and seeing how the final site fits together. This book does not describe every detail of the website, and it will be a lot clearer if you look at the final site first.

> The code and database are available from **www.wrox.com**. Once you've downloaded and unzipped it, look at the readme file to see how to get it working in Visual Studio .NET. You will get far more from the book if you look at the project *before* reading on.

In the next chapter we will start to build the foundations for the rest of the site.

2

Foundations

Laying foundations is one of the first steps we need to take when starting any non-trivial programming project. Foundations include things like code and documentation conventions, and the structure and design of the backend. In a formal development process, the foundations also typically include a vision statement of some kind, and a project plan.

Developers often have opposing views on how much work to do at this stage. Many want to sit in front of a keyboard and start coding straight away, while others want to spend weeks developing pages of rules and standards. Somewhere between the two extremes lies a fairly good medium. We don't want to get caught in an endless loop of designing, but we also don't want to write any code before we've figured out what our architecture and design is going to be like.

If we are building a house, and we build the foundations on sand, the house is likely to come tumbling down before the building is finished. On the other hand, if the ground is too hard then laying the foundations can be a major task in itself, placing unnecessary restrictions on the rest of the project.

This chapter will demonstrate a sensible compromise between the two extremes – building a solid but unrestrictive foundation for an ASP.NET website. First we will discuss the common problems facing an ASP.NET website architect in building the foundation. Then we will delve into designing a solution to these problems. Finally we'll implement these designs, and even get to work on some code. This chapter is geared towards both architects and developers alike. We will cover broad, high-level issues such as design and architecture, and we will also take a look at the code used to implement a solid foundation for an ASP.NET website.

The Problem

Building a solid foundation can be a daunting task. It requires a good understanding of how the application will operate before we've gone into the detailed design of each component. If we build a good foundation, everything else will seem to fall into place. But if the foundation is poor, the site will take an extraordinary amount of work and time to complete, if it's completed at all.

Building the foundation of a website is really a collection of smaller, inter-related tasks. There are many aspects of the website's development that need to be part of the initial foundation's design. One such aspect is the development environment – for example team size and working style, and the tools that will be used to build the site. The type of team that will work on the project is an important factor in developing the foundation, as the latter should be developed to support the needs of the team. For example, a small team in a single office might work well with a fairly loose foundation, because they can easily make small changes here and there. But a large, distributed team will benefit if the foundation is set in stone, since negotiating a change could be a mammoth task. For the website in this book, the development team consisted of only two people. However, these two people were on opposite sides of the world. For this reason, the foundation needed to provide a stable basis for plugging in the different modules that each developer was working on.

In addition to the *development* needs, we need to determine the requirements of the website in its *deployment* environment. A website can have many different types of requirements, including:

- ❑ **Physical** – the software and hardware environment in which the final website will run. Requirements such as these typically dictate whether the website needs to be in a certain directory, or on a certain machine, or in a certain network infrastructure. Physical requirements also dictate the specific type of database to be used to support the system. We need to plan ahead for what type of system we're going to use to store our back-end data. Will it be a relational database management system (RDBMS) like Oracle or SQL Server, or are we pulling information from a mainframe, from a web service, or even from a collection of XML files? While you can code your data services tier to be as source-agnostic as possible, it isn't an excuse to spend less time on the definition of your data requirements.

- ❑ **Architectural** – we need to know how we plan on structuring our application. We need to know where the physical and logical separations are, and we need to consider things like firewalls and networking considerations. The website may need to be designed to support a certain type of development style, or modification by authorized third parties.

- ❑ **Logical** – these requirements are those that, for example, dictate that a website will consist of three layers of servicing components on top of a layer of database stored procedures.

The deployment environment includes both the server and the client browser. Many websites recommend, or even require, a particular browser in order to function correctly. Sometimes this is appropriate, but often it isn't. When laying the foundations of the site, a strategic decision needs to be made about what type and version of browser your website must support. This will affect the HTML and client-side scripts that your developers can work with, and hence be part of the coding standard. As far as ThePhile.com is concerned, we will not be dictating the use of any particular browser. We will try to code the pages so that any recent browser that supports the latest HTML standards can use them.

We also need to consider what the purpose of the website is, and who will be the users. Many businesses, ranging from the small start-up business to the huge worldwide corporation, provide services and applications for their employees on their intranet. There are many different types of applications that fall into this category, including:

❑ HR applications – many large corporations provide systems on the web to automate many tasks for dealing with the employee's day-to-day business, such as time sheets and benefits tracking. These applications require high security and availability.

❑ Internal support applications – as well as creating software that is deployed to their customers, companies have various departments that often have 'in-house' software designed to support their own needs. These applications require security, reliability, availability, and often a high degree of support from the programming staff.

These types of applications have specific deployment issues, which often arise due to a wide disparity in system configuration and type across the employees requiring the software. Other deployment concerns arise simply due to the large number of employees that must make use of this software. It is also becoming more common for web application vendors to create an application, build a deployment program, place it on a CD, and then sell that CD to customers who then deploy that application throughout *their* intranet. For example, there are several companies that provide defect tracking solutions that are essentially websites you install from a CD to support your programming intranet. The possibilities are extremely wide and varied. You may not know your particular solution for deployment at the time you are defining your problem, but you should definitely be aware that it must be a core part of the design of your website foundation.

Finally, our website wouldn't look very much like a website without a user interface. So we obviously need some type of UI. Putting some effort into the design of the user interface before a lot of code has been written can have extremely large payoffs. We will need to take into consideration our audience when we design the look and feel of our website, as well as the navigation and flow of the site, to make it easy for the target audience to use and traverse.

Now that we've covered a little bit about the overall problems that face ASP.NET website architects, let's take a look at the problem statement we came up with for the foundation of our website. We had special needs for ours, because the developers of our website have never physically been in the same room.

The Problem Statement

For our purposes the problem statement includes stating the problem we are attempting to solve, and the constraints that we must conform to in solving that problem. Our problem statement is divided into two sections: a vision (or purpose) and a set of requirements. Depending on what particular software development process you use, your problem statements may vary significantly from the one we will present here. If you are a fan of the Microsoft Solutions Framework (MSF) then you might already be used to producing a vision document and a requirements document.

We'll present our vision statement and then list the requirements for our product. It is absolutely imperative that you do not start a single line of code or actual design until you have adequately defined these for your project. In many iterative processes, you may be satisfied with only partially defining the requirements, because you know you will revisit the requirements document multiple times throughout the lifetime of your project.

The Vision

We are endeavoring to build a complete, content-driven website that illustrates the importance of modular building and will hopefully illustrate a few ASP.NET 'best practices' along the way. We will develop a solid, scalable foundation on which to build the modules that will be developed throughout the rest of this book. A secondary goal is to provide a foundation that can be used by multiple programmers with diverse experience and still produce a coherent, cohesive solution.

The Requirements

It is important that we keep our requirements separate from our purpose. The requirements are the rules to which our design must conform in order to produce the solution we set out to create. In an iterative process, the requirements generally change with each iteration. In our small development environment, we won't need an iterative process, so the following is the list of requirements that we defined for our project:

❑ **Scalability** – our solution must be scalable. It must be able to expand to meet increasing performance demands with a minimum of extra coding required. It's a lofty goal, but it is quite possible with the right design.

❑ **Flexibility** – our solution must be *agile*. This may be a buzzword, but there is some validity behind it. We must try to make the foundation of our website agile in such a way that changes encountered during the development of a module that require modification of the foundation will not drastically affect the rest of the site.

❑ **Reusability** – our solution for the core foundation of our website must be designed in such a way that it promotes code reuse. A strong emphasis should be placed on object hierarchies, inheritance, and reuse, starting with the foundation and carrying on through all of the modules in the website.

❑ **Separation** – our core foundation code should provide a solid foundation for the rest of the website, but it should not be so closely tied to it that changes to individual modules will have an impact on the core foundation code.

❑ **Deployment** – our application should be coded in such a way that it can be deployed on the Internet for public use, and also to workstations running Windows 2000 and XP to allow programmers to examine and learn from the source code.

❑ **Test plan** – as experienced programmers we know that developing a large project, even one that may appear simple on the outside, is going to be a difficult process. As such, we need to make sure that we have an organized way in which we test our code so that we can be reasonably confident that there are no bugs in it when it is released to production.

In summary, the foundation for our website, ThePhile.com, needs to provide a stable, solid, scalable foundation that will give us the flexibility to make changes throughout the development process and later, as well as provide enough standardization and convention to allow a team of programmers to build portions of the website separately, allowing for easy integration of individual modules.

The Design

Now that we have formally defined the problem of building our application's foundation, we can begin the design process. Our design should reach a happy medium, providing enough foundation and structure to produce cohesive results, without getting so bogged down in design that we end up producing nothing.

Our discussion of the design process is going to look at some of the most common tasks in building the foundation of a website. Then we'll apply that general concept to our specific application by actually designing the various pieces of The Phile's foundation. The following list of items illustrates some of the concepts at the core of good foundation design:

- ❏ Naming and coding conventions

- ❏ Programming language choice

- ❏ Folder structure

- ❏ Designing the database(s)

- ❏ Building a data-services tier

- ❏ Building a business-services tier

- ❏ Providing for effective error handling

- ❏ Deployment and maintenance

- ❏ User interface design

Naming and Coding Conventions

Coding conventions can be unpopular, particularly where they are imposed on a team by a non-programmer and contain dated or restrictive rules. Every programmer has their own opinion about the usefulness of naming guidelines, coding conventions, and other code-related rules. The opinions range from those who think that any coding convention ruins the programmer's creative style, to those who thrive on the structure that conventions and standards provide.

Once again, we're faced with finding a compromise that benefits everybody. Standardization not only allows teams of programmers to produce code that follows the same conventions, making it easier to read and maintain, but it allows for the same programmer to write consistent code. Far more often than we like to admit, programmers will use one convention one day, and another convention the next. Without some sense of enforced structure to the programming, the infamous spaghetti code will rear its ugly head and make life miserable for everyone involved. Another common practice that ensures solid, standardized code is the use of **code reviews**. Code reviews are where other programmers (or managers, depending on skill distribution) review their peers' code for accuracy, efficiency, and compliance to coding standards and conventions. Some programmers resist this kind of practice, but it can be extremely valuable and productive.

The guidelines here tend to match the recommendations that Microsoft issues to its own .NET development teams. If we haven't pointed out a difference between our standards and Microsoft's, then they're essentially the same. When in doubt, it is generally a good idea to favor established methods that developers are already familiar with. Change can often bring with it benefits; however, it can also be a thing that programmers resist strongly.

Naming Guidelines

Naming guidelines actually cover two things: **naming** and **casing**. The following is a list of generic guidelines that apply to both naming and casing. Microsoft strongly recommends the use of a capitalization scheme called **Pascal casing**. Pascal casing is a scheme where all words in an identifier have the first letter capitalized and there is no separation character between words. Another type of capitalization scheme is called **camel casing**. This is where the first letter of the identifier is lowercased, and thereafter the first letter of each word is capitalized. The following table is a summary of Microsoft's capitalization suggestions:

Type	Case	Additional Information
Class	PascalCase	Examples: *MyClass, Utility, DataHelper*
Enum value	PascalCase	Examples: *Colors.Red, PossibleValues.ValueOff*
Enum type	PascalCase	Examples: *Colors, PossibleValues*
Event	PascalCase	Examples: *MouseClick, ButtonDown*
Exception class	PascalCase	Class name ends with `Exception` suffix, for example: *MyCustomException, WebServiceException*
Interface	PascalCase	Interface name is prefixed with the letter `I`, for example: *ICar, ISerializable*
Method	PascalCase	Examples: *GetItemData, UpdateModifiedValue*
Namespace	PascalCase	Examples: *Company.NewApplication.DataTier*
Property	PascalCase	Examples: *ItemValue*
Parameter	camelCase	Examples: *itemArray, valueData, purchasePrice*
Private member variable	camelCase	Microsoft makes no recommendation on this; however, it is useful to distinguish private member variables from other identifiers

In addition to the above summary of capitalization rules, the following guidelines apply to naming classes, interfaces, and namespaces:

❑ Do *not* use class names that overlap with namespaces, especially those namespaces that are supplied by Microsoft. So stay away from naming your classes things like `System`, `UI`, `Collections`, or `Forms`.

❑ Do *not* use the underscore character. Many of us who have been writing C++ code for a long time have developed the habit of using a preceding underscore to indicate a private member variable within a class. This practice has fallen from grace, and is now discouraged.

❑ Do *not* use identifier names that conflict with keywords. Most languages won't let you anyway!

❑ Do *not* use abbreviations in your identifiers. Also, where you use an acronym, treat it as a word – don't use all uppercase. For example, the .NET Framework has namespaces such as `SqlClient` (not `SQLClient`).

❑ *Do* follow the casing conventions in brand names. For example, if you place your company name in a namespace, and your company name has a specifically branded capitalization scheme (for example NeXT or IBM, both of which have a capitalization scheme that doesn't coincide with the casing recommendations) you should retain your company's branding. So, you would not reduce IBM in a namespace to `Ibm`, nor would you reduce NeXT in a namespace to `Next`.

❑ *Do* use nouns and noun phrases when naming your classes and namespaces. This is highly recommended and preferred over using verbs. For example, use `Parser` as a namespace or class name, rather than `Parse` or `Parsing`. Verbs should be used for method names only

❏ Do *not* use Hungarian notation when naming things. For example, in classic VB, controls were often given names like `btnConfirm`, which would immediately tell the reader that it was a button. Microsoft's style guidelines are now recommending that people do not prefix their variable names with anything related to that variable's data type. Microsoft feels that the development tools (specifically VS.NET) should provide information pertaining to a given member's data type by such means as intelligent hovering pop-up dialogs. A better purpose for a variable name is to describe its use rather than its data type. Interestingly enough, Microsoft *does* recommend the usage of Hungarian notation prefixes on static member names.

There are a lot of code conventions to remember, and for some people it is a radical switch in development style. The important thing is to have guidelines, even if they are different from those given here. If two programmers agree to follow guidelines, then there is a very good chance that they will produce code that looks similar and is just as easy to read. You can find all the information you need on Microsoft's recommended design, naming, and coding convention guidelines in the MSDN documentation that comes with the .NET Framework SDK. Some topic names to look up include:

❏ Parameter naming guidelines

❏ Property naming guidelines

❏ Event usage guidelines

❏ Method usage guidelines

❏ Field usage guidelines

❏ Static field naming guidelines

It's a good idea to follow the Microsoft guidelines wherever possible. Microsoft code samples all follow these guidelines, including those in the .NET documentation. Writing code using this style will make it easier to read other code in that style.

Namespace Hierarchy

If you haven't worked on large projects with .NET, designing the **namespace** hierarchy may seem alien. Namespaces in .NET are logical containers for classes, enumerations, and so on. One namespace can span multiple assemblies and modules.

> *An assembly is essentially a container for .NET components. Multiple .NET components can reside in a single assembly. To keep things familiar and to provide easier backwards compatibility, typical assemblies retain the familiar DLL extension.*

> *Modules are collections of components that can be compiled outside an assembly and then merged into an assembly later. For the most part (especially if you're using Visual Studio .NET) you will be working in a model that only has one module per assembly.*

Namespaces are conceptually similar to folders. One useful purpose of folders is to distinguish between two files of the same name – two classes with the same name can be distinguished by their namespace. For example, if we have a class named `Car`, and some other vendor has a class named `Car`, we can distinguish our car from theirs by using a different namespace.

However, folders are also useful because they enable us to organize our files. Namespaces allow us to organize our classes in a logical, memorable way. If all of the developers on the team know the namespace hierarchy, and the namespace hierarchy is logical and consistent, then any developer sitting down to start working on the application should have no trouble finding any code they need to get their job done. A well-organized namespace hierarchy can be a massive help towards building an application that is easy to maintain and enhance.

Now that we've determined that a well-organized namespace hierarchy is essential to any good core foundation design, let's design the namespace hierarchy for ThePhile.com.

Before we actually try to draw out the tree structure, we'll identify the primary areas of our website's functionality. These areas should give us an idea of what kind of namespaces we will need, and from there we can organize them into a tree and further sub-divide them if needed. One thing to be aware of when building a namespace hierarchy is that it is very easy to go overboard. Detailing namespaces down to too fine a degree of granularity will actually hinder the development process rather than enhance it. It is best to find a middle ground where there is enough categorization to make sense, but not so much that it confuses the programmers.

The areas of functionality are listed below in no particular order:

- ❑ E-mail newsletter
- ❑ News and content system
- ❑ Opinion polls (voting)
- ❑ Forums
- ❑ Users and security (accounting)
- ❑ Advertising
- ❑ Website basics (homepage, navigation, headers, footers, etc.)
- ❑ Administration (uploading changes to files)

Microsoft recommends that the namespace hierarchy strategy should always begin with the company name. In our case, the company name is "Wrox", so we're going to make sure that `Wrox` is our root namespace. Then, the second recommendation is that immediately beneath the company name should be the application (or technology) name. In our case, our application is called "The Phile", so we'll have another namespace underneath `Wrox` called `ThePhile`. Note that we're keeping in line with our naming convention rules and using Pascal casing and no underscores.

As we mentioned in the requirements listing, our design must allow us to separate the core functionality of the website (for example the core server controls, navigation, and pages) from the extra modules that we are building into it (forums, advertising, etc.). This way, we can logically separate each individual module from the core of the website, creating a plug-in feel for the other modules.

In order to do this, we'll create another namespace for all of the additional modules being developed for this application throughout this book. We're going to call this namespace `WebModules`. We are trying to make sure that everything we do conforms to the standards and casing conventions we came up with earlier. This namespace will be underneath the main root of `Wrox`.

If we take the above list of features and turn them into namespace names by following our naming convention, we get the following namespaces:

- ❑ `MailingLists`
- ❑ `NewsManager`
- ❑ `Polls`
- ❑ `Forums`
- ❑ `Accounts`
- ❑ `AdsManager`
- ❑ `FileManager`

So underneath our root namespace we have the namespace `WebModules`, beneath which we will have a namespace for each web module. Within each of these we will have a namespace called `Web` for our website skeleton. This namespace will hold each of the code-behind classes. Each of the `Web` namespaces can have a child namespace called `Controls` that will hold all of the user or server controls for that module. The `Wrox.ThePhile` namespace is structured in a similar way to an individual web module. There's room for expansion here, too – if we decide to make room for `WebServices`, we can add another child namespace to the `Web` namespace and call it `Services`. It could hold all the code-behind classes for the web services functionality for a given module.

Now that we've decided on the names, and we have some idea of where we want everything to flow, let's take a look at the diagram that our website designers came up with for the namespace hierarchy:

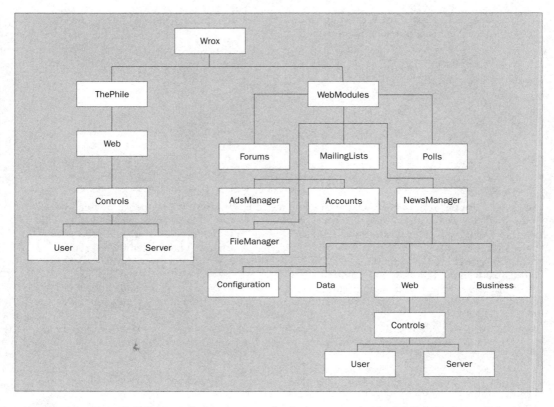

This diagram only fully expands the namespace for the NewsManager module, but other modules will have a similar structure.

The fact that we have three namespaces under each module looking very much like a standard three-tier architecture (with a presentation tier, business services tier, and data services tier) is far from coincidence. We also have the Configuration namespace, which we can use to logically contain any code that is required for the configuration of that particular module.

Having this hierarchy laid out early in the development can help with documenting and planning the project. For example, we can use the namespace hierarchy as a to-do list of things to design, implement, and document.

The modules we're building in this book are designed to be easily reusable so they can be plugged into other websites with little or no work and hassle, which will become more evident as we look into each module throughout this book. That is the main reason why the additional modules have been separated into their own namespaces, so they have no direct requirement of belonging to any given website.

Microsoft provides a few guidelines for building a namespace hierarchy. The general format is Company.Technology.Product. Therefore, you might see a namespace like Microsoft.Office.Word at some point in the future.

Programming Language

One of the things we need to decide early in our design phase is which programming language to use. With the CLR and .NET, the choice of programming language has become one of personal preference rather than necessity. With certain exceptions, most languages running under the CLR will perform similarly, so the choice is less driven by performance requirements than in previous legacy projects.

In our case, the application was originally entirely written in C#. For this edition of the book, the entire application was ported to Visual Basic .NET. In a real-world environment, however, it is entirely possible that a project team might choose to use both VB.NET and C#, with the language choice left up to each individual programmer. Because both C# and VB.NET are compiled to the same Intermediate Language, most of the components should co-operate just fine even if their main language is different.

> *There will be exceptions to this, if components make use of language features that are not supported by the CLR, or CLR features not supported by the language. For example, VB.NET does not have support for operator overloading, while it's an almost natural process in C#.*

Folder Structure

Just like a poorly organized namespace hierarchy, or a poorly defined set of coding standards, a poorly organized folder structure can hinder the maintainability of the application.

The easiest thing to do is take the namespace hierarchy diagram that we produced for the previous step and simply convert it into a tree of directories, making allowances for a few things like directories for images, stylesheets, XSLT files, and such like.

The following directory structure is the result of converting the namespace hierarchy into a directory tree:

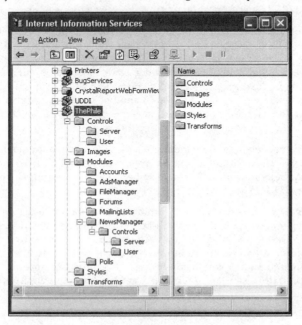

This doesn't include all of the repetitive sub-directories (Controls and Services) for each of the solutions we'll be building for the website. Only the NewsManager directory appears in full.

If you've worked with Visual Studio .NET for creating an ASP.NET application, you will know that any time you create a web form, the code-behind class is created in the same directory as that form. This will be the case for our solution too (at least in the version we distribute with source code). As you can tell, the ThePhile directory is the main application root. Below that, we have a directory that will house the code and .ascx files for our server and user controls. Also, there is a generic Images directory that is, obviously, designed to house our graphics. Each of the modules we will be developing throughout the rest of this book will be primarily contained in its own sub-directory in the Modules directory. There is a Styles directory that will contain any stylesheets we use, and a Transforms directory for our XSLT files.

Designing the Database

When we come to design the core components of the website, we will look at database design – the tables and relationships that we need to model. Each new module will lead to different demands so new tables and relationships will be added as the site progresses.

At this stage we need to make the decisions that will leave us with an appropriately constructed empty database. Before we can do this, we need to make important decisions about:

❑ **Hardware** – typically this covers the machine and what kind of hardware it sports, such as RAID hardware, hot-swappable drives, and multiple processors.

❑ **Network topology** – this covers considerations such as firewalls, security, backbone bandwidth, and speed (for example, will your middle tier encounter bandwidth bottlenecks in trying to reach your RDBMS?), and isolation to prevent various forms of network attacks and intrusions.

❑ **Database size and growth rate** – this is one area that is typically managed by the database administrator (DBA), but we aren't all fortunate enough to have a DBA around to do this for us. If you are warehousing data then you need to consider extreme growth rates in your data, whereas if you're serving up a fixed product catalog and not much else, you don't need to be too worried about database growth and size. In the past this was a huge concern, but in these modern days where we can simply drop in another massive hard drive into a logical partition, it is becoming less and less of a concern in terms of space. However, there are performance concerns with data growth that we won't go into here.

❑ **Disaster recovery** – every good database needs a backup. There needs to be some kind of plan in place that will allow for failures in the system so we can restore data to a previously good state. This can be done with full or differential backups, redundant storage, and other options that might be RDBMS-specific, such as clustering or managing mirrored tables.

❑ **Database quantity** – one decision that often gets overlooked in the design phase is whether or not everything you're going to need will be in the same physical database. With many modern RDBMSs like Oracle and SQL Server, each database is handled by a different running process (often referred to as an *instance* of the database), offering a potentially very large performance benefit if your web application needs access to two different stores of data, but not necessarily at the same time (for example, when you don't need to join data from one source to the other).

❑ **Security** – one thing you definitely don't want is people having unauthorized access to your system. Even if your database is safely tucked away behind a firewall, there are still ways of hijacking trusted resources on the other side that can 'spoof' their way into your database. A good way of preventing this kind of thing is by securing your database. For example, one *really* good idea might be to change the default password of the system administrator accounts for your RDBMS (such as 'sa' for MS SQL Server).

Now that we've looked at some database creation issues, we'll go over what we did for our particular application. It is important that third-party hosting companies and home-office Windows 2000 Professional machines can host ThePhile. This makes MS SQL Server an obvious choice.

All we need to do is create a database called ThePhile with all of the default options (meaning that it will automatically grow and automatically truncate the log file when necessary). Later on, as we develop the individual modules of the application, we'll start creating data structures in the database.

ThePhile.com uses a single database for the whole site, rather than a different one for each module. This is because third-party application hosts usually provide their customers with only a single database. We'll design our application modules so that they can easily be configured to run on their own separate databases if those resources are available, however.

> **In order to install and run the application we'll be developing throughout this book, you'll need to have at least an evaluation copy of SQL Server 7 or SQL 2000 installed on your machine. These are available from the Microsoft website.**

Building the Data-Services Tier

In many applications, programmers will often have a single tier between the presentation logic and the actual back-end database. They tend to lump both business logic and data access into the same logical tier. This will work, but it's usually a bad idea. It's better to separate the code that enforces business rules and performs multi-step business processes from the database-access code. This leaves us with a data-services tier, giving many benefits, including:

❑ **Scalability** – using a data-services tier can make an application far more scalable. Even if the data services tier isn't hosted in COM+ or MTS, there is still a large added benefit. Let's say we have a data services component that obtains inventory information by simply querying the database. Because our business logic is separate from the data component, we can upgrade the data component to use a stored procedure without changing any of the business code. Now assume we want to upgrade it even further by adding in the summary of transactions stored in an MSMQ queue; again all we need to do is place the new code into the data services component and drop it in. The user interface and the business rules are still the same and require no changes. Distinctly separating your code across tiers also allows you to scale the solution by adding more hardware to handle increased demand without having to modify existing code.

❑ **Availability** – separating the data services from the business services can help an application to be more fault-tolerant, and so more available to clients. By distinguishing separate units of business and data logic and placing them in separate components, you further separate your application from the classic 'monolithic' application model (which can tear everything down even if only a small problem occurs in a small subsystem). If a portion of your application breaks using an n-tier architecture, you will be able to isolate, identify, and replace the defective component far more easily and with less disruption than if you had been working with a monolithic application.

❑ **Maintainability** – as we mentioned when we talked about scalability, if you need to make a change to your data back end, all you need do is make the change to the data-services tier components that are affected and you're all set. If coded properly, the business tier and presentation tiers should be entirely unaffected by this change. For example, if you suddenly decided that your user information needed to come from an Oracle database, while your purchase history information needed to come from a DB2 database on a Unix mainframe, you could easily make the changes to the data services components and not have to worry about crashing the rest of your application. Another benefit in terms of development is the fact that the data source is literally plug-and-play. You can, for instance, make a minor configuration change and move a test application to a production database, or a production application to a test database, without significant impact to the overall application.

❑ **Performance** – in classic ASP, three tiers was almost a requirement because of the limitations of VBScript in the presentation tier (such as not being able to early bind to COM objects). With .NET there really is no performance benefit from splitting into the third tier, unless we're using COM+. Hosting business and/or data services components with COM+ allows us to pool our objects and take advantage of services like just-in-time (JIT) activation and object pooling. COM+ and related concepts are a little out of scope for this book, as our simple content application is just going to use standard components.

In the following sections we will look at creating a single base class for every object in a given tier. What this essentially means is that every data-access object will inherit from a common data-access object. In addition, every business class will inherit from a common business class. Typically, when designing a data-services tier, there are two main ideas people adopt: building a single helper class, which performs all data access on behalf of all components in the data tier, or building a data object for every type of entity that needs access to the database. For our purposes, we're going to go with the latter method. An entire book could be written about all of the different arguments people have both for and against each of these methods.

This technique further enhances scalability and maintainability. For example, if we want to change where every single data services component obtains its connection string, we just make a single change to the base class for the data services tier.

For more information on the benefits of creating base classes for related or similar groups of classes, consult a good object-oriented programming manual. There are many examples of these, including *Object-Oriented Analysis and Design with Applications* by Grady Booch (ISBN 0-8053-5340-2).

We will look at creating the base class for our data services tier in the Solution section of this chapter.

Building the Business-Services Tier

The business-services tier provides a layer of abstraction that rests atop the low-level components that compose the data services tier. It is often hard to see the purpose in splitting the business logic from the data-services tier, but once it's done, the benefits are massive. Keep in mind that we are talking about layers of abstraction, not actual physical layers or separations between components and component tiers.

We've already discussed maintainability as one of the benefits of this split. If the business rules and business logic rest in a layer above the data services, then the underlying data-access mechanisms, code, and even server or server location can all change without breaking any of the code in the business-services tier. As we mentioned earlier, this ability often produces the useful side effect of being able to 'switch' an application from a live data source to a debug or test data source with little or no visible consequence to the application itself.

The other main benefit is for modeling of business processes and rules. By separating your data access from your business tier, your designers can devote their full attention to determining how the application should function with the business rules in place. They won't need to concern themselves with whether or not a given field in a database table is a short or a long integer.

The bonus is in the modeling and design. The presentation tier is modeled to be close to what the user expects to see, for example, we have a class for each page the user can see. The data-services tier often ends up producing a close ratio of components to tables. The business-services tier generally produces something in the middle, modeling processes, rules, and logical abstractions rather than data-dependent components.

This diagram is a typical example of the dispersal of components across a three-tier model. It shows the difference in design patterns used in developing classes, or components, for each of the tiers:

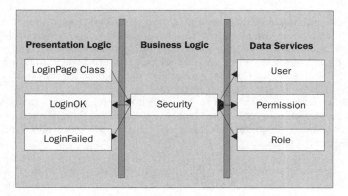

As we can see from the above diagram, a sample user might hit the login page for a simple web application. From there, an instance of the LoginPage class might invoke the Authenticate method in the business class for a particular username and password combination. The Security class is a model for the business processes relating to security. It first requests that an instance of the data-services class User validate that a given user exists with that username and password combination. Again, keep in mind that if we changed where and how we were storing user information, all we'd have to do is change our User component, leaving the business and presentation tiers unharmed. Then, assuming we have a fairly robust security scheme, the Security class instance checks to see what roles that user belongs to, and whether any of those roles has been given permission to log in.

From all this, the key point is that the presentation logic is modeled to be very close to what the user sees and interacts with; the business tier is modeled around business processes and rules; and the data-services tier is modeled around finite sets of data.

Even with these benefits, it might seem tedious to take on this extra work when modeling simple processes. However, applications grow – sometimes into things we never intended (this is typically where marketing and sales get involved). With a solid architecture, we have the room to scale our application with the demand of our customers, consumers, and even our sales department!

We are building our application in a number of modules. Each module will have its own presentation, business, and data tiers. This way we can drop a complete module into other web applications. Each chapter that deals with a specific module will cover the classes for that module.

Error Handling and Fault Tolerance

If we have been following good software development practices, then our code has received extensive testing before we release it to the public or to production. Typically, each individual component receives unit testing that is outlined in the project plan, and then each component is integration-tested in the larger application as a whole. However, no matter how good our testing plans are, we can't account for all possible unexpected occurrences. We can't program to expect hardware failures or other failures caused by effects that weren't part of our testing lab scenario. In these cases, we rely on the last resort: **exception handling**.

Many websites do not handle exceptions well. This results in users seeing low-level error messages, including the line number within the ASP page that caused the exception. This kind of thing is highly unprofessional, and any time you see it, you know that someone hasn't done their homework or enough testing.

If something unexpected happens, then the application should gracefully inform the user. It might also give them a phone number or e-mail address to send information about the problem. Windows XP, Office XP, and Visual Studio .NET all have a feature built-in that allows users to transmit debug information directly to Microsoft. While we can't all aspire to this level of fault tolerance, we should take a hint from this and strive for the best we can get out of our web application.

When an error does occur, the site should store as much information as it can about the error and inform the user that something went wrong. This way the user is told politely that an error occurred, without seeing any technical detail. Meanwhile, the administrators get detailed information that helps to track down and repair the failure.

In the Solution section we're going to start coding. As part of that, we will look at what kind of information we can store and how we can store it. We'll also look at how to provide an environment where programmers can track down bugs, even in a live system that can't be brought down for debugging.

Deployment Issues

You might be wondering why you need to consider deployment at the design stage. Isn't deploying the application done after you've completed all of the code? Well, yes and no. The physical deployment of the application does indeed take place when an iteration of the development phase has completed.

However, the choice of development design can radically affect the options available when building the application itself. There are many things to consider when designing your deployment strategy, such as the target platform, hardware requirements, software pre-requisites (such as requiring the .NET Framework or XML v3.0 on the destination machine), network deployment, and much, much more. We won't cover all the possible things you can consider when designing a deployment strategy here, as that could fill a book of its own.

For our deployment design, we decided to keep it as simple as possible. We are going to allow our application to be deployed via the Windows Installer to a programmer's machine. In addition, you can use XCopy deployment and some supplied database scripts to deploy the system to a third-party hosting company. We'll discuss all this and actually show you the solution to our deployment design at the end of the book, in Chapter 11, once we've developed all of the modules.

User Interface Design

We won't go into too much detail here, as we're just building the non-visible core foundation of code for this chapter. However, in the next chapter we'll take a look at some in-depth design of user interface elements and we'll cover some ideas for designing reusable interface controls. For now, it's sufficient to include in our design the requirement that our user interface should be professional and easy to navigate, but not so professional that our site looks like an accounting application.

The Solution

Now that the foundation has been designed, we can start writing some code. To recap, a few of the things that we covered in our design were:

❑ Naming and coding guidelines – we set out the conventions to be used throughout the project

❑ Programming language choice – the original application was built in C# but was then ported to VB.NET

❑ Folder structure – we designed a namespace hierarchy and a corresponding folder structure for all the modules of the website

❑ Designing the database – we chose SQL Server as our core database

❑ Building the data-services tier and the business-services tier – we talked about the importance of n-tier design and architecture, and about the usefulness of creating a base class for each tier

This next section will cover the code and implementation of each tier's base class, as well as a custom exception class that we're going to build.

Of course, the implementation we create here might have unforeseen limitations that we will discover later. We might find ourselves changing these classes throughout the development. At this point, we have to continue with what we already know, and build what's best at this point.

To create the solution for this chapter, we're going to create a new VB.NET Class Library project in Visual Studio .NET, and name it Core. We're going to make some minor changes to its properties and to the AssemblyInfo.vb file. Right-click the project and choose **Properties**. Then make sure that the **Assembly Name** property is set to Wrox.WebModules.Core, and the **Default Namespace** property is set to Wrox.WebModules.

The next thing we need to do is make sure that our project is **strong-named**. Since this is the first project in the entire web application, we get to make our **SNK file**. The SNK file is a file that contains a digital signature encrypted using the RSA algorithm. In order to make sure that all of our assemblies appear as though they're coming from the same vendor, they all need to have the same **public key**. The only way to accomplish this is to compile each of the assemblies against the same SNK file.

To create our digital signature file, we go to the command prompt and type:

SN –K ThePhile.SNK

Note that you won't be able to use **SN** from any directory unless you've launched the Visual Studio .NET command prompt, which pre-configures your path statement to allow you access to all of the useful .NET command-line tools.

The command creates a new digital signature file. Copy this file to some safe, common location on your hard drive. All of our examples use \Wrox\Keys\ThePhile.SNK as the location. This way we don't have to worry about the drive letter, only that the file is in the \Wrox\Keys directory on the same physical drive as the project.

We can now modify our AssemblyInfo.vb file to include a full version number and a reference to the digital signature file, which is required in order to create a strongly named assembly. AssemblyInfo.vb should contain the following (the comments have been removed to save space, but otherwise this is the complete file):

```
<Assembly: AssemblyTitle("ThePhile.com Web UI")>
<Assembly: AssemblyDescription("Web UI Forms for ThePhile.com")>
<Assembly: AssemblyCompany("Wrox Press Ltd")>
<Assembly: AssemblyProduct("Wrox.ThePhile")>
<Assembly: AssemblyCopyright("(C) 2002 Wrox Press Ltd")>
<Assembly: AssemblyTrademark("")>
<Assembly: CLSCompliant(True)>
<Assembly: AssemblyCulture("")>
<Assembly: AssemblyVersion("1.0.0.0")>
<Assembly: AssemblyKeyFile("\Wrox\Keys\ThePhile.snk")>
<Assembly: AssemblyKeyName("")>
<Assembly: AssemblyDelaySign(False)>
```

As well as the usual description and a title, there is an entry for company, product, and copyright. This is all just additional information that can be useful, but non-essential. The key components of the strong name are Culture, Version, and KeyFile. Our assembly isn't language-specific, so we've left the culture blank. An assembly built for the "en-us" culture is *not* considered the same as an identically versioned assembly built for the "en-uk" culture. These two assemblies would have different strong names, and components that reference the assemblies will be able to tell the difference between the two.

Each of the next three classes we're going to cover will be in the Wrox.WebModules.Core.DLL assembly that we just set up.

The DbObject Class

The first set of code we're going to produce is a base class for the data services tier. We've already explored the benefits of using a base class – it enables us to rapidly and easily change an aspect of behavior that is common to all data services classes, without having to change the code in every single class.

For our class we are going to provide a couple of support functions, as well as automatic instantiation and configuration of the SqlConnection object. One of the things we have already mentioned in our design is a preference for not using in-line SQL, and using stored procedures instead. In addition to speed improvements, the use of stored procedures allows us to make changes to the SQL and low-level data-access code without having to modify any classes in our core component library. In a situation where in-line SQL queries are not being used, it becomes apparent that there are two activities that most data-services classes will need to do:

❑ Execute a stored procedure and obtain a number – for inserting, updating, or deleting records. The number usually represents the number of records modified.

❑ Execute a stored procedure and obtain a `SqlDataReader` – for selecting records. This kind of stored procedure is typically executed with the `ExecuteReader` method of a `SqlCommand` instance. We're going to use a `SqlDataReader` for our core functions because our data needs are simple. We'll never be returning more than one related table from any given method, so we can make do with the faster, leaner `DataReader` object.

To create this class, remove the default one created with the Class Library project, and add a new one called `DbObject`. Let's take a look at the code for our `DbObject` base class. Inline comments have been removed to save space. We start by declaring it as an abstract class, which means that this class can act as a basis for other classes, but that we cannot instantiate it:

```
Imports System
Imports System.Data
Imports System.Data.SqlClient

Namespace WebModules.Data

   Public MustInherit Class DbObject
```

In the code below, we create two member variables. The first is to hold our SQL connection. It is protected, which means that only those classes deriving from this class can access this variable. If a class inherits from this one, it may provide a method that requires the `Connection`. The connection string is hidden from child classes, preventing them from too closely relying on any given underlying implementation:

```
      Protected myConnection As SqlConnection
      Private myConnectionString As String
```

Next we see our constructor. This constructor takes a connection string and instantiates a new connection based on that string. We don't open the connection at this point. Leaving a connection open for longer than required for the operation is wasteful and could slow down the application:

```
      Public Sub New(ByVal newConnectionString As String)
         myConnectionString = newConnectionString
         myConnection = New SqlConnection(myConnectionString)
      End Sub
```

This next routine, `BuildIntCommand`, automates the instantiation of a `SqlCommand` object. It does this by taking the name of the stored procedure and an array of `IDataParameter` objects. From there, it builds a SQL command using those parameters. Then, once those parameters have been added, it creates a new parameter to store the numeric return value of the stored procedure. The method returns the new command after it has been built:

```
      Private Function BuildIntCommand( _
         ByVal storedProcName As String, _
         ByVal parameters As IDataParameter()) _
         As SqlCommand
```

```
        Dim command As SqlCommand = _
          BuildQueryCommand(storedProcName, parameters)
        Dim parameter As New SqlParameter()

        With parameter
          .ParameterName = "ReturnValue"
          .DbType = SqlDbType.Int
          .Size = 4
          .Direction = ParameterDirection.ReturnValue
          .IsNullable = False
          .Precision = 0
          .Scale = 0
          .SourceColumn = String.Empty
          .SourceVersion = DataRowVersion.Default
          .Value = Nothing
        End With
        command.Parameters.Add(parameter)

        Return command

    End Function
```

The above method calls `BuildQueryCommand` to create a new SQL command object. This new command will typically be used for returning the results of SELECT statements in stored procedures to either a `DataSet` or a `DataReader`. The following is the listing for the `BuildQueryCommand` method:

```
    Private Function BuildQueryCommand( _
      ByVal storedProcName As String, _
      ByVal parameters As IDataParameter()) _
      As SqlCommand

        Dim command As New SqlCommand(storedProcName, myConnection)
        command.CommandType = CommandType.StoredProcedure

        Dim parameter As SqlParameter
        For Each parameter In parameters
          command.Parameters.Add(parameter)
        Next

        Return command

    End Function
```

The method below, `RunProcedure`, takes as arguments the name of the stored procedure to execute, an array of parameters, and an out integer parameter. The out parameter will contain the number of rows affected by the stored procedure after the method completes. This method helps execute Insert, Update, or Delete queries, and returns a numeric condition code that indicates success or some degree of failure. This method does not interpret these codes, so the class inheriting from DbObject can use any enumerations for its status codes and not interfere with any other classes. Calling `BuildIntCommand` will enable us to do this, as we've just seen. Then, the `ExecuteNonQuery` method is invoked, which returns the number of rows affected by the stored procedure. Finally, the method returns the value in the `ReturnValue` parameter (we saw that this parameter is added automatically by the `BuildIntCommand` method).

```
    Protected Overloads Function RunProcedure( _
       ByVal storedProcName As String, _
       ByVal parameters As IDataParameter(), _
       ByRef rowsAffected As Integer) _
       As Integer
       Dim result As Integer

       myConnection.Open()
       Dim command As SqlCommand = BuildIntCommand(storedProcName, parameters)
       rowsAffected = command.ExecuteNonQuery()
       result = CInt(command.Parameters("ReturnValue").Value)
       myConnection.Close()

       Return result

    End Function
```

The next code snippet contains an overload of the RunProcedure method. This overload is responsible for creating a SQL command (using BuildQueryCommand), executing it, and placing the results of the executed stored procedure into a SqlDataReader. This method will be called by inheriting classes that need fast, high-performance, forward-only access to data:

```
    Protected Overloads Function RunProcedure( _
       ByVal storedProcName As String, _
       ByVal parameters As IDataParameter()) _
       As SqlDataReader

       Dim returnReader As SqlDataReader

       myConnection.Open()
       Dim command As SqlCommand = _
          BuildQueryCommand(storedProcName, parameters)
       command.CommandType = CommandType.StoredProcedure

       returnReader = command.ExecuteReader( _
          CommandBehavior.CloseConnection)
       ' Connection will be closed automatically

       Return returnReader

    End Function
```

The next overload of the RunProcedure method (shown below) takes the usual arguments of the name of the stored procedure and the IDataParameter array. However, this one also takes the name of a table as an argument. This method runs the stored procedure, obtains the result set, and then stores that result set in a newly instantiated DataSet, in a table with the name indicated by the tableName parameter. A DataSet provides a read-write cache of data in a database, useful for more complex data manipulation. Here is the code:

```
    Protected Overloads Function RunProcedure( _
       ByVal storedProcName As String, _
       ByVal parameters As IDataParameter(), _
       ByVal tableName As String) _
```

37

```
        As DataSet

        Dim dataSet As New DataSet()

        myConnection.Open()
        Dim sqlDA As New SqlDataAdapter()
        sqlDA.SelectCommand = BuildQueryCommand(storedProcName, parameters)
        sqlDA.Fill(dataSet, tableName)
        myConnection.Close()

        Return dataSet

    End Function
```

The fourth and final `RunProcedure` overload (shown below) is very similar. However, in this case the code assumes that the `DataSet` has already been created, and simply adds the result set to a table within the previously existing `DataSet`. This allows for incredible flexibility, because an object can fill one table from one source and another table from another source. Relationships between the different sources can then be established using the `DataSet` object's `Relations` collection. Here is the code:

```
    Protected Overloads Sub RunProcedure( _
        ByVal storedProcName As String, _
        ByVal parameters As IDataParameter(), _
        ByVal dataSet As DataSet, _
        ByVal tableName As String)

        myConnection.Open()
        Dim sqlDA As New SqlDataAdapter()
        sqlDA.SelectCommand = BuildIntCommand(storedProcName, parameters)
        sqlDA.Fill(dataSet, tableName)
        myConnection.Close()

    End Sub
```

So that's the code for our `DbObject` abstract base class. One thing you might have noticed is that for our data services base class we didn't do anything with MTS or COM+. This was intentional. One of the design goals of ThePhile.com is to make it easy to deploy the site onto one of the many third-party hosting services that offer .NET and SQL Server support. If the site depended on COM+ services it would be harder to deploy on those systems. Most third-party .NET-hosting companies don't provide any ability to access COM+, so we decided to not implement it in our solution in order to keep things simple. However, in your own solution you might want to upgrade to a COM+ solution to gain object pooling, JIT activation, and transaction support.

The BizObject Class

Right now, we're not sure what kind of common functionality we want to supply to the business-services tier, so we're essentially just going to create an empty shell of a base class, called `BizObject`. It is pretty straightforward at this point. This base class is, of course, abstract and public, allowing any class from any assembly to inherit from it.

If we were worried about others potentially abusing our code, then we could place code attributes into our code that would restrict inheritance of this class to only those assemblies that have a certain public key, and so come from a specific vendor. This would restrict inheritance of our unsealed classes to classes we write ourselves. Techniques like this are covered in other books such as *Professional ADO.NET* (ISBN 1-86100-527-X).

Here's the code for the `BizObject` class:

```
Imports System

Namespace WebModules.Business

   Public MustInherit Class BizObject

   End Class

End Namespace
```

The AppException Class

Many times, in many different programming languages, error-handling routines have become enormous, cumbersome, and difficult to maintain. Even in modern languages that support the throwing of exceptions, one problem remains: how do we make sure that there is a persistent record of every exception the system throws? This is an absolute necessity for a website on the Internet where the users may not see the problem (it could be something internal that causes subtle failures, such as rounding problems or bad numbers). Even if the user sees the problem, most will either log off the website angry, or hit the back button and move on to some other feature of the website. We cannot rely on users to detect our errors.

To get around this, we will create our own custom derivative of `System.ApplicationException`. This custom exception class will place an entry in the NT/2000 Application Event Log every single time an exception is thrown. This way, the website administrator and the programmers can find out the details and time of every error that occurs.

Let's take a look at the code for our custom exception class, `AppException`:

```
Imports System
Imports System.Diagnostics

Namespace WebModules
  Public Class AppException
    Inherits System.Exception
    Public Sub New()
      LogEvent("An unexpected error occurred.")
    End Sub

    Public Sub New(ByVal message As String)
      LogEvent(message)
    End Sub
```

In this next overload of the constructor, if an inner (or nested) exception is passed to this exception (this is often called 'bubbling', where exceptions throw exceptions with themselves as the inner exception, allowing the exception to 'bubble' all the way up to an outer error-handler) then the function will actually log the message of the inner exception as well as the main exception:

```
Public Sub New( _
   ByVal message As String, _
   ByVal myInnerException As Exception)

   LogEvent(message)

   If Not (InnerException Is Nothing) Then
     LogEvent(myInnerException.Message)
   End If
End Sub
```

This next method is the one that actually logs the information to the event log. If there is no event log source called `ThePhile.com` then it will create one. After that, it will proceed to write the exception information to the event log with an entry type of "Error", which appears as a red exclamation point in the Event Viewer on NT/2000/XP.

```
Private Sub LogEvent(ByVal message As String)
   If Not EventLog.SourceExists("ThePhile.com") Then
     EventLog.CreateEventSource("ThePhile.com", "Application")
   End If

   EventLog.WriteEntry("ThePhile.com", message, EventLogEntryType.Error)
End Sub
```

This custom exception is useful in many respects. The first and foremost is that it allows us to log as an event every exception thrown using this class. The other is that it allows other code throughout our application to derive its own custom exceptions from this class – allowing the other modules to inherit the ability to automatically use the event log, as well as perform other custom tasks that those modules might need.

Logging Events to a File

The event log is a good place to store errors by our website – it collects all the events in one place where we can view them through the Windows event viewer. There are some problems with using the event log though:

❑   We need to have the correct permissions to create a new event log and write events to it

❑   We need to have access to the event log in order to read the events

Some web hosting companies will not allow us to have this sort of access so we need an alternative to the event log for storing our error events.

One area that we can access is the file area of our site, so we can use a text file to store our error events. We will then be able to open the text file to read the errors.

The great thing about the approach we have taken to logging errors is that we just need to change the code in our `AppException` class and all our errors will be logged using the new code.

Here is a replacement for `LogError` that uses a text file rather than the event log:

```
Public Shared Sub LogError(ByVal message As String)

    ' Get the current HTTPContext
    Dim context As HttpContext = HttpContext.Current

    ' Get location of ErrorLogFile from Web.config file
    Dim filePath As String = context.Server.MapPath( _
      CStr(System.Configuration.ConfigurationSettings.AppSettings( _
        "ErrorLogFile")))

    ' Calculate GMT offset
    Dim gmtOffset As Integer = _
      DateTime.Compare(DateTime.Now, DateTime.UtcNow)

    Dim gmtPrefix As String
    If gmtOffset > 0 Then
      gmtPrefix = "+"
    Else
      gmtPrefix = ""
    End If

    ' Create DateTime string
    Dim errorDateTime As String = _
      DateTime.Now.Year.ToString & "." & _
      DateTime.Now.Month.ToString & "." & _
      DateTime.Now.Day.ToString & " @ " & _
      DateTime.Now.Hour.ToString & ":" & _
      DateTime.Now.Minute.ToString & ":" & _
      DateTime.Now.Second.ToString & _
      " (GMT " & gmtPrefix & gmtOffset.ToString & ")"

    ' Write message to error file
    Try
      Dim sw As New System.IO.StreamWriter(filePath, True)
      sw.WriteLine("## " & errorDateTime & " ## " & message & " ##")
      'sw.WriteLine(message)
      'sw.WriteLine()
      sw.Close()
    Catch
      ' If error writing to file, simply continue
    End Try
End Sub
```

This is the version that is included by default in the code download, in order to make it as easy as possible to get the code working.

Note that this code requires a setting in the web.config to tell it where to find the error log file:

```
<add key="ErrorLogFile" value="~/ErrorLog.txt" />
```

This should be inside the <appSettings> section.

Summary

This chapter has introduced the problem of coming up with the core of the website. After creating an initial design for the website, we went on to create a design for the foundation of our website. This included designing a namespace layout, a preliminary directory tree, and even specifying some coding standards and naming conventions. Then we discussed some of the core concepts of building a data-services tier and a business-logic tier, and the benefits of splitting functionality into three or more tiers. Finally, we discussed the design concept behind robust error handling and why it is so important to the success of a production website.

After designing the solution to our problem, we went ahead and got into the code, producing the assembly `Wrox.WebModules.Core.DLL`, which can be used by all facets of our website as the initial foundation from which much of the rest of our classes will be built. We even included an alternative `DbObject`, the `ServicedDbObject`, in case we want to make some data services components hosted by COM+ services.

Hopefully you've gained some of the following knowledge after reading this chapter:

❑ The benefits of a strong and cohesive namespace hierarchy

❑ The benefits of separating business logic from pure data services

❑ The benefits and details of robust error handling in a web application

You should also now know how to implement systems that have these benefits.

The classes we developed for the core of our solution can be compiled into the `Core` DLL at this point. However, as all we've done so far is build the core, we won't actually be putting this code to use until the next chapter, where we will be making use of the foundation code to help build our user interface elements.

3

Foundations for Style and Navigation

Now that we have spent some time discussing many of the issues involved in creating a web application, and have begun building our core foundation, we can move on to creating the foundation of our front-end, or **user interface** (**UI**). In this chapter we will first identify the initial problem we need to solve relating to our front-end. Then we will move on to designing a solution to this problem. Finally, we'll cover the actual code and implementation of this solution.

This chapter will give you a good look at some of the tasks that are typically considered part of the foundation-building, or setup, phase of website development. These include:

❑   Identifying and creating reusable interface components

❑   The purpose and implementation of a 'page inheritance hierarchy'

❑   The purpose, benefits, and implementation of cascading stylesheets

❑   Using XML and XSLT to create content that is quick and easy to maintain

The Problem

At some point we will need a front-end (user interface) for our website. It would be fairly easy (especially for those programmers who've already spent a lot of time building classic ASP pages) to just open up a favorite editor and start cranking out page after page of content. I'm sure many of us have been in this situation before, which is why many of us remember the pain and suffering involved when we were told to change the layout, the style, or some other fundamental UI feature after we'd already built dozens of ASP pages from scratch. There's nothing worse than having to go back and re-write ASP pages because of a color change or something else that should be equally trivial.

To avoid this kind of maintenance nightmare we want the UI to be simple to maintain and modify. In order to achieve this we should build the UI on a *solid foundation*. Without a solid foundation for the user interface, changes are incredibly difficult and painstaking to make, and maintenance of the front-end can be a laborious task.

We also want it to be a good UI in terms of user experience. Following good usability and user interface design principles is absolutely essential to the success of your website. If the users are annoyed with the display on their screen when they see your site, they won't come back. Likewise, if they find it too difficult to get what they want from your site because it doesn't flow properly, isn't intuitive, or doesn't have clearly labeled functionality, they will also avoid your site like the plague. One thing to always keep in mind is that, no matter how good your site is, you will always have competition on the Internet.

> *There are many books on the market today that cover topics such as designing your website to meet the needs of your users, including* User-Centered Web Design *by John Cato (ISBN 0-20139-860-5). Something else you might want to take into consideration are users with accessibility needs who might have difficulty navigating a website that doesn't make certain interfaces explicitly available to them.*

The Problem Statement and Requirements

Our problem has two different facets. The first is, of course, to provide a solid, functional foundation on which to build the rest of our user interface. This is actually the problem statement. The other facet, which we cannot ignore, is the requirement that our design for our UI fundamentals should strive toward the following common goals:

❑ Achieve maximum ease of use through well-planned UI elements and efficient use of web page 'real estate'. Real estate is the available space on a web page in which you can display meaningful information to a user. Examples of poor use of real estate are pages in which important information occurs in such a position as to force the user to scroll down (or off to the side) in order to see it.

❑ Provide maximum flexibility by allowing configuration changes of UI elements to take place with minimal or zero re-compilation of code.

❑ Keeping in mind that a site's look and feel is almost as important as its functionality; we want to make the website attractive and intuitive to our users.

So far we've created a design and initial implementation for our core middle-tier foundation. The problem that we are attempting to solve in this chapter is to build a solid foundation for our front-end too. There are several things we can do to make our front-end extremely flexible, to avoid maintenance headaches and to improve usability. In this chapter we'll cover some of the fairly simple things we can do early on in our development process to make maintenance and modification of our application easier.

The Design

Now that we've determined that our problem is the lack of a solid UI foundation, we can go about designing the basics of our user interface, or presentation layer. Anyone with any experience of a full software development lifecycle knows that no matter how much effort you put into an initial design, it probably won't cover every scenario. This is why many managers opt for the **Unified Process**, a very common and popular iterative process that makes allowances for changes in specification and design in the middle of a development project. Other managers, especially those producing Microsoft-based solutions, prefer the **Microsoft Solutions Framework** (**MSF**).

You can read more about the Unified Process in the book The Unified Software Development Process *by Jacobson, Booch, and Rumbaugh (ISBN 0-201-57169-2). You can find more information about the Microsoft Solutions Framework at* http://www.microsoft.com/msf.

While there are management processes that allow us to make room for changes in our design, specification, and requirements throughout the lifecycle of our project, there are some things we can do in terms of code and infrastructure to make the development of those changes easier as well. Some of the common things we can do to make our website code more agile are as follows:

- ❏ Use cascading stylesheets to 'classify' different types of UI elements, such as headers, footers, tables used for certain purposes, background colors, and font styles.

- ❏ Use an object inheritance hierarchy in our component model to encapsulate functionality, properties, and visual traits common to related groups of pages and UI elements.

- ❏ Use reusable controls (server and user) in order to encapsulate common or frequently displayed UI elements that may occur on many or all pages, and to provide a code-enforced uniform look and feel.

We mentioned in *The Problem* section the desire to create an attractive UI. If you build a website that provides amazing functionality, but the interface is dull, drab, and uninspired, then you're probably not going to be as successful as a competitor who provides fewer services with a nicer looking website. It is a sad, unfortunate fact, but it remains true. The other thing to keep in mind is that the development process is iterative, and you'll probably go through many iterations of your user interface design before any customer ever sees your website, so don't grow too attached to any one particular idea.

Typically, one of the first steps people take when designing the UI of a website is to create mock-ups or samples of what they think the website might look like during a typical user session. Remember, the purpose here is not to provide any functionality here, just a foundation on which to build the UI. We did the same thing when we built this website.

Being a programmer who learned HTML using Emacs on a Unix machine, I still prefer to do my HTML design in Notepad, and so the mock-ups we used to create samples of our user interface were done in simple, static HTML designed in Notepad. However, a lot of people prefer using WYSIWYG editors like FrontPage.

The following is a screenshot of one of the sample mockups that were used in building the 'look and feel' of the website. The black and white format doesn't do it justice, but you should be able to gain some useful information from it:

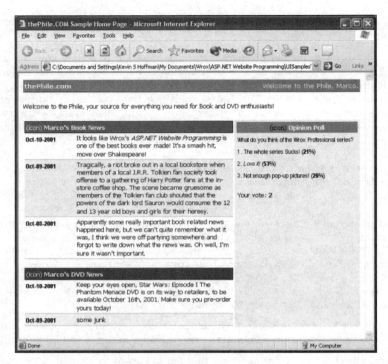

We can see that our page will include various types of content (for example news and opinion polls) and that we'd like to have a welcoming header to make the user feel comfortable with the site. Now that we have some ideas about what we want our website to look like, we can move on to actually working on some of the other issues relating to designing our core navigation and UI for the site.

Cascading Stylesheets

We cannot stress enough the importance of using **cascading stylesheets** (**CSS**). These provide a method by which the site designers can abstract a set of display properties and information. This allows for commonly displayed types of information to inherit certain visual display traits.

For example, if you have a website where you always want to display a product in a table cell, and you want that cell to have a blue background, you could either do it all by hand (and make that cell blue every time you display a product), or you can use a stylesheet. To truly illustrate the benefit of a stylesheet, we will show one in action and then compare it to the 'old' way of doing things. This is, of course, not a chapter intended to teach you the functionality of stylesheets, so we'll keep the example brief (there is a detailed example of using CSS in the solution section of this chapter). You can judge for yourself which method you'd like to use.

First, here's a fragment of HTML with the display properties embedded:

```
<td style="border:1px; border-style:solid; border-color:#000000;
    border-top:0px; border-left:0px; border-right:0px;"
    bgcolor="#000088">
  <font face="Arial,Helvetica" size="2" color="#ffffff">
  <b><i>This is a Product</b></i>
</td>
```

Looks pretty ugly, doesn't it? Now imagine having to type that in every single time you want to display a product, *anywhere* on your website. Even worse, think about what you'd have to do if your boss came by and said "Actually, how about using a yellow background for all the product names?"

Let's now look at a section of HTML that makes use of a class defined in a stylesheet. All the graphical and display properties that belong to the `Product_Cell` class are stored somewhere else (typically in a `.css` file).

```
<td class="Product_Cell">
    This is a Product
</td>
```

The CSS file contains a definition for the `Product_Cell` style, so we don't have to repeat the details every time we want to use this style, and changes to the style properties need only be made once. Seems pretty straightforward, doesn't it?

So, in order to design our stylesheets, what we need to do is attempt to produce a list of common display types, or classes, that we know we're going to be displaying. We can implement the code for the stylesheet during our actual development phase. The nice thing about the stylesheet functionality is that it's easy to go back later and add new classes.

After looking at our mockup layout for the home page, we can see that we will need quite a few display classes:

❑ Site Header – the set of display properties associated with the site header. This applies to the top of the page in our sample home page layout.

❑ Poll Header – the style class corresponding to the header information for the poll display. In our sample layout, this is the cell and text within it reading **Opinion Poll**.

❑ Poll (Generic) – the style class corresponding to any unclassified UI element that belongs in the display of an opinion poll. This would include the results of the poll and list of questions.

❑ Book News Header – the style class corresponding to the header of the **Book News** section of the display. In our layout this is a bordered cell with a background and bold, white text.

❑ Book News (Generic) – the style class corresponding to any unclassified UI element that belongs in the display of book news.

❑ Book News Item (Left Side, Date Field) – the style class corresponding to the items that appear on the left side of the first, third, fifth, etc., row in the display of book news items. In our sample layout this is the text representing the date of the news item for these rows.

❑ Book News Item (Right Side, Description Field) – same as above, only this style class applies to the items on the right side of the row, in other words the text representing the news item.

❑ Alternating Book News Item (Left Side, Date Field) – same as the Book News Item style class, only this item represents the second, fourth, sixth, etc., rows in the display.

❑ Alternating Book News Item (Right Side, Description Field) – same as the above, with the exception that this style class covers the text displayed on the right side of the news item row display.

❏ DVD News Header – the style class that represents the header of the DVD News display section.

❏ DVD News (Generic) – the style class that represents any unclassified UI element that belongs in the display of DVD News.

❏ DVD News Item (Left Side) – just like the style class for Book News Item, only this applies to DVD News.

❏ DVD News Item (Right Side) – same as above, only this applies to the right side of the text displayed in the news item row.

❏ Alternating DVD News Item (Left Side) – just like the style class for Alternating Book News Item, only this applies to DVD News.

❏ Alternating DVD News Item (Right Side) – same as above, only this applies to the right side of the text displayed in the news item row.

❏ Site Footer – the style class that applies to any UI element in the site footer.

This list of style classes that we plan on implementing for our website should be sufficient for now. Keep in mind that we will probably discover the need for more UI elements as our development and design progresses and we uncover new and unexpected common UI display classes or types, such as styles for our navigation menus, etc. In more complex implementations of CSS, you will see styles *cascade*, which means that one style inherits visual traits from another style, and that style might inherit traits from yet another style. For example, you might have a style called "Error", which inherits traits from the "Warning" style, which inherits traits from the "Red" font style, etc.

XSLT

Another way in which we will serve up dynamic content is through the use of **XSLT** (**Extensible Stylesheet Language Transformations**). You might be wondering, then, what is the difference between a cascading stylesheet and XSLT? CSS is designed to dynamically configure at run time (or display time) the visual traits of HTML elements displayed in a browser. XSLT, on the other hand, is far more versatile and has many more uses. One of its many uses is to take raw XML and convert that XML into static HTML elements.

The reason why this is important is that instead of using XSLT to convert XML into an incredibly lengthy set of HTML elements, including font tags, colors, and tables, we can instead use it to convert XML into HTML that utilizes CSS. For example, if we have the following code:

```
<Product Name="A bigger better ball of blue batter" ID="12"/>
```

XSLT can be used to convert it into the following HTML that utilizes stylesheets:

```
<TD><A style="Product" href="product.asp?ID=12">A bigger better ball of blue
batter</a></TD>
```

So, as you can see, XSLT and CSS are both used in helping render user interfaces, but they contribute to the user interface end result in entirely different ways. These can be combined to create an incredibly dynamic and powerful user-interface engine. One enormous benefit of using both XSLT and CSS in the generation of UI elements is that, in many cases, you won't have to re-compile a single line of code to change any of the display options. You can simply modify the XSLT and CSS files to tweak the user interface as you see fit.

The Page Base Class

In classic ASP, when programmers wanted to indicate that certain pages had functionality in common, they would simply make all of those ASP pages perform a server-side include of the file that contained the common functionality (using `<!--#include ...-->`).

Now that we are developing with the .NET Framework and ASP.NET, we can incorporate the full power of a true class inheritance hierarchy in our ASP.NET web pages. If you are using the code-behind functionality of ASP.NET (which is the default if you're using Visual Studio .NET to build your pages), then you no doubt have noticed that all of these code-behind pages inherit from a single class, `System.Web.UI.Page`. This class provides the basic functionality necessary to drive the most generic ASP.NET web page.

What we'd like to do is create our own class, which inherits from `System.Web.UI.Page`, and which will provide all of our web pages with a common set of functionality related to our application (ThePhile). This is more of a pre-emptive measure than anything else. At the moment, we can't think of too much functionality that *all* of our pages are going to require, but we know that the moment we start developing without this concept of a **page base class**, we'll find something and be unprepared for it. One thing that we expect we will need this base page class for is some common functionality involving user authentication, which we'll be discussing later in the book. We would rather be prepared, with a nearly empty base class, than unprepared, staring at a mountain of re-writes that we need in order to implement common functionality.

Our page class (to start with) will do two things:

❑ Contain a method that is called before the standard `Page_Load` event, allowing us to add functionality to every single page if we need to, simply by modifying this method.

❑ Provide us with a base on which we can add expanded functionality common to all pages, such as identifying and authenticating users.

A Reusable Navigation Control

My hat goes off to any of you who have succeeded in (or even attempted) implementations of a navigation control using classic ASP include files. The maintenance of such a system is typically a nightmare and often results in full-blown re-writes. The reason for this is that often such a system is implemented using server-side include files, which can be extremely difficult to maintain, as every single page must include the file, and must properly call the function (or set up an initial state) in order to properly display the navigation interface.

However, no one can dispute the necessity for users to be able to navigate your website. We discussed in the first chapter of this book that one goal of your website should be to foster the easiest possible communication between user and website. This includes making it straightforward and free of frustration for the user to navigate through the various features of your website.

Just as the high-functionality website could potentially lose visitors with an unpleasant-looking UI, it could also lose visitors if there is no easy and clear way to navigate to all of those features. Typically, websites provide some kind of *toolbar* implementation, where a section of a page is dedicated to a **navigator** of some kind that displays a list of links to the user. Our design calls for this as well.

When designing our navigation control, we are faced with a few questions:

❑ Where is the data going to come from that feeds the control?

❑ How are we going to convert that data into HTML?

❑ How are we going to implement this control?

Remembering that one of our goals is to make it so that we can reconfigure much of our website with little or no re-compilation, we decided to use an XML file on disk as the source for the navigation information. This XML file will be placed in a directory somewhere and will contain a list of links that the user can click. The main factor that led us to this decision was reliability. If the database goes down, we should still be able to present the user with a menu that allows them to navigate to the support page where they can e-mail us and complain. If, however, our navigation entries are stored entirely in the database, then we can't very well present a "Contact Us" link if our database is down.

To spruce it up a bit and make the control a bit more flexible, we decided to include categories in our navigation control to make links even easier to find on the control. Each of these categories will also have an icon that will be displayed next to the category name. Having categories will give us more flexibility to organize more complex navigation menus and allow us to create a nice user interface experience with the control.

We will discuss the format of the XML file when we actually get into implementing this control. One other thing we need to decide is how we're going to convert this XML into HTML. The first thing that comes to mind is to use an XSL transformation, especially since we know that the classes provided with the .NET Framework provide us with this ability in an easy-to-use XslTransform class.

As we did when we first started the design process, we can create a mockup, or a sample user interface, to demonstrate what we'd like our navigation control to look like. Having this on hand when we implement the control will make the coding easier and more straightforward. Here is a screenshot of this sample navigation control:

This should give you a good overview of the general idea. We have two categories, with a font style that is obviously different from that of the links themselves.

Looking at the mockup, it's apparent that in order to make this navigation control as configurable as possible we should create a stylesheet for it. This way, if we want to change the background color of the navigation control, we can simply change the color in the CSS file and not have to worry about re-compiling the control itself.

We can identify the following style elements from the above sample navigation control:

❑ **Main Table** – the style class representing the table itself. This will be used to provide the thin black border that surrounds the control.

❑ **Header Cell** – the style class representing the header. This is where the text thePhile.COM appears in the sample.

❑ **Category Cell** – the style class representing the category cell. This is where each category is displayed in bold and italics.

❑ **Item Cell** – the style class representing the cell for an individual item. This dictates the font and so on for an individual navigation item.

❑ **Item Link** – the style class representing the link to an individual item. This dictates behaviors such as the color of the link while the mouse is hovering over it, etc.

Headers and Footers

Two other extremely common user interface elements that we should provide for in our design are **headers** and **footers**. Essentially, a header is some UI element that sits atop every (or nearly every) page served to the client. The footer is a UI element that finishes off nearly every page served to the client. There are quite a few uses for these – we'll discuss a couple of them here and go into more detail about expanding the functionality of the header later in the book, such as in Chapters 5 and 7 on users and advertising.

The most important purpose of the header is for **branding**. Branding is incredibly important to every website, regardless of size, purpose, function, or form. Every page that the user sees should be in some way associated with your brand, which could involve including the company name, logo, or some other identifying mark. If the user forgets who is providing the web page they're currently viewing, then they probably won't remember where to go if they want to come back to that site.

Footers, on the other hand, traditionally have a far more utilitarian purpose. They are typically there to provide copyright and trademark information, as well as a list of links that might not fit in anywhere else on the site. This might include links to a list of available jobs, a tech support page, a contact or feedback page, and other miscellaneous navigation items that might not be visible to the user when they're looking at the top of a long web page.

Another purpose for the header that we'll talk about later in the book is for **advertising**. Advertising banners need to be displayed in a prominent place so that users viewing the page will see them. This prominent place is typically right at the top of the page above all other content.

Our design is going to call for a header that displays our branding (logo), as well as a customized greeting that displays a message to the user. This message will greet the user personally if they have logged in. In Chapter 5 we'll expand this header so that it can provide a link to a login form if the user has not yet authenticated.

There are also many other users for header controls. In our particular case, we're not going to make use of as many as we could. For example, if your website provides a search engine that allows users to search through your content, a quick-search type of control could be placed in the header to allow them quick access to your content database. Also, e-commerce sites typically have links in the header to the shopping cart and wish-list features.

Error Handling

When we were building the core foundation of our website, in Chapter 2, we built our own custom exception class, AppException. We did this in order to have an exception class that we could throw that would guarantee the writing of an event log entry. We can also extend this class later to add e-mail functionality to our custom errors without tracking down every single line of code that throws an exception.

As you've been working with ASP.NET you've probably seen the default exception screen. It isn't exactly pretty and our application loses control at that point. What this means is that if we don't trap exceptions properly and they display using ASP.NET's default mechanism, we can't guarantee that any of our code will execute. For this reason, we want to make sure that we're exerting strict control over the exception handling system. For our design, we would like to develop an error trapping system where we control the display of the error information to the users. We aren't quite sure how we're going to accomplish this at this point, but we're certain that we need to implement some form of error trapping system in the core of our presentation tier, especially if errors are going to 'bubble up' from the business tier or data-services tier at some point.

The Solution

This chapter has presented a problem – the need for creating a solid foundation for the presentation tier of our web application. After identifying the problem, we went on to discuss the concerns involved in designing a solution to this problem. Now that we have our basic design, and we have a good idea of what we plan on doing to create our presentation-tier foundation, let's get into the code and create some user interface elements.

We are going to be working with three projects, all of them within our main VS.NET Solution:

❑ ThePhile – the solution's default project, containing the site's homepage, and stylesheets. As we develop modules, it will need to reference to the presentation layer of each module. For now it should reference Core, Controls, and PhilePageBase.

❑ Controls – containing site-wide user controls: a header, footer, and navigator.

❑ PhilePageBase – containing a base class for all pages that we create for the site.

Let's look first of all at our stylesheets.

Styles

As we discussed in the design section, we know that we're going to need a stylesheet that provides user-interface element templates, or **classes**, for our website. As we discussed earlier, we're going to have one main stylesheet to aid in providing a consistent look and feel, and then we'll create another stylesheet for our navigator control.

The true benefit of these classes is that any time we decide to make a change to any of the user interface elements (this includes when sales or marketing decide to make this change, too!) all we have to do is modify the entries in the CSS file, and we don't have to worry about tracking down each and every page that displays the particular UI element we're modifying.

Here is the listing for our main stylesheet source file (`ThePhile.css` – this file should be created in the `Styles` directory directly under the main application directory, in other words `/ThePhile/Styles/ThePhile.css`). First we have the style definition for `<BODY>` elements:

```
BODY {
   background-color: #ffffff;
   font: x-small Verdana, Arial, sans-serif;
   font-size: 10;
}
```

In this next line, we're going to override the default behavior of the `<A>` element, making the link appear in dark blue instead of whatever the user has set in their browser configuration (to give the site a consistent look and feel):

```
A {
   color: darkblue;
}
```

By providing some style information for the `<TD>` element, we provide a default font and display size for all information that appears in table cells. This allows us to avoid filling our HTML output with dozens of redundant `<font>` elements.

```
TD
{
   font: x-small Verdana, Arial, sans-serif;
   font-size: 12;
   line-height: 17px;
}
```

In this next section, we're overriding the hover style of the A class.

Anytime you work with a pre-defined class (A, TD, etc.) they come with their own default styles that are defined by the user's browser options and the browser. The styles that begin A: are used to refine the styling that will be applied to <A> elements when a certain event occurs, such as hovering over such an element with a mouse pointer.

By indicating just the standard blue color here, the effect will be a dark blue link that grows slightly brighter when the mouse hovers over it. It should add a subtle and professional touch to our pages.

```
A:hover {
   color: blue;
}
```

We then have further style definitions that we'll be using later on, including those identified in our design section. To save space we won't show the entire code here, just the list of styles:

```
.Button

.TextBox

.Site_Header

.Poll_Header

.Poll_General

.Book_News_General

.Book_News_Header

.Book_News_Item_Left

.Book_News_Item_Right

.Book_News_AlternatingItem_Left

.Book_News_AlternatingItem_Right

.DVD_News_General

.DVD_News_Header

.DVD_News_Item_Left

.DVD_News_Item_Right

.DVD_News_AlternatingItem_Left

.DVD_News_AlternatingItem_Right
```

At this point we're pretty sure that we're going to need some administrative functionality added to this website. Each of the modules that we develop in this book is going to have its own administration section, which we'll cover in those modules' respective chapters. However, to provide a consistent look and feel we can include some stylistic templates here that each individual administrative section can adhere to. Again, the full code for each definition is not listed here, but can be seen in the ThePhile.css file in the code download. These are the styles we've included:

```
.Admin_MenuTable

.Admin_MenuRow

A.Admin_MenuItem

A.Admin_MenuItem:hover
```

You will notice that some are sub-styles of a pre-defined style (for the A tag in this case) but others are style groupings specific to our application, and don't have any foundation in existing HTML.

We know we're going to have errors (or at least that our users are going to make errors), so it won't hurt to provide a style that we can use for displaying them. At the moment we're only using red, but at a later date we can always come back and add more style to this class if we want the error messages to really stand out:

```
.ErrorMessage {
  color: red;
}
```

The use of cascading stylesheets should be fairly straightforward. Essentially what we're doing is defining some reusable display properties for all elements that belong to a certain class or category of display type, such as an administrative menu item, or the header for the DVD news section, etc.

Now let's look at the skeleton source for the stylesheet file we're going to use for our navigator control (found in /ThePhile/Styles/Navigator.css, relative to the root of the website). The full style definitions are not shown here, just the list of styles corresponding to those we identified in *The Design* section:

```
.Navigator_Table

.Navigator_Header_Cell

.Navigator_Category_Cell

.Navigator_Item_Cell

A.Navigator_Item_Link

A.Navigator_Item_Link:Hover
```

The PhilePage Class

As we mentioned in our design, we want a base class from which all pages on our website will either directly or indirectly inherit. This will allow us to either restrict or provide functionality to the entire site with minimal code changes. This kind of functionality might include providing some standard utility methods that we know will be called by many pages, as well as possibly providing some base code for user identification and authentication. At the moment we don't have anything in the base class, but once we set up its core structure, it should be fairly easy to add site-wide functionality to any of our pages.

To create this class, we add a class library project called PhilePageBase to our main solution. The default namespace should be Wrox.ThePhile.Web, and the class file is called PhilePage.vb. Let's take a look at the source code for this class:

```
Imports System
Imports System.Web
Imports System.Web.UI
Imports System.Diagnostics
Imports Wrox.WebModules
Imports Wrox.WebModules.Accounts.Business

Namespace ThePhile.Web

  Public Class PhilePage
    Inherits System.Web.UI.Page
```

`OnInit` (shown below) is an important method. What we're doing with our override is calling the `OnInit` method in the base class (`System.Web.UI.Page`) and then adding our custom page-load event handler (`PhilePage_Load`) to the `Load` delegate holder:

```
Protected Overrides Sub OnInit(ByVal e As EventArgs)

   MyBase.OnInit(e)
   AddHandler Me.Load, AddressOf PhilePage_Load

End Sub
```

Now that we have this base class for pages, we can create new pages that derive from `PhilePage` rather than `Page`.

> **If you notice any differences between the code in the download and the code shown here, the reason is that we will be adding to this class in Chapter 5, when we will be using the `PhilePage_Load` method to load the profile of users.**

The Navigator Control

The navigator control is one of those things that takes only a few lines of code, but is actually quite powerful. We're going to use a *server* control rather than a *user* control, as this will allow us greater influence over the class. It will completely encapsulate the implementation of the navigation system.

To create our navigator, we first need to decide on a format for the XML file from which the information would be loaded. We decided that a standard XML file was appropriate (as opposed to storing a `DataSet` serialization or something similar), but the beauty of encapsulating the functionality into a control is that if we decide to use something other than a file later on, then the change should be easy and straightforward.

Let's take a look at a sample XML file that feeds our navigator. (You can find this file in `/ThePhile/Config/NavMenu.xml` relative to the web root).

```xml
<?xml version="1.0"?>
<NavMenu title="ThePhile.COM">
  <Category title="DVDphile" icon="/ThePhile/images/DVDlogo.gif">
    <MenuItem title="Link1" link="/ThePhile/DVD/default.aspx"/>
  </Category>
  <Category title="Bibliophile" icon="/ThePhile/images/Booklogo.gif">
    <MenuItem title="Link2" link="/ThePhile/Books/default.aspx"/>
  </Category>
</NavMenu>
```

We can see that the document element, `<NavMenu>`, has a single attribute, which is the title of the navigation menu. Beneath that we have a list of categories, each indicated by a single `<Category>` node. Finally, at the lowest level in the tree, each of these categories is composed of `<MenuItem>` nodes. This form of maintaining the list of links for the navigation control is not only incredibly versatile and flexible, but it allows site administrators to make a quick change to a text file and affect possibly hundreds of pages throughout the site without recompiling anything.

Now that we know what data we're going to have in our XML file we can decide how we're going to transform that data into HTML. We discussed earlier that we wanted to use the `XslTransform` class to do our HTML transformation for us. The first thing we need to do in that case is actually build an XSLT file.

Further information on XSLT, including XPath, can be found in several Wrox books, including Professional XML for .NET Developers *(ISBN 1-86100-531-8) and* XSLT Programmer's Reference 2nd edition *(ISBN 1-86100-506-7).*

The following is the listing of the XSLT file (found in `/ThePhile/Transforms/NavMenu.xslt`, again relative to the web root). You might notice that instead of embedding all kinds of cell formatting, alignment, font sizing, and coloration directly into our XSLT file, we are simply referencing the classes defined in the CSS file we just built. This gives us many advantages. The first and foremost is that if we plan on changing the color scheme for our navigator, we don't have to change our XSLT file as well. Another is that this file is much easier to read and interpret, because all you're looking at is the HTML and associated CSS classes, and you don't have to sift through mountains of `<font>` tags.

```xml
<?xml version="1.0"?>
<xsl:stylesheet xmlns:xsl="http://www.w3.org/1999/XSL/Transform"
                version="1.0">

<xsl:template match="/NavMenu">
  <table width="150" border="0" cellspacing="0" cellpadding="0"
         class="Navigator_Table">
    <tr>
      <td colspan="2" class="Navigator_Header_Cell">
        <xsl:value-of select="@title"/>
        </td>
      </tr>
```

After we're done displaying the header for the navigator, we then use the `<xsl:for-each>` element to iterate through each `<Category>` element that we find beneath the `<NavMenu>` element. This allows us to create a loop of transformation that is performed on each category:

```xml
      <xsl:for-each select="Category">
      <!-- CATEGORY START -->
        <tr>
          <td width="40" align="center">
            <img align="absmiddle">
```

Something that often confuses people is the use of the `<xsl:attribute>` element. This allows you to set the value of a given attribute to a value obtained dynamically through an XPath `select` statement in the `<xsl:value-of>` element. Here, we're using this to dynamically set the `src` attribute of the `<img>` element. Our XPath expression is retrieving the value of the `icon` attribute (@ signifies an attribute):

```xml
            <xsl:attribute name="src">
              <xsl:value-of select="@icon"/>
            </xsl:attribute>
          </img>
        </td>
        <td width="110" class="Navigator_Category_Cell">
          <xsl:value-of select="@title"/>
        </td>
      </tr>
```

While we're in the master loop (iterating through each `<Category>` element contained within the `<NavMenu>` document element), we will create a nested loop for each item belonging to each category. This allows us to iterate through the list of items assigned to each category, giving us the ability to transform each item into its own set of HTML elements:

```
        <xsl:for-each select="MenuItem">
        <!-- MENU ITEM START -->
        <tr>
          <td width="40">
            <br/>
          </td>
          <td width="110" class="Navigator_Item_Cell">
            <a class="Navigator_Item_Link">
              <xsl:attribute name="href">
                <xsl:value-of select="@link"/>
              </xsl:attribute>
              <xsl:value-of select="@title"/>
            </a>
          </td>
        </tr>
        <!-- MENU ITEM END -->
        </xsl:for-each>
      <!-- CATEGORY END -->
      </xsl:for-each>
    </table>
  </xsl:template>

</xsl:stylesheet>
```

One of the things that many people find they have trouble understanding about XSLT is that it *must produce well-formed XML*. Even though the HTML 4.0 specification looks a lot like XML, it is far more lax in its requirements. For instance, HTML allows you to simply supply a `<br>` tag and be done with it. However, the XML output from an XSLT transformation *must* produce a completed element, either by producing a `<br>` and a `</br>` or by producing a `<br/>`. This is just something to keep in mind when building your XSLT files. As you can see in the XSLT above, we are producing `<br/>` tags rather than `<br></br>` tag pairs.

Now that we've created not only a sample XML source file, but also a working XSLT transformation file, we're ready to start writing the server control that we're going to use to make the transformation happen. To create this server control, we first create a new project (VB .NET Class Library, called `Controls`) that is part of our main solution that already contains our `Core` project and our `ThePhile` web application project. We then set the default namespace of this project to `Wrox.ThePhile.Web.Controls`, and set the output file to `Wrox.ThePhile.Web.Controls` (Visual Studio .NET will append the DLL to the filename for you, so you don't have to type that). The code for the `Navigator.vb` class begins as follows:

```
Imports System
Imports System.Web
Imports System.Web.UI
Imports System.Web.UI.HtmlControls
Imports System.Xml
Imports System.Xml.XPath
Imports System.Xml.Xsl


Namespace ThePhile.Web.Controls.Server
```

In the above code, you'll notice that we're using `System.Xml.XPath` and `System.Xml.Xsl`, two namespaces that provide us with basic XSLT functionality. All server controls inherit from `System.Web.UI.Control`, and our `Navigator` class is no exception:

```
Public Class Navigator
    Inherits System.Web.UI.Control
    Private myTransformFilePath As String
    Private mySourceFilePath As String
```

The `TransformFile` and `SourceFile` properties (shown below) are properties that we can assign within the navigator's server-side ASP.NET tag itself when we place it on our web page. These properties indicate the XML source file path (URL) and the XSLT transformation file path (also a URL).

```
    Public Property TransformFile() As String
      Get
        Return myTransformFilePath
      End Get
      Set(ByVal value As String)
        myTransformFilePath = value
      End Set
    End Property


    Public Property SourceFile() As String
      Get
        Return mySourceFilePath
      End Get
      Set(ByVal value As String)
        mySourceFilePath = value
      End Set
    End Property
```

The `OnInit` method simply calls the `OnInit` method of the base class.

```
    Protected Overrides Sub OnInit(ByVal myEvent As EventArgs)
      MyBase.OnInit(myEvent)
    End Sub
```

This next method, `Render`, is where the actual work of the control takes place. `Render` is the basic method of a `System.Web.UI.Control` that is responsible for producing the HTML that represents the control. For more information on building ASP.NET controls, see the Wrox book *Professional ASP.NET 1.0* (ISBN 1-86100-703-5).

The first thing we do is open the source XML file as an `XPathDocument`. The `XPathDocument` provides phenomenal transformation performance, so we've chosen it over a standard XML document. We use `Context.Server.MapPath` in order to translate the URL into a physical filename (on the local machine) that we can use for the `XPathDocument` constructor. From there, we instantiate an `XslTransform` object and output the results of the transformation to the `HtmlTextWriter` stream.

```
    Protected Overrides Sub Render(ByVal writer As HtmlTextWriter)

  Dim xDoc As New XPathDocument(Context.Server.MapPath(mySourceFilePath))
  Dim xslt As New XslTransform()

  With xslt
    .Load(Context.Server.MapPath(myTransformFilePath))
    .Transform(xDoc, Nothing, writer)
  End With
End Sub
```

In the above code, the most important line is the one in which the actual transformation takes place. We call the `Transform` method of the `XslTransform` instance, supplying the XPath document and an `HtmlTextWriter` onto which the results of the transformation will be placed:

```
    .Transform(xdoc, Nothin, writer);
```

So, at this point we have a cascading stylesheet that controls the visual appearance of our navigation UI elements, we have an XSLT file that dictates how the source XML file is to be transformed into HTML, and we have the source XML file that actually defines the navigation menu structure. We've seen what the navigator will look like when displayed in the browser, so to see how our XSLT transformation is looking, let's take a look at the HTML generated by this control (you can just do View | Source from any page with the navigator on it to see this):

```
<?xml version="1.0" encoding="utf-8"?>
<table width="150" border="0" cellspacing="0" cellpadding="0"
      class="Navigator_Table">
  <tr>
    <td colspan="2" class="Navigator_Header_Cell">
      ThePhile.COM
    </td>
  </tr>
  <tr>
    <td width="40" align="center">
      <img align="absmiddle" src="/ThePhile/images/DVDlogo.gif"></img>
    </td>
    <td width="110" class="Navigator_Category_Cell">
      DVDphile
    </td>
  </tr>
  <tr>
    <td width="40">
      <br />
    </td>
    <td width="110" class="Navigator_Item_Cell">
      <a class="Navigator_Item_Link"
          href="/ThePhile/DVD/default.aspx">Link1</a>
    </td>
  </tr>
  <tr>
    <td width="40" align="center">
      <img align="absmiddle" src="/ThePhile/images/Booklogo.gif"></img>
    </td>
```

```
      <td width="110" class="Navigator_Category_Cell">
        Bibliophile
      </td>
    </tr>
    <tr>
      <td width="40">
        <br />
      </td>
      <td width="110" class="Navigator_Item_Cell">
        <a class="Navigator_Item_Link"
          href="/ThePhile/Books/default.aspx">Link2</a>
      </td>
    </tr>
  </table>
```

If you compare the above output to the output you actually see when you examine the source code for any of the pages using this control, you'll notice that we prettied up the HTML considerably. The transformation we're performing doesn't actually include any whitespace within the elements. Remember that, while whitespace may mean something to the viewer or the reader of the XML or HTML files, whitespace between the end of a parent element and the beginning of a child element is going to be ignored in the resulting output. Thankfully this whitespace removal doesn't have any impact on how the client browser interprets the HTML, it just makes the HTML source a bit painful to read.

The SiteHeader Control

The SiteHeader control that we're going to build is a user control. One main difference between a server control and a user control is that while the server control is purely a class inheriting from a control, the user control is actually a mini-ASPX page (with an extension of .ascx) and a code-behind class. To build the code for this, we're going to go back to our main web application project (ThePhile), and create a new directory (if you haven't already) called Controls.

> *At the time of the current release of Visual Studio .NET, we can't easily define code-behind files that belong to different assemblies other than the target assembly of the website, so we won't cover that method. As such, all of our user controls are actually part of ThePhile.DLL, produced as a website project.*

The following is the code listing for the control 'page' (found in /ThePhile/Controls/SiteHeader.ascx):

```
<%@ Control Language="vb" AutoEventWireup="false"
        Codebehind="SiteHeader.ascx.vb"
        Inherits="Wrox.ThePhile.Web.Controls.User.SiteHeader"
        TargetSchema="http://schemas.microsoft.com/intellisense/ie5"%>

  <link href="/ThePhile/Styles/ThePhile.css" rel="stylesheet">

  <table width="100%" border="0" class="Site_Header">
    <tr>
      <td width="50%">
        <a href="/ThePhile/default.aspx">
          <img src="/ThePhile/images/ThePhile.gif" border="0"
              alt="ThePhile.COM">
```

```
        </a>
      </td>
      <td align="right" valign="bottom">
        <asp:Label id=Greeting runat="server"></asp:Label>
      </td>
    </tr>
  </table>
```

Now for the code-behind class for this header (found in
/ThePhile/Controls/SiteHeader.ascx.vb):

```
Imports System
Imports System.Data
Imports System.Drawing
Imports System.Web
Imports System.Web.UI.WebControls
Imports System.Web.UI.HtmlControls
Imports System.Web.Security

Imports Wrox.WebModules.Accounts.Business


Namespace ThePhile.Web.Controls.User

  Public MustInherit Class SiteHeader
    Inherits System.Web.UI.UserControl

    Protected Greeting As Label
```

Here we're kind of sneaking ahead in the book. We know that we're going to be implementing some
form of authentication system, and we know that the Context.User object is going to house that
information for us. Therefore, we can code our header now to greet the user personally if they've logged
in. Later on in the book, in Chapter 5 on users and authentication, we'll add some more to this page to
provide a link to a login or registration form if the user has not authenticated.

```
Private Sub Page_Load(ByVal sender As Object, _
      ByVal e As EventArgs) Handles MyBase.Load

  Greeting.Text = "Welcome, "
  If Context.User.Identity.IsAuthenticated Then
    Greeting.Text = Greeting.Text & Context.User.Identity.Name
  Else
    Greeting.Text = Greeting.Text & "Guest User."
  End If
End Sub
```

*For convenience we've removed the web form designer code that ordinarily would be displayed above
after the Page_Load event handler.*

The SiteFooter Control

The `SiteFooter` control is going to have a similar structure to the `SiteHeader` control. Essentially, we're just making a simple user control that we will use to display miscellaneous links, copyright notices, and additional information to the users, and to provide a feeling of closure to the page itself. Without even just a small footer, many users become confused and wonder if a portion of the page might have been broken or is not displaying for some reason. The following is the listing of the user control presentation (found in `/ThePhile/Controls/SiteFooter.ascx`). There is no code to speak of in the corresponding code-behind class so we won't bother listing that here.

```
<%@ Control Language="vb" AutoEventWireup="false"
        Codebehind="SiteFooter.ascx.vb"
        Inherits="Wrox.ThePhile.Web.Controls.User.SiteFooter"
        TargetSchema="http://schemas.microsoft.com/intellisense/ie5"%>
<table width="100%" border="0" cellspacing="0" cellpadding="0">
  <tr>
    <td align="middle">
      <font face="arial" size="1">
        <br><br><br>
        <i>Copyright &copy; 2001-2002 Wrox Press Ltd.</i><br>
        <a href="Contact.aspx">Contact Us</a> | Support | FAQ | Forums |
                            Newsletter | Voting | Your Account
      </font>
    </td>
  </tr>
</table>
```

Error Handling

After doing some research on how ASP.NET provides for error handling, we've come up with a solution that will allow us to provide a rich, robust solution that is also easy to maintain and extend.

> *For more information on error handling practices for ASP.NET, consult the MSDN .NET Framework SDK documentation or the aforementioned Professional ASP.NET.*

Page classes have the ability to trap events through **event handlers**. One such event is the `Error` event. Pages can provide a custom method that deals with the handling of this error. ASP.NET also provides the ability to define an application-wide event handler for the `Error` event in the case where the page may not have trapped the error.

This works out to be in our favor, because we have just finished creating a base class for all of our pages. We developed the base class for cases where we need to add the same functionality to every single page, so that they can inherit it from this base class (theoretically, this should be all of our pages). To allow each and every one of our pages to handle errors in a graceful manner, we're going to provide a default error handler event method that can be overridden, if needs be, by inheriting classes.

In order to add our custom error handling method to the list of delegates to be invoked in the event of an error, we need to modify our `OnInit` method. Remember from earlier that we modified this to create a custom 'pre-load' method that we could use in case we needed it. The following is the new version of our `OnInit` method:

```
Protected Overrides Sub OnInit(ByVal e As EventArgs)

    MyBase.OnInit(e)
    AddHandler Me.Load, AddressOf PhilePage_Load
    AddHandler Me.Error, AddressOf PhilePage_Error

End Sub
```

You can see that we've added a new line to the method, which sets up our event handler to be called in the case of a page exception. Now let's take a look at the code that gets launched in response to the error event:

```
Protected Sub PhilePage_Error(ByVal sender As Object, ByVal e As EventArgs)

    Dim currentError As Exception = Server.GetLastError()

    ' Write error to log file if not already done by AppException
    If Not (TypeOf currentError Is AppException) Then
       AppException.LogError(currentError.Message.ToString)
    End If

    ' Show error on screen
    ShowError(currentError)

    ' Clear error so that it does not buble up to Application Level
    Server.ClearError()

End Sub
```

The following line of code:

```
If Not (TypeOf currentError Is AppException) Then
```

tests to see if the currentError variable can be cast to an AppException. In other words, if currentError is of type AppException, or it is a *descendant* of AppException, this condition will evaluate to true. The reason we're making this test is that if the currentError is one of our own custom exceptions, we know that it has already logged its error information into the event log, so we don't need to log it again. On the other hand, if the exception came from somewhere else, for example a class in the SqlClient namespace, we need to log that error so that we have a record of it. We do that by calling the LogError shared method of our AppException class.

This is a good example of the advantages of building reusable classes – we are able to call the AppException.LogError method rather than adding code to actually do the logging here. If we want to change the way that errors are logged, we only have to do so in one place.

After dealing with logging the error, we need to display some sort of error message on the user's screen. You probably noticed in the PhilePage_Error event handler that we did this by calling the ShowError method. Here is that method:

```
Public Shared Sub ShowError(ByVal currentError As Exception)
   Dim context As HttpContext = HttpContext.Current

   context.Response.Write( _
     "<link rel=""stylesheet"" href=""/ThePhileVB/Styles/ThePhile.css"">" & _
     "<h2>Error</h2><hr/>" & _
     "An unexpected error has occurred on this page." & _
```

```
    "The system administrators have been notified.<br/>" & _
   "<br/><b>The error occurred in:</b>" & _
     "<pre>" & context.Request.Url.ToString & "</pre>" & _
   "<br/><b>Error Message:</b>" & _
     "<pre>" & currentError.Message.ToString & "</pre>" & _
   "<br/><b>Error Stack:</b>" & _
     "<pre>" & currentError.ToString & "</pre>")
End Sub
```

We simply output a friendly message and the details of the error.

> **Note – when we launch our site to the public, we would probably want to remove the details of the error from this error message and use the error log to get error details. This is because we may not want to expose information from errors to potentially malicious users. It is good practice to keep the exposure of technical information to a minimum.**

To test and make sure that our custom error trapping is working properly, we first need to build our solution to make sure that the pre-compiled code-behind classes are all up to date, and then we can place some code into our home page that we know is going to cause it to fail. In my case, I placed a line of code in the home page that attempts to open a connection to SQL Server without first having specified the connection string (of course, none of us have ever done this for real, right?). The following is a screenshot of the output I got when attempting to view a page that had this bad code in the `Page_Load` event:

Well, the output is still a little technical, but at least it is now in our control so that if we decide to do something fancier with it at a later date, it is simply a matter of changing a single method in a single class rather than modifying every single web page in our entire application. We're starting to see some of the solid benefits of sub-classing in ASP.NET.

As our needs, and the complexity of the application, expand, we may want to change the way in which we log errors, for example logging specific numeric event IDs for certain types of sub-classed exceptions, as well as sending e-mail to administrators in response to certain (or all) un-trapped exceptions. Many pagers these days can receive e-mail, and this would be a remarkably easy way to instantly notify the on-call administrator or programmer of possible application failures.

Home Page Draft

Now that we have laid down a good, solid foundation for our user interface, or presentation tier, let's put all of that together and build the first iteration of our website's home page (found in /ThePhile/default.aspx and /ThePhile/default.aspx.vb). We do this by adding a web form to our existing web application project (ThePhile). We start with the following lines of code:

```
<%@ Register TagPrefix="WroxUser" TagName="SiteHeader"
          Src="Controls/SiteHeader.ascx" %>
<%@ Register TagPrefix="WroxUser" TagName="SiteFooter"
          Src="Controls/SiteFooter.ascx" %>
<%@ Register TagPrefix="Wrox" Namespace="Wrox.ThePhile.Web.Controls.Server"
          Assembly="Wrox.ThePhile.Web.Controls" %>
```

The three special lines above tell the ASP.NET parser that we're going to be using some controls in our page. The first two elements, which indicate that we're using the TagPrefix of WroxUser, specify two controls using the TagName SiteHeader and SiteFooter respectively. The Src attribute allows us to reference the code in the specified files for the given user controls. Server controls use the Assembly attribute to locate the code. The third line above sets up a TagPrefix for our navigator server control, indicating that it can be found in the namespace Wrox.ThePhile.Web.Controls.Server, in the Assembly (which must be in the website's /bin directory) Wrox.ThePhile.Web.Controls.DLL.

Moving on, we have some fairly standard start-of-page code:

```
<%@ Page language="vb" Codebehind="Default.aspx.vb" AutoEventWireup="false"
        Inherits="Wrox.ThePhile.Web._Default" %>
<!DOCTYPE HTML PUBLIC "-//W3C//DTD HTML 4.0 Transitional//EN" >
<html>
  <head>
    <title>Default</title>
    <meta name="GENERATOR" Content="Microsoft Visual Studio 7.0">
    <meta name="CODE_LANGUAGE" Content="C#">
    <meta name=vs_defaultClientScript content="JavaScript">
    <meta name=vs_targetSchema
          content="http://schemas.microsoft.com/intellisense/ie5">
```

Then, in the next two lines of HTML, we're simply including the two stylesheets that we developed earlier in this chapter; one that is common to all pages throughout the site, and the other that supplies the necessary styles for our navigator:

```
    <link href="Styles/Navigator.css" rel="stylesheet">
    <link href="Styles/ThePhile.css" rel="stylesheet">
  </head>
<body >

    <form id="Default" method="post" runat="server">
```

On this next line we're simply including the `SiteHeader` user control at the very top of our output:

```
<WroxUser:SiteHeader id="Header" runat="server"/>
<br/>
<table width="100%" border="0" cellspacing="4" cellpadding="2">
  <tr>
    <td width="100%" valign="top">
      Greetings,<br/>
         <b>ThePhile.COM</b> is an example website
      written by Wrox authors to illustrate the principles of
      design, specification, and implementation of a content-based
      website in ASP.NET. This website is the example that is built
      progressively in the <a href="http://www.wrox.com">Wrox Press
      </a>book, <i>ASP.NET Website Programming</i>. <br/><br/>

      <table width="100%" border="0" style="border:1px;
            border-color:#000000; border-style:solid;">
        <tr>
          <td>
            Dynamic content will more than likely go here...
          </td>
        </tr>
      </table>

    </td>
    <td align="right">
```

Placed in a table cell aligned to the right of the page, we include our `Navigator` control and indicate the paths (relative URLs) to the source file and the transformation XSLT file:

```
      <Wrox:Navigator id="MenuNav"
                      SourceFile="Config/NavMenu.xml"
                      TransformFile="Transforms/NavMenu.xslt"
                      runat="server"/>
    </td>
  </tr>
</table>

<WroxUser:SiteFooter id="Footer" runat="server"/>

  </form>
 </body>
</html>
```

When ASP.NET has finished processing our page we receive output that looks something like the following web page. There are a couple of other things that we've done to the system that might not be all that obvious. First, we've placed several images in the /ThePhile/Images directory, which will contain all of our graphics. Secondly, you'll need to make sure that /ThePhile is a valid IIS application and that you have verified that it has the proper FrontPage extensions (otherwise Visual Studio .NET won't work with it properly). Also, the Core DLL needs to be built as well as the Controls DLL. If you've been using the solution approach in Visual Studio .NET, then it should automatically copy all necessary assemblies to /ThePhile/bin. If you've been doing it manually, you'll need to copy those assemblies yourself.

You can see in the following screenshot that the SiteHeader, Navigator, and SiteFooter controls have all been seamlessly integrated into the web page, with the end user having no knowledge as to the actual control implementations we're using:

Summary

This chapter began with an introduction to the problem: the need to provide a clear, consistent, solid, and scalable foundation for the presentation tier of our web application. We then worked through the design of this foundation, discussing stylesheets, sub-classing the default page class, creating a navigation control, creating headers and footers, and error handling within ASP.NET. After having read this chapter, you should now be familiar with the following concepts:

❑ Identifying and creating reusable interface components by creating user and server controls

❑ The purpose and implementation of a page inheritance hierarchy, using a base page class to save time and promote consistency

❑ How to dynamically render HTML using data styled with cascading stylesheets

❑ How to use XSLT to transform XML into HTML and other forms of data, and the difference between XSLT and CSS

In the next chapter we'll take the core foundation that we've been building and use it as a platform on which to build our first module, a module that allows for administration and maintenance of the site's files remotely via the web.

Maintaining the Site

Any real website is generally made up of a lot of pages, images, XML/XSL files, stylesheets, databases, and other types of document. It's very common to have many hundreds or even thousands of files for a single website. During development of the site these files will usually be modified several times. This will also continue after deployment, since no application is ever really finished – particularly when we can redeploy to all users in one go. As a result, an integral part of any development work is having some kind of maintenance system.

In this chapter we'll explain why it's useful to have an online site management system, and we'll design and build one that allows us to easily maintain the site's files and directories.

Our solution will provide file uploads over HTTP connections, a useful technique that is not limited to site maintenance. For example, web-based e-mail sites use the method to upload attachments, and many community sites use it to upload images for user profiles.

We will also build an online text editor, so that we can edit our ASPX files right in the web browser.

Our tools will really be for administrators or developers to use. But with a simplified, restricted front-end we could use this technique to build a maintenance system for even the most technically inept client!

The Problem

During the development of our site, we'll need to add, copy, and move files, change the source code of ASP.NET pages, edit the stylesheets, and generally fix things here and there. Since we're working on a test machine, and as we're all familiar with doing such common operations, this does not pose any problems. Managing the SQL Server database is easy as well, because even if we don't have the program installed on our development machine, through the Enterprise Manager we can do everything we could if we had the SQL Server on our local computer.

After development will come the time to upload everything and to test the website online. We'll almost certainly need to make further changes, upload additions, move files around, and perform other file management operations. The same applies to the database: we'll need to add, edit, or delete records, run and edit stored procedures, and backup the data. If we had an in-house server, we wouldn't expect to encounter any problems here, as we would just need to move everything to the production system. Maintaining the site would be as easy as it was on our development machine. Having an in-house server offers maximum control over the system, and this is important when we need to install additional software, register COM+ components, change the IIS default settings, and so on – in fact, whenever we want to configure things according to *our* needs. However, often we do not require all this power, especially for small and medium sized sites. Also, with ASP.NET, deployment and configuration has been made much easier and more flexible (take for example the use of `web.config` to change settings that would previously have required direct access to an IIS snap-in in ASP). Lastly, in-house or dedicated servers are expensive, and not all companies can and/or want to afford them, unless their purpose is very unusual.

Therefore, if we have budget limitations or we simply don't need full control over the system, the common solution for publishing our website is to a rent a shared server from a hosting company. We decided to choose this solution for our website, because we don't really need a deep level of system customization – `web.config` settings are enough for this. Also, we wanted to present an example that would be useful to the majority of readers, and that means using shared hosting.

FTP Versus Online File Management

Now that we've chosen to use a third-party hosting service for our site, we should also consider the additional implications that this choice has on the ease of site maintenance. Uploading files is not a problem – we need nothing more than a simple FTP client to upload, download, rename, and perform most of the other necessary operations on the files. There are lots of them on the market, many available for free. On the other hand, using FTP to update every changed file can be slow and boring, especially when you need to upload the same very large file several times for minor changes, perhaps affecting only a single line of code each time. Sometimes FTP can be slow or even inaccessible when the server is busy (remember that we chose to use a *shared* server) or because the FTP server is temporarily down. Imagine another situation, where you're traveling or visiting a client's place without your laptop: you show the project to your client and are asked to make a quick modification. Something simple; it should take a few seconds, but how do you do it if you don't have your ASP.NET source code available, and if you don't have an FTP program to upload your changes? Often company networks have firewalls or proxies that prevent full FTP access.

Some of these issues might not seem important and you may be thinking that we could just ignore them. Admittedly, these situations are not the rule, but they *do* happen, and having a reserve plan can turn out to be a good precaution. So, what is this reserve plan? It is having a web application that serves as a **file manager** for the web site's files and physical structure (that is, the structure of sub directories). Such a file manager should allow us to do most of the operations that we would normally do through the FTP utility, plus something else that FTP can't provide. That extra something is that, if we have such a tool for our website, we'll be able to explore our files and resources with nothing more than a web browser and an Internet connection. We'll also be able to edit text files (source code) from the web browser itself, so small changes can be made instantly without a download and subsequent upload.

In short, a file manager tool is pretty handy for site maintenance in some situations.

Database Management

ThePhile.com is a database-driven website that runs against SQL Server 2000. During development we can use the Enterprise Manager to create tables and stored procedures, add/edit/delete records, and set properties on everything. We could do everything with T-SQL scripts written by hand but, to be honest, the Enterprise Manager is so handy that everyone quickly gets used to it and performs most of the required creation and maintenance operations with its help.

However, when we deploy a website and replicate the database to the remote server, we can't always continue to use Enterprise Manager on the shared server. Some hosting plans do not allow webmasters to use Enterprise Manager, due to security reasons. This implies that we should resort to good old T-SQL to do everything, from simple operations such as adding records, to the creation and modification of tables and stored procedures, or the setting of various database options. Although all of this is possible with T-SQL code, it's not as quick as with Enterprise Manager, not to mention that coding long T-SQL statements is more error-prone. This is especially true for those commands that you never use in Enterprise Manager because you just need to select a checkbox or fill a textbox, and also because you don't see a handy list of all the available tables, columns, stored procedures, and other objects).

So, it seems that there is space for third-party tools here! And, in fact, third-party tools for general (or SQL-specific) database management are not that difficult to find. There are nice tools made up of a set of pages that allow you to see all the database objects, edit many properties, and in general manage the database in such a way that you won't miss the Enterprise Manager quite as much.

The Design

Now that we're aware of the usefulness of having maintenance tools, let's start designing our file manager module by writing down the list of features we want to implement. A typical utility of this type includes the following functionality:

❑ Starting from the web root, the file manager should allow the administrator to see the list of subdirectories and files, and to navigate the structure by clicking a directory name to go one level down, or an arrow at the top of the list to go one level up.

❑   It should display information about each file-system item (file or directory) in our application. This will include a pre-defined icon that describes the item type, size (of all the subdirectories and files if the item is a directory), attributes, creation date, and the date of last modification.

❑   There should be the ability to upload and download files.

❑   It should offer the ability to create, rename, copy, move, and change the attributes of any directories and files.

❑   It should enable us to view and edit the content of text files.

This list includes most of the basic commands that we would expect from any file manager for Windows. We want to reproduce them with a web interface running on a browser, which will allow us to perform common operations without the need for any external tools.

We want this application to respect a couple of basic requirements:

❑   It should be easy to integrate the tool into other existing websites

❑   It should not be possible for an anonymous Internet user to access the file manager; it must have a reliable authentication/authorization system

Let's look at some details to better explain the design choices.

Implementation Design

Most applications are data-driven and have a set of business rules to respect. In this case, as we said in Chapter 2, the first concern for a developer would be to decide how to split the application into several layers: data, business, and user presentation. This application, though, is of a different type – it has no database and the data to be shown is part of the structure of the file system. The components for working with the file system and performing all the required I/O operations are already provided by the huge collection of classes within the .NET Framework, so we don't have to worry about this either. Therefore, what we have to write is only the presentation layer – that is, a set of ASP.NET pages and custom controls.

This is the first *module* we're going to develop for ThePhile.com. By module, we mean a web application that is site-independent, so we should design it in a way that makes it easy to integrate this module with any other site. This is a requirement that all the other modules we'll see in the book should also meet. On the other hand, our designers do want to integrate this module with the rest of the site, so it should have the same color schemes and a similar layout. For this reason we'll make use of the shared stylesheet that we built in Chapter 2 for the entire site, so that if we change the style for an element or a style class, all the pages of our module will automatically change without any further manual intervention. In Chapter 2 we also built header and footer user controls that can be inserted into any page in order to have the same layout without having to manually copy and paste the common HTML code into each page. However, this module does not need the site-wide header and footer controls, since it really is an independent and external tool accessed by administrators only, so we'll avoid using these two shared controls.

The file manager will comprise only two ASP.NET pages: one for navigating the folder structure, uploading, deleting, renaming, copying, and moving files and directories, the other a simple text editor for creating a new file or editing an existing one.

Security Design

Most sites have an administration section that allows us to update a database or perform other operations that normal users are not allowed to do, and they usually also have other parts that are for registered members only. So, securing a website is often a major task that must be taken very seriously during the design phase. ASP.NET offers several types of security, which should be used in different situations. You should already know something about this if you've ever developed for the web with .NET, so let's just review them briefly:

❑ **Windows authentication**: based on IIS authentication and the NTFS file permissions of Windows 2000. After a user is authenticated, they access the protected resources under the context of that account, with its rights and limitations.

❑ **Forms-based authentication**: the user logs in via a custom ASP.NET page and their credentials are validated against the values stored in the web.config file, a database, an XML file, or some other data source.

❑ **Passport authentication**: the user is authenticated by an external web service powered by Microsoft at www.passport.com. This service, born in 1999 but not widely used yet, requires a paid subscription.

Each of these types of authentication is best suited to particular situations. Forms-based authentication allows a great deal of customization, and is best suited when you need to add, remove, and manage an unknown number of users quite frequently, and without touching IIS and Windows settings. This type of authentication will be explained in much more detail in the next chapter, where we'll build a users module for the management of the site's members and the administrators of the other modules that we'll present through the book.

On the other hand, Windows authentication requires the server administrator to set up a group and a number of users from the Computer Management snap-in, and to associate them with the resources to protect. It offers the opportunity to associate different permissions to different users. It is best suited when we're building a system based on an intranet, or when we know in advance the number of users for whom we should create an account. For the file manager module, we have a fixed number of administrators that we want to allow to manage the site's resources, so we can create a few accounts and use Windows authentication. However, with the User Accounts module we build later, you'll see how we could integrate our system with that.

The Solution

Now that we have a clear idea about what we're going to build, we can start creating the project with VS.NET. The files for the presentation layer are part of the main ThePhile project, and sit in the Modules\FileManager folder. Unless otherwise stated, all classes for this module should be part of the Wrox.WebModules.FileManager.Web namespace.

Classes to Work with Files and Directories

In *The Design* section of the chapter we mentioned that the .NET Framework provides quite a lot of classes to easily manipulate and retrieve information about the file system's items. The System.IO namespace contains all the classes that have to do with the IO operations for any backing store, and some classes that allow to do advanced stuff such as monitoring the file system and listening for changes (this was pretty hard to do with the Windows API). Since we'll use some of these classes throughout the chapter, it's worth giving a brief description of the most used IO classes:

Class	Description
Directory	Provides static (shared) methods for enumerating directories and logical drives, creating/deleting/moving directories and files, and retrieving/editing such as the creation date or the last access date.
DirectoryInfo	Used to work with a specified directory and its sub-directories.
File	Like Directory, but provides static methods for working with files: this includes opening or checking the existence of a file, and appending text data to a file.
FileInfo	Used to work with a specific file.
Path	Performs operations such as extracting the root or the file name from the specified path or combining two path strings.
FileSystemWatcher	Monitors the file system and raises events to handle changes.
Stream	Base class used to read from and write a backing store, such as the file system or network.
StreamReader	Used in conjunction with a stream to read characters from a backing store.
StreamWriter	Used in conjunction with a stream to write characters to a backing store.
TextReader	Abstract class used to define methods for reading characters from any source (backing store, string, and so on).
TextWriter	Abstract class used to define methods for writing characters to any source (backing store, string, and so on).
BinaryReader	Used to read primitive types such as string, integer, and Boolean from a stream.
BinaryWriter	Used to write primitive types such as string, integer, and Boolean to a stream.
FileStream	Used to read and write data in the file system.
MemoryStream	Used to read and write data in a memory buffer.

For a more complete listing of the System.IO namespace's classes and their methods, you can refer to *Professional ASP.NET* (Wrox Press ISBN 1-86100-703-5)

Header and Footer Controls

We start our coding with the module-specific controls – in other words the header and the footer. Create a new user control, named Header.ascx, and write the following code in the HTML tab of the IDE:

```
<%@ Control Language="vb" AutoEventWireup="false"
    Codebehind="Header.ascx.vb"
    Inherits="Wrox.WebModules.FileManager.Web.Controls.User.Header"%>
<a name="top">
  <table class="MenuTable" border="0" width="100%">
    <tr>
      <td>
        <b><u>FileManager - Wrox WebModule</u></b>
      </td>
      <td align="right">
        <a href="#bottom">
          <img Alt="Go to the bottom of the page"
               src="./Images/GoDown.gif" border="0" />
        </a>
      </td>
    </tr>
  </table>
```

This is simply HTML code (no need to use ASP.NET controls if we don't need to dynamically program them) that creates a title bar and a hyperlink image. This image links to an anchor placed at the bottom of the page, providing a quick way to scroll the page. Note that we associate the MenuTable style to the HTML table. In Chapter 3 we created a stylesheet, ThePhile.css, and began to define styles for use throughout the site. We have now added several new style definitions that we need for our FileManager module. We won't go into the code here – the modified file is available in code download, and you should refer back to Chapter 3 for an explanation of how cascading styles work. This stylesheet is imported by the page that will use this custom control.

The only modification we need to make in the code-behind is to change the namespace to Wrox.WebModules.FileManager.Web.Controls.User, which follows the conventions we discussed in Chapter 2.

The footer control, similarly, defines a link to jump to the top of the page. It contains an anchor that links from the icon to the header control. Here's the code for Footer.ascx:

```
<%@ Control Language="vb" AutoEventWireup="false"
    Codebehind="Footer.ascx.vb"
    Inherits="Wrox.WebModules.FileManager.Web.Controls.User.Footer"%>
<div align="right" Width="100%">
  <a href="#top">
    <img src="./Images/GoUp.gif"
         Alt="Go to the top of the page" border="0" />
  </a>
</div>
<a name="bottom">
```

Also, modify the namespace in the code-behind for `Footer.ascx` in exactly the same way as we did for the header control. In this particular module the header and footer controls are not really necessary, since we have only two pages, but it's a good practice to build them now, since we might want to add new features and thus other pages in the future.

The File Manager's Main Page

Before starting to write the code for this page, which is quite long, let's see how the page will look like when it is finished. The screenshot below shows the main page of the finished FileManager, while it is browsing the content of the ThePhile web directory:

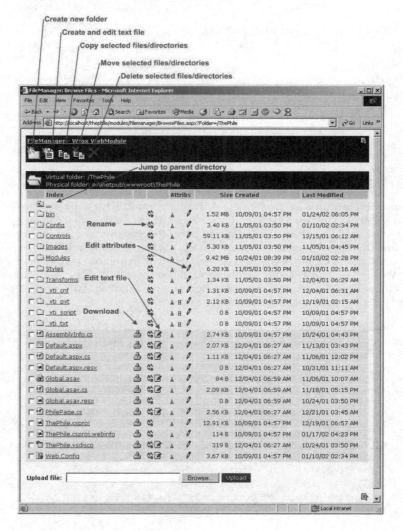

The page lists the directories first and then the files. Clicking the name of an item navigates to that sub-directory or file. For each item the page shows quite a lot of information, aligned in several columns, and some image buttons that allow us to rename the item, edit its attributes, edit a file's content, or download a file. The screenshot describes all the links so you should have no problems understanding how this interface works.

We can now start writing the page that will actually allow the administrator to navigate the site. We'll develop it piece by piece, starting from a simple explorer that just shows the directories and files, and progressively adding more and more information and commands.

First of all, create a new web form called `BrowseFiles.aspx`, and add the following code:

```
<%@ Page language="vb" Codebehind="BrowseFiles.aspx.vb"
    AutoEventWireup="false"
    Inherits="Wrox.WebModules.FileManager.Web.BrowseFiles" %>
<%@ Register TagPrefix="FileManager" TagName="Footer" src="Footer.ascx" %>
<%@ Register TagPrefix="FileManager" TagName="Header" src="Header.ascx" %>
<!DOCTYPE HTML PUBLIC "-//W3C//DTD HTML 4.0 Transitional//EN" >
<html>
  <head>
    <title>FileManager: Browse Files</title>
    <link rel="stylesheet" href="/ThePhile/Styles/ThePhile.css"
        type="text/css">
    <meta name="CODE_LANGUAGE" Content="vb">
  </head>
  <body>
    <form id="BrowseFiles" method="post" runat="server">
      <FileManager:Header ID="Title" runat="server" />
      <br>
      <asp:Table runat="server"
          CssClass="Grid_Header_Thin" Width="100%">
        <asp:TableRow>
          <asp:TableCell Width="36">
            <asp:Image runat="server" Height="32" Width="32"
                ImageUrl="./Images/OpenFolder.gif" />
          </asp:TableCell>
          <asp:TableCell>
            <asp:Label runat="server" ID="FolderDescription"/>
          </asp:TableCell>
        </asp:TableRow>
      </asp:Table>

      <asp:Table ID="FoldersAndFiles" runat="server"
          CssClass="Grid_General" Width="100%">
        <asp:TableRow CssClass="Grid_Header">
          <asp:TableCell Text="Index" />
        </asp:TableRow>
      </asp:Table>

      <br>
      <asp:Label ID="StatusMessage" runat="server"
          CssClass="StatusMessage" Visible="False" Width="100%" />
      <asp:Label ID="FolderStyle" runat="Server"
```

```
            Text="Grid_Item" Visible="false" />
        <asp:Label ID="FileStyle" runat="Server"
            Text="Grid_AlternatingItem" Visible="false" />
    </form>
    <FileManager:Footer ID="Footer" runat="server" />
  </body>
</html>
```

At this point the page does not contain many controls (we'll add others along the way); however, it's worth describing each of them briefly here:

❑ The table at the top of the page has two columns. The first one shows an icon representing an open folder, while the cell on the right has a label that will be set dynamically to show the virtual and physical path of the folder whose content is currently listed on the page.

❑ The second table, named FoldersAndFiles, is the table where we'll actually show the current folder's subdirectories and files. At this point it has just one column for the item name (file or directory). Later in the chapter we'll add more columns for item attributes and command buttons.

❑ The StatusMessage label is used to display text representing errors and exceptions.

❑ The FileStyle and FolderStyle controls are two invisible labels. They are only used to store the name of the style for the rows that will be dynamically created from the code-behind class, to display files or folders respectively. Instead of hard coding such settings in the compiled assembly, we want to leave them in the ASPX page (which can be easily modified without the need to recompile anything) and retrieve them later in the code-behind.

Listing the Contents of a Folder

It's time to write the code that shows the contents of the selected folder in the table. Most of the following code-behind code, BrowseFile.aspx.vb, is auto-generated by VS.NET. The procedure we need to focus on is Page_Load.

The virtual path of the folder to scan is passed along with the page URL, as a parameter called Folder. If not specified, the website root is taken as the default. The procedure gets the parameter value, stores it in a private variable, folderPath, and shows the virtual and physical path in the description table at the top of the page.

A second routine, called FillFoldersAndFilesTable, is then executed, and that is the one that finally scans the folder. Even though at this point the result just shows the folder and file names, with no additional information, the code for FillFoldersAndFilesTable is quite long, so we've left it out for the time being. Here is the remainder of the class:

```
Imports System
Imports System.Collections
Imports System.ComponentModel
Imports System.Data
Imports System.Drawing
Imports System.Web
Imports System.Web.SessionState
Imports System.Web.UI
```

```vbnet
Imports System.Web.UI.WebControls
Imports System.Web.UI.HtmlControls
Imports System.IO

Namespace WebModules.FileManager.Web

  Public Class BrowseFiles
    Inherits System.Web.UI.Page

    Protected TableHeader As Table
    Protected FolderDescription As Label

    Protected FoldersAndFiles As Table
    Protected UploadedFile As HtmlInputFile

    Protected StatusMessage As Label
    Protected FolderStyle As Label
    Protected FileStyle As Label

    Private folderPath As String

    Private Sub Page_Load( _
      ByVal sender As Object, _
      ByVal e As EventArgs) _
      Handles MyBase.Load

      ' Extract from the querystring the path to scan
      folderPath = Request.Params("Folder")

      If folderPath = "" Or folderPath = "/" Then
        folderPath = Request.ApplicationPath.ToString()
      ElseIf folderPath.EndsWith("/") Then
        folderPath = folderPath.Substring(0, folderPath.Length - 1)
      End If

      FolderDescription.Text = _
          "Virtual Folder: " & folderPath & "<br />" & _
          "Physical Folder: " & Server.MapPath(folderPath)

      FillFoldersAndFilesTable()

    End Sub

    Private Sub FillFoldersAndFilesTable()
       'to be added next…
    End Sub

    Private Sub Page_Init( _
      ByVal sender As Object, _
      ByVal e As EventArgs) _
      Handles MyBase.Init
      InitializeComponent()
    End Sub
```

Let's now fill in the code for the `FillFoldersAndFilesTable` procedure, one part at a time. It begins by retrieving the collection of child files and subdirectories for the folder stored in the private `folderPath` variable:

```
Private Sub FillFoldersAndFilesTable()

  ' Declare local variables to hold dir and file information
  Dim location As String
  Dim parentDir As DirectoryInfo
  Dim childDirs As DirectoryInfo()
  Dim childFiles As FileInfo()

  ' Get dir and file information
  Try
    parentDir = New DirectoryInfo(Server.MapPath(folderPath))
    childDirs = parentDir.GetDirectories()
    childFiles = parentDir.GetFiles()
  Catch exc As Exception
    StatusMessage.Text = exc.Message
    StatusMessage.Visible = True
    Return
  End Try
```

The code is protected within a `Try...Catch` block, so in cases where the `folderPath` folder does not exist an error message is shown and the procedure exits gracefully.

Next, the procedure checks whether the current folder is the site root. If it is not, the first row in the table must be a link to the parent folder, whose path is retrieved by removing the part after the last "/" character (remember that we're working with a virtual path here, so we cannot use `Directory.GetParent` as we would do with a physical path):

```
Dim rowItem As TableRow
Dim cellItemLink As TableCell
Dim linkItem As HyperLink

Dim styleFolderRow As Style = New Style()
styleFolderRow.CssClass = FolderStyle.Text

Dim styleFileRow As Style = New Style()
styleFileRow.CssClass = FileStyle.Text

Dim styleLink As Style = New Style()
styleLink.CssClass = "GridLink"

' Add row for parent dir (if not the site root)
If folderPath <> Request.ApplicationPath.ToString() Then
  rowItem = New TableRow()
  cellItemLink = New TableCell()
  linkItem = New HyperLink()

  linkItem.Text = "..."
  Dim lastSlashIndex As Integer = folderPath.LastIndexOf("/")
    location = folderPath.Substring(0, lastSlashIndex)
```

```
         If location.Length = 0 Then
            location = Request.ApplicationPath.ToString()
         End If
     linkItem.ApplyStyle(styleLink)
     cellItemLink.Controls.Add(linkItem)

     ' add the cell to the new row
     rowItem.Cells.Add(New TableCell())

     'add the row to the table
     rowItem.ApplyStyle(styleFolderRow)
     FoldersAndFiles.Rows.Add(rowItem)
   End If
```

Now we cycle through the `childDirs` collection and add the names of all the child directories. The name text links to `BrowseFiles.aspx`, with the `Folder` parameter set to the `folderPath` plus the name of the `childDirs` collection's current folder:

```
     Dim childDir As DirectoryInfo
     For Each childDir In childDirs

        location = folderPath
        If location.EndsWith("/") Then
          location = location & childDir.Name
        Else
          location = location & "/" & childDir.Name
        End If

        ' Define Link and add to link cell
        linkItem = New HyperLink()
        With linkItem
          .Text = childDir.Name
          .NavigateUrl = "BrowseFiles.aspx?Folder=" & location
          .ApplyStyle(styleLink)
        End With

        cellItemLink = New TableCell()
        cellItemLink.Controls.Add(linkItem)

        'add the cell to the new row
        rowItem = New TableRow()
        rowItem.Cells.Add(cellItemLink)

        rowItem.ApplyStyle(styleFolderRow)

        ' Add row to table
        FoldersAndFiles.Rows.Add(rowItem)
     Next
```

Note that, as for the previous piece of code, the dynamically created cell is added to a new row, which is added to the table's `Rows` collection.

The code that cycles through the collection of child files is very similar to the code just shown, except that the link behind the name of each file opens a new window to display the file (letting the web browser select *how* to display it):

```
Dim childFile As FileInfo
Dim extensionIndex As Integer

For Each childFile In childFiles

  location = folderPath
  If location.EndsWith("/") Then
    location = location & childFile.Name
  Else
    location = location & "/" & childFile.Name
  End If

  linkItem = New HyperLink()
  With linkItem
     .Text = childFile.Name
     .NavigateUrl = location
     .ApplyStyle(styleLink)
  End With

  cellItemLink = New TableCell()
  cellItemLink.Controls.Add(linkItem)

  rowItem = New TableRow()
  rowItem.Cells.Add(cellItemLink)

  rowItem.ApplyStyle(styleFileRow)

  ' Add row to table
  FoldersAndFiles.Rows.Add(rowItem)
  Next
End Sub
```

The code that allows the basic navigation functionality is now complete, and we can finally compile the assembly, and run the page. If you set BrowseFiles.aspx as the **Start Page** (right-click on the file in the Solution Explorer and click the respective command) the project is automatically compiled and the page is run when you press *F5*. Otherwise open Internet Explorer and navigate to http://localhost/ThePhile/Modules/FileManager/BrowseFiles.aspx.

The screenshot opposite represents what you should see if you use the file manager to navigate to the ThePhile folder:

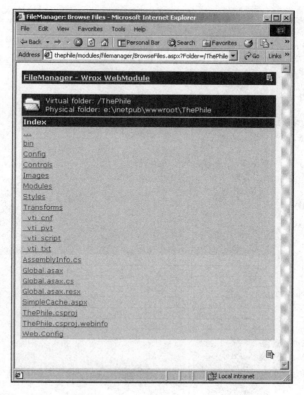

Displaying Additional Attributes

Just displaying the names of the child directories and files is not enough. We want to display much more information: an icon to describe the type of item, the attributes size, the date of creation, and date of last modification. The first thing to do is to create new columns in the `FolderAndFiles` table in `BrowseFiles.aspx`:

```
<asp:Table ID="FoldersAndFiles" runat="server"
    CssClass="Grid_General" Width="100%">
  <asp:TableRow CssClass="Grid_Header">
    <asp:TableCell Width="36px" />
    <asp:TableCell Text="Index" />
    <asp:TableCell Text="Attribs" Width="50px" />
    <asp:TableCell Text="Size" Width="80px" HorizontalAlign="Right" />
    <asp:TableCell Text="Created" Width="140px" />
    <asp:TableCell Text="Last Modified" Width="140px" />
  </asp:TableRow>
</asp:Table>
```

We also need to declare new cells and controls in the `FillFolderAndFilesTable` procedure in the code-behind, `BrowseFiles.aspx.vb`:

```
Dim rowItem As TableRow
Dim cellItemLink As TableCell
Dim linkItem As HyperLink
Dim cellSize As TableCell
Dim cellDownload As TableCell
Dim cellAttributes As TableCell
Dim cellCreated As TableCell
Dim cellLastModified As TableCell
Dim labelAttributes As Label
Dim imageItemIcon As WebControls.Image
```

Now we have to actually create, set, and add these new cells for each directory and file shown in the table. We're going to present the code required for the new columns, one column at a time.

Displaying the Item Icon

Creating the icon for the subdirectories and the link to the parent directory is straightforward, since we use a fixed icon. We just create the Image control named imgItemIcon, set its ImageUrl property, and add it to the first cell. Here's the code for the parent link block, in BrowseFiles.aspx.vb:

```
If folderPath <> Request.ApplicationPath.ToString() Then
   rowItem = New TableRow()
   cellItemLink = New TableCell()
   linkItem = New HyperLink()

   ' Create the cell with the folderup icon
   imageItemIcon = New WebControls.Image()
   imageItemIcon.ImageUrl = "./Images/ParentFolder.gif"

   cellItemIcon = New TableCell()
   cellItemIcon.Controls.Add(imageItemIcon)
   cellItemIcon.HorizontalAlign = HorizontalAlign.Right

   linkItem.Text = "..."
   Dim lastSlashIndex As Integer = folderPath.LastIndexOf("/")
       location = folderPath.Substring(0, lastSlashIndex)
       If location.Length = 0 Then
         location = Request.ApplicationPath.ToString()
       End If
   linkItem.ApplyStyle(styleLink)
   cellItemLink.Controls.Add(linkItem)

   ' Add the cells to the new row
   rowItem = New TableRow()
   With rowItem.Cells
     .Add(cellItemIcon)
     .Add(cellItemLink)
   End With

   'add the row to the table
   rowItem.ApplyStyle(styleFolderRow)
   FoldersAndFiles.Rows.Add(rowItem)
End If
```

The code for each child directory is very similar:

```
Dim childDir As DirectoryInfo
For Each childDir In childDirs

  location = folderPath
  If location.EndsWith("/") Then
    location = location & childDir.Name
  Else
    location = location & "/" & childDir.Name
  End If

  imageItemIcon = New WebControls.Image()
  imageItemIcon.ImageUrl = "./Images/ClosedFolder.gif"
  cellItemIcon = New TableCell()
  cellItemIcon.Controls.Add(checkItem)
  cellItemIcon.Controls.Add(imageItemIcon)
  cellItemIcon.HorizontalAlign = HorizontalAlign.Right

  ' Define Link and add to link cell
  linkItem = New HyperLink()
  With linkItem
    .Text = childDir.Name
    .NavigateUrl = "BrowseFiles.aspx?Folder=" & location
    .ApplyStyle(styleLink)
  End With

  cellItemLink = New TableCell()
  cellItemLink.Controls.Add(linkItem)

  rowItem = New TableRow()
  With rowItem.Cells
    .Add(cellItemIcon)
    .Add(cellItemLink)
  End With

  rowItem.ApplyStyle(styleFolderRow)

  ' Add row to table
  FoldersAndFiles.Rows.Add(rowItem)
Next
```

So far, so good. Now here's the more interesting part – adding an icon for each file. If we only wanted to differentiate files from folders, we could just associate a fixed icon for all the files (different from the one used for the folders). But we want to do something more. We want to display the icon that is usually shown in Windows Explorer to describe the file *type*. In Windows each file extension is identified by an icon, which is provided by the associated program. This icon is usually stored within a binary EXE or DLL file, and its index is stored in the registry. There are API functions to programmatically retrieve the icon index within a file, and then show the icon through the Windows ListView control, based on the icon's handle.

This is very tricky in ASP.NET, since the src attribute of an <img> tag should point directly to an image file.

It is possible to extract the icon associated with the file extension from a binary file, save it to disk, and show it with the `<img>` tag, or even directly send a binary stream to the browser. However, this would require a lot of work, would slow down the execution, and would not bring about any valuable improvements to the application, so we decided not to cover this method here.

We will create a predefined set of fixed images for the most common files used for a website. These images will be assigned to the files based on their extension. If we name such images according to the file extensions (for example, `aspx.gif`, `html.gif`, `ascx.gif`, `zip.gif`, `bmp.gif`, `gif.gif`, etc.) we'll just need to check if there is an image with a name corresponding to the file extension, and if so show it. If there is no image with that name, we'll show a predefined image, `unknown.gif`. The file icons for many extensions are in the code download, but of course you can add your own.

To speed up the test that verifies the existence of a certain icon, we define an array of extensions for which we've created the appropriate image, and the check is done against this array. Here's how the array is defined, as a private variable for the `BrowseFiles` class:

```
Private extensions() As String = { _
    ".arj", ".asa", ".asax", ".ascx", ".asmx", ".asp", ".aspx", ".au", _
    ".avi", ".bat", ".bmp", ".cab", ".chm", ".com", ".config", ".cs", _
    ".css", ".disco", ".dll", ".doc", ".exe", ".gif", ".hlp", ".htm", _
    ".html", ".jpg", ".inc", ".ini", ".log", ".mdb", ".mid", ".midi", _
    ".mov", ".mp3", ".mpg", ".mpeg", ".pdf", ".ppt", ".sys", ".txt", _
    ".tif", ".vb", ".vbs", ".vsdisco", ".wav", ".wri", ".xls", ".xml", _
    ".zip"}
```

You can add any others appropriate to your site's requirements.

Thanks to the `Array.IndexOf` shared method (which returns the index of the element being searched for in the array), checking whether the extension of a file is present within the `extensions` array is a matter of a single line of code. Here is the updated block that adds all the child files to the table:

```
For Each childFile In childFiles

    location = folderPath
    If location.EndsWith("/") Then
      location = location & childFile.Name
    Else
      location = location & "/" & childFile.Name
    End If

        extensionIndex = Array.IndexOf(extensions, _
          childFile.Extension.ToLower())
        imageItemIcon = New WebControls.Image()
        If extensionIndex > -1 Then
          imageItemIcon.ImageUrl = "./Images/" & _
            childFile.Extension.Substring(1) + ".gif"
        Else
          imageItemIcon.ImageUrl = "./Images/unknown.gif"
        End If

        cellItemIcon = New TableCell()
        cellItemIcon.Controls.Add(checkItem)
```

```
            cellItemIcon.Controls.Add(imageItemIcon)
            cellItemIcon.HorizontalAlign = HorizontalAlign.Right

        linkItem = New HyperLink()
        With linkItem
          .Text = childFile.Name
          .NavigateUrl = location
          .ApplyStyle(styleLink)
        End With

        cellItemLink = New TableCell()
        cellItemLink.Controls.Add(linkItem)

        rowItem = New TableRow()
        rowItem.Cells.Add(cellItemLink)

        rowItem.ApplyStyle(styleFileRow)

        ' Add cells to row
        rowItem = New TableRow()
        With rowItem.Cells
          .Add(cellItemIcon)
          .Add(cellItemLink)
    Next
```

Displaying the Item Attributes

Let's go ahead with the creation of the third column, the one that displays a list of attributes for the sub-directories and files. The modifications for the block that adds the directories and the block that adds the files are exactly the same. For the first row, which points to the parent directory (if any), we just add an empty cell. This is shown in the following code:

```
    If folderPath <> Request.ApplicationPath.ToString() Then

        'Code to create icon and link not included here (see earlier)

        ' Add the cells to the new row
        rowItem = New TableRow()
        With rowItem.Cells
          .Add(cellItemIcon)
          .Add(cellItemLink)
          .Add(New TableCell())
        End With

        'add the row to the table
        rowItem.ApplyStyle(styleFolderRow)
        FoldersAndFiles.Rows.Add(rowItem)
    End If

Dim childDir As DirectoryInfo
    For Each childDir In childDirs

        ' Create the link that points to this sub-directory
        ' Code not included here
```

```
        'Create icon
         'Code not included here


    ' Define Link and add to link cell
    'Code not included here

    ' Define attributes and add to attributes cell
    labelAttributes = New Label()
    labelAttributes.Text = GetAttributesDescription(childDir.Attributes)
    labelAttributes.Font.Name = "Courier"

    cellAttributes = New TableCell()
    cellAttributes.Controls.Add(labelAttributes)
    cellAttributes.Controls.Add(linkSetAttributes)

    ' Add cells to row
    rowItem = New TableRow()
    With rowItem.Cells
      .Add(cellItemIcon)
      .Add(cellItemLink)
      .Add(cellAttributes)
    End With
    rowItem.ApplyStyle(styleFolderRow)

    ' Add row to table
    FoldersAndFiles.Rows.Add(rowItem)

  Next
```

If you look back at this code, you'll see that the font of the label displaying the attribute description is set to Courier. This is because Courier is a fixed-width font, meaning that, for example, 'i' and 'z' have the same width. Another reason for using Courier is that spaces have the same width as letters, and this allows us to create virtual columns and have all the A letters in the column aligned, and the same for the letters R, H, and S. If an attribute is not set for an item, you see a blank space as large as the letter above it, and then the other attribute letters (if any).

You may also wonder why we created a Label control instead of directly setting the cell's Text property. The reason is that we'll add another control to this column later in the chapter, and it's easier to add two controls to the Controls collection than to set a very long string for the cell's Text property.

As you can see, the string that describes the item's attributes is not built directly in the code above, but is returned by a custom procedure called GetAttributesDescriptions, which receives as input the value of the Attributes property, exposed by both the DirectoryInfo and FileInfo data type. Here is its code:

```
Protected Function GetAttributesDescription( _
   ByVal attributes As FileAttributes) As String

   Dim itemAttributes As String = ""
```

```
' Check if the 'Archive' attribute is set
If ((attributes And FileAttributes.Archive) = _
  FileAttributes.Archive) Then
  itemAttributes = itemAttributes & "A"
Else
  itemAttributes = itemAttributes & " "
End If

' Check if the 'ReadOnly' attribute is set
If ((attributes And FileAttributes.ReadOnly) = _
  FileAttributes.ReadOnly) Then
  itemAttributes = itemAttributes & "R"
Else
  itemAttributes = itemAttributes & " "
End If

' Check if the 'Hidden' attribute is set
If ((attributes And FileAttributes.Hidden) = _
  FileAttributes.Hidden) Then
  itemAttributes = itemAttributes & "H"
Else
  itemAttributes = itemAttributes & " "
End If

' Check if the 'System' attribute is set
If ((attributes And FileAttributes.System) = _
  FileAttributes.System) Then
  itemAttributes = itemAttributes & "S"
Else
  itemAttributes = itemAttributes & " "
End If

Return itemAttributes

End Function
```

This procedure checks four attributes: Archive, ReadOnly, Hidden, and System. If the attribute being checked is set, the procedure adds its first letter to the description string that will be returned. Otherwise, if the attribute is not set, a space is added. So, for example, the string "A S" means Archive + System, while "ARH " means Archive + ReadOnly + Hidden.

Displaying the Item Size

The next column we want to add displays the size of the item. It is easy to get this information for the files, since the FileInfo class exposes a Length property. As the DirectoryInfo class does not have a Length property, we need to calculate the size of a directory by summing the size of all its child files. Here is a procedure that uses recursion to sum the child files of all subdirectories and obtain the overall size of the directory:

```
Protected Function GetDirectorySize(ByVal thePath As String) As Long

  Dim dirSize As Long
  Dim dir As DirectoryInfo = New DirectoryInfo(thePath)
```

```
    ' Add the size of each file
    Dim theFile As FileInfo
    For Each theFile In dir.GetFiles()

        dirSize = dirSize + theFile.Length

        ' Add the size of each subdirectory, retrieved by
        ' recursively calling this same function
        Dim subDir As DirectoryInfo
        For Each subDir In dir.GetDirectories
            dirSize = dirSize + GetDirectorySize(subDir.FullName)
        Next

    Next

    Return dirSize

End Function
```

Now we can easily get the size for both the files and the directories. But the size is returned in bytes, and a series of six or seven figures is not very readable. It would be better to show the size in bytes, Kilobytes, or Megabytes according to the number of bytes, as follows:

❏ Less than 1,024 bytes: show the size in bytes

❏ Between 1,024 and 1,048,576 bytes: show the size in KB (for example 2.52 KB, instead of 2,580 bytes)

❏ 1,048,576 bytes and above: show the size in MB

The following procedure accepts the size in `double` format, and returns a string with the size formatted in bytes, KB, or MB by following the rules above:

```
Protected Function FormatSize(ByVal fileSize As Double) As String

    If fileSize < 1024 Then
        Return String.Format("{0:N0} B", fileSize)
    ElseIf (fileSize < 1024 * 1024) Then
        Return String.Format("{0:N2} KB", fileSize / 1024)
    Else
        Return String.Format("{0:N2} MB", fileSize / (1024 * 1024))
    End If

End Function
```

Now that we can get the size for a directory, and format any size in the proper way, let's add the **Size** column for each item. As we've done for the **Attributes** column, we're going to insert an empty cell for the first row, which links to the parent folder, and a new cell with the size for all files and folders. Here are the necessary updates:

```
If folderPath <> Request.ApplicationPath.ToString() Then

    ' Create the cell with the folderup icon
    ' Code Not included here

    ' Add the link that points to the parent directory
    ' Code Not included here
```

```
        ' Add the cells to the new row
        rowItem = New TableRow()
        With rowItem.Cells
          .Add(cellItemIcon)
          .Add(cellItemLink)
          .Add(New TableCell())
          .Add(New TableCell())
                    End With

        ' Add the row to the table
        FoldersAndFiles.Rows.Add(rowItem)

    End If


    ' Add rows for directories
    '----------------------------------------------------------------
    Dim childDir As DirectoryInfo
    For Each childDir In childDirs

        ' Create the link that points to this sub-directory
        ' Code not included here

        ' Define Link and add to link cell
        ' Code not included here

        ' Define attributes and add to attributes cell
        ' Code not included here


        ' Define size cell
        cellSize = New TableCell()
        cellSize.Text = _
          FormatSize(GetDirectorySize(childDir.FullName)) & " "
        cellSize.HorizontalAlign = HorizontalAlign.Right

        ' Add cells to row
        rowItem = New TableRow()
        With rowItem.Cells
          .Add(cellItemIcon)
          .Add(cellItemLink)
          .Add(cellAttributes)
          .Add(cellSize)
        End With

        rowItem.ApplyStyle(styleFolderRow)

        ' Add row to table
        FoldersAndFiles.Rows.Add(rowItem)

    Next
```

```
' Add rows for files
'----------------------------------------------------------------
Dim childFile As FileInfo
Dim extensionIndex As Integer
For Each childFile In childFiles

    ' Find current directory location
    ' Code not included here


    ' Define check box and image icon (based on extension of the file)
    '  and add to ItemIcon cell
    ' Code not included here

    ' Define Link and add to link cell
    ' Code not included here

    ' Define size
    cellSize = New TableCell()
    cellSize.Text = FormatSize(childFile.Length) & " "
    cellSize.HorizontalAlign = HorizontalAlign.Right


    ' Add cells to row
    rowItem = New TableRow()
    With rowItem.Cells
        .Add(cellItemIcon)
        .Add(cellItemLink)
        .Add(cellAttributes)
        .Add(cellSize)
    End With
    rowItem.ApplyStyle(styleFileRow)

    ' Add row to table
    FoldersAndFiles.Rows.Add(rowItem)

Next
```

Displaying the Creation and Last Modification Dates

The last two columns we want to fill are the Created and Last Modified columns. We're lucky here as
there's almost nothing to do, since this information is returned by the `CreationTime` and
`LastWriteTime` properties exposed by the `DirectoryInfo` and `FileInfo` classes.

Here's the code to add:

```
If folderPath <> Request.ApplicationPath.ToString() Then

        ' Create the cell with the folderup icon
        ' Code not included here - see earlier


        ' Add the link that points to the parent directory
        ' Code not included here - see earlier
```

```vb
      ' Add the cells to the new row
      rowItem = New TableRow()
      With rowItem.Cells
        .Add(cellItemIcon)
        .Add(cellItemLink)
        .Add(New TableCell())
        .Add(New TableCell())
        .Add(New TableCell())
      End With
      rowItem.ApplyStyle(styleFolderRow)

      ' Add the row to the table
      FoldersAndFiles.Rows.Add(rowItem)

    End If


    ' Add rows for directories
    '-------------------------------------------------------------------
    Dim childDir As DirectoryInfo
    For Each childDir In childDirs

      ' Create the link that points to this sub-directory
      ' Code not included here - see earlier

      ' Define Link and add to link cell
      ' Code not included here - see earlier

      ' Define attributes and add to attributes cell
      ' Code not included here - see earlier

      ' Define size cell
      ' Code not included here - see earlier

      ' Define created and last modified cells
      cellCreated = New TableCell()
      cellCreated.Text = " " & _
        String.Format("{0:MM/dd/yy hh:mm tt}", childDir.CreationTime)

      cellLastModified = New TableCell()
      cellLastModified.Text = " " & _
        String.Format("{0:MM/dd/yy hh:mm tt}", childDir.LastWriteTime)


      ' Add cells to row
      rowItem = New TableRow()
      With rowItem.Cells
        .Add(cellItemIcon)
        .Add(cellItemLink)
        .Add(cellAttributes)
        .Add(cellSize)
        .Add(cellCreated)
        .Add(cellLastModified)
      End With
```

```
        rowItem.ApplyStyle(styleFolderRow)

        ' Add row to table
        FoldersAndFiles.Rows.Add(rowItem)

    Next


    ' Add rows for files
    '------------------------------------------------------------------
    Dim childFile As FileInfo
    Dim extensionIndex As Integer
    For Each childFile In childFiles

        ' Find current directory location
        ' Code not included here - see earlier


        ' Define check box and image icon (based on extension of the file)
        '  and add to ItemIcon cell
        ' Code not included here - see earlier


        ' Define Link and add to link cell
        ' Code not included here - see earlier

        'Define attributes and add to attributes cell
        ' Code not included here - see earlier


        ' Define size
        ' Code not included here - see earlier


        ' Define created and last modified cells
        cellCreated = New TableCell()
        cellCreated.Text = " " & _
           String.Format("{0:MM/dd/yy hh:mm tt}", childFile.CreationTime)

        cellLastModified = New TableCell()
        cellLastModified.Text = " " & _
           String.Format("{0:MM/dd/yy hh:mm tt}", childFile.LastWriteTime)


        ' Add cells to row
        rowItem = New TableRow()
        With rowItem.Cells
           .Add(cellItemIcon)
           .Add(cellItemLink)
           .Add(cellAttributes)
           .Add(cellSize)
           .Add(cellCreated)
           .Add(cellLastModified)
```

```
        End With
        rowItem.ApplyStyle(styleFileRow)

        ' Add row to table
        FoldersAndFiles.Rows.Add(rowItem)

    Next
```

We're finally done with the code for displaying the information about items! If you now recompile the assembly, and refresh the page in the browser, you should see something similar to the screenshot below:

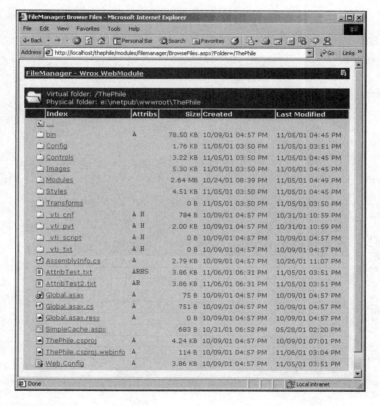

Downloading Files

When you click on an item's link, the file manager opens a new browser window and redirects to that file. If the file is an image or HTML file then you'll see it loaded and displayed by the browser. Instead, if it is a file that the browser is not able to open, such as a ZIP file, it will ask you if you want to download it. However, there are other file types that the browser will neither load nor allow you to download. For example, with `web.config` or `global.asax` you'll get an error page containing the message "This type of page is not served". Other files, particularly ASPX files, are processed on the server – so you'll see the result of the processing, not the source code.

We need to find a way to download a file or view its content without resorting to FTP. We can solve this with streams.

> **Using Streams, we can provide a file to the user 'as is' – without the interference of IIS.**

We need a separate ASPX file, called `download.aspx`. This takes a filename as a parameter, and returns the content of that file – unprocessed by the Web server. The ASPX file has no user interface – everything is done in the code-behind. Here's the code for `download.aspx.vb` `Page_Load` method:

```
Private Sub Page_Load( _
  ByVal sender As Object, _
  ByVal e As EventArgs) _
  Handles MyBase.Load

  ' Retrieve the path of the file to download, and create a
  ' FileInfo object to read its properties
  Dim thePath As String = Server.MapPath(Request.Params("File"))
  Dim theFile As System.IO.FileInfo = New System.IO.FileInfo(thePath)

  ' Clear the current output content from the buffer
  Response.Clear()

  ' Add the header that specifies the default filename
  ' for the Download/SaveAs dialog
  Response.AddHeader("Content-Disposition", "attachment filename=" _
    & theFile.Name)

  ' Add the header that specifies the file size, so that the
  ' browser can show the download progress
  Response.AddHeader("Content-Length", theFile.Length.ToString())

  ' Specify that the response is a stream that cannot be read _
  ' by the client and must be downloaded
  Response.ContentType = "application/octet-stream"

  ' Send the file stream to the client
  Response.WriteFile(theFile.FullName)

  ' Stop the execution of this page
  Response.End()

End Sub
```

We now need to add a download button to our `BrowseFiles.aspx` table. The button needs to point to `Download.aspx` with the appropriate parameter:

In the `BrowseFiles.aspx` file we need to add a new column to the `FoldersAndFiles` table:

```
<asp:Table ID="FoldersAndFiles" runat="server"
  CssClass="Grid_General" Width="100%">
  <asp:TableRow CssClass="Grid_Header">
    <asp:TableCell Width="36px" />
```

```
        <asp:TableCell Text="Index" />
        <asp:TableCell Width="25px" />
        <asp:TableCell Text="Attribs" Width="50px" />
        <asp:TableCell Text="Size" Width="80px" HorizontalAlign="Right" />
        <asp:TableCell Text="Created" Width="140px" />
        <asp:TableCell Text="Last Modified" Width="140px" />
    </asp:TableRow>
</asp:Table>
```

In `FillFoldersAndFilesTable` in the code-behind we have to create and add an empty cell for the first row, which points to the parent folder, as we did for other columns that are not appropriate for the parent folder. We are not going to repeat that code here.

We also have to add an empty cell to the rows for folders:

```
        rowItem = New TableRow()
        With rowItem.Cells
          .Add(cellItemIcon)
          .Add(cellItemLink)
          .Add(New TableCell()) ' No download link for folder
          .Add(cellAttributes)
          .Add(cellSize)
          .Add(cellCreated)
          .Add(cellLastModified)
        End With
```

For the file rows we create a new cell and an image that links to `Download.aspx`, with the appropriate parameter:

```
Dim childFile As FileInfo
        Dim extensionIndex As Integer
        For Each childFile In childFiles

            ' Find current directory location
            ' Code not included here - see earlier


            ' Define check box and image icon (based on extension of the file)
            ' Code not included here - see earlier


            ' Define Link and add to link cell
            ' Code not included here - see earlier


            ' Define download link and add to download cell
            linkDownload = New HyperLink()
            linkDownload.Text = "<img src=""./Images/Download.gif"" " & _
              "border=""0"" height=""16"" width=""16"" Alt=""Download"">"
            linkDownload.NavigateUrl = "Download.aspx?File=" & location

            cellDownload = New TableCell()
            cellDownload.Controls.Add(linkDownload)
```

```
            'Define attributes and add to attributes cell
            ' Code not included here - see earlier


            ' Define size
            ' Code not included here - see earlier


            ' Define created and last modified cells
            ' Code not included here - see earlier
            ' Add cells to row
            rowItem = New TableRow()
            With rowItem.Cells
              .Add(cellItemIcon)
              .Add(cellItemLink)
              .Add(cellDownload)
              .Add(cellAttributes)
              .Add(cellSize)
              .Add(cellCreated)
              .Add(cellLastModified)
            End With
            rowItem.ApplyStyle(styleFileRow)

            ' Add row to table
            FoldersAndFiles.Rows.Add(rowItem)

        Next
```

Now when we click the download icon, the source file will be downloaded – regardless of the file type.

Uploading Files

In addition to downloading files, we also want to *upload* files. Although we would certainly use FTP if we had to upload lots of files, this tool can be quite handy if you just need to upload a couple of files or if FTP is not available.

To select the file to upload we can use the standard HTML input control of type `file`. This comprises a textbox and a **Browse** button, which when pressed opens the **Choose File** dialog that allows the user to select a file. This control can be used and accessed in ASP.NET by adding the `runat="server"` attribute.

> In order to accept the submitted file, the form must be declared with the attribute `enctype="multipart/form-data"`.

Let's update our `BrowseFiles.aspx` page by adding this control and a button to submit the file:

```
<form id="BrowseFiles" method="post" runat="server"
    enctype="multipart/form-data">
<!-- other controls as above here -->
...
<asp:Table ID="FoldersAndFiles" runat="server" CssClass="Grid_General"
    Width="100%">
```

```
    <asp:TableRow CssClass="Grid_Header">
      <asp:TableCell Width="36px" />
      <asp:TableCell Text="Index" />
      <asp:TableCell Width="25px" />
      <asp:TableCell Text="Attribs" Width="50px" />
      <asp:TableCell Text="Size" Width="80px" HorizontalAlign="Right" />
      <asp:TableCell Text="Created" Width="140px" />
      <asp:TableCell Text="Last Modified" Width="140px" />
    </asp:TableRow>
  </asp:Table>
  <br>
  <asp:Table runat="server">
    <asp:TableRow>
      <asp:TableCell Width="80px" Font-Bold="True" Text="Upload file:" />
      <asp:TableCell>
        <input type="file" ID="UploadedFile" runat="server" size="35">
      </asp:TableCell>
      <asp:TableCell>
        <asp:Button ID="Upload" runat="server" Text="Upload"
            CssClass="Button" OnClick="Upload_Click" />
      </asp:TableCell>
    </asp:TableRow>
  </asp:Table>
  <!-- other controls as above here -->
  ...
  </form>
```

If we now save the file, VS.NET should add the following declaration to the code-behind:

```
Public Class BrowseFiles
    Inherits System.Web.UI.Page
    Protected UploadedFile As HtmlInputFile
```

The following code is for the Upload_Click event handler, which uploads the selected file to the current directory, but only if a file has been selected:

```
Protected Sub Upload_Click(ByVal sender As Object, ByVal e As EventArgs)

    ' Process only if a file has been specified
    If (Not UploadedFile.PostedFile Is Nothing) _
      And (UploadedFile.PostedFile.FileName.Length > 0) Then

      Dim destDir As String = Server.MapPath(folderPath)

      Try

        ' Save to the current directory
        Dim fileName As String = _
          Path.GetFileName(UploadedFile.PostedFile.FileName)
        UploadedFile.PostedFile.SaveAs(Path.Combine(destDir, fileName))

        ' Refresh the page
        Response.Redirect("BrowseFiles.aspx?Folder=" & folderPath)

      Catch exc As Exception
```

103

```
          StatusMessage.Text = exc.Message
          StatusMessage.Visible = True

      End Try

    End If

  End Sub
```

The code is straightforward, but you should note one point: after the file is uploaded to the server, we refresh the table by reloading the entire page. This is necessary because in Page_Load the table was filled, so if we called FillFoldersAndFilesTable again here we would get all the rows twice. Since the redirection is done on the server before any HTML code is sent to the client browser, this does not cause much overhead.

Also note that the code that uploads the file is protected by a Try...Catch block. If an exception occurs, for example because the current user does not have permission to write on this directory, an error message is shown in the StatusMessage label.

> Note that by default the maximum size of the uploaded file is 4MB. If you try to upload a bigger size you'll get an error page. You may want to increase this value, for example because you have ZIP, AVI, or MP3 files bigger than 4MB. To do so, set the maxRequestLength attribute of the <httpRuntime> setting in the ThePhile's web.config file. The size is specified in KB, so <httpRuntime maxRequestLength="8192" /> sets the maximum file size to 8MB.

It's time to recompile everything and jump to the browser to test the updated file manager. In the screenshot overleaf you can see both the new icons added to the files to download or open them, as well as the file input control and the **Choose** file dialog:

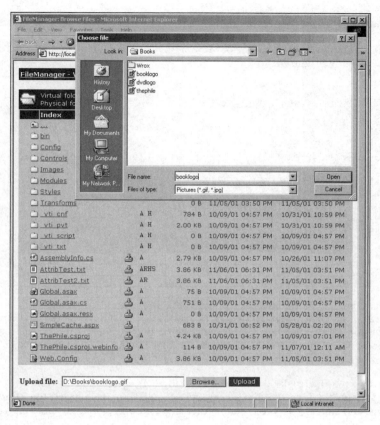

Creating Directories

So far we've seen the features of a typical file explorer (with the addition of a file uploader), but since we're building a file manager, we should also add functionality that will allow us to *change* the content and the structure of the site. We're going to implement many features in this category of commands; the first we'll see is the command to create a new directory.

Our designers want to create a toolbar with a link that, when pressed, pops up a dialog and asks for the name of the directory to create. As you might guess, this is not done by ASP.NET code, but rather by client-side JavaScript code, through the `prompt` function. If the user presses Cancel, nothing happens, but if the user types the name of the folder they want to create and presses OK, we have to pass this parameter back to the ASP.NET page that will actually create the directory and refresh the table.

The first thought might be to redirect to the current page and add the folder to create as a parameter in the URL. But ASP.NET is great because of its event procedures that handle the postbacks generated by specific controls, so why not use this cool feature? To do so, we need to have a clear understanding about the way the form is posted back when a button or a hyperlink control is pressed.

To demonstrate this we created a test page, which is not part of the final application. In it we placed a `HyperLink` control, as follows:

```
<asp:LinkButton ID="test" runat="server" Text="Demo" OnClick="Test_Click" />
```

Next, we wrote an empty `Test_Click` procedure in the code-behind, compiled, and then ran the page. This is the HTML code produced:

```
...
<a id="Test" href="javascript:__doPostBack('Test','')">Demo</a>
...
<input type="hidden" name="__EVENTTARGET" value="" />
<input type="hidden" name="__EVENTARGUMENT" value="" />
<script language="javascript">
<!--
    function __doPostBack(eventTarget, eventArgument) {
      var theform = document.BrowseFiles;
      theform.__EVENTTARGET.value = eventTarget;
      theform.__EVENTARGUMENT.value = eventArgument;
      theform.submit();
    }
// -->
</script>
...
```

As you can see, there is nothing magic here. When the link is pressed, instead of redirecting to another page, the __doPostBack JavaScript function is called. The first parameter that the function requires is the name of the control that is going to post back the form and generate the event on the server. The second parameter may contain additional information for the event, but it is empty in this case, and in fact the `Click` event has no additional information in the standard e parameter.

What the __doPostBack actually does is to set two hidden input controls, with the values passed in the input. Then it submits the form. On the server, the ASP.NET engine extracts the values of those two hidden controls, and calls the server event handler. Again, nothing magic – but very cool!

In conclusion, all the server controls do to post back the form is to call the __doPostBack function, but we can also do this by writing the HTML code by hand.

Back to our original problem: we can create a link that, when clicked, calls a JavaScript function. This function pops up the prompt dialog asking for a name. If the user presses OK, the function can save the specified folder name in a hidden field, and call the __doPostBack function to post back the form. All done then? Almost. Remember that the first parameter of the function is the name of the server control whose `Click` event (in this case, it might be a different event for other controls) will be raised. This control must actually exist on the page, but we can avoid setting its `Text` property and so make it invisible, and we add it just to use its associated `Click` event.

Let's look at the code in the ASP.NET page, `BrowseFiles.aspx`, to better explain how to do this. The code contains the JavaScript that asks for the new directory, the LinkButton, and the hidden control declaration:

```
...
<html>
  <head>
    <title>FileManager: Browse Files</title>
    <link rel="stylesheet" HREF="/ThePhile/Styles/ThePhile.css"
        TYPE="text/css" />
    <meta name="CODE_LANGUAGE" Content="VB">
```

```
    <script language="javascript">
      function CreateDir()
      {
        dirName = prompt('Type the name of the directory you want to
            create:','');

        if ((dirName) && (dirName!=""))
        {
          document.forms['BrowseFiles'].elements['funcParam'].value =
                                                          dirName;
          __doPostBack('CreateDir', '');
        }
      }
    </script>
  </head>
  <body>
    <form id="BrowseFiles" method="post" runat="server"
        enctype="multipart/form-data">
      <FileManager:Header ID="Title" runat="server" />
      <input type="hidden" id="funcParam" runat="server">
      <table class="MenuTable" border="0" width="100%">
        <tr>
          <td>
            <a href="javascript:CreateDir();">
              <img border="0" src="./Images/NewFolder.gif"
                  Alt="Create a new directory" height="28" width="28" />
            </a>
            <asp:LinkButton ID="CreateDir" runat="server"
                OnClick="CreateDir_Click" />
          </td>
        </tr>
      </table>
      <br>
      <asp:Table runat="server" CssClass="Grid_Header_Thin"
          Width="100%" ID="Table1">
        <asp:TableRow>
          <asp:TableCell Width="36">
            <asp:Image runat="server" Height="32"
                Width="32" ImageUrl="./Images/OpenFolder.gif" />
          </asp:TableCell>
```

The rest is unchanged.

You might be wondering why we completely avoided setting the **Text** property instead of simply setting its **Visible** property to **False**. The reason is that we need at least one control recognized by ASP.NET as a control that generates postbacks through a call to **__doPostBack**. Otherwise ASP.NET detects that there is no need for the **__doPostBack** function and does not include it in the generated HTML code for the client, which would cause an error when our **CreateDir** function calls it. A control with the **Visible="False"** attribute is not created in the HTML, and so neither is **__doPostBack**. Therefore, we need to declare the control, leaving out the **Text** property, so that the JavaScript function is created. Once we have this control, the other similar **LinkButton** controls we'll use later can be made invisible by the **Visible="False"** attribute.

In the code-behind we first declare the hidden control used to store the new folder name:

```
Protected funcParam As HtmlInputHidden
```

Then we have the `Click` event handler for the `CreateDir ButtonLink`:

```
Protected Sub CreateDir_Click( _
  ByVal sender As Object, _
  ByVal e As EventArgs)

  ' Build the complete path (current path + new dir name)
  Dim thePath As String = folderPath
  If thePath.EndsWith("/") Then
    thePath = thePath & funcParam.Value
  Else
    thePath = thePath & "/" & funcParam.Value
  End If

  Try

    ' Create the directory
    Directory.CreateDirectory(Server.MapPath(thePath))

    ' Refresh Page
    Response.Redirect("BrowseFiles.aspx?Folder=" & folderPath)

  Catch exc As Exception

    StatusMessage.Text = exc.Message
    StatusMessage.Visible = True

  End Try

End Sub
```

As usual, the possible exception is handled and an error message is shown. If the new directory is created successfully, the page is refreshed and the table re-filled with the updated content.

In this example we've taken advantage of both the client-side script and the ASP.NET event handling mechanism. The following screenshot shows the updated file manager and its dialog to enter the new directory name:

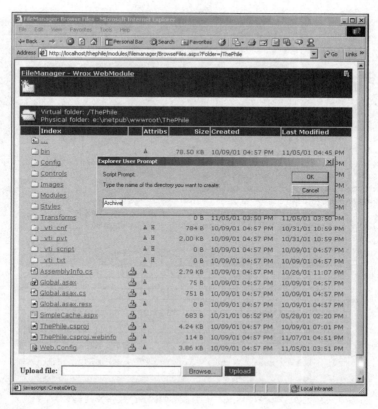

Creating Text Files

If we allow the administrator to create directories, we must also provide the opportunity to create text files (not empty text files of course, but files with some content). The approach is exactly the same as we used to implement the last command: manually calling the `__doPostBack` function from a JavaScript routine executed by an image link. The new code in the ASPX page is as follows:

```
...
<head>
  <title>FileManager: Browse Files</title>
  <link rel="stylesheet" HREF="/ThePhile/Styles/ThePhile.css"
      TYPE="text/css" />
  <meta name="CODE_LANGUAGE" Content="VB">
  <script language="javascript">

  function CreateDir()
  {
  ... unchanged from above ...
  }

  function CreateFile()
  {
```

```
            fileName = prompt('Type the name of the file you want to create:','');

            if ((fileName) && (fileName!=""))
            {
              document.forms['BrowseFiles'].elements[
                'funcParam'].value = fileName;
              __doPostBack('CreateFile', '');
            }
          }
        </script>
      </head>
      <body>
        <form id="BrowseFiles" method="post" runat="server"
            enctype="multipart/form-data">
          <FileManager:Header ID="Title" runat="server" />
          <input type="hidden" id="funcParam" runat="server">
            <table class="MenuTable" border="0" width="100%">
              <tr>
                <td>
                  <a href="javascript:CreateDir();">
                    <img border="0" src="./Images/NewFolder.gif"
                      Alt="Create a new directory" height="28" width="28" />
                  </a>
                  <asp:LinkButton ID="CreateDir" runat="server"
                      OnClick="CreateDir_Click" />
                  <a href="javascript:CreateFile();">
                    <img border="0" src="./Images/NewFile.gif"
                        Alt="Create a new text file" height="28" width="28">
                  </a>
                  <asp:LinkButton ID="CreateFile" runat="server"
                      OnClick="CreateFile_Click" Visible="False"/>
                </td>
              </tr>
            </table>
            ...
```

And here's the addition for the code-behind:

```
      Protected Sub CreateFile_Click( _
        ByVal sender As Object, _
        ByVal e As EventArgs)

        ' Build the complete path (current path + new dir name)
        Dim thePath As String = folderPath
        If thePath.EndsWith("/") Then
          thePath = thePath & funcParam.Value
        Else
          thePath = thePath & "/" & funcParam.Value
        End If

        ' If the file already exists, do not go to the text editor
        If File.Exists(Server.MapPath(thePath)) Then
          StatusMessage.Text = "The file you specified already exists."
```

```
      StatusMessage.Visible = True
   Else
      Response.Redirect( _
         "EditFile.aspx?File=" & thePath & "&CreateFile=True")
   End If

End Sub
```

The code above first of all checks if the specified file already exists (the whole path is retrieved by combining the current path and the name specified). If so, it just shows an error message – later in the chapter we'll add the possibility to edit an existing file. Otherwise it redirects to `EditFile.aspx` with the full virtual path of the file to create as a parameter, and another parameter, `CreateFile`, set to `true`. We're going to write this new page in the next section.

Building the Text File Editor

We want to build a very simple text editor that allows us to create a new file and also to edit an existing file. The editor will just have a multi-line textbox, a textbox for the destination path, a button to create or update the file, and another button to discard the changes and go back to the file manager.

In VS.NET create a new web form, named `EditFile.aspx`, and edit its content as follows:

```
<%@ Page language="VB" Codebehind="EditFile.aspx.vb" AutoEventWireup="false"
   Inherits="Wrox.WebModules.FileManager.Web.EditFile" %>
<%@ Register TagPrefix="FileManager" TagName="Header" src="Header.ascx" %>
<%@ Register TagPrefix="FileManager" TagName="Footer" src="Footer.ascx" %>
<!DOCTYPE HTML PUBLIC "-//W3C//DTD HTML 4.0 Transitional//EN" >
<html>
  <head>
    <title>FileManager: text editor</title>
    <link rel="stylesheet" HREF="/ThePhile/Styles/ThePhile.css"
        TYPE="text/css" />
    <meta name="CODE_LANGUAGE" Content="VB">
  </head>
  <body>
    <FileManager:Header ID="Title" runat="server" />
    <form ID="EditFile" method="post" runat="server">
      <asp:Table runat="server" CssClass="Grid_General" Width="100%">
        <asp:TableRow CssClass="Grid_Header">
          <asp:TableCell HorizontalAlign="Center" Text="EDIT TEXT FILE" />
        </asp:TableRow>
        <asp:TableRow>
          <asp:TableCell HorizontalAlign="Center">
            <asp:TextBox runat="server" Width="99%" Rows="20"
              TextMode="MultiLine" ID="FileContent" CssClass="TextBox" />
          </asp:TableCell>
        </asp:TableRow>
        <asp:TableRow>
          <asp:TableCell HorizontalAlign="Right" Text="Save As:">
            <asp:TextBox runat="server" Width="350px"
                ID="SaveAsPath" CssClass="TextBox" />
            <asp:Button runat="server" Text="Save" ID="Save"
                CssClass="Button" Width="80px" OnClick="Save_Click"
```

111

```
                            /> 
                <asp:Button runat="server" Text="Back to FileManager" ID="Back"
                    CssClass="Button" Width="150px"
                    OnClick="Back_Click" CausesValidation="False" />
            </asp:TableCell>
        </asp:TableRow>
        <asp:TableRow>
            <asp:TableCell HorizontalAlign="Right">
                <asp:RequiredFieldValidator ID="ValidateSaveAsPath"
                    runat="server" ControlToValidate="SaveAsPath"
                    Display="dynamic">* The Save As path is required
                </asp:RequiredFieldValidator>
                <asp:Label runat="server" ID="StatusMessage"
                    CssClass="StatusMessage" Visible="False" Width="100%" />
            </asp:TableCell>
        </asp:TableRow>
    </asp:Table>
    <br>
</form>
<FileManager:Footer ID="Footer" runat="server" />
</body>
</html>
```

We added a RequiredFieldValidator control that ensures that the SaveAsPath field is not empty when the form is submitted. Also, when we press the **Back to FileManager** button the form should not be validated, and that's why we set its CausesValidation property to False.

The Code-behind for EditFile.aspx

The code-behind for this page is not long, and is quite simple, but we'll show it piece by piece, starting from the beginning and including the Page_Load procedure:

```
Imports System
Imports System.Collections
Imports System.ComponentModel
Imports System.Data
Imports System.Drawing
Imports System.Web
Imports System.Web.SessionState
Imports System.Web.UI
Imports System.Web.UI.WebControls
Imports System.Web.UI.HtmlControls
Imports System.IO

Namespace WebModules.FileManager.Web

  Public Class EditFile
    Inherits System.Web.UI.Page

    Private Sub Page_Load( _
      ByVal sender As Object, _
      ByVal e As EventArgs) _
      Handles MyBase.Load
```

```
        If Not IsPostBack Then

          Dim filePath As String = Request.Params("File")

          If Not filePath Is Nothing Then

            If (Request.Params("CreateFile") Is Nothing) _
              Or (Request.Params("CreateFile") = "False") Then

              Try

                Dim reader As New StreamReader( _
                  File.Open(Server.MapPath(filePath), FileMode.Open))
                FileContent.Text = reader.ReadToEnd
                reader.Close()

              Catch myException As Exception

                StatusMessage.Text = myException.Message
                StatusMessage.Visible = True

              End Try

            End If

            ' Set the SaveAs textbox to the path specified in the Querystring
            SaveAsPath.Text = filePath

          End If

        End If

      End Sub
```

The `Page_Load` procedure extracts the path of the file to create or edit from the `QueryString`. Then it checks if the `CreateFile` parameter is set to `False`, or not present at all. In both these cases it means that the file is already present and the user does not want to create it, but rather to *edit* it. So the procedure opens the file, reads its content, and shows it in a large textbox (this code is protected within a `Try...Catch` block as usual).

The next block of code is the procedure called when the **Back to FileManager** button is pressed. Basically, it extracts the parent folder of the file passed in the `QueryString`, and redirects to `BrowseFiles.aspx`, pointing to the folder to browse:

```
      Protected Sub Back_Click(ByVal sender As Object, ByVal e As EventArgs)

        ' redirect to the referrer URL or to the BrowseFile.aspx page
        ' if the referrer is null
        Dim filePath As String = Request.Params("File")

        If Not filePath Is Nothing And filePath <> "/" Then
```

```
        Dim lastSlashIndex As Integer = filePath.LastIndexOf("/")
        Dim folderPath As String = filePath.Substring(0, lastSlashIndex + 1)

        Response.Redirect("BrowseFiles.aspx?Folder=" & folderPath)

    Else

        Response.Redirect("BrowseFiles.aspx")

    End If

End Sub
```

Finally, the last procedure is executed when the user presses the **Save** button. The file is created or updated with the new content:

```
Protected Sub Save_Click(ByVal sender As Object, ByVal e As EventArgs)

    ' Save the text to the specified file (the file is created
    ' anew even if it already exists)
    Try

        Dim filePath As String = SaveAsPath.Text
        If Not filePath.StartsWith("/") Then
            filePath = "/" & filePath
        End If

        Dim writer As StreamWriter = File.CreateText(Server.MapPath(filePath))
        writer.Write(FileContent.Text)
        writer.Close()

        StatusMessage.Text = "File successfully saved"

    Catch myException As Exception

        StatusMessage.Text = myException.Message

    End Try

    StatusMessage.Visible = True

End Sub
```

Note that the file is created from scratch in all cases. In other words, if the file already exists it is overwritten by a new file.

At this point we can recompile the assembly with the new page and switch to the browser. Click the **Create a new text file** icon on the toolbar, specify any file name you want (for example MyTestFile.txt) and confirm. This displays a page like this:

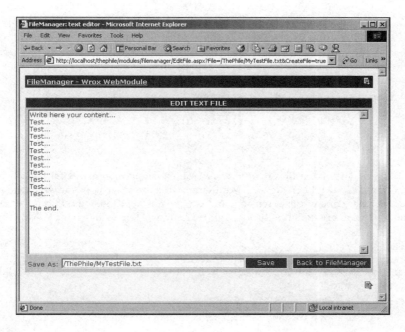

Editing Files

So, we've developed a page that allows the user to create and edit a new text file. We will now go back to the BrowseFiles.aspx page and add a new column with a link to the file editor for *all* the text files.

Here's the new column for the FoldersAndFilesTable table (this is the last time you need to change it, I promise):

```
<asp:Table ID="FoldersAndFiles" runat="server"
    CssClass="Grid_General" Width="100%">
  <asp:TableRow CssClass="Grid_Header">
    <asp:TableCell Width="36px" />
    <asp:TableCell Text="Index" />
    <asp:TableCell Width="25px" />
    <asp:TableCell Width="45px" />
    <asp:TableCell Text="Attribs" Width="50px" />
    <asp:TableCell Text="Size" Width="80px" HorizontalAlign="Right" />
    <asp:TableCell Text="Created" Width="140px" />
    <asp:TableCell Text="Last Modified" Width="140px" />
  </asp:TableRow>
</asp:Table>
```

Then, in the FillFoldersAndFilesTable routine in the code-behind file, add a new empty column (cellOperations) for the first row, which links to the parent folder, and for all directory rows. (This is not shown here; look at the code earlier in the chapter to see how to add columns, for example in the *Displaying the Item Attributes* section). We're going to add a link for any text files that are not read-only or system files. We won't add a link for the other files (we can't edit a GIF with a text editor).

115

The easiest way to decide whether a file is a text file is by looking at its extension. If the extension is .txt, .log, .bat, .vb, .config, .aspx, or some other well known text file extension, then we should be reasonably sure that the file is a text file. We define an array – private for the entire class – of known extensions, as we did for associating the extensions with an icon:

```
Private textExtensions() As String = { _
    ".asa", ".asax", ".ascx", ".asmx", ".asp", ".aspx", ".bat", _
    ".config", ".cs", ".css", ".disco", ".htm", ".html", ".inc", _
    ".ini", ".log", ".sys", ".txt", ".vb", ".vbs", ".vsdisco", _
    ".xls", ".xml"}
```

We could handle the list of text files in other ways, which would integrate with the system of assigning icons to extensions. We would create an XML file that lists the extensions for which we have an icon, where the tag has the name of the extension, and can have a "text" attribute that indicates whether the files with that extension are editable through our text editor. Here is an example XML file:

```
<filetypes>
    <filetype extension=".txt" icon="txt.gif" text="true">
    <filetype extension=".gig" icon="gif.gif" text="false">
</filetypes>
```

Note that we have **not** implemented this approach in the book example.

This solution would provide the flexibility to add, edit, and delete extensions without the need to recompile the assembly. However, working with an XML file is much slower than working with an array in a local private variable, and requires more code and resources. Considering that once you've set up a complete list of extensions you want to support you won't need to update it frequently, employing the XML solution is probably not worth the effort – but it's an option if you want the maximum flexibility and ease of use for the site administrator.

Now, in the code block that adds the child files to the table, we declare the new cell, and check if the current file's extension is listed in the array and if the file is write-enabled. If both conditions are satisfied the new icon link is added to the column:

```
' Define download link and add to download cell
linkDownload = New HyperLink()
linkDownload.Text = "<img src=""./Images/Download.gif"" " & _
    "border=""0"" height=""16"" width=""16"" Alt=""Download"">"
linkDownload.NavigateUrl = "Download.aspx?File=" & location

cellDownload = New TableCell()
cellDownload.Controls.Add(linkDownload)


' Define operations link and add to operations cell
cellOperations = New TableCell()

' - Operation 1: Edit (If this file is a text file and is
' write-enabled, add image link that point to EditFile.aspx)
extensionIndex = Array.IndexOf(textExtensions, _
    childFile.Extension.ToLower)
```

```
        If ((extensionIndex > -1) _
            And ((childFile.Attributes And FileAttributes.ReadOnly) _
                <> FileAttributes.ReadOnly) _
            And ((childFile.Attributes And FileAttributes.System) _
                <> FileAttributes.System)) Then

            Dim linkEditFile As HyperLink = New HyperLink()
            linkEditFile.Text = "<img src=""./Images/Write.gif"" " & _
            "height=""16"" width=""16"" border=""0"" alt=""Edit this file"">"
            linkEditFile.NavigateUrl = "EditFile.aspx?File=" & location
            cellOperations.Controls.Add(linkEditFile)
        End If


        'Define attributes and add to attributes cell
        labelAttributes = New Label()
        labelAttributes.Text = GetAttributesDescription(childFile.Attributes)
        labelAttributes.Font.Name = "Courier"
```

Renaming Files and Directories

The next command to implement is one for renaming files or directories. We're going to add a new button to each row in the table, except the first one, if it is the one that points to the parent folder. When pressed, the button will pop up a prompt dialog. If the new name is confirmed then an event will be raised on the server and handled by the proper procedure.

We've already seen how to use JavaScript for postbacks when we showed how to create a new directory or file. What's new here is that we're going to have an unknown number of buttons (one for each row, used to rename the item represented by the row where it is located) that will all raise the same event on the server. This does not make any difference to the actual implementation – we don't need to identify which row was clicked, just the original path name.

The other difference is that we need to submit two pieces of information – the original path name, and the new name. Although we could pack both of these parameters into a single control, adding a new hidden control produces no overhead and makes it simpler to extract the information.

In the ASPX page we just create the new hidden control, the JavaScript function that asks for the new name, and the invisible LinkButton control. The links that call this function are dynamically created in the code-behind for each file and directory.

Here's the additional code for BrowseFiles.aspx:

```
...
<head>
  <title>FileManager: Browse Files</title>
  <link rel="stylesheet" HREF="/ThePhile/Styles/ThePhile.css"
      TYPE="text/css" />
  <meta name="CODE_LANGUAGE" Content="VB">
  <script language="javascript">

    function CreateDir()
    {
```

```
      ...
    }

    function CreateFile()
    {
      ...
    }

    function Rename(path)
    {
      newName = prompt('Type the new name for this file/folder:','');

      if ((newName) && (newName!=""))
      {
        document.forms['BrowseFiles'].elements['funcParam'].value = path;
        document.forms['BrowseFiles'].elements['funcExtraParam'].value =
            newName;
        __doPostBack('Rename', '');
      }
    }
  </script>
</head>
<body>
  <form id="BrowseFiles" method="post" runat="server"
      enctype="multipart/form-data">
    <FileManager:Header ID="Title" runat="server" />
    <input type="hidden" id="funcParam" runat="server">
    <input type="hidden" id="funcExtraParam" runat="server">
    <table class="MenuTable" border="0" width="100%">
      <tr>
        <td>
          ... other LinkButtons and links for the Toolbar commands
          <asp:LinkButton ID="Rename" runat="server"
              OnClick="Rename_Click" Visible="False" />
        </td>
      </tr>
    </table>
    ...
```

We don't need to add a new column, as we're going to add the new link to the column with the Edit File icon. However, in the code-behind we need to create and add this column for the directories too, because the last time we modified it we just added an empty column.

Here are the additions for the code-behind, starting with `FillFoldersAndFilesTable`:

```
Dim childDir As DirectoryInfo
    For Each childDir In childDirs

        ' Create the link that points to this sub-directory
        ' Code not included here - see earlier

        ' Define check box and image icon and add to ItemIcon cell
        checkItem = New CheckBox()
        ' Code not included here - see earlier
```

```
' Define Link and add to link cell
' Code not included here - see earlier


' Define operations link and add to operations cell
cellOperations = New TableCell()

' - Operation 1: Edit (Not applicable to directories)

' - Operation 2: Rename (The 'D' before the file location
' denotes that the path identifies a directory)
linkRename = New HyperLink()
linkRename.Text = "<img src=""./Images/Rename.gif"" " & _
  "height=""16"" width=""16"" border=""0"" alt=""Rename this file"">"
linkRename.NavigateUrl = "javascript:Rename('D" & location & "');"

cellOperations.Controls.Add(linkRename)


' Define attributes and add to attributes cell
' Code not included here - see earlier


' Define size cell
' Code not included here - see earlier


' Define created and last modified cells
' Code not included here - see earlier


' Add cells to row
rowItem = New TableRow()
With rowItem.Cells
  .Add(cellItemIcon)
  .Add(cellItemLink)
  .Add(New TableCell()) ' No download link for folder
  .Add(cellOperations)
  .Add(cellAttributes)
  .Add(cellSize)
  .Add(cellCreated)
  .Add(cellLastModified)
End With
rowItem.ApplyStyle(styleFolderRow)

' Add row to table
FoldersAndFiles.Rows.Add(rowItem)

Next


' Add rows for files
'-------------------------------------------------------------------
Dim childFile As FileInfo
```

```vbnet
Dim extensionIndex As Integer
For Each childFile In childFiles

  ' Find current directory location
  ' Code not included here - see earlier


  ' Define check box and image icon (based on extension of the file)
  '  and add to ItemIcon cell
  ' Code not included here - see earlier

  ' Define Link and add to link cell
  ' Code not included here - see earlier


  ' Define download link and add to download cell
  ' Code not included here - see earlier


  ' Define operations link and add to operations cell
  cellOperations = New TableCell()

  ' - Operation 1: Edit (If this file is a text file and is
  ' write-enabled, add image link that point to EditFile.aspx)
  extensionIndex = Array.IndexOf(textExtensions, _
    childFile.Extension.ToLower)
  If ((extensionIndex > -1) _
      And ((childFile.Attributes And FileAttributes.ReadOnly) _
        <> FileAttributes.ReadOnly) _
      And ((childFile.Attributes And FileAttributes.System) _
        <> FileAttributes.System)) Then

    Dim linkEditFile As HyperLink = New HyperLink()
    linkEditFile.Text = "<img src=""./Images/Write.gif"" " & _
      "height=""16"" width=""16"" border=""0"" alt=""Edit this file"">"
    linkEditFile.NavigateUrl = "EditFile.aspx?File=" & location
    cellOperations.Controls.Add(linkEditFile)
  End If

  ' - Operations 2: Rename (The 'F' before the file location
  ' denotes that the path identifies a file)
  linkRename = New HyperLink()
        linkRename.Text = "<img src=""./Images/Rename.gif"" " & _
  "height=""16"" width=""16"" border=""0"" alt=""Rename this file"">"
    linkRename.NavigateUrl = "javascript:Rename('F" & location & "');"
    cellOperations.Controls.Add(linkRename)

  'Define attributes and add to attributes cell
  ' Code not included here - see earlier


  ' Define size
  ' Code not included here - see earlier
```

```
' Define created and last modified cells
' Code not included here - see earlier


' Add cells to row
rowItem = New TableRow()
With rowItem.Cells
  .Add(cellItemIcon)
  .Add(cellItemLink)
  .Add(cellDownload)
  .Add(cellOperations)
  .Add(cellAttributes)
  .Add(cellSize)
  .Add(cellCreated)
  .Add(cellLastModified)
End With
rowItem.ApplyStyle(styleFileRow)

' Add row to table
FoldersAndFiles.Rows.Add(rowItem)

    Next
```

The only peculiarity in the code above is that a 'D' or 'F' is added to the path passed to the JavaScript Rename function. The whole string will then be passed to the server event handler, which will determine if the path identifies a file or a folder by extracting the first letter. This is, of course, necessary because there are two different classes – one for working with folders and one for files.

You can see this in the following procedure:

```
Protected Sub Rename_Click(ByVal sender As Object, ByVal e As EventArgs)

    ' The first char of the first param is F is the path identifies
    '  a file, D otherwise. Extract the first char to determine this.
    Dim isFile As Boolean = funcParam.Value.StartsWith("F")

    ' Extract the source path
    Dim sourcePath As String = Server.MapPath(funcParam.Value.Substring(1))

    Dim destinationPath As String
    Try

      If isFile Then

        Dim sourceFile As FileInfo = New FileInfo(sourcePath)

        ' Create the destination path: source path dir + new name
        destinationPath = _
          Path.Combine(sourceFile.Directory.FullName, funcExtraParam.Value)

        ' Move the file
        sourceFile.MoveTo(destinationPath)

      Else
```

121

```
            Dim sourceDir As DirectoryInfo = New DirectoryInfo(sourcePath)

            ' Create the destination path: source path dir + new name
            destinationPath = _
              Path.Combine(sourceDir.Parent.FullName, funcExtraParam.Value)

            ' Move the directory
            sourceDir.MoveTo(destinationPath)

          End If

          ' Refresh page
          Response.Redirect("BrowseFiles.aspx?File=" & folderPath)

        Catch exc As Exception

          StatusMessage.Text = exc.Message
          StatusMessage.Visible = True

        End Try

      End Sub
```

The item is moved to the current path but with a different name, therefore it is renamed. At the end of the procedure, if no exceptions have been raised, the table is filled with the updated content. The exception handling is very important here: you may have loaded the page with the list of files fifteen minutes ago, and in the meantime another administrator might have deleted or moved some files. But you still see the old content as long as you don't refresh the page, and if you try to rename a file/directory that no longer exists an exception will be generated. In that case it is handled and a message explaining the problem is shown.

Modifying the Attributes of Files and Directories

Earlier in the chapter we added a column to show the attributes of the items, by reading the Attributes property. That property can be read *and* set, so why not add functionality to edit the attributes? Now that we know the trick to pop up a prompt dialog and raise server events, this is a no-brainer problem.

Let's add the new JavaScript to the <script> section, and the respective LinkButton control, in the BrowseFiles.aspx page:

```
...
<script language="javascript">
  function CreateDir()
  { ... }

  function CreateFile()
  { ... }

  function Rename(path)
  { ... }
```

```
    function SetAttributes(path)
    {
      attribs = prompt('Type the new attributes for the
          file/folder.\nA=Archive, R=ReadOnly, H=Hidden, S=System:','');

      if ((attribs) && (attribs!=""))
      {
        document.forms['BrowseFiles'].elements['funcParam'].value = path;
        document.forms['BrowseFiles'].elements['funcExtraParam'].value +
            = attribs;
        __doPostBack('SetAttributes', '');
      }
    }
  </script>
</head>
<body>
...
  <asp:LinkButton ID="SetAttributes" runat="server"
      OnClick="SetAttributes_Click" Visible="False" />
...
```

The `funcParam` hidden control is used to store the path of the item to update, while `funcExtraParam` stores the new attributes. Attributes are specified as a string of characters, where 'A' means `Archive`, 'R' `Read Only`, 'H' `Hidden`, and 'S' `System`. So, for example, "RS" means `Read Only + System`.

The column for the attributes is already present in the rows for both directories and files, so the additions for the `FillFoldersAndFilesTable` procedure in the code-behind are limited. Here are the changes for the directory display part:

```
        ' Define attributes and add to attributes cell
        labelAttributes = New Label()
        labelAttributes.Text = GetAttributesDescription(childDir.Attributes)
        labelAttributes.Font.Name = "Courier"

        linkSetAttributes = New HyperLink()
        linkSetAttributes.Text = "<img src=""./Images/Edit.gif"" " & _
        "height=""16"" width=""16"" border=""0"" Alt=""Edit Attributes"" />"
        linkSetAttributes.NavigateUrl = _
          "javascript:SetAttributes('" & location & "');"

        cellAttributes = New TableCell()
        cellAttributes.Controls.Add(labelAttributes)
        cellAttributes.Controls.Add(linkSetAttributes)
```

Here are the changes for the part that displays files:

```
        'Define attributes and add to attributes cell
        labelAttributes = New Label()
        labelAttributes.Text = GetAttributesDescription(childFile.Attributes)
        labelAttributes.Font.Name = "Courier"
```

```
       linkSetAttributes = New HyperLink()
       linkSetAttributes.Text = "<img src=""./Images/Edit.gif"" " & _
       "height=""16"" width=""16"" border=""0"" Alt=""Edit Attributes"" />"
       linkSetAttributes.NavigateUrl = _
         "javascript:SetAttributes('" & location & "');"

       cellAttributes = New TableCell()
       cellAttributes.Controls.Add(labelAttributes)
       cellAttributes.Controls.Add(linkSetAttributes)
```

There is nothing new to explain here, as the code is very similar to the code we added for the **Rename** command. There is a difference in the JavaScript we call and we just pass the plain item path. There is no need to prefix a 'D' or 'F' to identify the path as a directory or a file – we'll see the reason for this in a moment. Look at the code called on the server when the user confirms the new attributes:

```
  Protected Sub SetAttributes_Click( _
    ByVal sender As Object, _
    ByVal e As EventArgs)

    Dim thePath As String = Server.MapPath(funcParam.Value)
    Dim attributes As String = funcExtraParam.Value.ToUpper()
    Dim fileAttributes As FileAttributes = fileAttributes.Normal

    ' Search the 'A' (Archive) attribute in the descriptive string
    If attributes.IndexOf("A") > -1 Then
      fileAttributes = fileAttributes Or fileAttributes.Archive
    End If

    ' Search the 'R' (ReadOnly) attribute in the descriptive string
    If attributes.IndexOf("R") > -1 Then
      fileAttributes = fileAttributes Or fileAttributes.ReadOnly
    End If

    ' Search the 'H' (Archive) attribute in the descriptive string
    If attributes.IndexOf("H") > -1 Then
      fileAttributes = fileAttributes Or fileAttributes.Hidden
    End If

    ' Search the 'S' (ReadOnly) attribute in the descriptive string
    If attributes.IndexOf("S") > -1 Then
      fileAttributes = fileAttributes Or fileAttributes.System
    End If


    Try

      ' Set the new attributes. This works with directories as well.
      File.SetAttributes(thePath, fileAttributes)

      ' Refresh the page
      Response.Redirect("BrowseFiles.aspx?Folder=" & folderPath)

    Catch exc As Exception
```

```
            StatusMessage.Text = exc.Message
            StatusMessage.Visible = True

        End Try

    End Sub
```

The procedure checks if the 'A', 'R', 'H', and 'S' letters are present in the user-specified string, and the respective attribute for each occurrence found is added to a variable, of type FileAttributes. As a last step the procedure sets the new attributes by calling the File's SetAttributes shared method. As you have probably guessed, there was no need to prefix the path with a 'D' or 'F' letter because the SetAttributes method works fine with both directories and files, so there is no need to differentiate our code according to the item type.

The following screenshot shows how the file manager looks after these additions. You can see the new icons in the new columns, and the dialog for specifying the new attributes for a file or directory:

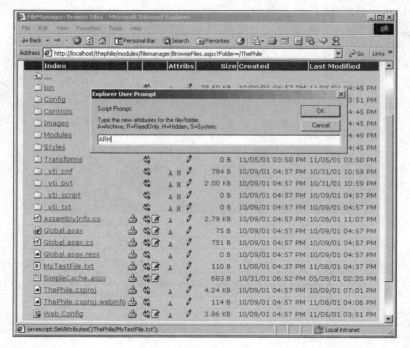

Deleting Files

What we want to implement now is a delete command. We could easily add a further link to the right of each item and associate a server procedure that deletes that item. However, so far we've implemented commands that work on individual files: at the moment we can create *one* file at time, rename *one* file at time, change the attributes of *one* directory at time, etc. Let's say that we want to delete twenty files – it would take twenty reloads to complete the operation, and that would be quite boring. If we take any file manager as a model, we can see that commands like rename work on an individual item, since they are based on the current properties (name, attributes, etc.) of the item. But if we want to delete, copy, or move a set of files, we can select more than one file and deal with them in a single step, saving time.

We want to follow the general guidelines of any good file manager, so we will do things that way as well. First problem: allowing the user (administrator) to select the files or directories they want to delete. The solution is to add a checkbox for each item, so that when the user presses the Delete link all the items whose checkbox is selected are deleted.

In our application this simply translates to dynamically adding a checkbox in the first column, before the item icon, in the `FillFoldersAndFilesTable` procedure in the code-behind file. In the `BrowseFiles.aspx` page we add JavaScript that asks the user to confirm the operation, the link on the toolbar, and a new invisible `LinkButton` for the server event handler:

```
<script language="javascript">
  function CreateDir()
  { ... }

  // other javascript functions
  ...

  function Delete()
  {
    if (confirm('Do you want to delete the selected folder(s) ' +
                                       'and/or file(s)?'))
    __doPostBack('Delete','');
  }
</script>
</head>
<body>
  ...
  <table class="MenuTable" border="0" width="100%">
    <tr>
      <td>
        ...
        <a href="javascript:Delete();">
          <img border="0" src="./Images/Delete.gif"
              Alt="Delete the selected files/directories"
              height="28" width="28">
        </a>
        <asp:LinkButton ID="Delete" runat="server"
            OnClick="Delete_Click" Visible="False" />
        ...
      </td>
    </tr>
  </table>
  ...
```

In the `FillFoldersAndFilesTable` procedure in the code-behind file, first of all we add the code for creating a checkbox for each folder:

```
Dim childDir As DirectoryInfo
For Each childDir In childDirs

  ' Create the link that points to this sub-directory
  location = folderPath
```

```
If location.EndsWith("/") Then
  location = location & childDir.Name
Else
  location = location & "/" & childDir.Name
End If



' Define check box and image icon and add to ItemIcon cell
checkItem = New CheckBox()
checkItem.Attributes("Path") = location
checkItem.Attributes("IsFile") = "false"

imageItemIcon = New WebControls.Image()
imageItemIcon.ImageUrl = "./Images/ClosedFolder.gif"

cellItemIcon = New TableCell()
cellItemIcon.Controls.Add(checkItem)
cellItemIcon.Controls.Add(imageItemIcon)
cellItemIcon.HorizontalAlign = HorizontalAlign.Right
```

and also for each file:

```
' Add rows for files
'----------------------------------------------------------------------
Dim childFile As FileInfo
Dim extensionIndex As Integer
For Each childFile In childFiles

  ' Find current directory location
  location = folderPath
  If location.EndsWith("/") Then
    location = location & childFile.Name
  Else
    location = location & "/" & childFile.Name
  End If


  ' Define check box and image icon (based on extension of the file)
  '  and add to ItemIcon cell
  checkItem = New CheckBox()
  checkItem.Attributes("Path") = location
  checkItem.Attributes("IsFile") = "true"

extensionIndex = Array.IndexOf(extensions, _
  childFile.Extension.ToLower())
imageItemIcon = New WebControls.Image()
If extensionIndex > -1 Then
  imageItemIcon.ImageUrl = "./Images/" & _
    childFile.Extension.Substring(1) + ".gif"
Else
  imageItemIcon.ImageUrl = "./Images/unknown.gif"
End If
```

You will notice that the item's path and type (file or directory) are stored as checkbox `Attributes`. The code in the `Delete_Click` procedure will get this information from all the selected checkboxes, and will accordingly use the `Directory` or `File` classes to delete those items. Here's this procedure:

```
Protected Sub Delete_Click(ByVal sender As Object, ByVal e As EventArgs)

    Dim isRedirect As Boolean = True

    Dim row As TableRow
    For Each row In FoldersAndFiles.Rows

        If (row.Cells(0).Controls.Count = 2) Then

            ' Get a reference to the checkbox
            Dim checkItem As CheckBox = _
                CType(row.Cells(0).Controls(0), CheckBox)

            If checkItem.Checked Then

                Try

                    Dim thePath As String = _
                        Server.MapPath(checkItem.Attributes("Path").ToString())

                    ' Is this item as file?
                    If Convert.ToBoolean(checkItem.Attributes("IsFile") = True) Then
                        File.Delete(thePath)
                    Else
                        Directory.Delete(thePath)
                    End If

                Catch exc As Exception

                    StatusMessage.Text = exc.Message
                    StatusMessage.Visible = True
                    isRedirect = False
                End Try
            End If
        End If
    Next
    ' Refresh page
    If isRedirect Then
        Response.Redirect("BrowseFiles.aspx?Folder=" & folderPath)
    End If
End Sub
```

For each row in the table the procedure checks if the first cell has two child controls. If there is only one, it means that this row has only the icon and link to jump to the parent directory. Therefore it does not represent a file system item, and so the code does nothing. If there are two controls, the procedure gets a reference to the checkbox control, and looks to see if the control is checked. If it is checked then it goes ahead, by extracting the path of the item and the attribute specifying if the item is a file or a directory, in order to use the appropriate class to delete the item.

Note that here we don't refresh the page after the operation is performed for just one item, but only when we're finished with *all* the selected items. Therefore we have to redirect just before the end of the procedure, based on the value of the `redir` variable, which is `true` when it is declared and set to `false` if an exception is thrown.

Copying and Moving Files

We're close to completing the features of our file manager, but what's still missing is the possibility to copy or move a set of files and folders. We already have the infrastructure for selecting multiple items; what we need to add are the JavaScript function that asks for the destination path, a `LinkButton` control, and the respective event handler. Copying and moving items are very similar operations, thus we'll handle both of them with the same event handler and the same JavaScript.

As usual, we start by showing the additions to the `BrowseFiles.aspx` page:

```
<script language="javascript">
  function CreateDir()
  { ... }

  // other javascript functions
  ...

  function CopyMove(op)
  {
    destPath = prompt('Type the destination virtual path:','');

    if ((destPath) && (destPath!=""))
    {
      document.forms['BrowseFiles'].elements['funcParam'].value = destPath;
      document.forms['BrowseFiles'].elements
          ['funcExtraParam'].value = op;
      __doPostBack('CopyMove', '');
    }
  }
</script>
</head>
<body>
  ...
  <table class="MenuTable" border="0" width="100%">
    <tr>
      <td>
        ...
        <a href="javascript:CopyMove('copy');">
          <img border="0" src="./Images/Copy.gif"
              Alt="Copy the selected files/directories"
              height="28" width="28">
        </a>
        <a href="javascript:CopyMove('move');">
          <img border="0" src="./Images/Move.gif"
              Alt="Move the selected files/directories"
              height="28" width="28">
        </a>
        <asp:LinkButton ID="CopyMove" runat="server"
            OnClick="CopyMove_Click" Visible="False" />
```

```
      ...
    </td>
  </tr>
</table>
  ...
```

In the event handler we can find out if the user wants to copy or move the file by looking at the value of the `funcExtraParam` hidden control, which can be "copy" or "move". The other control is used to pass the destination path. Here is the event handler code:

```
Protected Sub CopyMove_Click(ByVal sender As Object, ByVal e As EventArgs)

    Dim isRedirect As Boolean = True

    ' Extract the destination directory
    Dim theFolder As String = funcParam.Value

    ' Extract the operation to perform: can be "copy" or "move"
    Dim operation As String = funcExtraParam.Value

    ' If the user did not specify an absolute virtual directory,
    '   get the absolute version of it
    If Not theFolder.StartsWith("/") Then
      If folderPath.EndsWith("/") Then
        theFolder = folderPath & theFolder
      Else
        theFolder = folderPath & "/" & theFolder
      End If
    End If


    ' Now get the absolute physical path
    theFolder = Server.MapPath(theFolder)


    Dim row As TableRow
    For Each row In FoldersAndFiles.Rows

      If row.Cells(0).Controls.Count = 2 Then

        Dim checkItem As CheckBox = _
          CType(row.Cells(0).Controls(0), CheckBox)

        ' Go ahead only if the checkbox is selected
        If checkItem.Checked Then

          Dim destPath As String = _
            Path.Combine(theFolder, _
            CType(row.Cells(1).Controls(0), HyperLink).Text)
          Dim sourcePath As String = _
            Server.MapPath(checkItem.Attributes("Path").ToString())

          Try
```

```
      If Convert.ToBoolean(checkItem.Attributes("IsFile")) = True Then

          ' Copy or move this file
          If operation = "move" Then
            File.Move(sourcePath, destPath)
          Else
            File.Copy(sourcePath, destPath, True)
          End If

      Else

          ' Copy or move this directory
          If operation = "move" Then
            Directory.Move(sourcePath, destPath)
          Else
            CopyDirectory(sourcePath, destPath, True)
          End If

      End If

    Catch exc As Exception

      StatusMessage.Text = exc.Message
      StatusMessage.Visible = True
      isRedirect = False

    End Try

  End If

  End If

Next

' Refresh the page
If isRedirect Then
  Response.Redirect("BrowseFiles.aspx?Folder=" & folderPath)
End If

End Sub
```

The user can specify a relative or an absolute virtual directory as the destination. If the specified path begins with "/" it means that the path is absolute, so nothing extra needs to be done. Otherwise it is a relative path, and it is added to the current path. Then we get the respective physical path, which is the one we work with.

The other point to note is that both the File and Directory classes expose the Move method, but only the File class exposes a Copy method. Honestly, I don't know why the Directory class does not have a Copy method, but this is not a problem that can scare us – we can always write our custom CopyDirectory function, right?

No sooner said than done, here's the code for CopyDirectory:

```
      Private Sub CopyDirectory( _
        ByVal sourcePath As String, _
        ByVal destPath As String, _
        ByVal overwrite As Boolean)

        Dim sourceDir As New DirectoryInfo(sourcePath)
        Dim destDir As New DirectoryInfo(destPath)

        ' The source directory must exist, if not raise an exception
        If sourceDir.Exists Then

            ' If destination directory parent does not exist, throw an exception
            If Not destDir.Parent.Exists Then

            Throw New AppException("Destination directory does not exist: " & _
                destDir.Parent.FullName, New DirectoryNotFoundException())

            If Not destDir.Exists Then
              destDir.Create()
            End If

            ' Copy all the files of the current directory
            Dim theFile As FileInfo
            For Each theFile In sourceDir.GetFiles()

                If overwrite Then

                    theFile.CopyTo( _
                        Path.Combine(destDir.FullName, theFile.Name), True)

                Else

                    ' If overwrite = False, copy the file only if it does not exist.
                    ' This is done to avoid an IOException if a file already exists.
                    ' This way the other files can be copied anyway.

                If Not File.Exists( _
                Path.Combine(destDir.FullName, theFile.Name)) Then
                theFile.CopyTo(Path.Combine(destDir.FullName, theFile.Name), False)
                    End If
                End If
            Next
            End If

            ' Recursively call this procedure to copy the subdirectories
            Dim dir As DirectoryInfo
            For Each dir In sourceDir.GetDirectories()
                CopyDirectory(dir.FullName, _
                    Path.Combine(destDir.FullName, dir.Name), overwrite)
            Next
        Else
            Throw New AppException("Source directory does not exist: " & _
                sourceDir.FullName, New DirectoryNotFoundException())
        End If
      End Sub
    End Class
End Namespace
```

The procedure accepts the source and destination directories as input, plus a third parameter that specifies whether the files with the same name in the destination directory will be overwritten. The procedure first copies all the child files, and then uses recursion for each sub-directory. If the destination directory does not exist, an exception is thrown through the `AppException` class, which we built in Chapter 2. In order to use this class we have to add a reference to the `Core.dll` assembly, or the `Core` project if it is part of the solution. To add a reference, click the **References** command under the **Project** menu, and select from the list.

Our file manager is finally feature-complete! In the following screenshot you can see the final version, with the checkboxes for all items, the new command links in the toolbar, and the dialog asking for the destination directory for a copy operation:

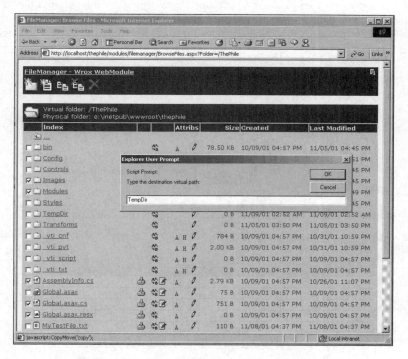

Securing the File Manager Using Windows Security

In the design section of this chapter we explained why security is a fundamental requirement and why we chose to use Windows security. Creating our own forms-based security system will be covered in the next chapter, and later chapters will show how to use it. It would be easy to apply this method to the file manager, and might be the best solution on other sites. But for ThePhile, Windows security is best.

IIS provides security control against IP, user, virtual directory, and NTFS resources. The IP-blocking mechanism allows the administrator to block or process requests coming from a selected range of IP addresses, and is very useful when you know in advance the IPs of the allowed computers, such as when you are working with an intranet, or when you're using a static IP. IIS also allows you to grant or deny read and execute privileges to a virtual directory and all the folders underneath, and to limit the rights of the anonymous user who accesses and browses the site (you typically allow this user to read the pages of a public section, but prevent any writing). Windows NT security is administered through the ACL (Access Control List), a list of permissions for every resource on NTFS partitions (FAT partitions are not supported). In this case we'll be using only the basic Windows NTFS security, but if you have the ability to do so, then you can also set up IP blocking, encryption, and any other available security mechanisms.

First of all we create a new user from the Computer Management console: choose the name, description, and password, and when you're done you'll see the new user added to the list. In our test we have created a user named ThePhileMaster, as shown in the list:

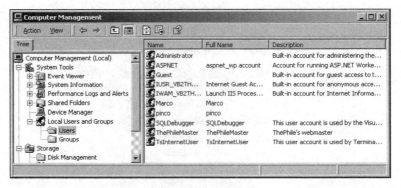

Now create a new group, name it ThePhile_FileManagerAdmins, and add the ThePhileMaster user to the list, as illustrated:

Now we have to declare permissions on the website folder and content. To do this, open Windows Explorer, select the physical directory of /localhost/ThePhile (`E:\Inetpub\wwwroot\ThePhile` on my system) and go to its properties through File | **Properties**. Switch to the **Security** tab, and select all the permissions for the ThePhile_FileManagerAdmins group, as follows:

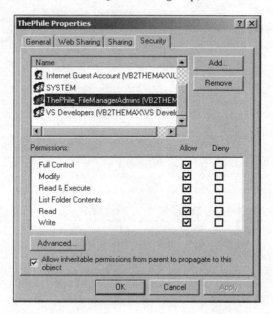

It's worth noting that although we can grant permissions to a specific user and not to the entire group, if we give a group permission to access a resource then we can later add users to that group without having to manually give every single user permissions to the resource. From the same dialog in Windows Explorer we remove the permissions of the IUSR_MACHINENAME user, that is, the Internet anonymous user. Finally, go to the IIS management console, and set the Integrated Windows Security for the **FileManager** folder. Note that the integrated security will only work with Microsoft browsers, unless basic authentication, or forms authentication is used. This is not a big issue in this case, though, as you can force the few administrators to use Internet Explorer. It would be a much more serious problem if we were planning to use this type of security to authenticate/authorize thousands of users that we don't even know.

Now when we try to open the `BrowseFiles.aspx` page from a browser, we get the login dialog asking for our username and password, as shown in the following screenshot:

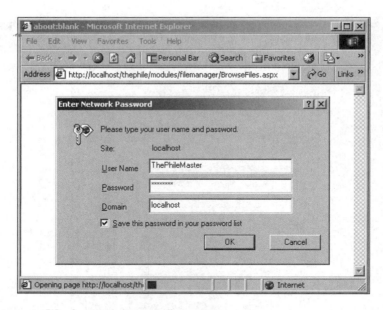

There's a lot more to Windows security – such as impersonation, anonymous access and other authentication methods, use of certificates, encryption and SSL – but here we just want a working solution for our web module. However, you should seriously consider security and all the available ways to enhance it. *Professional ASP.NET Security* ISBN 1-86100-620-9 covers IIS Windows security and how we an integrate it with ASP.NET.

Remember that Windows security can be set up through the `web.config` file, but we can't have more than one form of authentication/authorization in the same application. In the next chapter we'll be implementing forms-based authentication, so we can't have a different mode for the file manager. Since you need to access the IIS and folder settings only once to enforce Windows security in the traditional way, this is not a big problem. However, should you need to frequently or dynamically add/edit/remove administrators, then read the next chapter and integrate the accounts/security module to use forms-based authentication here as well.

Summary

This chapter presented the design and implementation of a web module, called `FileManager`, which provides functionality to:

- ❑ List and navigate folder contents
- ❑ Create directories
- ❑ Create and edit text files
- ❑ Download files
- ❑ Upload files

❑   Rename files and directories

❑   Modify file/directory attributes

❑   Delete files

❑   Copy and move files

This tool can help you to effectively manage your site files, resources, and directory structure. For all but very major updates, we can now rely on this tool without the need for external FTP clients or other tools.

We also saw how to set up Windows security to protect the `FileManager` module from unauthorized access.

Before concluding, here are a few new features that you could add to enhance the `FileManager`:

❑   Support for multiple file uploads. This would require the addition of other `HtmlInputFile` controls, and the use of the `Request.Files` collection to handle the uploaded files.

❑   A sort facility that allows the user to click on the grid's columns to sort the directories and files by name, size, or creation date.

❑   Logging the most significant operations, such as file or directory deletion, and adding a page to enable certain administrators to easily access this information (the logged events, their details, and the responsible users).

❑   Creating different levels of administrators that each have different permissions. With Windows security you can create users that cannot, for example, write or list files. But we could push this one step further, and show or hide the links for creating, deleting, and editing elements according to the current user and the group they belong to. For some purposes, we might also want to integrate the security for this module with the security system we will develop in the next chapter.

In the next chapter we'll look at building a module that allows administrators to manage the site's users and their roles, granting or denying them access to particular sections and features.

Users and Authentication

One of the most important aspects of a content-based website, or any website for that matter, is *community building*. As we discussed earlier in this book, a website with a strong, enthusiastic community can survive and profit far longer than other websites that might have greater funding, more development staff, or even a bigger advertising or marketing budget.

The first step towards building a thriving community is to give each user an **identity**. Each website has different needs in this area, but a few things are fairly common. The first step is to provide users with an **account** – a password-protected identity that can be used to represent the user on the website. These accounts allow us to add personalization, e-commerce facilities, targeted advertising, direct news delivery, and mailing list participation.

This chapter will first identify some of the issues and problems involved with providing user accounts. Once we've defined the problems, we will produce an initial design for a solution to this problem. Finally we will write the software to implement this solution.

We will also look at how we can secure some of the facilities and pages of our website, and how we can make provisions for administrators and power users.

The Problem

ThePhile.com provides content to users, and also allows users to contribute to the site in several ways, such as forums for example, which will be covered in Chapter 10. We also want our site to be able to serve different content to different users. All of these features rely on our site being able to identify its users, and determine what features they are allowed to access. In order to do this, the website must **authenticate** the user in some way, to prevent another person from using a particular user's account. For all this to work, **user accounts** will need to be created and maintained, and users will need to be correctly identified by their account.

Many features of the site will need to be administered remotely, so we need to allow for administrative users who will be given particular privileges. For example, some users might be able to remove offensive forum postings. However we might not want these users to access every administrative feature on the site – only those features required to moderate the forum. We might want to give another user – the main Webmaster, say – access to everything. So this is more complex than simply differentiating between a set of normal users and a set of super users.

Another thing that we feel very strongly about, that should be listed as part of our problem, is the concept of **user-friendliness**. The authentication and authorization system of a content website should be as unobtrusive as possible. The users should be barely aware of the fact that the website has recognized them, and the process of logging into the website should be quick and painless.

> *In many other situations, such as an e-commerce website or a secured intranet application, the authentication system should be very visible, and very, very strong. In our case, however, we want the authentication system to remain in the background to prevent it from slowing down the site and confusing or distracting our users.*

Now that we've described what we are trying to build, we can move on to designing a system that meets these needs.

The Design

With most desktop or intranet applications we can prevent users from accessing the application until they log in. This means that the developer can assume that the user of an application can always be identified. Most websites don't work this way. Many websites don't require the user to supply a password until the very last possible minute. For example, the user is often recognized through a *cookie*, goes shopping for a while, and just after they click the Check Out button, they are prompted for their security credentials.

Our site will follow the same policy. It will be completely acceptable for an anonymous user, or a user identified with a cookie but not authenticated with a password, to browse the site and use many of its features. If the user is identified with a cookie, some personalization can take place, as long as it doesn't compromise the user's privacy. For those parts of the site where authentication is required, the user will be forced to authenticate, otherwise they will be denied access.

In addition to building several *new* components that will drive our user authentication and security module, we should make sure that our design accounts for changes to the existing code. First of all, we're going to want to provide a link to log in, a page that allows logins, and a customized greeting in the site header that identifies the user by name.

The following UML use case diagram illustrates the process of authenticating a user. As you can see, at all times, any user (anonymous or authenticated) can follow a 'normal', or unsecured, link. This simply loads a new page and the process begins again. However, if the user chooses to authenticate, they can do this by either creating a new user account or by supplying the password information for an existing account. Finally, you can see from the diagram that it is possible to recognize a previously authenticated user without forcing them to manually authenticate. We will do this using the cookie-based system supplied with ASP.NET's forms-based authentication.

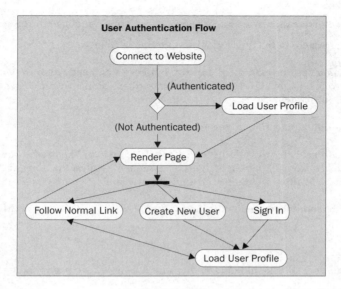

Our site will be using forms-based authentication, which is entirely based on cookies. But there are other ways to authenticate website users. For example, in order to truly secure the administrative portions of our application, we are going to use standard NT/2000 domain security (Windows authentication). This has the benefit of adding the requirement of domain membership (or trust) before the user can even attempt to view the page. Securing the administrative directories and only giving access to a particular *group* (as defined by the 'User Administrator for Domains' program), places the burden of only giving access to appropriate users onto the network administrator. We will see more about *how* we are going to implement the security once we've completed our design.

As with the other elements of our website, we'll design a 3-tiered module, with a presentation layer, business layer, and data layer. We'll need a database to store information about our users and the permissions available, and will design stored procedures to assist the interaction between the data layer classes and the database itself. The rest of this design section will walk you through the design decisions we made in creating our `Accounts` module.

The reason why we've chosen to call the module `Accounts` *is that often the 'users' of websites are not individual users at all but are in fact login accounts assigned to companies, groups, or large organizations.*

Forms Authentication

We decided to use ASP.NET Forms authentication on our site. We could have chosen other authentication methods, including Windows authentication and Passport, but we decided to opt for Forms authentication because it allows us to:

- ❑ Store the users' details in our own database
- ❑ Define our own logic for placing users into roles and granting permissions to roles
- ❑ Use our own login page

❑   Build an authentication system that will work with a wide range of browsers

❑   Extend the system in the future if we want to make changes

We could have built a custom solution of our own but Forms authentication provides most of the functionality that we need and allows us to extend it, so there didn't seem to be any reason to develop the functionality from scratch.

So, what does forms authentication do for us?

Forms authentication provides us with the ability to set a cookie on the user's browser when they log in to our website. This cookie will be sent with each subsequent request that they make to our website. The Forms Authentication Module will then pick up the cookie and use it to identify the user.

The important thing about forms authentication is that the cookie that is set on the users browser is protected in two ways:

❑   It is encrypted

❑   It has some special data added to it to ensure it cannot have been modified

We will see the specifics of how we make use of forms authentication later in the chapter but for now the important thing to understand is that forms authentication will provide us with the ability to identify users once they have logged in.

Designing the Database

Shown opposite is a diagram representing the database schema for the user accounting module of our sample website, ThePhile.com. It is fairly straightforward – we have three core data structures: users, permissions, and roles. A **role** is a logical grouping of permissions. For example, there might be a role called 'Administrator' that contains a different, more advanced set of permissions than a role entitled 'New User'. Roles can be associated with permissions and users, while permissions are associated with permission categories to allow for visible grouping of related permissions in the user interface. We will prefix every table name with the module name, `Accounts`, so that there is no conflict with other database tables.

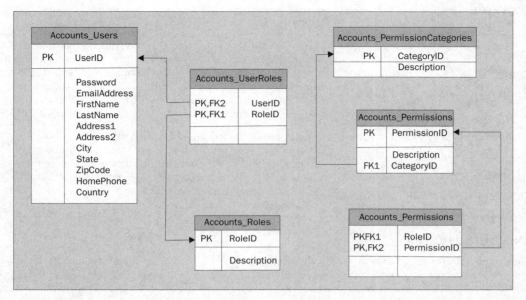

We can't stress enough the importance of a good application design when building your database schema. Because we spent the extra time to make sure that we had thought of as much as possible during the design phase, the creation of the database schema was fairly quick and painless.

The following is a brief description of each of the tables and how they relate to the other tables within the database. As with the other modules in this book, these tables will be added to the main database that we set up in Chapter 2. However, the module will be designed in such a way that, if the need arises, all of its data can come from an entirely separate data source. Full details of the columns, datatypes, keys, and nullabilities will be given in *The Solution* section later in this chapter.

Table	Description
Accounts_Users	This table is the core table for storing user information. Its primary key is the UserID, which is referenced by the Accounts_UserRoles table. It contains basic user information including password, e-mail address, and home contact information.
Accounts_Roles	This table is the core table for storing roles. RoleID is its primary key, which is referenced by the Accounts_RolePermissions table and the Accounts_UserRoles table.
Accounts_UserRoles	This is a mapping table used for cross-referencing roles and users. It essentially stores user membership within roles. Note that, since the combination of the UserID and RoleID form the primary key, it is possible for a user to be part of more than one role, allowing for some fairly advanced security techniques to be utilized.

Table continued on following page

Table	Description
Accounts_Permissions	This is the core table that stores verbose descriptions for each of the permissions. Note that when the code checks permissions, it checks them against a **hard-coded enumeration**. This table is used for user-friendly listing and querying of permission names and information. Its primary key is PermissionID, which is referenced by the Accounts_RolePermissions table.
Accounts_RolePermissions	This is another mapping table much like Accounts_UserRoles. It is responsible for mapping membership of permissions within roles. Again, note that, because of the dual primary key, a given permission can be granted to more than one role at a time, allowing for advanced security techniques.

Stored Procedures

Stored procedures are an integral part of the back-end data store for any web application. We could have the software in our data tier access the tables directly. However, it will keep our data-tier simpler and easier to maintain, as well as give higher performance, if we include some procedures within the database.

Fortunately for us, we're not doing anything overly complex with our stored procedures. Our procedures essentially mirror the functionality provided by the methods in the data-tier components, which we'll look at next. The following is a summarized list of the stored procedures we'll be using in this solution:

Stored Procedure Name	Description
sp_Accounts_CreateRole	Creates a new role in the database.
sp_Accounts_DeleteRole	Deletes an existing role, including removing all permissions from the role, and un-assigning all users from this role.
sp_Accounts_UpdateRole	Updates the description of a given role.
sp_Accounts_GetRoleDetails	Executes a SELECT, obtaining all pertinent details for a given role.
sp_Accounts_GetAllRoles	Obtains all roles in the entire system.
sp_Accounts_AddPermissionToRole	Adds a given permission to a given role.
sp_Accounts_RemovePermissionFromRole	Removes a given permission from a given role.
sp_Accounts_ClearPermissionsFromRole	Clears all permissions from a given role.
sp_Accounts_CreateUser	Creates a new user. Accepts only encrypted password arguments.
sp_Accounts_GetStateList	Utility function for obtaining list of all states for populating drop-down list UI control.

144

Stored Procedure Name	Description
sp_Accounts_UpdateUser	Updates pertinent details for a given user.
sp_Accounts_ValidateLogin	Validates a given e-mail address/encrypted password combination. If combination is valid, returns the numeric ID of valid user.
sp_Accounts_TestPassword	Tests a given encrypted password against the encrypted form of the given user ID's password.
sp_Accounts_GetPermissionCategories	Obtains a list of all permission categories in the entire system.
sp_Accounts_GetPermissionCategoryDetails	Obtains all detailed information (currently just a description) of the given category as indicated by the category ID parameter.
sp_Accounts_AddUserToRole	Assigns the given role to the given user.
sp_Acounts_RemoveUserFromRole	Removes the given user from the given role.

The Data Tier

The following is a summary of the design definitions for each of the data tier classes we think we'll need:

User Class Member	Description
Create	Creates a new user in the data store. This method accepts all of the arguments necessary for populating the appropriate database fields.
Retrieve	Retrieves a single user as indicated by the numeric user ID argument passed to the method. Returns a DataRow instance. Also has an overload allowing an e-mail address to be used to retrieve a user.
Update	Commits changes to a given user to the database. All arguments to this method correspond to database fields.
Delete	Removes a specific user from the data store as indicated by the numeric user ID passed to the method.
ValidateLogin	Returns a Boolean indicating whether or not a specific e-mail address and encrypted password is a valid login.
GetUserList	Obtains a completely unfiltered list of all users in the system. This function is intended for administrative purposes and for performance reasons should never be called by any UI function. Returns a DataSet.

Table continued on following page

User Class Member	Description
GetUserRoles	Returns an ArrayList indicating the list of roles to which the supplied user ID belongs.
GetEffectivePermissionList	Returns an ArrayList indicating the list of all permissions that the user has been granted based on their role membership.
TestPassword	Tests whether a supplied encrypted password is the same as the encrypted password in the data store for the given user.

Role Class Member	Description
Create	Creates a new role in the data store.
Update	Updates an existing role in the data store.
Delete	Removes an existing role in the data store. Removal of the role also causes all role membership records for this role to be removed, and all role-permission references to be removed.
Retrieve	Retrieves information on a single role in the form of a DataRow.
GetRoleList	Retrieves a list of roles in the system.
AddPermission	Adds a permission to the given role.
RemovePermission	Removes a permission from the given role.
ClearPermissions	Removes all permissions assigned to the role.

Permission Class Member	Description
Retrieve	Retrieves information on a single permission in the form of a DataRow.
GetPermissionList	Retrieves a list of permissions in the system. Returns a DataSet with relations providing a parent/child placing of permissions in categories.
GetPermissionList(role)	Retrieves a DataTable with a list of permissions belonging to a given role.

PermissionCategory Class Member	Description
Retrieve	Retrieves information on a single PermissionCategory in the form of a DataRow.
GetPermissionsInCategory	Retrieves a list of permissions belonging to a given category.
GetCategoryList	Retrieves a list of all permission categories in the system.

The Business Tier

Our business tier contains all the code that encapsulates business logic, workflow, process flow, non-data utility classes, and more. This next section will go through each of the specific things we will be designing for the implementation of the business tier of this module.

We're going to build two main classes as well as two more classes that will allow us to integrate with and extend the existing security system implemented by the ASP.NET core:

❑ The User class – we'll use this class to represent a user of the system.

❑ The Role class – we'll use this class to represent a single role within the system.

❑ SitePrincipal and SiteIdentity – these two classes, which we will discuss in greater detail later, will be used to integrate our custom security system into the existing security system already in place within ASP.NET.

The User Class

The User class encapsulates a user as they interact with the web application. This class is used specifically for loading information about a specific user, as well as creating, updating, and deleting users.

The User class is not used in authentication schemes – it is used to store general information about the user. We will use this class when users are logging into the system and either creating a new account or updating information on their existing account. We will look at the design for handling authentication schemes in the *Extending .NET Framework User Handling* section later in this chapter.

The following is a detailed description of the features and functionality we have designed into our User class:

User Class Member	Description
UserID	Property indicating the database ID of the given user.
FirstName	Property to set or get the first name of the user.
LastName	Property to set or get the last name of the user.
Address1	Property to set or get the first line of the user's address.
Address2	Property to set or get the second line of the user's address.
City	Property allowing read/write access to the user's city.
State	Property allowing read/write access to the user's state.
ZipCode	Property allowing read/write access to the user's zip code.
Country	Property allowing read/write access to the user's country.
EmailAddress	Property to set or get the e-mail address of the user.
Create()	Method that will create a new user by adding a new record to the database based on the supplied parameters.

Table continued on following page

User Class Member	**Description**
Update()	Method that will update the user's persisted information based on the values of the properties of the current user.
User()	Default constructor.
User(int)	Constructs a new instance of a user based on the numeric database user ID provided as the sole argument.
User(SitePrincipal)	Creates a new instance of a user based on an instance of the SitePrincipal class. So User((SitePrincipal)HttpContext.User) will return information about the currently logged in user.

The Role Class

A content-based web site is only as good as its content. In a site such as the one we are building, it is extremely important that we provide new and fresh content. To do this we need to maintain a pool of regular contributors. These contributors are typically responsible for obtaining, arranging for, or creating content.

Many of the site's users need to be able to create content. For example, a website that provides video game reviews needs to allow a team of reviewers to enter in new game reviews. A separate group of people might need to be allowed to upload screenshots of games not yet on the market, and yet another set of site visitors might need the ability to upload game previews or interviews with game publishers and developers. However, in each case we might not want to give all these abilities to all members of staff.

What this all boils down to is the need for roles. A role is a classification of a responsibility, duty, or job. Giving administrators the opportunity to create roles, and assign privileges to these roles, we allow for the type of flexibility we need in order to provide a fully functional content site. This also allows us to support a situation where a single user might have more than one duty. For example, many game review sites have reviewers who also need to post screenshots and interviews. However, there might be others who only need to post screenshots. A flexible system of roles enables this.

So any user can have a number of roles. To encapsulate a role, we will create a Role class with the following members:

Role Class Member	**Description**
RoleID	Property containing the numeric database identifier for the given instance of the role.
Description	Property containing the verbose (string) description of the particular instance of a role.
Permissions	Property containing the list/array of permissions granted to the role.
Create()	Creates a new role based on the values of the properties of the current instance.
Delete()	Deletes the current role, removing all associated permissions and un-assigning all appropriate users from the role.

Role Class Member	Description
Update()	Updates the current role based on the values of the properties of the current instance.
AddPermission(int)	Adds a given numeric permission identifier to the role, effectively granting that permission to all users who belong to the role.
RemovePermission(int)	Removes a given numeric permission identifier from the role, effectively removing that permission from all users who belong to the role.
ClearPermissions()	Removes all permissions from the current instance of a role.
Role()	Default constructor. Used when building a new role for the first time.
Role(int)	Constructor. Creates a new instance of a role based on that role's numeric database identifier.

Extending .NET Framework User Handling

One of the hardest aspects of .NET Framework programming is determining whether the Framework already provides a feature that we need, or whether we need to build it ourselves. If Microsoft already provides features for what we want to do, we should seriously consider using Microsoft's implementation.

The harder decisions appear when Microsoft has implemented something *similar* to what we need. This decision boils down to deciding whether to create our own implementation, or extend the Framework to suit our needs. It is worth spending some time looking for candidates to extend before developing our own solution from scratch.

This is true of our custom security for the website. The built-in user authentication support in ASP.NET is great. It automatically populates a property called User in the Context object. This property gives us access to all kinds of information, including whether or not the user has been authenticated, the type of authentication used to verify the user, and even the name of the user. Whether we use forms-based or Windows authentication, we can still use the User object in the current HttpContext instance, represented by the Context object.

> The Context.User object provided by the .NET Framework is not the same as the User class described earlier. Context.User is concerned with authentication, while our User class is concerned with encapsulating general information about a particular user.

However, Microsoft's implementation doesn't provide a way to obtain permission levels from a database. Microsoft's implementation is designed to use whatever role-based security mechanism is available to it. This means using NT groups when Windows authentication is enabled, etc. But we can extend Microsoft's system, so that our custom security does everything we need.

Before we spend more time discussing how we plan to extend it, we should talk a little about the existing Framework itself. Security within .NET (not just ASP.NET) is based around the concept of a **principal**. A principal object is a representation of the security context of the user on whose behalf the code is running. So, if I am running a program, then the principal is my security context for the duration of that program. One level lower than the principal is the **identity**. The identity represents the user who is executing the code. Therefore, every principal has an identity. This idea of a common principal and identity is used in forms-based authentication, Windows authentication, and is even used to pass credentials to websites and remoting hosts in other aspects of .NET programming. We decided that rather than implement our own security system, we would create our own concept of a principal and identity that snugly snapped into place within Microsoft's existing security framework. To allow programmers to easily adapt the existing security system, Microsoft provided the IPrincipal and IIdentity interfaces.

The object assigned to HttpContext.User must implement the IPrincipal interface. One of the properties defined by IPrincipal is Identity, which must implement the IIdentity interface. So if we write our own custom classes that implement these interfaces, we can add any capabilities we need. This is one of the beauties of having an extensive, inheritable framework – once we get familiar with it then we find that a lot of our work is already done.

Creating two classes that implement IPrincipal and IIdentity, called SitePrincipal and SiteIdentity, we can snap our classes into the existing framework. The following table shows the members of the SitePrincipal and SiteIdentity classes. Members defined by the standard interfaces are in normal type, while the new ones that we have created have their names in bold:

SitePrincipal Class Members (available through HttpContext.User)	
Identity	Property that gets the identity of the current principal. Returns an object implementing the IIdentity interface.
IsInRole	Method that returns a Boolean indicating whether or not the current principal belongs to a given role, specified with a string. We will be providing our own custom version of this method that queries our list of custom roles from our database.
Permissions	An array of PermissionIDs that the user has been granted indirectly through membership in various roles.
Roles	An array containing a list of roles to which the current principal belongs. Note that these roles are roles stored in our custom database, and are not to be confused with COM+ roles.
ValidateLogin	A method used to validate a specific set of login credentials, which include an e-mail address and a password.
HasPermission	A method used to query whether or not the principal belongs to a given role, as indicated by the supplied RoleID integer.
EncryptPassword	A method used to encrypt a plain text string representing a password.

The SitePrincipal class will enable the site to tell what a user is allowed to do. The Identity property will also tell us who the user is. In normal operation, the Framework itself will determine the identity of the user that owns the security context. In our situation, we will manually set the identity of the principal by using forms-based authentication in ASP.NET.

SiteIdentity Class Members (available through HttpContext.User.Identity)	
AuthenticationType	A string property representing the type of authentication used to obtain the current identity.
IsAuthenticated	Boolean value indicating whether or not the current identity is an authenticated user.
Name	A string property representing the name of the current identity.
FirstName	First name of the user identity; used in various UI controls for providing personalized user greetings.
LastName	Last name of the user identity; used in various UI controls for providing personalized user greetings.
EmailAddress	E-mail address of the user identity.
Password	Encrypted, binary form of the user's password.
UserID	Integer representing the database ID of the user identity.
TestPassword(string)	Method that takes a plain text string representing the user's password and compares it against the encrypted form stored in the database. Returns Boolean true if the password matches, false otherwise.

In *The Solution* section we get to look at the code implementation of the above security classes, and their relationship to the rest of the module, the website itself, and the existing security framework will become more clear.

Module Configuration

One of the main goals of this book is to illustrate the use and integration of multiple modules that provide different, unique functionality. These modules that we are developing throughout this book are all designed in such a way that they can either use their own database or share a central database. This is accomplished by allowing the modules to be configured through the use of XML configuration files and the Web.Config file provided by ASP.NET. These configuration files also allow us to specify module-specific configuration settings in a way that is easy for us to modify and maintain.

Some of this next section may not be all that familiar to you unless you have used XML class **serialization** and **de-serialization** using the .NET Framework. Serialization is the process of converting an instance of a class to a file on disk, or a stream, in the form of XML. De-serialization is converting an XML stream or file into an instance of a class. Every one of the modules we're developing has its own configuration. This configuration is stored in a special XML file for the module itself. In order for the modules to find their own configuration files, they will use the central site configuration file (Web.Config). In this central configuration file we will store the location of the module-specific configuration files.

Let's take a look at what a snippet of the Web.Config file looks like, with the location of our user module file in it (if you're coding along while reading, you'll want to add the following to your copy of the Web.Config file in your ThePhile web application):

```
<!-- LOCAL APPLICATION SETTINGS -->
<appSettings>
 <add key="Accounts_SettingsFile" value="/ThePhile/Config/Accounts.Config"/>
</appSettings>
```

This is found at the bottom of our `Web.Config` file, immediately after the `<system.web>` node, but still within the `<configuration>` node.

The essential core of our design is that we're going to create two classes. The first class, `ModuleConfig`, is a helper class that we'll use to retrieve and save (serialize and de-serialize) instances of our `ModuleSettings` class. The `ModuleSettings` class is nothing more than a serializable container of properties that represent **keys** in our custom XML configuration file. These keys are the string keys that are paired with the values in typical name-value pair fashion.

The ModuleConfig Class

As we mentioned above, the `ModuleConfig` class is a helper class that we use to create instances of the `ModuleSettings` class based on our custom XML configuration file, as well as take modified instances of the `ModuleSettings` class and save them back to XML, allowing for programmatic and user-driven changes to the configuration file.

The following is the design definition of our `ModuleConfig` class. As we progress throughout the book, you'll see this concept of the configuration-settings class pair used extensively.

ModuleConfig Class Member	Description
GetSettings()	Shared class method that returns an instance of the `ModuleSettings` class, properly de-serialized according to the values contained in the custom XML configuration file.
SaveSettings(ModuleSettings)	Shared class method that takes an instance of the `ModuleSettings` class and serializes it into the custom XML configuration file for our module.

The ModuleSettings Class

The `ModuleSettings` class, as we stated above, is simply a class that exposes public, serializable properties. The class *must* be designed so that its state is entirely preserved throughout a serialization and de-serialization. In other words, there can be no 'one-way' (write-only or read-only) properties, or the class will not function properly.

Each `ModuleSettings` class for each module is going to vary in that some modules require more administrative configuration than others (for example, `Forums` and `Advertising`). However, all of the modules are going to require that at least one setting be maintained. That setting is the database connection string used by the data tier in order to communicate with the database.

The following is a sample XML configuration file (`/ThePhile/Config/Accounts.Config`) defining a single serializable property for use by the module, `ConnectionString`. Again, if you're coding along with the chapter, you'll want to create this file now and populate it with the well-formed XML below. Note that this is simply a supporting data file, and there is no need to place this file in Visual Studio .NET:

```
<?xml version="1.0"?>
<ModuleSettings xmlns:xsi="http://www.w3.org/2001/XMLSchema-instance"
                xmlns:xsd="http://www.w3.org/2001/XMLSchema">
  <ConnectionString>
    server=(local);database=ThePhile;uid=sa;pwd=;
  </ConnectionString>
</ModuleSettings>
```

We'll show how to configure a class for XML serialization in *The Solution* section of this chapter. The following is the simple definition of our `ModuleSettings` class:

ModuleSettings Class	Description
ConnectionString	String property to set or get the value of the database connection string for the given module.

You'll have plenty of opportunity to see how the configuration classes are utilized when we cover the source code for this module (and as you examine the source code for virtually any module developed throughout this book).

We've now covered pretty much all of the classes that we plan on building for this particular module, so let's move on to briefly discuss the front-end design.

Administration

There isn't all that much to design in terms of the administration of the `Accounts` module. At a basic level, we will be providing site administrators with the ability to use a set of web pages to create new roles, update existing roles, grant/revoke permissions on roles, and grant/revoke roles on users. For security and confidentiality reasons, we've decided that administrative staff should not have the ability to edit users' personal information. Instead we will allow users to edit their own information on-line.

> *Of course, in a more realistic, real-world situation, the administrative staff of the site should have some kind of back-end tool that allows them to change e-mail addresses for users. Also, most successful large-scale websites include a feature that allows a user have their password e-mailed to them if they have forgotten it.*

You will see further coverage of how we're planning to administer the security system in the next section, where we will go through the sample source code for the administration pages.

The Solution

We have spent some time looking at our design, and will now start to build the software. To recap, we are implementing a traditional three-tier solution with distinct presentation, business logic, and data services tiers.

We'll start by implementing the database changes, and then work our way up through the data tier and the business tier to the presentation tier.

The Database

We've already looked at the table structure that we'll use for this part of the database. We can choose whether to construct it using visual tools or SQL scripts. In Chapter 6 we'll look at the Enterprise Manager's visual tools; for now we'll present the SQL scripts that can be run in the Query Analyzer. The scripts required are as follows:

```
CREATE TABLE [dbo].[Accounts_PermissionCategories] (
                    [CategoryID] [int] IDENTITY (1, 1) NOT NULL,
                    [Description] [varchar] (50) NOT NULL )
  ON [PRIMARY]
GO

CREATE TABLE [dbo].[Accounts_Permissions] (
                    [PermissionID] [int] NOT NULL,
                    [Description] [varchar] (50) NOT NULL,
                    [CategoryID] [int] NOT NULL )
  ON [PRIMARY]
GO

CREATE TABLE [dbo].[Accounts_RolePermissions] (
                    [RoleID] [int] NOT NULL,
                    [PermissionID] [int] NOT NULL )
  ON [PRIMARY]
GO

CREATE TABLE [dbo].[Accounts_Roles] (
                    [RoleID] [int] IDENTITY (1, 1) NOT NULL,
                    [Description] [varchar] (50) NOT NULL )
  ON [PRIMARY]
GO

CREATE TABLE [dbo].[Accounts_StateCodes] (
                    [Description] [varchar] (60) NOT NULL,
                    [StateCode] [char] (2) NOT NULL )
  ON [PRIMARY]
GO

CREATE TABLE [dbo].[Accounts_UserRoles] (
                    [RoleID] [int] NOT NULL,
                    [UserID] [int] NOT NULL )
  ON [PRIMARY]
GO

CREATE TABLE [dbo].[Accounts_Users] (
                    [UserID] [int] IDENTITY (1, 1) NOT NULL,
                    [EmailAddress] [varchar] (255) NOT NULL,
                    [FirstName] [varchar] (30) NOT NULL,
                    [LastName] [varchar] (50) NOT NULL,
                    [Address1] [varchar] (80) NOT NULL,
                    [Address2] [varchar] (80) NOT NULL,
                    [City] [varchar] (40) NOT NULL,
                    [State] [char] (2) NOT NULL,
```

```
                              [ZipCode] [varchar] (10) NOT NULL,
                              [HomePhone] [varchar] (14) NOT NULL,
                              [Password] [binary] (20) NOT NULL,
                              [Country] [varchar] (50) NOT NULL )
      ON [PRIMARY]
   GO
```

Stored Procedures

There are quite a few stored procedures employed in this module. Rather than going through each one, we will look at two representative examples. The full code for all procedures is included in the website's database available in the code download.

The following is the code for creating the sp_Accounts_GetEffectivePermissionList stored procedure. Again, this script can be run in the Query Analyzer. This stored procedure retrieves the list of all permissions granted to a user by virtue of their role membership:

```
CREATE PROCEDURE sp_Accounts_GetEffectivePermissionList @UserID int
AS
   SELECT DISTINCT PermissionID
     FROM Accounts_RolePermissions
     WHERE RoleID IN
       (SELECT RoleID FROM Accounts_UserRoles WHERE UserID = @UserID)
```

One of the more complex procedures is sp_Accounts_GetPermissionList. This procedure effectively obtains the sum of all permissions granted to a role. It performs a **join** (a way of looking up related data from more than one table) in order to obtain the verbose description of each permission assigned to the given role:

```
CREATE PROCEDURE sp_Accounts_GetPermissionList @RoleID int = NULL
AS
   IF @RoleID IS NULL
     SELECT PermissionID, Description
       FROM Accounts_Permissions
       ORDER BY Description
   ELSE
     SELECT ap.PermissionID, ap.Description
       FROM Accounts_Permissions ap
       INNER JOIN Accounts_RolePermissions apr
       ON ap.PermissionID = apr.PermissionID
       WHERE apr.RoleID = @RoleID
       ORDER BY ap.Description
```

Note the use of table name aliases (ap for Accounts_Permissions *and* apr *for* Accounts_RolePermissions*) to avoid having to type out the full table names each time we use them.*

The Data Tier

Now that we've seen an overview of the database implementation, we will look at the classes residing in our data services tier: User, Role, Permission, PermissionCategory, and a helper class.

User

The User class provides the basic CRUD (Create, Retrieve, Update, Delete) functionality required for any data entity. It does this with methods alone – it has no maintained state – and simply acts as a bridge between the business tier and the database.

The following is the source code listing for the User class. The full code is in the User.vb file from the AccountsData project in the code download. We start by importing namespaces, and declaring that we will extend Wrox.WebModules.Data.DbObject – our data-services base class:

```
Imports System
Imports System.Collections
Imports System.Data
Imports System.Data.SqlClient
Imports Wrox.WebModules.Accounts

Namespace WebModules.Accounts.Data

  Public Class User
    Inherits Wrox.WebModules.Data.DbObject
```

We want to make use of the functionality of the constructor in the parent class, DbObject, so we simply derive the constructor from it:

```
    Public Sub New(ByVal newConnectionString As String)
      MyBase.New(newConnectionString)
    End Sub
```

The following method creates a new user record, based on the supplied parameters. Firstly we create an array of SqlParameter objects, and construct each element appropriately. Then we assign them the value given by the corresponding method parameter. We then run the procedure in a try block. If the try fails, we catch the error.

```
    Public Function Create( _
        ByVal emailAddress As String, _
        ByVal password As Byte(), _
        ByVal firstName As String, _
        ByVal lastName As String, _
        ByVal address1 As String, _
        ByVal address2 As String, _
        ByVal city As String, _
        ByVal state As String, _
        ByVal zipCode As String, _
        ByVal homePhone As String, _
        ByVal country As String) As Integer


      Dim rowsAffected As Integer
      Dim parameters As SqlParameter() = { _
        New SqlParameter("@EmailAddress", SqlDbType.VarChar, 255), _
        New SqlParameter("@Password", SqlDbType.Binary, 20), _
```

```
        New SqlParameter("@FirstName", SqlDbType.VarChar, 30), _
        New SqlParameter("@LastName", SqlDbType.VarChar, 50), _
        New SqlParameter("@Address1", SqlDbType.VarChar, 80), _
        New SqlParameter("@Address2", SqlDbType.VarChar, 80), _
        New SqlParameter("@City", SqlDbType.VarChar, 40), _
        New SqlParameter("@State", SqlDbType.VarChar, 2), _
        New SqlParameter("@ZipCode", SqlDbType.VarChar, 10), _
        New SqlParameter("@HomePhone", SqlDbType.VarChar, 14), _
        New SqlParameter("@Country", SqlDbType.VarChar, 50), _
        New SqlParameter("@UserID", SqlDbType.Int, 4)}

    parameters(0).Value = emailAddress
    parameters(1).Value = password
    parameters(2).Value = firstName
    parameters(3).Value = lastName
    parameters(4).Value = address1
    parameters(5).Value = address2
    parameters(6).Value = city
    parameters(7).Value = state
    parameters(8).Value = zipCode
    parameters(9).Value = homePhone
    parameters(10).Value = country
    parameters(11).Direction = ParameterDirection.Output


    Try

        RunProcedure("sp_Accounts_CreateUser", parameters, rowsAffected)

    Catch exc As SqlException
```

If an error occurred we check the procedure's return value – otherwise we pass the exception up the call stack. If the return value is 2601, it matches our code for "primary key already exists" (in other words we tried to violate a unique index). We return a value from our enumeration – AccountAlreadyOnFile. This allows our user interface to intelligently trap a duplicate user entry failure.

```
        If exc.Number = 2601 Then
          Return CInt(ProcResultCodes.AccountAlreadyOnFile)
        Else
          Throw New AppException("An error occurred while executing" & _
            "the Accounts_CreateUser stored procedure", exc)
        End If

    End Try

    Return CInt(parameters(11).Value)

End Function
```

The next method retrieves a record from the database, based on a userID:

```
Public Overloads Function Retrieve(ByVal userId As Integer) As DataRow

  Dim parameters As SqlParameter() = { _
    New SqlParameter("@UserID", SqlDbType.Int, 4)}
  parameters(0).Value = userId

  Dim users As DataSet
  Try
    users = RunProcedure( _
      "sp_Accounts_GetUserDetails", parameters, "Users")
    Return users.Tables(0).Rows(0)
  Finally
    If Not users Is Nothing Then
      users.Dispose()
    End If
  End Try

End Function
```

You can see here that we use a `Try ... Finally ... End Try` block to ensure that an object is disposed of immediately after we have used it. The code in the `Finally` section will always run, even after the `Return` statement has been encountered.

The next method is an overload of `Retrieve` that retrieves details based on an e-mail address instead of a `userID`:

```
Public Overloads Function Retrieve( _
  ByVal emailAddress As String) _
  As DataRow

  Dim parameters As SqlParameter() = { _
    New SqlParameter("@EmailAddress", SqlDbType.VarChar, 255)}
  parameters(0).Value = emailAddress

  Dim users As DataSet
  Try
    users = RunProcedure( _
      "sp_Accounts_GetUserDetailsByEmail", parameters, "Users")

    If users.Tables(0).Rows.Count = 0 Then
      Throw New AppException("No user found on file for Email: " & _
        emailAddress)
    Else
      Return users.Tables(0).Rows(0)
    End If
  Finally
    If Not users Is Nothing Then
      users.Dispose()
    End If
  End Try

End Function
```

The Update method passes the user's details and updates the database accordingly. The return parameter confirms that the row was updated:

```
Public Function Update( _
    ByVal userId As Integer, _
    ByVal emailAddress As String, _
    ByVal password As Byte(), _
    ByVal firstName As String, _
    ByVal lastName As String, _
    ByVal address1 As String, _
    ByVal address2 As String, _
    ByVal city As String, _
    ByVal state As String, _
    ByVal zipCode As String, _
    ByVal homePhone As String, _
    ByVal country As String) As Boolean

    Dim rowsAffected As Integer
    Dim parameters As SqlParameter() = { _
        New SqlParameter("@EmailAddress", SqlDbType.VarChar, 255), _
        New SqlParameter("@Password", SqlDbType.Binary, 20), _
        New SqlParameter("@FirstName", SqlDbType.VarChar, 30), _
        New SqlParameter("@LastName", SqlDbType.VarChar, 50), _
        New SqlParameter("@Address1", SqlDbType.VarChar, 80), _
        New SqlParameter("@Address2", SqlDbType.VarChar, 80), _
        New SqlParameter("@City", SqlDbType.VarChar, 40), _
        New SqlParameter("@State", SqlDbType.VarChar, 2), _
        New SqlParameter("@ZipCode", SqlDbType.VarChar, 10), _
        New SqlParameter("@HomePhone", SqlDbType.VarChar, 14), _
        New SqlParameter("@Country", SqlDbType.VarChar, 50), _
        New SqlParameter("@UserID", SqlDbType.Int, 4)}

    parameters(0).Value = emailAddress
    parameters(1).Value = password
    parameters(2).Value = firstName
    parameters(3).Value = lastName
    parameters(4).Value = address1
    parameters(5).Value = address2
    parameters(6).Value = city
    parameters(7).Value = state
    parameters(8).Value = zipCode
    parameters(9).Value = homePhone
    parameters(10).Value = country
    parameters(11).Value = userId

    RunProcedure("sp_Accounts_UpdateUser", parameters, rowsAffected)

    Return CBool(rowsAffected = 1)

End Function
```

The Delete method deletes the specified user, and returns a Boolean indicating whether the operation was useful:

159

```
      Public Function Delete(ByVal userID As Integer) As Boolean

        Dim rowsAffected As Integer
        Dim parameters As SqlParameter() = { _
          New SqlParameter("@UserID", SqlDbType.Int, 4)}

        parameters(0).Value = userID

        RunProcedure("sp_Accounts_DeleteUser", parameters, rowsAffected)

        Return CBool(rowsAffected = 1)

      End Function
```

The following method takes an e-mail address and an encrypted password – the password is always encrypted before it's marshaled across tiers. If the user details are valid, it returns the user's ID:

```
      Public Function ValidateLogin( _
        ByVal emailAddress As String, _
        ByVal encPassword As Byte()) _
        As Integer

        Dim rowsAffected As Integer
        Dim parameters As SqlParameter() = { _
          New SqlParameter("@EmailAddress", SqlDbType.VarChar, 255), _
          New SqlParameter("@EncryptedPassword", SqlDbType.Binary, 20)}

        parameters(0).Value = emailAddress
        parameters(1).Value = encPassword

        Return RunProcedure( _
          "sp_Accounts_ValidateLogin", parameters, rowsAffected)

      End Function
```

The next method, listed below, takes a specific userID (the numeric identity column in SQL Server) and an encrypted password. If the password matches the password belonging to the user as indicated by the database, the method returns a 1, otherwise a 0. This is accomplished by executing the sp_Accounts_TestPassword stored procedure.

```
      Public Function TestPassword( _
        ByVal userId As Integer, _
        ByVal encPassword As Byte()) _
        As Integer

        Dim rowsAffected As Integer
        Dim parameters As SqlParameter() = { _
          New SqlParameter("@UserID", SqlDbType.Int, 4), _
          New SqlParameter("@EncryptedPassword", SqlDbType.Binary, 20)}

        parameters(0).Value = userId
        parameters(1).Value = encPassword
```

```
        Return RunProcedure( _
          "sp_Accounts_TestPassword", parameters, rowsAffected)

    End Function
```

The following method executes the sp_Accounts_GetUserRoles stored procedure. It obtains a SqlDataReader containing the list of all roles assigned to a given user. This SqlDataReader is then converted into an ArrayList and returned to the calling tier to be utilized in a property of the User class.

```
    Public Function GetUserRoles(ByVal userId As Integer) As ArrayList

      Dim roles As New ArrayList()
      Dim parameters As SqlParameter() = { _
        New SqlParameter("@UserID", SqlDbType.Int, 4)}

      parameters(0).Value = userId

      Dim tempReader As SqlDataReader = _
        RunProcedure("sp_Accounts_GetUserRoles", parameters)

      ' The 'SqlDataReader.Read' method returns 'True' if there
      ' are more rows to read
      While tempReader.Read
        roles.Add(tempReader.GetString(1))
      End While

      tempReader.Close()

      Return roles

    End Function
```

The method listed below calls the sp_Accounts_GetEffectivePermissionList stored procedure. This stored procedure returns a SqlDataReader indicating all permissions granted to a user by virtue of their role memberships. This SqlDataReader is then iterated through, converted into an ArrayList, and returned up to the User class in the business tier.

```
    Public Function GetEffectivePermissionList( _
      ByVal userId As Integer) _
      As ArrayList

      Dim permissions As New ArrayList()
      Dim parameters As SqlParameter() = { _
        New SqlParameter("@UserID", SqlDbType.Int, 4)}

      parameters(0).Value = userId

      Dim tempReader As SqlDataReader = _
        RunProcedure("sp_Accounts_GetEffectivePermissionList", parameters)

      While tempReader.Read
        permissions.Add(tempReader.GetInt32(0))
      End While
```

```
    tempReader.Close()

    Return permissions

End Function
```

The method below returns a list of all users in the database in the form of a `DataSet` object:

```
Public Function GetUserList() As DataSet

  Return RunProcedure( _
    "sp_Accounts_GetUsers", New IDataParameter() {}, "Users")

End Function
```

Finally, we have two methods that allow us to add or remove the user from a specified role:

```
Public Function AddRole( _
  ByVal userId As Integer, _
  ByVal roleId As Integer) _
  As Boolean

  Dim rowsAffected As Integer
  Dim parameters As SqlParameter() = { _
    New SqlParameter("@UserID", SqlDbType.Int, 4), _
    New SqlParameter("@RoleID", SqlDbType.Int, 4)}

  parameters(0).Value = userId
  parameters(1).Value = roleId

  RunProcedure("sp_Accounts_AddUserToRole", parameters, rowsAffected)

  Return CBool(rowsAffected = 1)
End Function


Public Function RemoveRole( _
  ByVal userId As Integer, _
  ByVal roleId As Integer) _
  As Boolean

  Dim rowsAffected As Integer
  Dim parameters As SqlParameter() = { _
    New SqlParameter("@UserID", SqlDbType.Int, 4), _
    New SqlParameter("@RoleID", SqlDbType.Int, 4)}

  parameters(0).Value = userId
  parameters(1).Value = roleId

  RunProcedure( _
    "sp_Accounts_RemoveUserFromRole", parameters, rowsAffected)

  Return CBool(rowsAffected = 1)
End Function
```

Role

The Role class in the data services tier is responsible for making all changes to the database relating to roles, as well as retrieving single and multiple roles at a time from the database.

We will now look at the source code listing for the Role class, which can be found in the Role.vb file from the AccountsData project.

Like the User class, we based Role on our DbObject base class and make use of its constructor:

```
Imports System
Imports System.Data
Imports System.Data.SqlClient


Namespace WebModules.Accounts.Data

  Public Class Role
    Inherits Wrox.WebModules.Data.DbObject

    Public Sub New(ByVal newConnectionString As String)
      MyBase.New(newConnectionString)
    End Sub
```

The method below takes a description of a new role and creates that role in the database. As usual, all database access takes place via stored procedures:

```
Public Function Create(ByVal description As String) As Integer

    Dim rowsAffected As Integer
    Dim parameters As SqlParameter() = { _
      New SqlParameter("@Description", SqlDbType.VarChar, 50)}

    parameters(0).Value = description

    Return RunProcedure("sp_Accounts_CreateRole", parameters, rowsAffected)

End Function
```

In this next method, a role is deleted by supplying the numeric ID of the role. This is facilitated by the sp_Accounts_DeleteRole stored procedure:

```
Public Function Delete(ByVal roleId As Integer) As Boolean

    Dim rowsAffected As Integer
    Dim parameters As SqlParameter() = { _
      New SqlParameter("@RoleID", SqlDbType.Int, 4)}

    parameters(0).Value = roleId

    RunProcedure("sp_Accounts_DeleteRole", parameters, rowsAffected)

    Return CBool(rowsAffected = 1)

End Function
```

This next method updates an existing role. We supply the existing role's numeric ID and the new description of the role, and the sp_Accounts_UpdateRole stored procedure is called to commit the changes to the database:

```
Public Function Update( _
  ByVal roleId As Integer, _
  ByVal description As String) _
  As Boolean

  Dim rowsAffected As Integer
  Dim parameters As SqlParameter() = { _
      New SqlParameter("@RoleID", SqlDbType.Int, 4), _
      New SqlParameter("@Description", SqlDbType.VarChar, 50)}

  parameters(0).Value = roleId
  parameters(1).Value = description

  RunProcedure("sp_Accounts_UpdateRole", parameters, rowsAffected)

  Return CBool(rowsAffected = 1)

End Function
```

The method below retrieves a single role by requesting it from the database using the role's numeric ID. The data for the role is placed in a single DataRow instance.

```
Public Function Retrieve(ByVal roleId As Integer) As DataRow

  Dim rowsAffected As Integer
  Dim parameters As SqlParameter() = { _
    New SqlParameter("@RoleID", SqlDbType.Int, 4)}

  parameters(0).Value = roleId

  Dim roles As DataSet
  Try
    roles = RunProcedure( _
      "sp_Accounts_GetRoleDetails", parameters, "Roles")
    Return roles.Tables(0).Rows(0)
  Finally
    If Not roles Is Nothing Then
      roles.Dispose()
    End If
  End Try

End Function
```

This next method returns a DataSet populated with a list of all the roles in the database. This list is sorted alphabetically by the sp_Accounts_GetAllRoles stored procedure.

```
Public Function GetRoleList() As DataSet

    Dim roles As DataSet
    Try
        roles = RunProcedure( _
            "sp_Accounts_GetAllRoles", New IDataParameter() {}, "Roles")
        Return roles
    Finally
        If Not roles Is Nothing Then
            roles.Dispose()
        End If
    End Try
End Function
```

This next method adds a permission to an existing role. By supplying the role identifier and the numeric ID for the permission, the Accounts_RolePermissions table is modified by calling the sp_Accounts_AddPermissionToRole stored procedure. If the permission is already part of the role, the method simply does nothing (the stored procedure exits successfully without making any changes).

```
Public Sub AddPermission( _
    ByVal roleId As Integer, _
    ByVal permissionId As Integer)

    Dim rowsAffected As Integer
    Dim parameters As SqlParameter() = { _
        New SqlParameter("@RoleID", SqlDbType.Int, 4), _
        New SqlParameter("@PermissionID", SqlDbType.Int, 4)}

    parameters(0).Value = roleId
    parameters(1).Value = permissionId

    RunProcedure( _
        "sp_Accounts_AddPermissionToRole", parameters, rowsAffected)

End Sub
```

This next method is essentially the opposite of the previous. By supplying a role identifier and a permission identifier, we effectively remove the permission from the role. If the permission is not currently part of the role, then the method simply does nothing.

```
Public Sub RemovePermission( _
    ByVal roleId As Integer, _
    ByVal permissionId As Integer)

    Dim rowsAffected As Integer
    Dim parameters As SqlParameter() = { _
        New SqlParameter("@RoleID", SqlDbType.Int, 4), _
        New SqlParameter("@PermissionID", SqlDbType.Int, 4)}

    parameters(0).Value = roleId
    parameters(1).Value = permissionId
```

```
        RunProcedure( _
          "sp_Accounts_RemovePermissionFromRole", parameters, rowsAffected)

    End Sub
```

The following method will completely remove all permissions from a given role by calling the
`sp_Accounts_ClearPermissionsFromRole` stored procedure:

```
    Public Sub ClearPermissions(ByVal roleId As Integer)

      Dim rowsAffected As Integer
      Dim parameters As SqlParameter() = { _
        New SqlParameter("@RoleID", SqlDbType.Int, 4)}

      parameters(0).Value = roleId

      RunProcedure( _
          "sp_Accounts_ClearPermissionsFromRole", parameters, rowsAffected)
    End Sub
  End Class
End Namespace
```

Permission

What each permission does is defined by database administrators and programmers of the website. This
class cannot change the permissions themselves. It provides an overloaded method called
`GetPermissionList`, which can either obtain an unfiltered list of all permissions in the system, or a
list of all permissions belonging to a given role. Both of these methods return a hierarchical `DataSet`
with a parent-child relationship already defined. This means we can traverse it in a data-bound control.

The following is the source code listing for the `Permission` class, found in the `Permission.vb` file –
part of the `AccountsData` project:

```
Imports System
Imports System.Data
Imports System.Data.SqlClient


Namespace WebModules.Accounts.Data

  Public Class Permission
    Inherits Wrox.WebModules.Data.DbObject

    Public Sub New(ByVal newConnectionString As String)
      MyBase.New(newConnectionString)
    End Sub
```

The following method loads a single permission by calling the
`sp_Accounts_GetPermissionDetails` and storing the results in an instance of the `DataRow` object:

```
    Public Function Retrieve(ByVal permissionId As Integer) As DataRow

      Dim parameters As SqlParameter() = { _
        New SqlParameter("@PermissionID", SqlDbType.Int, 4)}

      Dim permissions As DataSet
      Try
        RunProcedure( _
          "sp_Accounts_GetPermissionDetails", parameters, "Permissions")
        If permissions.Tables(0).Rows.Count = 0 Then
          Throw New AppException( _
            "No such permission found on file (" & permissionId & ").")
        Else
          Return permissions.Tables(0).Rows(0)
        End If
      Finally
        If Not permissions Is Nothing Then
          permissions.Dispose()
        End If
      End Try

    End Function
```

The following method loads all permissions in the database into a `DataSet` instance by calling the `sp_Accounts_GetPermissionCategories` stored procedure. The categories are then placed into the permissions `DataSet`. Then, the `sp_Accounts_GetPermissions` stored procedure is called to obtain all permissions in the database. Once both the permissions and categories are stored in the `DataSet`, we create a `DataRelation` to establish a parent-child relationship between permission categories and permissions.

```
    Public Overloads Function GetPermissionList() As DataSet

      Dim parameters As SqlParameter() = { _
        New SqlParameter("@RoleID", SqlDbType.Int, 4)}

      Dim permissions As DataSet
      Try

        permissions = RunProcedure( _
          "sp_Accounts_GetPermissionCategories", _
          New IDataParameter() {}, _
          "Categories")

        RunProcedure( _
          "sp_Accounts_GetPermissionList", _
          parameters, _
          permissions, _
          "Permissions")

        Dim permissionCategories As New DataRelation( _
          "PermissionCategories", _
          permissions.Tables("Categories").Columns("CategoryID"), _
          permissions.Tables("Permissions").Columns("CategoryID"))
```

```
            permissions.Relations.Add(permissionCategories)

         Return permissions

      Finally
         If Not permissions Is Nothing Then
            permissions.Dispose()
         End If
      End Try

   End Function
```

The other overload of GetPermissionList performs the same task as the previous method, but this time the results are filtered to only include those permissions that belong to a given role:

```
      Public Overloads Function GetPermissionList( _
         ByVal roleId As Integer) _
         As DataSet

         Dim parameters As SqlParameter() = { _
            New SqlParameter("@RoleID", SqlDbType.Int, 4)}

         parameters(0).Value = roleId

         Dim permissions As DataSet
         Try

            permissions = RunProcedure( _
               "sp_Accounts_GetPermissionCategories", _
               New IDataParameter() {}, _
               "Categories")

            RunProcedure( _
               "sp_Accounts_GetPermissionList", _
               parameters, _
               permissions, _
               "Permissions")

            Dim permissionCategories As New DataRelation( _
               "PermissionCategories", _
               permissions.Tables("Categories").Columns("CategoryID"), _
               permissions.Tables("Permissions").Columns("CategoryID"))

            permissions.Relations.Add(permissionCategories)

            Return permissions

         Finally
            If Not permissions Is Nothing Then
               permissions.Dispose()
            End If
         End Try
```

```
      End Function


   End Class

End Namespace
```

PermissionCategory

Just as with permissions, permission categories do not change. Permission categories are in the database only to allow for visible grouping of related permissions by the user interface. Beyond that, the permission categories serve no security-related purpose. The PermissionCategory class provides read access to the list of permission categories in the database.

The following is the source code listing for the PermissionCategory class. This can be found in the PermissionCategory.vb file, also part of the AccountsData project.

```
Imports System
Imports System.Data
Imports System.Data.SqlClient


Namespace WebModules.Accounts.Data

  Public Class PermissionCategory
    Inherits Wrox.WebModules.Data.DbObject

    Public Sub New(ByVal newConnectionString As String)
      MyBase.new(newConnectionString)
    End Sub
```

The following method retrieves a single permission category from the database and returns it in the form of a DataRow instance:

```
    Public Function Retrieve(ByVal categoryId As Integer) As DataRow

      Dim parameters As SqlParameter() = { _
        New SqlParameter("@CategoryID", SqlDbType.Int, 4)}

      parameters(0).Value = categoryId

      Dim categories As DataSet
      Try
        categories = RunProcedure( _
          "sp_Accounts_GetCategoryDetails", parameters, "Categories")
        Return categories.Tables(0).Rows(0)
      Finally
        If Not categories Is Nothing Then
          categories.Dispose()
        End If
      End Try

    End Function
```

The following method obtains a list of all permissions that belong to a given category, returning the results in the form of an instance of the `DataSet` class:

```
    Public Function GetPermissionsInCategory( _
      ByVal categoryId As Integer) _
      As DataSet

      Dim parameters As SqlParameter() = { _
        New SqlParameter("@CategoryID", SqlDbType.Int, 4)}

      parameters(0).Value = categoryId

      Dim permissions As DataSet
      Try
        permissions = RunProcedure( _
          "sp_Accounts_GetPermissionInCategory", parameters, "Categories")
        Return permissions
      Finally
        If Not permissions Is Nothing Then
          permissions.Dispose()
        End If
      End Try
    End Function
```

The following method obtains a list of all of the categories in the database, sorted alphabetically by the `sp_Accounts_GetPermissionCategories` stored procedure:

```
    Public Function GetCategoryList() As DataSet
      Dim categories As DataSet
      Try
        categories = RunProcedure( _
          "sp_Accounts_GetPermissionCategories", New IDataParameter() {}, _
            "Categories")
        Return categories
      Finally
        If Not categories Is Nothing Then
          categories.Dispose()
        End If
      End Try
    End Function
  End Class
End Namespace
```

AccountsTool

Occasionally we need to access a set of data, or some configuration information not directly related to any given model. In these cases, programmers typically employ a tool or helper class. This is the purpose of the `AccountsTool` class: for handling the miscellaneous tasks that we don't necessarily need a pure object model to handle.

Our `AccountsTool` class in the business layer will provide the following static methods, all returning datasets:

❑   GetStates – returns a list of states used to populate a drop-down list when the user sets
    their address

❑   GetAllPermissions – returns a list of all permissions in the system

❑   GetRoleList – returns a list of all roles in the database

The only one of these that does not have its data-access needs provided by another data-tier class is
GetStates, so Accounts.Data.AccountsTool (found in AccountsTools.vb) contains the
following method:

```
Public Function GetStateList() As DataSet
  Return RunProcedure( _
    "sp_Accounts_GetStateList", New IDataParameter() {}, "States")
End Function
```

This executes a stored procedure in the database, returning all states.

The Business Tier

This next section will take you through the source code for the business tier classes, starting with the
implementation of our SitePrincipal and SiteIdentity classes.

SitePrincipal

The SitePrincipal class snaps into the existing ASP.NET forms-based authentication. This class
implements the System.Security.Principal.IPrincipal interface, and adds additional
functionality to allow pages aware of our customizations to query additional security information. By
obeying the standards in the interface, we ensure that components and pages not aware of our
customizations will also be able to use our objects.

Here is the source code listing for the SitePrincipal class, from the SitePrincipal.vb file in the
AccountsBusiness project:

```
Imports System
Imports System.Collections
Imports System.Security
Imports System.Security.Cryptography
Imports System.Text

Imports Wrox.WebModules.Accounts

Namespace WebModules.Accounts.Business

  Public Class SitePrincipal
    Inherits Wrox.WebModules.Business.BizObject
    Implements System.Security.Principal.IPrincipal
```

Here we create some private member variables to hold our internal data. Referring to the requirements
of the IPrincipal interface, we know that we must implement an Identity property that returns an
instance of an IIdentity interface. Knowing this, we also put in a member variable to hold the
identity for this instance of IPrincipal:

171

```
  Protected myIdentity As Principal.IIdentity
  Protected myPermissionList As ArrayList
  Protected myRoleList As ArrayList
```

The following set of constructors initializes an instance of the SitePrincipal class. There are two ways we can construct this class – by user ID or e-mail address:

```
Public Sub New(ByVal userId As Integer)

  Dim moduleSettings As Configuration.ModuleSettings = _
    Configuration.ModuleConfig.GetSettings()
  Dim dataUser As New Data.User(moduleSettings.ConnectionString)

  myIdentity = New SiteIdentity(userId)
  myPermissionList = dataUser.GetEffectivePermissionList(userId)
  myRoleList = dataUser.GetUserRoles(userId)

End Sub

Public Sub New(ByVal emailAddress As String)

  Dim moduleSettings As Configuration.ModuleSettings = _
    Configuration.ModuleConfig.GetSettings()
  Dim dataUser As New Data.User(moduleSettings.ConnectionString)

  myIdentity = New SiteIdentity(emailAddress)
  myPermissionList = dataUser.GetEffectivePermissionList( _
    CType(myIdentity, Business.SiteIdentity).UserId)
  myRoleList = dataUser.GetUserRoles( _
    CType(myIdentity, Business.SiteIdentity).UserId)
End Sub
```

We then implement the property and method required by the IPrincipal interface:

```
Public ReadOnly Property Identity() As Principal.IIdentity _
  Implements Principal.IPrincipal.Identity

  Get
    Return myIdentity
  End Get

End Property

Public Function IsInRole(ByVal role As String) As Boolean _
  Implements Principal.IPrincipal.IsInRole

  Return myRoleList.Contains(role)
End Function
```

(Note that these are not next to each other in the source code file in the code download, as the source files are organized by member type rather than by the order in which they were added).

This next method, `HasPermission`, is one of the methods we have added:

```
Public Function HasPermission(ByVal permissionId As Integer) As Boolean
    Return myPermissionList.Contains(permissionId)
End Function
```

As long as we typecast properly, we can always have access to this method even though Microsoft's code is handing around pointers to the `IPrincipal` instance.

We also want some properties to provide access to the roles and permissions that are associated with the user:

```
Public ReadOnly Property Roles() As ArrayList
  Get
    Return myRoleList
  End Get
End Property

Public ReadOnly Property Permissions() As ArrayList
  Get
    Return myPermissionList
  End Get
End Property
```

Notice that these properties are read only as we don't want the roles or permissions associated with a `SitePrincipal` to be changed 'on the fly'. Changes to roles or permissions must take place through changes to the details in the database.

In this next method, in order to validate the user's plain text ASCII password without transmitting it across a wire in that format, we encrypt it first and then pass it to the data-services tier for validation against the encrypted password stored in the database:

```
Public Shared Function ValidateLogin( _
   ByVal emailAddress As String, _
   ByVal password As String) _
   As SitePrincipal

   Dim moduleSettings As Configuration.ModuleSettings = _
     Configuration.ModuleConfig.GetSettings()
   Dim newId As Integer
   Dim cryptPassword As Byte() = EncryptPassword(password)
   Dim dataUser As New Data.User(moduleSettings.ConnectionString)
```

In this next `if` block, we evaluate the result of the `ValidateLogin` method in the data-services user component. If the result is greater than -1, then we assume that the result was the numeric identity of the user attempting to log in. If the result was equal to -1, then we assume the login failed and we return `null`, indicating that the login failed.

```
   newId = dataUser.ValidateLogin(emailAddress, cryptPassword)
   If newId > -1 Then
     Return New SitePrincipal(newId)
```

```
            Else
                Return Nothing
            End If
        End Function
```

SiteIdentity

`SiteIdentity` implements the `System.Security.Principal.IIdentity` interface. We use this interface so that our class can snap into the existing authentication framework provided by ASP.NET.

We will now look at the source code listing for the `SiteIdentity` class, which you can find in the `SiteIdentity.vb` file in the `AccountsBusiness` project:

```
Imports System
Imports System.Collections
Imports System.Data
Imports System.Security
Imports System.Security.Cryptography
Imports System.Text

Imports Wrox.WebModules.Accounts

Namespace WebModules.Accounts.Business

  Public Class SiteIdentity
    Inherits Wrox.WebModules.Business.BizObject
    Implements System.Security.Principal.IIdentity

    Private myFirstName As String
    Private myLastName As String
    Private myEmailAddress As String
    Private myPassword As Byte()
    Private myUserId As Integer
```

The `IIdentity` interface requires us to provide three properties:

```
        Public ReadOnly Property AuthenticationType() As String _
          Implements Principal.IIdentity.AuthenticationType

          Get
            Return "Custom Authentication"
          End Get
        End Property

        Public ReadOnly Property IsAuthenticated() As Boolean _
          Implements Principal.IIdentity.IsAuthenticated

          Get
            ' Assumption: All instances of a SiteIdentity have
            ' already been authenticated.
            Return True
```

```
      End Get
   End Property

   Public ReadOnly Property name() As String _
      Implements Principal.IIdentity.Name
      Get
         Return myFirstName & " " & myLastName
      End Get
   End Property
```

You may have noticed the assumption in the IsAuthenticated property, that all instances of SiteIdentity are authenticated. Why can we make this assumption? Well, we will only be using SiteIdentity along with SitePrincipal, which will in turn only be used when we have authenticated a user.

Like SitePrincipal, SiteIdentity also has two constructors – one for e-mail address and one for user ID:

```
   Public Sub New(ByVal currentEmailAddress As String)

      Dim moduleSettings As Configuration.ModuleSettings = _
         Configuration.ModuleConfig.GetSettings()
      Dim dataUser As New Data.User(moduleSettings.ConnectionString)
      Dim userRow As DataRow = dataUser.Retrieve(currentEmailAddress)

      myFirstName = CStr(userRow("FirstName"))
      myLastName = CStr(userRow("LastName"))
      myEmailAddress = currentEmailAddress
      myUserId = CInt(userRow("UserId"))
      myPassword = CType(userRow("Password"), Byte())

   End Sub

   Public Sub New(ByVal currentUserId As Integer)

      Dim moduleSettings As Configuration.ModuleSettings = _
         Configuration.ModuleConfig.GetSettings()
      Dim dataUser As New Data.User(moduleSettings.ConnectionString)
      Dim userRow As DataRow = dataUser.Retrieve(currentUserId)

      myFirstName = CStr(userRow("FirstName"))
      myLastName = CStr(userRow("LastName"))
      myEmailAddress = CStr(userRow("EmailAddress"))
      myUserId = CInt(userRow("UserId"))
      myPassword = CType(userRow("Password"), Byte())

   End Sub
```

We now add a method for checking a user's password against the database. The really great thing about having this method is that, should we decide to change how we store or encrypt users' credentials, we can simply change this method.

```vb
Public Function TestPassword(ByVal password As String) As Integer

  Dim moduleSettings As Configuration.ModuleSettings = _
    Configuration.ModuleConfig.GetSettings()
  Dim encoding As New UnicodeEncoding()
  Dim hashBytes As Byte() = encoding.GetBytes(password)

  Dim sha1 As New SHA1CryptoServiceProvider()
  Dim cryptPassword As Byte() = sha1.ComputeHash(hashBytes)

  Dim dataUser As New Data.User(moduleSettings.ConnectionString)

  Return dataUser.TestPassword(myUserId, cryptPassword)

End Function
```

Finally, we add a series of properties to provide access to the details of the user. These are read-only properties as we do not want to ensure that the details in the `SiteIdentity` are the same as those drawn from the database when the object was constructed.

```vb
Public ReadOnly Property FirstName() As String
  Get
    Return myFirstName
  End Get
End Property


Public ReadOnly Property LastName() As String
  Get
    Return myLastName
  End Get
End Property
```

We've removed a couple of the property definitions from this code listing because they are all very similar.

User

Of course, in a module that provides user authentication and account storage, the `User` class is going to be the main class in the module. This class provides a model that represents a single user, and can be used to create or update a single user. Do not confuse the `User` class with either the `SitePrincipal` or `SiteIdentity` classes, as they represent two distinct sets of functionality. The latter two classes are for integrating with ASP.NET security.

The following is a partial source-code listing for the `User` class. The full version is available in `User.vb` in the `AccountsBusiness` project.

```vb
Imports System
Imports System.Data
```

```
Namespace WebModules.Accounts.Business

  Public NotInheritable Class User
    Inherits Wrox.WebModules.Business.BizObject

    Private myModuleSettings As Configuration.ModuleSettings
    Private myUserId As Integer
    Private myFirstName As String
    Private myLastName As String
    Private myAddress1 As String
    Private myAddress2 As String
    Private myCity As String
    Private myState As String
    Private myZipCode As String
    Private myHomePhone As String
    Private myEmailAddress As String
    Private myPassword As Byte()
    Private myCountry As String
```

We provide three constructors, one to create a fresh User object, one to create a User based on a user ID, and one to create a User based on a SitePrincipal object.

```
Public Sub New()
  myModuleSettings = Configuration.ModuleConfig.GetSettings()
End Sub

Public Sub New(ByVal existingUserId As Integer)
  myModuleSettings = Configuration.ModuleConfig.GetSettings()
  myUserId = existingUserId
  LoadFromId()
End Sub

Public Sub New(ByVal existingPrincipal As SitePrincipal)
  myModuleSettings = Configuration.ModuleConfig.GetSettings()
  myUserId = CType(existingPrincipal.Identity, SiteIdentity).UserId
  LoadFromId()
End Sub
```

Two of these constructors use a private method that populates the User object based on a user ID:

```
Private Sub LoadFromId()

  Dim dataUser As New Data.User(myModuleSettings.ConnectionString)
  Dim userRow As DataRow = dataUser.Retrieve(myUserId)

  myFirstName = CStr(userRow("FirstName"))
  myLastName = CStr(userRow("LastName"))
  myAddress1 = CStr(userRow("Address1"))
  myAddress2 = CStr(userRow("Address2"))
  myCity = CStr(userRow("City"))
  myState = CStr(userRow("State"))
  myZipCode = CStr(userRow("ZipCode"))
```

```
      myHomePhone = CStr(userRow("HomePhone"))
      myEmailAddress = CStr(userRow("EmailAddress"))
      myPassword = CType(userRow("Password"), Byte())
      myCountry = CStr(userRow("Country"))
End Sub
```

The constructor that uses an existing `SitePrincipal` is a really useful shortcut for creating a new `User` object based on the details of a user who is logged into our site.

Next, we add methods that will cause our `User` object to make calls to the data layer to actually store changes in the database. The first method creates a new entry in the database for the user:

```
Public Function Create() As Integer
   Dim dataUser As New Data.User(myModuleSettings.ConnectionString)

   myUserId = dataUser.Create( _
       myEmailAddress, _
       myPassword, _
       myFirstName, _
       myLastName, _
       myAddress1, _
       myAddress2, _
       myCity, _
       myState, _
       myZipCode, _
       myHomePhone, _
       myCountry)

   Return myUserId
End Function
```

The other one updates the database with changes made to the user's details:

```
Public Function Update() As Boolean
   Dim dataUser As New Data.User(myModuleSettings.ConnectionString)

   Return dataUser.Update( _
       myUserId, _
       myEmailAddress, _
       myPassword, _
       myFirstName, _
       myLastName, _
       myAddress1, _
       myAddress2, _
       myCity, _
       myState, _
       myZipCode, _
       myHomePhone, _
       myCountry)
End Function
```

We also have two methods that manipulate the roles that the user belongs to:

```
        Public Function AddToRole(ByVal myRoleId As Integer) As Boolean

          Dim dataUser As New Data.User(myModuleSettings.ConnectionString)
          Return dataUser.AddRole(myUserId, myRoleId)

        End Function


        Public Function RemoveRole(ByVal myRoleId As Integer) As Boolean

          Dim dataUser As New Data.User(myModuleSettings.ConnectionString)
          Return dataUser.RemoveRole(myUserId, myRoleId)

        End Function
```

The code continues to define get/set properties for each private member variable declared above. By now this syntax should be second nature, so we won't include it here. The properties removed from the listing to keep the chapter length manageable are all simple get/set accessors for the first name, last name, address, and so forth.

Role

The Role class in the business tier is for administration. All of the information about the permissions and roles granted to a logged in user is contained in the identity-principal pair. This class is used to create and update roles, as well as grant/revoke permissions on the role.

The following is the source-code listing for the Role class, which is in Role.vb, part of the AccountsBusiness project:

```
Imports System
Imports System.Data
Imports Wrox.WebModules.Accounts

Namespace WebModules.Accounts.Business

  Public Class Role
    Inherits Wrox.WebModules.Business.BizObject

    Private myRoleId As Integer
    Private myDescription As String
    Private myPermissions As DataSet

    Public Sub New()
    End Sub
```

This constructor will instantiate a Role object based on the ID of an existing role:

```
        Public Sub New(ByVal currentRoleId As Integer)

          Dim moduleSettings As Configuration.ModuleSettings = _
            Configuration.ModuleConfig.GetSettings()
          Dim dataRole As New Data.Role(moduleSettings.ConnectionString)
```

```
    Dim roleRow As DataRow

    roleRow = dataRole.Retrieve(currentRoleId)
    myRoleId = currentRoleId
    myDescription = CStr(roleRow("Description"))

    Dim dataPermission As New _
      Data.Permission(moduleSettings.ConnectionString)
    myPermissions = dataPermission.GetPermissionList(currentRoleId)

End Sub
```

Like in the `User` class, we have methods for making changes to the database (through the data-layer objects):

```
Public Function Create() As Integer
   Dim moduleSettings As Configuration.ModuleSettings = _
     Configuration.ModuleConfig.GetSettings()
   Dim dataRole As New Data.Role(moduleSettings.ConnectionString)

   myRoleId = dataRole.Create(myDescription)

   Return myRoleId
End Function

Public Function Update() As Boolean
   Dim moduleSettings As Configuration.ModuleSettings = _
     Configuration.ModuleConfig.GetSettings()
   Dim dataRole As New Data.Role(moduleSettings.ConnectionString)

   Return dataRole.Update(myRoleId, myDescription)
End Function
```

We also include a method to delete the role:

```
Public Function Delete() As Boolean

   Dim moduleSettings As Configuration.ModuleSettings = _
     Configuration.ModuleConfig.GetSettings()
   Dim dataRole As New Data.Role(moduleSettings.ConnectionString)

   Return dataRole.Delete(myRoleId)

End Function
```

The next two methods deal with the permissions that a role has – adding or removing them.

```
Public Sub AddPermission(ByVal myPermissionId As Integer)

   Dim moduleSettings As Configuration.ModuleSettings = _
     Configuration.ModuleConfig.GetSettings()
   Dim dataRole As New Data.Role(moduleSettings.ConnectionString)
```

```
        dataRole.AddPermission(myRoleId, myPermissionId)

    End Sub


    Public Sub RemovePermission(ByVal myPermissionId As Integer)

      Dim moduleSettings As Configuration.ModuleSettings = _
        Configuration.ModuleConfig.GetSettings()
      Dim dataRole As New Data.Role(moduleSettings.ConnectionString)

      dataRole.RemovePermission(myRoleId, myPermissionId)

    End Sub
```

This next method removes *all* permissions currently associated with the current role instance:

```
    Public Sub ClearPermissions()

      Dim moduleSettings As Configuration.ModuleSettings = _
        Configuration.ModuleConfig.GetSettings()
      Dim dataRole As New Data.Role(moduleSettings.ConnectionString)

      dataRole.ClearPermissions(myRoleId)

    End Sub
```

We want to provide read-only access to the ID of the role and to the permissions that the role has:

```
    Public ReadOnly Property RoleId() As Integer
      Get
        Return myRoleId
      End Get
    End Property

    Public ReadOnly Property Permissions() As DataSet
      Get
        Return myPermissions
      End Get
    End Property
```

We do not want to provide write access to these properties for different reasons in each case. We do not want the ID to be changed at all – once a Role object is instantiated, its ID should stay the same. We want changes to the permissions of the role to take place through the methods we provided earlier so we do not allow write access through the property.

We also want to provide access to the description of the role. This property should provide write access as it is through this property that the description will be updated.

```
      Public Property Description() As String
        Get
          Return myDescription
        End Get
        Set(ByVal value As String)
          myDescription = value
        End Set
      End Property
```

AccountsTool

The following is the source-code listing for the `AccountsTool` class, a utility class that allows us to obtain lists that do not fit into the object model. This class is in the `AccountsTool.vb` file in the `AccountsBusiness` project:

```
Imports System
Imports System.Data

Namespace WebModules.Accounts.Business

  Public Class AccountsTool
    Inherits Wrox.WebModules.Business.BizObject

    Public Shared Function GetStates() As DataSet
      Dim tool As New Data.AccountsTool( _
        Configuration.ModuleConfig.GetSettings().ConnectionString)
      Return tool.GetStateList
    End Function

    Public Shared Function GetAllPermissions() As DataSet
      Dim dataPermission As New Data.Permission( _
        Configuration.ModuleConfig.GetSettings().ConnectionString)
      Return dataPermission.GetPermissionList()
    End Function

    Public Shared Function GetRoleList() As DataSet
      Dim dataRole As New Data.Role( _
        Configuration.ModuleConfig.GetSettings().ConnectionString)
      Return dataRole.GetRoleList()
    End Function

  End Class

End Namespace
```

As you can see, this performs some functions that do not fit neatly into any of our other classes – getting a list of allowed states for users, getting all the available permissions, and getting all the available roles.

We could have added these methods as shared members of other classes but collecting them here makes it easy to remember where they are.

Configuration Classes

In the design section, we described two classes, `ModuleConfig` and `ModuleSettings`, which will manage the configuration of the accounts module.

Let's have a look at how these classes are implemented.

ModuleSettings

This class is very simple:

```
Namespace WebModules.Accounts.Configuration
  Public Class ModuleSettings

    Private myConnectionString As String

    <XmlElement()> _
    Public Property ConnectionString() As String
      Get
        Return myConnectionString
      End Get
      Set(ByVal value As String)
        myConnectionString = value
      End Set
    End Property
  End Class
End Namespace
```

It consists of a single private member and accompanying public property. Note the `<XmlElement()>` attribute that is attached to the property. We use this attribute to specify that when the class is serialized as XML, the `ConnectionString` property will be represented as an XML element.

ModuleConfig

In the design section, we described the two shared methods that this class should provide. The first deserializes a `ModuleSettings` object from instances our XML configuration file:

```
Public Shared Function GetSettings() As ModuleSettings

  Dim context As HttpContext = HttpContext.Current
  Dim data As ModuleSettings = _
    CType(context.Cache("Accounts_Settings"), ModuleSettings)

  If data Is Nothing Then
    Dim serializer As New XmlSerializer(GetType(ModuleSettings))

    Try

      Dim fileName As String = _
        HttpContext.Current.Server.MapPath(GetSettingsFile())

      ' Create a filestream to read the XML document
      Dim fileStream As New FileStream(fileName, FileMode.Open)
```

```
            ' Use the Deserialize method to retrieve the object state
            data = CType(serializer.Deserialize(fileStream), ModuleSettings)
            fileStream.Close()

            context.Cache.Insert("Accounts_Settings", data, _
              New CacheDependency(fileName))

         Catch exc As System.IO.FileNotFoundException

            ' If the file is not found, return an empty class
            data = New ModuleSettings()
         End Try
      End If
      Return data
End Function
```

The other method does the reverse operation – it serializes a `ModuleSettings` object and stores it in the configuration file:

```
      Public Shared Sub SaveSettings(ByVal settings As ModuleSettings)

         Dim fileName As String = _
           HttpContext.Current.Server.MapPath(GetSettingsFile())
         Dim serializer As New XmlSerializer(GetType(ModuleSettings))

         ' Serialize the object
         Dim fs As New FileStream(fileName, FileMode.Create)
         serializer.Serialize(fs, settings)
         fs.Close()

      End Sub
```

As you may have noticed, both of these methods use a method, `GetSettingsFile`, to get the filename of the configuration file. Here is that method:

```
      Public Shared Function GetSettingsFile() As String

         Dim context As HttpContext = HttpContext.Current

         ' Get the file path from the cache
         Dim filePath As String = CStr(context.Cache("Accounts_SettingsFile"))

         ' If Path is null, get it from web.config
         If filePath Is Nothing Then

            ' Retrieve the value
            filePath = ConfigurationSettings.AppSettings("Accounts_SettingsFile")

            ' Save into the cache
            context.Cache("Accounts_SettingsFile") = filePath

         End If
```

```
     ' Return the connection string
     Return filePath

  End Function
```

Modifying the UI to Support Authentication

If you remember back to Chapter 3 where we built the core foundation of the user interface, we created several standardized UI elements for use in our `ThePhile` web application project. Two of these elements were a base class for pages and a user control to display a site header at the top of every page. Both of these were implemented assuming that some kind of authentication would be taking place, but without knowing the exact implementation.

In this section we will change the `PhilePage` class and the `SiteHeader` user control in order to take full advantage of our authentication system. These changes are going to make use of the `SiteIdentity` and `SitePrincipal` classes, which we discussed earlier.

Modifying the SiteHeader Control

Another facet of our website that will become a bit more robust with our user authentication solution is our site header control.

One thing we know about user controls is that they each have their own `Page_Load` event, since ASP.NET considers them almost as 'micro pages'. We know that the parent page, if it inherits from `PhilePage`, will have already created an appropriate `SitePrincipal` in the `Context.User` property. Therefore, to obtain a more user-friendly greeting, all we have to do is modify the site header control (`/ThePhile/Controls/SiteHeader.ascx.vb` file in the `ThePhile` project) in the following way:

```
     Private Sub Page_Load(ByVal sender As Object, _
       ByVal e As EventArgs) Handles MyBase.Load

       Greeting.Text = "Welcome, "

       If Context.User.Identity.IsAuthenticated Then
         Dim id As SiteIdentity = CType(Context.User.Identity, SiteIdentity)
         Greeting.Text = Greeting.Text & "<b>" & id.name & "</b>"
         UserLink.Text = "My Account"
         UserLink.NavigateUrl = _
           "/ThePhileVB/WebModules/Accounts/MyAccount.aspx"
         SignOut.Visible = True
       Else
         Greeting.Text = Greeting.Text & "Guest User."
         UserLink.Text = "Click to Login"
         UserLink.NavigateUrl = "/ThePhileVB/WebModules/Accounts/Login.aspx"
         SignOut.Visible = False
       End If
     End Sub
```

This not only provides a user-friendly greeting, but it intelligently decides which link to display to the user. If they have already logged in, then they are given a link to the `"My Account"` page, which allows them to make changes to their personal information and preferences. If they have not logged in (no authentication cookie was found), then they are given a link to the login page.

185

If the user is logged in, we also display the sign out option. We need to provide a event handler for when this option is clicked:

```
Private Sub SignOut_Click(ByVal sender As Object, _
   ByVal e As EventArgs) Handles SignOut.Click

   FormsAuthentication.SignOut()
   Response.Redirect("/ThePhileVB")

End Sub
```

We use the `SignOut` method of `FormsAuthentication` to delete the user's authentication cookie and then redirect them back to the root of the application.

The Login Page

The following is a screenshot of the new login page, the code for which is available as /ThePhile/Modules/Users/Login.aspx. The top of the page shows the modified `SiteHeader` control, which has recognized the user and is displaying that user's first and last names:

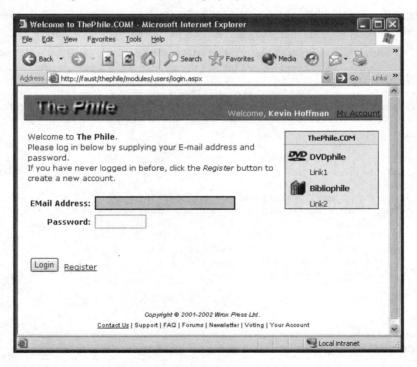

There are two interesting parts in the code-behind for this page.

Firstly, in the `Page_Load` event handler, we have the following code:

```
         Private Sub Page_Load(ByVal sender As Object, ByVal e As EventArgs)

           If (Request("ShowError") = "true") _
             Or (Request("ShowError") = "1") Then

             AuthRedirectFailure.Text = "You did not have sufficient " & _
                "permission to view the previous page. Please login below."
             AuthRedirectFailure.Visible = True
           Else
             AuthRedirectFailure.Visible = False
           End If
         End Sub
```

This allows us to pass the ShowError parameter to this page and have an error message displayed. We will use this in the rest of the site when the user tries to do something that they do not have permission for.

The really important part of the login page is the event handler for the click event of the Login button:

```
         Private Sub Submit_Click( _
           ByVal sender As Object, _
           ByVal e As EventArgs) _
           Handles Submit.Click

           Dim newUser As SitePrincipal = _
             SitePrincipal.ValidateLogin(EmailAddress.Text, Password.Text)

           If newUser Is Nothing Then
             LoginResult.Text = "Login failed for " & EmailAddress.Text
             LoginResult.Visible = True
           Else
             Context.User = newUser
             FormsAuthentication.SetAuthCookie(EmailAddress.Text, True)
             Response.Redirect("/ThePhileVB/Default.aspx")
           End If
         End Sub
```

First we use the ValidateLogin method that we defined in our SitePrincipal class to check the username and password that have been entered against our database.

If the login fails, we display an error message. If the login was successful, we use the FormsAuthentication.SetAuthCookie method to create a new encrypted authentication cookie and attach it to our response to the browser. We then redirect the user back to the site default page.

It is this code that sets up the authentication cookie that is used in subsequent requests to identify the user.

Picking up the Authentication Cookie in Subsequent Requests

Our login page sets the authentication cookie and sends it to the user's browser. Their browser will then send it back to our website with each subsequent request. Our application will then pick up the cookie and use it to identify the user – but how does it do this?

The good news is that we don't have to do any coding for this – all we have to do is activate the Forms Authentication Module and it will take care of it for us.

When activated, the Forms Authentication Module taps into the `AuthenticateRequest` event that fires once for each page request that is made. It looks for the authentication cookie and, if it finds one, it will decrypt the information and use it to populate the `Context.User` object with a `GenericPrincipal` object that in turn contains a `FormsIdentity` object.

We want to use our own principal and identity objects (`SitePrincipal` and `SiteIdentity`) objects rather than `GenericPrincipal` and `GenericIdentity` so we have to a little more work as we will discuss in the *Modifying the PhilePage Class* section below.

Configuring Forms Authentication

Activating the forms authentication module is very simple. We simply need to add the following section to our `web.config` file (in the root folder of our website)

```
<authentication mode="Forms" >
    <forms
        name="ThePhile"
        path="/"
        loginUrl="/ThePhileVB/WebModules/Accounts/Login.aspx"
        protection="All"
        timeout="30">
    </forms>
</authentication>
```

Here you can see that we specify that we want to use forms authentication, that we would like the cookie to be named `"ThePhile"` and that we would like users to log in through our `login.aspx` page.

That's all there is to it!

Modifying the PhilePage Class

In order to use our customized `SiteIdentity` and `SitePrincipal` classes for the rest of the website, including all of the other modules being developed for this book, we decided to make a slight change to the `PhilePage` class by enhancing its `PhilePage_Load` method. Here is the new version of that method, in the `PhilePage.vb` file in the main `ThePhile` project:

```
Private Sub PhilePage_Load(ByVal sender As Object, ByVal e As EventArgs)

    If Context.User.Identity.IsAuthenticated Then

        If Not (TypeOf context.User Is SitePrincipal) Then

            Dim newUser As New SitePrincipal(Context.User.Identity.Name)
            Context.User = newUser

        End If
    End If
End Sub
```

Essentially, this is the 'load profile' portion of the user authentication flow diagram that we saw earlier in the chapter. At the very beginning of the load process of the page a check is made to see if the user is authenticated. If the authenticated user *is not* already one of our custom `SitePrincipal` instances, then we simply create a new instance of the `SitePrincipal` class based on the current user identity name (we're using the e-mail address as the 'name'). Once the new instance is created, we assign that instance back to the `Context.User` property. This loads a complete user profile into the authentication framework provided by ASP.NET.

The User Details Page

Finally, let's take a look at a screenshot of the user profile page. This is the page that the user sees when they want to modify their own personal information. A very similar version of this page is displayed when the user is first registering as a new account:

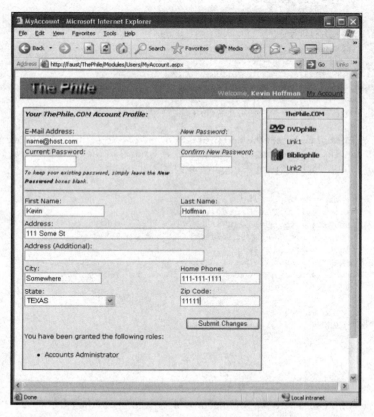

This form is accomplished using some fairly standard and simple ASP.NET data-binding techniques. For demonstration purposes, it is sometimes helpful to show how to do things both ways, so in the code for this form (which you can find in `/ThePhile/Modules/Users/MyAccount.aspx.vb`) we've shown how to manually set the value of the textboxes rather than use data binding. In the administration section (discussed later) we use some more complex data binding to show you the difference in code size and readability.

The following is the Page_Load event for the page displayed above:

```
        Private Sub Page_Load(ByVal sender As Object, ByVal e As EventArgs)

    RoleList.Visible = False
    SaveMessage.Visible = False

    If Not Page.IsPostBack Then

      Dim states As DataSet
      If Context.User.Identity.IsAuthenticated Then

        Dim currentUser As New AccBusiness.User( _
          CType(Context.User, SitePrincipal))

        FirstName.Text = currentUser.FirstName
        EmailAddress.Text = currentUser.EmailAddress
        LastName.Text = currentUser.LastName
        Address1.Text = currentUser.Address1
        Address2.Text = currentUser.Address2
        ZipCode.Text = currentUser.ZipCode
        City.Text = currentUser.City
        HomePhone.Text = currentUser.HomePhone
```

The previous few lines of codes set the text property of the page's TextBox controls. The following code block uses data binding to bind a DropDownList control to the list of states available. This list includes a 'blank' state for those people logging in from outside the US:

```
        states = AccountsTool.GetStates()
        StateDropDown.DataSource = states
        StateDropDown.DataTextField = "Description"
        StateDropDown.DataValueField = "StateCode"
        StateDropDown.DataBind()
        StateDropDown.SelectedIndex = StateDropDown.Items.IndexOf( _
          StateDropDown.Items.FindByValue(currentUser.State))

      Else

        mainPanel.Visible = False

      End If

    End If
```

This is another example of where our architecture of expanding on the existing security system is going to pay off. Here, we simply ask the Context.User object if it has any roles assigned to it. If it does, then we will iterate through them, building an HTML unordered list to display those roles.

```
        If CType(Context.User, SitePrincipal).Roles.Count > 0 Then

      RoleList.Visible = True
```

```
         Dim roles As ArrayList = CType(Context.User, SitePrincipal).Roles
         RoleList.Text = _
           "You have been granted the following roles:  <ul>"

         Dim idx As Integer
         For idx = 0 To (roles.Count - 1)
          RoleList.Text = RoleList.Text & "<li>" & roles(idx) & "</li> "
         Next

         RoleList.Text = RoleList.Text & "</ul>"

      End If

   End Sub
```

Administering Roles and Accounts

The administration of the roles and accounts system is fairly straightforward. The `Admin` directory of the `User` module has been secured by `NTFS`, which allows us to ensure that nobody without the specific permissions defined on that directory will be able to access those files. If someone attempts to access this directory without the appropriate account, the browser will simply report that it cannot access the files.

> *If you have downloaded the sample code, then more than likely your `Admin` directory will not be secured. For testing purposes, that's fine. However, to secure it, simply right-click it in your file explorer and administer the permissions as you would any other directory. Consult your Windows 2000 or XP manual or reference guide for more information on NTFS permissions.*

The `Accounts` administration module provides a *role editor*. This role editor will allow administrative users to create new roles, as well as edit existing ones. The following screenshot shows a sample of the administration screen that administrative users are greeted with when they first open up the page (they'll have to type in the URL manually, as there are no links to this page):

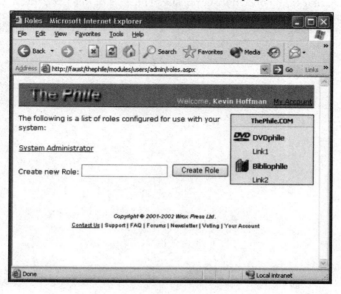

The following is the listing for the Page_Load event from the above page (found in /ThePhile/Modules/Users/Admin/Roles.aspx.vb, again, still in our ThePhile application):

```
Private Sub Page_Load(ByVal sender As Object, ByVal e As EventArgs)

    If (TypeOf Context.User Is SitePrincipal) _
       AndAlso CType(Context.User, SitePrincipal).HasPermission( _
         CInt(AccountsPermissions.CreateRoles)) Then

      NewRoleButton.Visible = True
      NewRoleDescription.Visible = True

    Else

      NewRoleButton.Visible = False
      NewRoleDescription.Visible = False

    End If

    myRoles = AccountsTool.GetRoleList()
    RoleList.DataSource = myRoles.Tables("Roles")
    RoleList.DataBind()
End Sub
```

As you can see, we are controlling the visibility of the **Create Role** button based on whether or not the currently logged in user has the AccountsPermissions.CreateRoles permission. Beyond that, we simply bind our DataList control, RoleList, to the Roles table returned from the GetRoleList method.

As shown in the previous screenshot, it is a pretty simple interface. Selecting an existing role presents an interactive screen similar to the one shown opposite. The core of this particular UI is the side-by-side listboxes. By clicking on a category in the left listbox, the child list of permissions is filled into the listbox on the right. Then, by clicking on the entry for a permission item, the option to remove that permission automatically becomes available. There is also the option to delete the current role:

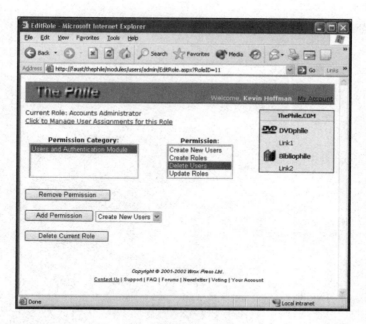

Let's examine the code-behind source code for this page (`EditRole.aspx.vb`). In order to get all of this to work, the `ListBox` that contains the permission categories must automatically post back any time an event on it triggers. This allows us to respond to the event on the server side and obtain more data from the data source to populate the second `ListBox` for the permissions themselves.

```
Namespace WebModules.Accounts.Web

    Public Class EditRole
        Inherits Wrox.ThePhile.Web.PhilePage

        Private myCurrentRole As Role

        Protected MenuNav As Wrox.ThePhile.Web.Controls.Server.Navigator

        Protected WithEvents ManageAssignmentsLink As LinkButton
        Protected WithEvents CategoryList As ListBox
        Protected WithEvents PermissionList As ListBox
        Protected WithEvents RemovePermissionButton As Button
        Protected WithEvents AddPermissionButton As Button
        Protected WithEvents RemoveRoleButton As Button

        Protected RoleLabel As Label
        Protected PermissionDropList As DropDownList
```

We knew in advance that there would be several different occasions when we were going to need to configure the data-binding properties of this page (each time an event fires that causes a server postback, we need to make sure that our data is returned to the appropriate state after responding to the event). So we placed all of that code into a separate function to be called by any event that needs to. We called this function `DoInitialDataBind`:

```
Private Sub DoInitialDataBind()

  myCurrentRole = New Role(Convert.ToInt32(Request("RoleId")))
  RoleLabel.Text = "Current Role: " & myCurrentRole.Description

  PermissionList.Items.Clear()
  RemovePermissionButton.Visible = False
  CategoryList.DataSource = myCurrentRole.Permissions.Tables("Categories")
  CategoryList.DataTextField = "Description"
  CategoryList.DataValueField = "CategoryID"
  CategoryList.DataBind()

  Dim allPermissions As DataSet = AccountsTool.GetAllPermissions()
  PermissionDropList.DataSource = allPermissions.Tables("Permissions")
  PermissionDropList.DataTextField = "Description"
  PermissionDropList.DataValueField = "PermissionId"
  PermissionDropList.DataBind()

End Sub
```

Here is the Page_Load event handler. First, we test to see if the user has the right permissions to be viewing this page. If they don't, we simply stop the process and end the Response. Otherwise, we test to see if this is the first time the page has been loaded. If so, then we must perform the initial data binding. If it is a postback, then we know that each control is having its state rebuilt by the ASP.NET server process automatically, so there is no need to re-bind:

```
Private Sub Page_Load(ByVal sender As Object, ByVal e As EventArgs)
  If TypeOf Context.User Is SitePrincipal _
    AndAlso CType(Context.User, SitePrincipal).HasPermission( _
      CInt(AccountsPermissions.UpdateRoles)) Then
    If Not Page.IsPostBack Then
      DoInitialDataBind()
    End If
  Else
    Response.Write( _
      "You don't have sufficient permission to be using this page.")
    Response.End()
  End If
End Sub
```

In order for our web form to appear as though its state is being properly maintained we need to respond to events. One task we perform over and over again is selecting the category. This method is designed to select a given category as well as populate the permissions DropDownList accordingly:

```
Private Sub SelectCategory( _
  ByVal categoryId As Integer, _
  ByVal forceSelection As Boolean)

  If forceSelection Then
    CategoryList.SelectedIndex = CategoryList.Items.IndexOf( _
      CategoryList.Items.FindByValue(categoryId.ToString()))
  End If
```

```
        myCurrentRole = New Role(Convert.ToInt32(Request("RoleID")))
        Dim categories As DataTable = _
          myCurrentRole.Permissions.Tables("Categories")

        ' The DataTable categories must have a primary key before its
        ' Find method can be used, hence the line below.
        categories.PrimaryKey = _
          New DataColumn() {categories.Columns("CategoryID")}
        Dim currentCategory As DataRow = _
          categories.Rows.Find(categoryId)
        If Not currentCategory Is Nothing Then

          Dim permissions As DataRow() = _
            currentCategory.GetChildRows("PermissionCategories")

          PermissionList.Items.Clear()

          Dim currentRow As DataRow
          For Each currentRow In permissions
            PermissionList.Items.Add(New ListItem( _
                CStr(currentRow("Description")), _
                Convert.ToString(currentRow("PermissionId"))))
          Next
        End If
      End Sub
```

We now need an event handler that will fire when the item that is selected in the drop-down list has changed:

```
    Private Sub CategoryList_SelectedIndexChanged( _
      ByVal sender As Object, _
      ByVal e As EventArgs) _
      Handles CategoryList.SelectedIndexChanged

      SelectCategory(Convert.ToInt32(CategoryList.SelectedItem.Value), False)

    End Sub
```

As you can see, it simply calls the `SelectCategory` method that we just defined.

We have set up an event to handle the **Remove Permission** button click, for when we want to remove a permission item from our `DropDownList` of permissions. This works fine, but the category list loses its state – because its state is populated in the initial binding, which we don't need to do in a postback. To account for this, we use the `SelectCategory` method, forcing a selection of the current category after a permission has been removed:

```
    Private Sub RemovePermissionButton_Click( _
      ByVal sender As Object, _
      ByVal e As EventArgs) _
      Handles RemovePermissionButton.Click

      Dim myCurrentRole As Integer = Convert.ToInt32(Request("RoleID"))
```

```
      Dim bizRole As Role = New Role(myCurrentRole)

    bizRole.RemovePermission( _
      Convert.ToInt32(PermissionList.SelectedItem.Value))
    DoInitialDataBind()
    SelectCategory(Convert.ToInt32(Request("CategoryList")), True)
  End Sub
```

By default, the **Remove Permission** button is invisible. To reveal the button after a permission is selected in the appropriate ListBox, we respond to the SelectedIndexChanged event by making the **Remove Permission** button visible:

```
    Private Sub PermissionList_SelectedIndexChanged( _
      ByVal sender As Object, _
      ByVal e As EventArgs) _
      Handles PermissionList.SelectedIndexChanged

      RemovePermissionButton.Visible = True
    End Sub
```

This next event handler responds to the **Add Permission** button's Click event. This will add the currently selected permission to the role currently being edited. While it is physically possible for us to use purely client-side methods to accomplish this same thing visibly, we're going to avoid that. Instead, we're going to use the event model that ASP.NET provides us. The main reason for this is that server-side code is guaranteed to work on all browsers. If we round-trip for this action, we don't care about the client support for JavaScript (ever seen a DHTML page try to run on a WebTV box or a Sega Dreamcast web browser?). By doing all the work on the server side, we take an initial latency penalty, but since all of the data is already available to the web page to begin with, the performance loss we suffer is negligible and our gains in browser compatibility are well worth it.

```
    Private Sub AddPermissionButton_Click( _
      ByVal sender As Object, _
      ByVal e As EventArgs) _
      Handles AddPermissionButton.Click

      Dim myCurrentRole As Integer = Convert.ToInt32(Request("RoleID"))
      Dim bizRole As Role = New Role(myCurrentRole)

      bizRole.AddPermission( _
        Convert.ToInt32(PermissionDropList.SelectedItem.Value))
      DoInitialDataBind()
      SelectCategory(Convert.ToInt32(Request("CategoryList")), True)
    End Sub
```

This next event handler will delete the current role (the stored procedure will also remove all data dependent on that role) and then transfer control to the Roles.aspx page, as the current role will no longer exist.

```
    Private Sub RemoveRoleButton_Click( _
      ByVal sender As Object, _
      ByVal e As EventArgs) _
      Handles RemoveRoleButton.Click
```

```
    Dim myCurrentRole As Integer = Convert.ToInt32(Request("RoleID"))
    Dim bizRole As Role = New Role(myCurrentRole)

    bizRole.Delete()
    Server.Transfer("roles.aspx")
End Sub
```

If the user clicks the option to manage user assignments, we want to transfer them to the role assignments page:

```
Private Sub ManageAssignmentsLink_Click( _
  ByVal sender As Object, _
  ByVal e As EventArgs) _
  Handles ManageAssignmentsLink.Click

  Server.Transfer("RoleAssignments.aspx?RoleID=" & Request("RoleID"))

End Sub
```

Finally, as the last part of our user accounting administration section, let's take a look at the source code of the page that manages the user memberships of given roles. Here is a screenshot of this page in action:

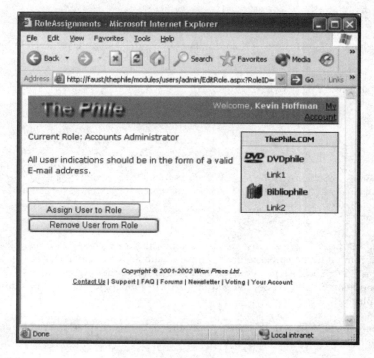

This page works in a fairly straightforward manner. The user of the page, who would typically be a system administrator, supplies an e-mail address and can then either click the **Assign User to Role** button or the **Remove User from Role** button. If the user is already in the role when being added, no error is displayed. If the user is not in the role when being removed from the role, then no error message is displayed. The reason for not displaying any messages is that if your desired state is *already* the way you intend it, then we shouldn't have to report that the code did nothing to get you to that state. If you want to remove a user who isn't there, why bother telling you we didn't remove a user that wasn't there? Obviously, we could make the administration system more user-friendly by giving more verbose reports, but that's typically something we would work on after the system is fully functional.

Let's take a look at the code-behind for this page (`/ThePhile/Modules/Users/Admin/RoleAssignments.aspx.vb`). Instead of listing the entire source code, we'll just include the important method definitions and web form designer code:

```vb
Private Sub Page_Load(ByVal sender As Object, ByVal e As EventArgs)

    If Not Page.IsPostBack Then

        Dim currentRole As New Role(Convert.ToInt32(Request("RoleID")))
        CurrentRoleLabel.Text = "Current Role: " & currentRole.Description

    End If
End Sub
```

This next event handler is executed in response to clicking the **Assign User to Role** button:

```vb
Private Sub AssignUserButton_Click( _
    ByVal sender As Object, _
    ByVal e As EventArgs) _
    Handles AssignUserButton.Click

    Dim tempPrincipal As New SitePrincipal(EmailAddress.Text)
    Dim tempUser As New Business.User(tempPrincipal)

    tempUser.AddToRole(Convert.ToInt32(Request("RoleID")))
    StatusLabel.Text = "User " & EmailAddress.Text & " Granted Role.<br/>"
    StatusLabel.Visible = True
End Sub
```

First, we obtain a `SitePrincipal` instance by instantiating the `SitePrincipal` class with an e-mail address as an argument to the constructor. Then we obtain an instance of a `User` class by passing in the instance of `SitePrincipal` we just created. Once this is done then we can invoke the `AddToRole` method on that object. Finally, we set the text of a `Label` control, to inform the administrative user of what just took place.

The last method we will look at in this class (and, indeed, in this chapter) is fired when the user clicks the **Remove** button:

```vb
Private Sub RemoveUserButton_Click( _
    ByVal sender As Object, _
    ByVal e As EventArgs) _
```

```
Handles RemoveUserButton.Click

Dim tempPrincipal As New SitePrincipal(EmailAddress.Text)
Dim tempUser As New Business.User(tempPrincipal)

tempUser.RemoveRole(Convert.ToInt32(Request("RoleID")))
StatusLabel.Text = "User " & EmailAddress.Text & " Removed from Role.<br/>"
 StatusLabel.Visible = True

End Sub
```

Just as we did in the last event handler, we obtain an instance of a `SitePrincipal` class by supplying the e-mail address contained in the form. Once we've accomplished this we can instantiate a `User` object by passing the new `SitePrincipal` instance to the `User` constructor. Once we have an instance of the `User` class, we can simply call `RemoveRole` on that instance and we're done.

Summary

This chapter started off by presenting a problem that many websites today are faced with: that of identifying, authenticating, remembering, and persisting user accounts. We then went through a design for a solution to this problem. Finally, we looked at the extensive source code for an expandable, powerful implementation.

In this chapter we covered quite a few topics and took a look at a fair amount of code. We covered some important concepts, such as the uses and benefits of role-based security, and the importance of integrating into existing systems rather than creating entirely new infrastructures. We covered a complex system of assigning permissions to roles, and assigning users to those roles, and showed how we can create a fully functioning authentication system around this concept.

Hopefully, you have found this chapter useful, and you will understand the following important concepts that you can use in your own projects and sample applications:

❑   The issues surrounding user identification

❑   Issues involved in user authentication

❑   Issues involved in securing all or some of a web application

❑   Provisions for administrative or 'power' users

Now that we have our `Accounts` module we can move on and implement other modules that rely on it for user identification and authentication. In the next chapter we'll begin to look at modules relating to the *content* of our site, beginning with one to manage news articles.

6

News Management

The site we're building is basically a content site focused on DVDs and books. Content can be in the form of news, articles, reports of special events, reviews, and so on. In this chapter we're going to point out some of the content-related problems that should be considered for sites of this type. We'll then design and develop an online news manager to enable complete management of our site's content – acquiring news, adding, activating, and removing news, sharing news with others, and so on. While we will focus on managing news, many of these techniques will be relevant when dealing with other types of content.

The Problem

There are several ways to gather information and news for our site's content: we might hunt for news ourselves, get news directly from the users (a great example of this is the Add Your News link at www.aspwire.com), or rely upon a company, such a Reuters, whose business it is to gather and organize news and distribute it to third-party sites. Another common technique is to keep an eye on other news sites, and scrape articles together from information available on the Internet. Many sites (for example www.wired.com) also provide links to suggested stories elsewhere. It doesn't matter which methods we use, we still need fresh and updated content if your site is to be successful and entice users to return. No user will come regularly to a site if they never, or very seldom, find some new content.

Once we have news sources, a second problem arises: how to add news and articles to our site. We can immediately rule out manually updating or adding static HTML pages – if we have to add news several times a day, or even just several times every week, creating and uploading pages and editing all the links is not practicable in most cases. In cases where it is practicable, we don't need to write a new management system!

For our site, we need a much more flexible system, one that allows the site administrators to easily publish news without requiring special HTML tools or a knowledge of HTML. We want it to have many features, such as enabling us to organize news in categories and show abstracts, and allowing the site users to post their own news. We'll see the complete list of features we're going to implement in *The Design* section. For now it's sufficient to say that we must be able to manage the content online, without any other tool. Think about what this implies: you can add or edit news as soon as it is available, in a few minutes, even if you're not in your office and even if you don't have access to your own computer; all you need is a connection to the Internet and a browser; and this can work the same way for your news contributors and partners. They won't need to e-mail the news to you and then wait for you to publish it – they can submit and publish content without your intervention (although in our case we will give the administrator the option to approve or edit the content before publication). A good example of this is www.codeproject.com, which provides article categories plus an "unedited section" for the user-submitted articles that have not been edited yet.

For small content sites, or for sites where news and articles are not the main business, simply showing news and other resources is sufficient. But others may want to take this one step further, and decide to offer the news they have gathered/written and organized to other sites. Such sites might not want to spend time finding and formatting articles, may not have people who look after a news management system, but might want to fuel their site with some fresh content automatically updated on a regular basis. In many cases, paying a fee for such a service can be relatively cheap and very easy, since the site administrator doesn't have to worry at all about the content, and they'll be able to focus on the site's main business (commerce of goods related to the published news, for example). Therefore we decided to find a way to offer our news to other companies. We also wanted this data to be available not only for web browsers, but for Windows client applications too.

The last problem is the implementation of security. We want to give full control to one or more administrators, allow a specific group of users to submit news, and allow normal users to just read the news. We could even prevent them from reading the content if they have not registered with the site.

So, to summarize the problem, we need:

❑ A source of news and articles

❑ An online tool for managing news content

❑ A method of allowing other sites and applications to use our content

❑ A system that allows various users different levels of access to the site's content

The Design

In this section we're going to work on the design of our online tool for acquiring, managing, and sharing the news content of our site. Specifically we will:

❑ Provide a full list of the features we want to implement

❑ Design the database tables for this module

❑ Write down a list and a description of the stored procedures that provide access to the database

❑ Describe the object models of the data and business layers

- ❏ Describe the user interface services specific to news management, such as the site pages, reusable user controls, and web services
- ❏ Explain how we will ensure security for the administration section and for other access-restricted pages

Features to Implement

Let's start our discussion by writing down a list of the features that the news manager module should provide in order to be flexible and powerful, but still easy to use. We might decide to add more features later, but these are the things we definitely need to implement:

- ❏ A news item can be added to the database at any time, with the option to not publish it until a specified release date. In addition, the person submitting the news must be able to specify an expiration date, after which the news will be retired. If these dates are not specified then the news should be immediately published and remain active indefinitely.

- ❏ News items or articles can have an approved status. If it is the administrator who submits the news item, it should be approved directly. If we allow other people, such as staff or users of the site, to post their own news, then it should be added to the database in a "pending" state. The site administrator will then take care of controlling this content, applying any required modifications, and finally approving the news for publishing once it is considered suitable.

- ❏ The system should track *who* originally submitted an article or news item. This is important as it provides information on whether a contributor is active, who is responsible for incorrect content, whom to contact for further details if the news is particularly interesting, and so on.

- ❏ There should be multiple categories, allowing all news items and articles to be organized in different virtual folders.

- ❏ The user should have a page with the available categories as a menu. Each category should be linked to a page that shows a short abstract for each news item. The administrator will use a protected page to define the length of the abstracts. By clicking on the abstract the user can read the whole text.

- ❏ We want to expose the news through a web service, so that we can offer content to external sites, and provide a Windows client that downloads the news or links to the respective online pages.

- ❏ Above all, the news manager must be integrated with the existing site. In our case this means that the pages must tie in with the current layout, and that we must take advantage of the current authentication/authorization system to protect each section and to identify the author of the submitted content.

Having this list of features is very important when designing the database tables, as we now know what information we need to store, and the information that we should retrieve from existing tables.

Database Design

As we saw in Chapter 2, we are using a single database for all the modules of this site. So, we need to use module-specific prefixes for the tables, stored procedures, and the other objects of our modules. The prefix for the news manager module is News_.

We have only two tables, one for the categories and the other for the actual news content. The following diagram shows how they are linked to each other and to the Accounts_Users table that we created in Chapter 5:

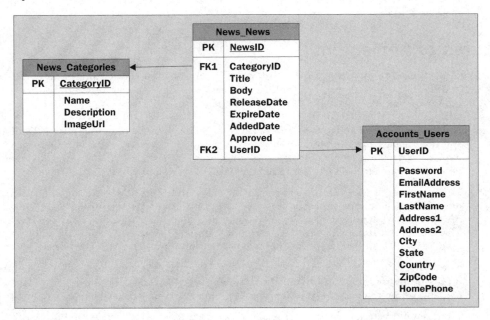

Let's start describing these tables and their relationship in more detail.

The News_Categories Table

Unsurprisingly, the News_Categories table stores the name, a description, and an image for each category:

Column Name	Type	Size	Allow Null	Description
CategoryID	int – Identity primary key	4	No	The unique ID for the category.
Name	varchar	50	No	The name of the category.
Description	varchar	250	Yes	The description of the category.
ImageUrl	varchar	100	Yes	The URL of an image that graphically describes the category. It might be used in menus, for example.

This system supports a single-level category, meaning that we cannot have subcategories. Enhancing the system to support subcategories is left as an exercise to the reader but, as a suggestion, the DB would only require an additional `ParentCategoryID` column containing the ID of the parent category.

The News_News Table

This table contains the content and all further information for all the news items in all categories. It is structured as follows:

Column Name	Type	Size	Allow Null	Description
NewsID	int – Identity Primary key	4	No	The unique ID for the news item.
CategoryID	int Foreign key	4	No	The ID of the category to which the news item belongs.
Title	varchar	250	No	The title of the news item.
Body	text		Yes	The body of the news item, in HTML format.
ReleaseDate	datetime	8	No	The date that the news can be released. We use `datetime` instead of `smalldatetime`, to provide compatibility with ASP 3.
ExpireDate	datetime	8	No	The date that the news will expire.
AddedDate	datetime	8	No	The date that the news was added.
Approved	bit	1	No	The approved status of the news item. If `false`, the administrator has to approve the news before it is actually published and available to readers.
UserID	int Foreign key	4	Yes	The ID of the user who submitted or added this news. It should match an ID in the `Accounts_Users` table of the `Accounts` module.

As noted, the `UserID` field refers to a table of the `Accounts` module. Although this would be possible even if the `Accounts_Users` table were in a separate database, having all these tables in the same database allows easier integration between modules.

Stored Procedures

To manage the database we will build a set of stored procedures, which we'll run later in the data layer classes to do everything from the addition of categories and news, to the update of single fields. The stored procedures we need, and their parameters, are listed here (we'll be writing the code later in the chapter in *The Solution* section):

Stored Procedure	Parameters	Description
Sp_News_GetCategories		Returns the entire content of the News_Categories table.
sp_News_GetCategoryDetails	@CategoryID int	Returns the complete row identified by the specified ID.
sp_News_InsertCategory	@Name varchar(50), @Description varchar(250), @ImageUrl varchar(250), @CategoryID int OUTPUT	Inserts a new category. If the specified Name already exists then the output parameter @CategoryID will be -1, otherwise it will be set to the new category ID.
sp_News_DeleteCategory	@CategoryID int	Deletes the category identified by CategoryID.
sp_News_UpdateCategory	@CategoryID int, @Name varchar(50), @Description varchar(250), @ImageUrl varchar(100)	Updates all the fields of the category specified by CategoryID.
sp_News_GetNews	@CategoryID int, @CurrentApprovedOnly bit = 0, @AbstractLength int = -1	Returns all news items for the specified category. If @CurrentApprovedOnly is true it returns only the news items whose Approved field is 1 (true), and for which the current date is between ReleaseDate and ExpireDate. The last parameter is the length for the partial body content that is returned. If @AbstractLength is -1 the whole of the Body is returned.
sp_News_GetNewsDetails	@NewsID int	Returns the complete row for the specified news item. This also includes the whole Body field content.

Stored Procedure	Parameters	Description
sp_News_GetHeadlines	@CategoryID int	Returns only the NewsID, Title, and ReleaseDate for the current and approved news items of the specified category.
sp_News_InsertNews	@CategoryID int, @Title varchar(250), @Body text, @ReleaseDate datetime, @ExpireDate datetime, @Approved bit, @UserID int, @NewsID int OUTPUT	Inserts a news item. If there is already a row with the specified CategoryID, Title, ReleaseDate, and ExpireDate then the output parameter @NewsID is set to –1, and no changes are made. Otherwise it is set to the added news ID.
sp_News_DeleteNews	@NewsID int	Deletes the news item identified by the specified ID.
sp_News_UpdateNews	@NewsID int, @Title varchar(250), @Body text, @ReleaseDate datetime, @ExpireDate datetime, @Approved bit	Updates all the fields of the specified news item.
sp_News_SetNewsApproved	@NewsID int, @Approved bit	Changes the value of the Approved field for the specified news item.

Most of these stored procedures are pretty standard – procedures to insert, update, return, and delete rows. However, it's worth noting some design decisions that will impact on the performance of the site:

❑ The sp_News_GetNews procedure has a parameter that allows us to specify the length of the Body text we want to retrieve. Instead of storing the news abstracts in a separate field, we retrieve an abstract by returning the first @AbstractLength characters of the Body field. The Body field is of type text, thus it can contain very long articles. As we only need to list the available news items, it would be a tremendous waste of time and traffic to retrieve the body text for all the news items. It's therefore a good idea to completely avoid retrieving the body, or, as we did, add a parameter to specify how many characters to retrieve. Also, we included the option to retrieve all the news from the specified table, or only the current and approved news. We'll need to retrieve all the news in cases such as the administration section, where we must be able to see and edit any news. In the pages for the end user we'll only be interested in the active news.

It's worth noting that the method we employ to retrieve the news abstracts assumes that the beginning of each piece of news contains useful information, or at least something that allows the user to understand what the news is about. This is standard practice in journalism – the first sentence or paragraph typically summarizes the entire article. If we couldn't be sure of useful information appearing at the beginning of the text, we could use a separate abstract field instead. This way we can organize the news text anyway we like. This chapter does not show how to implement this alternative method, but implementing it would not be difficult – we'd just need to add another column to the News_News table and code to make use of it.

❑ The sp_News_GetNewsDetails procedure returns all the details (fields) of the specified news item. This includes the whole Body text, and so the procedure is used when we need to display the whole newsitem in its own dynamically filled page.

❑ The sp_News_GetHeadlines procedure returns only selected information about the current and approved news item, such as the title, ID, and the release date. This information will be useful for a headlines box that we might want to show on the homepage, for example. The ID is enough for us to provide a link to the full article.

Designing the Data Layer

Now that we have a clear idea of what the database tables store, and how we retrieve data through the stored procedures, we can design the data services. We will simply create classes with methods that wrap the calls to the stored procedures one by one.

These classes will be part of an assembly of their own, called Wrox.WebModules.NewsManager.Data, and they will all be grouped by this namespace. In Chapter 2 we created a database class in the Wrox.WebModules.Core module. We'll use this DbObject class as the base for all data classes in this module, as DbObject provides methods for creating a connection, and running stored procedures using just a few lines of code. We'll see how easy it is to develop the data classes by inheriting from the DbObject base in *The Solution* section later in the chapter.

Before we look at each of the classes in turn, here is a UML diagram that shows the classes we need in the data layer:

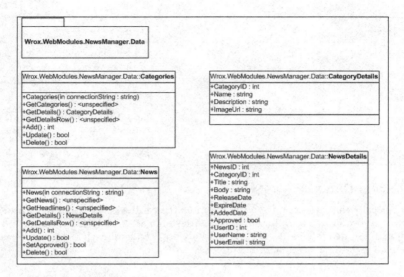

Wrox.WebModules.NewsManager.Data

Wrox.WebModules.NewsManager.Data::Categories

+Categories(in connectionString : string)
+GetCategories() : <unspecified>
+GetDetails() : CategoryDetails
+GetDetailsRow() : <unspecified>
+Add() : int
+Update() : bool
+Delete() : bool

Wrox.WebModules.NewsManager.Data::CategoryDetails

+CategoryID : int
+Name : string
+Description : string
+ImageUrl : string

Wrox.WebModules.NewsManager.Data::News

+News(in connectionString : string)
+GetNews() : <unspecified>
+GetHeadlines() : <unspecified>
+GetDetails() : NewsDetails
+GetDetailsRow() : <unspecified>
+Add() : int
+Update() : bool
+SetApproved() : bool
+Delete() : bool

Wrox.WebModules.NewsManager.Data::NewsDetails

+NewsID : int
+CategoryID : int
+Title : string
+Body : string
+ReleaseDate
+ExpireDate
+AddedDate
+Approved : bool
+UserID : int
+UserName : string
+UserEmail : string

The CategoryDetails Class

This class has no methods, just four public properties that map the fields of the News_Categories table. It does nothing by itself – the properties will be set by the calling functions that use this class simply as a data type to return from the Categories class. Doing this will make our business layer simpler.

The Categories Class

This class wraps the calls to the stored procedures that manage the categories. It has only methods, no properties, and it returns an instance of CategoryDetails to return the details of a specific category. Since there are no relationships with other classes (except one method that returns an instance of CategoryDetails), at this point it's easy to provide a list of the methods and their definitions:

Method Name	Description
Categories	Class constructor taking the connection string as a parameter.
GetCategories	Returns a DataSet containing the names of all the categories.
GetDetails	Returns an instance of CategoryDetails that describes the specified category.
GetDetailsRow	Returns the DataRow of the category identified by the specified ID.

Table continued on following page

Method Name	Description
Add	Adds a new category, and returns the ID of the new record. Returns -1 if the record was already present, and does not change the database.
Update	Updates all the fields of the specified category.
Delete	Deletes the specified category.

The NewsDetails Class

This class is basically the same as `CategoryDetails` but for the `News_News` table instead of the `News_Categories` table. It has only public properties such as `NewsID`, `CategoryID`, `Title`, and `Body`, which map all the table fields. All are set by external code; this class only serves as the data type for a function we're going to see in a moment.

The News Class

This class wraps the calls to all the stored procedures that manage the news items and their attributes. Like the `Categories` class, this class has a `GetDetails` method that returns an instance of `NewsDetails` containing everything from the specified news record. Here is a complete list of the methods to implement:

Method Name	Description
News	Class constructor taking the connection string as a parameter.
GetNews	Returns the news item for the specified category. The other two parameters are the same as we defined for the `sp_News_GetNews` stored procedure.
GetHeadlines	Returns the `NewsID`, `Title`, and `ReleaseDate` for the current and approved news items of the specified category.
GetDetails	Returns an instance of `NewsDetails` that describe the specified news item.
GetDetailsRow	Returns the `DataRow` of the news item identified by the specified ID.
Add	Adds a news item, and returns the ID of the new record. Returns -1 if the record was already present. See the description of `sp_News_InsertNews` for more details.

210

Method Name	Description
Update	Updates all the fields of the specified news record.
SetApproved	Changes the Approved status of the specified news item.
Delete	Deletes the specified news item.

Designing the Business Layer

The data layer is made up of two classes with methods that call the stored procedures, but they don't represent an entity in a real object-oriented way. This is done by the classes of the business layer, which use the data layer classes to access the database, and represents the data as useful objects. These classes will be part of an assembly, Wrox.WebModules.NewsManager.Business, and will inherit from the BizObject class, as decided in Chapter 2. This means that if we can add methods to every business object in the application in one go, by modifying BizObject. We'll look at each of our classes in turn. But first, here is the UML diagram that describes the classes. To save space, some method overloads are not included:

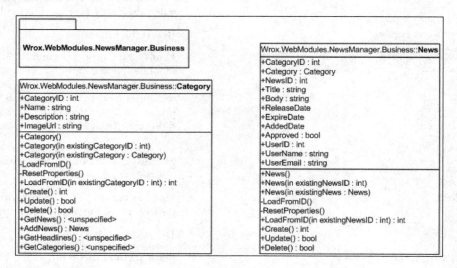

The Category Class

This class has properties that fully describe a news category, with methods to create, update, or delete one category, or add news child items. The following table shows the declaration and description of each member:

Member Name	Description
ID	Read-only property; the category's ID.
Name	Gets/sets the name of the category.
Description	Gets/sets the description of the category.
ImageUrl	Gets/sets the image URL of the category.
Category	Class constructor with no parameters. Resets property values.
public Category(existingCategoryID as Integer)	Class constructor that sets the properties to the category identified by the input ID.
public Category(existingCategory as Catgory)	Class constructor that sets the properties to describe the category identified by an existing Category object.
LoadFromID	Loads the properties of the category identified by a private ID variable. This method is called by the constructors or when the data has to be refreshed.
ResetProperties	Resets the properties.
LoadFromID(existingCategoryID as Integer)	Loads all the properties of the category identified by the input ID. This method allows us to load a different category after the object has been created, or to load the properties if we created an object but didn't specify an ID for the constructor.
Create	Creates a new category, and sets the properties of the object to represent the new record.
Update	Updates the current category with the new values of the public properties.
Delete	Deletes the category.
GetCategories	Static method that returns all the categories in a Dataset.
GetNews	Returns all the child news items in a Dataset.

Member Name	Description
GetNews(currentApprovedOnly as Boolean)	Overloaded method that can return only the approved child news items.
GetHeadlines	Returns the NewsID, Title, and ReleaseDate for the current and approved news items in the category, plus the full URL of the whole news page.
AddNews	Adds a child news item.

You might be wondering why the Create method requires all the properties for the new category as input, instead of retrieving them from the public variables. This is because in other classes we might require values that are exposed as read-only properties, so we would need to get them through input parameters. So for consistency with future classes, we require all the values as parameters, and then set the properties accordingly. Also note that the AddNews method returns an object of type News, which is described in the next section.

The most notable method here is GetHeadlines. It not only calls the homonymous method of the data layer, but it also adds a column to the table of the returned DataSet. The value of this column is the complete URL of the page where the user can read the whole news, and not just its abstract. The complete path is made up of a base path of the ASPX page, plus the NewsID attribute as a parameter. For example, say that the page is ShowNews.aspx, and that the base path is localhost/ThePhile/Modules/NewsManager/ShowNews.aspx, then the URL for a news item would be something like localhost/ThePhile/Modules/NewsManager/ShowNews.aspx?NewsID=4.

Adding this column is really important for providing the ability to share headlines with external sites and to browse the news with programs other than a web browser. What we're going to do later in the chapter, in fact, is to build a Windows application that shows the current headlines, and that opens a browser and loads the whole news item when a headline is clicked. The client application does not have to do anything to find the URL to which it must redirect, as it is given along with the other data in the table, and the client developer is not required to know the path of the ShowNews.aspx page in advance. In addition to being easier for the client developer, this also means that if the webmaster moves the page or changes its name, the client application will continue to work fine as soon as it downloads an updated DataSet, without requiring any modification to the code.

We could have returned only the NewsID from the business layer, and had the presentation layer objects construct a URL link themselves. This would be a purer way of building an n-tier system, but would require slightly more code. So in this case it's best to compromise our n-tier architecture a little.

The News Class

This class describes and manipulates a news record, using the following properties and methods:

Member Name	Description
ID	Read-only property that returns the ID of the news item represented by the object.
CategoryID	Read-only property that returns the ID of the parent category.
Category	Returns the parent category.
Title	Gets/sets the title of the news item.
Body	Gets/sets the body of the news item.
Approved	Gets/sets the Approved status.
ReleaseDate	Gets/sets the release date.
ExpireDate	Gets/sets the expiry date.
AddedDate	Read-only property that returns the date when the news item was added to the database.
UserID	Read-only property that returns the ID of the user who submitted the news item.
UserName	Read-only property that returns the name of the user who submitted the news.
UserEmail	Read-only property that returns the e-mail address of the user who submitted the news.
News	Class constructor with no parameters. It only resets the properties.
News(existingNewsID as Integer)	Class constructor that sets the properties to describe the news item identified by the input ID.
News(existingNews as News)	Class constructor that sets the properties to describe the news item identified by an existing news object.
LoadFromID	Loads the properties of the news item identified by a private ID variable. This method is called by the constructors, or when the data has to be refreshed.

Member Name	Description
ResetProperties	Resets the properties.
LoadFromID(existingNewsID as Integer)	Loads all the properties of the news item identified by the input ID. This method allows us to load a different news item after the object has been created, or to load the properties if we created an object but didn't specify an ID for the constructor.
Create	Creates a news item, and sets the properties of the object to represent the new record.
Update	Updates the current news item with the new values of the public properties.
Delete	Deletes the news item.

It's worth noting that here the Create method requires input values such as the parent category and the user ID. These values are exposed by read-only variables, so we need to pass them as parameters. As mentioned above, we decided to pass all the necessary parameters to the Create methods of other classes as well, to avoid confusion.

Storing and Retrieving Settings

In addition to categories and news, our module also has some settings to store, such as the database connection string. In the previous chapter we discussed the advantages of storing the settings as an XML file produced by serializing a class. We've seen how to de-serialize the content of that same file to create a class instance with the state it had in the previous session. With this module we're going to use exactly the same method. We have a Wrox.WebModules.NewsManager.Configuration.dll assembly and a namespace with the same name. It will include two classes. ModuleConfig gets and sets the settings, by de-serializing the file to an object or serializing an object to a file. ModuleSettings exposes the settings as public properties, and whose state will be serialized or de-serialized. The ModuleSettings class has three properties:

❏ ConnectionString: the connection string that all the data classes use to access the database

❏ NewsUrl: the URL of the ShowNews.aspx page, necessary to build the full links from the headlines to the whole news

❏ AbstractLength: the number of characters that make up an abstract by truncating the news item's Body

Here is the UML diagram that represents this component:

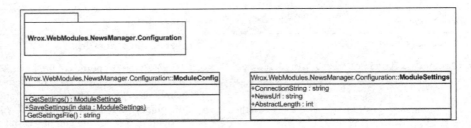

Designing the Presentation Layer

The design of the ASP.NET pages is nothing really special, so there's not much to discuss. We have a set of pages, some for the administrators and some for the end users, which allow us to manage news, and navigate through categories and read news, respectively.

The main consideration is that we must integrate these module-specific pages into the rest of the site, but this is easily possible by adding the site-wide header and footer controls to our pages, and by using a common CSS file.

Let's focus on some of the more news-specific needs: plugging headlines into other parts of the site, and providing headlines as a web service.

Plug-in Headlines

The first new issue here is that we need a way to quickly add the headlines to any page we want. It's not enough to just have entirely new pages – we want to plug the headlines into *existing* pages. A user control is the best solution in this case, because it will allow us to add news and customize appearance with a single line in an ASPX page.

Our headlines control must expose properties that select the headlines we want to show, and define the style and size of the control on the page. We could add many more graphical properties, but these are enough for a fully working and useful control.

The control will connect to the database with a connection string that is automatically retrieved. The Webmaster will only need to know the appearance they want to assign to the control, and the ID of news category they want to display. This way, we can insert the control into a page with just a couple of lines of code, and without knowledge of the underlying object model.

The Headlines Web Service

We said earlier that we want to allow other sites to use our headlines, and also build non-browser applications (such as a Windows client) to show the headlines. If we were planning to distribute the whole of the news item, we would probably want to make some money from it, but we will take a different approach. Instead of giving away the whole news item, we will share only the headlines. Any external site and program can get them for free, with a link to our own site for the full story. This page with the full news text is only available on our site. What this means is that if we allow everybody to insert our headlines into their sites, and if a lot of sites take up this opportunity, we're going to have lots of advertising and new traffic *for free*! Whenever a user clicks on a title they will be redirected to ThePhile.com, and they will probably end up generating page views (which can lead to revenue if we're selling advertisement space). They may visit some other sections of the site, or buy something if we're selling products or services. If nothing else, our site will gain a better reputation and a larger audience.

Later, if this service is successful, we could push things further and offer an extended service that allows external sites to insert the whole news item into their own pages. But this time for a fee!

However, for this book's scope the first type of service is enough, so let's go ahead and see what it should provide. This web service only needs a couple of methods for what we plan to do:

Method Name	Description
GetCategories	Returns all the available categories
GetHeadlines	Returns ID, title, and URL for all published news from the specified category

Providing such a service is really easy in VS.NET (and also with the .NET Framework without the help of the VS.NET's wizards): a web service takes care of all the details, and plumbing code deals with the communication protocols and SOAP messages. Thus, designing a simple web service is very simple and similar to designing a class. There are many differences between web services and classes, of course, such as the fact that they can be called remotely, and they are stateless, but essentially a web service is still a class that exposes some public methods.

We remember that the data classes accept the connection string as input in the constructor method, and then use it in all the other methods. Here we can't do this, due to the fact that the web service is stateless and can't store the connection string with a private variable. The easy solution is to get the connection string every time a method is called. We have only two methods, so there isn't much work, and the connection string is cached (we'll show how to do this in the implementation of the Settings assembly), so there is no overhead.

The Need for Security

The news manager module divides into two basic parts:

❑ The administration section, which allows the webmaster or someone else to add, delete, or edit the categories, publish news, and change the module's settings

❑ The end-user section, which has pages to navigate through the categories and read the news, or see the headlines on the homepage

The division is made more complex because of the page where users can post their own news. The administrator can decide to allow any user to access this page, or select a group of trusted people and block access to everybody else. So this page could be for end-users, or for administrators.

In the previous chapter we developed a very flexible module that allows us to administer the registered users, read or edit their profile, and dynamically assign permissions for certain operations. For the news manager we'll have a NewsManagerPermissions enumeration, with the following three permissions that we can assign to users:

❑ AdministerNews: the user has full power over the news system. They can add, edit, or delete categories, approve and publish news items, and change the settings. Only one person (or at least very few people) should have this permission.

❑   SubmitNews: the user can submit their own news items, but these won't be published until the administrator approves them. We could give this permission to any user, if we want to gather as much news as possible, or a selected group of people otherwise.

❑   PublishNews: the user can submit their own news items, and these will be immediately published. There is no need for any intervention by the administrator. Only a selected group of trusted people should have this permission, because everything they send will be available straight away. You must be pretty sure that they won't send incorrect content and that what they write won't require any editing.

Enforcing these security rules is a simple task with the help of the Users module, which also provides a GUI tool for changing the permissions of users. We can integrate it in the solution and then allow the general administrator to choose trusted people and give them the appropriate rights.

The Solution

We've discussed just about every aspect of the design, and we are now ready to produce the solution. We'll follow the same pattern as in *The Design* section: from the creation of database tables and stored procedures, to the implementation of security, passing through the data access and user interface services coding.

Working on the Database

Creating the database tables is straightforward, using the Enterprise Manager, so we won't cover it here. The best way to set up the database is to use the backed-up version in the code download.

Now let's look at how to create the relationships between the tables and write some stored procedures, although these already exist in the backup.

Relationships Between the Tables

We create a new diagram in the Enterprise Manager, and by following the wizard we add the News_Categories, News_News, and Accounts_Users tables. As soon as the three tables are added to the underlying window, the Enterprise Manager should recognize a relationship between News_Categories and News_News and automatically add a connection with the correct properties. However, if it does not, click on the News_News table's CategoryID field and drag and drop the icon that appears over the News_Categories table. Once you release the button, a dialog with the relationship's properties appears. You should set the options as shown in the following screenshot:

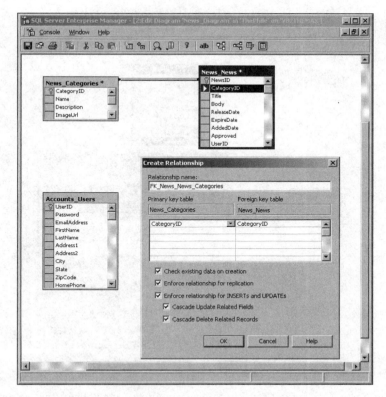

The **Cascade Update Related Fields** option ensures that if we change the `CategoryID` primary key in the `News_Categories` table, this change is propagated to the foreign keys in the `News_News` table.

> *The primary key should never be changed, since it is used for identification. The administration pages won't allow us to change it, but it's a good idea to select this option anyway.*

The **Cascade Delete Related Records** option ensures that if we delete a category, all the related news items are deleted as well. This option is very important and must be checked, because otherwise we'll end up with a database filled with unreachable news (since the parent category will no longer exist).

Now we have to create a relationship between `News_News` and `Acounts_Users`, based on the `UserID` field of both tables. As before, click the `News_News` table's `UserID` field, drag and drop the icon over the `Accounts_Users` table, and complete the **Properties** dialog as follows:

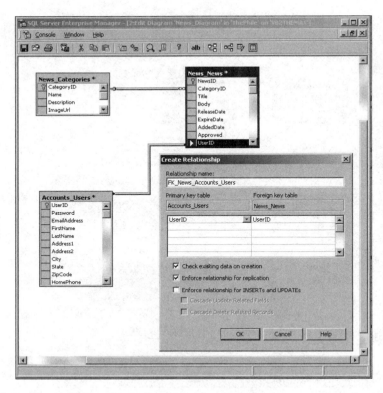

Things are a bit tricky with this relationship and, as you might have noticed, the settings are different from before: we don't select the **Enforce relationship for INSERTs and UPDATEs** option. In the first relationship we built, we wanted all dependent news items to be deleted whenever a category was deleted. Here, when we delete a user we don't want to delete all their news items too. That user might be a former employee of our company, or they might have unregistered from the site, but we want to keep their news in the database.

> *If we select the Enforce relationship for INSERTs and UPDATEs option but not the Cascade Delete Related Records option, if we try to delete a user then we'll get an error. This is because we have a constraint that ensures that the foreign key can't point to a non-existent row in the referenced table. If we don't select the former option we still have the foreign key, but we can also delete a user without automatically deleting the respective news.*

We're not finished yet. We can't leave a foreign key to a row that no longer exists, because if we change another user's ID or add a new user with the same ID as the deleted user, the news will end up referencing not a non-existent user, but the wrong user. We simply need to 'reset' (set to null) the UserID field in the News_News table for the news whose author has been deleted from the Accounts_Users table. This issue can be easily resolved with a **trigger**, which we're going to see in the next section.

A Trigger for the UserID Foreign Key

To create the trigger that sets the UserID foreign key to null when a user is deleted, go back to the Enterprise Manager main window (save the diagram before closing the designer), right-click the Accounts_Users table, and click **All Tasks | Manage Triggers**. A dialog pops up with the textbox for the trigger text, which is as follows:

```
CREATE TRIGGER SetNewsAuthorToNull ON [dbo].[Accounts_Users]
FOR DELETE
AS

UPDATE News_News
   SET UserID = NULL
   WHERE UserID = (SELECT UserID FROM Deleted)
```

This code creates a trigger named SetNewsAuthorToNull, which is raised when a record in the Accounts_Users table is deleted. It sets the rows in News_News that were linked to the deleted row to null.

Creating the Stored Procedures

In this section we'll show the code for some of the stored procedures. We won't cover all of them, since the code is actually very similar regardless of whether we are adding, editing, or deleting a category or a news item. The stored procedures that work with the news items are more elaborate than the respective procedures that manage the categories, because they have to join two tables and usually have more parameters, so these are the ones we'll look at.

sp_News_GetNews

Here's the code to create the procedure that returns the news item:

```
CREATE PROCEDURE sp_News_GetNews
@CategoryID       int,
@CurrentApprovedOnly    bit,
@AbstractLength int
AS

-- if @AbstractLength is not -1 return the first @AbstractLength
-- chars of the Body field, otherwise return the whole news body
IF @AbstractLength <> -1
  BEGIN
  IF @CurrentApprovedOnly = 1
    BEGIN
    SELECT NewsID, Title,
        LEFT(CAST(Body AS varchar(1000)), @AbstractLength)  +
            '...' AS Abstract,
        ReleaseDate, ExpireDate, AddedDate, Approved,
        News_News.UserID, (FirstName + ' ' + LastName) AS UserName,
        EmailAddress AS UserEmail
      FROM News_News LEFT JOIN Accounts_Users
        ON News_News.UserID = Accounts_Users.UserID
      WHERE CategoryID = @CategoryID AND Approved = 1 AND
        ReleaseDate <= GETDATE() AND ExpireDate >= GETDATE()
```

```
      END
    ELSE
      BEGIN
      SELECT NewsID, Title,
          LEFT(CAST(Body AS varchar(1000)), @AbstractLength)  +
            '...' AS Abstract,
          ReleaseDate, ExpireDate, AddedDate, Approved,
          News_News.UserID, (FirstName + ' ' + LastName) AS UserName,
          EmailAddress AS UserEmail
        FROM News_News LEFT JOIN Accounts_Users
            ON News_News.UserID = Accounts_Users.UserID
        WHERE CategoryID = @CategoryID
      END
    END
  ELSE
    BEGIN
    IF @CurrentApprovedOnly = 1
      BEGIN
      SELECT NewsID, Title, Body AS Abstract, ReleaseDate, ExpireDate,
          AddedDate, Approved, News_News.UserID,
          (FirstName + ' ' + LastName) AS UserName,
          EmailAddress AS UserEmail
        FROM News_News LEFT JOIN Accounts_Users
            ON News_News.UserID = Accounts_Users.UserID
        WHERE CategoryID = @CategoryID AND Approved = 1 AND
            ReleaseDate <= GETDATE() AND ExpireDate >= GETDATE()
      END
    ELSE
      BEGIN
      SELECT NewsID, Title, Body AS Abstract, ReleaseDate, ExpireDate,
          AddedDate, Approved, News_News.UserID,
          (FirstName + ' ' + LastName) AS UserName,
          EmailAddress AS UserEmail
        FROM News_News LEFT JOIN Accounts_Users
            ON News_News.UserID = Accounts_Users.UserID
        WHERE CategoryID = @CategoryID
      END
    END
  END
  GO
```

Although the procedure is quite long, it is really very simple. It executes different SELECT queries according to the passed parameters. If we want to retrieve only the current and approved news items then one query is run, if we want all the news items then a less restrictive query is run instead. The same applies for the abstract length: if it is not -1 we must truncate the Body field after the specified characters, otherwise we simply return the whole content (aliased as Abstract).

sp_News_GetNewsDetails

This procedure is simpler, since it has no parameters except for the NewsID, and it returns the whole row:

```
CREATE PROCEDURE sp_News_GetNewsDetails
@NewsID int
AS
```

```
SELECT NewsID, CategoryID, Title, Body, ReleaseDate, ExpireDate, AddedDate,
    Approved, News_News.UserID,
    (FirstName + ' ' + LastName) AS UserName, EmailAddress AS UserEmail
  FROM News_News LEFT JOIN Accounts_Users
    ON News_News.UserID = Accounts_Users.UserID
  WHERE NewsID = @NewsID
GO
```

sp_News_GetHeadlines

This procedure returns a few fields for the active news only, so this is very short and easily understandable:

```
CREATE PROCEDURE sp_News_GetHeadlines
@CategoryID     int
AS

SELECT NewsID, Title, ReleaseDate
  FROM News_News
  WHERE CategoryID = @CategoryID AND Approved = 1 AND
    ReleaseDate <= GETDATE() AND ExpireDate >= GETDATE()
  ORDER BY ReleaseDate DESC
GO
```

sp_News_InsertNews

The following code inserts a new row in the News_News table, and returns the ID of the added row as the output parameter. If a news record with that ID exist, the procedure does nothing:

```
CREATE PROCEDURE sp_News_InsertNews
@CategoryID int,
@Title          varchar(250),
@Body           text,
@ReleaseDate    datetime,
@ExpireDate datetime,
@Approved    bit,
@UserID int,
@NewsID int OUTPUT
AS

DECLARE @CurrID int

-- see if the news already exists
SELECT @CurrID = NewsID
  FROM News_News
  WHERE CategoryID = @CategoryID AND Title = @Title AND
    ReleaseDate = @ReleaseDate AND ExpireDate = @ExpireDate

-- if not, add it
IF @CurrID IS NULL
  BEGIN

  INSERT INTO News_News
```

```
          (CategoryID, Title, Body, ReleaseDate, ExpireDate,
       AddedDate, Approved, UserID)
     VALUES (@CategoryID, @Title, @Body, @ReleaseDate, @ExpireDate,
         GETDATE(), @Approved, @UserID)

  SET @NewsID = @@IDENTITY

  IF @@ERROR > 0
    BEGIN
    RAISERROR ('Insert of News failed', 16, 1)
    RETURN 99
    END
  END
ELSE
  BEGIN
  SET @NewsID = -1
  END
GO
```

sp_News_UpdateNews

This procedure updates all the fields of a row, except for the ID of course. It runs within a **transaction**, so that the changes can be rolled back if an error occurs:

```
CREATE PROCEDURE sp_News_UpdateNews
@NewsID int,
@Title       varchar(250),
@Body        text,
@ReleaseDate     datetime,
@ExpireDate datetime,
@Approved    bit
AS

BEGIN TRANSACTION UpdateNews

UPDATE News_News
  SET
    Title = @Title,
    Body = @Body,
    ReleaseDate = @ReleaseDate,
    ExpireDate = @ExpireDate,
    Approved = @Approved
  WHERE NewsID = @NewsID

IF @@ERROR > 0
  BEGIN
  RAISERROR ('Update of News failed', 16, 1)
  ROLLBACK TRANSACTION UpdateNews
  RETURN 99
  END

COMMIT TRANSACTION UpdateNews
GO
```

Running the SQL commands within a transaction ensures that the data is updated correctly, and that **atomicity** is maintained. A transaction is atomic if all statements must complete, or all fail. Say that we need to execute three UPDATEs, and that the last one generates an error and does not complete correctly. If you run all the three statements within a transaction you'll be able to roll back the transaction, returning the data to its original state. If all statements run fine, you can commit the transaction to persist the changes.

Transactions are a complex topic, beyond the scope of this book. To find out more about this subject, you can refer to *Professional SQL Server 2000* (ISBN 1-86100-448-6).

sp_News_SetNewsApproved

This procedure works in a similar way to the procedure above, but with the difference that only the Approved field is updated. This is useful when the administrator only needs to approve a currently inactive news item, or to disapprove a news item already published, without having to supply the current values for all the other fields to the procedure, as was the case above:

```
CREATE PROCEDURE sp_News_SetNewsApproved
@NewsID int,
@Approved   bit
AS

BEGIN TRANSACTION UpdateNews

-- update the news item's approved state
UPDATE News_News
  SET Approved = @Approved
  WHERE NewsID = @NewsID

IF @@ERROR > 0
  BEGIN
  RAISERROR ('Update of News failed', 16, 1)
  ROLLBACK TRANSACTION UpdateNews
  RETURN 99
  END

COMMIT TRANSACTION UpdateNews
GO
```

sp_News_DeleteNews

This is the easiest procedure. It deletes the row with the specified ID:

```
CREATE PROCEDURE sp_News_DeleteNews
@NewsID int
AS

DELETE FROM News_News
  WHERE NewsID = @NewsID
GO
```

Implementing the Data Access Assembly

Now that the database is complete, let's go ahead and start writing the .NET code for the data-access component. We create a **Class Library** project within the ThePhile solution, with the assembly name and the default namespace `Wrox.WebModules.NewsManager.Data`. The `AssemblyInfo.vb` file needs editing as follows:

```
Imports System.Reflection
Imports System.Runtime.InteropServices

<Assembly: AssemblyTitle("ThePhile.com NewsManager Module - Data Tier")>
<Assembly: AssemblyDescription("Data Tier for the NewsManager Module of
ThePhile.com")>
<Assembly: AssemblyCompany("Wrox Press Ltd")>
<Assembly: AssemblyProduct("Wrox.WebModules")>
<Assembly: AssemblyCopyright("(C) 2001 Wrox Press Ltd")>
<Assembly: AssemblyTrademark("")>
<Assembly: CLSCompliant(True)>
<Assembly: AssemblyCulture("")>

<Assembly: AssemblyVersion("1.0.0.0")>

<Assembly: AssemblyKeyFile("\Wrox\Keys\ThePhile.snk")>
<Assembly: AssemblyKeyName("")>
<Assembly: AssemblyDelaySign(False)>
```

We need a reference to the assembly of the `Core` project, and to the `System.Data.Dll` assembly, in order to use the `DBObject` base class developed in Chapter 2, and the ADO.NET classes, respectively.

The project consists of two class files, `Categories.vb` and `News.vb`. We will only look at `News.vb` here, because `Categories.vb` is very similar – there's no point in going over both. It's easy to complete the code for the other class, and the complete code is available in the code download.

The News Class

This simple class provides methods that closely map all the available stored procedures that manage news. We'll look at each method in turn. The class's file name is `News.vb` and the namespace must be `Wrox.WebModules.NewsManager.Data`. The name should already be correct if the default namespace is set in the project properties.

We need an `Imports` directive in order to use the types in the `System.Data` and `SystemData.SqlClient` namespaces without having to specify the namespaces. We're going to be using classes and enumerations of these namespaces very often in the code for this class, and it's quicker to write only the class name and not the full namespace as the prefix.

The `News` class must inherit from the `DbObject` class of the `Core` assembly, and the constructor method must call the base constructor. So a skeleton of our class would be:

```
Imports System
Imports System.Data
Imports System.Data.SqlClient
```

```
Public Class News
  Inherits Wrox.WebModules.Data.DbObject

  Public Sub New(ByVal newConnectionString As String)
    MyBase.New(newConnectionString)
  End Sub
```

Now let's take a look at the methods.

The GetNews Method

This method wraps the call to the stored procedure sp_News_GetNews. It accepts as input exactly the same parameters as the stored procedure. It creates an array of SqlParameter objects (one for each input parameter), calls the RunProcedure function to execute the stored procedure, and returns the resulting DataSet:

```
Public Function GetNews( _
    ByVal categoryId As Integer, _
    ByVal currentApprovedOnly As Boolean, _
    ByVal abstractLength As Integer) _
    As DataSet

  ' Create the parameters
  Dim parameters As SqlParameter() = { _
    New SqlParameter("@CategoryID", SqlDbType.Int, 4), _
    New SqlParameter("@CurrentApprovedOnly", SqlDbType.Bit, 1), _
    New SqlParameter("@AbstractLength", SqlDbType.Int, 4)}

  ' Set the values
  parameters(0).Value = categoryId
  parameters(1).Value = currentApprovedOnly
  parameters(2).Value = abstractLength

  Return RunProcedure("sp_News_GetNews", parameters, "News")
End Function
```

The DbObject class is very useful, and spares us having to manually create and use a SqlDataAdapter. The RunProcedure function also uses the SqlConnection it has instantiated in the base constructor, so we don't need to create and store our own instance. All of this allows us to speed up the code development for methods like this and the following ones, and the resulting code is also more readable.

The GetHeadlines Method

This method simply retrieves all the headlines (ID, ReleaseDate, and Title of the active news) by calling the sp_News_GetHeadlines stored procedure:

```
Public Function GetHeadlines(ByVal categoryId As Integer) As DataSet
  Dim parameters As SqlParameter() = { _
    New SqlParameter("@CategoryID", SqlDbType.Int, 4)}
  parameters(0).Value = categoryId
```

```
      Return RunProcedure( _
        "sp_News_GetHeadlines", parameters, "Headlines")
    End Function
```

The GetDetails Method

This method retrieves only the row for the specified ID, and returns an instance of a custom
`NewsDetails` class. As previously said, this class only exposes a set of public fields, and is used as a
return type. Here is the class, which is located in the same file, just below the namespace declaration
and before we declare the `News` class:

```
Public Class NewsDetails
    Public NewsId As Integer
    Public CategoryId As Integer
    Public Title As String
    Public Body As String
    Public ReleaseDate As DateTime
    Public ExpireDate As DateTime
    Public AddedDate As DateTime
    Public Approved As Boolean
    Public UserId As Integer
    Public UserName As String
    Public UserEmail As String
End Class
```

We could have used public properties here, but we don't need any processing or checks of validity
before modifying state, so public fields are sufficient in this case.

Here is the code that gets the specified news record, creates an instance of `NewsDetails`, and returns it:

```
Public Function GetDetails(ByVal newsId As Integer) As NewsDetails

    ' Create the parameter
    Dim parameters As SqlParameter() = { _
      New SqlParameter("@NewsID", SqlDbType.Int, 4)}
    parameters(0).Value = newsId

    Dim theNews As DataSet
    Try
      theNews = RunProcedure( _
        "sp_News_GetNewsDetails", parameters, "News")

      ' If the record was found, set the properties of the class instance
      Dim details As New NewsDetails()
      If theNews.Tables(0).Rows.Count > 0 Then
        Dim rowNews = theNews.Tables(0).Rows(0)
        details.NewsId = CInt(rowNews("NewsID"))
        details.CategoryId = CInt(rowNews("CategoryID"))
        details.Title = rowNews("Title").ToString()
        details.Body = rowNews("Body").ToString()
        details.ReleaseDate = Convert.ToDateTime(rowNews("ReleaseDate"))
        details.ExpireDate = Convert.ToDateTime(rowNews("ExpireDate"))
```

```
            details.AddedDate = Convert.ToDateTime(rowNews("AddedDate"))
            details.Approved = Convert.ToBoolean(rowNews("Approved"))
            If rowNews("UserID") Is DBNull.Value Then
              details.UserId = -1
            Else
              details.UserId = CInt(rowNews("UserID"))
            End If
            details.UserName = rowNews("UserName").ToString()
            details.UserEmail = rowNews("UserEmail").ToString()
          Else
            details.NewsId = -1
          End If
          Return details
        Finally
          theNews.Dispose()
        End Try
      End Function
```

You can see that the `DataSet` returned by `RunProcedure` is defined within the scope of some `try …`
`finally` statements. This way the `DataSet` variable will be disposed of as soon as the `try` statement's
scope ends. The code then creates an instance of `NewsDetails`, but sets its fields only if the `DataSet`
variable contains a row. Otherwise it means that there is no news with the specified ID and so we set the
`NewsID` field to `-1`, as an indication for the code that called the method. Each `DataRow` field is
converted to the type of the respective `NewsDetails` field.

We remember that the `UserID` field may be null (if the user has been deleted) If it is null, it can't be
converted to an `Integer` value. We must check if the field is null by comparing it to `DBNull.Value`
and in that case we set the `NewsDetails` field to `-1`.

The GetDetailsRow Method

This method is a simpler version of the previous method. It obtains the details of the specified news
item, without any processing, by returning the respective `DataRow`:

```
      Public Function GetDetailsRow(ByVal newsId As Integer) As DataRow
        Dim parameters As SqlParameter() = { _
          New SqlParameter("@NewsID", SqlDbType.Int, 4)}
        parameters(0).Value = newsId

        Dim news As DataSet
        Try
          news = RunProcedure("sp_News_GetNewsDetails", parameters, "News")
          Return news.Tables(0).Rows(0)
        Finally
          news.Dispose()
        End Try
      End Function
```

Although not used in this module, this method will be useful if we want to add this row to a custom
table. Later, in Chapter 8, we'll see why and how to use a method like this in an effective way.

The Add Method

This method passes all the input parameters to the sp_News_InsertNews stored procedure, and returns the ID of the added news item. This value is returned by the last parameter, which is declared as an output parameter by setting its Direction property to ParameterDirection.Output:

```
Public Function Add( _
    ByVal categoryId As Integer, _
    ByVal title As String, _
    ByVal body As String, _
    ByVal releaseDate As DateTime, _
    ByVal expireDate As DateTime, _
    ByVal approved As Boolean, _
    ByVal userID As Integer) As Integer

Dim rowsAffected As Integer

' Create the parameters
Dim parameters As SqlParameter() = { _
    New SqlParameter("@CategoryID", SqlDbType.Int, 4), _
    New SqlParameter("@Title", SqlDbType.VarChar, 50), _
    New SqlParameter("@Body", SqlDbType.Text), _
    New SqlParameter("@ReleaseDate", SqlDbType.DateTime), _
    New SqlParameter("@ExpireDate", SqlDbType.DateTime), _
    New SqlParameter("@Approved", SqlDbType.Bit, 1), _
    New SqlParameter("@UserID", SqlDbType.Int, 4), _
    New SqlParameter("@NewsID", SqlDbType.Int, 4)}

' Set the values
parameters(0).Value = categoryId
parameters(1).Value = title.Trim()
parameters(2).Value = body.Trim()
parameters(3).Value = releaseDate
parameters(4).Value = expireDate
parameters(5).Value = approved
parameters(6).Value = userID
parameters(7).Direction = ParameterDirection.Output

RunProcedure("sp_News_InsertNews", parameters, rowsAffected)

Return CInt(parameters(7).Value)
End Function
```

It's worth noting that although we use RunProcedure as before, this is actually an overloaded version that executes a non-query command (a command that does not return a set of rows). The last parameter, rowsAffected, is an output parameter that we can use to determine the number of rows affected by the command. In this method the value is not used, because we always add one at a time. It will be in the next method, as we'll see in a moment.

The Update Method

The code of this method is very similar to the code above, except that here we also specify the ID of the news item to update, and the method returns a Boolean value to indicate whether the command was successfully executed. This will be True when at least one record is affected by the query:

```
        Public Function Update( _
            ByVal newsId As Integer, _
            ByVal title As String, _
            ByVal body As String, _
            ByVal releaseDate As DateTime, _
            ByVal expireDate As DateTime, _
            ByVal approved As Boolean) As Boolean

        Dim rowsAffected As Integer

        ' Create the parameters
        Dim parameters As SqlParameter() = { _
            New SqlParameter("@NewsID", SqlDbType.Int, 4), _
            New SqlParameter("@Title", SqlDbType.VarChar, 50), _
            New SqlParameter("@Body", SqlDbType.Text), _
            New SqlParameter("@ReleaseDate", SqlDbType.DateTime), _
            New SqlParameter("@ExpireDate", SqlDbType.DateTime), _
            New SqlParameter("@Approved", SqlDbType.Bit, 1)}

        ' Set the values
        parameters(0).Value = newsId
        parameters(1).Value = title.Trim()
        parameters(2).Value = body.Trim()
        parameters(3).Value = releaseDate
        parameters(4).Value = expireDate
        parameters(5).Value = approved

        RunProcedure("sp_News_UpdateNews", parameters, rowsAffected)

        Return CBool(rowsAffected = 1)
    End Function
```

The SetApproved Method

This is basically a wrapper procedure for the sp_News_SetNewsApproved stored procedure, and has nothing in particular that needs further explanation. Here is the code:

```
        Public Function SetApproved( _
            ByVal newsId As Integer, _
            ByVal approved As Boolean) _
            As Boolean

        Dim rowsAffected As Integer

        ' Create the parameters
        Dim parameters As SqlParameter() = { _
            New SqlParameter("@NewsID", SqlDbType.Int, 4), _
            New SqlParameter("@Approved", SqlDbType.Bit, 1)}

        ' Set the values
        parameters(0).Value = newsId
        parameters(1).Value = approved
```

```
      RunProcedure("sp_News_SetNewsApproved", parameters, rowsAffected)

      Return CBool(rowsAffected = 1)
  End Function
```

The Delete Method

Similar to the method above, this just wraps a call to sp_News_DeleteNews:

```
  Public Function Delete(ByVal newsId As Integer) As Boolean

    Dim rowsAffected As Integer

    ' Create the parameter
    Dim parameters As SqlParameter() = { _
      New SqlParameter("@NewsID", SqlDbType.Int, 4)}
    parameters(0).Value = newsId

    RunProcedure("sp_News_DeleteNews", parameters, rowsAffected)

    Return CBool(rowsAffected = 1)
  End Function
```

This is all we need to do for the News and NewsDetails classes. Category and CategoryDetails are very similar to this, so we won't go over them here – they can be found in the code download.

The Configuration Assembly

The next step in the development of the news manager module should be the implementation of its business layer. However, the business layer needs a configuration component to retrieve the connection string and the other settings (we want the business classes to get the required settings by themselves, instead of being passed them as parameters when the object is created), so we'll examine the configuration assembly first. We've already seen how to create this assembly for another module in Chapter 5, so we will be fairly brief here. For the ModuleConfig class the code is almost the same, while the ModuleSetting class will contain new properties specific to this module.

We use a new **Class Library** project, with the namespace and assembly name Wrox.WebModules.NewsManager.Configuration. The AssemblyInfo.vb file is the same as for the data assembly. Now let's look at the code.

The ModuleSettings Class

In the design section we've already discussed what settings we're going to store and use for this module. They are ConnectionString, AbstractLength, and the ShowNews.aspx path. We give these properties the XmlElement attribute, so that they are serialized to XML elements. Here is the class:

```
  Public Class ModuleSettings
      Private myConnectionString As String
      Private myNewsUrl As String
      Private myAbstractLength As Integer
```

```
    <XmlElement()> _
    Public Property ConnectionString() As String
      Get
        Return myConnectionString
      End Get
      Set(ByVal value As String)
        myConnectionString = value
      End Set
    End Property

    <XmlElement()> _
    Public Property NewsUrl() As String
      Get
        Return myNewsUrl
      End Get
      Set(ByVal value As String)
        myNewsUrl = value
      End Set
    End Property

    <XmlElement()> _
    Public Property AbstractLength() As Integer
      Get
        Return myAbstractLength
      End Get
      Set(ByVal value As Integer)
        myAbstractLength = value
      End Set

    End Property
End Class
```

The ModuleConfig Class

As we said earlier, this class is very similar to the ModuleConfig class in the previous chapter. What's different here is the name of the settings file, and the entry name used to store a ModuleSettings instance in the cache. The following code highlights the lines that differ:

```
Imports System.Configuration

Namespace WebModules.NewsManager.Configuration

  Public Class ModuleConfig
    Public Shared Function GetSettings() As ModuleSettings
      Dim context As HttpContext = HttpContext.Current
      Dim data As ModuleSettings = _
        CType(context.Cache("NewsManager_Settings"), ModuleSettings)

      If data Is Nothing Then
        Dim serializer As New XmlSerializer(GetType(ModuleSettings))
        Try

          Dim fileName As String = _
            HttpContext.Current.Server.MapPath(GetSettingsFile())
```

```vbnet
            ' Create a filestream to read the XML document
            Dim fs As New FileStream(fileName, FileMode.Open)

            ' Use the Deserialize method to retrieve the oject state
            data = CType(serializer.Deserialize(fs), ModuleSettings)
            fs.Close()

            context.Cache.Insert( _
              "NewsManager_Settings", data, New CacheDependency(fileName))

        Catch exc As System.IO.FileNotFoundException

            ' If the file is not found, return an empty class
            data = New ModuleSettings()

        End Try

    End If

    Return data
End Function


Public Shared Sub SaveSettings(ByVal data As ModuleSettings)
    Dim fileName As String = _
       HttpContext.Current.Server.MapPath(GetSettingsFile())
    Dim serializer As New XmlSerializer(GetType(ModuleSettings))

    ' Serialize the object
    Dim fs As New FileStream(fileName, FileMode.Create)
    serializer.Serialize(fs, data)
    fs.Close()
End Sub

Private Shared Function GetSettingsFile() As String
    Dim context As HttpContext = HttpContext.Current
    ' Get the file path from the cache
    Dim filePath As String = _
      CStr(context.Cache("NewsManager_SettingsFile"))

    ' If Path is null, get it from web.config
    If filePath Is Nothing Then

      ' Retrieve the value
      filePath = ConfigurationSettings.AppSettings( _
        "NewsManager_SettingsFile")

      ' Save into the cache
      context.Cache("NewsManager_SettingsFile") = filePath

    End If

    ' Return the connection string
    Return filePath
  End Function
  End Class
End Namespace
```

The Settings File

If the settings file is not present then the module automatically builds it. However, since the connection string is needed to access the database and it is stored in the settings file, we must have it before testing the pages we'll be building. Here is a typical example – the connection string and server name (in NewsUrl) will be different on some machines:

```xml
<?xml version="1.0"?>
<ModuleSettings xmlns:xsi="http://www.w3.org/2001/XMLSchema-instance"
    xmlns:xsd="http://www.w3.org/2001/XMLSchema">
  <ConnectionString>
    server=(local);database=ThePhile;uid=sa;pwd=;
  </ConnectionString>
  <NewsUrl>
    http://localhost/thephile/modules/newsmanager/shownews.aspx
  </NewsUrl>
  <AbstractLength>100</AbstractLength>
</ModuleSettings>
```

This file is called NewsManager.Config under /ThePhile/Config. We can store this file anywhere we like, provided we specify it in Web.Config as follows:

```xml
<?xml version="1.0" encoding="utf-8" ?>
<configuration>
  <appSettings>
    <add key="NewsManager_SettingsFile"
        value="/ThePhile/Config/NewsManager.Config" />
  </appSettings>
  ...
</configuration>
```

Implementing the Business Classes

In this section we'll be building the Business classes for this module. These will get data from the data layer we've just looked at and give it to the presentation layer in an object-oriented, business-centered way. Again we have a Class Library project within our ThePhile solution, with all the usual settings and modifications to the AssemblyInfo.vb file. We need to reference Core, NewsManager.Data, and NewsManager.Configuration projects. The News and Categories business layers are similar – we will focus on News again.

The News class is located in the News.vb file, while Category is in Category.vb. We also have a class named News in a file called News.vb in the data access project. This is not a problem because the files are placed in different folders and have different namespaces.

The News Class

To start off, we declare the News class and define its private, and public read/write or read-only properties.

```vb
Imports System
Imports System.Data
Imports System.Data.SqlClient
```

```
Namespace WebModules.NewsManager.Business

  Public NotInheritable Class News
    Inherits Wrox.WebModules.Business.BizObject

    Private mySettings As Configuration.ModuleSettings
    Private myNewsId As Integer
    Private myCategoryId As Integer
    Private myTitle As String
    Private myBody As String
    Private myReleaseDate As DateTime
    Private myExpireDate As DateTime
    Private myAddedDate As DateTime
    Private myApproved As Boolean
    Private myUserId As Integer
    Private myUserName As String
    Private myUserEmail As String
```

We won't bother showing all of the property definitions here – they are all just simple read or read/write properties.

It's worth noting that the class is defined as `NotInheritable`, meaning it can't be inherited from. We do this since we know we won't need to create derived classes.

The Constructors

We have three different constructors for this class: one with no parameters that just resets the properties to their default values, one that takes the news ID as input and loads the corresponding news item, and one that takes an existing `News` object and initializes itself based on the passed news item's ID. Here's the code:

```
Public Sub New()
  mySettings = Configuration.ModuleConfig.GetSettings()
  ResetProperties()
End Sub


Public Sub New(ByVal existingNewsId As Integer)
  mySettings = Configuration.ModuleConfig.GetSettings()
  myNewsId = existingNewsId
  LoadFromId()
End Sub


Public Sub New(ByVal existingNews As News)
  mySettings = Configuration.ModuleConfig.GetSettings()
  myNewsId = existingNews.Id
  LoadFromId()
End Sub
```

Each one of these constructors retrieves the settings through the `Configuration` assembly, and saves the `ModuleSettings` instance to the private variable.

Loading and Resetting the Properties

The constructors also set the object properties with the attributes of the specified news item or, in the case of the parameter-less constructor, reset them. Here's the code of the LoadFromID and ResetProperties private methods:

```
Private Sub LoadFromId()
    Dim news As New Data.News(mySettings.ConnectionString)
    Dim details As Data.NewsDetails = news.GetDetails(myNewsId)

    myNewsId = details.NewsId
    myCategoryId = details.CategoryId
    myTitle = details.Title
    myBody = details.Body
    myReleaseDate = details.ReleaseDate
    myExpireDate = details.ExpireDate
    myAddedDate = details.AddedDate
    myApproved = details.Approved
    myUserId = details.UserId
    myUserName = details.UserName
    myUserEmail = details.UserEmail
End Sub

Private Sub ResetProperties()
    myNewsId = -1
    myCategoryId = -1
    myTitle = ""
    myBody = ""
    myReleaseDate = New DateTime()
    myExpireDate = New DateTime()
    myAddedDate = New DateTime()
    myApproved = False
    myUserId = -1
    myUserName = ""
    myUserEmail = ""
End Sub
```

It's worth noting that the LoadFromID method also reads the NewsID field of the NewsDetails object returned by Data.News.GetDetails, and stores the value in the private newsID variable. Why is this required? We already had the newsID, in fact we used it to retrieve all the other properties! The reason is that the ID passed to the class constructor might not be present in the database (because the news has been deleted, or simply because the caller specified an invalid ID value). In this case, we don't want to have all the properties reset, and the NewsID property returns a wrong ID. Thus, we also reset the newsID variable: if a record was found, its value remains valid, otherwise it is set to -1.

We also have a public LoadFromID method that takes as input the ID of the news item we want to load, and which can be used instead of the constructor to specify the ID:

```
Public Function LoadFromId(ByVal existingNewsId As Integer) As Integer
    myNewsId = existingNewsId
    LoadFromId()
    Return myNewsId
End Function
```

Create, Update, and Delete a News Item

Finally, we have three methods to manipulate the news. Firstly the Create method:

```
Public Function Create( _
    ByVal newsCategoryId As Integer, _
    ByVal newsTitle As String, _
    ByVal newsBody As String, _
    ByVal newsReleaseDate As DateTime, _
    ByVal newsExpireDate As DateTime, _
    ByVal newsApproved As Boolean, _
    ByVal newsUserId As Integer) As Integer
  Dim theNews As New Data.News(mySettings.ConnectionString)
  myNewsId = theNews.Add( _
    newsCategoryId, _
    newsTitle, _
    newsBody, _
    newsReleaseDate, _
    newsExpireDate, _
    newsApproved, _
    newsUserId)
  LoadFromId()
  Return myNewsId
End Function
```

This method calls the Data.News.Add method to create the new record, and then calls LoadFromID to refresh the properties and refresh the news item just created. If for some reason the news item is not added, for example because it is duplicated, the Add method returns -1, and the properties are reset.

The Update method simply takes the current values of the object properties, and passes them to Data.News.Update:

```
Public Function Update() As Boolean
  Dim theNews As New Data.News(mySettings.ConnectionString)
  Return theNews.Update( _
    myNewsId, _
    myTitle, _
    myBody, _
    myReleaseDate, _
    myExpireDate, _
    myApproved)
End Function
```

The Delete method works in the same way:

```
Public Function Delete() As Boolean
  Dim theNews As New Data.News(mySettings.ConnectionString)
  Dim ret As Boolean = theNews.Delete(myNewsId)
  ResetProperties()
  Return ret
End Function
```

The Category Class

This class (saved in `Category.vb`) has methods for loading, creating, updating, and deleting a category, just like the `News` class. But it also has some other methods to create a child news item, return all the child headlines or news items, and return all the available categories. We'll briefly look at these new methods here.

The GetCategories Method

There's nothing special about this method expect that it is declared as `static`. This is because it applies to all categories (the entire category class, not a category object):

```
Public Shared Function GetCategories() As DataSet
   Dim settings As Configuration.ModuleSettings = _
     Configuration.ModuleConfig.GetSettings()
   Dim theCategories As New Data.Categories(settings.ConnectionString)

   Return theCategories.GetCategories()
End Function
```

It's worth noting that since this is a static method, the settings are not retrieved in the class constructor when it is called, so we must get them from inside this function.

Adding and Returning Child News Items

To return the child news items, we use the `Data.News.GetNews` method. Below we see the small amount of code required, and also an overloaded version of the function. This passes `False` as the default parameter to the first version, meaning that we want to retrieve all the news, and not just the current and active news:

```
Public Overloads Function GetNews( _
   ByVal currentApprovedOnly As Boolean) _
   As DataSet

   Dim theNews As New Data.News(mySettings.ConnectionString)
   Return theNews.GetNews( _
     myCategoryId, currentApprovedOnly, mySettings.AbstractLength)
End Function

Public Overloads Function GetNews() As DataSet
   Return GetNews(False)
End Function
```

To add a child news item we don't have to directly access the data layer. We create a new `Business.News` instance and use its `Create` method:

```
Public Function AddNews( _
    ByVal newsTitle As String, _
    ByVal newsBody As String, _
    ByVal newsReleaseDate As DateTime, _
    ByVal newsExpireDate As DateTime, _
    ByVal newsApproved As Boolean, _
    ByVal newsUserID As Integer) As News
```

```
     Dim theNews As New Business.News()
     theNews.Create( _
       myCategoryId, _
       newsTitle, _
       newsBody, _
       newsReleaseDate, _
       newsExpireDate, _
       newsApproved, _
       newsUserID)

   Return theNews
End Function
```

The GetHeadlines Method

This method calls the `GetHeadlines` method of the data layer, but it also adds a new custom field to the table – the full URL of the page showing the whole news story. The field value is made up of the base page URL retrieved from the settings, plus the `NewsID` as a parameter appended to this URL:

```
Public Function GetHeadlines() As DataSet

   Dim theNews As New Data.News(mySettings.ConnectionString)
   Dim headlines As DataSet = theNews.GetHeadlines(myCategoryId)

   ' Add the NewsUrl column that is a link to the page that shows
   ' the entire news body
   Dim url As String = "'" & mySettings.NewsUrl & "?NewsId=' + newsId"
   headlines.Tables(0).Columns.Add( _
     "NewsUrl", System.Type.GetType("System.String"), url)

   Return headlines
End Function
```

It's worth noting that the new column is named `NewsUrl`, and the pages or programs that will call this method will use the value of this column to show the whole news item in a web browser when the headline's title is clicked.

The User Interface

The database, data-access, business, and configuration classes are complete, and so much of the work is done. We'll now look at the user interface, which will sit on top of our business layer, and complete the application.

Administration

We'll start by looking at the administration system. Then we can use it to populate the database with some stories, and look at how we display them to readers. But before looking at the ASP.NET and VB.NET code for the pages, let's see a small part of the result we want to achieve:

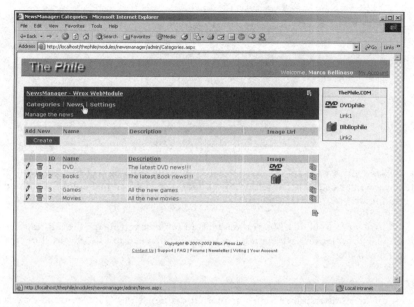

The page shown above is part of the administration console, and allows the administrator to see the available categories, create, delete, or edit a category, and jump to other pages in the application.

The table displays all the categories that it gets from the database, shows their properties, and gives the opportunity to sort them by their ID, Name, or Description. The icons on the left and right of the grid are hyperlinks to other pages to do something else related to the category of that row. Specifically, the icon on the far left representing a pencil puts the grid into edit mode (we'll see what this means shortly), the recycle bin deletes a record, and the group of sheets on the far right is used to jump directly to the page to manage the news for the category. The grid, the menu bar, and the other controls are plugged into the site layout, with the title bar at the top and the menu box on the right.

Let's look at the code now. In the main ThePhile project, we create a new folder under /ThePhile/Modules/ called NewsManager. We need to add references to NewsManager.Business, and NewsManager.Configuration. We don't need to reference NewsManager.Data, since the presentation layer never directly accesses the data layer.

Creating the Header and Footer User Controls

In the previous chapters we've already talked about the advantages of having reusable user controls for the interface, so we won't do it again here. With regard to a shared site-wide layout, in Chapter 2 we saw our site-wide header and footer user controls. These can be inserted into any page in order to have the same layout without having to manually copy and paste the common HTML code onto each page. This module follows exactly the same design pattern, and additionally has its own two private controls. The trick to easily plug the module into the existing layout is to insert the site-wide header at the top of the module-specific header, and the site-wide footer at the bottom of the module-specific footer. The following picture illustrates the various pieces that form the final page:

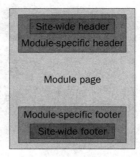

This way, with a few lines we'll get our module to fit into the existing website structure. If the site layout changes later, we won't need to do anything to the module, as it will just continue to load the updated site header and footer.

For this module, we want to have different header and footer controls for the administration section and for the end-user section, because we want the administration section's header to show the menu bar with links to the protected pages.

Admin Header

Let's start with the administration section's header: add a new User Control to the NewsManager project and name it AdminHeader.ascx. This control renders the site-wide title bar at the very top of the page, and then the module's title and menu. Let's look at the complete HTML code first, and then we'll discuss it:

```
<%@ Control Language="vb" AutoEventWireup="false"
    Codebehind="AdminHeader.ascx.vb"
    Inherits="Wrox.WebModules.NewsManager.Web.Controls.User.AdminHeader"%>
<%@ Register TagPrefix="WroxUser" TagName="SiteHeader"
    Src="/ThePhile/Controls/SiteHeader.ascx" %>
<WroxUser:SiteHeader id="Header" runat="server" />
<br>
<table width="100%" border="0" cellspacing="4" cellpadding="2">
  <tr>
    <td width="100%" valign="top">
      <script language="JavaScript1.2">
        function SetStatusBarText(text)
        {
          StatusBar.innerHTML = text;
        }
      </script>

<a name="top" />
  <table class="MenuTable" border="0" width="100%">
    <tr>
      <td>
        <table class="MenuTable" border="0" width="100%">
          <tr>
            <td>
              <b><u>NewsManager - Wrox WebModule</u></b>
            </td>
```

```
                     <td align="right">
                        <a href="#bottom"><img Alt="Go to the bottom of the page"
                            src="./Images/GoDown.gif" border="0" /></a>
                     </td>
                  </tr>
                </table>
            </td>
          </tr>
          <tr>
            <td>
              <table border="0" width="100%">
                <tr>
                  <td>
                    <a class="MenuItem"
                        onMouseOver="SetStatusBarText('Manage the categories');"
                        onMouseOut="SetStatusBarText('');" href="Categories.aspx">
                      Categories
                    </a>
                  </td>
```

Similar table entries follow, providing links to News.aspx and Settings.aspx. There's no point in repeating them here. Here's the final section:

```
                  </tr>
                </table>
            </td>
          </tr>
          <tr>
            <td width="100%">
              <div align="left" id="StatusBar">
            </td>
            <td>
               
            </td>
          </tr>
        </table>
```

This is just plain HTML (except for the site-wide header at the beginning). There is no need to use ASP.NET controls if we want to produce static and non-programmable content, and plain HTML is faster to process. The code is pretty simple and shouldn't require much explanation. We create a table – the first row shows the title, the second row contains a further table with columns for each menu item and separator. The last row has a container (an HTML <div> element). Each hyperlink of the menu points to another ASPX page, and calls the SetStatusBarText method when the mouse enters or leaves its area. SetStatusBarText sets the content of our HTML <div> element to the specified string.

Admin Footer

The footer user control is called AdminFooter.ascx (a new **Web User Control** in VS.NET) and is composed of only a few lines of code:

```
<%@ Control Language="vb" AutoEventWireup="false"
    Codebehind="AdminFooter.ascx.vb"
    Inherits="Wrox.WebModules.NewsManager.Web.Controls.User.AdminFooter"%>
<%@ Register TagPrefix="Wrox" Namespace="Wrox.ThePhile.Web.Controls.Server"
    Assembly="Wrox.ThePhile.Web.Controls" %>
<%@ Register TagPrefix="WroxUser" TagName="SiteFooter"
```

```
        Src="/ThePhile/Controls/SiteFooter.ascx" %>

<br>
<div align="right" Width="100%">
  <a href="#top"><img src="./Images/GoUp.gif" Alt="Go to the top of the
      page" border="0">
  </a>
</div>
<a name="bottom"></a>
</td>
<td align="right" valign="top">
  <Wrox:Navigator id="MenuNav" SourceFile="/ThePhile/Config/NavMenu.xml"
      TransformFile="/ThePhile/Transforms/NavMenu.xslt" runat="server" />
</td>
</tr></table>
<WroxUser:SiteFooter id="Footer" runat="server" />
```

Here we add a new column to the table opened in the header to create the page layout, insert the site menu, and finally close that table and insert the site-wide footer.

We change the namespace to `Wrox.WebModules.NewsManager.Web.Controls.User`, according to our conventions from Chapter 2.

The Categories Manager Page

The previous screenshot shows how the categories management page appears when it is loaded. The display changes, however, according to the action we want to perform. For example, this is what you get when you press the pencil icon at the far left to edit a category:

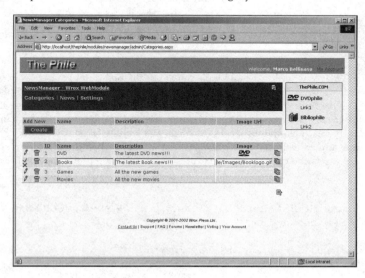

The current `Name`, `Description`, and `ImageUrl` of the category are displayed inside three textboxes. The administrator can change these values and click the green tick icon to update the values in the database, or click the X to abort the operation. The ID column is not editable, because the ID is a counter column whose value cannot be changed. By default the categories are sorted by ID. Sorting is done by clicking on the header of the column you want to sort by.

To add a new category the administrator clicks the **Create** button at the top-left of the main page, and this is the result:

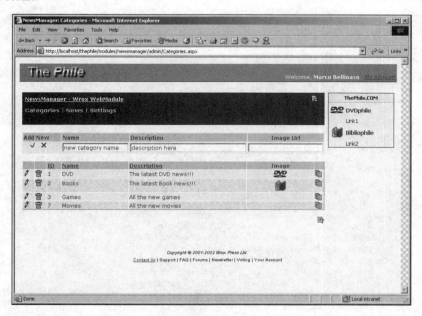

Three empty textboxes are shown, and the administrator fills them with the name, description, and path of an image for the category to be created. The action can be confirmed or canceled by clicking on one of the two icons on the left side. In both cases, and this is true for editing too, the textboxes are hidden and the display returns to how it was. While this effect is done almost automatically when we click the icon to edit a new row, we need to handle the events of the controls and show or hide the textboxes by ourselves when adding a new row. However, this process is much simpler than it might seem at first glance – only a few lines of code are needed, which we'll see in just a minute.

The Categories.aspx Page

This is the ASP.NET page where the user interface is defined. The source code of the page is too long to be shown all at once, so we'll look at it piece by piece.

The page starts with the declaration of the code-behind file and the <head> section. There's nothing new here, lets go in at the <body> element:

```
<body>
  <form method="post" runat="server" ID="Categories">
    <!-- Insert the menu user control -->
    <NewsManager:AdminHeader ID="Menu" runat="server" />
```

First we open a new form, and add our `AdminHeader` control. Moving on, we reach a table with four columns and a **Create** button. When this button is pressed, two textboxes and the icons for confirming or canceling the operation appear, as shown previously, while the rest of the display remains the same. All these controls are defined in the page, but only the button is visible at the beginning – the rest have `Visible` set to `False`:

```
<asp:Table id="TableNewCategory" runat="server" CssClass="Grid_General"
    Width="100%">
  <asp:TableRow CssClass="Grid_Header">
    <asp:TableCell Width="85px" Text="Add New" />
    <asp:TableCell Width="150px" Text="Name" />
    <asp:TableCell Text="Description" />
    <asp:TableCell Width="170px" Text="Image Url" />
  </asp:TableRow>
  <asp:TableRow ID="CreateNewRow">
    <asp:TableCell HorizontalAlign="Center">
      <asp:Button runat="server" Text="Create" ID="Create"
          CssClass="Button" OnClick="Create_Click" Width="80px" />
    </asp:TableCell>
    <asp:TableCell ID="AddNewResultCell" ColumnSpan="3">
      <asp:Label runat="server" CssClass="Error" ID="AddNewError"
          Text="This item was already present" Visible="false" />
    </asp:TableCell>
  </asp:TableRow>
  <asp:TableRow ID="AddNewControlsRow" Visible="false">
    <asp:TableCell VerticalAlign="Top">
      <asp:Image ImageURL="./Images/Spacer.gif" Width="15px"
          Height="1px" runat="server" ID="Image1" />
      <asp:LinkButton ID="AddNew" runat="server"
          Text="<img border=0 src=./Images/OK.gif Alt='Add new list'>"
          OnClick="AddNew_Click" />
      <asp:Image ImageURL="./Images/Spacer.gif" Width="15px"
          Height="1px" runat="server" ID="Image2" />
      <asp:LinkButton ID="CancelAddNew" runat="server"
          CausesValidation="false"
          Text="<img border=0 src=./Images/Cancel.gif Alt='Cancel
          editing mode'>" OnClick="CancelAddNew_Click" />
    </asp:TableCell>
    <asp:TableCell VerticalAlign="Top">
      <asp:TextBox runat="server" CssClass="TextBox"
          ID="NewCatName" Width="150px" />
      <asp:RequiredFieldValidator Id="ValidateNewName" runat="server"
          ControlToValidate="NewCatName" Display="dynamic">
        <br>* Name is required
      </asp:RequiredFieldValidator>
    </asp:TableCell>
    <asp:TableCell VerticalAlign="Top">
      <asp:TextBox runat="server" CssClass="TextBox"
          ID="NewCatDescr" Width="100%" />
    </asp:TableCell>
    <asp:TableCell VerticalAlign="Top">
      <asp:TextBox runat="server" CssClass="TextBox"
          ID="NewCatImageUrl" Width="100%" />
    </asp:TableCell>
  </asp:TableRow>
</asp:Table>
```

Note that all the server controls that will need to be accessed programmatically have an ID attribute, and that all the code is placed within a server-side form. Also note that the name of the category is required when a new category is created, and this is ensured by a `RequiredFieldValidator` control. The meaning of the `ControlToValidate` property is clear, and the `Display` property, set to `dynamic`, specifies that the space to show the error message will be created dynamically.

We use a `DataGrid` control to display the categories. This is one of the most useful ASP.NET controls. If you haven't used it before it's well worth investigating – see the .NET Framework documentation, or *Professional ASP.NET 1.0* from Wrox (ISBN 1-86100-703-5) for more information.

Here is the declaration for the `DataGrid` in our page:

```
<asp:DataGrid id="CatGrid" runat="server"
    Width="100%"
    CssClass="Grid_General"
    HeaderStyle-CssClass="Grid_Header"
    ItemStyle-CssClass="Grid_Item"
    AlternatingItemStyle-CssClass="Grid_AlternatingItem"
    AllowSorting="True"
    AutoGenerateColumns="False"
    DataKeyField="CategoryID"
    OnEditCommand="CatGrid_Edit"
    OnCancelCommand="CatGrid_CancelEdit"
    OnUpdateCommand="CatGrid_Update"
    OnDeleteCommand="CatGrid_Delete"
    OnSortCommand="CatGrid_Sort">
```

The `DataGrid` does a lot of the work for us. After setting its appearance, we set `AllowSorting` to True. That's all we need to do to let the user sort the table anyway they like – a big job in ASP 3!

To enable `DataGrid` editing, we need to specify the primary key of the data in the grid – that way the `DataGrid` can communicate which row to edit/update back to the server. We use the `DataKeyField` property for this. The last lines define the event procedures that are called to handle the operations of the grid. We'll see how to write these event procedures shortly, when looking at the code-behind class.

Back to our ASPX – we need to manually declare how each column has to be rendered. We need the following columns:

- ❑ A clickable image to edit the row

- ❑ A clickable image to delete the row

- ❑ A column to display the category's name

- ❑ A column to display the category's description

- ❑ A column to display the category's image when the grid is in normal display mode, or the URL of the image during editing

- ❑ A clickable image to jump to the page that shows the news items for the category of the current row

Here's the code needed for the first two columns:

```
<Columns>
  <asp:EditCommandColumn
      ItemStyle-Width="25px"
      EditText="<img border=0 Alt='Edit' src=./Images/Edit.gif>"
      CancelText="<img border=0 src=./Images/Cancel.gif>"
      UpdateText="<img border=0 src=./Images/OK.gif>"
  />
  <asp:ButtonColumn
      ItemStyle-Width="25px"
      Text="<img border=0 Alt='Delete' src=./Images/Delete.gif>"
      CommandName="delete"
  />
```

The EditCommandColumn is a specific column with a link to begin the editing, while ButtonColumn creates normal buttons or links whose Click event must be handled to perform any operation you need. Note that we render the graphical buttons by including an <img> tag in the Text property of the column. If we write a normal string instead of the HTML, we get a standard button with that string as its caption.

Here is the code for the columns that display the list's ID, name, description, and image:

```
<asp:BoundColumn HeaderText="ID"
    ItemStyle-Width="30px" DataField="CategoryID"
    ReadOnly="True" SortExpression="CategoryID"
/>
<asp:TemplateColumn HeaderText="Name"
    SortExpression="Name" ItemStyle-Width="150px">
  <ItemTemplate>
    <asp:Label runat="server"
        Text='<%# DataBinder.Eval(Container.DataItem, "Name") %>'
    />
  </ItemTemplate>
  <EditItemTemplate>
    <asp:TextBox ID="EditCatName" runat="server"
        Text='<%# DataBinder.Eval(Container.DataItem, "Name") %>'
        CssClass="TextBox" Width="150px"
    />
    <asp:RequiredFieldValidator Id="ValidateEditName"
        runat="server" ControlToValidate="EditCatName"
        Display="dynamic">* Name is required
    </asp:RequiredFieldValidator>
  </EditItemTemplate>
</asp:TemplateColumn>
<asp:TemplateColumn HeaderText="Description"
    SortExpression="Description">
  <ItemTemplate>
    <asp:Label runat="server" Text='<%#
        DataBinder.Eval(Container.DataItem, "Description") %>'
    />
  </ItemTemplate>
  <EditItemTemplate>
    <asp:TextBox ID="EditCatDescr" runat="server" Text='<%#
        DataBinder.Eval(Container.DataItem, "Description") %>'
        CssClass="TextBox" Width="100%"
```

```
          />
        </EditItemTemplate>
      </asp:TemplateColumn>
      <asp:TemplateColumn HeaderText="Image"
          ItemStyle-Width="150px" ItemStyle-HorizontalAlign="Center">
        <ItemTemplate>
          <asp:Label runat="server" Text='<%# GetImage(
              DataBinder.Eval(Container.DataItem, "ImageUrl")) %>'
          />
        </ItemTemplate>
        <EditItemTemplate>
          <asp:TextBox ID="EditCatImageUrl" runat="server" Text='<%#
              DataBinder.Eval(Container.DataItem, "ImageUrl") %>'
              CssClass="TextBox" Width="100%"
          />
        </EditItemTemplate>
      </asp:TemplateColumn>
```

The first column is defined as a normal, non-editable column and there isn't much to say about it. The other three are more interesting because they show how to create a templated column that uses a label to show the value, or a textbox to edit it. The proper view is automatically set when we enter or exit the editing mode for a row. Note that the text of the label and textboxes is handled by the `DataBinder.Eval` method, which returns the value of a column for the row being read, and that the list's name is required, as shown earlier in the table, to add a new category.

Of even more interest is the final column, which shows an image when in normal mode, and its path in a textbox when in editing mode. Since the `ImageUrl` can be `null`, we call the external function `GetImage`. This accepts the field value and returns an empty string or a complete `<img>` tag, depending on whether the field is `null` or not.

The last column on the far right shows the icon to jump to the details page:

```
      <asp:HyperLinkColumn ItemStyle-Width="20px"
          DataNavigateUrlField="CategoryID"
          DataNavigateUrlFormatString="News.aspx?CategoryID={0}"
          DataTextFormatString="<img border=0 Alt='Show news'
              src=./Images/Group.gif>"
        DataTextField="CategoryID"
      />
    </Columns>
```

It is a non-editable hyperlink rendered as an image, and the URL which it points to is built with a string template defined in the `DataNavigateUrlFormatString`: the ID of each row will replace the `{0}` marker.

The page ends with the closing tag for the `DataGrid` control, the footer control, and the closing tag for the form:

```
      </asp:DataGrid>
      <!-- Insert the footer -->
      <NewsManager:AdminFooter ID="Footer" runat="server" />
    </form>
  </body>
</html>
```

The Code-behind for Categories.aspx

Finally we can start looking at the code that handles the execution of the page. The code-behind file (Categories.aspx.vb) was automatically created by VS.NET together with the page itself. Again, we'll examine it one section at a time.

After the namespace declaration (which we change to Wrox.WebModules.NewsManager.Web) and the controls declaration, we come to where the page functionality is implemented. Here is the handler that it runs when the page is loaded:

```
Private Sub Page_Load(ByVal sender As Object, ByVal e As EventArgs)
   If Not Page.IsPostBack Then

      ' Bind the page's controls
      BindGrid()
   End If
End Sub
```

(You may notice that the code in the download has some extra lines in this event handler. We will explain the addition of these lines later in the chapter, in the *Securing the Module* section.)

Then there is the BindGrid method, called by the above routine, which fills the grid with the categories:

```
Private Sub BindGrid()
   ' Get all the categories
   Dim categoriesDataView As DataView = _
      Business.Category.GetCategories().Tables(0).DefaultView
   ' Sort the data according to the SortExpression value
   If Not (CatGrid.Attributes("SortExpression") Is Nothing) Then
      categoriesDataView.Sort = CatGrid.Attributes("SortExpression")
   End If
   CatGrid.DataSource = categoriesDataView
   CatGrid.DataBind()
End Sub
```

The function is only called if the page's IsPostBack property is False: when the page is loaded for the first time or manually refreshed by the user with the browser's Refresh/Reload command. It is not called when the page is reloaded because the user posted some data to the form. In fact, when that page is posted back, the state of the controls is stored in a hidden HTML control (named __VIEWSTATE) and then automatically restored, avoiding the need for re-executing a query on the database. The content of this hidden field is passed back and forth between the client to the server, which can cause a significant overhead in the case of big grids or lots of controls that must maintain their state.

BindGrid is the core function of this page, because it gets the data from the database and displays the records through the DataGrid. The first line gets a DataView with all the available categories, by calling the GetCategories static method of Business.Category. The DataView is then sorted according to a DataGrid attribute, which is a custom attribute set by our code later: the first time the function is called this attribute is null and the DataView is not sorted. The last two lines associate the DataView to the DataSource property, and call the DataBind method to display the rows.

Talking about data binding, we remember that a column in the `DataGrid` calls a `GetImage` method to create an `<img>` tag and show the category's image, if the `ImageUrl` field is not `null`. The code is really simple – the only important point is that the function must be declared as `public`:

```
Public Function GetImage(ByVal imageUrl As Object) As String
   If imageUrl.ToString().Length > 0 Then
      Return "<img border=""0"" src=""" + imageUrl.ToString() + """>"
   Else
      Return ""
   End If
End Function
```

Sorting the Categories

When a column header is clicked, the `CatGrid_Sort` function is called on the server, which looks like this:

```
Protected Sub CatGrid_Sort( _
   ByVal sender As Object, _
   ByVal e As DataGridSortCommandEventArgs)
   AddNewError.Visible = False
   ShowAddNewControls(False)
   CatGrid.EditItemIndex = -1

   ' Set the SortExpression attribute that will be used to
   ' actually sort the data in the BindGrid method
   CatGrid.Attributes("SortExpression") = e.SortExpression.ToString()
   BindGrid()
End Sub
```

The function first of all hides the controls for adding a new category, or displaying an error message. Then it disables the editing mode of a row, if enabled. Finally it gets from the input parameter the sort expression to use to actually sort the data, and refreshes the `DataGrid`'s content by calling `BindGrid`.

Editing and Updating Categories

Now we will implement the methods that deal with the editing and updating of rows. The first puts the relevant row in edit mode, the second cancels the current edit:

```
Protected Sub CatGrid_Edit( _
   ByVal sender As Object, _
   ByVal e As DataGridCommandEventArgs)

   AddNewError.Visible = False
   ShowAddNewControls(False)

   ' start editing
   CatGrid.EditItemIndex = CInt(e.Item.ItemIndex)
   BindGrid()

End Sub

Protected Sub CatGrid_CancelEdit( _
```

```
        ByVal sender As Object, _
        ByVal e As DataGridCommandEventArgs)

        CatGrid.EditItemIndex = -1
        BindGrid()
    End Sub
```

CatGrid_Edit hides the controls for adding a row, and sets the EditItemIndex property to the index of the row to edit: this value is retrieved from the Item object, which is exposed as a property of the object e passed as a parameter to the function. Finally, BindGrid is called again to bind the data for that row to the three textboxes. When the X icon is pressed, the EditItemIndex is simply set to –1 and the grid is refreshed.

Now let's look at CatGrid_Update, which does most of the work:

```
    Protected Sub CatGrid_Update( _
        ByVal sender As Object, _
        ByVal e As DataGridCommandEventArgs)

    If Page.IsValid Then
        ' Get the new values from the textboxes
        Dim catName As String = _
            CType(e.Item.FindControl("EditCatName"), TextBox).Text
        Dim catDescr As String = _
            CType(e.Item.FindControl("EditCatDescr"), TextBox).Text
        Dim catImageUrl As String = _
            CType(e.Item.FindControl("EditCatImageUrl"), TextBox).Text
        Dim categoryId As Integer = _
            CInt(CatGrid.DataKeys(e.Item.ItemIndex))

        ' Update the values
        Dim updatedCategory As New Business.Category(categoryId)
        updatedCategory.Name = catName
        updatedCategory.Description = catDescr
        updatedCategory.ImageUrl = catImageUrl
        updatedCategory.Update()

        CatGrid.EditItemIndex = -1
        BindGrid()
    End If
End Sub
```

Firstly, note that the code is executed only if the page is valid, that is when the rules of the validator controls are observed. In this case the Name textbox must be filled with a valid (not null) name. If this check succeeds, the execution goes ahead and gets the current values of the three textboxes. The reference to each textbox control is returned by the FindControl method of Item, and then the content is read from the Text property. Note that that the generic Control object returned by FindControl does not have a Text property, so we need to manually cast the returned object to a TextBox. The last parameter we need is the ID of the row to update, which is very easy to get because this column was set as the primary key for the DataGrid, so our work is reduced to reading in a property value. Finally, we create a Business.Category object for the selected category, set its properties, and call the Update method to persist the changes to the database. As a last step we refresh the DataGrid to reflect the changes.

Deleting a Category

The procedure for the `CatGrid_Delete` event follows exactly the same structure as the previous ones, although it is simpler. We create a `Business.Category` object for the category identified by the category ID returned by the `DataKeys` enumerator property, and then call its `Delete` method:

```
Protected Sub CatGrid_Delete( _
  ByVal sender As Object, _
  ByVal e As DataGridCommandEventArgs)

  AddNewError.Visible = False
  ShowAddNewControls(False)
  CatGrid.EditItemIndex = -1

  ' Get the ID of this record and delete it
  Dim deletedCategory As New Business.Category( _
    CInt(CatGrid.DataKeys(e.Item.ItemIndex)))
  deletedCategory.Delete()

  ' Re-bind
  BindGrid()
End Sub
```

Creating a Category

The last task is adding a new row. When the **Create** button is pressed, three textboxes and the respective icons for confirming or canceling the operation are shown, while the **Create** button is made invisible. The `DataGrid`'s `EditItemIndex` property is also set to −1, to stop any editing operation from taking place. Here is the code for this event, and for the function that shows or hides the controls according to the passed Boolean parameter:

```
Protected Sub Create_Click(ByVal sender As Object, ByVal e As EventArgs)
  ' Show the textboxes and buttons for adding a new record
  AddNewError.Visible = False
  ShowAddNewControls(True)
  CatGrid.EditItemIndex = -1
  BindGrid()
End Sub

Private Sub ShowAddNewControls(ByVal showControls As Boolean)

  ' Show/hide the controls for adding a new record
  NewCatName.Text = ""
  NewCatDescr.Text = ""
  NewCatImageUrl.Text = ""

  AddNewControlsRow.Visible = showControls
  CreateNewRow.Visible = Not showControls
End Sub
```

The method is called when the user confirms the new row, by clicking the 'tick' icon:

```
        Protected Sub AddNew_Click(ByVal sender As Object, ByVal e As EventArgs)
          If Page.IsValid Then

            Dim newCategory As New Business.Category()

            ' Add the new record
            If newCategory.Create(NewCatName.Text, _
              NewCatDescr.Text, NewCatImageUrl.Text) < 0 Then

              ' If Add returned -1, the category was already present
              AddNewError.Visible = True
            End If

            ShowAddNewControls(False)
            BindGrid()
          End If
        End Sub
```

If the data is valid (it obeys the rules enforced by the validators declared in the `Categories.aspx`
page), the code gets the content of the three textboxes and passes these strings to the `Create` method of
a `Business.Category` object. In this case the code is simpler because we can directly reference the
two textboxes, since they are uniquely identified by name. If the `Category.Create` method returns -1
it means that a category with the same name was already present in the database and it can't be added
twice. Therefore we show the `AddNewError` label on `Categories.aspx`, with the `Text` property set
to an error message that explains the problem.

The icon for canceling the addition is a `ButtonLink` control, which when clicked restores the grid to
the default display. Here's the code for its `Click` event:

```
        Protected Sub CancelAddNew_Click( _
          ByVal sender As Object, _
          ByVal e As EventArgs)

          ShowAddNewControls(False)
        End Sub
```

There is one important point to note here. When a button is pressed it causes the page to be posted
back. The control for the category's name is validated when a page is posted back, which would cause
the posting to be stopped if the new category's name were missing. Since we are canceling, and don't
care what the user has typed, we set the button's `CausesValidation` property to `False`.

The code for the categories management page is now complete. This page particularly shows how much
better ASP.NET is than classic ASP – to build a grid like this in ASP 3 would take hundreds, perhaps
thousands, of lines of code.

Managing the News

The page for managing the news in each category has a very similar structure to the page just analyzed,
but it also has some additions that we're going to highlight. The following image shows the page while
adding a news item. The administrator has attempted to add a news item but has specified an invalid
release date in the From textbox, so the validator controls tell the user why the form can't be submitted
and the news added:

254

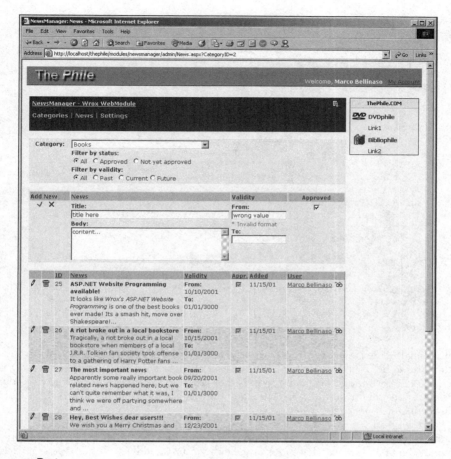

The News.aspx Page

The above screenshot shows how this page differs from the previous one. We have a different number of columns and grid content, a drop-down list where we can select a category to view its news, and radio button controls so that the administrator can filter the news.

The ASPX is fairly similar to Categories.aspx. We will only look at the notable differences. The first major differences are the DropDownList control for the categories, and the set of controls to filter the grid rows:

```
<asp:table Width="100%" ID="TableNews" runat="server"
    CssClass="Grid_General">
  <asp:TableRow>
    <asp:TableCell Width="85px" HorizontalAlign="Center"
        VerticalAlign="Top" Font-Bold="True" Text="Category:" />
    <asp:TableCell>
      <asp:DropDownList runat="server" ID="CatDropDown" Width="300px"
          DataTextField="Name" DataValueField="CategoryID"
          CssClass="TextBox" AutoPostBack="True"
```

```
            OnSelectedIndexChanged="CatDropDown_IndexChanged"
        />
        <br>
        <b>Filter by status:</b><br>
        <asp:RadioButton runat="server" ID="ShowAll"
            GroupName="ShowByStatus" Text="All"
            Checked="True" AutoPostBack="True"
            OnCheckedChanged="ShowNews_CheckedChanged"
        /> 
        <asp:RadioButton runat="server" ID="ShowApproved"
            GroupName="ShowByStatus" Text="Approved"
            Checked="False" AutoPostBack="True"
            OnCheckedChanged="ShowNews_CheckedChanged"
        /> 
        <asp:RadioButton runat="server" ID="ShowPending"
            GroupName="ShowByStatus" Text="Not yet approved"
            Checked="False" AutoPostBack="True"
            OnCheckedChanged="ShowNews_CheckedChanged"
        />
        <br>
        <b>Filter by validity:</b><br>
        ...the other RadioButtons go here...
    </asp:TableCell>
  </asp:TableRow>
</asp:table>
```

The main thing to note is that the drop-down list has the `AutoPostBack` property set to `True`, which causes the form to be posted back every time the user changes the selected item. This event raises the `OnSelectedIndexChanged` event and so calls the `CatDropDown_IndexChanged` procedure. Also, the `RadioButtons` set this property to `True`, and they all use the same `ShowNews_CheckedChanged` procedure to handle the event.

The rest of the page is similar to what we have seen before, but the `DataGrid`'s columns are used more fully than for the previous page. Let's look at the extra or updated lines of the `DataGrid` declaration:

```
<asp:DataGrid ID="NewsGrid" runat="server"
    DataKeyField="NewsID"
    OnEditCommand="NewsGrid_Edit"
    OnCancelCommand="NewsGrid_CancelEdit"
    OnUpdateCommand="NewsGrid_Update"
    OnDeleteCommand="NewsGrid_Delete"
    OnSortCommand="NewsGrid_Sort"
    AllowPaging="True"
    PageSize="20"
    PagerStyle-HorizontalAlign="Right"
    PagerStyle-PageButtonCount="20"
    PagerStyle-Mode="NumericPages"
    OnPageIndexChanged="NewsGrid_PageChanged"
    OnSelectedIndexChanged="NewsGrid_SelectionChanged"
    SelectedItemStyle-CssClass="Grid_SelectedItem"
```

The new lines say that the data will be displayed in pages of twenty rows each, and that the user will be able to navigate the pages through the page numbers on the bottom right side. An event procedure to handle the page changing is defined. The last two lines define an event handler and the style for the selected item. We're going to add an icon on the far right side of the grid that, when clicked, will highlight the row and show the whole news text in a label at the bottom of the page.

Let's also look at the declaration of some of the columns, as there are a few new bits. The following code adds the column for the news title and abstract:

```
<asp:TemplateColumn HeaderText="News" SortExpression="Title">
  <ItemTemplate>
    <asp:Label runat="server"
        Text='<%# DataBinder.Eval(Container.DataItem, "Title") %>'
        Font-Bold="True" />
    <br>
    <asp:Label runat="server"
        Text='<%# DataBinder.Eval(Container.DataItem, "Abstract") %>' />
  </ItemTemplate>
  <EditItemTemplate>
    <b>Title:</b>
    <br>
    <asp:TextBox runat="server" CssClass="TextBox"
        Text='<%# DataBinder.Eval(Container.DataItem, "Title") %>'
        ID="EditTitle" Width="100%" />
    <asp:RequiredFieldValidator runat="server"
        ControlToValidate="EditTitle" Display="dynamic">
        * Title is required
    </asp:RequiredFieldValidator>
    <br>
    <b>Body:</b>
    <br>
    <asp:TextBox runat="server" CssClass="TextBox"
        TextMode="MultiLine" Rows="5" Text='<%#
        GetNewsText(int.Parse(DataBinder.Eval(
            Container.DataItem, "NewsID").ToString())) %>'
        ID="EditBody" Width="100%" />
  </EditItemTemplate>
</asp:TemplateColumn>
```

The first thing we note is that we can add all the controls to the same column, but this is not a special feature. The important point here is that in normal display mode the column shows the news abstract by binding to the Abstract field (which is, as you might remember, dynamically created by the stored procedures by truncating the Body field), whereas in editing mode we use a custom GetNewsText function to retrieve the whole news text. We've already said that we get the whole text only when it is strictly necessary, while that field is not returned by the standard procedure because it would be slow.

Next, we add the columns for the release and expiry dates:

```
<asp:TemplateColumn HeaderText="Validity"
    SortExpression="ReleaseDate" ItemStyle-Width="100px">
  <ItemTemplate>
    <b>From:</b>
```

```
    <br>
    <asp:Label runat="server" Text='<%# DataBinder.Eval(
        Container.DataItem, "ReleaseDate", "{0:MM/dd/yyyy}") %>' />
    <br>
    <b>To:</b>
    <br>
    <asp:Label runat="server" Text='<%# DataBinder.Eval(
        Container.DataItem, "ExpireDate", "{0:MM/dd/yyyy}") %>' />
  </ItemTemplate>
  <EditItemTemplate>
    <b>From:</b>
    <br>
    <asp:TextBox runat="server" CssClass="TextBox" Text='<%#
        DataBinder.Eval(Container.DataItem, "ReleaseDate",
        "{0:MM/dd/yyyy}") %>' ID="EditReleaseDate" Width="100%" />
    <asp:CompareValidator runat="server"
        ControlToValidate="EditReleaseDate" Type="Date"
        Operator="DataTypeCheck" Display="dynamic">
        * Invalid format
    </asp:CompareValidator>
    <asp:CompareValidator runat="server" ControlToValidate="EditReleaseDate"
        ControlToCompare="EditExpireDate" Type="Date"
        Operator="LessThanEqual" Display="dynamic">
        * Invalid value
    </asp:CompareValidator>
    <br>
    <b>To:</b>
    <br>
    <asp:TextBox runat="server" CssClass="TextBox" Text='<%#
        DataBinder.Eval(Container.DataItem, "ExpireDate",
        "{0:MM/dd/yyyy}") %>' ID="EditExpireDate" Width="100%" />
    <asp:CompareValidator runat="server"
        ControlToValidate="EditExpireDate" Type="Date"
        Operator="DataTypeCheck" Display="dynamic">
        * Invalid format
    </asp:CompareValidator>
  </EditItemTemplate>
</asp:TemplateColumn>
```

This column's code isn't of particular interest except for the validator controls that ensure the dates are in a valid format, and that the expiry date is after the release date. The dates aren't required, and if they are not specified we'll insert default values; if they are supplied they can't contain invalid characters.

Now we have the column that shows and allows editing of the Approved field. This is a bit special because it uses a read-only CheckBox in normal display mode, and a writable CheckBox in edit mode:

```
<asp:TemplateColumn HeaderText="Appr." SortExpression="Approved"
    ItemStyle-Width="30px" HeaderStyle-HorizontalAlign="Center"
    ItemStyle-HorizontalAlign="Center">
  <ItemTemplate>
    <asp:CheckBox runat="server" Enabled="false"
        Checked='<%# Convert.ToBoolean(
        DataBinder.Eval(Container.DataItem, "Approved")) %>'
```

```
        />
      </ItemTemplate>
      <EditItemTemplate>
        <asp:CheckBox ID="EditApproved" runat="server"
            Checked='<%# Convert.ToBoolean(
                DataBinder.Eval(Container.DataItem, "Approved")) %>'
        />
      </EditItemTemplate>
    </asp:TemplateColumn>
```

To determine whether the control has to be checked, we convert the field value to a Boolean value by using the ToBoolean shared method of the Convert class.

We'll skip the Added column as it really has nothing new to be shown. Let's move straight to the User column, which shows a hyperlink that opens the default program to send an e-mail to the writer's e-mail address. Here is its declaration:

```
<asp:TemplateColumn HeaderText="User"
    SortExpression="UserName" ItemStyle-Width="100px">
  <ItemTemplate>
    <asp:HyperLink runat="server" NavigateUrl='<%#
        "mailto:" + DataBinder.Eval(Container.DataItem, "UserEmail") %>'
        Text='<%# DataBinder.Eval(Container.DataItem, "UserName") %>'
        CssClass="GridLink"
    />
  </ItemTemplate>
</asp:TemplateColumn>
```

The code above creates a HyperLink control and sets its NavigateUrl and Text properties to the user's e-mail address and user's full name, respectively.

Lastly, we have the column that, when clicked, highlights the row and shows the whole news text at the bottom:

```
<asp:ButtonColumn CommandName="Select" ItemStyle-Width="20px"
    Text="<img border=0 Alt='View news' src=./Images/View.gif>"
/>
```

Its CommandName property is set to Select, and this means that when it is clicked it raises the OnSelectedIndexChanged event.

The Codebehind for News.aspx

The structure of the code-behind for the News page is the same as for the Categories page. There are a few more lines of code to handle the new controls added. Here's the code that executes when the page loads:

```
        Private Sub Page_Load(ByVal sender As Object, ByVal e As EventArgs)
            ' Get the CategoryId from the QueryString
            Dim categoryId As String = Request.Params("CategoryId")
            NewsGrid.Attributes("CategoryId") = categoryId
```

```
         If Not Page.IsPostBack Then

            ' Load all the available lists in the DropDown control
            Dim categoriesDataView As DataView = _
               Business.Category.GetCategories().Tables(0).DefaultView
            CatDropDown.DataSource = categoriesDataView
            CatDropDown.DataBind()

            If Not (categoryId Is Nothing) Then

               ' select the DropDown element according to the CategoryId
               CatDropDown.SelectedIndex = CatDropDown.Items.IndexOf( _
                  CatDropDown.Items.FindByValue(categoryId))

            End If
            ' Bind the page controls
            BindGrid()
         End If
      End Sub
```

First we have security code that is very similar to that from the Categories page.

The second part of the event handler is a little more complex. On the Categories.aspx page, the right side of each grid's row contained a button that passed the user to the News.aspx page to see the news for that category. To do this, the button pointed to the News.aspx page and added the category's ID as a parameter in the query string. This value is retrieved from the query string and saved as an attribute of the DataGrid control, because it is used to create a Business.Category object, needed to get its child news items.

In addition to the usual BindGrid call, this time there is also a drop-down list to fill with the available categories. This is done directly within Page_Load by calling the GetCategories static method of the Business.Category class and assigning the resulting table to the DataSource for the dropdown. Then we use the ID in the page's querystring to select the correct item in the dropdown.

The BindGrid method for this page has code to read the category's ID for which we want to retrieve the news, and also filters the results as specified by the RadioButtons at the top of the page:

```
      Private Sub BindGrid()
         Dim categoryId As Integer
         ' Get the CategoryId value from the Grid's attributes
         If Not (NewsGrid.Attributes("CategoryId") Is Nothing) Then
            categoryId = Integer.Parse(NewsGrid.Attributes("CategoryId"))
         Else
            categoryId = Integer.Parse(CatDropDown.SelectedItem.Value)
         End If

         ' Get all the news of this category
         Dim categoriesDataView As DataView = New _
            Business.Category(categoryId).GetNews(False).Tables(0).DefaultView

         ' Sort the records according to the SortExpression value
         ' in the Grid's attributes
```

```
          If NewsGrid.Attributes("SortExpression") <> "" Then
            categoriesDataView.Sort = NewsGrid.Attributes("SortExpression")
          End If

          ' Show only the approved/pending news, as specified in the options
          If ShowApproved.Checked Then
            categoriesDataView.RowFilter = "Approved = 1"
          Else
            If ShowPending.Checked Then
              categoriesDataView.RowFilter = "Approved = 0"
            Else
              categoriesDataView.RowFilter = "1 = 1"
            End If
          End If

          ' Show only the past/current/future news, if specified in the options
          If ShowPast.Checked Then
            categoriesDataView.RowFilter &= _
              " AND ExpireDate < '" & DateTime.Today + "'"
          Else
            If ShowCurrent.Checked Then
              categoriesDataView.RowFilter &= " AND ReleaseDate <= '" & _
                DateTime.Today & "' AND ExpireDate >= '" & DateTime.Today & "'"
            Else
              If ShowFuture.Checked Then
                categoriesDataView.RowFilter &= _
                  " AND ReleaseDate > '" & DateTime.Today & "'"
              End If
            End If
          End If
          NewsGrid.DataSource = categoriesDataView
          NewsGrid.DataBind()
        End Sub
```

The records are filtered as specified by the user, by appending conditional expressions to the RowFilter property of the DataView. The BindGrid function is called every time a RadioButton is selected, so that the records are immediately filtered accordingly:

```
        Protected Sub ShowNews_CheckedChanged( _
          ByVal sender As Object, _
          ByVal e As EventArgs)
          UnselectGridItem()
          ' Filter the news for the grid
          BindGrid()
        End Sub
```

The following function handles the selection of an item in the drop-down list:

```
        Protected Sub CatDropDown_IndexChanged( _
          ByVal sender As Object, _
          ByVal e As EventArgs)
          ' Reload the page to show the news for the selected category
```

```
              ' This will also hide the controls to add a news if they were visible
              Response.Redirect(("News.aspx?CategoryID=" & _
                CatDropDown.SelectedItem.Value))
        End Sub
```

This redirects the browser to the same page, but with the ID of the selected item, in order to load the correct subscribers the next time `BindGrid` is called.

When the user navigates to another of the grid's pages, we need to cancel editing mode – which means that before rebinding the grid we have to hide the controls for adding a new row, and hide the error message that would be shown when the news we want to add is already present in the category. Of course we also have to set the `CurrentPageIndex` property to the new value to actually change the current page:

```
        Protected Sub NewsGrid_PageChanged( _
          ByVal sender As Object, _
          ByVal e As DataGridPageChangedEventArgs)
          ' The DataGrid page is changed, so hide the controls for
          ' adding a new record if they were visible
          UnselectGridItem()
          AddNewError.Visible = False
          ShowAddNewControls(False)
          ' Change the current page
          NewsGrid.CurrentPageIndex = e.NewPageIndex
          BindGrid()
        End Sub
```

Next we have the procedure that executes when we select an item:

```
        Protected Sub NewsGrid_SelectionChanged( _
          ByVal sender As Object, _
          ByVal e As EventArgs)

          ShowAddNewControls(False)

          ' Get the ID of the selected row
          Dim newsId As Integer = _
            Integer.Parse(NewsGrid.DataKeys(NewsGrid.SelectedIndex).ToString())

          ' Show the Body text in the Preview label
          NewsPreview.Text = New Business.News(newsId).Body
          NewsPreview.Visible = True

          NewsGrid.EditItemIndex = -1
          BindGrid()

        End Sub
```

This gets the ID of the clicked row, retrieves the whole body of the news, and shows it in a label. If the news body is in HTML format, it will be shown in HTML format, so there is no limitation to what we can store and show. By the way, the `GetNewsText` method does almost the same thing, but it is used in the ASP.NET page to show the full text for editing mode. Here we see a highlighted row, with the corresponding label at the bottom of the page:

		ID	News	Validity	Appr.	Added	User	
✎	🗑	25	**ASP.NET Website Programming available!** It looks like *Wrox's ASP.NET Website Programming* is one of the best books ever made! Its a smash hit, move over Shakespeare!...	From: 10/10/2001 To: 01/01/3000	☑	11/15/01	Marco Bellinaso	🔗
✎	🗑	26	**A riot broke out in a local bookstore** Tragically, a riot broke out in a local bookstore when members of a local J.R.R. Tolkien fan society took offense to a gathering of Harry Potter fans ...	From: 10/15/2001 To: 01/01/3000	☑	11/15/01	Marco Bellinaso	🔗
✎	🗑	27	**The most important news** Apparently some really important book related news happened here, but we can't quite remember what it was, I think we were off partying somewhere and ...	From: 09/20/2001 To: 01/01/3000	☑	11/15/01	Marco Bellinaso	🔗
✎	🗑	28	**Hey, Best Wishes dear users!!!** We wish you a Merry Christmas and the happiest new year!!! Remember not to drink too much!!!...	From: 12/23/2001 To: 01/05/2002	☑	11/15/01	Marco Bellinaso	🔗
✎	🗑	29	**I have something to say!** Well, I HAD something so say...I am afraid I forgot it!!! I'm sorry if I wasted your time......	From: 11/16/2001 To: 05/01/2002	☐	11/16/01	Marco Bellinaso	🔗

1

Tragically, a riot broke out in a local bookstore when members of a local J.R.R. Tolkien fan society took offense to a gathering of Harry Potter fans at the in-store coffee shop. The scene became gruesome as members of the Tolkien fan club shouted that the powers of the dark lord Sauron would consume the 12 and 13 year old boys and girls for their heresy.

The methods for deleting, updating, and adding a row are very similar to the ones we've seen earlier for the `Categories.aspx` page. However, there are some additions, especially to the method for adding news items, which we'll look at now:

```
Protected Sub AddNew_Click(ByVal sender As Object, ByVal e As EventArgs)

  If Page.IsValid Then

    Dim categoryId As Integer = _
      Integer.Parse(CatDropDown.SelectedItem.Value)
    Dim title As String = NewTitle.Text
    Dim body As String = NewBody.Text
    Dim approved As Boolean = NewApproved.Checked

    ' Set predefined release/expire dates, in case they are not specified
    Dim releaseDate As DateTime = DateTime.Today
    Dim expireDate As New DateTime(3000, 1, 1)

    ' If the dates are supplied, take them, otherwise keep the predefined
    If NewReleaseDate.Text.Trim().Length > 0 Then
      releaseDate = DateTime.Parse(NewReleaseDate.Text)
    End If

    If NewExpireDate.Text.Trim().Length > 0 Then
      expireDate = DateTime.Parse(NewExpireDate.Text)
    End If
```

```
        ' Add the news
        Dim newsCategory As New Business.Category(categoryId)
        Dim currUser As SiteIdentity = _
          CType(Context.User.Identity, SiteIdentity)
        If newsCategory.AddNews( _
          title, _
          body, _
          releaseDate, _
          expireDate, _
          approved, _
          currUser.UserId _
          ).Id < 0 Then

          ' If the call to the Add method returned -1, it means that this
          ' news was already present, so show the label that tells this
          AddNewError.Visible = True

        End If

        ' Hide the controls for adding a news
        ShowAddNewControls(False)
        BindGrid()

      End If

    End Sub
```

You may remember that the release and expiry date are not required when adding a news item, but they are required in the database. If we don't specify a release date, we want to have the current date as the default. If we don't specify an expiry date then we'll take 1/1/3000 as the default, which practically means forever. We set the variables to these default values first, and then replace them if the dates are supplied.

The other very important point is that the last parameter of the AddNews method is the ID of the user currently logged in. We don't need to retrieve a name or e-mail address, only the ID, as the other information is already present in the Accounts_Users table. Retrieving the current user's ID is a simple task, thanks to the Business component of the Accounts module we developed in the previous chapter. To use it, we have to add a reference to that project, and we also reference the namespace at the top of the file, with the following line of code:

```
Imports Wrox.WebModules.Accounts.Business
```

At this point we can cast the Context.User.Identity object to the SiteIdentity type, and save a reference to it, as follows:

```
Dim currUser As SiteIdentity = _
  CType(Context.User.Identity, SiteIdentity)
```

The value currUser.UserID is the ID we were looking for, and we can pass it to the AddNews method.

Modifying the Settings Online

So far we've used some of the values stored in the `NewsManager.Config` XML file, as we set them when we created the file. But if the administrator wants to change some values, then a web page is needed to enable the online modification of these settings, to avoid having to sit down at the web server and manually update the file. The page is represented below:

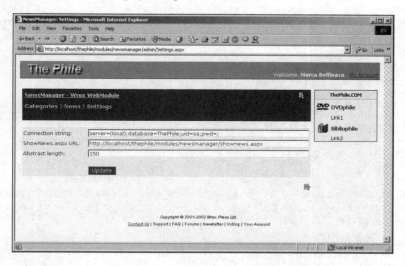

The Settings.aspx Page

The ASP.NET page is formed by a set of controls that show and allow the editing of the respective settings contained in the XML file. The values are not directly bound in a declarative method in the ASPX page, as they were in the previous pages. Here we have three textboxes identified by unique names, and we can easily set their `Text` property from the code-behind in the `Page_Load` event. There's very little that's new in the ASPX file, except the validator we use on the `AbstractLength` field:

```
<asp:TextBox runat="server" Width="100%"
    ID="AbstractLength" CssClass="TextBox" />
<asp:CompareValidator runat="server"
    ControlToValidate="AbstractLength" Type="Integer"
    Operator="DataTypeCheck" Display="dynamic">
  <br>* Invalid format</asp:CompareValidator>
```

Here we ensure that the value supplied is a number. If other characters are inserted it doesn't allow the form to be submitted. We used this same control in the `News.aspx` page to validate the dates; the difference here is that the `Type` property is set to `Integer`.

Now let's move straight on to the code-behind.

The Codebehind for Settings.aspx

The code-behind for Settings.aspx is composed of two procedures: Page_Load and Update_Click.

Page_Load retrieves the settings from the XML file (or from the cache if this is not the first time we have requested them) using the ModuleConfig and ModuleSettings classes in the Configuration assembly. Let's start by looking at the code that sets the textboxes to the current values when the page loads:

```
Private Sub Page_Load(ByVal sender As Object, ByVal e As EventArgs)
    If Not IsPostBack Then
        ' Load all the settings
        Dim settings As Configuration.ModuleSettings = _
            Configuration.ModuleConfig.GetSettings()
        ConnectionString.Text = settings.ConnectionString
        NewsURL.Text = settings.NewsUrl
        AbstractLength.Text = settings.AbstractLength.ToString()
    End If
End Sub
```

The second procedure is Update_Click. It gets the new settings from the controls, sets the properties of a new ModuleSettings object, and finally calls ModuleConfig.SaveSettings to serialize the settings object to the XML file:

```
Protected Sub Update_Click(ByVal sender As Object, ByVal e As EventArgs)
    Dim settings As New Configuration.ModuleSettings()
    ' Aet the new properties values and update everything
    settings.ConnectionString = ConnectionString.Text.Trim()
    settings.NewsUrl = NewsURL.Text.Trim()

    ' If no abstract length is specified (textbox empty),
    ' set to -1 (whole news body)
    If AbstractLength.Text.Trim().Length > 0 Then
        settings.AbstractLength = Integer.Parse(AbstractLength.Text)
    Else
        AbstractLength.Text = "-1"
        settings.AbstractLength = -1
    End If
    ' Save the new settings
    Configuration.ModuleConfig.SaveSettings(settings)
End Sub
```

As explained in the comments, if the AbstractLength is not supplied it is set to -1, and -1 is also shown in the textbox (remember that we didn't create a validator control that requires us to specify this setting).

Summary of the Administration Console

The administration section is complete and fully functional. We now have facilities to:

❑ View, add, delete, and edit categories of news. The data is shown through a grid that also shows the category's image when in view mode, or its path during editing. The grid also has a link for each row, allowing the administrator to jump directly to the page showing the news items for the selected category.

❑ View, add, delete, and edit the news articles. The user can filter the articles on whether they are released, and whether they have been approved. In addition to the news item's title, the grid shows the abstract for each news item, made up from the specified number of characters from the article.

❑ Change the application's settings, such as the DB connection string. Using this page, the administrator need not manually edit the configuration file and re-upload it to the server.

Now let's look at how we display the news to users.

Showing News to the User

We can now add news content to the database, but now we need a way for the users to read it. In this section we're going to build a small set of pages that will allow the user to navigate through the available categories, and read abstracts or entire news articles. Later we'll also see how to build a user control to plug the headlines into any page we want.

These pages use another set of header/footer controls, named `Header.ascx` and `Footer.ascx`: their content is the same as the admin controls, except that here the header does not show the menu bar. We want to keep them separate so that future changes to the admin header or footer do not affect the user end of the site. We won't show the code here, because they are so similar to the admin controls.

Showing the Categories

First of all we write the page that lists the categories, called `ShowCategories.aspx`. The interface is made up of a single control: a `DataList` that shows the categories in two columns, together with their image and description. Here's the ASPX code for the datalist:

```
<asp:DataList id="CategoriesList" runat="server">
  <ItemTemplate>
    <table cellpadding="2" width="100%">
      <tr>
        <td valign="top" width="20px">
          <asp:Label runat="server" Text='<%# GetImage(
              DataBinder.Eval(Container.DataItem, "ImageUrl")) %>'
          />
        </td>
        <td valign="top">
          <asp:HyperLink runat="server" Text='<%#
              DataBinder.Eval(Container.DataItem, "Name") %>'
              NavigateUrl='<%# "ShowAbstracts.aspx?CategoryID=" +
              DataBinder.Eval(Container.DataItem, "CategoryID") %>'
              Font-Bold="True" Font-Size="12" CssClass="GridLink"
          />
          <br>
          <asp:Label runat="server" Text='<%# DataBinder.Eval(
              Container.DataItem, "Description") %>' />
        </td>
      </tr>
    </table>
  </ItemTemplate>
</asp:DataList>
```

As in the `DataGrid`, the `ItemTemplate` section gets repeated for each record in the bound table. The difference is that here it's up to us to create all the HTML code, whereas the strength of the `DataGrid` is that it creates all of the HTML required for the grid structure.

The code-behind for this page only binds the categories returned by the `GetCategories` static method of the `Business.Category` class to the `DataList`. It's nothing new, so we won't show it here – you can find the full code listings in the download.

Here are the results you should get if you run this new page:

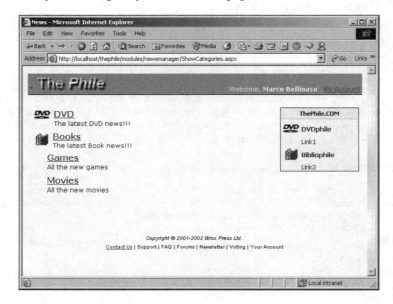

There is something to consider, though. The content of this page won't change frequently, as new categories are rarely added, so why query the database every time if we know that we'll likely get the same results every time? We could create a static HTML page, but this would make the admin systems useless. ASP.NET offers a new feature called **dynamic output caching** that allows us to store a page in the cache for a certain amount of time, if certain conditions are met (such as the client browser or URL of the page being the same, for example). This means that the first time the page is requested we access the database and create the HTML to send to the client. This HTML is then stored in the server cache, and sent as a response to subsequent requests, saving processing time and cycles.

Of course, this feature is applicable when we know that the content for the page does not change for some time, which is exactly the case for this page. To add this feature to our existing page, just add the following line at the top of the page:

```
<%@ OutputCache Duration="600" VaryByParam="none" %>
```

Setting the `Duration` parameter to `600` specifies that the page will be cached for ten minutes. Setting `VaryByParam` to `none` means that the cached page does not depend on the URL's parameters (useful in cases, like this one, where any parameters provided are ignored).

If you'd like to show a box with the news categories in more than one page, or maybe plug a box directly into the shared site layout, you could move the code of this page to a custom control. The code that binds the data to the `DataList`, and the `DataList` declaration, would be exactly the same.

Showing the Abstracts

We now write the `ShowAbstracts.aspx` page, called by `ShowCategories.aspx` when the user clicks a category name. This page is as simple as the previous one; let's look at the main code:

```
<%@ OutputCache Duration="600" VaryByParam="*" %>
```

The opening tags for the page, such as `<html>`, `<head>`, `<body>`, `<form>`, and the header control go here – we have seen them many times, so let's jump straight to the datagrid:

```
<asp:DataGrid ID="NewsGrid" runat="server"
    BorderWidth="0" Width="100%" PagerStyle-CssClass="Grid_Item"
    PageSize="20" AllowPaging="True" PagerStyle-HorizontalAlign="Right"
    PagerStyle-PageButtonCount="20" PagerStyle-Mode="NumericPages"
    AutoGenerateColumns="False" OnPageIndexChanged="NewsGrid_PageChanged">
  <Columns>
    <asp:TemplateColumn>
      <ItemTemplate>
        <br>
        <asp:HyperLink runat="server" Text='<%#
            DataBinder.Eval(Container.DataItem, "Title") %>'
            NavigateUrl='<%# "ShowNews.aspx?NewsID=" +
            DataBinder.Eval(Container.DataItem, "NewsID") %>'
            CssClass="GridLink"
        />
        <asp:Label runat="server" Text='<%#
            DataBinder.Eval(Container.DataItem, "ReleaseDate",
            "{0:MM/dd/yy}") %>' ForeColor="DarkBlue" Font-Size="8" />
        <br>
        <asp:Label runat="server" Text='<%#
            DataBinder.Eval(Container.DataItem, "Abstract") %>' />
        <br>
        <hr>
      </ItemTemplate>
    </asp:TemplateColumn>
  </Columns>
</asp:DataGrid>
// Add footer control and close the page here.
```

The abstracts are shown in a read-only `DataGrid`, with links that point to the `ShowNews.aspx` page – the same way that `ShowCategories.aspx` links to `ShowAbstract.aspx`.

The `VaryByParam` parameter of the @ `OutputCache` is now set to `'*'`. This means that the page is processed if a parameter in the URL changes. This is what we want, because we need to get the abstracts directly from the database if the `CategoryID` parameter is not the same as the value in a previous call to the page. The ASP.NET cache feature is smart enough to detect when the parameters on the URL change, and hold a different cache entry for different parameters.

The HTML output is cached on the server, which could lead to a memory overhead that can impact on the server's performance. This can happen when:

❑ We try to cache hundreds of different ASP.NET pages

❑ We cache a few ASP.NET pages, but these can have many different parameter values; each different value is like having a completely different page, and the full HTML text is cached

In our case we have a few pages, with one or no parameters at all, so it's not a big issue. It's just a question of balancing the cost of hitting the database more often, with the cost of occupying more memory. The right decision will vary from site to site.

In the following screenshot you can see the result you should get in your browser when you click a category name. The current and approved news items are displayed from the newest to the oldest:

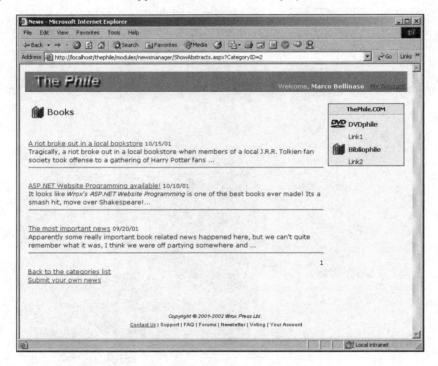

Showing the Whole News Item

The ShowNews.aspx page shows the whole text of the specified news item, and of course the title and release date. It is probably the simplest page we've built so far. Let's just look at the code for the body:

```
<asp:Label runat="server" ID="Title" ForeColor="Navy"
    Font-Bold="True" Font-Size="15" />
<asp:Label runat="server" ID="ReleaseDate"
    ForeColor="DarkBlue" Font-Size="8" />
<br>
```

```
<asp:Label runat="server" ID="Body" Width="100%" />
<br>
<a href="javascript:history.back();">Go back</a>
```

In the code-behind file we create an instance of `Business.News` by passing to the constructor the ID specified, along with the URL, and we set the labels to the respective values. Here is the finished page:

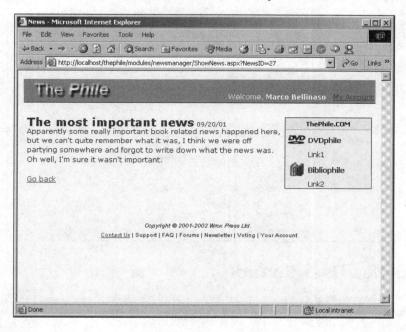

User-Submitted News

We've already discussed why we might want to allow the users (or maybe our external contributors who have no access to the administration section) to post their own news. We need to build a form for users to submit news to the server.

This page, called `SubmitNews.aspx`, does almost the same as the administration `News.aspx` but is only for adding new articles. It also hides the `Approved` value passed to the `AddNews` method of the `Business.Category` class. If the current user has permission to publish a news item, it will be added to the database with the `Approved` status set to `True`, otherwise it will be `False`. We'll come back and show how to do this shortly, while discussing the implementation of security. But the rest of the code is exactly the same so we won't show it here (it is available in the code download). You can see the result in the following screenshot:

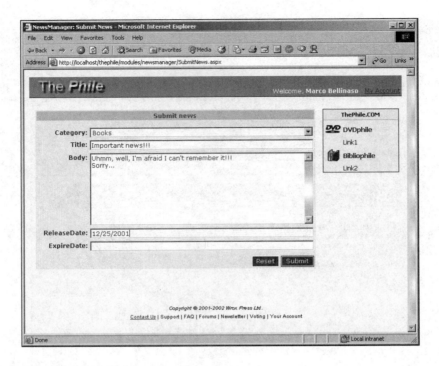

The Headlines User Control

The administration section is complete, and the users can browse the news in each category. Now what? Well, currently the news items are only shown in their own page. We also want a user control that will allow us to easily plug a headlines grid into any page we want with just a couple of lines of code. It seems that we've got something new to do, finally!

Although user controls are a powerful feature of ASP.NET, they are as easy to develop as ASP.NET pages. There's not much difference between a control and a page, except that they use a @Control directive instead of @Page, and they should almost never contain a web form or the <body> tag, because these are present in the page that hosts the control.

Headlines.ascx, part of the NewsManager project, has the following code:

```
<%@ OutputCache Duration="300" VaryByParam="none" %>
<asp:Label ID="HeadlinesHeader" runat="server" />
<asp:DataGrid ID="HeadlinesGrid" runat="server"
    ShowHeader="False" AutoGenerateColumns="False">
  <Columns>
    <asp:TemplateColumn ItemStyle-Width="100px">
      <ItemTemplate>
        <asp:Label runat="server" Font-Bold="True" Text='<%#
            DataBinder.Eval(Container.DataItem,
            "ReleaseDate", "{0:MM/dd/yy}") %>'
        />
```

```
        </ItemTemplate>
      </asp:TemplateColumn>
      <asp:TemplateColumn>
        <ItemTemplate>
          <asp:HyperLink runat="server" NavigateUrl='<%#
              DataBinder.Eval(Container.DataItem, "NewsUrl") %>'
              Text='<%# DataBinder.Eval(Container.DataItem, "Title") %>'
          />
        </ItemTemplate>
      </asp:TemplateColumn>
    </Columns>
  </asp:DataGrid>
```

There is really nothing new to explain here. There is a `DataGrid` that displays the release date and title of the news article, and when clicked it redirects to the page with the whole article.

Let's look at the code-behind file. This class should be in the `Wrox.WebModules.NewsManager.Web.Controls.User` namespace:

```
Namespace WebModules.NewsManager.Web.Controls.User

  Public MustInherit Class Headlines
    Inherits System.Web.UI.UserControl

    Private myCategoryId As Integer
    Protected HeadlinesGrid As DataGrid
    Protected HeadlinesHeader As Label
```

There are several properties exposed here. They simply provide access to member variables, or properties of `HeadlinesGrid`. Let's move on to the methods:

```
    Private Sub Page_Load(ByVal sender As Object, ByVal e As EventArgs) _
      Handles MyBase.Load

      If Not IsPostBack Then
        DataBind()
      End If
    End Sub

    Public Overrides Sub DataBind()
      ' Get the row describing this category
      Dim theCategory As New Business.Category(myCategoryId)

      ' Set the image and the category name
      HeadlinesHeader.Text = New Categories().GetImage(theCategory.ImageUrl)
      HeadlinesHeader.Text = HeadlinesHeader.Text & theCategory.Name

      ' Show all the headlines of this category
      Dim categoriesDataView As DataView = _
        theCategory.GetHeadlines().Tables(0).DefaultView
      HeadlinesGrid.DataSource = categoriesDataView
      HeadlinesGrid.DataBind()

    End Sub
```

The core procedure is DataBind, which overrides the implementation of the base class and binds the headlines table to the grid. There is also the Page_Load event that calls DataBind if the page that hosts the control is not posted back. We could avoid implementing the Page_Load event, and leave the host page with the task of calling the control's BindData method, as we've done for controls in the previous pages. However, this is a special control because it gets the records and sets the DataGrid's properties on its own, so it makes sense that it also binds the data to the grid without any external intervention.

Testing the Control

To test the control we create a ShowHeadlines.aspx file with an external text editor. We don't want to create a new page in VS.NET because it would be added to the project and its code-behind compiled into the assembly, which is not what we want since this is just a test page and not a class to compile and reuse. Here is the content for the page:

```
<%@ Page Inherits="Wrox.ThePhile.Web.PhilePage" %>
<%@ Register TagPrefix="NewsManager" TagName="Headlines"
    src="Headlines.ascx" %>
<%@ Register TagPrefix="NewsManager" TagName="Header" src="Header.ascx" %>
<%@ Register TagPrefix="NewsManager" TagName="Footer" src="Footer.ascx" %>

<html>
<head>
  <title>NewsManager: NewsHeadlines</title>
  <link rel="stylesheet" HREF="/ThePhile/Styles/ThePhile.css" />
  <link href="/ThePhile/Styles/Navigator.css" rel="stylesheet">
  <meta name="CODE_LANGUAGE" Content="VB">
</head>

<body>
  <!-- Insert the menu user control -->
  <NewsManager:Header ID="Menu" runat="server" />

  <!-- Insert the headlines boxes -->
  <NewsManager:Headlines
      ID="DVD"
      runat="server"
      CssClass="DVD_News_General"
      HeaderStyle="DVD_News_Header"
      ItemStyle="DVD_News_Item"
      AlternatingItemStyle="DVD_News_AlternatingItem"
      Width="100%"
      CategoryID="1"
  />
  <br><br>
  <NewsManager:Headlines
      ID="Books"
      runat="server"
      CssClass="Book_News_General"
      HeaderStyle="Book_News_Header"
      ItemStyle="Book_News_Item"
      AlternatingItemStyle="Book_News_AlternatingItem"
      Width="500px"
      CategoryID="2"
```

```
  />

  <!-- Insert the footer -->
  <NewsManager:Footer ID="Footer" runat="server" />

</body>
</html>
```

We declare two Headlines controls, set the properties for the style (the two controls have different header and item styles, and a different width), and select a different category for each. Here is the result:

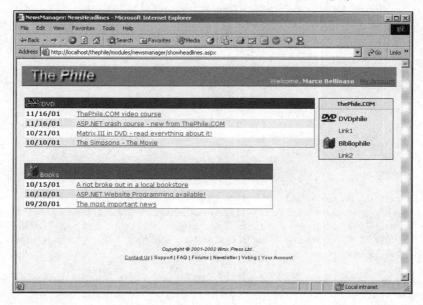

The user interface section is now functionally complete – we just need to develop the security system. After that, we will look at how to provide our news content to other sites and applications.

Securing the Module

Now that the administration console and the user side of things are complete, but before going ahead with the web service and the Windows client, we should think about the implementation of security. In the design section we discussed the three permissions we need, so now we only have to define the enumeration that contains them, and perform the proper checks when the pages are loaded. We need to add these to the Enums.vb file of the Core module, as we did for the Accounts permissions in Chapter 5:

```
Namespace WebModules.NewsManager
  Public Enum NewsManagerPermissions
    AdministerNews = 200
    PublishNews = 201
    SubmitNews = 202
  End Enum
End Namespace
```

Now, when any administration page loads, we must ensure that the current user has the AdministerNews permission. To do this, we added the following code to the Page_Load event of those pages (Categories.aspx, News.aspx, and Settings.aspx):

```
Private Sub Page_Load(ByVal sender As Object, ByVal e As EventArgs)

    ' If user is not authenticated or does not have authority to manage
    ' news categories, redirect to login page
    If Not (TypeOf Context.User Is SitePrincipal) _
        OrElse Not CType(Context.User, SitePrincipal).HasPermission( _
            CInt(NewsManagerPermissions.AdministerNews)) Then

        Response.Redirect( _
            "/ThePhileVB/WebModules/Accounts/Login.aspx?ShowError=true", True)

    End If

    If Not Page.IsPostBack Then

        . . .

    End If

End Sub
```

We cast the Context.User object to SitePrincipal, which exposes the HasPermission method. This is necessary because if we tried to access the page before logging-in, the page would generate an exception, because it could not cast Context.User object to SitePrincipal. If either condition of the If block returns False, the user is redirected to the login page, where an error message will inform them that they don't have permission to view the page.

The code above has to be added to all of the administration pages. For the SubmitNews.aspx page we instead want to grant access to anyone who has any of the three possible permissions:

```
If Not (TypeOf Context.User Is SitePrincipal) _
    OrElse Not CType(Context.User, SitePrincipal).HasPermission( _
        CInt(NewsManagerPermissions.AdministerNews)) _
    OrElse Not CType(Context.User, SitePrincipal).HasPermission( _
        CInt(NewsManagerPermissions.PublishNews)) _
    OrElse Not CType(Context.User, SitePrincipal).HasPermission( _
        CInt(NewsManagerPermissions.SubmitNews)) Then

    Response.Redirect( _
        "/ThePhileVB/WebModules/Accounts/Login.aspx?ShowError=true", True)
End If
```

Then, when the news is added to the database, if the user has the AdministerNews or PublishNews permissions the news will be approved immediately, otherwise it will be added in the pending state, with Approved = false:

```
        Dim currPrincipal As SitePrincipal = _
          CType(Context.User, SitePrincipal)
        Dim currUser As SiteIdentity = _
          CType(Context.User.Identity, SiteIdentity)

        Dim selectedCategory As New _
          Business.Category(Integer.Parse(CatDropDown.SelectedItem.Value))
        Dim canPublish As Boolean = _
          currPrincipal.HasPermission(CInt(NewsManagerPermissions.PublishNews))
        Dim canAdminister As Boolean = _
          currPrincipal.HasPermission(CInt(NewsManagerPermissions.AdministerNews))

        Dim addedNews As Business.News = selectedCategory.AddNews( _
            NewTitle.Text, _
            NewBody.Text, _
            releaseDate, _
            expireDate, _
            (canPublish Or canAdminister), _
            currUser.UserId)
```

That's all! Pretty simple, isn't it? Now you can test the module with different users, or try removing and adding permissions to your user account through the `Accounts` administration module developed in the previous chapter. (Remember that you have to manually add the new permissions to the database first.)

The Headlines Web Service

The last thing we have to implement for this module is the web service that will allow us to share the headlines with any other website or program that can send and receive XML/SOAP packages.

We have a new web service called `Headlines.asmx`. There is nothing in the ASMX file, just the declaration of the code-behind file, whose incredibly short content is listed here in its entirety:

```
Imports System
Imports System.Data
Imports System.Data.SqlClient
Imports System.Web.Services

Namespace WebModules.NewsManager.Web.Services

  Public Class Headlines
    Inherits System.Web.Services.WebService

    <WebMethod(Description:="Returns the headlines for the current and approved _
      News of the specified category")> _
    Public Function GetHeadlines(ByVal categoryId As Integer) As DataSet
      Return New Business.Category(categoryId).GetHeadlines()
    End Function

    <WebMethod(Description:="Returns all the categories")> _
    Public Function GetCategories() As DataSet
      Return Business.Category.GetCategories()
    End Function
```

277

```
    End Class

End Namespace
```

We've changed the namespace to `Wrox.WebModules.NewsManager.Web.Services`, following the guidelines given in Chapter 2. The `Headlines` class inherits from `System.Web.Services.WebService`, and although it has the same name as the class for the `Headlines` user control, the two classes don't clash because they are located in different namespaces. The web service exposes two methods, `GetHeadlines` and `GetCategories`, which simply return the result of the calls to the methods in the `Business.Category` class. The small detail that turns two normal methods into web-accessible methods is the `<WebMethod>` attribute, which also has a parameter to specify a description.

Testing the Web Service

It's easy to test web services. Just jump to the `Headlines.asmx` file with your browser, and you'll get the following:

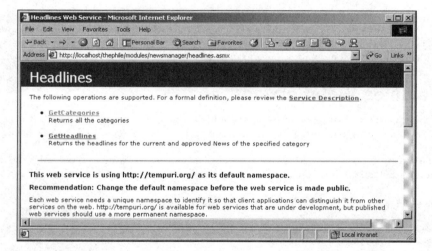

You can see the two web methods listed on the page, together with their description. Click on a link to test that method. For example, click the `GetHeadlines` link and you'll get this page:

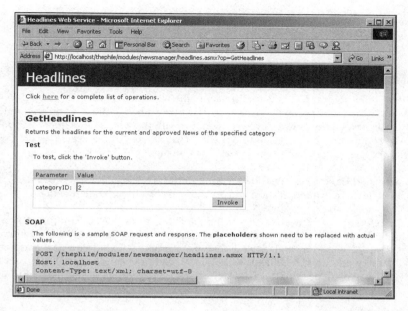

The method is detected to require a parameter, so the page provides a textbox where you can enter the ID of a category. Press **Invoke** and you'll finally execute the method. This is the result produced for a `categoryID` of 2:

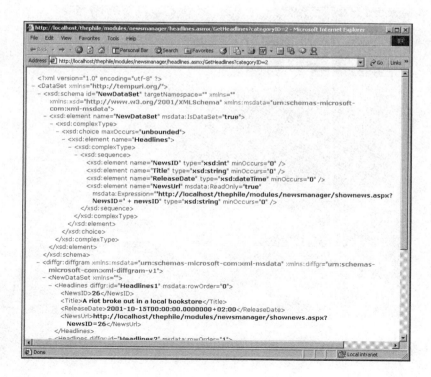

We get a page with XML/SOAP output that represents a `DataSet`. The `DataSet` includes one table containing the headlines. The web service seems to work very well, so we can now go ahead and build the client.

The News Ticker Application

We can build different types of clients that consume the web service, such as a web page or a desktop program. To show how to access web services, we'll build a small Windows application for browsing the headlines by category, and opening a browser window with the whole news body by double-clicking on a headline. We could offer this program to our site's visitors, so that they can check if there are new headlines without typing the URL in the browser and manually refreshing the page.

We add a new **Visual Basic .NET Windows Forms** project to the solution (we could create this application anywhere we wanted, it's just convenient to keep all our code together).

We then add a reference to the web service using the **Project | Add Web Reference...** menu option. We specify the full URL of the web service file, and clicking **Add Reference** VS.NET automatically creates a proxy class to access the web service. Note that in the Solution Explorer a new entry has been added under **Web References**, called localhost, and underneath it you can see the WSDL and the discovery files created. We renamed localhost to ThePhile, but it isn't really important, it is just the name we'll use to access the proxy class.

The form contains a `DropDownList` for listing the categories, a `DataGrid` to show the headlines, a button to refresh the headlines, and a timer to automatically refresh the headlines after a certain amount of time. You should place the controls as shown in the following screenshot:

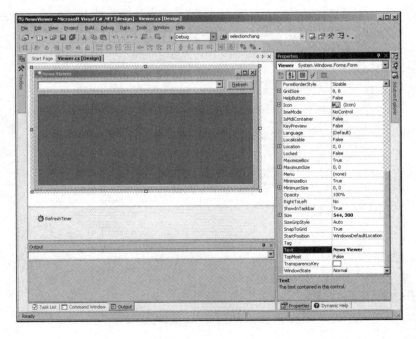

Explaining how to create Windows Forms in detail is beyond the scope of this book, but we'll quickly look at the code piece by piece:

```
Private Sub Viewer_Load(ByVal sender As Object, ByVal e As EventArgs) _
    Handles MyBase.Load

    ' Get the categories and the headlines for the first category
    myCategoriesDataset = New ThePhile.Headlines().GetCategories()

    ' Bind categories to the ComboBox, display the Name and keep the
    ' CategoryId as value for each item
    Categories.DataSource = myCategoriesDataset.Tables(0).DefaultView
    Categories.DisplayMember = "Name"
    Categories.ValueMember = "CategoryID"
    categoriesLoaded = True

    ' Fill the grid with headlines
    FillHeadlinesGrid()
End Sub
```

In the `Viewer_Load` event (which corresponds to `Page_Load` in ASP.NET pages) we retrieve the categories and save them to a private `DataSet` variable. We then bind them to the `DropDownList`, and call another routine to get the headlines and fill the grid:

```
Private Sub FillHeadlinesGrid()

    ' If the categories have not been loaded yet, or if there is no
    ' category in the ComboBox, then exit now
    If Not categoriesLoaded Or Categories.Items.Count = 0 Then Return

    ' Get the headlines for the selected category
    Dim headlines As New ThePhile.Headlines()
    myHeadlinesDataset = headlines.GetHeadlines( _
        CInt(Categories.SelectedValue))

    ' Remove the current grid columns (if any)
    HeadlinesGrid.TableStyles.Clear()

    ' Bind myHeadlinesDataset to the grid, and show the ReleaseDate
    ' and Headline titles in two custom columns
    HeadlinesGrid.SetDataBinding(myHeadlinesDataset, "Headlines")
    Dim tableStyle As New DataGridTableStyle()
    tableStyle.MappingName = "Headlines"
    tableStyle.AlternatingBackColor = Color.LightGray

    ' Add the ReleaseDate column
    Dim textCol As New DataGridTextBoxColumn()
    textCol.MappingName = "ReleaseDate"
    textCol.HeaderText = "Release Date"
    textCol.Width = 80
    tableStyle.GridColumnStyles.Add(textCol)
```

```
' Add the Headline's title column
Dim titleCol As New DataGridTextBoxColumn()
titleCol.MappingName = "Title"
titleCol.HeaderText = "Headline"
titleCol.Width = 400
tableStyle.GridColumnStyles.Add(titleCol)

' Add the (hidden) NewsUrl column
Dim urlCol As New DataGridTextBoxColumn()
urlCol.MappingName = "NewsUrl"
urlCol.Width = 0
tableStyle.GridColumnStyles.Add(urlCol)

' Finally add the table to the grid
HeadlinesGrid.TableStyles.Add(tableStyle)

End Sub
```

The code above creates a new column for each column of the data table, and binds these columns to the respective fields. When the user clicks a row header of the grid, we want to open the default browser and redirect to the page that shows the whole news story. The URL of the news item is one of the columns in the data table, and opening the default browser is done with a single line, thanks to the `System.Diagnostic.Process` class. The following code checks if the user double-clicks on a row header and in that case loads the news page within the browser:

```
Private Sub HeadlinesGrid_DoubleClick( _
  ByVal sender As Object, _
  ByVal e As EventArgs) _
  Handles HeadlinesGrid.DoubleClick

  ' Get the current cursor position relative to the HeadlinesGrid
  Dim pt As Point = HeadlinesGrid.PointToClient(Cursor.Position)

  ' Navigate to the link only if the user clicked on the row header
  If HeadlinesGrid.HitTest(pt.X, pt.Y).Type = _
    DataGrid.HitTestType.RowHeader Then

    Dim bmGrid As BindingManagerBase
    bmGrid = BindingContext(myHeadlinesDataset, "Headlines")

    ' Open the default browser and navigate to the Url of the
    ' currently selected row
    System.Diagnostics.Process.Start( _
      CType(bmGrid.Current, DataRowView)("NewsUrl").ToString())
  End If
End Sub
```

The last three procedures are called, respectively, at the timer's interval, when the user selects another category, or when the user presses the Refresh button. All of them simply call the `FillHeadlinesGrid` procedure to refresh the grid:

```
Private Sub RefreshTimer_Tick( _
  ByVal sender As Object, _
  ByVal e As EventArgs) _
  Handles RefreshTimer.Tick

  FillHeadlinesGrid()
End Sub

Private Sub Categories_SelectedIndexChanged( _
  ByVal sender As Object, _
  ByVal e As EventArgs) _
  Handles Categories.SelectedIndexChanged

  FillHeadlinesGrid()

End Sub

Private Sub RefreshButton_Click( _
  ByVal sender As Object, _
  ByVal e As EventArgs) _
  Handles RefreshButton.Click

  FillHeadlinesGrid()
End Sub
```

All the code is finally complete, and if you run the application you'll get the following form:

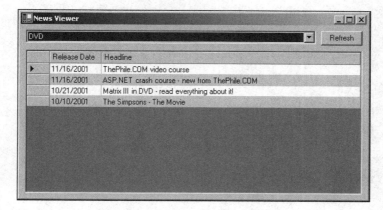

You might also want to test this application in detail, by adding some news through the NewsManager administration section, and then waiting a few minutes to see if the grid is automatically refreshed (or manually refill it by clicking Refresh).

Summary

In this long chapter we have seen how to build a complex and feature-rich module to completely manage the site's news and articles. We've provided numerous features through the chapter:

❑ A tool for managing the database

❑ Pages for browsing the published content

❑ Integration with the `Accounts` module to secure the module and track the authors of the news items

❑ A user control for showing the headlines on the homepage or in any other page

❑ A web service that can share the headlines with any site or program that can use and understand XML/SOAP messages

❑ A Windows client program that uses the web service to show the headlines of all the available categories, and that opens a browser and shows the whole news item when a title is clicked.

This system should be flexible enough to be successfully plugged into many real-world applications. When customized to fit a particular site's needs, it could become very powerful.

7

Advertising

No matter how wonderful the website, how amazing the look, how talented the programmers, or how useful the service – a site will not last long without a consistent source of funding. Some sites are maintained by volunteers who donate their own time and money, others get subscription fees from readers. Many of these sites try to supplement their revenue with advertising, and other sites rely on it entirely.

Many sites use banner advertisement-style features even when they don't sell advertising space. For example, some sites exchange links with other sites. Others (for example www.play.com) use banner advertising to provide links to areas of their product catalogue that the viewer would not necessarily go looking for.

In this chapter we will present an overview of the problems involved with advertising and some common design patterns in overcoming those problems. We'll develop a reusable advertising module that we'll plug into our website and that we can easily adapt to our future needs.

The Problem

There are two main concepts you need to be familiar with to provide advertising on a website: impressions and hits.

Impressions

An **impression** occurs when a particular advertisement is displayed on a web page to a single user. Website owners, administrators, and marketing managers should consider impressions a commodity – chips to bargain with when obtaining lucrative advertising contracts.

Consider this scenario: a popular content website receives over a million hits a day. For the sake of example, imagine that it is a fan club website dedicated to a popular video game. Its audience consists of a wide range of browsers from older adults to young teenagers and pre-teens. An impression on this site would be considered an extremely valuable commodity to a video game manufacturer. However, a manufacturer of a popular brand of craft glue would probably not find those impressions particularly valuable.

Impressions are *yours* to sell, and you should look for a buyer for your impressions that would be most interested in your target audience. Therefore, you *must* know the audience of your website in order to market your impressions to the right audience.

Typically, impressions are sold in bulk. A typical advertising contract will consist of the advertising buyer paying for a mathematical or statistical guarantee that a certain number of impressions of a given ad will be displayed in a given time period (usually measured in weeks or months).

Hits

While impressions are yours to sell, **hits** are to be considered rewards or prizes. An impression occurs when an advertisement appears on the user's page. If the user is particularly interested in what the advertisement has to offer, then the user will click the advertisement. This is called a hit. Just to confuse things more, virtually every dotcom company has a different term for hits, including clicks, click-throughs, scores, buy-ins, and more. No matter what term is used – it all boils down to the simple act of the user clicking on the advertisement.

This is where advertising gets more profitable. Hits are worth more than impressions. Advertising contracts typically pay percentages of sales resulting from banner advertisement hits, or they pay a flat rate per hit.

When designing an advertising system we need to keep track of the following:

- ❑ Impression counts
- ❑ Hit counts
- ❑ Community demographics – *who* is using your web site, what they do and don't have in common, their interests, etc.

Earlier in the book we discussed community building and mentioned that opinion polls provide a fun way for users to interact with your site. They also provide an easy way for you to obtain valuable demographics that you might be able to use to land that advertising contract you might not have otherwise been able to get. For example, if you put up a poll asking users what their favorite DVD is, and 75% of them say that their favorite DVD is *Star Wars: Episode I*, then chances are you could use that information to strike a pretty lucrative advertising deal with a DVD on-line retailer.

Requirements

There are many things that we need to cover in the design of our advertising module. We want to make sure that it takes care of all of our needs and solves our problem – which is that we need to generate revenue, so we need impression/hit data to attract advertisers, and a way of putting adverts in our pages. In addition, we want to make it flexible and scalable enough so that if our advertising needs increase in the future, it should be easy enough to create more code and functionality to deal with this.

In short, our design is going to need to take care of the following issues for us:

❑ **Database design** – we need to make sure that we have a database that can track all necessary information, and provide the reporting capabilities we know we're going to need.

❑ **Layout and display** – we need to make sure that we have a good place to put our advertisement and a layout in mind that won't intrude on or interfere with the existing interface.

❑ **Auditing** – we need to track as much information as possible about the advertisements, and make that information available in such a way that we can obtain useful reports whenever we need them.

❑ **Administration** – our website administrators, who may not necessarily be located in the office, need to be able to log in to some administration console to make changes and additions to the advertising data.

Administrative users should be able to perform the following tasks:

❑ Create new advertisements

❑ Edit/view existing advertisements

❑ Add details of new advertising companies

❑ View all current advertisements

❑ Generate reports to show advertising activity

Design

Now that we have specified the broad requirements of our advertising system, let's lay down a design for it. Once again ASP.NET provides a component that almost does what we want – the AdRotator. So before we look at the components we are going to build, let's look at how the AdRotator works and what impact using it will have on the rest of our design.

Using the AdRotator

The AdRotator handles a lot of the work associated with displaying an advert. It will save us time overall if we use it, but it has its own foibles that we need to overcome.

We would like to store all data for our application in the database, but AdRotator only supports an XML file. So we will need to find a way to work around this. Information required by the AdRotator will go in the XML file, while related data will go in the database. We will need a way to tell which entry in the database relates to which entry in the XML file.

Another limitation is that the AdRotator doesn't come with the ability to record hits or impressions. It doesn't expose a click event that we could use ourselves to record hits, so we'll have to implement this functionality ourselves. However, it does fire an event every time an ad is displayed – so we can use this to record an impression.

The XML file for an AdRotator stores the following details:

Property	Description
ImageUrl	Absolute or relative URL to an image to be displayed as the banner advertisement.
NavigateUrl	The URL of the page to go to if a user clicks the ad.
AlternateText	Text to display in the image's ALT attribute.
Keyword	An optional keyword for the advertisement, to allow filtering. We won't be using this feature here; consult the MSDN documentation for more information on this property.
Impressions	This number indicates the *relative* importance of this advertisement with respect to all other ads in the rotator's XML file. The larger this number, the more frequently the ad will be displayed. This number will typically be adjusted based on how much the advertiser is paying.

So, we will store this information in the XML file, and anything else in the database. Here's an example of a single ad in the XML file. Note that the properties listed above have all been serialized as XML elements.

```
<Advertisements>
  <Ad>
    <ImageUrl>http://localhost/thephile/images/wroxbanner.jpg</ImageUrl>
    <NavigateUrl>/ThePhile/Modules/AdsManager/PassThrough.aspx?AD=9
    </NavigateUrl>
    <AlternateText>Wrox Press</AlternateText>
    <Keyword>wrox</Keyword>
    <Impressions>1</Impressions>
  </Ad>
  <!-- more advertisements here, each with the Ad element. -->
</Advertisements>
```

> *For more information on the AdRotator control, consult the MSDN .NET Framework SDK Developer's Guide entry for AdRotator. It's available at http://msdn.microsoft.com/library/default.asp?url=/library/en-us/cpgenref/html/cpconadrotatorwebcontrol.asp.*

The Database

One of the first steps in any database design, from the smallest to the largest, is an **entity list**. Before figuring out what kind of columns we need, what data types we need, etc., we need to know the basic list of the *things* we need to keep track of. The following is a list of the entities that we need in order to maintain an effective advertising database:

❑ Advertisements

❑ Companies

❑ Impressions

❑ Hits

We need to store some basic descriptive information about the advertisement in the database. Because we know a little bit about how ASP.NET's `AdRotator` control works, we know we're not going to need to store things like image file names and relative importance in the database.

As for other modules in this book, all tables will be given a unique prefix (`AdsManager_`). The database will use the following schema:

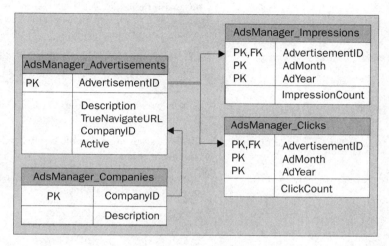

The `AdsManager_Advertisements` table is pretty straightforward. It has `AdvertisementID` as the main primary key/identity field. From there we get to the `AdsManager_Impressions` and `AdsManager_Clicks` tables. Each of these uses as a primary key the combination of the `AdvertisementID`, the `AdMonth`, and the `AdYear` fields. The `AdYear` and `AdMonth` fields are simple number fields that contain the month and year during which the click count or impression count was accumulated. This allows monthly summaries to be generated without bogging the database down with slow and complex date calculations.

The interesting thing about this design is that we're doing a little bit of warehousing in the way we're storing our data. It would be inefficient to add a row to the database every time someone sees or clicks a banner ad. So we've taken inspiration from data warehousing, and we just store *summary* information. Data warehousing is basically the storage of summary (or otherwise calculated) data separately from the live (also called transactional) data. We store monthly totals of both clicks and impressions for a given advertisement. As opposed to storing each click in its own row with a pinpoint time/date stamp, like this:

```
2/02/2002 05:34 1
2/02/2002 05:36 2
```

we instead store the total sum of all the clicks for February 2002 as follows:

```
02      2002    85
```

This way, to retrieve all clicks for February, we retrieve one row, without calculation, saving us an immense amount of effort. Because each advertisement belongs to a single company, it becomes very easy to obtain reports of monthly activity for all the advertisements for the same company or group of companies.

In addition to the database tables, our database will also contain several stored procedures. These will make the system slightly more efficient, and simplify our data layer.

Stored Procedure	Description
sp_AdsManager_CreateAdvertisment	Creates a new advertisement in the database. This only creates the in-database portion of the advertisement. The XML stored in the AdRotator's config file is handled by the data-services component itself.
sp_AdsManager_CreateCompany	Creates a new company profile in the database. Currently we only store the company's name, but the module can be adapted to store more information.
sp_AdsManager_GetAdList	Retrieves a full list of all advertisements in the database. Used for administration.
sp_AdsManager_GetAdvertDetails	Obtains all of the available details concerning a given advertisement.
sp_AdsManager_GetCompanyList	Obtains an alphabetically sorted list of all companies in the database.
sp_AdsManager_GetCompanyReport	Data is formatted and retrieved to provide a company with all the relevant information as to the progress and history of its advertising campaigns. Can be used to support a billing process by being fed into a reporting tool such as Crystal Reports.
sp_AdsManager_RecordClick	Records the event in which a user *clicks* on an ad banner.
sp_AdsManager_RecordImpression	Records the event in which a user *sees* an ad banner.
sp_AdsManager_UpdateAdvertisement	Updates the pertinent information about a given advertisement.

The Data Services Layer

As with other modules, our data services layer will consist of stateless classes that provide access to the data source. However, because we're using the AdRotator, we have two data stores – the database and the XML file. We want to keep this complication hidden from the business layer, so our data services objects will need to aggregate the information from the different sources.

We will use two classes in the data layer:

❑ AdMaster – deals with data requests that do not refer to a single advert: manipulating companies, or returning a list of all ads in the database.

❑ Advertisement – deals with data requests referring to a particular advert: creating, updating, and retrieving ads, and recording click-throughs and impressions.

The Business Layer

With a solid data layer, the business layer can safely ignore the complication of having two data sources.

The AdMaster class in the business tier will simply call methods in the data tier, which in turn call stored procedures in the database. Like the AdMaster data class, it is stateless.

The Advertisement class in the business tier provides an abstraction of a single advert. When we instantiate it, we can provide an ID to identify a given advert. We then have methods and properties to manipulate that advert. This class does maintain state during the lifetime of its instantiation.

Alternatively we can instantiate a new advert and save it. The data layer will create a new database record and XML entry.

The Presentation Layer

We now have all the data and logic that we need to make the advertisement system work, and can move on to looking at the presentation layer. The presentation layer needs to do two things:

❑ Display the advertisement, and record an impression

❑ Handle a hit (click) – record it, and pass the user to the appropriate site

We will display the advert using the AdRotator, which will automatically select an advert based on a weighting. However, the AdRotator does not record impressions. To do that, we can catch the AdCreated event, and use that to record the impression.

The AdRotator control simply provides a link – it does not expose a click event. So if we link directly to the target site, we will not know when a user has clicked the advert. To record hits, we will use a **pass-through page**. This is a page on our own site that uses the business components to record which advertisement was clicked, and then forwards the browser on to the eventual target. The AdRotator link points to the pass-through page, not the target site.

Advertising Administration

Also in the presentation layer is our administration system. Our design is fairly straightforward. We will provide administrators with a web interface for administering the banner ads and their related properties. We also want to have a stored procedure for feeding a reporting tool, such as Crystal Reports, for supplying data to advertisers in a professional, easy-to-read format.

Configuration

As with the previous modules described in this book, there are two configuration classes used to abstract access to and from a configuration file: ModuleConfig and ModuleSettings. ModuleConfig is a utility class designed to de-serialize an instance of ModuleSettings from the appropriate file and serialize that same class back into the file if changes are necessary.

The Solution

As with any project, we hope that by the time we're ready to code we've created a good, solid, effective design. In our design we covered the data services and business layer classes that we would need to create. We also discussed the fact that we would be using the AdRotator control.

This is actually a very simple control to use, and is the core of our advertising solution. You just put the AdRotator control onto your ASP.NET page and indicate where it can find the advertisement files – it then handles everything else. In this section we'll show you how we use this control to record impressions and hits, two things that it doesn't have built-in support for recording. We'll also show you how we've implemented the rest of our design to support the advertising solution.

The Database Tables

Before building our database, we need to decide on the details of the tables. Here is a fuller schema, which we will use to build the database.

AdsManager_Advertisements Table

Column Name	Data Type	Description
AdvertisementID	int – Identity primary key	Unique ID for the advertisement
Description	varchar	Description of the advertisement
CompanyID	int foreign key	ID of company owning the advertisement
Active	bit	Boolean flag indicating whether the advertisement is active
TrueNavigateUrl	varchar	URL where the user will be redirected from the pass-through page

AdsManager_Companies Table

Column Name	Data Type	Description
CompanyID	int – Identity primary key	Unique ID for the company
Description	varchar	Description of the company

AdsManager_Impressions Table

Column Name	Data Type	Description
AdvertisementID	int	Advertisement ID for the given impression count
AdMonth	int	Month for the given impression count
AdYear	int	Year for the given impression count
ImpressionCount	int	Actual impression count for an ad/year/month

AdsManager_Clicks Table

Column Name	Data Type	Description
AdvertisementID	int	Advertisement ID for the given click count
AdMonth	int	Month for the given click count
AdYear	int	Year for the given click count
ClickCount	int	Actual click count for a given month/year/ad ID

Stored Procedures

The scripting source for all the stored procedures is in the code download. We don't have the space to list the source code for all of the stored procedures, so we've selected a few samples that represent some of the most frequently performed tasks.

sp_AdsManager_CreateAdvertisement

The sp_AdsManager_CreateAdvertisement stored procedure takes a few simple arguments and returns as an output parameter the ID of the created advertisement:

```
CREATE PROCEDURE sp_AdsManager_CreateAdvertisement
                @CompanyID int,
                @Description varchar(255),
                @TrueNavigateUrl varchar(255),
                @AdvertisementID int output
AS
   INSERT INTO AdsManager_Advertisements(CompanyID, Description,
                                                     TrueNavigateUrl)
     VALUES(@CompanyID, @Description, @TrueNavigateUrl)

   SET @AdvertisementID = @@IDENTITY
GO
```

sp_AdsManager_GetAdList

The sp_AdsManager_GetAdList stored procedure obtains a list of all advertisements in the database. It uses an inner join to combine details of the ad with details of the company:

```
CREATE PROCEDURE sp_AdsManager_GetAdList
AS
SELECT ad.AdvertisementID,
       ad.Description,
       ad.CompanyID,
       cp.Description as CompanyName
  FROM AdsManager_Advertisements ad
  INNER JOIN AdsManager_Companies cp ON ad.CompanyID = cp.CompanyID
  ORDER BY CompanyName ASC, ad.Description ASC
GO
```

sp_AdsManager_GetCompanyReport

The sp_AdsManager_GetCompanyReport stored procedure queries the database to provide a history of all of the advertising campaigns for a given company during a certain time period. Clicks and impressions are stored as a month-by-month count, rather than by creating a new record for each click or impression:

```
CREATE PROCEDURE sp_AdsManager_GetCompanyReport
                @CompanyID int,
                @StartMonth int,
                @StartYear int,
                @EndMonth int,
                @EndYear int
AS
  SELECT adimp.AdvertisementID, adimp.ImpressionCount, adimp.AdMonth,
         adimp.AdYear, adclick.ClickCount, ad.Description
    FROM AdsManager_Impressions adimp
    INNER JOIN AdsManager_Advertisements ad
      ON adimp.AdvertisementID = ad.AdvertisementID
    LEFT JOIN AdsManager_Clicks adclick
      ON adimp.AdvertisementID = adclick.AdvertisementID
    WHERE ad.CompanyID = @CompanyID AND
      (adclick.AdYear >= @StartYear AND
      adclick.AdYear <= @EndYear AND
      adimp.AdYear >= @StartYear AND
      adimp.AdYear <= @EndYear) AND
      (adclick.AdMonth >= @StartMonth AND
      adclick.AdMonth <= @EndMonth AND
      adimp.AdMonth >= @StartMonth AND
      adimp.AdMonth <= @EndMonth)

    ORDER BY adimp.adYear ASC, adimp.adMonth ASC
GO
```

This stored procedure facilitates reporting but we have not implemented a user interface for it. This user interface can easily be implemented in a reporting tool such as Crystal Reports or by a program written for an advertising manager. The following is the output summarizing a brand new company's ad campaign history:

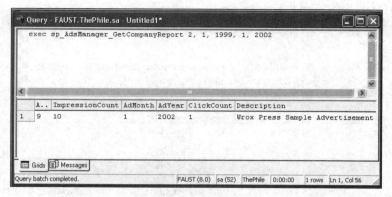

The data shows each company's advertising campaigns. Each campaign will have a single row for each month during the time specified by the stored procedure. This makes it incredibly easy to create a grouping in a reporting tool that allows sub-reports and other interactive features, or in an ASP.NET web page. As you can see, the above ad campaign had ten impressions and one click during January 2002. If this campaign had been created during December 2001, there would be another row for that month, also summarizing that month's activity.

The Data Services Layer

Now that we've taken a look at the format of our data in SQL Server and we've seen what stored procedures we're going to be working with, it will be fairly easy to turn that into a set of methods that the data services layer requires.

Let's take a look at the source code for each of the required classes. We'll also examine some of the decisions that went into choosing a particular code style or algorithm. To get started, we'll create a new Class Library project (in Visual Basic .NET) and call it `AdsManagerData`. We'll make sure that the default namespace for this project is `Wrox.WebModules.AdsManager.Data`, as well as making sure that the output filename is `Wrox.WebModules.AdsManager.Data`. One last thing before we start looking at the source code for the classes is to add a reference to the `Core` project.

The AdMaster Class

The `AdMaster` class is pretty straightforward. It provides a front-end to the stored procedures in the database for performing operations that don't belong to the `Advertisement` class. As with all the other data services classes in this book, this class inherits from `Wrox.WebModules.Data.DbObject`, which we looked at in Chapter 2. The following code is found in `AdMaster.vb`:

```
Imports System
Imports System.Data
Imports System.Data.SqlClient

Imports Wrox.WebModules.Data

Namespace WebModules.AdsManager.Data

  Public Class AdMaster
    Inherits Wrox.WebModules.Data.DbObject
```

```
Public Sub New(ByVal newConnectionString As String)
  MyBase.New(newConnectionString)
End Sub
```

The method below will retrieve a list of companies from the database by using the
`sp_AdsManager_GetCompanyList` stored procedure, and will store the results in a `DataSet`:

```
Public Function GetCompanyList() As DataSet
  Dim companies As DataSet = RunProcedure( _
    "sp_AdsManager_GetCompanyList", New SqlParameter() {}, "Users")

  Return companies
End Function
```

This next method retrieves the master list of all advertisements in the database into a `DataSet`:

```
Public Function GetAdList() As DataSet
  Dim ads As DataSet = RunProcedure( _
    "sp_AdsManager_GetAdList", New SqlParameter() {}, "Advertisements")

  Return ads
End Function
```

The following method uses a stored procedure to create a new company in the database given the name
of the company as an argument:

```
Public Sub CreateCompany(ByVal companyName As String)
  Dim rowsAffected As Integer
  Dim parameters As SqlParameter() = { _
    New SqlParameter("@Companyname", SqlDbType.VarChar, 255)}
  parameters(0).Value = companyName

  RunProcedure("sp_AdsManager_CreateCompany", parameters, rowsAffected)
End Sub
```

The Advertisement Class

Now we add a class called `Advertisement` to the `AdsManagerData` project we created earlier. This
class has a bit more functionality than the previous class. It is responsible for loading the details for a
single advertisement, updating the details for an advertisement, creating a new advertisement, and
recording clicks and impressions for an existing advertisement. The tricky part of this class comes in
completely abstracting the source of the data. As you'll see, the data for a single 'advertisement' entity is
split between both a database and an XML file. The business layer above, however, has no idea that this
split exists. This allows us flexibility in upgrading the class to obtain more information from more
sources. In pure OOP terms, this concept is called **information aggregation** or **information hiding**.

> *Note that the `Retrieve` method in the business object accesses the XML file directly. Strictly
> speaking, if we wanted to be true to the tier-separation model, even though we're only accessing a
> text file, we should still do all data access (regardless of the storage medium) in the data-services
> tier. So the data layer `Retrieve` method could integrate data from the XML file, and we could
> add columns to the row that the data object returns programmatically, so it will appear to the
> business tier that it all came from one database. We won't take this approach here but bear in mind
> that it is an option.*

The Advertisement class has no properties and provides the following methods:

- **Create** – creates a new advertisement in the database, as well as populating the AdRotator XML file with the appropriate data. Invokes the sp_AdsManager_CreateAdvertisement procedure.

- **RecordClick** – records in the summary tables that a click occurred on a given advertisement. Invokes the procedure sp_AdsManager_RecordClick.

- **RecordImpression** – records in the summary tables that an impression occurred on a given advertisement. Invokes the procedure sp_AdsManager_RecordImpression.

- **RetrieveAd** – obtains all the relevant details for a given advertisement. Pulls information from the database via the sp_AdsManager_GetAdvertDetails stored procedure.

- **Update** – saves changes to an existing advertisement by calling the sp_AdsManager_UpdateAdvertisement stored procedure and by modifying the XML configuration file.

Let's take a look at the source for Advertisement.vb (found in the project for the Wrox.WebModules.AdsManager.Data namespace, which is in the AdsManagerData class library we've been working with up to this point). Most of the code is straightforward, providing methods to retrieve details of an ad, and for recording an impression or click:

```vb
Imports System
Imports System.Data
Imports System.Data.SqlClient
Imports System.Xml
Imports Wrox.WebModules.Data
Imports Wrox.WebModules.AdsManager


Namespace WebModules.AdsManager.Data

  Public Class Advertisement
    Inherits Wrox.WebModules.Data.DbObject

    Public Sub New(ByVal newConnectionString As String)
      MyBase.New(newConnectionString)
    End Sub

    Public Function RetrieveAd(ByVal advertisementId As Integer) As DataRow

      Dim parameters As SqlParameter() = { _
        New SqlParameter("@AdvertisementID", SqlDbType.Int, 4)}
      parameters(0).Value = advertisementId

      Dim ads As DataSet
      Try
        ads = RunProcedure( _
          "sp_AdsManager_GetAdvertDetails", parameters, "Advertisements")
        Return ads.Tables(0).Rows(0)
      Finally
```

```
            ads.Dispose()
        End Try

    End Function

    Public Sub RecordImpression(ByVal advertisementId As Integer)

        Dim rowsAffected As Integer

        Dim parameters As SqlParameter() = { _
            New SqlParameter("@AdvertisementID", SqlDbType.Int, 4)}
        parameters(0).Value = advertisementId

        RunProcedure( _
            "sp_AdsManager_RecordImpression", parameters, rowsAffected)

    End Sub


    Public Sub RecordClick(ByVal advertisementId As Integer)

        Dim rowsAffected As Integer

        Dim parameters As SqlParameter() = { _
            New SqlParameter("@AdvertisementID", SqlDbType.Int, 4)}
        parameters(0).Value = advertisementId

        RunProcedure("sp_AdsManager_RecordClick", parameters, rowsAffected)

    End Sub
```

The Create method is a little more complex . We have seen that the AdRotator gets its data from an XML file. We want to keep this, as much as possible, secret from the business layer. So, when the business layer issues a call to create an advert, we need to synchronize entries between the database and the XML file.

The start of the method deals with adding details of the advertisement to the database:

```
    Public Sub Create( _
        ByVal imageUrl As String, _
        ByVal trueNavigateUrl As String, _
        ByVal alternateText As String, _
        ByVal keyword As String, _
        ByVal companyId As Integer, _
        ByVal description As String, _
        ByVal rotatorFile As String)

        Dim rowsAffected As Integer

        Dim parameters As SqlParameter() = { _
            New SqlParameter("@CompanyID", SqlDbType.Int, 4), _
            New SqlParameter("@Description", SqlDbType.VarChar, 255), _
            New SqlParameter("@TrueNavigateUrl", SqlDbType.VarChar, 255), _
```

```
            New SqlParameter("@AdvertisementID", SqlDbType.Int, 4)}

    parameters(0).Value = companyId
    parameters(1).Value = description
    parameters(2).Value = trueNavigateUrl
    parameters(3).Direction = ParameterDirection.Output

    RunProcedure( _
      "sp_AdsManager_CreateAdvertisement", parameters, rowsAffected)
```

We then need to add the advertisement to the XML file that drives the AdRotator control. We also want the link taken when the user clicks an ad to be to the pass-through page. There we need to retrieve the true destination, and forward the user to it. These are issues for the presentation layer, but it does mean that when we create an ad entry we need to enter the link to the pass-through, and not the true target, into the AdRotator's XML file. The link to the pass-through needs to provide all the information we need to record the click and pass the user on to the correct site.

So the link we use as NavigateUrl in the XML file will include the ad ID as a parameter, which the pass-through page can use to obtain full details from the database.

Below, we're going to use some standard XML code to create the appropriate elements and save them in the AdRotator's XML file. The location of this XML file is stored in our config file (AdsManager.Config) and retrieved using the standard configuration classes. When we add the advert to the database, the stored procedure returns the new ad's ID. We use that in the XML file's NavigateUrl:

```
    Dim settings As Configuration.ModuleSettings = _
        Configuration.ModuleConfig.GetSettings()

    Dim rotatorDom As New XmlDocument()
    rotatorDom.Load(rotatorFile)

    Dim temp As XmlElement
    Dim newAd As XmlElement = rotatorDom.CreateElement("Ad")

    temp = rotatorDom.CreateElement("ImageUrl")
    temp.InnerText = imageUrl
    newAd.AppendChild(temp)

    temp = rotatorDom.CreateElement("NavigateUrl")
    temp.InnerText = settings.PassThroughPage & "?AD=" & _
      parameters(3).Value.ToString()
    newAd.AppendChild(temp)

    temp = rotatorDom.CreateElement("AlternateText")
    temp.InnerText = alternateText
    newAd.AppendChild(temp)

    temp = rotatorDom.CreateElement("Keyword")
    temp.InnerText = keyword
    newAd.AppendChild(temp)
```

```
        temp = rotatorDom.CreateElement("Impressions")
        temp.InnerText = "1"
        newAd.AppendChild(temp)

        rotatorDom.DocumentElement.AppendChild(newAd)
        rotatorDom.Save(rotatorFile)

    End Sub
```

The Update method is very similar to the Create method that we just looked at. Like the Create method, it starts with code to make the changes to the database:

```
    Public Sub Update( _
      ByVal advertisementId As Integer, _
      ByVal imageUrl As String, _
      ByVal trueNavigateUrl As String, _
      ByVal alternateText As String, _
      ByVal keyword As String, _
      ByVal description As String, _
      ByVal impressions As Integer, _
      ByVal active As Boolean, _
      ByVal rotatorFile As String)

      Dim rowsAffected As Integer

      Dim parameters As SqlParameter() = { _
        New SqlParameter("@AdvertisementID", SqlDbType.Int, 4), _
        New SqlParameter("@TrueNavigateUrl", SqlDbType.VarChar, 255), _
        New SqlParameter("@Description", SqlDbType.VarChar, 255), _
        New SqlParameter("@Active", SqlDbType.Bit)}

      parameters(0).Value = advertisementId
      parameters(1).Value = trueNavigateUrl
      parameters(2).Value = description
      parameters(3).Value = active

      RunProcedure( _
        "sp_AdsManager_UpdateAdvertisement", parameters, rowsAffected)
```

In this next section of this method, we update the information contained in the AdRotator's XML file. This is a bit trickier than creating the original <Ad> element in the Create method. In order to update a single element in a database or file, we need to *locate* the item we're updating. In an RDBMS we do this by supplying a key, or some information about the row that is entirely unique to that row only.

The AdRotator XML file doesn't contain any support for numeric identifiers. We didn't want to modify the format of the AdRotator XML file – that would negate the purpose of reusing an existing control. However, we do know that the database ID of an advertisement is stored in the NavigateUrl element. Therefore, we're going to use the NavigateUrl element as our unique key and we'll use a little XPath to find the appropriate element:

```
        Dim settings As Configuration.ModuleSettings = _
          Configuration.ModuleConfig.GetSettings()

        Dim rotatorDom As New XmlDocument()
        rotatorDom.Load(rotatorFile)

        ' Must locate the right XML element to update. This is the one
        ' containing a NavigateUrl element with "?AD=NNN", where NNN is
        ' the advertisementId passed to this method.
        Dim temp As XmlElement
        Dim xPathFind As String = "//Ad[NavigateUrl=""" & _
          settings.PassThroughPage & "?AD=" & _
          advertisementId.ToString() & """]"
        Dim currentAd As XmlElement = _
    CType(rotatorDom.DocumentElement.SelectSingleNode(xPathFind), XmlElement)

        temp = CType(currentAd.SelectSingleNode("ImageUrl"), XmlElement)
        temp.InnerText = imageUrl

        temp = CType(currentAd.SelectSingleNode("AlternateText"), XmlElement)
        temp.InnerText = alternateText

        temp = CType(currentAd.SelectSingleNode("Keyword"), XmlElement)
        temp.InnerText = keyword

        temp = CType(currentAd.SelectSingleNode("Impressions"), XmlElement)
        temp.InnerText = impressions.ToString()

        rotatorDom.Save(rotatorFile)
    End Sub
```

The Business Layer

The advertising module only deals with keeping track of advertisements, and as such shouldn't have an overly complex object model. Our business tier is also a small one, consisting of only two main classes: AdMaster and Advertisement. The following sections give a detailed description and source listing of each of the classes in our business layer. But before we get into the source code for the classes in this project, let's actually create the project. To do this, we create a new Class Library and add it to the current solution (ThePhile). Then, we set the default namespace and output file to Wrox.WebModules.AdsManager.Business.

The AdMaster Class

The AdMaster class in the business layer is a layer of abstraction on top of the AdMaster class in the data-services tier. It implements four methods:

❑ Default constructor.

❑ **GetCompanyList** – this method obtains a list of all companies in the system. It is sorted alphabetically. It is a simple forwarded call to the data tier to populate a DataSet.

❑ **GetAdList** – this method obtains a list of all advertisements in the system. It is a forwarded call to the data tier to populate a DataSet.

303

❑ **CreateCompany** – a method with no return value that creates a new company in the database by forwarding the call to the data tier.

These methods just make simple requests to the data layer so they don't really need much explanation. Here is the full class:

```
Imports System
Imports System.Data

Imports Wrox.WebModules.AdsManager

Namespace WebModules.AdsManager.Business

  Public Class AdMaster

    Public Sub New()
    End Sub

    Public Function GetCompanyList() As DataSet

      Dim admaster As AdsManager.Data.AdMaster = _
        New AdsManager.Data.AdMaster( _
          Configuration.ModuleConfig.GetSettings().ConnectionString)
      Return admaster.GetCompanyList()
    End Function

    Public Function GetAdList() As DataSet

      Dim admaster As AdsManager.Data.AdMaster = _
        New AdsManager.Data.AdMaster( _
          Configuration.ModuleConfig.GetSettings().ConnectionString)
      Return admaster.GetAdList()
    End Function

    Public Sub CreateCompany(ByVal companyName As String)
      Dim admaster As AdsManager.Data.AdMaster = _
        New AdsManager.Data.AdMaster( _
          Configuration.ModuleConfig.GetSettings().ConnectionString)
      admaster.CreateCompany(companyName)
    End Sub
  End Class
End Namespace
```

The Advertisement Class

The `Advertisement` class is the core component in our business tier. It is added as a new class in our `AdsManagerBusiness` project. It is responsible for handling all of the activities that can take place with regard to an advertisement, such as creation, deletion, updating, and recording clicks and impressions. Most calls are forwards to the data tier, though some logic often takes place before the call to the data-services component.

We start with the private members that will hold the details of the advertisement and a default constructor for creating an empty advertisement object.

```
Imports System
Imports System.Web
Imports System.Data
Imports System.Xml

Imports Wrox.WebModules.AdsManager

Namespace WebModules.AdsManager.Business

  Public Class Advertisement
    Inherits Wrox.WebModules.Business.BizObject

    Private myImageUrl As String
    Private myNavigateUrl As String
    Private myAlternateText As String
    Private myKeyword As String
    Private myImpressions As Integer
    Private myTrueNavigateUrl As String

    Private myAdvertisementId As Integer
    Private myCompanyId As Integer
    Private myIsActive As Boolean
    Private myDescription As String

    Public Sub New()
      ' Constructor used when creating an empty instance.
    End Sub
```

Our other constructor is rather more complex. It takes the ID of an advert and populates the object with the correct details, by making calls to the data layer.

```
    Public Sub New(ByVal advertId As Integer)

      Dim context As HttpContext = HttpContext.Current
      Dim settings As Configuration.ModuleSettings = _
        Configuration.ModuleConfig.GetSettings()
      Dim xPathFind As String = "//Ad[NavigateUrl=""" & _
        settings.PassThroughPage & "?AD=" & advertId.ToString() & """]"

      Dim ad As New Data.Advertisement(settings.ConnectionString)
      Dim advertData As DataRow = ad.RetrieveAd(advertId)

      myAdvertisementId = advertId
      myDescription = CStr(advertData("Description"))
      myTrueNavigateUrl = CStr(advertData("TrueNavigateUrl"))
      myIsActive = CBool(advertData("Active"))
      myCompanyId = CInt(advertData("CompanyId"))

' Now fill up the rest of the properties with information from the XML file.
      Dim adDom As New XmlDocument()
      adDom.Load(context.Server.MapPath(settings.RotatorXmlFile))
      Dim adCurrent As XmlElement = CType( _
        adDom.DocumentElement.SelectSingleNode(xPathFind), XmlElement)
```

```
    If adCurrent Is Nothing Then
      Throw New InvalidOperationException( _
        "Advertisement Selected Does not Exist in Rotator XML Source")
    End If

  myImageUrl = adCurrent.SelectSingleNode("ImageUrl").InnerText
  myNavigateUrl = adCurrent.SelectSingleNode("NavigateUrl").InnerText
  myAlternateText = adCurrent.SelectSingleNode("AlternateText").InnerText
  myKeyword = adCurrent.SelectSingleNode("Keyword").InnerText
  myImpressions = Convert.ToInt32( _
    adCurrent.SelectSingleNode("Impressions").InnerText)

End Sub
```

The methods for recording impressions and clicks, creating a new advertisement and updating the data layer are all very simple:

```
Public Sub RecordImpression()
  Dim settings As Configuration.ModuleSettings = _
    Configuration.ModuleConfig.GetSettings()
  Dim currentAd As New _
    Data.Advertisement(settings.ConnectionString)

  currentAd.RecordImpression(myAdvertisementId)
End Sub


Public Sub RecordClick()
  Dim settings As Configuration.ModuleSettings = _
    Configuration.ModuleConfig.GetSettings()
  Dim currentAd As New _
    Data.Advertisement(settings.ConnectionString)

  currentAd.RecordClick(myAdvertisementId)
End Sub

Public Sub Create()
  Dim context As HttpContext = HttpContext.Current
  Dim settings As Configuration.ModuleSettings = _
    Configuration.ModuleConfig.GetSettings()
  Dim newAd As New Data.Advertisement(settings.ConnectionString)

  newAd.Create( _
      myImageUrl, _
      myTrueNavigateUrl, _
      myAlternateText, _
      myKeyword, _
      myCompanyId, _
      myDescription, _
      context.Server.MapPath(settings.RotatorXmlFile))
End Sub


Public Sub Update()
```

```
                 Dim context As HttpContext = HttpContext.Current
                 Dim settings As Configuration.ModuleSettings = _
                   Configuration.ModuleConfig.GetSettings()
                 Dim currentAd As New Data.Advertisement(settings.ConnectionString)

                 currentAd.Update( _
                     myAdvertisementId, _
                     myImageUrl, _
                     myTrueNavigateUrl, _
                     myAlternateText, _
                     myKeyword, _
                     myDescription, _
                     myImpressions, _
                     myIsActive, _
                     context.Server.MapPath(settings.RotatorXmlFile))
             End Sub
```

The class also includes publicly exposed properties to allow us to access and alter the details of an advertisement. We won't bother showing these here.

The Presentation Layer

Our presentation layer consists of several ASP pages and the code-behind classes that support them. Keep in mind that all our changes and additions to the presentation tier take place in the original ThePhile web application project that is part of our main solution. In addition, we've made some changes to the SiteFooter control in order to facilitate the display of our banner ads. The following is a list of the elements that compose our presentation tier:

❑ Admin.aspx [.vb] – main page of the advertising administration system. Displays the list of advertisements in a data grid and contains links for creating ads and entries for companies.

❑ AdDetail.aspx [.vb] – web page and related code-behind class to display and edit the details of a given advertisement.

❑ NewAd.aspx [.vb] – web form for creating a new advertisement.

❑ NewCompany.aspx [.vb] – web form for creating a new entry for a company.

❑ Passthrough.aspx [.vb] – pass-through page (discussed next) facilitating proper auditing of hits on banner advertisements.

The Pass-through Page

Despite the fact that this page has absolutely no user interface, it is the most important part of the entire advertising module. Without this page the advertising module cannot function at all.

The purpose of this page is to accept an incoming request that contains a single URL parameter, called AD. This parameter contains the numeric ID of a particular advertisement that has been clicked. The page then looks up the advertisement in the database to find out the *actual* destination intended for the advertisement. Once this information has been obtained, the page records a click on the advertisement in the database and re-directs the user to the appropriate advertiser's product or home page.

To see how this works, take a look at the `Page_Load` event of the `Passthrough.aspx.vb` file:

```
Private Sub Page_Load(ByVal sender As Object, ByVal e As EventArgs)
  Dim currentAd As New _
    AdsBusiness.Advertisement(Convert.ToInt32(Request("AD")))

  currentAd.RecordClick()
  Response.Redirect(currentAd.TrueNavigateUrl)
End Sub
```

The New SiteFooter Control

In order to get the advertisements to appear all over our site without having to re-write too much of our existing code, we're going to modify the `SiteFooter` control. Because we built all of the pages to use the footer control to begin with, only a few changes are required in order to display our `AdRotator` control.

Take a look at the new code for the `SiteFooter` control (`SiteFooter.ascx`), which replaces the original:

```
<%@ Control Language="vb" AutoEventWireup="false"
           Codebehind="SiteFooter.ascx.vb"
           Inherits="Wrox.ThePhile.Web.Controls.User.SiteFooter"
           TargetSchema="http://schemas.microsoft.com/intellisense/ie5" %>
<table width="100%" border="0" cellspacing="0" cellpadding="0">
<tr>
  <td align="middle">
    <font face="arial" size="1">
      <br><br>
      <asp:AdRotator ID=Rotator Runat=server
                 AdvertisementFile="/ThePhile/Config/AdRotator.xml"/>
      <br>
      <i>Copyright &copy; 2001-2002 Wrox Press Ltd.</i><br>
      <a href="Contact.aspx">Contact Us</a> | Support | FAQ | Forums |
                        Newsletter | Voting | Your Account
    </font>
  </td>
</tr>
</table>
```

We've added an `<asp:AdRotator>` control, given it a name (`ID`), and pointed it to the appropriate XML file.

Putting the `AdRotator` in the page as we've shown above gives us the ability to track clicks and display the ad, but it isn't quite complete if we need to track impressions (displays). In order to do that, we need to provide a handler for the `AdCreated` event, which is listed below (found in the code-behind class in `SiteFooter.ascx.vb`):

```
Private Sub Rotator_AdCreated(ByVal sender As Object, _
    ByVal e As AdCreatedEventArgs) Handles Rotator.AdCreated

    Dim advertId As Integer
    Dim adNumber As String
```

```
      Dim eqPos As Integer

      eqPos = e.NavigateUrl.IndexOf("=")
      adNumber = _
        e.NavigateUrl.Substring(eqPos + 1, e.NavigateUrl.Length - eqPos - 1)
      advertId = Convert.ToInt32(adNumber)

      Dim currentAd As New AdsBusiness.Advertisement(advertId)
      currentAd.RecordImpression()
    End Sub
```

In the code above, we need to determine *which* advertisement has been displayed. As we said earlier, the default implementation of the AdRotator control doesn't support numbering or keying of individual advertisements. Therefore, to find the database ID of the advertisement that was displayed we need to extrapolate it from other information. For the duration of this event, we have access to the standard information about the advertisement, such as the NavigateUrl property. We know that this property contains the AD parameter to send to the pass-through page. The above code extracts that value from the URL and uses it to create a new instance of the advertisement class in order to record the impression.

You may have noticed by now that the RecordImpression and RecordClick methods both eventually call the database. This means that every time the SiteFooter control is displayed on the bottom of a page, a call to the stored procedure is made to record an impression. This is a little on the inefficient side. As an exercise, you might want to consider ways to speed up this process and make it more efficient for recording clicks and impressions. One option might be to maintain an in-memory cache of clicks and impressions, and periodically flush that cache to the database rather than make a database call every single time an impression or a click takes place.

Administering Advertisements

There are two things we can do with advertisements: display them and administer them. We've already seen how to display the advertisements, and we've seen the business and data components that enable the administration. Now let's take a look at implementing the administration system.

Admin.aspx

This page should be treated as the default page for the administration section of the advertising module. It displays a list of all of the advertisements in the database in a DataGrid that is coded to support data paging. It also allows us to click a link in that DataGrid to drill down into a detailed view page. There are links to create companies and advertisements from here. Here is a screenshot of the advertisement administration main page:

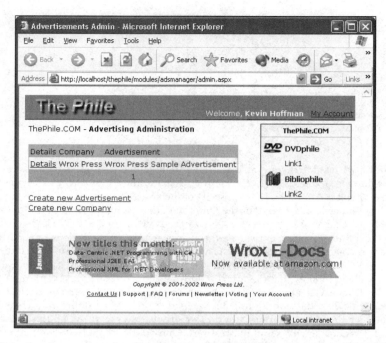

You can see from the above screenshot that there is a single advertisement currently in the database. This particular advertisement is one that links back to the Wrox Press home page. You can see the advertisement indicated by the DataGrid displayed at the bottom of the page in the SiteFooter control.

Let's take a look at the HTML code in the ASPX page that creates the DataGrid:

```
<asp:DataGrid id="adsGrid" runat="server"
      AutoGenerateColumns="False"
      BorderColor="Tan"
      BorderWidth="1px"
      BackColor="LightGoldenrodYellow"
      CellPadding="2"
      GridLines="None"
      AllowPaging="True"
      PageSize="15"
      ForeColor="Black">
    <SelectedItemStyle
          ForeColor="GhostWhite"
          BackColor="DarkSlateBlue" />
    <AlternatingItemStyle BackColor="PaleGoldenrod" />
    <HeaderStyle Font-Bold="True" BackColor="Tan" />
    <FooterStyle BackColor="Tan" />
    <Columns>
        <asp:ButtonColumn
              Text="Details"
              HeaderText="Details"
              CommandName="Details" />
        <asp:BoundColumn
```

```
                         DataField="CompanyName"
                         HeaderText="Company" />
              <asp:BoundColumn
                         DataField="Description"
                         HeaderText="Advertisement" />
              <asp:BoundColumn
                         Visible="False"
                         DataField="AdvertisementId" />
       </Columns>
       <PagerStyle
              HorizontalAlign="Center"
              ForeColor="DarkSlateBlue"
              BackColor="DarkKhaki"
              Mode="NumericPages" />
</asp:DataGrid>
```

The DataGrid uses a ButtonColumn, has defined a PagerStyle, and has enabled the
AllowPaging flag.

The ButtonColumn is a custom templated column that allows programmers to place a button in a
DataGrid column and give the button access to the information contained within the DataGrid. In
our case, the ButtonColumn re-directs the user to the AdDetail.aspx page, allowing the user to edit
an existing advertisement. It does this by providing a handler for the ItemCommand event in the
DataGrid, which is triggered when a command-button is clicked on a row. Here is the method that
handles the ItemCommand event in Admin.aspx.vb:

```
    Private Sub adsGrid_ItemCommand( _
      ByVal source As Object, _
      ByVal e As DataGridCommandEventArgs) _
      Handles adsGrid.ItemCommand

      If e.CommandName = "Details" Then

         Dim Id As String = e.Item.Cells(3).Text
         Response.Redirect(("AdDetail.aspx?AD=" + Id))

      End If
    End Sub
```

Only one ItemCommand event handler is used for the entire DataGrid, regardless of how many
ButtonColumns are used. The items differentiate themselves by providing a CommandName property.
Therefore, we check if the CommandName property of the command was "Details". If so, then we can
continue. The first thing we do is to obtain the ID of the advertisement clicked. This is accomplished by
getting the value of the last bound column in the row. This particular column is hidden, allowing us to
make the ID easily available without cluttering up our display with information the end user might find
useless or confusing.

Next we need to support paging across a large result set. The stored procedure for obtaining the list of
advertisements pulls the entire set, so it is possible that the UI would get cluttered extremely fast
without providing support for paging. Just simply enabling the AllowPaging property on the
DataGrid isn't quite enough to support paging. We need to provide a handler for the
PageIndexChanged event, which is listed next:

```
Private Sub adsGrid_PageIndexChanged( _
  ByVal source As Object, _
  ByVal e As DataGridPageChangedEventArgs) _
  Handles adsGrid.PageIndexChanged

  adsGrid.CurrentPageIndex = e.NewPageIndex
  DoDataBind()
End Sub
```

First we obtain the new page index, and then we bind the DataGrid accordingly, having set its current page index to the new page. This allows the grid to move to the right page within the data set. The following is a listing for the DoDataBind method in Admin.aspx.vb, which binds the data to the DataGrid:

```
Private Sub DoDataBind()
  Dim admaster As New AdsBusiness.AdMaster()
  Dim adsSet As DataSet = admaster.GetAdList()

  adsGrid.DataSource = adsSet.Tables(0)
  adsGrid.DataBind()
End Sub
```

AdDetail.aspx

We've seen how the main page, which displays a list of advertisements and allows us to drill-down to edit an existing one, was made. Now let's take a look at the AdDetail.aspx page. After clicking the Details link on the DataGrid, the user is presented with a pre-populated web form like this:

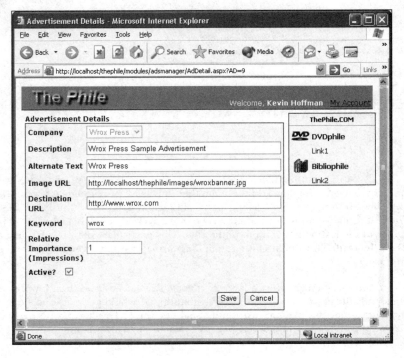

It looks like a pretty standard input form. It presents the user with all the fields they can edit (as well as displaying a read-only company dropdown, an example of the UI enforcing a business rule) and then presents the user with **Save** and **Cancel** buttons. The **Cancel** button takes the user back to the `Admin` page, while the **Save** button will commit the changes both to the database and to the rotator XML file. The UI makes no visible distinction as to which data is stored in the XML file and which data is stored in the database. That boundary is completely invisible to the presentation layer.

Let's take a look at the code that sets up the pre-population for the form:

```
Private Sub DoDataBind()
  Dim currentAd As New _
    AdsBusiness.Advertisement(Convert.ToInt32(Request("AD")))
  Dim admaster As New AdsBusiness.AdMaster()
  Dim companies As DataSet = admaster.GetCompanyList()

  lbCompanies.DataSource = companies.Tables(0)
  lbCompanies.DataTextField = "Description"
  lbCompanies.DataValueField = "CompanyId"
  lbCompanies.DataBind()
  lbCompanies.SelectedIndex = lbCompanies.Items.IndexOf( _
    lbCompanies.Items.FindByValue(currentAd.CompanyId.ToString()))

  Description.Text = currentAd.Description
  ImageUrl.Text = currentAd.ImageUrl
  TrueNavigateUrl.Text = currentAd.TrueNavigateUrl
  Keyword.Text = currentAd.KeyWord
  Impressions.Text = currentAd.Impressions.ToString()
  AlternateText.Text = currentAd.AlternateText
  Active.Checked = currentAd.IsActive
End Sub
```

The method is called `DoDataBind` more out of convention than anything else – not much binding is going on. The `Text` property of the input controls is being manually set to the data retrieved from the instance of the advertisement. The only binding happening is the binding of the company drop-down list to the list of companies retrieved by the `AdMaster` object. Because we are editing a single record, and will only ever save or cancel, the 'pre-populate' approach is better.

When editing an advertisement, the company drop-down listbox is disabled. This establishes a business rule preventing the company ownership of an advertisement campaign.

When the user has finished making changes, they click the **Save** button and trigger the following event (`SaveChanges_Click`, a button click handler):

```
Private Sub SaveChanges_Click( _
  ByVal sender As Object, _
  ByVal e As EventArgs) _
  Handles SaveChanges.Click

  Dim advertId As Integer = Convert.ToInt32(Request("AD"))
  Dim currentAd As New AdsBusiness.Advertisement(advertId)
```

```
        currentAd.AlternateText = AlternateText.Text
        currentAd.Description = Description.Text
        currentAd.ImageUrl = ImageUrl.Text
        currentAd.Impressions = Convert.ToInt32(Impressions.Text)
        currentAd.IsActive = Active.Checked
        currentAd.KeyWord = Keyword.Text
        currentAd.TrueNavigateUrl = TrueNavigateUrl.Text
        currentAd.Update()

        Response.Redirect("Admin.aspx")
    End Sub
```

NewAd.aspx

This page works much like the `AdDetail.aspx` page. However, it doesn't allow you to set the value of the `Impressions` property (that is set to 1 for all newly created advertisements). It also doesn't allow you to choose the `Active` checkbox because a newly created advertisement is considered active by default. The following is a screenshot of the "New Advertisement" web form:

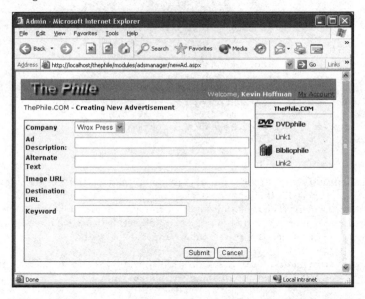

Again, the only binding we're going to use on this form is going to be for the drop-down list. This is done in our `DoInitialDataBind` method, shown below (from `NewAd.aspx.vb`):

```
    Private Sub DoInitialDataBind()
      Dim adMaster As New Wrox.WebModules.AdsManager.Business.AdMaster()

      myCompanies = adMaster.GetCompanyList()
      lbCompanies.DataSource = myCompanies.Tables(0)
      lbCompanies.DataTextField = "Description"
      lbCompanies.DataValueField = "CompanyId"
      lbCompanies.DataBind()
    End Sub
```

When the user has completed the form and is ready to create the new advertisement, this code handles the `Click` event of the Submit button:

```
        Private Sub OKButton_Click( _
          ByVal sender As Object, _
          ByVal e As EventArgs) _
          Handles OKButton.Click

          Dim newAd As New Ads.Business.Advertisement()

          newAd.ImageUrl = ImageUrl.Text
          newAd.Description = Description.Text
          newAd.TrueNavigateUrl = NavigateUrl.Text
          newAd.KeyWord = Keyword.Text
          newAd.AlternateText = AlternateText.Text
          newAd.CompanyId = Convert.ToInt32( _
            lbCompanies.Items(lbCompanies.SelectedIndex).Value)
          newAd.Create()

          Response.Redirect("Admin.aspx")
        End Sub
```

Module Configuration

As with the previous modules we have a configuration file that is identified in the main `Web.Config` in the following way:

```
    <!-- LOCAL APPLICATION SETTINGS -->
      <appSettings>
        <add key="Accounts_SettingsFile"
             value="/ThePhile/Config/Accounts.Config"/>
        <add key="AdsManager_SettingsFile"
             value="/ThePhile/Config/AdsManager.Config"/>
      </appSettings>
```

The `AdsManager.Config` file contains the following entries:

```
    <?xml version="1.0"?>
    <ModuleSettings xmlns:xsi="http://www.w3.org/2001/XMLSchema-instance"
                    xmlns:xsd="http://www.w3.org/2001/XMLSchema">
      <ConnectionString>server=(local);database=ThePhile;uid=sa;pwd=;
      </ConnectionString>
      <RotatorXmlFile>/ThePhile/Config/AdRotator.Xml</RotatorXmlFile>
      <PassThroughPage>/ThePhile/Modules/AdsManager/PassThrough.aspx
      </PassThroughPage>
    </ModuleSettings>
```

As you can see, it contains its own database connection string to allow for maximum flexibility. If, for some reason, an administrator wanted the advertising database to be separate from all the others, then the only requirement would be to change the connection string in this config file. There are definitions for the rotator XML file (which we have already covered in detail) and for the pass-through page.

The source code for the module configuration class files has been covered already in this book and by now you should be able to determine what the property definitions for the `ModuleSettings` class might look like for the above XML file. Of course, the complete class is available in the download if you want to have a look.

Summary

Advertising is an interesting and exciting facet of doing business on the web. Many websites pay their bills by offering advertising. Website owners and administrators can track the demographics of their audience and use that information to convince advertisers that paying for impressions on their site is a worthwhile investment. Those same administrators can also keep track of how many impressions and clicks a particular advertisement receives and use that information to bill the client (advertiser).

After reading this chapter, you should have a solid understanding of:

❑ Storing information on advertisements by aggregating both XML and RDBMS data in the data layer, hiding the distinction from the business layer.

❑ Keeping audit trails of clicks and impressions by trapping events in the `AdRotator` control and doing some data warehousing in the database.

❑ Providing sufficient information to advertisers to prove ad effectiveness (or lack of) by providing a stored procedure designed to pull reporting information from the data warehouse.

So far we've looked at several ways of providing our site visitors with information. In the next chapter we'll show how to find out what our readers think, by implementing an opinion polls module.

8

Polls

In this chapter we'll discuss polls – which comprise questions with sets of optional responses that the user can select from and vote for. First we'll recap why polls are useful and important for different websites. We'll then demonstrate how to design and implement an easily pluggable and maintainable voting module for our ThePhile.com site. We'll also show how to make it accessible to external clients, such as other sites or Windows programs, via a web service.

The Problem

We briefly discussed the benefits of polls in Chapter 1. To recap, sites that provide a poll usually do so because they are interested in what people think. They use polls as a form of user-to-site communication because they want views on the products they sell or review, or opinions about the market in general, or they want to know who the users are, their age, their occupation, and other demographic information. Good polls always contain targeted questions that can help the site's managers to know who their users are and what they want to find on the site. This information can be used to identify which parts of the site to improve.

Polls are valuable for e-commerce sites too, because they can indicate for which products the interest and demand are higher. Armed with this information, e-commerce businesses can highlight those products, provide more detailed descriptions or case studies, or offer discounts to convince users to buy from their site.

Another use for the information is to attract advertising revenue. If you look on any middle to large site the chances are that you'll see an "Advertise with us" link, or something similar. On that page you'll probably find information about the age of the typical users, the region or country they live in, and sometimes also their average income. This information is often gathered by direct or indirect polls. The more details you provide about your typical audience, the more chance you have of finding a sponsor to advertise on your site.

Another benefit is user-to-user communication. Users generally like to know what their peers think about a product or a subject of interest to them, and maybe even how much they earn! I must admit that I'm usually curious when I see a poll on a website. Even if I don't have a very clear opinion about the question being asked, I vote, often because I want to know which is the most popular response! This explains why polls are usually well accepted, and why users generally vote quite willingly.

Another reason why users might be willing to vote is that they may feel that their choice has some significance for the people behind the scenes. The votes actually are important; as we've seen, the results can drive the future content of the site and other decisions.

That said, we want the benefits of a poll facility for ThePhile.com, and therefore want to implement some form of poll on the website. Now we should consider some further details about web polls, namely the problems that we must address to successfully run a polling system.

First of all, as for the news and other content, the same poll shouldn't remain active for too long. If we leave the same poll on the page for, say, two months, we might gather some more votes, but we risk losing the interest of users who voted early on. Neither can we keep a poll up for just a couple of days, at least not if we want to achieve significant results. The right duration depends mostly on the average number of visitors we have and how often they come back to visit the site. As a rough guide, if we know that several thousands of users regularly come to visit the site each week, then that is a good duration for the active poll. Otherwise, if we have less visitors, we can leave the poll for two or more weeks, but probably never longer than a month.

In case you're wondering how to get the information you need to make this decision, there are several services that allow you to easily retrieve statistics for your site, such as the frequency and the number of visitors, and much more. Some of these services are commercial, but you can also find some good ones for free: examples are www.extremetracking.com, www.sitemeter.com, and www.fastcounter.com, but there are others. Most of these services give you some information for free, while other statistics (such as visitors by search engine and search word, client browser information, traffic forecast, etc.) are subscription-based. Of course you could implement your own hit counter – it would be pretty easy to track visitors and generate some basic statistics, but to reproduce all the advanced features sold by specialized services would involve quite a lot of work, and it would probably be cheaper to subscribe to the professional/advanced plan of one of the services mentioned above.

When you change the active poll, a new question arises – what to do with the old questions and their results. Should we throw them away? Certainly not! They might be very interesting for new users who didn't take part in the vote, and the information will probably remain valid for some time, so we should keep them available for viewing. They can even be considered as part of the content of our site, and we should probably build an archive of past polls.

If we allow a user to vote however many times they want to, we'll end up with incorrect results. The vote will be biased towards that user's personal opinion. Having false results is just as useless as having no results at all, since we can't base any serious decisions on them. Therefore, in general we will want to prevent the user from voting more than once for the same question.

However, there are occasions when we might want to allow the user to vote several times. For example, during the development and testing stage, we may need to post many votes to see if the module works well. The administrator could just manually add some votes through the Enterprise Manager's table viewer, or by directly calling the appropriate stored procedure. But using the polling user interface that we'll build is a much more convenient method, that more thoroughly tests the module, so we want to leave this door open.

There are reasons for wanting to allow multiple votes after deployment too. Imagine that we are running a competition to select the best resource on any selected topic, and the list of these resources (external sites, our site's sections, downloads, etc.) is updated weekly, and the competition lasts one month. If we prevented multiple votes we would have to create a new poll for each of the four weeks, and after one month we would need to add together the results of the four distinct polls to get the final winner. There wouldn't be much extra work to do, but it's not very elegant. A better and quicker solution would be to have only one poll for the entire month, but allow the user to re-vote, with the limitation of one vote per week. This way, at the end of the month we will have the final results without doing anything else.

> *In this discussion we're talking about polls that only allow a single option to be selected (those poll boxes with a series of radiobuttons). However, there is also another type of poll that allows the user to vote for multiple options in a single step (the options are listed with checkboxes, and you can select more than one). This might be useful if you wanted to ask a question like "What do you usually buy online?" and you wanted to allow the user to answer "books, DVDs, games, etc." through multiple separate options. However, this type of poll is quite rare. The design of this type of poll would complicate our module, so we decided to leave it out. But be aware that they exist, and you may want to use them in situations like the one mentioned above.*

So in summary our problem definition is that we want to implement a poll facility on our site to gauge the opinions of our users and to generate a sense of community. We don't want users to lose interest but we want the results to be significant, so we will need to add new questions and change the current poll sufficiently often. We also want to generate content for our site, so we'd like to make all the results available for viewing. Finally, we want to control the voting so the results are as unbiased and accurate as possible.

In the next section we're going to discuss the design in more detail, and consider how we will solve these problems.

The Design

As usual, in this section we're going to work on the design of the solution. We'll be looking at how we can provide voting functionality for our site. This module – like most of the others presented in the previous chapters – stores the data (questions, answers, votes, etc.) in the database shared by all modules of this book. To easily access the database we'll need a set of stored procedures and a data-access layer, and a business layer to keep the presentation layer separate from the database and the details of its structure. Of course there will be some sort of user interface that allows the administrators to view and manage the data through their favorite browser.

To start with we'll list the features we want to implement, then we'll begin to design any database tables, stored procedures, data and business layers, user interface services, and security that we need for this module.

Features to Implement

Let's start our discussion by writing down a list of features that the polls module should provide:

❑ In order to easily change the current poll and add or remove questions, the administrator will need an access-protected administration console. It should allow multiple questions, and their options, to be added, edited, or removed. The ability to have multiple questions is important, because we might want to have different polls in different sections of our site. The administration pages should also show the current results for each option, and the total number of votes for each question.

❏ A user control that builds the poll box that can be inserted into any page. The poll box should display the question text and the available options (usually rendered as radio buttons to allow only one choice). Each question will be identified by a unique ID, which should be specified as a custom property for the user control, so that the webmaster can easily change the currently displayed question by setting the value for that property.

❏ We should prevent the user from voting multiple times for the same poll. Or, even better, we should be able to dynamically decide if we want to allow the user to vote more than once, and specify the period for which they will be prevented from voting again. We'll further discuss why we might want to do this in the next section.

❏ We can have only one poll (question) declared as current. When we set a question as being current, the question that was previously the current one should change its state. The current poll will be displayed unless we specify another question ID for the poll box. Any non-archived poll can be displayed. Of course we can have different polls on the site at the same time depending on the section (one for DVDs and one for books, for example), but setting the default question is useful because we'll be able to add a poll box without specifying the ID of the question to display (through the custom property mentioned above). We'll also be able to change the question through the administration console, without manually changing the page and re-uploading it.

❏ A poll should be archived when we decide that we no longer want to use it. Once archived, a question cannot be displayed even if we explicitly declare its ID for the poll box.

❏ A page that displays all the archived polls and their results. We don't need a page for the results of the current poll, since we want to show them in the poll box – instead of the list of options – when we detect that the user has already voted. This way, the users are forced to express their opinion if they want to see the current poll's results. (Once the poll expires it will be archived and anyone can see the results even if they haven't voted.) You can bet this will bring in more votes than if the current results were freely available to users that have not voted.

Shortly we'll see the database tables for this module, and the respective stored procedures. The administration pages don't require further discussion here. The ASP.NET pages of this section are merely a handy user interface for managing the database records through the stored procedures.

As for the user control that creates the poll box, it will be discussed in more detail a bit later, after describing the database tables and stored procedures. What we need to discuss at this point, before starting to think about the database design, is how to handle multiple votes.

Handling Multiple Votes

We discussed above that we want to be able to control whether users can cast multiple votes, and allow them to vote again after a specified period. It would be pretty cool to do this, and we like to implement cool things, so we decided to do it!

So, we want to give the administrator the ability to prevent multiple votes, or to allow multiple votes but with a specified lock duration (one week in the example above). We still have to find a way to ensure that the user does not vote more times than is allowed. The simplest solution is to write a **cookie** to the client that stores the ID of the question for which the user has voted. Then, when the poll box loads, it will first try to find a cookie matching the question. If a cookie is not found the poll box will display the options and the user can vote. Otherwise, the poll box will show the latest results and not allow the user to vote again. To allow multiple votes, the cookie must have an expiration date. If we set it to the current date plus seven days, it means that in seven days time the user will be allowed to re-vote.

Writing and checking cookies is really straightforward, and in most cases it is sufficient. In *most cases*, unfortunately not all cases. The drawback of this method is that the user can easily turn off cookies through a browser option, or delete the cookies from their machine, and then be allowed to vote however many times they want to. (Only a very small percentage of users keep cookies turned off– except for company users where security is a major concern – since they are used on many sites and are sometimes actually required.)

However, there is an alternative method for preventing multiple votes: **IP locking**. When the user votes, their computer's IP address can be retrieved and stored in the database together with the other vote details. Later, when the poll box loads or when the user tries to vote again, we can run a query that returns the records matching both the current computer's IP address and the question ID. If a record is found, the user has already voted and we can prevent further voting. The expiration date can be saved as an additional field in the database table.

There is yet another option. We could track the logged users through their ID, instead of their computer's IP address. However, this will only work if the user is registered. We don't want to limit the vote to registered users only, and will not cover this last method in practice in this chapter. It is an additional option you could add in future if required.

In our module we'll provide the option to employ both the cookie and IP locking methods, only one of them, or neither. Employing neither of them means that we will allow multiple votes with no limitations, and this should only be used during the testing stage. In a real scenario we might need to disable one method. Say that we run the application on an intranet, and that the computers that access the pages with the poll are in a lab. Several users share each computer (students for example, who don't have their own PC). Each user has his own account, so the cookies are not shared, but the IP is static. This means that if we employ IP checking, only the first user to access the application with that computer can vote. IP locking is usually fine when employed on a LAN where you can be reasonably sure that any user has their own computer. However, this will not prevent people from using multiple machines to vote multiple times if they really want to do so. Another issue about IP locking is that if the user gets a dynamic IP from their ISP, every time they disconnect and reconnect, they will get a new IP, so this locking strategy won't have any effect. Yet another case where IP locking causes problems is when someone is surfing with a group through a proxy, because they would always echo the IP of the proxy, regardless of the machine that they were surfing on. IP locking is fine on an intranet but on the Internet can be awkward for this reason. That is why we decided to let the administrator decide which methods should be employed, according to the particular situation.

In conclusion, the polls module will have the following options:

❑ Multiple votes can be allowed

❑ Multiple votes can be prevented with client cookies or IP locking or a combination of the two methods

❑ Limited multiple votes can be allowed, in which case the administrator can specify a lock duration for either method

This way, the polls module will be flexible and can be used with the options that best suit the particular situation.

Designing the Database Tables

Having a precise list of features to implement is fundamental to designing tables from scratch (although this might be impossible with large systems that grow over time). Basically, we need to store questions, options, and votes. At first we might think that two tables would be enough: one for the questions and another for the options, with a column for the number of votes, incremented every time a user votes for that option. However, we've said that we want to store information about the user that voted, such as the IP address and the date, and of course this additional data can't be stored together with the options – we must have a separate table that contains all the details of any vote. So we need at least three tables. You may also suggest a further **linking table** (also known as an associate table) in order to create a many-to-many relationship between the questions and the options tables. This could be useful if we wanted to use the same options, such as simple "yes" and "no" answers, for multiple questions. However, this would make it more difficult to store and retrieve the votes, because it would no longer be possible to identify an option by its ID, but it would be necessary to use the option's ID plus the question's ID, since the same option could be shared by several questions. Furthermore, short and general answers such as "yes" and "no" are not as useful as having more specific options. For these reasons, we decided to avoid the many-to-many relationship between the questions and options, and opted for a simpler one-to-many relationship. In conclusion, we need just three tables: one for the questions, one for the options for each question, and one for the votes. We have a good idea of the information we need to store in the database; now we're ready to design it.

As mentioned in previous chapters, we need a prefix for our module-specific tables, because we have only one SQL Server database, shared by the tables of all the modules in this project. The prefix for this module is `Polls_`. Let's see the diagram that shows the tables and their relationships, before describing them in more detail:

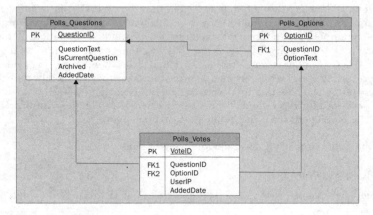

The Polls_Questions Table

The `Polls_Questions` table contains all the questions for the polls, and their attributes, such as whether they are the default question, and the archived status:

Column Name	Type	Size	Allow Null	Description
QuestionID	int – Identity primary key	4	No	The unique ID for the question.
QuestionText	varchar	150	No	The text of the question.
IsCurrentQuestion	bit	1	No	If true (1) this question is the default for the poll box, and is used when no other question ID is specified.
Archived	bit	1	No	If true (1) the question can no longer be used in the poll box but its results are still made accessible through an Archive page.
AddedDate	datetime	8	No	When the question was added.

The Polls_Options Table

The Polls_Options table contains the options (possible answers) for all the questions in the Polls_Questions table:

Column Name	Type	Size	Allow Null	Description
OptionID	int – Identity primary key	4	No	The unique ID for the option.
QuestionID	int foreign key	4	No	The ID of the question to which the option belongs.
OptionText	varchar	150	No	The text of the option.

This is a simple table that has a many-to-one relationship with the Polls_Questions table, through the QuestionID foreign key.

The Polls_Votes Table

The Polls_Votes table stores all the votes for each option, and some details that will be used to prevent multiple votes by the same user:

Column Name	Type	Size	Allow Null	Description
VoteID	int – Identity primary key	4	No	The unique ID for the vote.
QuestionID	int foreign key	4	No	The ID of the question for which the user has voted.
OptionID	int foreign key	4	No	The ID of the option to which the user has given their vote.
UserIP	varchar	15	No	The IP address of the user's computer.
AddedDate	datetime	8	No	When the vote was added.

We keep track of both the question and the specific option that the user has voted for. Both pieces of information are useful for counting how many votes there have been, for a question and for each option. You might think that retrieving the number of votes for each option by counting all the individual records with the specified `OptionID` is slower than incrementing a number in a field in the `Polls_Options` table (and the same for the total number of votes in the `Polls_Questions` table). However, our method makes the insertion of a new vote a bit faster, because we don't need to update other fields, and we also avoid the problems of potential concurrent updates – we actually add a new record for each new vote. Later in the chapter we'll also see how to avoid having to re-query the database every time we display the results in the poll box, in order to save the time that would be required to re-count the votes.

In addition, storing the ID of the question allows us to quickly count the total number of votes for a given question, and easily check if the user has already voted for it. Although we could find this out by looking at the `OptionID` they have voted for and matching this to a `QuestionID`, adding the extra ID directly to the `Options_Votes` table makes queries much faster. The user is identified by the IP address of their computer.

Finally, we store the date when the vote was added, and not the IP lock expiration date. This is more flexible, because we can dynamically change the lock duration and have the new duration applied not only to the future votes, but also to the current votes. In practice, the expiration date is calculated from the `AddedDate` column and a lock duration value supplied later in the code.

The Stored Procedures that Manage the Database

To manage the database we will build a set of stored procedures. We'll run these later in the data layer classes, to do everything from the addition or deletion of questions, options, and votes, to the update of single fields. Here is the complete list of the stored procedures we'll build later, with their parameters:

Stored Procedure	Description
sp_Polls_GetQuestions	Returns all the questions or just the archived questions, according to the @ArchivedOnly parameter. The questions are sorted by date, in descending order (from the newest to the oldest).
sp_Polls_GetQuestionDetails	Returns the complete row for the specified question.
sp_Polls_GetCurrentQuestionID	Returns the ID of the current question, which is used as the default for the poll box when no other ID is explicitly set.
sp_Polls_SetCurrentQuestionID	Changes the ID of the current question. This means setting the IsCurrentQuestion field of the specified question to 1, and the field for all the other questions to 0.
sp_Polls_InsertQuestion	Inserts a new question. If a question already exists with the same text, and it is not archived, the new question is not added and the output parameter is set to -1. Otherwise @QuestionID will be set to the new question's ID.
sp_Polls_UpdateQuestion	Updates all the fields of the question identified by the specified ID.
sp_Polls_SetQuestionArchived	Updates only the Archived field of the specified question.
sp_Polls_DeleteQuestion	Deletes the specified question.
sp_Polls_GetOptions	Returns all the options for the specified question.
sp_Polls_GetOptionDetails	Returns the complete row for the specified option.
sp_Polls_InsertOption	Inserts a new option for the specified question. If the question already has an option with the same text, the option is not added and @OptionID is set to -1, otherwise it is set to the added option's ID.
sp_Polls_UpdateOption	Updates all the fields of the specified option.
sp_Polls_DeleteOption	Deletes the specified option.

Stored Procedure	Description
sp_Polls_GetVotes	Returns all the votes for the specified question.
sp_Polls_GetVoteDetails	Returns the complete row for the specified vote.
sp_Polls_GetUserVoteID	Sets the output parameter to the ID of the vote for the specified question, posted by the user identified by the IP address. If @VoteID is set to -1, it means that the user has not yet voted for that question.
sp_Polls_InsertVote	Inserts a new vote for the specified question, and also stores the ID of the option selected by the user.

Most of these stored procedures are simple ones that return, insert, delete, or update records in the various tables. The descriptions in the table above are sufficient for most of them, but there are a few points that are worth a fuller explanation here before proceeding:

❑ sp_Polls_GetQuestions, sp_Polls_GetOptions, and the two procedures that return only a single row, are a bit more complex than a plain SELECT query. They all add a dynamically calculated column, TotalVotes, which contains the number of votes for the questions and the options, respectively. Later, in the implementation section, we'll see how to do this.

❑ sp_Polls_GetOptions and sp_Polls_GetOptionDetails return a calculated data column, in addition to the TotalVotes column. The column is called Percentage, and it contains the votes for each option as a percentage of the total votes for the question.

❑ sp_Polls_InsertVote inserts the vote for the specified question and option. It does not check if the user has already voted. In fact, we might have chosen to allow multiple votes. Multiple votes are prevented, if necessary, by the business component that we'll see later.

Designing the Data Layer

Now that we have a clear picture of what the database tables store, and how we retrieve data through the stored procedures, we can design the data services. These are nothing but a set of classes that wrap calls to the stored procedures. In fact, you'll see that the methods of the classes have exactly the same parameters as the respective stored procedures.

These classes will be part of an assembly called Wrox.WebModules.Polls.Data, all under the Wrox.WebModules.Polls.Data namespace. As we've done in previous chapters, we inherit the data classes from DbObject, the base class from the Core assembly that we built in Chapter 2.

The QuestionDetails Class

This class has no methods – it just exposes six public fields that map the values of the five physical fields of the Polls_Questions table, plus the calculated column, TotalVotes. This class is used as a return type for a GetDetails method that, instead of returning a DataRow type, returns an instance of an object that exposes the values in an immediately accessible way.

The Questions Class

This class wraps calls to the stored procedures that manage the questions. Contrary to the class above, this one has only methods, whose return values are the values of the output parameters of the respective stored procedures, or a Boolean indicating whether the query succeeded. One method returns an instance of QuestionDetails.

Method Name	Description
Questions	Class constructor taking the connection string as a parameter.
GetQuestions	Returns a DataSet containing all the questions.
GetDetails	Returns an instance of QuestionDetails that describes the specified question.
GetDetailsRow	Returns the DataRow of the question identified by the specified ID.
GetCurrentID	Returns the ID of the current/default question, or -1 if there is no current question.
Add	Adds a new question, and returns its ID, or -1 if the same question was already present.
Update	Updates all the fields of the specified question.
SetArchived	Changes the Archived state of the specified question.
Delete	Deletes the specified question.

> *Another way to retrieve all the polls or only those archived would have been to define two public methods with different names, such as GetAllQuestions and GetArchivedQuestions that, in turn, call a helper private method called GetQuestions(bool bArchivedOnly). However, if we later wanted to allow retrieval of polls archived in a certain interval of time, or with other properties, we would need to add further methods in addition to the new overloaded methods. More code would be needed, but without bringing significant advantages, since it should be already clear to the client what the overloaded methods do with different parameters.*

The OptionDetails Class

This class is basically the same as QuestionDetails but for the Polls_Options table instead. It has only public fields that map the physical fields of the table, plus the TotalVotes and Percentage fields that are calculated values returned by the sp_Polls_GetOptionDetails stored procedure.

The Options Class

This class wraps the calls to all the stored procedures that manage the options, in the same way as the Questions class does for the questions. Here is a complete list of the methods to implement:

Method Name	Description
Options	Class constructor taking the connection string as a parameter.
GetOptions	Returns the options for the specified question.
GetDetails	Returns an instance of OptionDetails that describes the specified option.
GetDetailsRow	Returns the DataRow of the option identified by the specified ID.
Add	Adds an option and returns the ID of the added record, or -1 if an option with the same text was already present for the specified question.
Update	Updates all the fields of the specified option.
Delete	Deletes the specified option.

The VoteDetails Class

This class is similar to the two xxxDetails classes above, with the following public fields: VoteID, QuestionID, OptionID, UserIP, and AddedDate.

The Votes Class

This class is similar to Questions and Options, but a bit simpler because here we don't need methods that update and delete votes. If this functionality is really necessary, for example during the testing stage, you should resort to the Enterprise Manager or some other database manager, like the one we discussed in Chapter 4, which allows the administrator to work online. Here are the methods for this last data-access class:

Method Name	Description
Votes	Class constructor taking the connection string as a parameter.
GetVotes	Returns all the votes for the specified question.
GetDetails	Returns an instance of VoteDetails that describes the specified vote.
GetDetailsRow	Returns the DataRow of the specified vote.
GetUserVoteID	Returns the ID for the vote for the specified question posted by the user whose computer's IP is userIP. Returns -1 if no record is found.
Add	Adds a vote for the specified question and option, and returns the ID of the added record. The record is always added; multiple votes, when not allowed, are prevented by a business class.

Storing and Retrieving Settings

Before showing the design of the business layer we'd better spend a moment thinking about the settings we want to offer, because they will be important for the logic of some of the business methods. The most obvious setting is the connection string for the database, but there are others relating to the methods to be employed to avoid unwanted multiple votes.

In the previous chapters we've already extensively discussed how to store and retrieve settings: we decided to use an XML file, written and read by a separate module-specific assembly with two classes. The assembly for this module should be named `Wrox.WebModules.Polls.Configuration.dll` and there should be a corresponding namespace for the classes. The first class is `ModuleConfig`, and this takes care of persisting and retrieving the settings to and from the XML file. The other class is `ModuleSettings`, which has public properties that expose the settings, and is used as source and destination for the serialization and de-serialization of the settings. This is achieved thanks to a great ASP.NET class, `XmlSerializer`, which we've already seen in action earlier.

The properties we need for `ModuleSettings` are as follows:

- ❑ `ConnectionString`: the connection string that all the data classes use to access the database.
- ❑ `LockByCookie`: Boolean property that, if `True`, means that we want to use cookies to prevent multiple votes.
- ❑ `LockByIP`: Boolean property that, if `True`, means that we want to use IP locking to prevent multiple votes.
- ❑ `LockDuration`: integer property that specifies the duration of the lock, during which the user is not allowed to vote more than once. The period is specified in days. If −1, it means that the lock never expires.

Designing the Business Layer

The data access classes are sufficient for administering the database, since there are no particular rules to respect when adding, editing, or deleting records. Simple rules, such as preventing the addition of a record that is already present, are applied within the stored procedures. However, we have more complex business rules to take care of, for example preventing the user from voting multiple times if the administrator has decided that this should not be possible, or writing and retrieving cookies when the user votes. In addition, we want to access the data in a more object-oriented way; the data layer basically provides a mere set of functions, without properties that describe the object and relationships between child and parent objects. Therefore we must create another couple of classes to do this, and so separate the business logic from the data layer. This is needed because a lower layer is not supposed to access information available to another layer – if you need such information it is supposed to be passed as a method parameter. The business layer is based on top of the data layer, and has classes that provide a completely object-oriented description of the entities (questions and options), as well as methods to manipulate them. It hides the details of the data layer, and prevents direct access to protected records, such as the votes.

We'll put the business classes in a new assembly, `Wrox.WebModules.Polls.Business`, whose classes will inherit from `BizObject` in the `Core` assembly.

The Question Class

This class fully describes a question, and is based on the data layer's `Questions`, `Options`, and `Votes` classes. It also provides methods that check if the current user is allowed to vote, add their vote, and add or return the possible options for a question:

Method Name	Description
ID	Read-only property that returns the ID of the question represented by the object.
Text	Gets/sets the question text.
IsCurrent	Gets/sets the IsCurrentQuestion status of the question.
Archived	Gets/sets the Archived status of the question.
TotalVotes	Read-only property that returns the number of votes for all the child options.
AddedDate	Read-only property that returns the date when the question was added to the database.
AllowVote	Read-only property that, based on the current settings, returns a value indicating whether the current user can vote for this question.
Question	Class constructor with no parameters. It just sets the public properties to default values. For example, the ID property is set to -1, indicating that no record is represented by the object, TotalVotes is 0, Text is an empty string, etc.
Question	Class constructor that sets the properties to describe the question identified by the input ID. We will also provide an overload that will accept a Question object.
LoadFromID	Loads the properties of the question identified by a private ID variable. This method is called by the constructors, or when the data has to be refreshed.
ResetProperties	Resets the properties.
LoadFromID	Loads all the properties of the question identified by the input ID. This method allows a different question to be loaded after the object has been created, or the properties to be loaded if we created an object but didn't specify an ID for the constructor.
LoadCurrent as int	Loads the question marked as current, and sets the properties accordingly.
Create	Creates a new question, and sets the properties of the object to represent the new record.
Update	Updates the current question with the new values of the public properties.
Delete()	Deletes the question.
GetQuestions	Static method that returns all the questions or only the archived ones.

Method Name	Description
GetCurrentID	Returns the ID of the question defined as the current/default question.
GetCurrent	Returns a DataSet with two tables: the first has a row that identifies the current/default question, and the second has all the child options.
GetOptions	Returns all the child options.
AddOption	Adds a child option.
Vote	Votes for the child option identified by the specified ID.
Vote	Votes for the option specified in the input. This overloaded version accepts an Option object instead of its ID, and is actually based upon the previous version.

Here we have quite a few interesting methods and properties, such as AllowVote, Vote, and GetCurrent. AllowVote determines whether the user is allowed to vote for the question according to the options set by the administrator and exposed by the configuration component explained above. It checks for the presence of a cookie on the client's system, and checks against the IP address to see if they have already voted. We'll be using this property from inside the Vote method, to find out if the current user has already voted, and therefore whether we should show the list of options and radio buttons for the question, or whether we should show the results.

The other interesting method is GetCurrent, but we'll describe it in more detail shortly, when discussing the design of the presentation layer, and specifically the design of the web service.

The Option Class

This is a simple class that describes a particular option and allows us to update, delete, or create a new one. Below is the list of methods and properties we'll be implementing:

Method Name	Description
ID	Read-only property that returns the ID of the option represented by the object.
QuestionID	Read-only property that returns the ID of the parent question.
Question	Returns the parent question.
Text	Gets/sets the text of the option.
TotalVotes	Read-only property that returns the number of votes this option received.
Percentage	Read-only property that returns the percentage of votes this option received, in relation to all the options of the parent question.
Option	Class constructor with no parameters. It just resets the properties. We also provide overloads that take an existing ID or an existing Option object and create a new object based on those details.

Table continued on following page

Method Name	Description
LoadFromID	Loads the properties of the option identified by a private ID variable. We will also provide an overload that will accept a different ID.
ResetProperties	Resets the properties.
Create	Creates a new option, and sets the properties of the object to represent the new record.
Update	Updates the current option with the new values of the public properties.
Delete	Deletes the option.

Designing the User Interface Services

In this section we'll discuss the user control that will allow us to insert the poll box into any page we want, with just a couple of lines of code. In addition, we'll also see the design of a web service that makes the current poll's question and results available to any client that can send and understand XML/SOAP messages (for example, another site, or a Windows or Linux application).

The Poll User Control

This control has two functions:

❑ If we detect that the user has not voted for the question yet, the control presents a list of radiobuttons with the various options, and a Vote button.

❑ If we detect that the current user has already voted, instead of the radiobuttons we have to show the results. We will show the percentage of votes for each option, as a number and also graphically as a colored bar.

In both cases the control can optionally show header text, and a link at the bottom that points to the Archive page. Some polls that you may have found around the web are simpler; they always show the options, and tell you that you can't vote again only when you try to do so. The results are displayed through a pop-up window when you vote, or with an explicit link. Our method is much better, as it doesn't need any additional window and it intelligently hides the radio buttons if the user can't vote. Why show the options and the Vote button if the user will get an error message when it is pressed?

Let's think a bit about the actual voting system: how do we handle the option posted by the user? We have two possibilities, both with advantages and disadvantages:

❑ We can use the ASP.NET postback events, and thus have all the required code in the code-behind of the user control. The advantage is that it is easy to implement, and similar to the normal ASP.NET pages we've already developed so far: just a RadioButtonList, a button, and its server-side Click event. The drawback is that the user control must be declared inside a server-side form to be able to handle postback events. This is not a problem when we want to insert the poll box in single pages that we know about in advance, but say that we want to insert the poll box in the site layout, the header or footer of the site, in order to show the box from every page. We'll have to be sure that the header/footer controls are declared inside the server form, and often this isn't the case. (It is not necessary when we are showing static HTML, only if we have to show server controls.)

❑ The other possibility is to work as in traditional ASP: we create a normal HTML `<form>` tag and post the selected option to a different ASP.NET page. The advantage of this solution is that we can easily insert the poll box outside a server form and into the site layout, maybe in a column that is always visible. The drawback is that to ensure that the form will correctly post the data it must be declared outside the server form, in case it exists. This is OK if we want to insert the box into an external column of the layout, but it is a problem if we want to insert the control into a particular page, with other controls that are declared in a server-side form. There are other drawbacks, such as the need to manually build the list of options (we can't use a `RadioButtonList` bound to a data source from outside a server form), and we need to have a separate page for processing the selected option being posted. In practice we lose all the advantages of ASP.NET.

As you can see, there isn't a perfect solution for every case, but the pure ASP.NET solution has many more advantages than the latter, and the drawback is limited, especially if we are aware of it! For these reasons we decided to build a real ASP.NET user control that posts back the form and handles the events on the server.

Having decided how to solve the most compelling issue, handling the vote posting, we can now complete the discussion of the user control with the list of properties we want to implement:

Property Name	Description
QuestionID	The ID of the question to ask within the poll box. If no ID is specified, the question with the IsCurrentQuestion field set to 1 will be used (if any).
ArchiveLinkVisible	If True, shows a link at the bottom of the control, pointing to the Archive page.
HeaderText	The text for the control's header bar.
Width	The width, in pixels or percentage, of the poll box.
HorizontalAlign	The alignment of the text inside the box.
CssClass	The CSS class for the box content. (CSS styles were discussed in Chapter 3.)
QuestionStyle	The CSS class for the question. If not specified then CssClass is used for the question as well.
HeaderStyle	The CSS class for the header bar. If not specified the CssClass is used for the header as well.
ButtonStyle	The CSS class for the Vote button.
LinkStyle	The CSS class for the link to the Archive page.
ResultsStyle	The CSS class for the result percentages (in numbers).
BarStyle	The CSS class for the results percentage bar.

We could add more properties for the graphical aspect, but these should be enough for a complete and functional example. The data will actually be shown in the control through a call to an overridden `DataBind` method.

The Poll Web Service

The site staff can discover the results of the current poll either by adding their own vote, or by accessing the administration section. However, instead of having to refresh the page from time to time to re-query the database and see the latest results, it would be cool if they could check the result with a small Windows client that connects to the site, downloads all the results from the polls, and shows them through different type of graphs. Or it could simply be something more appealing to show to a client!

For our example we're going to keep things simple: we'll just show the results for the current question, using a grid displaying the numerical percentages. Explaining a more complex Windows application is beyond the scope of the book, but it wouldn't be that much more difficult. The web service would still be structured in a very similar way.

The web service is a small piece of software that will allow our future Windows client to query the database on the server. We want to show the current poll, so we must retrieve the row describing the current question and the corresponding options. We could simply use two methods to do this. However, we've chosen to return a `DataSet`, because this will be disconnected from the physical data on the database, and the cursor can be moved through the records in any direction. Remember that a `DataSet` is basically a container for any number of tables (it can also include constraints and relationships among tables, but let's keep it simple for now) so we can return both the question and the options in a single step. We can get a `DataSet` with the options, and then add a table for the row of the parent question. This would also work fine if we wanted to return all the questions, not just the current one, as we would just add more rows to this table.

So, the web service will have only one method, defined as follows:

❑ public `DataSet GetCurrent`: returns a `DataSet` with a table called `Questions` containing the current question, and a table named `Options` containing all the options (and the results) for the current question. This method is based upon the static `GetCurrent` method of the `Business.Question` class that we mentioned earlier.

Of course we'll need to use the `[WebMethod]` attribute to make the method remotely accessible, while retrieving the required data will be straightforward through the use of the data-access component.

It's worth highlighting again that this method returns the question's details every time we call it. This is a little wasteful because, unlike the options, the question does not change between consecutive calls. Therefore there is no need to retrieve it again every time, we could just get it the first time and then only download the updated results. However, this is not a big issue in our case because we've decided to retrieve just the *current* question and its options/results, and we don't need to retrieve the questions very often as we only have a few administrators who need to access this information (we want to make the web service available to the site staff only). If, on the other hand, we were designing the web service to return any archived polls (maybe hundreds), and for a large number of clients, then the time required to retrieve the questions from the database and to send them to the client every time would be much more significant. In that case it would be better to have a method that returns all the questions, and have a separate method that returns the options/results for a particular question. This way the questions could be downloaded only when the client starts, and the options could be downloaded when the user changes the selected question. This is very similar to what we've done in Chapter 6, for the news manager's web service. If you think you need better performance for the polls web service, refer back to that chapter to see how to change the implementation presented in this chapter.

The Need for Security

The `Polls` module is basically split in two parts:

- ❑ The administration section that allows the webmaster (or someone else) to add, delete, or edit the questions and their options, and change the module's settings.

- ❑ The poll box control, the respective ASP.NET page that handles its data posted to the server to add the vote to the database, and the page that shows the archived polls' results.

The second part is freely accessible to the user, but we must protect access to the administration pages. Only one person, or a selected set of people, should be allowed to enter this section. In the previous chapters, especially in Chapters 6 and 7, we saw how to enforce security in a similar situation by using the `Accounts` module developed in Chapter 5.

We will follow exactly the same strategy here. We'll place the administration pages under an `Admin` directory, and allow only the users who have `AdministerPolls` permission to enter. If they do not have that permission, they will be redirected to the default login page.

The Solution

Now that we have a thorough design for the module, we can start the hands-on part – the implementation of the solution. We'll follow the same order as we did in the design section: starting with the implementation of the database tables, we'll move on to the data, configuration, and business assemblies, and finally we'll look at the presentation layer. This comprises the administration section, the poll user control, the web service, and the Windows web service consumer.

Working on the Database

With the help of the Enterprise Manager, creating the tables for our SQL Server database is such a simple task that it is not necessary to describe it in detail here. Earlier in this chapter we presented the complete lists of the columns for each table, along with the most significant properties, so you should have no problems creating them. (Alternatively, script files to create the tables are available in the code download, as is a complete backup of the database.)

You can create the new tables (or even a new database if you need to) right within Visual Studio .NET, without opening SQL Server. On the far left of the IDE, near the Toolbox, you find another tab called **Server Explorer**. This window allows the developer to explore the server components such as SQL Server databases, events logs, message queues, etc., through an easy-to-browse tree control. Under the SQL Server leaf are listed all the available databases. If you select and expand one you can see its tables, stored procedures, views, diagrams, and functions. You can edit or delete existing objects, or create new ones, by clicking the respective commands of the pop-up menu that appears when you right-click on a tree item. The following screenshot shows the IDE while displaying the data of the `Polls_Options` table:

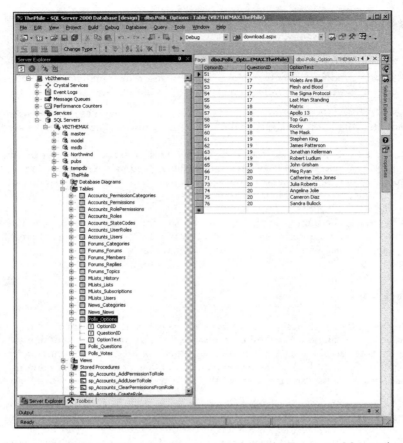

The data is displayed and edited with an interface very similar to the Enterprise Manager's editors, and the same is true for the table designers. What's even cooler is that you can drag and drop a table/view or a stored procedure over a form or control (Windows or web, it doesn't matter), and Visual Studio .NET will auto-generate the code for the respective `DataAdapter`, `SqlConnection`, and `SqlCommand` objects. Honestly, I don't like this feature very much because Visual Studio .NET generates code for any constructor parameter and for most properties – even if not required – and I prefer to write tighter code. But it's actually great if you just want to quickly test a stored procedure or fill a grid on the page, for example.

In the next sections we'll see the relationships we need to create between the tables, and the code for some of the stored procedures.

Creating the Relationships

After creating the tables, we have to create the relationships between them, as shown in the diagram in the design section. As we saw in Chapter 6, with the Enterprise Manager (or with Visual Studio .NET's Server Explorer) this is also a simple matter, so we won't go into details here. We need three relationships:

❏ A relationship between the question and the possible options that can be selected. This relationship, FK_Polls_Options_Questions, is between the QuestionID column of the Polls_Options table and the Polls_Questions table. The other settings are as shown:

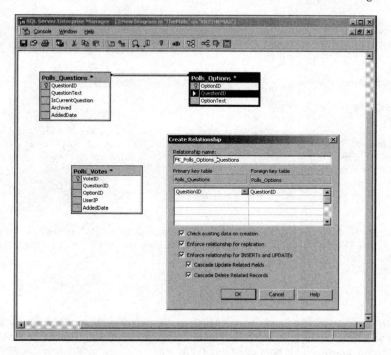

We select the Cascade Update and Cascade Delete options, so that if a question ID is changed (which shouldn't happen, since the QuestionID is an identity field) the QuestionID foreign key in the Polls_Options table will change accordingly, and if a question is deleted all the child options will be deleted as well.

❏ A relationship between the votes and the question. FK_Polls_Votes_Questions links the QuestionID column of the Polls_Votes table with the Polls_Questions table, and has the same settings as seen above.

❏ A relationship between the votes and the options. FK_Polls_Votes_Options links the OptionID column of the Polls_Votes table with the Polls_Options table, and again has the same settings.

All three relationships are many-to-one, since many options belong to the same question, and many votes refer to the same question and option.

Creating the Stored Procedures

The code for inserting, deleting, or updating a record is very similar for all three tables, and is similar to the respective procedures already seen in previous chapters, so here we'll only show the few procedures that differ somehow. You can easily derive the code for the other procedures, or use the scripts in the code download to create all the procedures.

sp_Polls_GetQuestions

Here's the code for the sp_Polls_GetQuestions procedure that returns the archived questions only, or all the questions, according to the input parameter:

```
CREATE PROCEDURE sp_Polls_GetQuestions
                @ArchivedOnly   bit = 0
AS

DECLARE @QuestionID int

IF @ArchivedOnly = 1
  BEGIN
  SELECT QuestionID, QuestionText, IsCurrentQuestion, Archived, AddedDate,
      (SELECT COUNT(*) FROM Polls_Votes WHERE QuestionID = Q.QuestionID)
      AS TotalVotes
    FROM Polls_Questions Q
    WHERE Archived = 1
  END
ELSE
  BEGIN
  SELECT QuestionID, QuestionText, IsCurrentQuestion, Archived, AddedDate,
      (SELECT COUNT(*) FROM Polls_Votes WHERE QuestionID = Q.QuestionID)
      AS TotalVotes
    FROM Polls_Questions Q
  END
GO
```

There are two distinct SELECT statements – which one is run depends on whether we are retrieving *archived* questions or *all* questions. The most important point to note is how we declare and calculate the new TotalVotes column. This contains the total number of votes for the row's question. Basically, we run a sub-query that counts the votes where the QuestionID field is equal to the QuestionID of the current row in the Polls_Questions table being queried, and the result is kept in a new column named TotalVotes.

sp_Polls_GetCurrentQuestionID

The sp_Polls_GetCurrentQuestionID procedure runs a simple SELECT to get the ID of the row that contains the current (non-archived) question. If no current question is found, the procedure returns -1, as an indication for the caller code:

```
CREATE PROCEDURE sp_Polls_GetCurrentQuestionID
                @QuestionID int OUTPUT
AS

SELECT @QuestionID = QuestionID
  FROM Polls_Questions
  WHERE IsCurrentQuestion = 1 AND Archived = 0

IF @QuestionID IS NULL
  SET @QuestionID = -1
GO
```

sp_Polls_SetCurrentQuestionID

The sp_Polls_SetCurrentQuestionID procedure is used to assign the current question. It can't just update the IsCurrentQuestion field of the selected question; it must also ensure that only one question is marked as current. So it first sets to 0 the IsCurrentQuestion field of all the rows, and then sets to 1 the field of the specified question:

```
CREATE PROCEDURE sp_Polls_SetCurrentQuestionID
                @QuestionID int
AS

-- first set IsCurrentQuestion = 0 for all questions
UPDATE Polls_Questions
  SET IsCurrentQuestion = 0

-- set the current question
UPDATE Polls_Questions
  SET IsCurrentQuestion = 1
  WHERE QuestionID = @QuestionID
GO
```

sp_Polls_InsertQuestion

The following code, sp_Polls_InsertQuestion, inserts a new row in the Polls_Questions table, and returns the ID of the added row through the output parameter. If the question already exists and it is not archived, it is not added again:

```
CREATE PROCEDURE sp_Polls_InsertQuestion
                @QuestionText varchar(150),
                @IsCurrentQuestion int,
                @Archived int,
                @QuestionID int OUTPUT
AS

DECLARE @CurrID int

-- see if the question already exists
-- (check only the non-archived questions)
SELECT @CurrID = QuestionID
  FROM Polls_Questions
  WHERE QuestionText = @QuestionText AND Archived = 0

-- if not, add it
IF @CurrID IS NULL
  BEGIN

  INSERT INTO Polls_Questions
      (QuestionText, IsCurrentQuestion, Archived, AddedDate)
      VALUES (@QuestionText, @IsCurrentQuestion, @Archived, GETDATE())

  SET @QuestionID = @@IDENTITY

  IF @@ERROR > 0
```

```
      BEGIN
      RAISERROR ('Insert of Question failed', 16, 1)
      RETURN 99
      END

    -- if @CurrentQuestion is 1, set this question as the active one.
    -- This could not be done in the Insert statement because we need to
    -- set CurrentQuestion = 0 for the other questions first
    IF @IsCurrentQuestion = 1
      EXEC sp_Polls_SetCurrentQuestionID @QuestionID

  END
ELSE
  BEGIN
  SET @QuestionID = -1
  END
GO
```

In the INSERT statement we specify the input value for the IsCurrentQuestion field. If the parameter is 0, we're done. If it is 1, we must ensure that the new row is the only one that has IsCurrentQuestion set to 1, and so we must call the sp_Polls_SetCurrentQuestionID procedure that does this, as we've seen earlier.

sp_Polls_UpdateQuestion

The sp_Polls_UpdateQuestion procedure updates all the fields of the specified question, except for the ID of course. If @IsCurrentQuestion is 1 then we must call sp_Polls_SetCurrentQuestionID, for the reason explained above:

```
CREATE PROCEDURE sp_Polls_UpdateQuestion
                @QuestionID int,
                @QuestionText varchar(150),
                @IsCurrentQuestion bit,
                @Archived bit
AS

BEGIN TRANSACTION UpdateQuestion

UPDATE Polls_Questions
  SET QuestionText = @QuestionText, IsCurrentQuestion = @IsCurrentQuestion,
      Archived = @Archived
  WHERE QuestionID = @QuestionID

-- if @CurrentQuestion = 1, call the sproc that unchecks the value
-- for all the other questions, and check this
-- if @CurrentQuestion = 0, it has already been updated by the command above
IF @IsCurrentQuestion = 1
  EXEC sp_Polls_SetCurrentQuestionID @QuestionID

IF @@ERROR > 0
  BEGIN
  RAISERROR ('Update of Question failed', 16, 1)
  ROLLBACK TRANSACTION UpdateQuestion
```

```
        RETURN 99
        END

COMMIT TRANSACTION UpdateQuestion
GO
```

sp_Polls_GetOptions

This procedure returns the options for the specified question, and the total number of votes. It also creates a new column that shows the votes for each option as a percentage of the votes for all the options of this question. Here's the code:

```
CREATE PROCEDURE sp_Polls_GetOptions
                @QuestionID int
AS

DECLARE @QuestionTotalVotes int

-- get the total of number votes for this question
SELECT @QuestionTotalVotes = COUNT(*) FROM Polls_Votes
  WHERE QuestionID = @QuestionID

IF @QuestionTotalVotes = 0
  SET @QuestionTotalVotes = 1

-- get the OptionID and OptionText
-- + count the total number of votes for each options
-- + calc the percentage for each option
SELECT OptionID, OptionText,
       (SELECT COUNT(*) FROM Polls_Votes WHERE OptionID = O.OptionID)
         AS TotalVotes,
       (CAST((SELECT COUNT(*) FROM Polls_Votes WHERE OptionID = O.OptionID)
         AS Decimal) * 100 / @QuestionTotalVotes)
         AS Percentage
  FROM Polls_Options O
  WHERE QuestionID = @QuestionID
GO
```

It first gets the total number of votes for all the options of this question, and saves this value in a variable. If no votes are found, it sets the variable to 1, because otherwise the forthcoming division would produce an error. Finally it executes the SELECT query and adds the Percentage column, with the following code:

```
(CAST((SELECT COUNT(*) FROM Polls_Votes WHERE OptionID = O.OptionID)
     AS Decimal) * 100 / @QuestionTotalVotes)
     AS Percentage
```

The number of votes for an option are multiplied by 100 and then divided by the total number of votes for the question. It's worth noting that the expression is CAST to Decimal, in order to achieve more accuracy than an integer percentage would provide.

The code of the sp_Polls_GetOptionDetails procedure is almost identical to this code, with two exceptions. It is restricted to a single record, and the question's ID is not provided as a parameter, but must be retrieved with a simple SELECT query to select the QuestionID field of the specified option.

343

Implementing the Data-Access Assembly

Now that the database is complete, let's go ahead and look at the .NET code for the data-access component. In Visual Studio .NET we add a new Class Library project called `Polls.Data` to our ThePhile solution, and using its **Properties** dialog set both the assembly name and the default namespace to `Wrox.WebModules.Polls.Data`. Then we edit the automatically created `AssemblyInfo.vb` file with the assembly's description, version, and other information, as we've already seen in previous chapters.

At this point you should rename the default `Class1.vb` file to `Questions.vb`, and we also need two other classes, for the options and the votes. These classes are simply wrappers for the stored procedures, as mentioned earlier, and their code is very similar to the code of the data-access classes described in Chapter 6. Therefore, to avoid useless repetition of code we will not show the code here, but of course you can download the finished assembly from the Wrox site.

The Configuration Assembly

In previous chapters we've already seen, more than once, the implementation of the configuration assembly, so we won't repeat all the details again here. Briefly, we create a new **Class Library** project, change the project's properties (the namespace and assembly name are both `Wrox.WebModules.Polls.Configuration`), and edit the `AssemblyInfo.vb` file as we did for the data assembly. We are then ready to write the classes.

The ModuleSettings Class

In the design section we listed the settings we need to store, and here you'll find the necessary code for the class:

```vb
Imports System
Imports System.IO
Imports System.Text
Imports System.Xml.Serialization
Imports System.Xml
Imports System.Configuration

Imports System.Web
Imports System.Web.Caching
Namespace WebModules.Polls.Configuration

  Public Class ModuleSettings
    Private myConnectionString As String
    Private myLockByIP As Boolean
    Private myLockByCookie As Boolean
    Private myLockDuration As Integer

    <XmlElement()> _
    Public Property ConnectionString() As String
      Get
        Return myConnectionString
      End Get
      Set(ByVal Value As String)
```

```
            myConnectionString = Value
        End Set
    End Property

    <XmlElement()> _
    Public Property LockByIP() As Boolean
      Get
         Return myLockByIP
      End Get
      Set(ByVal Value As Boolean)
         myLockByIP = Value
      End Set
    End Property

    <XmlElement()> _
    Public Property LockByCookie() As Boolean
      Get
         Return myLockByCookie
      End Get
      Set(ByVal Value As Boolean)
         myLockByCookie = Value
      End Set
    End Property

    <XmlElement()> _
    Public Property LockDuration() As Integer
      Get
         Return myLockDuration
      End Get
      Set(ByVal Value As Integer)
         myLockDuration = Value
      End Set
    End Property
  End Class
End Namespace
```

As you can see, it is a simple class – the key point is the use of [XmlElement]. This tells the serializer that the property state has to be serialized and de-serialized to and from the chosen settings file.

The ModuleConfig Class

This class differs from the implementations of the previous chapters in just a few lines, basically the name of the key in the site-wide web.config file – Polls_SettingsFile – and the name of the entry in the cache – Polls_Settings. You can actually copy and paste the code from the ModuleConfig class of a previous module, and replace the configuration and cache entry names with those values.

The Settings File

To see what the settings file looks like, we first implemented a simple page that created an instance of ModuleSettings with the settings we wanted, and then persisted it to a file with the ModuleConfig class. This created the file with the right format and values, and spared us the need to write it by hand. This is the file content produced:

```
<?xml version="1.0"?>
<ModuleSettings xmlns:xsi="http://www.w3.org/2001/XMLSchema-instance"
                xmlns:xsd="http://www.w3.org/2001/XMLSchema">
  <ConnectionString>server=(local);database=ThePhile;uid=sa;pwd=;
  </ConnectionString>
  <LockByIP>true</LockByIP>
  <LockByCookie>true</LockByCookie>
  <LockDuration>7</LockDuration>
</ModuleSettings>
```

We decided to name the file `Polls.Config`, but you can choose any name you want, as long as you store its path in the site-wide `web.config` file, as follows:

```
<?xml version="1.0" encoding="utf-8" ?>
<configuration>
  <appSettings>
    <add key="Polls_SettingsFile" value="/ThePhile/Config/Polls.Config" />
  </appSettings>
  ...
</configuration>
```

The Business Assembly

We create a Class Library project for the new business assembly, change the usual properties, and set the namespace and assembly name as `Wrox.WebModules.Polls.Business`. Also remember that we must add references to the `Core`, `Wrox.WebModules.Polls.Data`, and `Wrox.WebModules.Polls.Configuration` projects. We have two classes for this assembly, `Question` and `Option`. As we've said for the data-access assembly, the code of many methods is very similar to the code of the business classes of Chapter 6. For example, the methods for loading a specified record and exposing its values through the object's public properties, returning all the records, and adding, editing, or deleting a record, are actually almost the same. All that changes is the name of the data-access class to instantiate and the methods to call, and of course the number and type of parameters. We don't want to repeat here code already shown, so we'll only cover the methods that are really new to this module, namely those methods that implement the real business rules, such as checking if the user has already voted and is allowed to vote again, reading and writing cookies and IP addresses to remember a vote, etc. As always, the entire code of all the other methods is available in the code download.

The Question Class

This is the class that will be used most frequently, since it provides access to any question and the associated options and results. It also exposes methods to vote for a particular option and to check if the user can vote for the question represented by an instance of this class. In the following sections we'll see the implementation of most of the methods that are specific to this module and not as general as other methods mentioned above.

Managing the Child Options

We have a couple of methods for creating a child option, and for returning all the available child options already present. The first method does not directly access the data layer to create a new record, but it calls the `Create` method of an `Option` object. As a result it's quicker to update the business class if the data class changes, because we have less code that references it directly.

```
Public Function GetOptions() As DataSet
   Dim options As New Data.Options(mySettings.ConnectionString)

   Return options.GetOptions(myQuestionId)
End Function

Public Function AddOption(ByVal optionText As String) As Business.Option
   Dim voteOption As New Business.Option()

   voteOption.Create(myQuestionId, optionText)

   Return voteOption
End Function
```

The GetCurrent Method

Here things start to get more interesting. In the design section we decided to return both the question and the results through a single static method, GetCurrent, which returns a DataSet with two tables. The code is as follows:

```
Public Shared Function GetCurrent() As DataSet

   Dim settings As Configuration.ModuleSettings = _
     Configuration.ModuleConfig.GetSettings()

   ' Get the current question's Id
   Dim questions As New Data.Questions(settings.ConnectionString)
   Dim myQuestionId As Integer = questions.GetCurrentId()

   ' If there is no current questions, return an empty DataSet
   If myQuestionId = -1 Then
     Return New DataSet()
   End If

   ' Get the options for this question
   Dim options As New Data.Options(settings.ConnectionString)
   Dim currPoll As DataSet = options.GetOptions(myQuestionId)

   ' Get the current question's details
   Dim question As DataRow = questions.GetDetailsRow(myQuestionId)

   ' Clone its parent table's structure and add it to the DataSet
   currPoll.Tables.Add(question.Table.Clone())

   ' Import the details row into the new table
   currPoll.Tables("Questions").ImportRow(question)

   ' Return the Dataset with the two tables
   Return currPoll
End Function
```

If there is no current question, the method creates and returns an empty `DataSet`. Otherwise, it first retrieves the `DataSet` with a table called `Options` containing the options for the current question. Then it retrieves the row with the details of the question, and adds a new table, `Questions`, to the `DataSet` retrieved in the previous step. It does this by cloning the structure of the question row's parent table. Finally, it imports the question's details row to the `Questions` table. This might sound a bit intricate, but look again at the code and read the comments, and you'll see that it's actually quite straightforward.

When we clone a table it means that we clone its structure, namely the number and type of columns it has, and all its attributes. The normal way to add a new table to a `DataSet` (which if you remember is a collection of tables and relationships) would be to create a new `DataTable` object and add all the required columns by hand. However, this would require quite a lot of code to set all the attributes (data type, size, etc.) for any column. Instead, cloning an existing table that has the structure we want to reproduce is quite a nice trick, because it only requires a single line, and brings us to the same result.

The `GetDetailsRow` method of the `Data.Questions` class calls the `sp_Polls_GetQuestionDetails` stored procedure and puts the results in a table called `Questions`. When the table is cloned, the new table is also called `Questions` because the attributes are copied. This explains why we can easily access it by name rather than by index when we call its `Add` method to add the row that describes the current question.

The AllowVote Property

This property checks whether the user can vote for the specified question. The check is done against a client cookie and the IP address stored in the database. If the user has already voted, it also looks to see if the lock period for multiple votes has expired.

```
Public ReadOnly Property AllowVote() As Boolean
  Get
    Dim cookieOK As Boolean = False
    Dim ipOK As Boolean = False

    Dim request As HttpRequest = HttpContext.Current.Request
    Dim duration As Integer = mySettings.LockDuration

    ' If the lock period is 0, return true
    If duration = 0 Then Return True

    ' Check the cookie if necessary
    If mySettings.LockByCookie Then

      If Not (request.Cookies( _
        ("Polls_Question" & myQuestionId.ToString())) Is Nothing) Then

        Return False

      Else ' If the cookie is null, we're ok so far
        cookieOK = True
      End If

    Else
      cookieOK = True
```

```
        End If

        ' Check the Id if necessary
      If mySettings.LockByIP Then

        Dim votes As New Data.Votes(mySettings.ConnectionString)
        Dim voteId As Integer = votes.GetUserVoteID( _
          myQuestionId, request.UserHostAddress.ToString())

        ' If GetUserVoteId returned -1, the current user has never
        ' voted for this question
        If voteId = -1 Then
          ipOK = True
        Else

          ' If a vote for this question is found, and the duration time is
          ' -1 it means that it will never expire --> return false
          If duration = -1 Then
            Return False
          End If

          ' otherwise check if the LockDuration time has expired
          Dim myAddedDate As DateTime = votes.GetDetails(voteId).AddedDate
          ipOK = myAddedDate.AddDays(duration) <= DateTime.Today

        End If

      Else
        ipOK = True
      End If

      Return cookieOK AndAlso ipOK
    End Get
  End Property
```

As you can see, if the lock duration is 0 it means that multiple votes are allowed with no limitations, so the procedure returns True straight away, without performing any further checks. Otherwise, it starts by checking if the client has a cookie ending with the specified question's ID, if we enabled cookie locking in the settings. If the cookie exists, the user has already voted and so the routine returns False. Otherwise, we go ahead by checking in the database, looking for a vote for the specified question with the current user's IP address, if IP locking is employed. The IP address of the current user is returned by the UserHostAddress property of the HttpContext.Current.Request class. (Note that to use this class you need to reference the System.Web.dll assembly, which is not added by default in Class Library projects.) If both checks go well, the method ends by returning the final value of True.

It is also worth noting that we do not need to check the LockDuration setting for the cookie. In fact, when the cookie is created (we'll see how, when, and where, in a moment) it is given an expiration time equal to the LockDuration setting. When that time has passed the cookie is no longer valid, and is therefore not found by the server – the check succeeds. In the database we store the date the vote was added, so we also need to check if the specified time has passed since the AddedDate date.

The Vote Method

The Vote method is the one that actually adds votes to the database. It first calls AllowVote, discussed above, to check if the user has already voted for this question, and if so, to check if the lock period for multiple votes has expired. If the check returns True, the vote is saved to the database and a cookie is created on the client to record that the current user has voted for that question.

The trick to handling cookies for multiple polls is to name the cookie with a fixed string (Polls_Question in the code above) plus the ID of the question. This way different polls have different cookies and are not overwritten by each other. The cookie's value is the ID of the option voted for: this information could be useful later if we want to remind the user of their choice. The cookie is given an expiration time, which is the current date plus a number of days (specified by the LockDuration setting, or 365 days if the setting is −1).

> If LockDuration is −1 it is meant to be forever, but we considered one year as long enough. You can of course change LockDuration to any value you want.

Finally, the cookie is saved to the client computer using the Add method of the Cookies collection of the current Response object.

```
Public Overloads Function Vote(ByVal optionId As Integer) As Boolean

    ' Before voting, check if the user has already voted, and if so
    ' check also if the lock period for multiple votes has expired
    If AllowVote AndAlso myQuestionId <> -1 AndAlso optionId <> -1 Then

        Dim voteId As Integer
        Dim duration As Integer = mySettings.LockDuration

        If duration = -1 Then duration = 365

        ' Add the vote
        Dim votes As New Data.Votes(mySettings.ConnectionString)
        voteId = votes.Add(myQuestionId, optionId, _
          HttpContext.Current.Request.UserHostAddress)

        ' Add a new cookie for this question
        Dim voteCookie As New _
          HttpCookie("Polls_Question" & myQuestionId.ToString())
        voteCookie.Value = optionId.ToString()
        voteCookie.Expires = DateTime.Today.AddDays(duration)
        HttpContext.Current.Response.Cookies.Add(voteCookie)

        Return voteId <> -1

    Else
        Return False
    End If
End Function
```

We also have an overload of Vote that will accept an Option object. This simply extracts the ID from the Option and calls the overload that we just looked at:

```
Public Overloads Function Vote(ByVal voteOption As Business.Option) _
   As Boolean

   Return Vote(voteOption.Id)
End Function
```

The Administration User Interface

Even though we've already completed much of the work, we can't yet see any results in the browser. As with the rest of our site, designing and implementing good data and business components is of fundamental importance and has taken precedence here. Having taken care of the data and business layers we can now move on to our administration user interface. The presentation tier will directly use only the business layer to access and modify the data, and will have no dependency on the data layer. We just need to show the records and offer some way to call the business component's methods, which is a trivial task thanks to the powerful ASP.NET server controls available.

The ASPX files for this module should go into the modules\forums folder and be part of the main ThePhile project. Remember to add a reference to the Business and Configuration projects developed earlier.

Before starting to look at the code, let's see a screenshot of what we're going to produce:

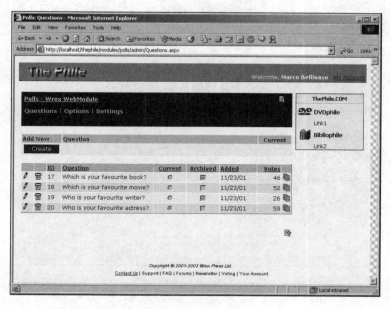

This page allows the administrator to see the available questions, change which is the current one, archive old questions, change the text, see the number total votes for any question, and add a new question. The 'group of sheets' icon on the far right is used to jump directly to the page that displays and manages the options for the question.

Creating the Header and Footer User Controls

As in previous chapters, we need a header control and a footer control for all the pages in this administration section. The header control includes the site bar and another menu bar, as can be seen in the previous screenshot. This menu bar contains the module name and links to the other administration pages. The footer bar is the same as for the other administration pages.

We add two user controls to the project and name them `AdminHeader.ascx` and `AdminFooter.ascx`. Their content is exactly the same as the header/footer we built for the `NewsManager` module in Chapter 6, except for the links of course, so refer back if you want to see the complete code. Except for the site header and footer, and the menu server control, the rest is plain HTML code for displaying the links, and a JavaScript function to show a short description when the mouse cursor hovers over a menu link. We don't need to add any code to the code-behind files, just change their namespace from the default value to `Wrox.WebModules.Polls.Controls.User`, according to the naming conventions described in Chapter 2.

The Questions Manager Page

The previous screenshot shows the records in the grid in normal display mode. To add a new question the administrator clicks the **Create** button at the top-left of the main page, and this is the result:

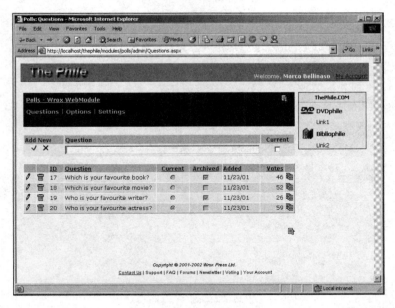

In 'new question mode' the administrator can type the text of the new question and check the checkbox if the new question is to be the current one. It is not possible to set the `Archived` attribute at this time, because it would not make sense to add a question and archive it immediately. The question is actually added to the database by pressing the green tick icon, or the operation can be canceled by pressing the red **X**.

You can see that the Current and Archived attributes are displayed in the grid with a radio button and a checkbox, respectively. We use a radiobutton for the **Current** column because only one question can be the current one, and radio buttons generally indicate that only one of a set of options can be selected. In this case this is more a graphical detail, because it is not possible to change the values anyway since the controls are in read-only mode. If you want to change the Archived/Current attributes, or edit the text of any question, press the pencil icon at the far left of the grid, and you'll get the grid changed as follows:

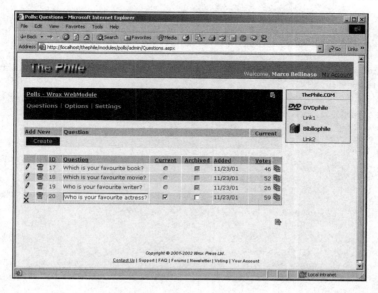

The clicked row has changed, and now displays a textbox with the current question's text, and two checkboxes. Note that the radio button has been replaced by a checkbox, to allow you to select or deselect it: it wouldn't be possible to deselect the radio button without selecting another one (and the others are not enabled anyway). Note also that some of the columns, namely **ID**, **Added**, and **Votes**, are not editable, because these values should not be manually amended. Once you've changed the values, you can confirm or cancel the update with the tick or the cross icon.

The Questions.aspx Page

This ASP.NET page is the place where the user interface is defined. We create Questions.aspx page in the modules\forums folder of the main ThePhile project. The page starts with the declaration of the code-behind file, the <head> section, the insertion of the header control, and the declaration of the server-side form:

```
<%@ Page language="vb" Codebehind="Questions.aspx.vb"
        AutoEventWireup="false"
        Inherits="Wrox.WebModules.Polls.Web.Questions" %>
<%@ Register TagPrefix="Polls" TagName="AdminHeader"
            src="AdminHeader.ascx" %>
<%@ Register TagPrefix="Polls" TagName="AdminFooter"
            src="AdminFooter.ascx" %>
<!DOCTYPE HTML PUBLIC "-//W3C//DTD HTML 4.0 Transitional//EN" >
```

```
<html>
  <head>
    <title>Polls: Questions</title>
    <link href="/ThePhile/Styles/ThePhile.css" rel="stylesheet" />
    <link href="/ThePhile/Styles/Navigator.css" rel="stylesheet" />
    <meta name="CODE_LANGUAGE" Content="VB">
  </head>
  <body>
    <form method="post" runat="server" ID="Questions">
      <!-- Insert the menu user control -->
      <Polls:AdminHeader ID="Menu" runat="server" />
```

Moving down into the body of the page, we come to the table for adding a new question when the Create button is pressed:

```
<asp:table runat="server" CssClass="Grid_General" Width="100%" >
  <asp:TableRow CssClass="Grid_Header">
    <asp:TableCell Width="85px" Text="Add New" />
    <asp:TableCell Text="Question" />
    <asp:TableCell Width="70px" Text="Current" HorizontalAlign="Center" />
  </asp:TableRow>
  <asp:TableRow ID="CreateNewRow">
    <asp:TableCell HorizontalAlign="Center">
      <asp:Button runat="server" Text="Create" ID="Create"
                  CssClass="Button" OnClick="Create_Click" Width="80px" />
    </asp:TableCell>
    <asp:TableCell ID="AddNewResultCell" ColumnSpan="2">
      <asp:Label runat="server" CssClass="Error" ID="AddNewError"
                 Text="This item was already present" Visible="false" />
    </asp:TableCell>
  </asp:TableRow>
  <asp:TableRow ID="AddNewControlsRow" Visible="false">
    <asp:TableCell VerticalAlign="Top">
      <asp:Image ImageURL="./Images/Spacer.gif" Width="15px"
                 Height="1px" runat="server" />
      <asp:LinkButton ID="AddNew" runat="server"
                 Text="<img border=0 src=./Images/OK.gif Alt='Add new list'>"
                 OnClick="AddNew_Click" />
      <asp:Image ImageURL="./Images/Spacer.gif" Width="15px"
                 Height="1px" runat="server" />
      <asp:LinkButton ID="CancelAddNew" runat="server"
                      CausesValidation="false"
      Text="<img border=0 src=./Images/Cancel.gif Alt='Cancel editing mode'>"
                      OnClick="CancelAddNew_Click" />
    </asp:TableCell>
    <asp:TableCell VerticalAlign="Top">
      <asp:TextBox runat="server" CssClass="TextBox"
                   ID="NewQuestionText" Width="100%" />
      <asp:RequiredFieldValidator runat="server"
                                  ControlToValidate="NewQuestionText"
                                  Display="dynamic">
        <br>* Question text is required
      </asp:RequiredFieldValidator>
```

```
      </asp:TableCell>
      <asp:TableCell VerticalAlign="Top" HorizontalAlign="Center">
        <asp:CheckBox runat="server" ID="NewIsCurrent" />
      </asp:TableCell>
    </asp:TableRow>
  </asp:table>
```

The controls for the question's text and its current state are made invisible in the declaration above – they will be shown later from the code-behind, in the Click event of the **Create** button.

Now let's look at the central part of the page: the grid that displays and edits the records. It's very similar to what we've already covered in previous chapters, but we'll show it again here in a few separate pieces. In the following code the grid is declared, and we create the first two columns, for editing and deleting a row:

```
<asp:DataGrid ID="QuestionsGrid" runat="server"
              CssClass="Grid_General"
              HeaderStyle-CssClass="Grid_Header"
              ItemStyle-CssClass="Grid_Item"
              AlternatingItemStyle-CssClass="Grid_AlternatingItem"
              AllowSorting="True" AutoGenerateColumns="False"
              DataKeyField="QuestionID"
              OnEditCommand="QuestionsGrid_Edit"
              OnCancelCommand="QuestionsGrid_CancelEdit"
              OnUpdateCommand="QuestionsGrid_Update"
              OnDeleteCommand="QuestionsGrid_Delete"
              OnSortCommand="QuestionsGrid_Sort"
              Width="100%">

  <Columns>
    <asp:EditCommandColumn
                      ItemStyle-Width="25px" EditText="<img border=0
                      Alt='Edit this question' src=./Images/Edit.gif>"
                      CancelText="<img border=0 src=./Images/Cancel.gif>"
                      UpdateText="<img border=0 src=./Images/OK.gif>"
    />
    <asp:ButtonColumn
                      ItemStyle-Width="25px" Text="<img border=0
                      Alt='Delete this question' src=./Images/Delete.gif>"
                      CommandName="delete"
    />
```

The grid allows us to sort the questions, set the QuestionID column as the primary key for the grid, and define some event handlers. The EditCommandColumn is a specific column with a link to begin the editing, while ButtonColumn creates normal buttons or links whose Click event must be handled to delete the question. Here is the code for the columns that display the question's ID, text, and other attributes that were visible in the last screenshot:

```
<asp:BoundColumn HeaderText="ID" ItemStyle-Width="30px"
                 DataField="QuestionID" ReadOnly="True"
                 SortExpression="QuestionID"
```

```
    />
  <asp:TemplateColumn HeaderText="Question"
                      SortExpression="QuestionText">
    <ItemTemplate>
      <asp:Label runat="server" Text='<%# DataBinder.Eval(
               Container.DataItem, "QuestionText") %>' />
    </ItemTemplate>
    <EditItemTemplate>
      <asp:TextBox ID="EditQuestionText" runat="server"
        Text='<%# DataBinder.Eval(Container.DataItem, "QuestionText") %>'
        CssClass="TextBox" Width="100%" />
      <asp:RequiredFieldValidator runat="server"
                                  ControlToValidate="EditQuestionText"
                                  Display="dynamic">
                                  * Question text is required
      </asp:RequiredFieldValidator>
    </EditItemTemplate>
  </asp:TemplateColumn>
<asp:TemplateColumn HeaderText="Current"
                    SortExpression="IsCurrentQuestion"
                    ItemStyle-Width="70px"
                    HeaderStyle-HorizontalAlign="Center"
                    ItemStyle-HorizontalAlign="Center">
  <ItemTemplate>
    <asp:RadioButton runat="server" Enabled="false" Checked='<%#
                     Convert.ToBoolean(DataBinder.Eval(
                          Container.DataItem, "IsCurrentQuestion")) %>' />
  </ItemTemplate>
  <EditItemTemplate>
    <asp:CheckBox ID="EditIsCurrent" runat="server" Checked='<%#
                  Convert.ToBoolean(DataBinder.Eval(
                          Container.DataItem, "IsCurrentQuestion")) %>' />
  </EditItemTemplate>
</asp:TemplateColumn>
<asp:TemplateColumn HeaderText="Archived" SortExpression="Archived"
                    ItemStyle-Width="70px"
                    HeaderStyle-HorizontalAlign="Center"
                    ItemStyle-HorizontalAlign="Center">
  <ItemTemplate>
    <asp:CheckBox runat="server" Enabled="false" Checked='<%#
                  Convert.ToBoolean(DataBinder.Eval(
                                    Container.DataItem, "Archived")) %>' />
  </ItemTemplate>
 <EditItemTemplate>
   <asp:CheckBox ID="EditArchived" runat="server" Checked='<%#
                 Convert.ToBoolean(DataBinder.Eval(
                                   Container.DataItem, "Archived")) %>' />
 </EditItemTemplate>
</asp:TemplateColumn>
<asp:TemplateColumn HeaderText="Added"
                    SortExpression="AddedDate" ItemStyle-Width="80px">
  <ItemTemplate>
    <asp:Label runat="server" Text='<%# DataBinder.Eval(
              Container.DataItem, "AddedDate", "{0:MM/dd/yy}") %>' />
```

```
        </ItemTemplate>
    </asp:TemplateColumn>
    <asp:BoundColumn HeaderText="Votes" ItemStyle-Width="50px"
                     DataField="TotalVotes" ReadOnly="True"
                     SortExpression="TotalVotes"
                     ItemStyle-HorizontalAlign="Right"
                     HeaderStyle-HorizontalAlign="Right"
    />
```

The first column is defined as a normal, non-editable column that shows the ID of the question. The second column has a label with the question text when in display mode, and a textbox for modifying the text when in editing mode.

The third and fourth columns show a radio button and a checkbox, respectively, when in display mode, and both of them show a checkbox in editing mode. There isn't much difference between using a radio button or a checkbox as they both have a Checked property, whose value is the value of the respective field converted to a Boolean value through the Convert.ToBoolean method. We use a radio button for the Current column because it indicates that only one question can be the current one.

The last two columns declared in the code above are read-only columns that display the AddedDate and TotalVotes field values, respectively.

The last column on the far right shows the icon to jump to the options page:

```
    <asp:HyperLinkColumn ItemStyle-Width="20px"
                DataNavigateUrlField="QuestionID"
                DataNavigateUrlFormatString="Options.aspx?QuestionID={0}"
                DataTextFormatString="<img border=0 Alt='Show options'
                                                  src=./Images/Group.gif>"
                DataTextField="QuestionID"
                ItemStyle-HorizontalAlign="Center"
    />
    </Columns>
</asp:DataGrid>
```

It is a non-editable hyperlink rendered as an image, and the URL which it points to is built with a string template defined in DataNavigateUrlFormatString: the ID of each row will replace the {0} marker.

The page ends with the closing tags for the DataGrid control, the form, and the footer control:

```
        <Polls:AdminFooter ID="Footer" runat="server" />
    </form>
  </body>
</html>
```

The Code-behind for Questions.aspx

Now we're going to write the code that drives the page's functionality, in the code-behind file automatically created by Visual Studio .NET, Questions.vb. The code of this file is very similar to the code-behind file we saw in Chapter 6, so we'll show the code here without repeating all the details already explained. Here is the handler that runs when the page is loaded:

```
Private Sub Page_Load(ByVal sender As Object, ByVal e As EventArgs)
   If Not Page.IsPostBack Then
      BindGrid()
   End If
End Sub
```

(Note that the code for this method in the code download has some additional code in it that we will be adding in the section on securing the module later in the chapter)

The code above calls the `BindGrid` method, which actually fills the grid with the database records. Here's the code for this procedure:

```
Protected Sub BindGrid()
   ' Get all the Questions
   Dim myDV As DataView = _
      Business.Question.GetQuestions().Tables(0).DefaultView

   ' Sort the data according to the SortExpression value
   If Not (QuestionsGrid.Attributes("SortExpression") Is Nothing) Then
      myDV.Sort = QuestionsGrid.Attributes("SortExpression")
   End If

   QuestionsGrid.DataSource = myDV
   QuestionsGrid.DataBind()
End Sub
```

The function uses the business component to retrieve all the questions, and assigns the resulting `DataView` to the `DataSource` property of the `QuestionsGrid`. The `DataView` is then sorted according to a custom attribute set by the code in the next section. By default, when the page is loaded for the first time or when the grid's `SortAttribute` is null anyway, the records are sorted by creation date. They are already returned sorted in that way by the `sp_Polls_GetQuestions` stored procedure, so we don't have to set the `Sort` property in this case.

Sorting the Questions

When a column header is clicked, the `QuestionsGrid_Sort` function is called:

```
Protected Sub QuestionsGrid_Sort( _
   ByVal sender As Object, _
   ByVal e As DataGridSortCommandEventArgs)

   ' Hide controls for new question or error, in case they are visible
   AddNewError.Visible = False
   ShowAddNewControls(False)

   ' Disable the edit mode of a row, if enabled
   QuestionsGrid.EditItemIndex = -1

   ' Set the SortExpression attribute that will be used to actually sort
   ' the data in the BindGrid method
   QuestionsGrid.Attributes("SortExpression") = _
      e.SortExpression.ToString()
   BindGrid()
End Sub
```

The function first of all hides the controls for adding a new question or displaying an error message, in case they are visible. Then it disables the editing mode of a row, if enabled. Finally it extracts the selected ordering field and saves it as a grid attribute, the one we've just used in the previous procedure. The BindGrid procedure is called to refresh the grid with the new order applied.

Editing and Updating Questions

Now we will implement the methods that deal with the editing and updating of rows. The first procedure hides the control for adding a record, if visible, and starts the editing mode for the selected row by setting the EditItemIndex property:

```
Protected Sub QuestionsGrid_Edit( _
  ByVal sender As Object, _
  ByVal e As DataGridCommandEventArgs)

  ' Hide controls for new question or error, in case they are visible
  AddNewError.Visible = False
  ShowAddNewControls(False)

  ' Start editing
  QuestionsGrid.EditItemIndex = CInt(e.Item.ItemIndex)
  BindGrid()
End Sub
```

The second procedure resets the same property to −1, which brings the grid back to the normal display mode:

```
Protected Sub QuestionsGrid_CancelEdit( _
  ByVal sender As Object, _
  ByVal e As DataGridCommandEventArgs)

  QuestionsGrid.EditItemIndex = -1
  BindGrid()
End Sub
```

The last procedure completes the updating of the row, as long as the validator controls find no error in the input values. It extracts the new values from the edit controls, updates the properties of a Business.Question object, and persists the changes by calling its Update method:

```
Protected Sub QuestionsGrid_Update( _
  ByVal sender As Object, _
  ByVal e As DataGridCommandEventArgs)

  If Page.IsValid Then

    ' Get the new values from the textboxes
    Dim questionText As String = _
      CType(e.Item.FindControl("EditQuestionText"), TextBox).Text
    Dim isCurrent As Boolean = _
      CType(e.Item.FindControl("EditIsCurrent"), CheckBox).Checked
    Dim archived As Boolean = _
      CType(e.Item.FindControl("EditArchived"), CheckBox).Checked
```

```
        Dim questionId As Integer = _
          CInt(QuestionsGrid.DataKeys(e.Item.ItemIndex))

        ' Update the values
        Dim question As New Business.Question(questionId)
        question.Text = questionText
        question.IsCurrent = isCurrent
        question.Archived = archived
        question.Update()

        QuestionsGrid.EditItemIndex = -1
        BindGrid()
    End If
```

Deleting a Question

This event handler has the same structure as the procedure above, but it's actually simpler because it just extracts the primary key of the clicked row, uses it to initialize a new Business.Question object, and calls its Delete method:

```
Protected Sub QuestionsGrid_Delete( _
    ByVal sender As Object, _
    ByVal e As DataGridCommandEventArgs)

    ' Hide controls for new question or error, in case they are visible
    AddNewError.Visible = False
    ShowAddNewControls(False)

    ' Put grid out of edit mode
    QuestionsGrid.EditItemIndex = -1

    ' Get the ID of this record and delete it
    Dim theQuestion As New Business.Question( _
      CInt(QuestionsGrid.DataKeys(e.Item.ItemIndex)))

    theQuestion.Delete()
    BindGrid()
End Sub
```

Creating a Question

The last part to see is how to add a new question. When the **Create** button is pressed, the textbox and checkbox controls and the respective icons for confirming or canceling the operation are shown, while the **Create** button is made invisible. Below you can see the code for this event and the support functions that show or hide the controls according to the passed Boolean parameter:

```
Protected Sub Create_Click(ByVal sender As Object, ByVal e As EventArgs)
    ' Show the textboxes and buttons for adding a new record
    AddNewError.Visible = False
    ShowAddNewControls(True)
    QuestionsGrid.EditItemIndex = -1
    BindGrid()
End Sub
```

```
Protected Sub ShowAddNewControls(ByVal ShowControls As Boolean)
    ' Show/hide the controls for adding a new record
    NewQuestionText.Text = ""
    NewIsCurrent.Checked = False

    AddNewControlsRow.Visible = ShowControls
    CreateNewRow.Visible = Not ShowControls
End Sub
```

The icon for adding a new list is a button with a click-event procedure:

```
Protected Sub AddNew_Click(ByVal sender As Object, ByVal e As EventArgs)
    If Page.IsValid Then

        ' Add the new record
        If New Business.Question().Create( _
            NewQuestionText.Text, NewIsCurrent.Checked, False) < 0 Then

            ' If Add returned -1, the question was already present
            AddNewError.Visible = True

        End If
        ShowAddNewControls(False)
        BindGrid()
    End If
End Sub
```

The above code calls the `Create` method of the `Business.Question` class with the values read from the input textbox and checkbox, and the value `False` for the `Archived` field. If the method returns `True` then it makes visible the label that tells the user that the question is already present.

The `LinkButton` control is for canceling the operation; when pressed it hides the controls for adding the question and shows the **Create** button:

```
Protected Sub CancelAddNew_Click( _
    ByVal sender As Object, _
    ByVal e As EventArgs)

    ShowAddNewControls(False)
End Sub
```

This button would cause the page to be validated, as does any control that handles a server event and submits the page, and would result in an error if the textbox were empty. To avoid this problem we set its `CausesValidation` property to `False` when we declared it in the ASPX page.

Managing the Options

The page for managing the options of the questions has a very similar structure to the page we've just completed. It is simpler because we have less information to show, and it only adds a `DropDownList` control to select the question for which we want to see and edit the available options. The following screenshot shows the page while we're adding an option for the currently selected question:

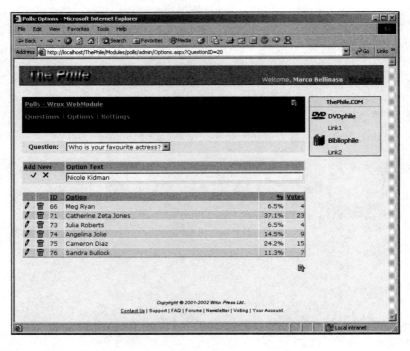

The Options.aspx Page

As we mentioned, the code for this page is similar to the previous one, so we'll only see the additions, which in this case is just the drop-down list of questions. Look at the code below to see how this is declared:

```
<asp:table Width="100%" ID="TableOptions"
           runat="server" CssClass="Grid_General">
  <asp:TableRow>
    <asp:TableCell Width="85px" HorizontalAlign="Center"
                   VerticalAlign="Top" Font-Bold="True" Text="Question:" />
    <asp:TableCell>
      <asp:DropDownList runat="server" ID="QuestionsDropDown"
                   DataTextField="QuestionText"
                   DataValueField="QuestionID"
                   CssClass="TextBox" AutoPostBack="True"
                   OnSelectedIndexChanged="QuestionsDropDown_IndexChanged"
      />
    </asp:TableCell>
  </asp:TableRow>
</asp:table>
```

The main thing to note is that the drop-down list has the AutoPostBack property set to True, which causes the form to be posted back every time the user changes the selected item. Remember that when a page is posted back its IsPostBack property is True – you can check this property to avoid filling the DropDownList of questions every time the form is posted back, since the control's state is maintained in subsequent calls of the page.

The rest of the page is mostly composed of the grid, which has four columns (`QuestionID`, `QuestionText`, `Percentage`, and `TotalVotes`) returned by the `sp_Polls_GetOptions` stored procedure. (Remember that `TotalVotes` and `Percentage` are calculated columns, but this does not make any difference here.) Only the question's text is an editable column, the others are read-only columns. There is really nothing in this grid that we haven't already seen in the `Questions.aspx` page and the previous chapters, so we won't repeat the code here. You can find the complete code in the download.

The Code-behind File for Options.aspx

As for the ASPX page, here we'll show only the differences from the previous page. The code for loading and binding the records to the grid is the same, as well as the code that adds, edits, and deletes the options. The difference here is that we also retrieve the questions and bind them to a `DropDownList` control, selecting the question with the ID that was specified in the `QueryString` passed along with the page URL. Here is the code that does all this, in the `Page_Load` event handler:

```
Private Sub Page_Load(ByVal sender As System.Object, ByVal e As EventArgs)

    ' Get the QuestionId from the QueryString
    Dim questionId As String = Request.Params("QuestionId")
    OptionsGrid.Attributes("QuestionId") = questionId

    If Not Page.IsPostBack Then

        ' Load all the avaible questions in the DropDown control
        Dim myDV As DataView = _
            Business.Question.GetQuestions().Tables(0).DefaultView
        QuestionsDropDown.DataSource = myDV
        QuestionsDropDown.DataBind()

        If Not (questionId Is Nothing) Then

            ' Select the DropDown element according to the questionId
            QuestionsDropDown.SelectedIndex = _
                QuestionsDropDown.Items.IndexOf( _
                QuestionsDropDown.Items.FindByValue(questionId))

        End If

        ' bind the page's controls
        BindGrid()

    End If

End Sub
```

(Note that the code in the download for this method has some additional code in it that we will be adding in the section on securing the module, later in the chapter)

If the ID retrieved from the `QueryString` is supplied, we select the corresponding item in the `DropDownList` after it has been filled.

Staying with the `QuestionsDropDown` control, here is the procedure that handles the `OnSelectedIndexChanged` event:

```
Protected Sub QuestionsDropDown_IndexChanged( _
  ByVal sender As Object, _
  ByVal e As EventArgs)

  Response.Redirect(("Options.aspx?QuestionId=" & _
    QuestionsDropDown.SelectedItem.Value))
End Sub
```

This redirects the browser to the same page, but with the ID of the selected question, in order to load that question's options the next time `BindGrid` is called.

Modifying the Settings Online

We've used the configuration component on several occasions so far, to get the settings, but whenever we wanted to change them we had to manually edit the `Polls.Config` file. It's not that big a deal, but why not provide a new page that allows the administrator to make all the changes through a web browser? This will avoid the need for editing the file and uploading it through FTP or with the tool we built in Chapter 4. The page, `Settings.aspx`, is presented below:

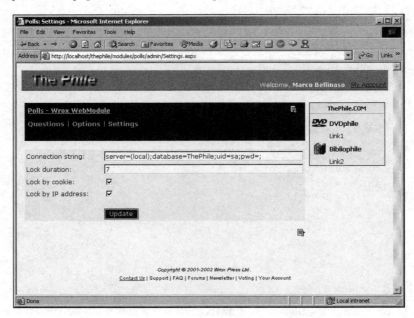

The Settings.aspx Page

This ASP.NET page is made up of a couple of textboxes, a couple of checkboxes, and the Update button, all aligned within a table. Once we've created the new `Settings.aspx` page, we fill it with the usual code for the page declaration, the header and the footer, and this server-side form in the middle:

```
<form method="post" runat="server" ID="Settings">
  <asp:table runat="server" CssClass="Grid_General" Width="100%">
    <asp:TableRow>
      <asp:TableCell Width="150px" Text="Connection string:" />
      <asp:TableCell>
        <asp:TextBox runat="server" Width="100%"
                     ID="ConnectionString" CssClass="TextBox" />
        <asp:RequiredFieldValidator runat="server"
                     ControlToValidate="ConnectionString" Display="dynamic">
          <br>* This field is required
        </asp:RequiredFieldValidator>
      </asp:TableCell>
    </asp:TableRow>
    <asp:TableRow>
      <asp:TableCell Text="Lock duration:" />
      <asp:TableCell>
        <asp:TextBox runat="server" Width="100%"
                     ID="LockDuration" CssClass="TextBox" />
        <asp:CompareValidator runat="server"
                         ControlToValidate="LockDuration" Type="Integer"
                         Operator="DataTypeCheck" Display="dynamic" >
          <br>* Invalid format
        </asp:CompareValidator>
      </asp:TableCell>
    </asp:TableRow>
    <asp:TableRow>
      <asp:TableCell Text="Lock by cookie:" />
      <asp:TableCell>
        <asp:CheckBox runat="server" ID="LockByCookie" />
      </asp:TableCell>
    </asp:TableRow>
    <asp:TableRow>
      <asp:TableCell Text="Lock by IP address:" />
      <asp:TableCell>
        <asp:CheckBox runat="server" ID="LockByIP" />
      </asp:TableCell>
    </asp:TableRow>
    <asp:TableRow VerticalAlign="Bottom" Height="40px">
      <asp:TableCell />
      <asp:TableCell>
        <asp:Button runat="server" Text="Update" ID="Update"
                 CssClass="Button" OnClick="Update_Click">
        </asp:Button>
      </asp:TableCell>
    </asp:TableRow>
  </asp:table>
</form>
```

The highlighted code declares the controls that show the current settings and allow changes to be made. There are two invisible controls, the validators, which ensure that the connection string is supplied and that if the (optional) lock duration is provided it is a number.

The Code-behind for Settings.aspx

The code-behind for modifying settings is composed of just two procedures. The first is Page_Load, which retrieves the settings from the XML file (or from the cache if this is not the first time we request them) by using the ModuleConfig and ModuleSettings classes in the Configuration assembly. The following code shows the current settings when the page is first loaded:

```
Private Sub Page_Load(ByVal sender As Object, ByVal e As EventArgs)
    If Not Page.IsPostBack Then

        ' Load all the settings
        Dim settings As Configuration.ModuleSettings = _
            Configuration.ModuleConfig.GetSettings()
        ConnectionString.Text = settings.ConnectionString
        LockDuration.Text = settings.LockDuration.ToString()
        LockByCookie.Checked = settings.LockByCookie
        LockByIP.Checked = settings.LockByIP

    End If

End Sub
```

(Note that the code in the download for this method has some additional code in it that we will be adding in the section on securing the module, later in the chapter)

The second procedure is Update_Click, raised when the **Update** button is clicked. It gets the new settings from the controls, sets the properties of a new ModuleSettings object, and finally calls the ModuleConfig's SaveSettings method to serialize the settings object to the XML file:

```
Protected Sub Update_Click(ByVal sender As Object, ByVal e As EventArgs)
    Dim settings As New Configuration.ModuleSettings()

    ' Set the new properties values and update everything
    settings.ConnectionString = ConnectionString.Text.Trim()
    settings.LockByCookie = LockByCookie.Checked
    settings.LockByIP = LockByIP.Checked

    If LockDuration.Text.Trim().Length > 0 Then
        settings.LockDuration = Integer.Parse(LockDuration.Text.Trim())
    Else
        settings.LockDuration = -1
        LockDuration.Text = "-1"
    End If

    ' Save the new settings
    Configuration.ModuleConfig.SaveSettings(settings)
End Sub
```

Note that the LockDuration setting is not required; if it is not supplied then the default value -1 is chosen, and also shown in the respective textbox.

We're done with the administration settings now. In the next sections we're going to discuss the end-user side of the module, such as the poll box, archive page, and the Windows client.

The Poll User Control

The administration system is complete, and now we can think about the implementation of the end-user part of the module. In the previous screenshots you will have noticed that a number of votes have been cast, but so far we have no way of posting a vote. In order to be able to test the grid in the administration pages we initially added some records to the Polls_Votes table manually. Now it's time to build the poll user control that we'll use in the homepage or other pages of the site. The poll box we want to create is represented in the following screenshot:

We add a new user control named Poll.ascx to the project, and enter the following code. The code is quite long, so we'll split it up and explain the individual pieces. The code below is all that is needed to create the poll box, and show the question and list of options:

```
<%@ Control Language="vb" AutoEventWireup="false" Codebehind="Poll.ascx.vb"
            Inherits="Wrox.WebModules.Polls.Web.Controls.User.Poll"%>
<asp:Table runat="server" ID="PollTable">
  <asp:TableRow>
    <asp:TableCell runat="server" ID="PollHeader"
                   HorizontalAlign="Center" />
  </asp:TableRow>
  <asp:TableRow>
    <asp:TableCell runat="server" ID="PollQuestion"
                   HorizontalAlign="Center" />
  </asp:TableRow>
  <asp:TableRow>
    <asp:TableCell HorizontalAlign="Center">
      <asp:RadioButtonList runat="server" ID="OptionsList"
                   DataTextField="OptionText" DataValueField="OptionID" />
      <asp:Label Runat="server" ID="PollError" Text="* Please select an
                 option" CssClass="Error" Visible="False" />
    </asp:TableCell>
  </asp:TableRow>
  <asp:TableRow>
    <asp:TableCell HorizontalAlign="Center">
      <asp:Button runat="server" Text="Vote" ID="Vote" CssClass="Button"
                  OnClick="Vote_Click" />
    </asp:TableCell>
  </asp:TableRow>
```

The header of the poll will be displayed by setting the Text property of the cell named PollHeader, and the question through the PollQuestion cell. Finally, the options are shown by the RadioButtonList called OptionsList. This works similarly to a DropDownListBox: it creates an item for each row in the data source and shows the content of the DataTextField field, and the added radio button has the value of the DataValueField field.

In a few lines we've already declared all the controls that show the options and post back the form with the selection. Now we need to declare other controls that show the results after the user has voted. We use a DataList for this, because it allows us to repeat custom HTML code or server controls for all the rows in the data source. The DataList control has many members in common with the DataGrid control, since they both inherit from BaseDataList – properties such as DataKeyField, DataKeys, DataSource, and DataMember and methods such as DataBind have exactly the same meaning in the two controls, and are used in the same way. The main difference between the two controls is that the DataList requires at least the <ItemTemplate> section, which contains the template code repeated for each item of the bound DataSource, while the DataGrid control can auto-generate HTML for rendering the data in columns. If you want to reproduce something like a grid, with multiple columns, you must do it by writing the <table>, <tr>, and <td> tags by yourself to create the grid layout; the DataList does not do that for you. Other templates supported by the DataList control are HeaderTemplate, AlternatingItemTemplate, EditItemTemplate, SelectedItemTemplate, SeparatorTemplate, and FooterTemplate, whose meaning should be clear (many of them are available for the DataGrid's templated columns too). A very interesting property for this control is RepeatColumns, which allows us to specify that the templated items will be repeated in one or more columns.

> *For complete examples of these properties and templates refer to* Professional ASP.NET 1.0 *(Wrox Press, ISBN 1-86100-703-5)*

The DataList in our page is declared as follows:

```
<asp:TableRow>
  <asp:TableCell HorizontalAlign="Center">
    <asp:DataList runat="server" ID="ResultsList">
      <ItemTemplate>
        <span class='<%# CssClass %>'>
          - <%# DataBinder.Eval(Container.DataItem, "OptionText") %>
          <br>
        </span>
        <span class='<%# ResultsStyle %>'>
          <%# DataBinder.Eval(Container.DataItem, "TotalVotes",
                                                    "({0} votes") %>
          - <%# DataBinder.Eval(Container.DataItem, "Percentage",
                                                    "{0:N1}%)") %>
        </span>
        <hr class='<%# BarStyle %>' width='<%# DataBinder.Eval(
            Container.DataItem, "Percentage", "{0:N0}%") %>' align="left">
      </ItemTemplate>
    </asp:DataList>
  </asp:TableCell>
</asp:TableRow>
```

The ItemTemplate section will be repeated for every row of the data source, as we said. For each data row we create the following elements:

- ❑ A <span> container for the option's text.

- ❑ A <span> container for the option's total number of votes and the corresponding percentage. (Both values are provided by the data source, and calculated by the sp_Polls_GetOptions stored procedure.)

- ❑ An <hr> line, whose width is set to the Percentage field of the data row currently being processed by the DataList. This way, creating the bars that graphically show the results for the options is really a no-brainer.

So, I guess that displaying the results and the graphical bars has turned out to be simpler than you might have thought.

It's worth noting that in the table in the previous piece of code, and in the code above, we set the class or CssClass properties of the HTML and server controls to public properties defined in the code-behind. No style is hard-coded in the control itself – everything (well, the most important parts at least) can be defined by the hosting page at design time or programmatically at run time, as we can do with any server control.

The file ends with a link to the ShowArchive.aspx page, and the closing tags for the parent table and the HTML form:

```
<asp:TableRow>
  <asp:TableCell HorizontalAlign="Center">
    <asp:HyperLink runat="server" ID="ArchiveLink" Text="[Archive]"
                   NavigateUrl="ShowArchive.aspx" />
  </asp:TableCell>
</asp:TableRow>
</asp:Table>
```

The Code-behind for the Poll User Control

In the code-behind for the poll user control, we change the namespace to Wrox.WebModules.Polls.Web.Controls.User. The class then starts with the declaration of the server-side control that Visual Studio .NET should have already added for us. Then we have to add the code for the public variables listed in the design section: the properties for the style of the header, question, results, and, most notably, the QuestionID property for specifying the ID of the question to load in the poll box. Here is the code for the private members and some of the properties:

```
Private myQuestionId As Integer = -2
Private myBarStyle As String
Private myResultsStyle As String

Public Property ArchiveLinkVisible() As Boolean
  Get
    Return ArchiveLink.Visible
  End Get
  Set(ByVal Value As Boolean)
    ArchiveLink.Visible = Value
  End Set
End Property
```

```
        Public Property BarStyle() As String
          Get
            Return myBarStyle
          End Get
          Set(ByVal Value As String)
            myBarStyle = Value
          End Set
        End Property
```

It's worth noting that most style properties, such as `HeaderStyle` or `ButtonStyle`, directly map properties of the server-side control:

```
        Public Property HeaderStyle() As String
          Get
            Return PollHeader.CssClass
          End Get
          Set(ByVal Value As String)
            PollHeader.CssClass = Value
          End Set
        End Property
```

Others, such as `BarStyle` and `ResultStyle`, need an auxiliary private property to keep the state of the respective property:

```
        Public Property BarStyle() As String
          Get
            Return myBarStyle
          End Get
          Set(ByVal Value As String)
            myBarStyle = Value
          End Set
        End Property
```

This is because the controls they will be used with are dynamically built by the `DataList` control at run time.

Now for the code that retrieves the data from the database, binds it to the proper controls, and either shows or hides the options or results (depending on whether the user has already voted for the question being asked):

```
        Public Overrides Sub DataBind()
          PollError.Visible = False

          ' If the QuestionId is not specified, get the current question's ID
          If myQuestionId = -2 Then
            myQuestionId = Business.Question.GetCurrentId()
          End If

          ' If there is a valid question
```

```vb
    If myQuestionId > -1 Then

      ' Get the details for the specified question
      Dim question As New Business.Question(myQuestionId)

      ' If this question does not exist, exit now
      If question.Id = -1 Then
        Vote.Visible = False
        Return
      End If

      ' Show the question text
      PollQuestion.Visible = True
      PollQuestion.Text = question.Text

      ' Get the options
      Dim options As DataView

      options = question.GetOptions().Tables(0).DefaultView

      ' If the user has not already voted, or is allowed
      ' to vote again anyway...
      If question.AllowVote Then
        ' Show the radiobutton options and hide the results
        OptionsList.Visible = True
        ResultsList.Visible = False
        OptionsList.DataSource = options
        OptionsList.DataBind()

        ' Show the Vote button only if there is at least 1 option
        Vote.Visible = options.Count >= 1
      Else

        ' Otherwise hide the RadioButtonList + Vote button,
        ' and show the results
        OptionsList.Visible = False
        Vote.Visible = False
        ResultsList.Visible = True
        ResultsList.DataSource = options
        ResultsList.DataBind()
        ' Add the number of total votes to the question text
        PollQuestion.Text &= "<br/>(" & question.TotalVotes & " votes)"
      End If
    Else
      ' If there is no current question, hide the controls
      PollQuestion.Visible = False
      OptionsList.Visible = False
      Vote.Visible = False
      ResultsList.Visible = False
    End If
End Sub
```

The core procedure is DataBind, which overrides the implementation of the base class. The code first gets the details of the specified question (if no QuestionID is supplied, it takes the current question by default). If the question is not found the procedure does not do anything else, otherwise it goes ahead by showing the question text in the respective table cell. Then, if it detects that the current user can vote (through the AllowVote property of the instance of Business.Question) it binds the question's options to the RadioButtonList control and shows it. Otherwise it hides the RadioButtonList control and binds the options to the DataList control, and shows this control instead. Also the Vote button is shown or hidden accordingly.

There is also the Page_Load event that calls DataBind if the page that hosts the control is not posted back. We could avoid having to implement the Page_Load event, and we could leave the task of calling the control's DataBind method up to the host page, as we've done for all controls in the previous pages. However, the control retrieves the connection string, gets the records, and sets all the controls' properties on its own, so it makes sense that it also actually binds the data to the proper controls without any external intervention. This is the same method we followed for the Headlines control in the NewsManagement module in Chapter 6. Here's the required code:

```
Private Sub Page_Load(ByVal sender As Object, ByVal e As EventArgs) _
   Handles MyBase.Load

   If Not Page.IsPostBack Then
     DataBind()
   End If
End Sub
```

> It's worth noting that in the code above we called the **DataBind** methods of this control. We can't use the **Page.DataBind** method to bind the data to all the controls, because this would also affect the controls on the page that hosts the user control, and this can cause unwanted behaviors. For example, say that the parent page has a listbox bound to a table, and that during its **Page_Load** event we selected an item. If we call **Page.DataBind** from the code above, the listbox would be reloaded and would of course deselect the item previously selected.

Handling the Postback Event

The code for the Vote_Click event is straightforward, thanks to the Business.Question's Vote method that takes care of checking if the user has already voted, and stores the vote in the database. We just have to get the ID of the selected option from the RadioButtonList, and pass it to the Vote method. If no option is selected, which is the case when the options are loaded and the user does not click any of them, then the control shows an error message instead. Here's the complete code:

```
Protected Sub Vote_Click(ByVal sender As Object, ByVal e As EventArgs)
   ' If there is no option selected, show the error label
   If OptionsList.SelectedItem Is Nothing Then
     PollError.Visible = True
   Else
     If myQuestionId = -2 Then
       myQuestionId = Business.Question.GetCurrentId()
     End If
```

```
        ' Add the user's vote. The business component will take care of
        ' checking if the user as already voted, setting the cookie etc.
        Dim theQuestion As New business.Question(myQuestionId)
        theQuestion.Vote(Integer.Parse(OptionsList.SelectedItem.Value))

        ' Re-bind, to show the results this time
        DataBind()
    End If
End Sub
```

Optimizing the Poll User Control

At this point the poll user control is fully functional. There is an issue though: every time we load the page that hosts the poll box we have to query the database to get the options and their details. Say that we want to insert the poll box into the site layout, into the header or footer maybe, and show the poll box from all the pages. This means that we would slow down execution of all the pages.

The content of the poll box does not change very often (at least as long as you don't have thousands of concurrent users with a large proportion actually voting), and once published it is very likely that the available options will remain the same. The first thing that comes to mind is to employ dynamic output caching, as we did in Chapter 6, since it allows us to easily cache pages and user control output for a given amount of time. However, after considering this option, we realized that this isn't the ideal solution in this case. In fact, dynamic caching saves the output every *n* seconds, or when the parameters in the URL or the form's controls change. But it does not refresh the cache based on custom rules defined within our control's code. In our case, we have to output different HTML depending on whether the user has or has not already voted for the current question. If we use dynamic output caching, the first time the control is displayed the whole output will be cached. Say that the user that requests the page with the poll box for the first time has already voted for the current question: the cached output would be the list of results. Now a second user, who has not voted yet, loads the page with the poll box: the ASP.NET engine detects that the output for the poll box is cached and displays it. Unfortunately, it displays the version with the results, and does not allow the user to vote! And a similar problem would occur if the first user had not voted yet; the output cached would display the list of options, and this would then be displayed to subsequent users, even those who should be prevented from voting again.

Well, this is the behavior of the standard control caching, but we can always employ our own implementation. Instead of caching the complete output, we will only cache the options data retrieved from the database – this is the operation that takes the longest time, and this data is the same in both cases (whether we're showing the results or the options list). When the user votes we delete the cached data, so that it is refreshed the next time someone loads the poll box.

Storing and reading data to and from the cache is really a no-brainer, thanks to the `Cache` object. Like the `Application` object, it is has a key-value pair `HashTable` to save and retrieve data, but also adds dependency-based expiration, lock management, and resource management (meaning that cached items not used are automatically removed). A dependency can be another cache key, a file, or a timestamp. When a dependency changes or expires, the respective cache item is invalidated and removed, so that the data must be retrieved again from its real source (file, database, return value of a function, etc.) the next time we need it. As mentioned, the `Cache` object manages concurrent requests and locks on its own, and unlike the `Application` object does not need the caller to use the `Lock` and `Unlock` methods.

Overleaf is the complete structure of the code-behind, with the added or modified code highlighted:

```csharp
public abstract class Poll : System.Web.UI.UserControl
{
  // controls declaration...

  private int cacheDuration = 5;

  public int CacheDuration
  {
    get { return cacheDuration; }
    set { cacheDuration = value; }
  }

  // other properties and private variables...

  public override void DataBind()
  {
    // if the QuestionID is not specified, get the current question's ID...

    // if there is a valid question
    if (QuestionID > -1)
    {
      ...
      // get the options
      DataView options;
      // if the options for this question are not cached,
      // retrieve and cache them, adding a dependency to a timestamp
      if (Cache["Polls_Question" + question.ID.ToString()]== null)
      {
        options = question.GetOptions().Tables[0].DefaultView;
        Cache.Insert("Polls_Question" + question.ID.ToString(), options,
                null, DateTime.Now.AddMinutes(CacheDuration), TimeSpan.Zero,
                System.Web.Caching.CacheItemPriority.High, null);
      }
      else
      {
        // otherwise extract the DataView from the cache
        options = (DataView)Cache["Polls_Question" +
                                            question.ID.ToString()];
      }

      // display the options or the results...
    }
    else
    {
      // if there is no current question, hide the controls...
    }
  }

  protected void Vote_Click(object sender, EventArgs e)
  {
      // add the user's vote...
      ...
      // reset the options cached
      ResetCache();
```

```
      // re-bind, to show the results this time
      DataBind();
    }
  }

    public void ResetCache()
    {
      if (QuestionID == -2) QuestionID = Business.Question.GetCurrentID();
      Cache.Remove("Polls_Question" + QuestionID.ToString());
    }
  }
```

First of all we added a public property called `CacheDuration`, which allows us to specify the number of minutes for which the data is cached (five minutes is the default).

```
      Private myQuestionId As Integer = -2
      Private myCacheDuration As Integer = 5
      Private myBarStyle As String
      Private myResultsStyle As String
```

Then, in `Page_Load` we check if the cache has a non-null entry for the current question. If so, the entry is cast to a `DataView` type and we can bind the data to the proper controls. Otherwise, we first retrieve the data and then insert it into the cache, specifying the expiration time by summing the `CacheDuration` minutes to the current time.

```
      Public Overrides Sub DataBind()
        PollError.Visible = False
        If myQuestionId = -2 Then
          myQuestionId = Business.Question.GetCurrentId()
        End If
        If myQuestionId > -1 Then
          Dim question As New Business.Question(myQuestionId)
          If question.Id = -1 Then
            Vote.Visible = False
            Return
          End If
          PollQuestion.Visible = True
          PollQuestion.Text = question.Text
          ' Get the options
          Dim options As DataView
          ' If the options for this question are not cached, retrieve
          ' and cache them
          If Cache(("Polls_Question" + question.Id.ToString())) Is Nothing Then

            options = question.GetOptions().Tables(0).DefaultView

            Cache.Insert( _
              "Polls_Question" & question.Id.ToString(), _
              options, _
              Nothing, _
              DateTime.Now.AddMinutes(myCacheDuration), _
              TimeSpan.Zero, _
```

```
              System.Web.Caching.CacheItemPriority.High, _
              Nothing)

        Else

            ' Otherwise extract the DataView from the cache
            options = CType(Cache( _
                ("Polls_Question" + question.Id.ToString())), DataView)

        End If
        If question.AllowVote Then
          OptionsList.Visible = True
          ResultsList.Visible = False
          OptionsList.DataSource = options
          OptionsList.DataBind()
          Vote.Visible = options.Count >= 1
        Else
          OptionsList.Visible = False
          Vote.Visible = False
          ResultsList.Visible = True
          ResultsList.DataSource = options
          ResultsList.DataBind()
        End If
      Else
        PollQuestion.Visible = False
        OptionsList.Visible = False
        Vote.Visible = False
        ResultsList.Visible = False
      End If
End Sub
```

Lastly, in `Vote_Click`, after adding the vote, we call `ResetCache`, which deletes the cached `DataView`, so that the updated options and results are retrieved again next time `DataBind` is executed. The `ResetCache` method has public visibility, so that the host page can call it by itself if there are special needs.

```
Protected Sub Vote_Click(ByVal sender As Object, ByVal e As EventArgs)
  If OptionsList.SelectedItem Is Nothing Then
    PollError.Visible = True
  Else
    If myQuestionId = -2 Then
      myQuestionId = Business.Question.GetCurrentId()
    End If
    Dim theQuestion As New business.Question(myQuestionId)
    theQuestion.Vote(Integer.Parse(OptionsList.SelectedItem.Value))

    ' Reset the options cached
    ResetCache()
    DataBind()
  End If
End Sub
```

```
      Public Sub ResetCache()

        If myQuestionId = -2 Then
          myQuestionId = Business.Question.GetCurrentId()
        End If

        Cache.Remove(("Polls_Question" & myQuestionId.ToString()))

      End Sub
```

Now we have an optimized control, which only queries the database every five minutes, or whatever duration you choose with the programmable CacheDuration property. This way we speed up all the pages that host the control.

Testing the Control

To test the control we add one poll box to the Questions.aspx page of the administration section. We want to test if the control correctly shows the current question when we change it from the administration page, and if it shows the updated text. It is also useful to have it here because we can add test votes without leaving the administration console. We register the control at the top of the page, and declare one at the bottom, just before the server form closing tag:

```
<%@ Page language="vb" Codebehind="Questions.aspx.vb"
         AutoEventWireup="false"
         Inherits="Wrox.WebModules.Polls.Web.Questions" %>
<%@ Register TagPrefix="Polls" TagName="Poll" src="..\Poll.ascx" %>
<%@ Register TagPrefix="Polls" TagName="AdminHeader"
         src="AdminHeader.ascx" %>
<%@ Register TagPrefix="Polls" TagName="AdminFooter"
         src="AdminFooter.ascx" %>
<html>
  <body>
    <form method="post" runat="server" ID="Questions">
      ...

      <Polls:Poll ID="CurrentPoll" runat="server"
                  CacheDuration="10"
                  Width="180px"
                  ArchiveLinkVisible="True"
                  HeaderText="Current Poll"
                  CssClass="Poll_Box"
                  BarStyle="Poll_Bar"
                  ResultsStyle="Poll_Results"
                  HeaderStyle="Grid_Header"
                  QuestionStyle="Poll_Question"
                  ButtonStyle="Button"
                  LinkStyle="PollLink"
                  HorizontalAlign="Center"
      />

      <!-- Insert the footer -->
      <Polls:AdminFooter ID="Footer" runat="server" />
    </form>
  </body>
</html>
```

We haven't supplied the QuestionID property, so the control will show the current question. We've instead set the other properties for the style (font, colors, etc.) of the various parts of the poll box, and set the duration for which the results will be cached.

As a possible enhancement, you could extend the ModuleSettings class and the Settings.aspx page to allow the administrator to change the default cache duration online, without the need to manually change the settings in the source code and re-upload the updated file.

We also have to modify the code-behind code, by adding the calls to CurrentPoll's DataBind method every time we delete, add, or edit a question. This is necessary if we want the poll box to always show the current question and the updated question text. Here are the modifications:

```
Protected Sub QuestionsGrid_Update( _
  ByVal sender As Object, _
  ByVal e As DataGridCommandEventArgs)

  If Page.IsValid Then
    ' Get the new values from the textboxes
    Dim questionText As String = _
      CType(e.Item.FindControl("EditQuestionText"), TextBox).Text
    Dim isCurrent As Boolean = _
      CType(e.Item.FindControl("EditIsCurrent"), CheckBox).Checked
    Dim archived As Boolean = _
      CType(e.Item.FindControl("EditArchived"), CheckBox).Checked
    Dim questionId As Integer = _
      CInt(QuestionsGrid.DataKeys(e.Item.ItemIndex))
    ' Update the values
    Dim question As New Business.Question(questionId)
    question.Text = questionText
    question.IsCurrent = isCurrent
    question.Archived = archived
    question.Update()

    QuestionsGrid.EditItemIndex = -1
    BindGrid()
    ' Rebind the CurrentPoll control, because the current
    ' poll might have changed
    CurrentPoll.DataBind()
  End If
End Sub


Protected Sub QuestionsGrid_Delete( _
  ByVal sender As Object, _
  ByVal e As DataGridCommandEventArgs)
  ' Hide controls for new question or error, in case they are visible
  AddNewError.Visible = False
  ShowAddNewControls(False)
  ' Put grid out of edit mode
  QuestionsGrid.EditItemIndex = -1
  ' Get the ID of this record and delete it
  Dim theQuestion As New Business.Question( _
    CInt(QuestionsGrid.DataKeys(e.Item.ItemIndex)))
```

```
      theQuestion.Delete()
      BindGrid()
      ' Rebind the CurrentPoll control, because the deleted poll
      ' could be the current one
      CurrentPoll.DataBind()
   End Sub


   Protected Sub AddNew_Click(ByVal sender As Object, ByVal e As EventArgs)

      If Page.IsValid Then
        ' Add the new record
        If New Business.Question().Create( _
          NewQuestionText.Text, NewIsCurrent.Checked, False) < 0 Then
          ' If Add returned -1, the question was already present
          AddNewError.Visible = True
        End If
        ShowAddNewControls(False)
        BindGrid()
        ' Rebind the CurrentPoll control, because the current
        ' poll might have changed
        CurrentPoll.DataBind()
      End If
   End Sub
```

Finally, here is how the Questions.aspx page looks with the poll user control within it:

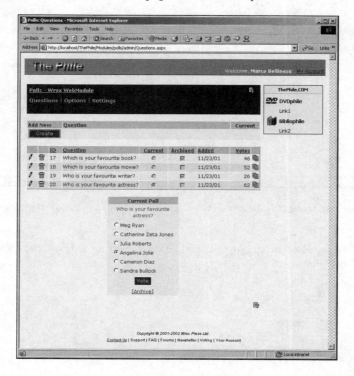

The screenshot above shows the `Polls` control with the radio buttons to allow the user to vote. The screenshot below shows the situation where the `Poll` control detects that the current user has already voted for the question, and so it automatically shows the results:

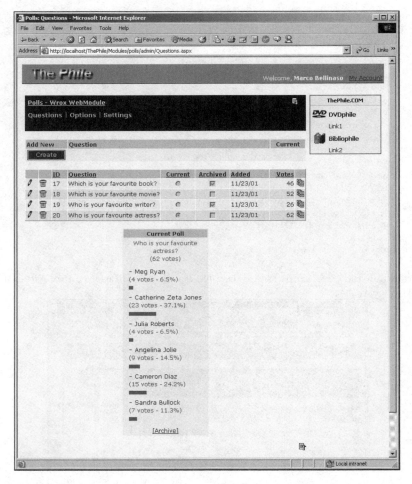

Of course, your results might be different – it's a matter of personal taste, and this was just an example. :-)

We only showed a single poll box here, but you could try creating a simple page with multiple boxes that ask different questions.

The ShowArchive.aspx Page

We've already mentioned a few times that we need a page that shows the results for the archived polls, and we added a link to it from within the poll box. Now it's time to develop the page. We want it to show all the questions, one per line, and when we click one it has to expand and display its options and results. We should be able to have multiple questions expanded at the same time if we want to. We will initially show them in 'collapsed' mode because we don't want to create a very long page, distracting the user and making it hard for them to search for a particular question. Displaying only the questions when the page is first loaded produces a clearer and more easily navigable page. The following screenshot shows the complete page with three archived polls (two expanded to show the results and one collapsed):

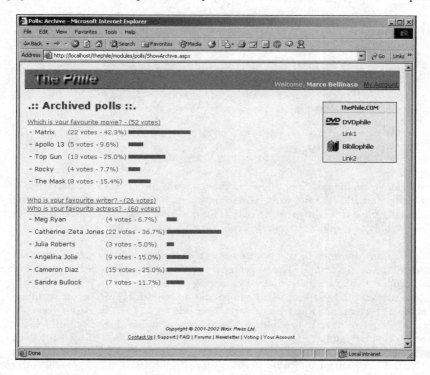

That said, here's the content of the ASPX page, ShowArchive.aspx:

```
<%@ Page language="vb" Codebehind="ShowArchive.aspx.vb"
        AutoEventWireup="false"
        Inherits="Wrox.WebModules.Polls.Web.ShowArchive" %>
<%@ OutputCache Duration="3600" VaryByParam="none" %>
<%@ Register TagPrefix="WroxUser" TagName="SiteHeader"
            Src="/ThePhile/Controls/SiteHeader.ascx" %>
<%@ Register TagPrefix="Wrox" Namespace="Wrox.ThePhile.Web.Controls.Server"
            Assembly="Wrox.ThePhile.Web.Controls" %>
<%@ Register TagPrefix="WroxUser" TagName="SiteFooter"
            Src="/ThePhile/Controls/SiteFooter.ascx" %>
<!DOCTYPE HTML PUBLIC "-//W3C//DTD HTML 4.0 Transitional//EN" >
```

```
<html>
  <head>
    <title>Polls: Archive</title>
    <link rel="stylesheet" HREF="/ThePhile/Styles/ThePhile.css" />
    <link href="/ThePhile/Styles/Navigator.css" rel="stylesheet" />
    <meta name="CODE_LANGUAGE" Content="VB">
    <script language="JavaScript1.2" type="text/javascript">
      function expandDiv(ctrl)
      {
        ctl = eval(ctrl);
        if (ctl.style.display == "none")
          ctl.style.display = "";
        else
          ctl.style.display = "none";
      }
    </script>
  </head>
  <body>
    <form method="post" runat="server" ID="Archive">
      <WroxUser:SiteHeader id="Header" runat="server" />
      <br>
      <table width="100%" border="0" cellspacing="4" cellpadding="2">
        <tr>
          <td width="100%" valign="top">
```

The code above defines the JavaScript function that expands or collapses the passed <div> element, inverting its state, and adds the site-wide header and menu box. Also note that we've used the @ OutputCache directive to cache the page output for one hour (you can change this value to suit your needs), which avoids querying the database every time the page is loaded.

The rest of the code, continued below, is a Repeater control that shows the question text and the total number of votes for each question. The Repeater control does not inherit from BaseDataList, but it does expose properties and methods that we've already seen in the DataGrid and DataList controls, such as DataSource and DataBind. This control has no built-in HTML layout at all; it just processes and repeats the Item template (the code is declared inside an <ItemTemplate> section) for each item of the specified source of data. It also does not have built-in support for selecting/deleting/editing items – if you need to do that you have to implement the mechanism by yourself by using the general ItemCommand event. This control is best suited when you don't need the advanced features of a DataGrid/DataList control, and want to generate as little HTML code as possible, to speed up the download from the server to the client. It is also used when you don't want to show the records in rows (for which you have to build a table by yourself, as we see in our page), but maybe you want to render the data as a continuous string, or with any other heavily customized layout.

This first Repeater also contains a second Repeater control. The DataSource of this nested Repeater is dynamically set by calling a public function declared in the code-behind, which accepts as input the ID of the question being processed by the parent Repeater. The called function returns a DataView with the child options and number of votes, which are shown as in the poll control. The only other difference is that here the nested Repeater is wrapped by a collapsed <div> element, refreshed when the question text is clicked.

```
<asp:Repeater runat="server" ID="ArchivedPolls">
  <ItemTemplate>
    <a class="Poll_Question" href="javascript:expandDiv('div<%#
                    DataBinder.Eval(Container.DataItem, "QuestionID") %>')">
      <%# DataBinder.Eval(Container.DataItem, "QuestionText") %>
      - <%# DataBinder.Eval(Container.DataItem, "TotalVotes",
                                                "({0} votes)") %>
    </a>
    <div style="display:'none'" ID="<%# "div" +
                    DataBinder.Eval(Container.DataItem, "QuestionID") %>">
    <table>
      <asp:Repeater id="MyRepeater" runat="server"
                    DataSource='<%# GetResultsSource(int.Parse(
                    DataBinder.Eval(Container.DataItem,
                    "QuestionID").ToString())) %>'>
        <ItemTemplate>
          <tr>
            <td class="Poll_Option">
              - <%# DataBinder.Eval(Container.DataItem, "OptionText") %>
            </td>
            <td class="Poll_Results">
              <%# DataBinder.Eval(Container.DataItem, "TotalVotes",
                                                    "({0} votes") %>
              - <%# DataBinder.Eval(Container.DataItem, "Percentage",
                                                    "{0:N1}%)") %>
            </td>
            <td width="300px">
              <hr class="Poll_Bar" width='<%# DataBinder.Eval(
                        Container.DataItem, "Percentage", "{0:N0}%") %>' >
            </td>
          </tr>
        </ItemTemplate>
      </asp:Repeater>
    </table>
    </div>
    <br>
  </ItemTemplate>
</asp:Repeater>
```

The page terminates with the site-wide footer control, and the other closing tags.

The Code-behind for ShowArchive.aspx

The following code retrieves all the questions and binds them to the `ArchivedPolls` Repeater control:

```
Private Sub Page_Load(ByVal sender As Object, ByVal e As EventArgs)
  ArchivedPolls.DataSource = _
    Business.Question.GetQuestions(True).Tables(0).DefaultView
  ArchivedPolls.DataBind()
End Sub
```

Note that on this occasion we pass True to the GetQuestions method, because we only want the archived questions. Here is the GetResultsSource method that returns the child options of the specified question:

```
Public Function GetResultsSource(ByVal questionId As Integer) As DataView
   Return New Business.Question(questionId).GetOptions().Tables(0).DefaultView
End Function
```

Securing the Module

For this module we're going to protect only the administration console, and leave the archive page freely accessible. However, if you plan to employ polls to gather marketing information, or if you receive several thousands of votes (making your results accurate enough to sell them), you might want to protect the archives too. You'll just need to add a new permission, or in the ShowArchive.aspx page add the code to check if the current user has the AdministerPolls permission.

First we declare the enumeration with the single permission, under the Wrox.WebModules.Polls namespace, in the Enums.vb file of the Core module:

```
Namespace WebModules.Polls
   Public Enum PollsPermissions
      AdministerPolls = 300
   End Enum
End Namespace
```

Then, in the Page_Load event of the administration pages, we add the following code:

```
Private Sub Page_Load(ByVal sender As Object, ByVal e As EventArgs)
   ' Check if the current user is allowed to administer the polls
   If Not (TypeOf Context.User Is SitePrincipal) _
      OrElse Not CType(Context.User, SitePrincipal).HasPermission( _
         CInt(PollsPermissions.AdministerPolls)) Then

      Response.Redirect( _
         "/ThePhileVB/WebModules/Accounts/Login.aspx?ShowError=true", True)

   End If

   If Not Page.IsPostBack Then
      'the rest of the page loading code usually goes here
   End If
End Sub
```

If Context.User will not cast to a SitePrinicpal then the user is not logged in and the method redirect the request to the login page. It does the same if the user is logged in but without the AdministerPolls permission. Refer back to Chapter 5 if you need more details about the way the Accounts.Business classes work.

The Poll Web Service

The last thing we have to implement is the web service that allows external clients to retrieve the current question and its results from our site. In the design section we decided to return both the question and the results through a single method, GetCurrent, in two tables of the same DataSet object. The web service's method simply wraps a call to the GetCurrent static method of the Business.Question class. So, we add a new web service to the project, name it Poll.asmx, and edit its code-behind file. (The web services created by Visual Studio .NET use the .asmx file only to declare the respective code-behind.) Apart from the use of the <WebMethod()> attribute, which permits remote calling of this method, the code is not particularly exciting and so we will not list it in full here:

```
<WebMethod()> _
Public Function GetCurrent() As DataSet
    Return Wrox.WebModules.Polls.Business.Question.GetCurrent()
End Function
```

This is another example of well contructed business classes allowing us to deliver information in different forms with the minimum of effort.

Testing the Web Service

After compiling the project the web service is now ready to be tested. If you browse to Poll.asmx, you'll get the list of the available web methods, just GetCurrent in this case. Click the GetCurrent link, and you'll see sample SOAP code for requests and responses, and a button to invoke the method. The following screenshot shows part of this window, and the window opened when the Invoke button is pressed, with the SOAP response that lists the question and the results:

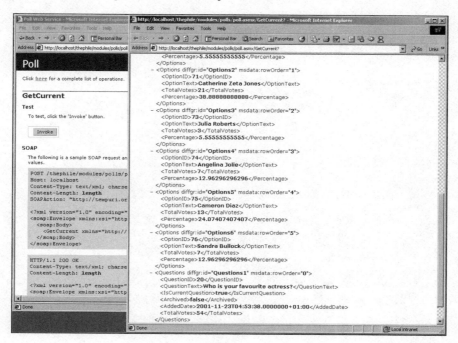

As you can see in the foreground window, the returned `DataSet` first lists the options, and then has all the details for the current question.

The Windows Client Application

In Visual Studio .NET we add a new Visual Basic .NET Windows Forms project to the solution. First we create a proxy class for using the `Poll` web service. We do this by adding a web reference to the project (Project | Add Web Reference). We just specify the full URL of the web service file, and Visual Studio .NET creates a proxy class to access the web service. The proxy class appears under Web References in the Solution Explorer. We rename it from `localhost` to `ThePhile`, to make its name more meaningful.

Now, through the visual designer, we drop some controls onto the form:

❏ A label to display the question

❏ A `DataGrid` to show the options and their percentages

❏ A timer and a button to automatically or manually refresh the results

The code we need to add is pretty simple. We retrieve the question and the options in a single call, then we get the question text from a table and show it in the label, and bind the other table to the grid to make it automatically display the results one per row. Here is the code you have to add to the Visual Studio .NET generated code of the form class:

```
Private Sub Viewer_Load(ByVal sender As Object, ByVal e As EventArgs) _
    Handles MyBase.Load

    FillOptionsGrid()
End Sub

Private Sub FillOptionsGrid()

    ' Get the dataset through the webservice
    Dim currPoll As New DataSet()
    Dim poll As New ThePhile.Poll()

    ' Set the web service timeout to 180 seconds
    poll.Timeout = 180

    Try

        currPoll = poll.GetCurrent()

    Catch exc As Exception

        ' If the call to GetCurrent throws an exception, disable the timer,
        ' show the exception message and close the app
        TimerRefresh.Enabled = False
        MessageBox.Show(exc.Message, "Error", MessageBoxButtons.OK, MessageBoxIcon.Error)
        Close()

    End Try
```

```
        Options.DataSource = currPoll.Tables("Options")

        ' Set the question title
        Question.Text = String.Format( _
          "{0}    ( {1} votes )", _
          currPoll.Tables("Questions").Rows(0)("QuestionText").ToString(), _
          currPoll.Tables("Questions").Rows(0)("TotalVotes").ToString())

        ' Remove the current grid columns
        Options.TableStyles.Clear()

        ' Bind Options table to the Grid, and show the OptionText,
        ' TotalVotes, and Percentage
        Options.SetDataBinding(currPoll, "Options")
        Dim ts As New DataGridTableStyle()
        ts.MappingName = "Options"
        ts.AlternatingBackColor = Color.LightGray

        ' Add the OptionText column
        Dim OptionCol = New DataGridTextBoxColumn()
        OptionCol.MappingName = "OptionText"
        OptionCol.HeaderText = "Option"
        OptionCol.Width = 300
        ts.GridColumnStyles.Add(OptionCol)

        ' Add the TotalVotes column
        Dim VotesCol = New DataGridTextBoxColumn()
        VotesCol.MappingName = "TotalVotes"
        VotesCol.HeaderText = "Votes"
        VotesCol.Width = 50
        VotesCol.Alignment = HorizontalAlignment.Right
        ts.GridColumnStyles.Add(VotesCol)

        ' Add the Percentage column
        Dim PercCol = New DataGridTextBoxColumn()
        PercCol.MappingName = "Percentage"
        PercCol.HeaderText = "%"
        PercCol.Width = 50
        PercCol.Alignment = HorizontalAlignment.Right
        ts.GridColumnStyles.Add(PercCol)

        ' Finally add the table to the grid
        Options.TableStyles.Add(ts)

End Sub

Private Sub RefreshTimer_Tick( _
  ByVal sender As Object, _
  ByVal e As EventArgs) _
  Handles TimerRefresh.Tick

    ' Refresh the grid
    FillOptionsGrid()
```

```
      End Sub

      Private Sub ButtonRefresh_Click( _
        ByVal sender As Object, _
        ByVal e As EventArgs) _
        Handles ButtonRefresh.Click


        ' Refresh the grid
        FillOptionsGrid()
      End Sub
```

The heart of the class is the `FillOptionsGrid` routine, which is called when the form loads, when the **Refresh** button is pressed, and when the time specified for the timer expires. As previously mentioned, the routine retrieves the `DataSet` returned by the web service's `GetCurrent` method, gets the question's text and total number of votes from the `Questions` table, and shows this information in the label. Then it binds the `Options` table to the grid, and creates columns for the option's text, total number of votes, and respective percentage, by mapping the database's columns to the grid's new columns. It's worth noting that the call to `GetCurrent` is protected inside a `Try...Catch` block, to catch exceptions that may occur, for example if the web service or a specific method is not found, or if the request times out. If an exception is caught we first disable the timer that updates the results by re-calling the `FillOptionsGrid` routine, and then show an error message with the exception's text – when the user closes the message box the application is terminated. If we didn't disable the timer then if the user does not close the message box soon and exits the application, the timer would continue to refresh the grid, opening further error dialogs.

Here is a screenshot of the application running:

The Web Service's Timeout and Url Properties

Before concluding the web service example it's worth introducing two very useful properties that every web service proxy exposes: `Timeout` and `Url`. The former allows us to set the interval of time before a request – a call to a method – times out. The default is 90 seconds, but you may want to choose a longer or shorter interval, according to the forecasted traffic and number of calls to the web service. The concept is exactly the same as the timeout interval for an ASP.NET page. This is a public property, so from the client code you can easily change the value as follows:

```
dim poll as ThePhile.Poll = new ThePhile.Poll()
' set the timeout to 180 seconds
poll.Timeout = 180;
```

The `Url` property allows the consumer of the web service to change the URL to which the proxy points. When we added a reference to the web service in Visual Studio .NET, the IDE saved for us a **WSDL** (**Web Service Description Languag**e) **file** and created the proxy, namely the local class that allows the client to access the web service as if it were on the local computer and not on a server on the Internet. Both the WSDL file and the proxy reference the web service with the URL specified in the **Add Web Reference** wizard. In the WSDL file the URL is defined in the `<soap:address>` tag as follows:

```
<service name="Poll">
  <port name="PollSoap" binding="s0:PollSoap">
    <soap:address
              location="http://localhost/ThePhile/Modules/Polls/poll.asmx" />
  </port>
  ...
</service>
```

While in the proxy it's defined in the constructor.

The code above saves the URL of the web service in the public variable `Url`, which is accessible from the client code too. This means that the client can change the value of this property and point to a web service in a different location, as long as it supports the same methods and parameters of course. This is quite important, because if we have deployed the web service on several servers and we find that one server is not available, we can easily change the proxy's `Url` property and point to the web service on another working server! Here's a quick example:

```
dim poll as ThePhile.Poll = new ThePhile.Poll()
poll.Url = "http://www.thephile2.com/Modules/Polls/poll.asmx"
```

As a last note, in this example we've referenced the web service on our local server. Of course when we deploy the site and the web service we must rebuild the proxy so that it points to the web service on the production server, or we can manually change the URL in the WSDL file and the proxy class.

If you want to know more about web services you can refer to Professional ASP.NET Web Services with VB.NET *(ISBN 1-86100-775-2)*

Summary

This chapter has presented a working solution for handling multiple dynamic polls on our website. The complete `Polls` module is made up of several parts:

- ❑ An administration console for managing the polls through a web browser
- ❑ Integration with the `Accounts` module to secure the administration pages
- ❑ A user control that enables us to show different polls in any page we want with just a couple of lines of code

- ❏ A web service that can be accessed by external clients to get the current poll's question and results

- ❏ A Windows client program that uses the web service to display the current poll and its results

This module can easily be employed in many real-world sites as it is now, but of course you can expand and enhance it. Here are just a few suggestions:

- ❏ Add more styles properties to the poll control, and the ability to remind the user which option they voted for. Currently they can see the results, but the control does not indicate how they voted.

- ❏ Add a `ReleaseDate` and `ExpireDate` to the polls, so that we can schedule the current poll to change automatically.

- ❏ Provide the option to allow only registered users to vote. Alternatively, keep the vote open to all, but allow only registered users to see the results and/or the archive page.

- ❏ Expand the web service and the respective Windows client so that it can display all the archived polls as well as the current one.

In the next chapter we're going to continue the development of ThePhile.com through the addition of another easily pluggable module. This new module will be used for managing multiple mailing lists and their subscribers, and for sending out newsletters.

9

Mailing Lists

In this chapter we'll discuss the design and implementation of a complete mailing list system. This will enable users to subscribe to receive regular newsletters, and will allow administrators to manage mailing lists and newsletter content. First we'll look at what mailing lists and newsletters can offer to websites like ours, and will consider various ways of making the mailing list administrator's life as easy as possible. By the end of the chapter we'll have developed a flexible mailing list module that can be plugged into most sites. In keeping with the rest of the project, we will aim to integrate this module into our ThePhile.com site through the reuse of familiar code and architecture where appropriate.

The Problem

Throughout this book we've mentioned that the key to a successful site is having good content. This content also needs to be logically organized to ease navigability, have an attractive design, and offer some interaction with the user. The content not only has to be interesting and accurate, but to ensure that users keep visiting the site it must always be fresh and regularly updated. To help us achieve this for our ThePhile.com website, we built the `NewsManager` module (in Chapter 6) to allow an administrator to easily manage and publish new content (for example an article, a new product for sale, or a new design).

But even if fresh content is frequently added to the site, not every user will be aware of it. They might not visit the site daily or weekly just to see the latest updates, especially if the site is updated on a random basis with no public announcement of when new material has been added. A good way to inform the user that some new content has been added to the site is to send an e-mail **newsletter** that lists all the new resources available on the site. Many sites offer the option of subscribing to a **mailing list**, which typically represents a group of users interested in a certain kind of news. A newsletter is sent to a mailing list to inform the community of users that the site is still worth visiting.

You should always keep in mind that you're offering a service to the user, and it must be a high quality service if you don't want to lose your subscribers. This means that you need to provide *targeted* content. So, you shouldn't send out a general content newsletter if you have a large site with different sections and different types of content. For example, at ThePhile.com we cover DVDs and books, and so we have news for two different topics. We should provide at least two different mailing lists, so that the users can get what they want and avoid getting what they are not interested in, which they may perceive as spam.

It's a nice touch to personalize every e-mail message, for example with the name of the subscriber if this information is available, because this can help to build a more personal relationship with the subscriber. However, in order to persuade users to subscribe to a mailing list the subscription process should be as straightforward as possible and they should not be forced to provide additional personal details. The most common way of subscribing to a list is to type your e-mail address in a form on the home page and press submit. This will allow only the e-mail address to be used to personalize the newsletter. In order to achieve more extensive personalization you have to ask the users to provide more details, such as their first and last names. For your websites the choice is up to you, but we want our module for ThePhile.com to support both a basic and extended subscription form, so that we can cater for users with different attitudes and so that managing the mailing list is as straightforward as possible in either case.

Some website visitors don't like to submit their e-mail address even to be informed about changes to the website. To encourage people to maintain their subscriptions, and to encourage more people to sign up, a webmaster can offer something extra that is only available to the mailing list's subscribers, for example a short tip, article, or some kind of discount for one of the site's products.

The primary purpose of a mailing list system is to inform the users that some new material is available online, and therefore convince them to visit the site again. But you could also make money from your mailing lists. Say that you have several thousands of subscribers; you could sell some space in your newsletters for **advertisement spots**. These shouldn't be anything too invasive, perhaps just a two to three line description of a partner site or company, or the manufacturer of a product you sell on your site. If you provide some valuable content in your newsletters (as mentioned above, an extra article or tip), and the advertisement is short and not invasive, the users won't complain about it. If you manage to sell space in the newsletter, remember that this space is very valuable for the sponsor. As users have elected to receive the newsletter, they will often read it thoroughly, and so the advertisement will get much more attention than it would receive through a common banner ad. Research shows that the average click-through from spots in newsletters is around 4-5%, compared to around 1% or less for banner ads.

However you decide to promote your website and get more people to subscribe, you will face the problem of managing all the details of your clients, such as e-mail addresses, keeping track of the messages you send, and building a system to allow the user to subscribe or unsubscribe easily. The user must have the right to unsubscribe at any time, so we should provide facilities that allow the user to easily do this, preferably without having to re-type their e-mail address. Some small sites manually collect subscriber e-mail addresses from an HTML form, create a group of contacts in Outlook or their messaging client, and use it to write to all the subscribers. This mostly applies to static sites, where ASP or other server-side code is not used. However, when the site starts to have a significant number of subscribers, manually adding or removing the users several times a week becomes a pain, and if the number is in the order of thousands, it is almost impossible.

The Problem Statement

This leads us to our problem statement: we risk losing traffic because we have no way of letting our users know that our content has been updated. So the aim for the chapter is to build a newsletter mailing list system so we can deliver targeted, personalized content to users who choose to subscribe. A secondary problem then arises – managing the system and personalizing newsletters could become time-consuming. So we want to include a subscription and administration system that automates most of the tasks and allows the administrator to complete the rest of the tasks much more easily.

Now we know what the problems are that we want to solve, we can move on to specifying the features we want our solution to have, in other words the requirements:

- ❑ A user interface where users can join/leave mailing lists without needing to register on the site.

- ❑ An administration console for managing multiple mailing lists. It should allow the administrator to add, remove, or modify lists and their properties.

- ❑ The administrator should also be able to manage the archive of newsletters previously sent to each list, reading the archived messages, and copying them. The copy facility will be useful for quickly creating new messages, or for manually sending a message to a recent subscriber who has requested an old newsletter.

- ❑ The ability to send e-mails to subscribers in plain text or HTML format, containing the message and other information about the list (such as the name and description).

- ❑ In each newsletter there should be a link to enable easy un-subscription.

- ❑ A facility for automatically customizing each e-mail message with the name and address of the user, even within the body of the message (the user feels this as a more personal relationship with the site's staff, even if we all know that it's not really personal, since the name is automatically replaced by a machine). We will also need a backup plan in case the user decides not to supply their name.

- ❑ The ability for the administrator to auto-generate HTML code for a form that will collect the user's data. This feature works like a wizard – we choose the list we want to create the form for, select a few other options, and the wizard generates the code for us. This can then be copied into any (static or dynamic) page where we want to show the subscription form.

- ❑ The facility to set options such as the sender's name and address that will be seen by the subscribers on the e-mails they receive, a signature that will be automatically added to each message, a default subject, and subscription and un-subscription messages.

- ❑ We want the administrator to be able to monitor website subscribers online, contact them, and even change the website layout from anywhere in the world – all that is needed is access to a computer with a Web browser and an Internet connection.

In the next section we're going to provide a more detailed discussion of the features we can implement to have a fully functional mailing list module.

The Design

From our requirements it's clear that we're going to be handling data about users and the lists they subscribe to. In keeping with the rest of the site we'll use our SQL Server database to store this information. We'll also need an interface for administrators to manage the lists, and an interface where users can subscribe. As with other modules we'll use a multi-tier approach and will make use of data access and business logic layers to keep the UI and database separate.

In this section we'll design the database tables for this module, and design the data and business layers that we'll use for managing the subscriptions from the administration console. The nice thing about the administration console is that we won't need to manually manage the group of subscribers – the application will automatically add or remove them to/from the database. For this we will make use of stored procedures called by methods in response to certain events.

Designing the Database Tables

As discussed in Chapter 2, all modules in our project require a prefix for the tables and stored procedures. For this module it will be `MLists_`. We need the four tables shown in the following diagram, which also indicates their relationships:

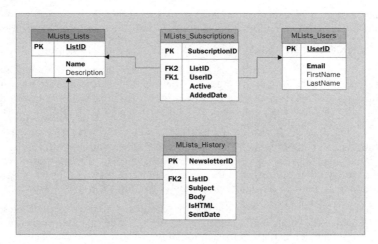

The MLists_Lists Table

The `MLists_Lists` table is used to store the information about each available mailing list:

Column Name	Type	Size	Allow Null	Description
ListID	int – Identity primary key	4	No	The unique ID for the mailing list.
Name	varchar	50	No	The name of the mailing list.
Description	varchar	250	Yes	The optional description of the mailing list.

The MLists_Users Table

The MLists_Users table stores the users' personal information:

Column Name	Type	Size	Allow Null	Description
UserID	int – Identity primary key	4	No	The unique ID for the user.
Email	varchar	50	No	The user's e-mail address. This column must have a unique constraint, to avoid multiple records with the same e-mail address.
FirstName	varchar	50	Yes	The user's first name.
LastName	varchar	50	Yes	The user's last name.

You may wonder why we need a new table for storing the user's e-mail address and name, since we already have an Accounts_Users table that can store this information (created in Chapter 5). That table stores information about users who have registered with the site, in order to gain access to protected areas or to personalize the site. But a visitor might not be interested in those advantages, and might just want to know when the site is updated. We can't force them to register and provide personal details if they only want to subscribe to the mailing list. Many sites follow this approach: subscribing to a mailing list often requires the e-mail address only, or at most the e-mail and subscriber's name. They have a different page that asks for a lot of personal details (most of which are not optional) that are required, for example, for shipping goods and invoicing in the case of an e-commerce site. We decided that it would be wiser to have two tables to separate registered users from those who have just subscribed to a mailing list. Furthermore, not depending on the Accounts module allows any site to easily plug in the mailing lists manager, even if it's already using another online manager to administer its customers/users, without requiring changes to the existing code. Of course, this does not prevent us from modifying the registration page written in Chapter 5 and allowing the user to register for both the site and the mailing list in a single step. Later we'll build a new data component that makes the addition of a subscription very easy.

Another thing you'll notice in this table is that we decided to allow the first and last names to be null. Having the first and last name would allow us to achieve some form of newsletter personalization, but most sites don't ask for this information, because users prefer to give as little information as possible. So we'll make it optional to supply this information. Later we'll see how we can replace some special marks in the newsletter with the user's information, so that they receive a newsletter customized with their name. This will contribute to making the user feel that they have a more personal relationship with the site's staff. If their name isn't supplied we'll use a generic 'name' instead, such as "List Reader".

This table does not store the lists to which the user is subscribed, because a single user can subscribe to several lists. This would require the user's data to be repeated, which is bad design, as it wastes space and makes it more difficult to update the user's details. Instead we treat each user-list pair as a subscription and store these in a separate table.

The MLists_Subscriptions Table

The MLists_Subscriptions table stores the subscriptions for all the lists:

Column Name	Type	Size	Allow Null	Description
SubscriptionID	int – Identity primary key	4	No	The unique ID for the subscription.
ListID	int foreign key	4	No	The ID of the list to which the user is subscribed, which should match an ID in the MLists_Lists table.
UserID	int foreign key	4	No	The ID of the user, which should match an ID in the MLists_Users table.
Active	bit	1	No	If false (0) the subscription is inactive, and the user will not receive newsletters for the ListID list.
AddedDate	datetime	8	No	The date of creation of this subscription.

This is the table where we maintain the relationship between the users and the mailing lists to which they have subscribed. In conjunction with MLists_Users, we have all the information for the subscription: for example the lists to which the user is subscribed, the e-mail address and name of the subscriber, and each subscription's activity state.

The Active column is included to allow the user to unsubscribe from a mailing list (and you must allow this), without deleting the subscription details. This is useful because you might still want to contact old subscribers in special circumstances. If a subscription record has 0 (false) in that field, it means that the subscription is inactive, namely that the user does not receive newsletters from the mailing list of that subscription. Later in the chapter we'll show how the administration console allows us to change the Active status of any subscription. We'll also give options for when a user wants to unsubscribe, that is, whether their subscription should be permanently deleted or just made inactive.

The MLists_History Table

The `MLists_History` table is used to store newsletters previously sent to the subscribers of a mailing list:

Column Name	Type	Size	Allow Null	Description
NewsletterID	int - Identity primary key	4	No	The unique ID for the message.
ListID	int foreign key	4	No	The mailing list to which the message was sent.
Subject	varchar	200	No	The subject of the message.
Body	text		No	The body of the message.
IsHTML	bit	1	No	If `True`, it means that the message was sent in HTML format.
SentDate	datetime	8	No	When the message was sent.

The Stored Procedures that Manage the Database

To manage the database we will build a set of stored procedures, that we'll run later in the data layer classes to do everything from the addition or deletion of lists and subscriptions, to the update of single fields. Here is the complete list of the stored procedures we'll be building, with their parameters:

Stored Procedure	Parameters	Description
sp_MLists_GetLists		Returns all the available mailing lists.
sp_MLists_GetListDetails	@ListID int	Returns the complete row identified by the specified ID.
sp_MLists_InsertList	@Name varchar(50), @Description varchar(250), @ListID int OUTPUT	Inserts a new list. If a list already exists with the same name, the new list is not added and the output parameter is set to -1. Otherwise @ListID will be set to the new list's ID.

Table continued on following page

Stored Procedure	Parameters	Description
sp_MLists_UpdateList	@ListID int, @Name varchar(50), @Description varchar(250)	Updates all the fields of the mailing list identified by the specified ID.
sp_MLists_DeleteList	@ListID int	Deletes the specified list.
sp_MLists_GetSubscriptions	@ListID int, @ActiveOnly bit	Returns the subscriptions (with all the details for both the subscriptions and the subscribers) for the specified list. If @ActiveOnly is 1, returns only the subscriptions where the Active field is 1.
sp_MLists_GetSubscriptionDetails	@SubscriptionID int	Gets all the details for the specified subscription.
sp_MLists_GetSubscriptionID	@ListID int, @Email varchar(50), @SubscriptionID int OUTPUT	Gets the ID of the subscription for the specified mailing list, with the specified e-mail address.
sp_MLists_InsertSubscription	@ListID int, @FirstName varchar(50), @LastName varchar(50), @Email varchar(50), @Active bit, @SubscriptionID int OUTPUT	Inserts a new subscription for the specified mailing list. If a subscription to this list already exists with the specified e-mail address, the new subscription is not added and the output parameter is set to -1. Otherwise @SubscriptionID will be set to the new subscription's ID.

Stored Procedure	Parameters	Description
sp_MLists_UpdateSubscription	@Subscription ID int, @FirstName varchar(50), @LastName varchar(50), @Email varchar(50), @Active bit	Updates all the fields of the specified subscription. This includes the fields of the subscriber (name and e-mail address).
sp_MLists_SetSubscriptionActive	@Subscription ID int, @Active bit	Updates only the Active field for the specified subscription.
sp_MLists_DeleteSubscription	@Subscription ID int	Deletes the specified subscription (but not the respective user, because they could be subscribed to other lists).
sp_MLists_GetNewsletters	@ListID int	Gets all the archived newsletters sent to the specified list.
sp_MLists_GetNewsletterDetails	@NewsletterID int	Gets all the details of the specified archived newsletter.
sp_MLists_InsertNewsletter	@ListID int, @Subject varchar(200), @Body text, @IsHTML bit, @NewsletterID int OUTPUT	Inserts a newsletter into the database and returns its ID. No check is performed to see if the newsletter is already present in the archive, since we can have as many newsletters with the same subject as we want. The value for the SentDate field is not passed as a parameter; the stored procedure takes care of retrieving and using the current date for that field, as the other Insert procedures do for the AddedDate fields.
sp_MLists_DeleteNewsletter	@NewsletterID int	Deletes the specified newsletter.

The stored procedures that manage the lists and the archived newsletters are pretty simple, while those that manage the subscriptions are a bit more complex, because they work on two tables, MLists_Subscriptions and MLists_Users. For example, when we retrieve all the subscriptions, using sp_MLists_GetSubscriptions, we need to *join* the two tables, in order to have rows with the complete details of the subscriptions, the parent list's ID, the active state of the subscription, and all the details of the subscribed user. The procedures that add and update a subscription also operate on the same two tables. In cases like this, having stored procedures that do the work will make it much easier to write the data component later, rather than writing SQL commands directly into the classes, because we write methods that map the stored procedures, and don't worry much about the relationships. This is even more evident when different teams are responsible for the database/stored procedure design and writing the data/business layers.

Designing the Data Services

Now that we understand what data is stored in the database tables, and we have designed a set of stored procedures to add, delete, and modify any row in the tables, we can design the data services. These are a set of classes in their own assembly and namespace (Wrox.WebModules.MailingLists.Data) that provide an object-oriented version of the stored procedures. In other words the data components have methods that exactly map the stored procedures, exposing them through a set of classes. We will look at each class in turn.

The ListDetails Class

The ListDetails class exposes three public fields that map the three fields of a row in the MLists_Lists table. This class is used as the return type for the GetDetails method in the Lists class, discussed next, that instead of returning a DataRow type returns an instance of an object that exposes the values in a more easily accessible way.

The Lists Class

This class has a set of methods that map the calls to the stored procedures that manage the mailing lists. The methods return the value of the output parameter of the respective stored procedure, or a Boolean value indicating whether the query succeeded. Here is a complete list of the methods we'll implement:

Method Name	Description
Lists	Class constructor taking the connection string as a parameter.
GetLists	Returns a DataSet with all the lists.
GetDetails	Returns an instance of ListDetails that describes the specified mailing list.
GetDetailsRow	Returns a DataRow containing details of the specified list.
Add	Adds a new mailing list, and returns its ID, or -1 if the same list was already present.
Update	Updates all the fields of the specified mailing list.
Delete	Deletes the specified mailing list.

The SubscriptionDetails Class

This class is basically the same as `ListDetails`, but for the `MLists_Subscriptions` and `MLists_Users` tables. It has only public fields that map the physical fields of the tables returned by the `sp_MLists_GetSubscriptionDetails` stored procedure.

The Subscriptions Class

This class wraps the calls to the stored procedures that manage the subscriptions and the respective users:

Method Name	Description
Subscriptions	Class constructor taking the connection string as a parameter.
GetSubscriptions	Returns a `DataSet` with all the subscriptions for a particular mailing list.
GetSubscriptions	The same as above, but here we have the opportunity to specify that we only want the *active* subscriptions.
GetDetails	Returns an instance of `SubscriptionDetails` that describes the specified subscription.
GetDetailsRow	Returns the `DataRow` of the specified subscription.
GetSubscriptionID	Returns the ID of the subscription for the specified mailing list, and with the specified e-mail address.
Add	Adds a new subscription, and returns its ID, or -1 if the same e-mail address was already subscribed for the specified list.
Update	Updates all the fields of the specified subscription. This includes fields in both the `MLists_Subscriptions` and `MLists_Users` tables.
SetActive	Changes only the `Active` state of the specified subscription.
Delete	Deletes the specified subscription.

The NewsletterDetails Class

This class is the same as the two `xxxDetails` classes above, but this time for the archived newsletters. It has fields corresponding to all the fields of the `MLists_History` table.

The Newsletters Class

This class is shorter than the previous ones, because it only provides methods to retrieve, add, and delete newsletters, and doesn't provide any methods for updating them:

Method Name	Description
Newsletters	Class constructor taking the connection string as a parameter.
GetNewsletters	Returns all the newsletters for a particular mailing list.
GetDetails	Returns an instance of NewsletterDetails that describes the specified newsletter.
GetDetailsRow	Returns the DataRow of the newsletter identified by the specified ID.
Add	Archives a newsletter, and returns the ID of the new record.
Delete	Deletes a newsletter.

Storing and Retrieving Settings

In previous chapters we've already designed a couple of classes that retrieve and store each module's settings in an XML file. This module has quite a lot of settings to store, because we want it to be as flexible as possible. This is the list of settings that will be persisted to and retrieved from the XML file:

Setting Name	Type	Description
ConnectionString	string	The connection string that all the data classes use to access the database.
SubscribeURL	string	The complete URL of the Subscribe.aspx page that actually adds or removes a user to or from a list.
SenderName	string	The name of the news sender.
SenderEmail	string	The e-mail address of the news sender.
NewsSubject	string	The default subject for the news. The administrator will be able to append any text to this default string, directly from the page where the message is written.
Signature	string	The signature that will automatically be appended at the end of the message.
SubscrSubject	string	The subject of the e-mail sent as the confirmation message for the subscription.
SubscrMessage	string	The body of the e-mail sent as the confirmation message for the subscription.
UnsubscrSubject	string	The subject of the e-mail sent as the confirmation message for the un-subscription.
UnsubscrMessage	string	The body of the e-mail sent as the confirmation message for the un-subscription.

Setting Name	Type	Description
UnsubscrAction	UnsubscrActionType custom enumeration	Specifies the action taken when a user un-subscribes from a mailing lists. They can be completely removed, or the subscription can just be set as inactive, by setting the respective field in the `MLists_Subscription` table.
SendSubscrEmail	bool	If `True`, the new subscriber will get a confirmation e-mail after subscribing to a list.
SendUnsubscrEmail	bool	If `True`, the existing subscriber will get a confirmation e-mail after un-subscribing from a list.

The `NewsSubject`, `[Un]SubscrSubject`, and `[Un]SubscrMessage` settings can contain special tags, such as `#SubscriberFirstName#` and `#ListDescription#`. These will be replaced with their respective values just before each mail is sent. We'll see more on this point later in the chapter.

Designing the Business Services

At this point we have all the calls to the stored procedures wrapped into easily accessible methods of the data-access layer. Now it's time to build the business classes upon the data-access classes, in order to provide a real object-oriented representation of the data and its relationships. However, the mailing list manager not only has to manage the data in the database, but it has other work to take care of too, such as actually sending out the newsletters to the active subscribers (the stored procedure only inserts the newsletter into the database, but does not send the e-mails), subscribing or unsubscribing someone and sending a confirmation message if required, and processing special list and subscription tags. One option would be to write the code to do this directly in the presentation layer: if we have data/business classes that simplify access to the database, the rest of the work will be quite easy. However, these methods are best placed in the business layer, since they are based upon business rules and the application's settings, stuff that the presentation layer doesn't need to know about. By also adding methods in the business layer to do the non-database work, in the presentation layer we'll be able to write only the code that manages the visual appearance of the site, plus a few lines to call the business assembly's methods. With this code separation we achieve better reusability and maintainability of the business rules, and it's easier to change the application's user interface, because we don't need to touch the business code.

The List Class

This class exposes most of the functionality we need: it allows us to manage the mailing lists, but also to send out newsletters, subscribe and un-subscribe someone, and return all the child records (both subscriptions and archived newsletters), although some of these methods just wrap the respective methods of the child objects.

Member Name	Description
ID	Read-only property that returns the ID of the list represented by the object.
Name	Gets/sets the list's name.
Description	Gets/sets the list's description.
List	Class constructor with no parameters. It only sets the default properties.
List	Class constructor that sets the properties to describe the list identified by the input ID.
List	Class constructor that sets the properties to describe the list identified by an existing List object.
LoadFromID	Retrieves the list record identified by a private ID variable, and loads the object's properties accordingly. This method is called by the constructors, or when the data has to be refreshed.
ResetProperties	Resets the properties.
LoadFromID	Loads all the properties of the question identified by the input ID.
Create	Creates a new mailing list, and sets the properties of the object to represent the new record.
Update	Updates the list with the new values of the public properties.
Delete	Deletes the list.
GetLists	Static method that returns all the mailing lists in a dataset.
GetNewsletters	Returns all the child archived newsletter in a dataset.
SendNewsletter	Sends out a newsletter to all the active subscribers of the mailing list.
GetSubscriptions	Gets the subscribers of the list; all of them or only those that are active.
GetSubscriptions	Overloads the above method, and returns *all* the subscriptions.
AddSubscription	Adds a new child subscription to the database.
Subscribe	Subscribes a new user to the mailing list. It differs from the AddSubscription method in that a confirmation is sent to the subscriber, if required in the settings.
Unsubscribe	Un-subscribes the user with the specified e-mail address. The output parameters are used to return the subject and body of the confirmation message.

You may be wondering why we need both the AddSubscription and the Subscribe methods. Well, the former simply wraps a call to the Add method of the Data.Subscriptions class to add a new record to the database, and is used by the administration console to manage the subscriptions. On the other hand, the Subscribe method adds a record to the database if the subscription is not present, or activates the existing subscription. It also sends a customized confirmation message to the user, if required. Consequently, the page that handles the mailing list subscription box uses this version and it is therefore available to any site visitor.

The Subscription Class

This is a simple class that describes a particular subscription. It allows us to update, delete, or create a new subscription, and also to subscribe/un-subscribe a user:

Method Name	Description
ID	Read-only property that returns the ID of the subscription represented by the object.
ListID	Read-only property that returns the ID of the parent mailing list.
List	Returns the parent mailing list.
UserID	Returns the ID of the user.
Active	Gets/sets the Active state of the subscription.
FirstName	Gets/sets the subscriber's first name.
LastName	Gets/sets the subscriber's last name.
Email	Gets/sets the subscriber's e-mail.
AddedDate	Returns the date when the subscription was added to the database.
LoadFromID	Retrieves the subscription record identified by a private ID variable, and loads the object's properties accordingly.
ResetProperties	Resets the properties.
LoadFromID	Loads all the properties of the subscription identified by the input ID.
LoadFromEmail	Loads all the properties of the subscription with the specified e-mail address.
Create	Creates a new subscription record in the database.
Update	Updates the current subscription with the new values of the public properties.
Delete	Deletes the subscription.
Subscribe	Creates a new subscription or reactivates a disabled one, and optionally (if required in the settings) sends a confirmation message. The last two output parameters return the subject and body of that message, customized with the list and subscriber's data.
Unsubscribe	Removes or inactivates a subscription, as specified in the settings, and optionally sends a confirmation message. The last two output parameters return the subject and body of that message.

The Subscribe and Unsubscribe methods are those used by the identically named methods of the List class. Subscribe adds a subscription for the specified mailing list if one with the same specified values is not already present, otherwise it ensures that its Active status is True. Unsubscribe removes a subscription, or deactivates it.

The Newsletter Class

The Newsletter class is even simpler than Subscription because, in addition to the usual LoadFromID, ResetProperties, and Update, it has only a Send method, and all the properties are read-only. This is because it doesn't make sense to modify a newsletter when it is archived.

Method Name	Description
ID	Returns the ID of the newsletter represented by the object.
ListID	Returns the ID of the parent mailing list.
List	Returns the parent mailing list.
Subject	Returns the newsletter's subject.
Body	Returns the newsletter's body.
IsHTML	Returns whether the newsletter is in HTML format.
SentDate	Returns the date when the newsletter was sent.
LoadFromID	Loads the properties of the option identified by a private ID variable.
ResetProperties	Resets the properties.
LoadFromID	Loads all the properties of the specified archived newsletter.
Delete	Deletes the newsletter.
Send	Sends out a newsletter with the specified subject, body, format, and priority to all the active subscribers of the specified mailing list.
Send	The same as the above version, but without the last output parameter.

The Send method requires as input all the parts of the newsletter (subject, body, priority) in order to archive the newsletter to the database. The interesting point is that the subject and body strings can contain special tags such as #ListName# or #SubscriberEmail#. These are processed and replaced with the respective values for each subscription to which the newsletter is sent. Read below for more details about the supported tags.

An alternative implementation of the Send method would be to set all the public parameters, and just call a Send() method without parameters. However, some properties are read only and this would create a bit of confusion when the user has to set them. Additionally, and this is the main reason, I personally prefer to pass all the parameters in a single line, rather than having to set one property per line. This same discussion applies to the Create methods of most of the business classes, which require as input all the values for a new record, instead of using the values of the public properties.

The Helper Class

The Helper class exposes some static methods that are not specific to any other class, but can be of general use, namely it exposes the methods to process and replace the special tags just mentioned above:

Method Name	Description
ProcessListTags	Replaces the list's special tags with the respective values.
ProcessSubscriptionTags	Replaces the subscription's special tags with the respective values.
ProcessSettingsTags	Replaces the settings' special tags with the respective values.

You may be wondering why there are three methods instead of only one. Each method requires the subscription ID or list ID as input and performs the necessary replacements. The reason for having three methods is as follows. When we build the administration console later in the chapter, we'll see that there are occasions when we only need to parse and replace the tags for the settings and the list, and not for the current subscription. For example, when we preview a message during its preparation with the editor that we'll provide, we can't replace the tags for the subscription. This is because there is no current subscription to parse; the preview is general, not specific to a particular subscription. This means that we wouldn't have a subscription ID to pass to a unique method. Sure, we could pass a value with the special meaning of "do not replace the tags for the subscription", but at this point it is easier to use separate methods.

The tags for the list can be inserted in both the body and the subject of the newsletters we send out, while the tags for the settings and the subscription are allowed within the body only. The newsletter's subject does not need to be customized for each subscriber, so we accept this limitation by design in order to speed up the execution of the Send method. In fact, we can spare thousands of calls to the ProcessSubscriptionTags and ProcessSettingsTags methods for the subject in this way, if we have thousands of subscriptions. This is another reason why it is simpler to provide three separate methods that parse the text and replace the tags: if we had only one method for all the replacements, we would need a further parameter to tell the method if the passed text is the subject, and whether we can skip the tags for the subscriber.

But which are the tags for the lists, subscriptions, and settings? Here is the complete list:

❑ List tags: #ListID#, #ListName#, #ListDescription#

❑ Subscription tags: #SubscriptionID#, #SubscriberFirstName#, #SubscriberLastName#, #SubscriberEmail#

❑ Settings tags: #SenderName#, #SenderEmail#, #SubscribeURL#

The settings should be self-explanatory, except for #SubscribeURL# maybe. This tag maps the SubscribeUrl setting, and refers to the full base URL (the URL without additional parameters) of the page that takes care of subscribing or un-subscribing a user based on the parameters passed along with its URL. At the end of each newsletter we should provide an opt-out link to allow the user to easily un-subscribe. The link points to that page, with some additional parameters that specify the current e-mail address, and the fact that we want to un-subscribe them from the mailing list. So we can use this tag and the other subscription tags to dynamically build the complete opt-out link customized for each subscriber.

Designing the User Interface Services

The user interface layer of this module is simpler than for the previous ones. Some of our other modules have numerous pages for the user, reusable user controls, web services, and also Windows clients that make use of the web services. In this case, most of the module is made up of the administration console. The end-user side of things includes a box for subscribing to a mailing list, and a page that either confirms the operation or reports an error.

We could think about implementing a web service to administer the mailing lists through a Windows client, but this wouldn't be really useful. The administrator only needs to access the administration console for sending out a newsletter once a week, every two weeks, or less frequently. There isn't a huge amount of work involved in administering subscriptions, since the users can subscribe and un-subscribe by themselves, with no help from the administrator. Therefore, unless you have dozens of different mailing lists and you are sending out newsletters every day, the mailing list administration pages won't be required very often. When you have to prepare a newsletter, you'll usually use a word processor or an HTML editor to write and format the content, then you'll copy and paste it to the module's administration page and send it out. In the HTML code you can also use <img> tags that reference images on your server, and these can be uploaded through the file manager tool presented in Chapter 4. Most of the time that is actually spent is on thinking about the organization of the content, but this has nothing to do with the module implementation. Therefore, we decided we don't need a web service and a Windows client to administer the newsletters section of the database.

Let's move on and think about the subscription box. Should we build a user control so we can insert it into any page? Well, that is a possible solution, but in this case there are other factors to consider:

- ❏ We aren't using any server controls bound to the data.

- ❏ We don't need the box to be dynamically programmable.

- ❏ The box is a simple HTML table that requires only a few lines of normal HTML code.

- ❏ When a user subscribes we want to point to a different page to handle the submitted data, because we also want to print a confirmation message or show an error message if the user has not supplied the required information. If we employed a user control, we would need to handle a server event and then redirect to another page to show those messages, because writing the messages directly into the box could possibly enlarge the subscription box and mess up the layout of the page that hosts the user control. We don't have this problem if we use a simple HTML form that points to a separate ASP.NET page to handle the submitted user's data and show the required messages.

- ❏ If we have partner sites, they may agree to host our mailing list subscription box on their own site. If they run on a Linux server or a Windows server without the .NET Framework installed, they won't be able to insert our user control box. We can avoid this problem by using HTML.

After considering all these points, we came to the conclusion that having a user control won't provide any significant advantages for this solution. In fact, it would actually make it more difficult to customize it, add JavaScript client-side validation of input, or show the confirmation/error messages. Also, a mailing-list box is something that we can plug into our layout and show in every page (maybe in the right-hand column in a typical site layout). However, our web developers might have got used to two-line implementations for things like this. So instead of forcing them to manually write the dozen lines of HTML code, in the administration console we'll provide a wizard that will create the necessary code for the box for the specified mailing list. Aren't we kind to our web developers? The wizard actually auto-generates the code for a basic subscription box that the developers can customize with images, JavaScript, other colors, etc., to make it best fit with the current site's layout and styles.

The Need for Security

As we just mentioned in the last section, the end-user side of this module is very limited, and most of the module is concerned with the administration console. Therefore, all that we need to do to protect this module is to check if the current user has the `AdministerData` permission for general administration tasks (adding, editing, and deleting records), and the `SendNewsletter` permission for sending out a newsletter. We'll be using the `Accounts` module from Chapter 5 to check the permissions, as we've already done in previous chapters for other administration pages.

The Solution

This module has a very similar structure to that of previous modules. The administration console has similar pages: the page for the mailing lists (questions or categories in the previous chapters), the page for the subscribers (options and news in the previous chapters), and the page for the settings. We won't list the code for these pages, as it is so similar to the code already seen – all of the code can be found in the download. The same applies to the data component. Thanks to the `DbObject` base class of the `Core` assembly, we can use the `RunProcedure` method to run the stored procedures and return a dataset or an output parameter. As we saw in *The Design* section, our data assembly has classes that almost exactly map the stored procedures, and there is nothing new to add that wasn't already discussed in previous chapters.

So what *are* we going to see? We'll look at the code of some of the stored procedures (to better understand the relationships between the tables), the business classes, the subscription box, and the pages required for subscribing.

Working on the Database

Looking at the diagram and the descriptions of the tables we provided earlier, you should have no problems building the tables for our SQL Server database and the relationships. (All three one-to-many relationships should have the Enforce Relationship for INSERTs and DELETEs options selected.) However, as for the previous chapters, you can go to the Wrox site and download the database backup with all the tables, stored procedures, triggers, and also some data that will allow you to test the module straight out of the download.

Creating the Stored Procedures and Triggers

In this section we won't cover the code of all the stored procedures, since in previous chapters we've already seen how the procedures for deleting and updating a record work. However, we'll show a few of the procedures for working with subscribers, because they are a bit more complex as they involve joins and relationship constraints.

Retrieving Subscriptions

Here's the code for the `sp_MLists_GetSubscriptions` procedure. It joins the `MLists_Subscriptions` and `MLists_Users` table, to return either all the details of the subscriptions for the specified mailing list, or just the details of those users with an active subscription:

```
CREATE PROCEDURE sp_MLists_GetSubscriptions
                @ListID int,
                @ActiveOnly bit
AS

IF @ActiveOnly = 0
  BEGIN
  SELECT SubscriptionID, MLists_Users.UserID, Active, FirstName, LastName,
                                       Email, AddedDate, ListID
    FROM MLists_Users
    INNER JOIN MLists_Subscriptions
      ON MLists_Users.UserID = MLists_Subscriptions.UserID
    WHERE MLists_Subscriptions.ListID = @ListID
  END
ELSE
  BEGIN
  SELECT SubscriptionID, MLists_Users.UserID, Active, FirstName, LastName,
                                       Email, AddedDate, ListID
    FROM MLists_Users
    INNER JOIN MLists_Subscriptions
      ON MLists_Users.UserID = MLists_Subscriptions.UserID
    WHERE MLists_Subscriptions.ListID = @ListID
          AND MLists_Subscriptions.Active = 1
  END
GO
```

There are two distinct SELECT statements, with or without the WHERE clause for the active subscriptions. The two tables are joined on the UserID field that is present in each table.

The sp_MLists_GetSubscriptionDetails procedure is very similar, it just has an additional WHERE clause for the specified SubscriptionID.

Retrieving Subscriptions by ID

This procedure, sp_MLists_GetSubscriptionID, also joins the two tables, as above, but only for the purpose of returning the information for the subscription with the specified e-mail address that points to the specified mailing list. If a row is found we return its SubscriptionID, or -1 otherwise:

```
CREATE PROCEDURE sp_MLists_GetSubscriptionID
                @ListID int,
                @Email varchar(50),
                @SubscriptionID int OUTPUT
AS

SELECT @SubscriptionID = SubscriptionID
  FROM MLists_Users
  INNER JOIN MLists_Subscriptions
    ON MLists_Users.UserID = MLists_Subscriptions.UserID
  WHERE MLists_Subscriptions.ListID = @ListID
        AND MLists_Users.Email = @Email

IF @SubscriptionID IS NULL
  SET @SubscriptionID = -1
GO
```

Inserting Subscriptions

sp_MLists_InsertSubscription is the most complex procedure. It has to add a row in both tables, but it also has to check that the subscription does not already exist. If it does not, it has to check if a user with the specified e-mail address already exists (which is the case when the user is already subscribed to another mailing list). If so, it gets their ID and uses it for the UserID field of the new row it creates in MLists_Subscription. Otherwise it first adds a new row in MLists_Users, gets the ID of the new row, and then adds a row in MLists_Subscriptions. The code below is well commented, so you should have no problems understanding the execution flow:

```
CREATE PROCEDURE sp_MLists_InsertSubscription
                 @ListID int,
                 @FirstName varchar(50),
                 @LastName varchar(50),
                 @Email varchar(50),
                 @Active bit,
                 @SubscriptionID int OUTPUT
AS

DECLARE @CurrSubscription int
DECLARE @CurrUser int

-- see if the subscription already exists
SELECT @CurrSubscription = SubscriptionID
  FROM MLists_Users
  INNER JOIN MLists_Subscriptions
    ON MLists_Users.UserID = MLists_Subscriptions.UserID
  WHERE MLists_Subscriptions.ListID = @ListID
        AND MLists_Users.Email = @Email

-- if not, go ahead
IF @CurrSubscription IS NULL
  BEGIN

  -- the subscription does not exist, but check if the user already exists
  SELECT @CurrUser = UserID
    FROM MLists_Users
    WHERE MLists_Users.Email = @Email

  -- if the user is not present, add it
  IF @CurrUser IS NULL
    BEGIN
    -- insert the User
    INSERT INTO MLists_Users
               (FirstName, LastName, Email)
               VALUES (@FirstName, @LastName, @Email)
    -- save the new UserID
    SET @CurrUser = @@IDENTITY

    IF @@ERROR > 0
      BEGIN
      RAISERROR ('Insert of User failed', 16, 1)
      RETURN 99
      END
```

413

```
    END

  -- add the new subscription
  INSERT INTO MLists_Subscriptions
          (ListID, UserID, Active, AddedDate)
          VALUES (@ListID, @CurrUser, @Active, GETDATE())
  -- save the new ID to be returned
  SET @SubscriptionID = @@IDENTITY

  IF @@ERROR > 0
    BEGIN
    RAISERROR ('Insert of Subscription failed', 16, 1)
    RETURN 99
    END

  END
ELSE
  SET @SubscriptionID = -1
GO
```

Deleting Subscriptions

To delete a subscription we have a simple stored procedure, sp_MLists_DeleteSubscription, defined as follows:

```
CREATE PROCEDURE sp_MLists_DeleteSubscription
              @SubscriptionID int
AS

DELETE FROM MLists_Subscriptions WHERE SubscriptionID = @SubscriptionID
GO
```

As you can see, this code only deletes the record in the MLists_Subscription table, and does not delete the respective user in the MLists_Users table. The same user can be subscribed to more than one mailing list, so if we wanted to delete it, we should first ensure that there are no other subscriptions that refer to it. This would be simple to do, and could be done from within the stored procedure above. However, if we deleted a subscription by directly executing a DELETE query, without calling the helper stored procedure, no check would be performed, and unused users could remain in the database. To be sure that the user is deleted and can have no more subscriptions when we delete a subscription, either via the stored procedure or with a direct query, we can write a **trigger**. This is the code to create it:

```
CREATE TRIGGER DeleteUser ON [dbo].[MLists_Subscriptions]
FOR DELETE
AS

DELETE MLists_Users
  FROM MLists_Users AS u
  JOIN Deleted AS d
    ON u.UserID = d.UserID
  LEFT JOIN MLists_Subscriptions AS s
    ON s.UserID = d.UserID
  WHERE s.UserID IS NULL
```

This trigger is executed when one or more records are deleted from the MLists_Subscription table. When records are deleted, they are copied into the Deleted table, a table managed by SQL Server behind the scenes, and that exists only within the scope of the trigger. Therefore, we can retrieve the deleted subscriptions from the Deleted table, join the two tables as you see above, and detect which users are no longer subscribed to any mailing list and can therefore be deleted.

> *If you want to know more about triggers, you can read about them in* Professional SQL Server 2000 *(Wrox Press, ISBN 1-86100-448-6).*
>
> *Note that if we were using the* Users *table of the* Accounts *module to store the users' contact information for the subscriptions, we wouldn't have this trigger. Although they aren't subscribed to anything they might still use the site and so we should keep their account in the database.*

Implementing the Data and Configuration Assemblies

At this point we should build the data and configuration assemblies, following the structure designed earlier. However, as we mentioned, the code required has the same structure as the respective assemblies of the previous chapters, with just the following differences:

- ❑ The names of the methods and stored procedures in the data component
- ❑ The site-wide web.config's custom key that stores the settings file name
- ❑ The entry name for the cached settings in the configuration component

The data component is an assembly named Wrox.WebModules.MailingLists.Data, the configuration assembly and namespace is Wrox.WebModules.MailingLists.Configuration, the new custom key for web.settings is MailingLists_SettingsFile, and the cache entry is MailingLists_Settings. You can refer back to Chapter 5 to see how these two assemblies are structured, and you can find the complete code for this module in the download.

Implementing the Business Layer

Just like the data assembly, some of the methods of the business layer are the same as in other modules. For example, those that load and reset the properties, and those that create, delete, and update a record. But there are also some things that are specific to this module, such as the methods for sending out a newsletter, subscribing/un-subscribing a user, and processing the special tags. We'll just look at these new methods here. In *The Design* section you can read the complete declaration of them all, and you can understand how they are implemented by looking at the respective methods in some of the previous chapters.

We start off by adding a new Class Library to the solution, name it MailingLists.Business, set its properties (set the assembly and default namespace name to Wrox.WebModules.MailingLists.Business) and edit its AssemblyInfo.cs file to specify the assembly key file. From reading the previous chapters you should already know how to complete all this without the need for further details, so let's go ahead and start coding the classes.

The Subscription Class

If you still have the default Class1.vb file in the project, rename it to Subscription.vb. The methods we're going to show for this class are Subscribe and Unsubscribe. These are also used by the corresponding methods of the List class.

The Subscribe Method

The Subscribe method takes care of all the details for the subscription of a new user. It checks if the user is already present on the chosen mailing list, but in inactive mode. In that case it sets the user as active, otherwise it adds a new record. Then, if required in the settings, it sends a confirmation message to the subscriber. Sending the notification e-mail requires a couple of classes of the .NET Framework, MailMessage and SmtpMail, which we'll explain when discussing the Send method of the current class. For now just be aware that they are needed to send e-mails.

The notification message can be personalized with the name, e-mail address, and other user or list information, thanks to the special tags explained earlier, which are replaced by the methods of the Helper class that we'll see shortly. The subject and the body of the confirmation message are also returned to the caller through two output parameters, in case the caller wants to print them on the page (that's exactly what we'll be doing later). Here's the code:

```
Public Function Subscribe( _
  ByVal subscrListId As Integer, _
  ByVal subscrFirstName As String, _
  ByVal subscrLastName As String, _
  ByVal subscrEmail As String, _
  ByRef subjectText As String, _
  ByRef messageText As String) _
  As Integer

  subjectText = ""
  messageText = ""

  If subscrEmail.Trim() = "" Then
    Return -1
  End If

  ' Get the subject/body of the subscription message
  subjectText = settings.SubscrSubject
  messageText = settings.SubscrMessage

  ' Get the subscription for this list, with the specified e-mail,if any
  Dim subscription As New _
    Business.Subscription(subscrListId, subscrEmail)

  ' If the subscription already exists...
  If subscription.Id <> -1 Then

    ' Set it myActive
    subscription.myActive = True
    subscription.Update()

  Else

    ' Otherwise add the subscription
    subscription.Create( _
      subscrListId, _
      subscrFirstName, _
      subscrLastName, _
      subscrEmail, _
```

```
         True)

    End If

    ' Replace the tags of this new subscriber
    messageText = Helper.ProcessSubscriptionTags( _
      messageText, subscription.Id)

    ' Replace the list's and settings tags
    subjectText = Helper.ProcessListTags(subjectText, subscrListId)
    messageText = Helper.ProcessListTags(messageText, subscrListId)
    messageText = Helper.ProcessSettingsTags(messageText)

    ' If a confirmation e-mail is required
    If settings.SendSubscrEmail Then

      ' Create a new message
      Dim mailMsg As New MailMessage()
      mailMsg.From = settings.SenderName & _
        " <" & settings.SenderEmail & ">"

      ' Set the "To" field to the subscriber's e-mail
      mailMsg.To = subscrEmail

      ' Set the Subject/body to the subject/body created for the
      ' confirmation(page)
      mailMsg.Subject = subjectText
      mailMsg.Body = messageText

      ' Send the mail
      SmtpMail.Send(mailMsg)

    End If

    If subscription.Id = -1 Then
      ResetProperties()
    Else
      LoadFromId(subscription.Id)
    End If
    Return mySubscriptionId
End Function
```

In order to save a round trip to the database, we could also add an overloaded version of
ProcessSubscriptionTags that accepts a Subscription object instead of the subscription's ID,
and pass in the existing Subscription object. But as this method isn't called very often (unless we
have 100 users registering every minute) the effect on performance will not be significant.

The Unsubscribe Method

The Unsubscribe method has the same structure as Subscribe. It first checks if the specified
subscriber is present: if not, the method returns False, otherwise it sets the subscription as inactive (the
subscriber won't receive any future newsletters for this mailing list), or completely removes the record
from the database, according to the options set by the administrator. It also sends the confirmation
message if required:

```
Public Function Unsubscribe( _
   ByVal subscrListId As Integer, _
   ByVal subscrEmail As String, _
   ByRef subjectText As String, _
   ByRef messageText As String) _
   As Boolean

   subjectText = ""
   messageText = ""

   If subscrEmail.Trim() = "" Then
     Return False
   End If

   ' Get the subscription for this list, with the specified e-mail,if any
   Dim subscription As New _
      Business.Subscription(subscrListId, subscrEmail)

   ' If the subscription does not exists...
   If subscription.Id = -1 Then

     subjectText = _
       "There is no subscription with the specified e-mail address"
     messageText = ""
     Return False

   End If

   ' Get the subject/body of the subscription message
   subjectText = settings.UnsubscrSubject
   messageText = settings.UnsubscrMessage

   ' Replace the tags of this subscription. This has to be done
   ' BEFORE removing the subscription
   messageText = Business.Helper.ProcessSubscriptionTags( _
     messageText, subscription.Id)

   ' Remove or inactivate the subscription, according to the
   ' UnsubscrAction(setting)
   If settings.UnsubscrAction = _
     Configuration.UnsubscrActionType.Remove Then

     subscription.Delete()

   Else

     subscription.myActive = False
     subscription.Update()

   End If

   ' Replace the list's and settings tags
   subjectText = Helper.ProcessListTags(subjectText, subscrListId)
   messageText = Helper.ProcessListTags(messageText, subscrListId)
```

```
        messageText = Helper.ProcessSettingsTags(messageText)

    ' If a confirmation subscremail is required
    If settings.SendUnsubscrEmail Then

      ' Create a new message
      Dim mailMsg As New MailMessage()
      mailMsg.From = settings.SenderName & _
        " <" & settings.SenderEmail & ">"

      ' Set the "To" field to the subscriber's subscremail
      mailMsg.To = subscrEmail

      ' Set the Subject/body to the subject/body created for
      ' the confirmation page
      mailMsg.Subject = subjectText
      mailMsg.Body = messageText

      ' Send the mail
      SmtpMail.Send(mailMsg)

    End If

    ResetProperties()
    Return True

  End Function
```

You can see that in both these methods we use the static methods of the `Helper` class to process and replace the special tags. In this second case, this is still required because even if the subscription is being deleted and the user won't receive any more newsletters from that mailing list, we need to show and/or send a last personalized confirmation message. We'll see the implementation of those helper methods shortly, but let's first have a look at the `Newsletter` class.

The Newsletter Class

The core of the `Newsletter` class is the `Send` method, which sends the newsletter to all the active subscribers for the specified list. The e-mails are sent through the default SMTP service installed with Windows 2000 Server, so we don't need anything special or any third-party server to send the messages. All we need is a reference to `System.Web.dll`, which is not added by default for this type of project. Before starting with the implementation of the methods, ensure that you've also added a reference to the `Core` project, inherited from `BizObject`, and added an `Imports` directive for the `System.Web.Mail` namespace.

How to Send E-Mails with the .NET Classes

In the `Subscribe` and `Unsubscribe` methods shown above we've used a couple of classes from the `System.Web.Mail` namespace to send the notification e-mails. Before going ahead with the `Send` method that actually sends out all the newsletters, it's worth taking a closer look at those classes.

The most important class is `SmtpMail`, which allows e-mail messages to be sent through the use of the **Collaboration Data Objects (CDO)** for Windows. The e-mails are delivered through any third-party server specified by the static property `SmtpServer` or, if this property is not set, through the default SMTP Server installed with Windows 2000 Server. In our case we'll always use the default server, so there is no need to supply a value for this property. The method that we actually use to send a mail is `Send`, which has two overloaded versions.

The first version accepts as input all the parameters needed to send an e-mail, namely the e-mail address of the sender and the receiver, and the subject and body text. The method is static, so we don't need to create an instance of the class to use it. Here's an example of its usage:

```
SmtpMail.Send("myemail@thephile.com", "youremail@thephile.com", _
              "Test", _
              "Hello! This is just to test the Send method")
```

This version works fine if we only want to send a message in plain text, and we don't need anything more than those four parameters; but what if we want to create an HTML e-mail, set its priority, and the CC and BCC properties? Well, for this there is the second overloaded version of the Send methods that takes a MailMessage object as its parameter.

The MailMessage object has properties such as From, To, Cc, Bcc, Subject, Text, Priority, BodyFormat, and Attachments. The meaning of these properties is clear; in the implementation of the Unsubscribe/Subscribe methods we've already seen how to create and use a MailMessage object and send the respective mail, and we'll see similar code again in the next section, for the implementation of Newsletter.Send. The only property that's worth a further example is Attachments, because it is not used anywhere in our module. Say that we've already created an instance of MailMessage called mailMsg, and set its basic properties (sender, recipient, subject, and text). The following code shows how to add a couple of attachments:

```
mailMsg.Attachments.Add(new MailAttachment("C:\file1.doc"))
mailMsg.Attachments.Add(new MailAttachment("C:\file2.bmp"))
```

We add new MailAttachment items through the Add method of the Attachments collection. The constructor of the MailAttachment class takes as input the path of the file to add to the e-mail. As a last step, the mail is sent with:

```
SmtpMail.Send(mailMsg)
```

The Send Method

The Send method requires as input the destination mailing list's ID, the newsletter's subject, body, format, and priority, and a parameter that tells whether the newsletter has to be archived to the database or not. It returns the number of sent e-mails through the last (output) parameter. Here is the complete code:

```
Public Overloads Function Send( _
    ByVal newsletterListId As Integer, _
    ByVal newsletterSubject As String, _
    ByVal newsletterBody As String, _
    ByVal newsletterIsHTML As Boolean, _
    ByVal priority As MailPriority, _
    ByVal saveToDB As Boolean, _
    ByRef totalNewsletters As Integer) _
    As Integer

    ' Reset the Id of the newsletter identifies by this object
    myNewsletterId = -1
```

```vbnet
' Replace the list's tags in the subject
newsletterSubject = Helper.ProcessListTags( _
  newsletterSubject, newsletterListId)

' Replace the list's and settings' tags in the body
newsletterBody = Helper.ProcessListTags( _
  newsletterBody, newsletterListId)
newsletterBody = Helper.ProcessSettingsTags(newsletterBody)

' Add a new record in the newsletters archive, if required
If saveToDB Then

  Dim news As New Data.Newsletters(mySettings.ConnectionString)
  myNewsletterId = news.Add( _
    newsletterListId, _
    newsletterSubject, _
    newsletterBody, _
    newsletterIsHTML)

End If

' Create a new mail message and set the common properties
Dim mailMsg As New MailMessage()

mailMsg.From = mySettings.SenderName & _
  " <" & mySettings.SenderEmail & ">"
mailMsg.Priority = priority
mailMsg.BodyFormat = CType(Convert.ToInt16(newsletterIsHTML), MailFormat)
mailMsg.Subject = newsletterSubject

' Get all the active subscribers of this list
Dim dt As DataTable = New _
  Business.List(newsletterListId).GetSubscriptions(True).Tables(0)

Dim i As Integer
For i = 0 To dt.DefaultView.Count - 1

  ' Replace the subscriber's special tags with their values
  mailMsg.To = CStr(dt.DefaultView(i)("Email"))
  mailMsg.Body = Helper.ProcessSubscriptionTags( _
    newsletterBody, CInt(dt.DefaultView(i)("SubscriptionId")))

  ' Send the mail to this subscriber
  SmtpMail.Send(mailMsg)

Next i

' Load the data for the sent newsletter in the current object
If myNewsletterId <> -1 Then
  LoadFromId()
Else
  ResetProperties()
End If
```

```
        ' Return the number of sent newsletters through an output parameter
        totalNewsletters = dt.DefaultView.Count

        ' Return the Id of the newsletter added to the archive, or -1
        ' if it has not been added
        Return myNewsletterId

    End Function
```

This code does quite a lot of things so let's break it down:

- ❑ The special tags for the list and the general settings are replaced with their values.

- ❑ If required, the newsletters is archived to the database through the Data.Newsletters class.

- ❑ A new MailMessage object is created, and its properties that are common for all the subscribers are set.

- ❑ A Business.List class instance is used to get all the active subscribers for the specified mailing list, through the GetSubscriptions method.

- ❑ For each subscription returned by the query, it replaces the subscription's special tags, sets its e-mail address as the destination address for the mail object, and sends the mail.

- ❑ The number of sent messages is saved and returned to the caller through the output parameter.

This method does not support attachments for the newsletters, but it would be quite easy to add a parameter array with the path of the files to send, and attach them through the MailMessage's Attachments collection (of course you would need to update the presentation layer as well, though).

One last thing that's worth noting in the code is that after sending the newsletter we call the LoadFromID method to set the object's properties with the values of the new record. This is exactly what we do in the Create methods of any other business class. Here the name of the method is different and we also do different work, but we still add a record to the database (if saveToDB is True) and so we also update the object's state before terminating the method.

For the sake of completeness, let's also look at the overloaded version of the Send method. This version takes the same parameters except for the last one, and it's useful because it is quicker to call if we're not interested in the number of sent messages. Here's the code:

```
    Public Overloads Function Send( _
        ByVal newsletterListId As Integer, _
        ByVal newsletterSubject As String, _
        ByVal newsletterBody As String, _
        ByVal newsletterIsHTML As Boolean, _
        ByVal priority As MailPriority, _
        ByVal saveToDB As Boolean) _
        As Integer

        Dim totalNewsletters As Integer

        Return Send( _
          newsletterListId, _
```

```
          newsletterSubject, _
          newsletterBody, _
          newsletterIsHTML, _
          priority, _
          saveToDB, _
          totalNewsletters)
   End Function
```

It just calls the first version we wrote, and passes as the last parameter a variable declared with a private scope. The Send method is also called by another business class (List) from its SendNewsletter method.

The Helper Class

The Helper class is the easiest to implement, as it only exposes three very short, static methods. The ProcessListTags method retrieves the details of the specified list through an instance of Business.List, and then replaces the special tags:

```
   Public Shared Function ProcessListTags( _
      ByVal message As String, _
      ByVal listId As Integer) _
      As String

      Dim list As New Business.List(listId)

      message = message.Replace("#ListId#", listId.ToString())
      message = message.Replace("#ListName#", list.Name)
      message = message.Replace("#ListDescription#", list.Description)

      Return message
   End Function
```

ProcessSubscriptionTags does the same, but for the subscription tags:

```
   Public Shared Function ProcessSubscriptionTags( _
      ByVal message As String, _
      ByVal subscrId As Integer) _
      As String

      ' If the subscriber does not exist, replace with empty strings
      If subscrId = -1 Then

         message = message.Replace("#SubscriptionId#", "")
         message = message.Replace("#SubscriberFirstName#", "")
         message = message.Replace("#SubscriberLastName#", "")
         message = message.Replace("#SubscriberEmail#", "")

      Else

         ' Otherwise get the details of this subscriber
         Dim subscription As New Business.Subscription(subscrId)

         ' And replace the tags
```

```
        message = message.Replace("#SubscriptionId#", subscrId.ToString())
        message = message.Replace( _
          "#SubscriberFirstName#", subscription.FirstName)
        message = message.Replace( _
          "#SubscriberLastName#", subscription.LastName)
        message = message.Replace("#SubscriberEmail#", subscription.Email)

      End If

    Return message
  End Function
```

In the code above there is one detail that's especially worth noting. If the subscriber's first name is empty, the #SubscriberFirstName# tag is replaced with "List Reader". This is because we might ask the subscriber to type and submit only the e-mail address, or, even if we asked for their name they could choose not to supply it (as long as we don't make it required of course, but that's not a good choice usually). The conclusion is that we might easily have subscriptions without the first/last names. If we then sent a newsletter with the #SubscriberFirstName# tag, someone would receive the message with a null string where their name should be (for example "Dear , how's it going?", instead of something like "Dear Marco, how's it going?"). To prevent this, we replace the tag with "List Reader" if the first name is not provided, so that the message would be "Dear List Reader, how's it going?". That is a more acceptable message.

> *It's better not to replace #SubscriberFirstName# with "List" and #SubscriberLastName# with "Reader", as you might think at first, because we may use only the first tag in the newsletter. However, if we use both, it's very probable that we won't have e-mails with "List Reader" plus a non-null last name (for example "Dear List Reader Bellinaso, ..."), because if the first name is not supplied then it's very likely that the last name won't be either. (Also, we might ask for the full name with a single field, and the value would be stored as first name only.)*

Lastly, ProcessSettingsTags processes and replaces the settings tags, retrieved through an instance of ModuleSettings:

```
  Public Shared Function ProcessSettingsTags( _
    ByVal message As String) _
    As String

    Dim settings As Configuration.ModuleSettings = _
      Configuration.ModuleConfig.GetSettings()

    ' Replace the tags
    message = message.Replace("#SenderName#", settings.SenderName)
    message = message.Replace("#SenderEmail#", settings.SenderEmail)
    message = message.Replace("#SubscribeURL#", settings.SubscribeUrl)

    Return message
  End Function
```

The Administration User Interface

The administration console is made up of a set of pages that allows us to add, remove, and edit the mailing lists, their subscriptions, and the subscribers' personal details. It also allows us to send out newsletters and consult the archive, and a few other things. The following screenshot shows the Lists.aspx page, which lists and manages the available mailing lists:

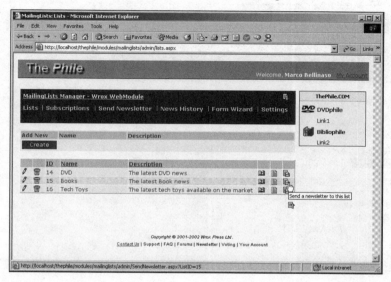

You can see that, in addition to the ID, name, and description of each mailing list, the grid also displays some icons, which allow us to directly jump to other pages to do something to the mailing list of the clicked row. Here is a list of the grid's icons with a description of the actions they perform:

Icon	Description
	Edit the record.
	Delete the record.
	Jump to the page that shows the subscribers of this mailing list.
	Jump to the page that shows the newsletters previously sent to this mailing list.
	Jump to the page to compose and send a new newsletter to the subscribers of this mailing list.

When you click the third icon of the table above you jump to the page to manage the subscriptions, `Subscriptions.aspx`, which looks like the following screenshot:

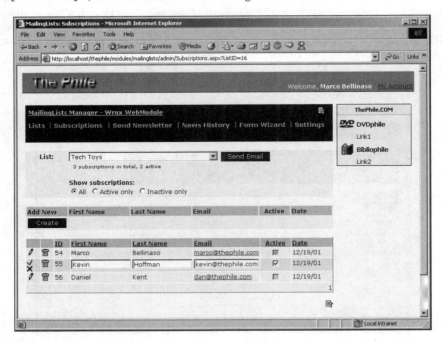

The code for these two web forms should be familiar if you've read the previous chapters. Maybe the only interesting new detail is that we use a `RegularExpressionValidator` control to validate the e-mail address for a new subscription or a subscription being edited. Here is how we define the textbox and the validators:

```
<asp:TextBox runat="server" CssClass="TextBox" ID="NewEmail" Width="100%" />
<asp:RequiredFieldValidator runat="server" ControlToValidate="NewEmail"
                            Display="dynamic"><br>* Email is required
</asp:RequiredFieldValidator>
<asp:RegularExpressionValidator runat="server"
                            ValidationExpression=".*@.*\..*"
                            ControlToValidate="NewEmail"
                            Display="dynamic">
                            <br>* This Email address is not valid
</asp:RegularExpressionValidator>
```

The expression `.*@.*\..*` means that the string must begin with a number of characters (`.*`), then it must contain an '@' character, some more characters, a period (escaped as `\.`), and finally more characters. For example, marco@thephile.com is a valid e-mail address, while marco@thephile and marco.thephile.com are invalid addresses.

The following tables summarize the most commonly used syntax constructs for the **regular expressions**. First of all let's see how to express the characters that we want to match:

Character Escapes	Description
ordinary characters	Characters other than .$^{[(|)*+?\ match themselves.
\b	Matches a backspace.
\t	Matches a tab.
\r	Matches a carriage return.
\v	Matches a vertical tab.
\f	Matches a form feed.
\n	Matches a newline.
\	If followed by a non-ordinary character (one of those listed in the first row), matches that character. For example, \+ matches a + character.

In addition to single characters, we can specify a class or a range of characters that can be matched in the expression. That is to say, we might want to allow any digit or any vowel in a position, and exclude all other characters. The following character classes enable this:

Character Class	Description
.	Matches any character except \n.
[aeiou]	Matches any single character specified in the set.
[^aeiou]	Matches any character not specified in the set.
[3-7a-dA-D]	Matches any character specified in the specified ranges (in the example the ranges are 3-7, a-d, and A-D).
\w	Matches any word character, that is, any alphanumeric character or the underscore (_).
\W	Matches any non-word character.
\s	Matches any whitespace character (space, tab, form-feed, newline, carriage return, or vertical feed).
\S	Matches any non-whitespace character.
\d	Matches any decimal character.
\D	Matches any non-decimal character.

Also, we can specify that a certain character or class of characters must be present at least once, or between two and six times, etc. The quantifiers are put just after a character or a class of characters, and allow us to specify how many times the preceding character/class must be matched:

Quantifier	Description
*	Zero or more matches.
+	One or more matches.
?	Zero or one matches.
{N}	N matches.
{N,}	N or more matches.
{N,M}	Between N and M matches.

To recap everything with another easy example, say that we have the expression `[aeiou]{2,4}\+[1-5]*`: this means that a string to correctly match this expression must start with two to four vowels, have a + sign, and terminate with zero or more digits between 1 and 5.

> *Regular expressions are a very powerful tool to validate the content of a control because they can be very detailed and complex. Furthermore, you can use them to do other advanced tasks, such as replacing or extracting the occurrences that match the expression, as we'll see in practice in the next chapter.*

You have to be aware, however, that the regular expression used to validate the e-mail address in the module only checks that the address is well formed. There's nothing to prevent someone from subscribing with an e-mail address that does not exist. To limit this you can at least improve the regular expression with other rules, such as checking that the domain name is at least two characters long and that it does exist, and that the extension is supported (consult www.icann.org to get a complete list). There are other rules, and although we kept it simple in our example, you'll find that a complete regular expression could be much longer than ours. If regular expressions are not enough for you (and they are not if you want to check the existence of a domain, for example), you can use a CustomValidator and write your own function to validate a value.

However, even with the most complete expression and other methods you can't be 100% sure that the address exists. The user can write an address with a real domain name, a real extension, but with a made-up name before the @. When the messages are sent out, you won't get any errors or exceptions at that time – the SMTP server does its work without letting you know about the result. However, messages sent to non-existent addresses usually come back to the sender with an error message saying that the message couldn't be successfully delivered because the address does not exist. These error messages are sent to the server's postmaster and then forwarded to the site's administrator. At this point, when you get such a message you can manually remove the address from the database. Alternatively you could write a program that parses the incoming messages to find the error messages, and automatically deletes the non-existent e-mail addresses by using the business classes of the MailingList module. This is beyond the scope of this book, and it is usually only provided by professional modules that must be able to handle tens or hundreds of thousands of e-mails, and automate any possible process. For most sites, though, our module is enough, and deleting the erroneous addresses from the database once a month or so is not such a big issue (how often you should do this actually depends on the frequency of your newsletters).

Sending out Newsletters to Subscribers

The console has a simple newsletter editor, basically a form with a textbox for the body, and the common fields you find in any e-mail client, such as Subject, To, Format, and Priority. You can type a newsletter, preview it, and finally send the message out to the selected mailing list's active subscriptions. The screenshot below represents the `SendNewsletter.aspx` page with the message preview:

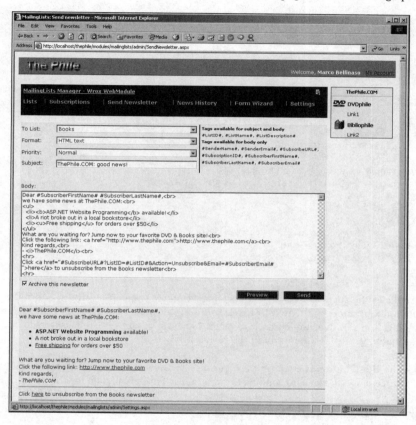

You can see that the settings tags (such as `#SubscribeURL#`) and the list tags (such as `#ListName#`) were processed for the preview, while the subscription tags were not. This is because they have different values for every subscription, and are actually processed only when the newsletter is sent to each subscriber.

The code for presenting the page is simple enough, so we won't show it. Instead, we'll have a look at the code-behind subroutine that shows the message preview, and actually sends out and archives the newsletter. First of all, in `Page_Load` there is some code that fills the `DropDownList` with the available mailing lists, and sets the default subject and signature as specified in the settings file. Then, when the **Preview** button is pressed, the following event handler is executed on the server:

```vb
Protected Sub Preview_Click(ByVal sender As Object, ByVal e As EventArgs)

  Dim msgText As String = Body.Text
  Dim listId As Integer = _
    Integer.Parse(ListsDropDown.SelectedItem.Value)

  ' Replace the list's and settings special tags with their values
  msgText = Business.Helper.ProcessListTags(msgText, listId)
  msgText = Business.Helper.ProcessSettingsTags(msgText)

  ' Encode the body if the format is not HTML
  If FormatDropDown.SelectedIndex = 0 Then

    msgText = HttpUtility.HtmlEncode(msgText)

    ' Replace the new lines with <br/>, to show the new lines
    ' in the Label
    msgText = msgText.Replace(ControlChars.Lf, "<br/>")

    ' Remove carriage returns
    msgText = msgText.Replace(ControlChars.Cr, "")

  End If

  ' Show the body in the preview label
  MsgPreview.Text = msgText
  MsgPreview.Visible = True
End Sub
```

This code replaces the special list and settings tags with their respective values, and if the selected format is plain text it encodes the text (for example <b> become <b>), replaces the new-lines with a <br> tag, and removes the carriage returns, because '\n' and '\r' characters are not recognized by HTML. Finally, it displays the body in the preview label.

The code for the **Send** button is even simpler, because the Newsletter business class does all the work required for processing the tags and sending out the mails. This is the code for the button's Click event:

```vb
Protected Sub Send_Click(ByVal sender As Object, ByVal e As EventArgs)
  Server.ScriptTimeout = 3600

  ' Send the newsletter and eventually save it to the DB
  Dim numSent As Integer
  Dim list As New Business.List( _
    Integer.Parse(ListsDropDown.SelectedItem.Value))

  list.SendNewsletter(Subject.Text, _
    Body.Text, _
    CBool(FormatDropDown.SelectedIndex = 1), _
    CType(PriorityDropDown.SelectedIndex, MailPriority), _
    ArchiveNewsletter.Checked, numSent)

  ' Show the number of sent mails
  MsgPreview.Text = String.Format( _
```

```
        "<b>{0} mail(s) have been sent</b>", numSent)

    ' If the newsletter has been archived, say this
    If ArchiveNewsletter.Checked Then
        MsgPreview.Text &= "<br/><b>The newsletter has been archived</b>"
    End If

    MsgPreview.Visible = True

End Sub
```

The last parameter of this method returns the number of mails that have been sent, and this is displayed at the bottom of the page, as a confirmation message. The only point that's worth noting here is the first line of code:

```
Server.ScriptTimeout = 3600
```

Sending a single message is a very quick task, but if you have thousands of subscribers this may take a while: several minutes or even some hours for large messages. Those of you who are already familiar with traditional ASP programming will know that by default a page has 90 seconds to execute the scripting code and to send all the generated HTML code to the browser. The IIS administrator can change this value or we can hard-code it into the page, which is exactly what we do here. We set the maximum time to complete the execution to an hour, but you can change it to a value that you consider to be long enough for your needs. If you have many thousands of subscriptions, you may even consider deploying the MailingLists module on a separate server, to avoid serious problems with the services that run on the primary server. You can have the module's engine on a server and the subscription box on another server, as long as the subscription box points to the Subscribe.aspx page on the first server. However, if you have a really large base of subscribers, some web hosting companies can offer a dedicated server with specific software that can handle tens or hundreds of thousands of e-mail addresses. This software should be able to process your newsletters asynchronously and provide some fault tolerance, by using transactions and messaging services such as MSMQ. It goes without saying that these extra services are quite expensive, and are not required for most sites.

Here is an example of the message generated, as received in Outlook Express:

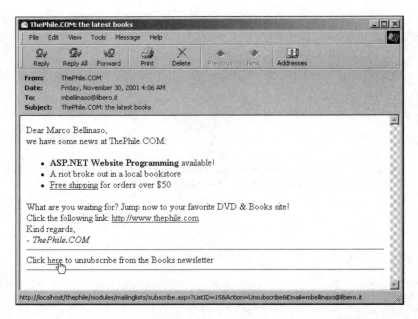

In the status bar of the window above you can see the URL pointed at by the link under the mouse cursor. It redirects to the `Subscribe.aspx` page with some parameters indicating that the user with the specified e-mail address wants to be un-subscribed from the specified mailing list. We'll be looking at this page and the required parameters shortly.

Managing the Newsletters Archive

The newsletters archive page, `NewsHistory.aspx`, displays all the messages previously sent to any mailing list, in plain text or HTML, according to the format they were sent in. Here is a screenshot of the page:

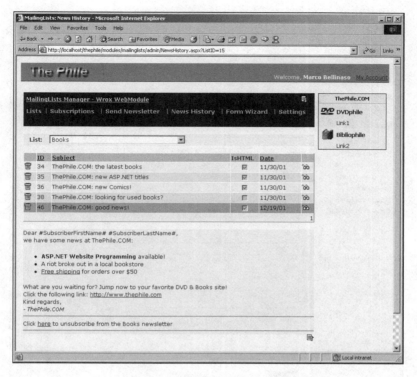

The code for the `DataGrid` has already been covered earlier in the book, so we'll skip it here. In this case the grid is even simpler because it does not have to handle the editing mode or additions of new rows. The code for displaying the newsletters is almost the same as the code shown in the previous section to display the preview of a message before sending it out.

Modifying the Settings Online

The `Settings.aspx` page makes use of the configuration classes to retrieve and show the current settings, and persist the new settings changed by the user. This is the user interface:

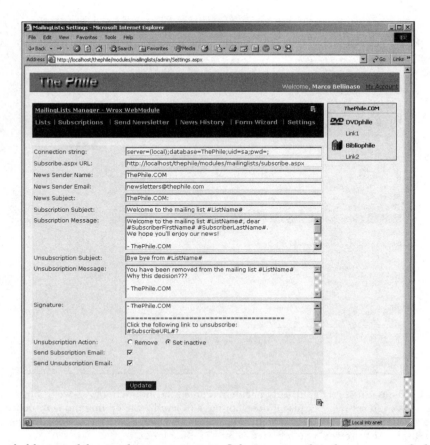

This is probably one of the simplest pages to write. It has a series of textboxes, some of which require a value and can't be left empty, and a few other controls. We've already seen the settings page for other modules. The one for this module is the longest, as this module has quite a lot of options, but it works in exactly the same way. In `Page_Load` we retrieve an instance of `ModuleSettings` through a call to the shared method `Configuration.ModuleConfig.GetSettings`, and fill the textboxes and other controls with the respective `ModuleSettings` properties. When the Update button is pressed we create a new instance of `ModuleSettings`, set its properties with the values currently present on the page, and call the shared method `Configuration.ModuleConfig.SaveSettings` to persist the new settings to the XML file.

Creating a Subscription Form for the User

All the pages to manage mailing lists and subscriptions, send e-mail messages, and change the settings are finally complete. So what's left? The subscription form to allow the end user to subscribe from the public part of the site, of course!

Instead of writing the HTML code for each mailing list (a boring task), it would be much better to add a further page that automates this operation. This involves generating the HTML code for the specified mailing list subscription form, as demonstrated in the following screenshot of our `FormWizard.aspx` page:

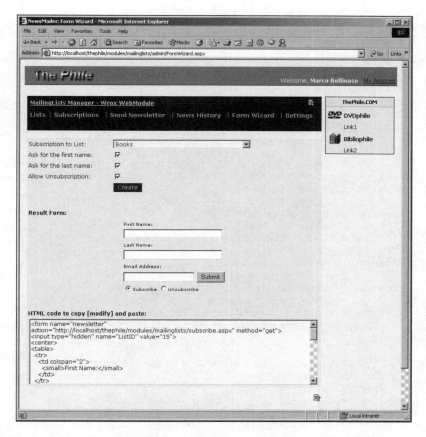

The administrator selects the mailing list for which they want to create the subscription form, specifies if the fields for the first and last name are required (these fields are not mandatory for a subscription, so the form can work without them), and chooses whether the form will have two option buttons to allow the user to subscribe and un-subscribe. When the Create button is pressed the HTML code is generated and appears within the textbox at the bottom, and a preview of the form is shown in the center of the page. At this point the administrator can copy the HTML and paste it into any HTML page.

The first part of the page, that has the drop-down list and the checkboxes, is built as usual, with the controls aligned using a table. The second part of the table shown above (the "Result Form:" part) is invisible by default, and is only displayed when the user presses the Create button. As this code consists almost entirely of ASP.NET controls, the like of which we have seen many times before, we will not show the code here.

The code-behind for this page simply uses the database to fill the drop-down list with the available mailing lists, and gets the URL of the Subscribe.aspx page from the settings file. The rest of the code, the Create_Click event handler, builds the HTML string, the content of which depends on the options selected by the administrators in the top of the page. Here's the code for this event handler:

```
Protected Sub Create_Click(ByVal sender As Object, ByVal e As EventArgs)
  Dim formHTML As String = ""

  ' Create the subscription controls (table, textbox to type the
  ' address, submit Button and a hidden field to store the destination
  ' ListId value)
  formHTML &= String.Format( _
    "<input type=""hidden"" name=""ListId"" value=""{0}"">", _
    ListsDropDown.SelectedItem.Value)
  formHTML &= ControlChars.Lf & "<center>" & ControlChars.Lf & "<table>"

  ' Add the Fist Name choice if the AskFirstName CheckBox is checked
  If AskFirstName.Checked Then
    formHTML &= ControlChars.Lf & _
      "  <tr>" & ControlChars.Lf & "    <td colspan=""2"">"
    formHTML &= ControlChars.Lf & _
      "      <small>First Name:</small>"
    formHTML &= ControlChars.Lf & _
      "    </td>" & ControlChars.Lf & "  </tr>"
    formHTML &= ControlChars.Lf & _
      "  <tr>" & ControlChars.Lf & "    <td colspan=""2"">"
    formHTML &= ControlChars.Lf & _
      "      <input type=""text"" name=""FirstName"" size=""30"">"
    formHTML &= ControlChars.Lf & _
      "    </td>" & ControlChars.Lf & "  </tr>"
  End If

  ' Add the Fist Name choice if the AskFirstName CheckBox is checked
  If AskLastName.Checked Then
    formHTML &= ControlChars.Lf & _
      "  <tr>" & ControlChars.Lf & "    <td colspan=""2"">"
    formHTML &= ControlChars.Lf & _
      "      <small>Last Name:</small>"
    formHTML &= ControlChars.Lf & _
      "    </td>" & ControlChars.Lf & "  </tr>"
    formHTML &= ControlChars.Lf & _
      "  <tr>" & ControlChars.Lf & "    <td colspan=""2"">"
    formHTML &= ControlChars.Lf & _
      "      <input type=""text"" name=""LastName"" size=""30"">"
    formHTML &= ControlChars.Lf & _
      "    </td>" & ControlChars.Lf & "  </tr>"
  End If

  ' Add the Email Address field and the Submit button
  formHTML &= ControlChars.Lf & _
    "  <tr><td><small>Email Address:</small></td></tr>"
  formHTML &= ControlChars.Lf & _
    "  <tr>" & ControlChars.Lf & _
    "    <td><input type=""text"" name=""Email"" size=""20""></td>"
  formHTML &= ControlChars.Lf & _
    "    <td><input type=""submit"" value=""Submit""></td>"
  formHTML &= ControlChars.Lf & _
    "  </tr>"
```

```
        ' Add the Unsubscribe choice if the AllowUnsubscription CheckBox
        ' is checked
        If AllowUnsubscription.Checked Then
            formHTML &= ControlChars.Lf & _
                "  <tr>" & ControlChars.Lf & _
                "    <td colspan=""2"">"
            formHTML &= ControlChars.Lf & _
                "      <small><input type=""radio"" name=""Action"" " & _
                "value=""Subscribe"" checked>Subscribe"
            formHTML &= ControlChars.Lf & _
                "      <input type=""radio"" name=""Action"" " & _
                "value=""Unsubscribe"">Unsubscribe</small>"
            formHTML &= ControlChars.Lf & _
                "    </td>" & ControlChars.Lf & "  </tr>"
        End If

        formHTML &= ControlChars.Lf & "</table>" & _
            ControlChars.Lf & "</center>"

        ' Show the table just created
        ResultForm.Text = formHTML

        ' Get the settings
        Dim settings As Configuration.ModuleSettings = _
            Configuration.ModuleConfig.GetSettings()

        ' Add the <form> tag and show the HTML code in the TextBox
        formHTML = String.Format( _
            "<form name=""newsletter"" action=""{0}"" method=""get"">" & _
                ControlChars.Lf & "{1}" & ControlChars.Lf & "</form>", _
            settings.SubscribeUrl, _
            formHTML)

        ResultFormHTML.Text = formHTML

        ' Show the result table and the HTML code
        TableResult.Visible = True
    End Sub
```

First of all the code creates the text for a hidden field in which the ID of the selected mailing list is stored. Then it creates the table and textboxes for the first and last name (if required, as indicated by the respective checkboxes) and the e-mail address, and finally the Submit button. As a last step, if the Allow Unsubscription checkbox is selected, it also adds two radio buttons to let the user specify if they want to subscribe or un-subscribe. The administrator may not want to add the Unsubscribe option to the form to prevent someone from un-subscribing someone else just by typing an e-mail address. Sure, they could do this anyway with the special un-subscription URL (the one which is often added at the bottom of each newsletter), but it is more difficult and less likely to be done by accident.

The HTML code just created is displayed in the ResultForm label to give a preview of the result. The pasted code is not a real form though, and if we press the Submit button nothing happens, because we didn't add the <form> tag. This tag wraps the previously created FormHTML string, specifying the Subscribe.aspx page as the target for the post operation, and then the closing tag is appended at the end of the string. The final string is set as the text of the textbox control, to let the user easily copy it.

437

In the following screenshot you can see a few examples of forms produced by this page:

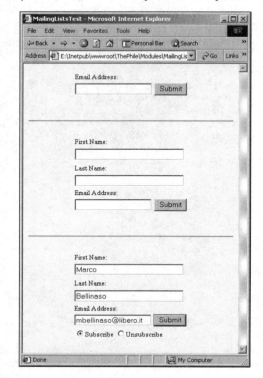

The first form in the above screenshot was produced by leaving all three options unchecked. The second was produced by selecting the first two options (ask for the first and last name), while the third was produced by checking all three options.

Since the code produced is simple HTML, you can customize the result as you wish: for example you may want to change the colors, the font, the width of the textboxes, add an image as a border or background, or a comment informing the client about the name of the mailing list they are subscribing to. A very useful change would be to add a JavaScript function to ensure that the e-mail address field is not empty before actually submitting the form.

Subscribing to a Mailing List

So far we've seen the entire application from the administrator's point of view, but what about the end user? We're now going to show how a visitor can come to our website and subscribe to a mailing list. The page with the subscription form can be located anywhere, even on a different server, because it points to the full URL of Subscribe.aspx stored in the settings.

It's now time to test one of the subscription forms shown in the last screenshot to subscribe a new user (we used the third form and chose the Books mailing list). If the Send Subscription Email setting option is selected in the administrator's page, which it is by default if you use the provided settings file, the subscriber receives the confirmation e-mail message customized with their information:

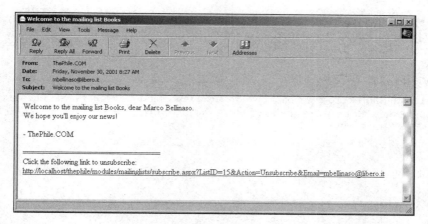

The last line is a link that, if clicked, will delete this subscriber from the mailing list. This link is dynamically built by replacing the tags of the following string:

```
#SubscribeURL#?ListID=#ListID#&Action=Unsubscribe&Email=#SubscriberEmail#
```

As you can guess from reading the string, what differentiates between a subscription and un-subscription is the Action parameter, which in this case is set to Unsubscribe. The link for the subscription is the same string but without the Action parameter, or with that parameter set to anything other than Unsubscribe. The other parameters of the link are the ID of the mailing list (stored in the hidden field in the form) and the e-mail address of the subscriber.

The confirmation e-mail is sent only if the respective setting is enabled. However, you always get a confirmation web page, containing the same text as the mail. The same applies to the un-subscription process. To also test this operation, click the link of the previous e-mail message – a browser instance will open and a message will be displayed, as follows:

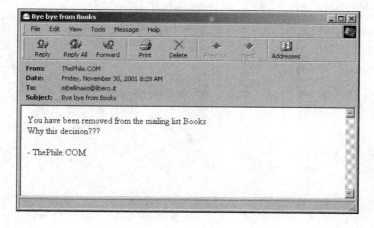

You would get exactly the same result by selecting the Unsubscribe option in the HTML form. Obviously, you can check if the subscriber is actually added or removed by viewing the Subscriptions.aspx page in the administration console.

The Subscribe.aspx Page

This page has the shortest code we have seen so far in this chapter. Except for the site header/footer and menu box, the controls we're interested in are the following:

```
<asp:Label ID="Subject" runat="Server" CssClass="SubscrSubject"
        Visible="false" />
<br>
<asp:Label ID="Message" runat="Server" CssClass="SubscrMessage"
        Visible="false" />
<asp:Label runat="server" ID="EmailRequired" Visible="false"
        Text="The Email address is required" CssClass="Error" />
```

There are three labels: one for the confirmation subject, one for the message body, and one for an error message in case the e-mail address is not specified. All these labels are invisible by default. They will be shown after the user subscribes or un-subscribes, according to the result of the operation.

The Code-behind for Subscribe.aspx

All the code of this code-behind class is located in the Page_Load procedure, because everything is done when the page is loaded – there aren't any forms or controls that raise other events. The complete code of this event handler is as shown:

```
Private Sub Page_Load(ByVal sender As Object, ByVal e As EventArgs)

    ' Get the ListId, FirstName, LastName, Email and the action to
    ' perform from the QueryString generated by the HTML form
    Dim listId As Integer = Integer.Parse(Request.Params("ListId"))
    Dim firstName As String = Request.Params("FirstName") + ""
    Dim lastName As String = Request.Params("LastName") + ""
    Dim email As String = Request.Params("Email") + ""
    Dim action As String = Request.Params("Action") + ""

    If email.Trim() = "" Then

        ' If the Email was not specified, show the error message and
        ' do not proceed
        EmailRequired.Visible = True

    Else

        Dim subjectText As String
        Dim messageText As String

        ' Remove/inactivate or add/activate a subscription, according
        ' to the Action param
        Dim list As New Business.List(listId)

        If action = "Unsubscribe" Then
```

```
            list.Unsubscribe(email, subjectText, messageText)
        Else
            List.Subscribe(firstName, lastName, email, subjectText, messageText)
        End If

        ' Show the message that confirms the action
        Subject.Text = subjectText
        Message.Text = messageText.Replace(ControlChars.Lf, "<br/>")
        Subject.Visible = True
        Message.Visible = True
    End If
End Sub
```

In the first lines the target list's ID and the subscriber's name and address are extracted from the query string and saved in local variables to make it easier to use them later in the procedure. Before going ahead with any other operation, the code checks if the e-mail parameter is empty. If it is then the EmailRequired error label is shown and the rest of the procedure is not executed. If the execution does proceed, we call the Subscribe or Unsubscribe method of the instance of Business.List for the target mailing list, according to the Action parameter. As we've seen earlier, these methods will take care of all the details and will operate according to the settings stored in the XML file. They will also return the confirmation message, so that we can show it on the page as an instant confirmation.

Securing the Module

In *The Design* section we decided that two permissions are adequate to provide security for the module: one for general administration, and the other for sending out a newsletter. We define these permissions in a new enumeration in the Enum.vb file of the Core module, as follows:

```
Namespace WebModules.MailingLists

    Public Enum MailingListsPermissions
        AdministerData = 400
        SendNewsletter = 401
    End Enum

End Namespace
```

Then we limit access to the administration pages by adding the following code at the beginning of the Page_Load event handler (remember that you must add a reference to the business component of the Accounts module for it to work):

```
        Private Sub Page_Load(ByVal sender As Object, ByVal e As EventArgs)

            ' Check if the current user is allowed to administer the lists
            If Not (TypeOf Context.User Is SitePrincipal) _
                OrElse Not CType(Context.User, SitePrincipal).HasPermission( _
                    CInt(MailingListsPermissions.AdministerData)) Then

                Response.Redirect( _
                    "/ThePhileVB/WebModules/Accounts/Login.aspx?ShowError=true", True)

            End If
```

```
    If Not Page.IsPostBack Then
       'other code generally goes here
    End If
End Sub
```

As we've already seen in some of the previous chapters, in the code above we first check if the user is authenticated: if not, the second half of the `if` block is not processed (thanks to short-circuiting) and we redirect to the login page (with the `ShowError` parameter set to `True`, to cause the login page to show an error message telling the user that they do not have the necessary permissions to load the page). Otherwise we check if the current user has the `AdministerData` permission, by casting `Context.User` to `SitePrincipal` (which implements the `IPrincipal` interface) and calling its `HasPermission` method. If the specified permission is not found in the user's profile, the user is redirected to the login page, as if they were not authenticated. Otherwise the execution of the page continues, and the data is retrieved from the database and shown in the grid and the other controls.

The code for protecting `SendNewsletter.aspx` is almost the same; the permission just needs to be changed from `AdministerData` to `SendNewsletter`. We don't need to add anything to the `Subscribe.aspx` page, as it must be freely accessible by the visitor when they post a subscription.

Summary

The aim of this chapter was to show how to design and build a full-featured mailing list manager that could be used as-is for many websites. We've implemented an administration console that allows us to:

❑   Add, edit, and delete mailing lists and their associated subscriptions

❑   Create and send newsletters (both in plain text and HTML format) and consult the archive of previously sent messages

❑   Modify the settings online

❑   Auto-generate the HTML code for the subscription box

Administration aside, we've developed the page that actually handles the subscription process. This used the business components developed at the beginning of the implementation section. Finally, we've used the `Accounts` business classes to ensure that only users with the appropriate permissions can administer the data and send out newsletters.

By doing all this we've learned some new techniques in this chapter, most notably:

❑   How to use the `SmtpMail` and `MailMessage` classes to send e-mails with the Windows SMTP Server

❑   The use of regular expressions to validate e-mail addresses (or, in general, any other string) against a given pattern

As for any other module presented in this book, you can add further features to make it even more powerful. Here are just a few ideas:

❑ Add the ability to create and handle subscription forms that allow the user to subscribe to *multiple* mailing lists in one step, giving their e-mail address only once. This would simply require a few changes to the HTML form that you paste in your pages, and to the `Subscribe.aspx` page that processes the data posted to the server. Adding a subscription to more than one list is really just a matter of a few lines of code, thanks to the business layer classes that handle the actual subscription process.

❑ Allow each user to choose whether to receive the newsletters in HTML or plain text format, and send different newsletters according to that choice.

❑ Add the ability to send attachments with the newsletters. This can be very useful if you want to send HTML newsletters with images. Currently, you can send mails with images by referencing the full URL of the image on your server, but it would be better to send them along with the message.

❑ Add a search engine to the administration console, which allows a specified e-mail address or contact name to be easily found. This would be useful if the administrator wants to see or change the properties of a particular subscriber.

❑ Add a double check on the subscription/un-subscription process. This consists of sending a notification e-mail to the subscriber, asking them to confirm that they want to subscribe/un-subscribe from/to the mailing list. The action will only be taken if they click a link to confirm. This feature is really useful if you want to be sure that someone does not subscribe someone else by posting a false e-mail address. You can't be 100% sure that this won't happen anyway, since (as always) someone could hack the link format and make false confirmations, but it's better than doing no checks at all!

❑ Add the option to have multiple administrators, with different rights. For example, a basic administrator could only see the current mailing lists and subscribers, a second level of administrator could also send out new newsletters, and an advanced administrator would have full rights, with permission to add, remove, and modify the mailing lists and subscribers.

In the last few chapters we've developed modules to strengthen the site-to-user communication, such as the polls module and this mailing lists manager. In the next chapter we're going to implement a module to manage forums, the most important form of user-to-user communication system.

10

Forums and Online Communities

A successful site should build a community of loyal visitors. Internet users like to feel part of a community of people with the same interests, to discuss their favorite subjects, and to ask questions and reply to those of others. Community members will return often to meet other people that they've already chatted with, or to find comments and opinions about their interests. In this chapter we'll outline some of the advantages of building such a virtual community. We'll then identify the goals for our website community, and step through the design and implementation of a new module for setting up and managing discussion boards (forums).

The Problem

User-to-user communication is important in many types of website. For example, in a content-based site relating to programming resources, programmers need to ask questions about problems they are facing and hear suggestions from their peers. E-commerce sites benefit from allowing users to review products online.

Two ways to provide user-to-user communication are opinion polls and discussion boards. We looked at opinion polls in Chapter 8. In this chapter we will talk about discussion boards, or **forums**.

Forums act as a source of content, and provide an opportunity for visitors to participate and contribute. Visitors can browse the various messages in the forums, post their questions and topics, reply to other people's questions, and share ideas and tips.

For our ThePhile.com site, we can offer discussion boards about books and DVDs. We will also want sub-groups within that, so that it is easier for visitors to read about what they are specifically interested in. For example, if we have a books category we can have sub-forums for programming books, classic literature, novels, and publishing.

Early web-forum systems often threw up long lists of messages on a single page, which took ages to load. We want to avoid this by displaying lists in pages, with each page containing a set number of messages.

Our website already has a way to identify users (the `Accounts` module we developed in Chapter 5), and our forums should support that. But we should also give users the opportunity to create a **profile**, so that they can post messages without revealing their true identity. These profiles should include a public name, an avatar image (a small picture that represents the user), a signature, and a homepage URL.

The administrator must be able to add, remove, or edit categories, forums, topics, and replies, and change the module's settings. If you're wondering what the difference is between a category and a forum, let's say that a category is a container for multiple forums. For example, we can have two categories: Books and DVD. The Books category can contain the following forums: programming books, books for children, school course books, spy stories, etc. The DVD category, on the other hand, will have child forums such as PC games, action movies, horror movies, cartoons, etc. In practice, a category allows better organization and keeps together forums with related subjects.

Cross-Site Scripting

One problem with forums is when users enter HTML or JavaScript code that somehow impairs the site. This could range from making the page look irritating (remember `<blink>`?), including large or offensive images, or automatically redirecting the browser to other sites. However, giving readers access to some simple tags can allow them to be far more expressive in their postings.

The problems we're trying to solve here are relatively simple. Our site will be nothing like the massive forum systems such as Slashdot or Plastic. In the site's design, we will try to get the best of both worlds – give users the flexibility to present their messages well, without allowing them to damage the site.

The Design

As usual, we will design our data layer first and work up to the presentation layer. The configuration system is quite important in this module, so we will look at the design for that before considering the business layer.

The Database

The design begins with the database tables needed to store all the categories, forums, topics, replies, and members. The prefix for the tables and stored procedure for this module is `Forums_`. We have five new tables (we also use `Accounts_Users`, created in Chapter 5), shown in the following diagram:

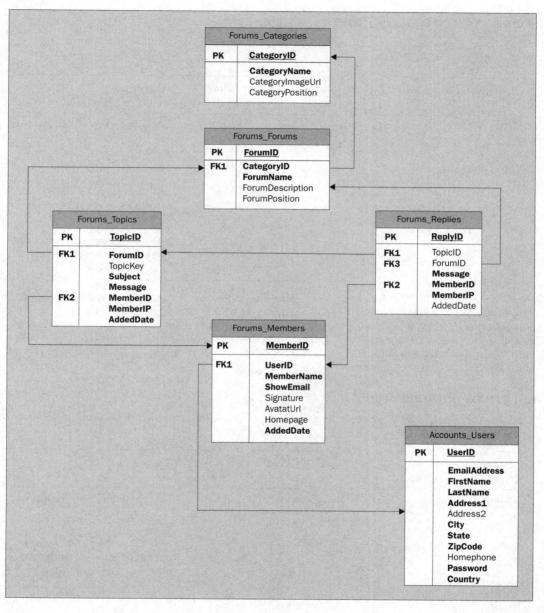

In the next sections we'll be explaining each table in detail, but remember that – as usual – you can download the complete database backup with the required tables, stored procedures, views, etc. from the Wrox site.

The Forums_Categories Table

The `Forums_Categories` table is used to store the name and image for the forum categories. It is structured as follows:

Column Name	Type	Size	Allow Null	Description
CategoryID	int – Identity primary key	4	No	The unique ID for the category.
CategoryName	varchar	100	No	The name of the category.
CategoryImageUrl	varchar	100	Yes	The optional URL of the category's descriptive image.
CategoryPosition	int	4	Yes	The ordinal position of the category. Later we'll return the categories ordered by this field, in ascending order.

At first, the `CategoryPosition` column might seem useless, but it's actually very handy. It allows the administrator to decide the position of the categories when they are all shown in a web page. For example, you may want to show a particular category at the top of the page, because it reflects the subject of the site's main business. We can't just use the ID column to order the categories, because it is an Identity column that's auto-incremented. It reflects the order in which the categories were created and not necessarily their importance.

The Forums_Forums Table

The `Forums_Forums` table stores information on specific forums, and their relationship with the parent categories. It is structured as follows:

Column Name	Type	Size	Allow Null	Description
ForumID	int – Identity primary key	4	No	The unique ID for the forum.
CategoryID	int foreign key	4	No	The ID of the parent category, matching a record in the `Forums_Categories` table.
ForumName	varchar	100	No	The name of the forum.
ForumDescription	varchar	250	Yes	An optional description of the forum.
ForumPosition	int	4	Yes	The ordinal position of the forum, used to control display order.

The Forums_Topics Table

The Forums_Topics table stores all the topics for all the forums. When a new topic is introduced, the message is stored in this table. Then responses are posted as replies to this message – our chat room does not allow true threading at this stage. Forums_Topics has the following columns:

Column Name	Type	Size	Allow Null	Description
TopicID	int – Identity primary key	4	No	The unique ID for the topic.
ForumID	int foreign key	4	No	The ID of the parent forum, matching a record in the Forums_Forums table.
TopicKey	varchar	15	Yes	An optional key for the topic.
Subject	varchar	100	No	The subject/title of the topic.
Message	text		No	The text of the topic.
MemberID	int foreign key	4	No	The ID of the member who authored this message. It matches a record in the Forums_Members table (presented shortly).
MemberIP	varchar	15	No	The IP address of the member who authored this message.
AddedDate	datetime	8	No	When the message was added to the database.

Two columns, TopicKey and MemberIP, are worth some more explanation. TopicKey enables us to associate a particular topic to other resources, such as a news article. It can contain the ID (but in string format) of a news article, or some identifier (of string type) of another resource, such as the ISBN for a book, for example. Later we'll see in practice how to employ this column to integrate the module with other parts of the site.

The MemberIP column stores the IP address of the member who submitted the topic. We already have the MemberID column to identify members, and can ban them if they post offensive messages. If a user posts something illegal, we might need to resort to legal means to identify them. Although difficult, it is sometimes possible to use IP to trace a specific user. In any case, it will act as a deterrent for serious misuse.

The Forums_Replies Table

Forums_Replies is similar to Forums_Topics, but stores messages sent in reply to the topics:

Column Name	Type	Size	Allow Null	Description
ReplyID	int – Identity primary key	4	No	The unique ID for the reply.
TopicID	int foreign key	4	No	The ID of the parent topic, matching a record in the Forums_Topics table.
ForumID	int foreign key	4	No	The ID of the parent forum. It matches a record in the Forums_Forums table.
Message	text		No	The text of the message.
MemberID	int foreign key	4	No	The ID of the member who authored this message. It matches a record in the Forums_Members table, presented below.
MemberIP	varchar	15	No	The IP address of the member who authored this message.
AddedDate	datetime	8	No	When the message was added to the database.

As you can see, this table has almost the same columns as Forums_Topics, except for TopicKey and Subject, which are not present here. We could just use one table for the topics and the replies, but using two separate tables makes retrieving a list of topics for a forum faster. We also want to calculate further columns for topics and replies, and this is much easier if they are stored in separate tables.

ForumID may seem unnecessary, since we could retrieve the parent forum's ID from the Forums_Topics table joined through the TopicID value. However, repeating the ForumID here helps us count the number of replies for the specified forum, which we will want to do later when displaying the page with the available forums.

It's also worth noting that this structure does not support **threaded discussions**, such as the newsgroup discussions that you can browse through your mail client. Threaded discussions allow a reply to any post, as a new topic or as a reply to an existing topic, and are represented through a tree structure. The structure for non-threaded discussions only allows replies directly to the main topic – there is no field in the database to keep a reference to another reply. The replies will be shown to the reader sorted by creation date, from the oldest to the newest. Both these two types of forum systems, threaded or not, have their pro and cons. Threaded discussions make it easier to follow replies to previous posts, but non-threaded discussions make it easier to follow the discussion with the correct temporal order. Furthermore, non-threaded discussions usually allow a previous reply to be quoted, making it quite easy for the reader to follow the discussion even if the referenced message is a number of posts above the new reply. I don't know if it is because non-threaded forums are a little easier to develop, but our investigations of the discussion boards used in quite a lot of popular sites show that non-threaded discussions seem to be used most often, so we've decided to go that way too.

The Forums_Members Table

The `Forums_Members` table stores the profiles of the registered forums' members:

Column Name	Type	Size	Allow Null	Description
MemberID	int – Identity primary key	4	No	The unique ID for the member.
UserID	int foreign key	4	No	The ID of the respective site's account that matches a record in the `Accounts_Users` table.
MemberName	varchar	15	No	The member's name.
ShowEmail	bit	1	No	If `true`, the e-mail address will be visible in the posts of this member.
Signature	varchar	300	Yes	The signature text, added at the bottom of every message from this member.
AvatarUrl	varchar	100	Yes	The URL of an image that will be shown together with the member name in all the member's posts.
Homepage	varchar	100	Yes	The URL of the member's homepage, if any.
AddedDate	datetime	8	No	The date when the user registered a profile for the forums.

This table is joined to the `Accounts_Users` table of the `Accounts` module, developed in Chapter 5, on the `UserID` column. This table contains information specific to forums, while other information such as the user's first and last name, e-mail address, etc., is already present in the `Accounts_Users` table. This also means that the user must create an account for the site first, and then register for the forums. This is good because this way the user is not required to insert the same information twice, but neither do we need to have a unique but larger table if the user does not want to use the forums. Of course, you can change the site's registration page to require all the information in a single place, and store the value for both tables.

Database Views

We need to return more information than that stored in the tables above, including the number of topics and posts (topics plus replies) to the forums, and the date of the most recent post to a forum or topic. We will provide this through views with dynamically calculated columns, so that it's easier to access the data from the stored procedures without repeating the required SQL code in all of them. We'll build some **views** for retrieving the data in `Accounts_Users` and `Forums_Members` in a single `SELECT` statement, so that we don't need to write the `JOINs` in the stored procedures, and it's easier to modify them if we need to do so. We'll see all the details about the added columns and the required `JOINs` in the solution section.

Stored Procedures

As usual, we'll use stored procedures to keep our application efficient and simplify the data layer. The complete list of the stored procedures that we'll build later is presented below.

Managing the Categories

We will build the following stored procedures for managing categories:

Stored Procedure	Description
sp_Forums_GetCategories	Returns all the available categories.
sp_Forums_GetCategoryDetails	Returns the complete row identified by the specified ID.
sp_Forums_InsertCategory	Inserts a new category. If a category already exists with the same name, the new category is not added and the output parameter is set to -1. Otherwise @CategoryID will be set to the new category's ID.
sp_Forums_UpdateCategory	Updates all the fields of the category identified by the specified ID.
sp_Forums_DeleteCategory	Deletes the specified category.

Managing the Forums

These procedures are the same as above, but this time for the Forums_Forums table:

Stored Procedure	Description
sp_Forums_GetForums	Returns all the forums underneath the specified category.
sp_Forums_GetForumDetails	Returns the complete row identified by the specified ID.
sp_Forums_InsertForum	Inserts a forum and returns its ID. If a forum with the same name already exists, returns -1.
sp_Forums_UpdateForum	Updates the specified forum record.
sp_Forums_DeleteForum	Deletes a forum.

Managing the Topics

The procedures for the Forums_Topics table are slightly more complex:

Stored Procedure	Description
sp_Forums_GetTopics	Returns all the topics of the specified forum.
sp_Forums_GetTopicsByPage	Returns the topics for the specified virtual page of the specified forum. The last parameter is the number of topics that make up a page.

Stored Procedure	Description
sp_Forums_GetTopicDetails	Returns the complete row identified by the specified ID.
sp_Forums_GetTopicID	Returns the ID of the topic identified by the specified key.
sp_Forums_InsertTopic	Inserts a new topic and returns its ID. Nothing is done to check if a topic with the same subject is already present, as this is perfectly possible in a forum.
sp_Forums_UpdateTopic	Updates a topic record. Note that not all fields can be updated, in fact we don't want to allow anybody to change the ID or the IP address of the user who posted the topic.
sp_Forums_DeleteTopic	Deletes the specified topic.

The most notable procedure here is sp_Forums_GetTopicsByPage, which instead of returning *all* the topics returns only the topics for a virtual page. We've already seen that it's important to display long discussions in pages. If we paginate the records through the auto pagination feature of the DataGrid or DataList controls, all the records are retrieved, and then only the records for the current page are shown. This works fine if we have a few records but it becomes inefficient when we have thousands of topics to retrieve. The sp_Forums_GetTopicsByPage procedure only returns the records of a specified page with a specified size, wasting no time retrieving records that we won't show.

sp_Forums_UpdateTopic doesn't update the member's ID and IP, because it is only the administrator who will update a topic – we want to preserve the information about the original sender. If an administrator wants to change the IP or member ID, they must use a SQL query through the online database manager presented in Chapter 4.

Managing the Replies

These procedures are very similar to the procedures above, but work against the Forums_Replies table:

Stored Procedure	Description
sp_Forums_GetReplies	Returns all the replies to the specified topic.
sp_Forums_GetRepliesByPage	Returns the replies for the specified virtual page of the specified topic.
sp_Forums_GetReplyDetails	Returns the complete row identified by the specified ID.
sp_Forums_InsertReply	Inserts a new topic and returns its ID.
sp_Forums_UpdateReply	Updates the message text of the specified reply.
sp_Forums_DeleteReply	Deletes the specified reply.

Managing the Members

These procedures work against the Forums_Members and Accounts_Users tables to manage those members who are current site users with a special profile for the discussion board:

Stored Procedure	Description
sp_Forums_GetMembers	Returns all the members.
sp_Forums_GetMemberDetails	Returns the complete row identified by the specified ID.
sp_Forums_GetMemberID	Returns the ID of the member registered against the specified user account.
sp_Forums_InsertMember	Inserts a new member. If a member already exists with the same name, the new member is not added and the output parameter is set to -1. Otherwise @MemberID will be set to the new member's ID.
sp_Forums_UpdateMember	Updates the member.
sp_Forums_DeleteMember	Deletes a member.

Designing the Data Services

As usual, the data layer will consist of classes whose members map one-by-one onto the stored procedures listed above. The parameters are the same as those of the respective stored procedure. Since the meaning of the methods is also the same as the stored procedure, we won't repeat the complete list of members here.

Configuration

As in the previous module, the Forums module will have a configuration component that exposes two classes to load, access, and save the settings. The classes are ModuleConfig and ModuleSettings, as before.

The table below lists all of the available settings, with their meaning:

Setting Name	Type	Description
ConnectionString	String	Database connection string.
TopicsPerPage	Integer	The maximum number of topics per page.
RepliesPerPage	Integer	The maximum number of replies per page.
HtmlEnabled	Boolean	If True, users can use HTML tags. Usually False.
SpecialTagsEnabled	Boolean	If True, the users can use special tags such as [:)], [B], and [/B] to format their messages and add 'smilies'.
SmiliesFolder	String	The virtual path of the folder where the 'smilies' images are stored. These images are shown if SpecialTagsEnabled is True, and replace some special tags such as [:)].

The Business Layer

The business layer of this module is not complex, but it is fairly big: six classes, with quite a lot of members, to manipulate the data in a good object-oriented way. All the classes except for `Helper`, which has a single static method, expose a set of public properties that describe a specified record and then have methods such as `Create`, `LoadFromID`, `ResetProperties`, and `Delete`. It's easy to guess that the meaning of these methods is always the same, so it's not worth showing the declaration for each class here. Instead, we'll look at the complete declarations for just a representative class, `Forum`, and the `Helper` class.

The Forum Class

A `Forum` object represents a single forum. Here are the members of the `Forum` class:

Method Name	Description
ID	Read-only property that returns the ID of the forum represented by the object.
CategoryID	Returns the ID of the parent category.
Category	Returns a `Category` object that represents the forum's parent category.
Name	Gets/sets the forum's name.
Description	Gets/sets the forum's description.
Position	Gets/sets the forum's position.
Topics	Returns the total number of topics for this forum. This information is dynamically calculated by a view, as we mentioned earlier.
Posts	Returns the total number of posts (topics plus replies) for this forum. This information is dynamically calculated by a view, too.
LastPostDate	Returns the date when the last post for this forum was added. As with the two properties above, this is a dynamically calculated value.
LoadFromID	Loads the properties of the list identified by a private ID variable. This method is called by the constructors, or when the data has to be refreshed.
ResetProperties	Resets the properties.
Create	Creates a new forum, and sets the properties of the object to represent the new record.
Update	Updates the forum with the new values of the public properties.
Delete	Deletes the forum.
GetTopics	Returns all the child topics.
GetTopics	Returns the child topics for the specified page. This method is employed for the custom pagination. The number of topics per page is retrieved internally through the configuration component.
AddTopic	Adds a child topic and returns a `Topic` object that represents the new record.

This class allows us to create, edit, and delete any forum, and to access its properties. It also provides direct access to all the properties and operations of the parent category, by exposing the `ParentCategory` property of type `Category`. Lastly, it has methods to directly retrieve the child topic or add a new topic. It's not like the data-access classes, where each class has methods to retrieve, add, edit, and delete only the records of the respective database table, and has no relationships with the other classes. The business classes really provide an object-oriented way to access records, by returning and linking to instances of other business classes.

The Helper Class

This class has a single static method, `ProcessSpecialTags`, which processes a given text string and replaces the special tags with the respective HTML tags. It's time to decide which tags we want to support, so here's the complete list:

❑   `[B]sometext[/B]` is replaced with `<b>sometext</b>`.

❑   `[I]sometext[/I]` is replaced with `<i>sometext</i>`.

❑   `[U]sometext[/U]` is replaced with `<u>sometext</u>`.

❑   `[:)]`, `[:D]`, `[8)]`, `[:(]`, `[:o]`, `[:x]` are all replaced with 'smilies' images, whose folder's path is stored in the settings file and is exposed by `ModuleSettings.SmiliesFolder` of the `Configuration` library.

❑   `[URL]http://www.thephile.com[/URL]` is replaced with `<a href="http://www.thephile.com" target="_blank">http://www.thephile.com</a>`.

❑   `[EMAIL]marco@thephile.com[/EMAIL]` is replaced with `<a href="mailto: marco@thephile.com ">marco@thephile.com</a>`.

❑   `[QUOTE]sometext[/QUOTE]` is replaced with `<blockquote>sometext</blockquote>`, and is used to indent the `sometext` part. This tag is still supported when `ProcessSpecialTags` is `False`, because quoting a message must always work – the other tags will still appear on screen.

Designing the User Interface Layer

All of the modules from previous chapters have two separate user interfaces: one for administrators, and one for normal users.

With the `Forums` module, we want administrators to see similar things to normal users. Instead of building a separate administration system, we will simply give users with special privileges access to features hidden from other users. Here are the relevant permissions, and the special facilities they will grant:

❑   `AdministerCategories`: the user is allowed to add, edit, or delete categories and forums

❑   `ModerateForums`: the user is allowed to add, edit, and delete topics and replies

❑   `EditSettings`: the user is allowed to edit the module's settings

That said, the following diagram describes all the various execution paths that an end user can follow in the forums application. This is useful to determine what pages to build:

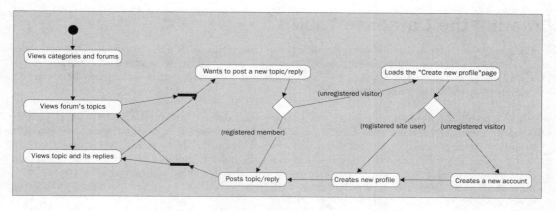

As you can see, first the user views the available categories and forums in one page, then in another page views the topics for the selected forum. One level below, again, and they read the complete topic and its replies. From the list of topics or from the complete topic the users may want to post their own message to the current forum, or to post a reply to the current topic. When they try to load the page to post the message, if they already have a profile for the Forums module the page loads correctly and they can post the message. Otherwise they are redirected to the page to register a new profile. But we already know that to create a new profile, a site account must be already present. This check is done when the registration page loads, and if the user is not logged in or the account is not present at all, the user is redirected immediately to the Login page developed in Chapter 5, where there is also a link to create the new account. Otherwise the profile is created, and the message sent.

This shows that we need to develop the following new pages:

- ❑ Default.aspx: lists categories and respective forums

- ❑ Forum.aspx: lists all topics in a selected forum

- ❑ Topic.aspx: displays a topic and its replies (in pages)

- ❑ PostMessage.aspx: posts a new topic or a reply to an existing topic

- ❑ MyProfile.aspx : creates or edits the user's profile

- ❑ Settings.aspx: enables the administrator to edit the module's settings online, without the need to manually edit and upload the settings file

The Solution

We've already developed several modules throughout the book, and we know the path to follow. We start by creating the database tables and the stored procedures, then we continue with the data and business classes, and finish with the ASP.NET pages for the presentation layer. In practice, we'll follow exactly the order of the design section. Much of the code required here is very similar to that of previous chapters, which was shown in great detail. So we'll skip the discussion of the common code, and try to focus on the new stuff.

Creating the Database Tables

We create the tables and relationships, and set all relationships to enforce cascade updates and deletes – except for the relationship between Forums_Replies and Forums_Members. This is because we already have a relationship between Forums_Topics and Forums_Members, and one between Forums_Replies and Forums_Topics.

When a member is deleted, all topics by that member are deleted, and all the replies of that topic are deleted as well. SQL Server can't handle a cascade delete of the same row when rows from two different tables are deleted, which would happen if we enforced a cascade update between Forums_Replies and Forums_Members. Exactly the same applies for the cascade update. So, when a member is deleted their topics are deleted, the replies of those topics are deleted, and we must ensure that the replies authored by that member for other topics are deleted as well. This can be done using a DELETE trigger, created on the Forums_Members table as follows:

```
CREATE TRIGGER DeleteForumsReplies ON [dbo].[Forums_Members]
  FOR DELETE
  AS

    DELETE Forums_Replies
      WHERE MemberID = (SELECT MemberID FROM Deleted)
```

Deleting all records of a user is an extreme measure. In most cases we would prevent a user from accessing the site by revoking all their permissions, but would leave their database entries intact.

Creating the Views

We now need to create views to add dynamically calculated columns, and create standard joins between tables.

The v_Forums_Forums View

This view joins the Forums_Categories and Forums_Forums table to return rows with information on the forums and their parent category as well. It also adds these calculated columns:

❑ ForumTopics: the total number of topics for the forum

❑ ForumPosts: the total number of posts (topics + replies) for the forum

❑ LastPostDate: the date when the last post for the forum was added

Here's the code used for this view:

```
SELECT Forums_Categories.CategoryID, Forums_Categories.CategoryName,
       Forums_Categories.CategoryImageUrl,
       Forums_Categories.CategoryPosition, Forums_Forums.ForumID,
       Forums_Forums.ForumName, Forums_Forums.ForumDescription,
       Forums_Forums.ForumPosition,
  (SELECT COUNT(*)
    FROM Forums_Topics
    WHERE Forums_Topics.ForumID = Forums_Forums.ForumID) AS ForumTopics,
  (SELECT COUNT(*)
```

```
    FROM Forums_Topics
    WHERE Forums_Topics.ForumID = Forums_Forums.ForumID) +
      (SELECT COUNT(*)
        FROM Forums_Replies
        WHERE Forums_Replies.ForumID = Forums_Forums.ForumID) AS ForumPosts,
  (SELECT MAX(AddedDate)
    FROM (SELECT ForumID, AddedDate FROM Forums_Topics
      UNION ALL
      SELECT ForumID, AddedDate FROM Forums_Replies) AS dates
    WHERE dates.ForumID = Forums_Forums.ForumID) AS ForumLastPostDate
  FROM Forums_Categories INNER JOIN Forums_Forums
  ON Forums_Categories.CategoryID = Forums_Forums.CategoryID
```

Except for the join between the two tables, it's pretty simple. The interesting thing is the code that calculates the other dynamic column. Let's see the code piece by piece. Here's the SQL that counts the topics for the forum:

```
(SELECT COUNT(*)
   FROM Forums_Topics
   WHERE Forums_Topics.ForumID = Forums_Forums.ForumID) AS ForumTopics
```

To count the number of posts, we copy the code above and add similar code to count the replies, then sum the two values:

```
(SELECT COUNT(*)
    FROM Forums_Topics
    WHERE Forums_Topics.ForumID = Forums_Forums.ForumID) +
      (SELECT COUNT(*)
        FROM Forums_Replies
        WHERE Forums_Replies.ForumID = Forums_Forums.ForumID) AS ForumPosts
```

The last column, LastPostDate, is the most complex to calculate:

```
(SELECT MAX(AddedDate)
    FROM (SELECT ForumID, AddedDate FROM Forums_Topics
      UNION ALL
      SELECT ForumID, AddedDate FROM Forums_Replies) AS dates
    WHERE dates.ForumID = Forums_Forums.ForumID) AS ForumLastPostDate
```

Here we extract the ForumID and AddedDate values from the Forums_Topics and Forums_Replies tables. All these values are placed in a temporary table by the UNION operator. The view then gets the date of the final post by calculating the latest date among the values in the temporary table, using the MAX function.

The v_Forums_Members View

This view joins the Accounts_Users and Forums_Members table, to view all user information together. Here's the code:

```
SELECT Forums_Members.MemberID, Forums_Members.UserID,
       Forums_Members.MemberName, Forums_Members.ShowEmail,
       Forums_Members.Signature, Forums_Members.AvatarUrl,
       Forums_Members.Homepage, Forums_Members.AddedDate,
       Accounts_Users.EmailAddress AS Email
  FROM Forums_Members INNER JOIN Accounts_Users
  ON Forums_Members.UserID = Accounts_Users.UserID
```

The v_Forums_Topics View

This joins the members and forums tables, and calculates the date of the last post for a topic. This way, in a single virtual table we can see all the information on topics, their authors, and their parent forums and categories. All this data will be retrieved by stored procedures and returned to the ASP.NET pages. Here's the complete code of the view:

```
SELECT v_Forums_Forums.CategoryID, v_Forums_Forums.CategoryName,
       v_Forums_Forums.CategoryPosition, v_Forums_Forums.ForumID,
       v_Forums_Forums.ForumName, v_Forums_Forums.ForumDescription,
       v_Forums_Forums.ForumPosition, v_Forums_Forums.ForumTopics,
       v_Forums_Forums.ForumPosts, Forums_Topics.TopicID,
       Forums_Topics.TopicKey, Forums_Topics.Subject,
       Forums_Topics.Message, Forums_Topics.AddedDate,
  (SELECT COUNT(*)
    FROM Forums_Replies
    WHERE Forums_Replies.TopicID = Forums_Topics.TopicID) AS TopicReplies,
  (SELECT MAX(AddedDate)
    FROM Forums_Replies
    WHERE Forums_Replies.TopicID = Forums_Topics.TopicID) AS
                                                      TopicLastReplyDate,
  (SELECT MAX(AddedDate)
    FROM (SELECT TopicID, AddedDate FROM Forums_Topics
    UNION ALL
    SELECT TopicID, AddedDate FROM Forums_Replies) AS dates
    WHERE dates.TopicID = Forums_Topics.TopicID) AS TopicLastPostDate,
       Forums_Topics.MemberID, v_Forums_Members.UserID,
       v_Forums_Members.MemberName, v_Forums_Members.ShowEmail,
       Forums_Topics.MemberIP,
       v_Forums_Members.Signature, v_Forums_Members.AvatarUrl,
       v_Forums_Members.Homepage, v_Forums_Members.Email,
       v_Forums_Forums.ForumLastPostDate
  FROM v_Forums_Forums INNER JOIN Forums_Topics
     ON v_Forums_Forums.ForumID = Forums_Topics.ForumID INNER JOIN
     v_Forums_Members ON Forums_Topics.MemberID = v_Forums_Members.MemberID
```

The v_Forums_Replies View

The code in this view is much simpler than in the previous one, because it has no columns to dynamically calculate – it just joins Forums_Replies with v_Forums_Members, v_Forums_Forums, and Forums_Topics:

```
SELECT v_Forums_Forums.CategoryID, v_Forums_Forums.CategoryName,
       v_Forums_Forums.ForumID, v_Forums_Forums.ForumName,
       Forums_Topics.TopicID, Forums_Topics.TopicKey,
```

```
            Forums_Replies.ReplyID, Forums_Replies.Message,
            Forums_Replies.MemberID, Forums_Replies.AddedDate,
            Forums_Replies.MemberIP, v_Forums_Members.UserID,
            v_Forums_Members.MemberName, v_Forums_Members.ShowEmail,
            v_Forums_Members.Signature, v_Forums_Members.AvatarUrl,
            v_Forums_Members.Homepage, v_Forums_Members.Email
    FROM Forums_Topics INNER JOIN Forums_Replies
      ON Forums_Topics.TopicID = Forums_Replies.TopicID
      INNER JOIN v_Forums_Forums
        ON Forums_Topics.ForumID = v_Forums_Forums.ForumID
        INNER JOIN v_Forums_Members
          ON Forums_Replies.MemberID = v_Forums_Members.MemberID
```

Creating the Stored Procedures

The stored procedures we need are similar to those in other modules. They add, edit, delete, and return records for all our tables. The following procedure returns all the topics of the specified forum:

```
CREATE PROCEDURE sp_Forums_GetTopics
                @ForumID int
AS

SELECT TopicID, Subject, AddedDate, TopicReplies, TopicLastReplyDate,
       TopicLastPostDate, MemberID, MemberName, Email, ShowEmail
  FROM v_Forums_Topics WHERE ForumID = @ForumID
  ORDER BY TopicLastPostDate Desc
GO
```

You see that even if the v_Forums_Topics view exposes many more columns, namely all the details of the parent forum and category, we don't need to return them all, and we take advantage of the fact that we don't need to calculate columns such as TopicReplies, TopicLastReplyDate, and TopicLastPostDate. The records are sorted by the TopicLastPostDate field in descending order, because we'll be displaying the topics from the one with the newest post to the one with the oldest post. Returning the details of a topic is just a matter of returning the complete row of the same view:

```
CREATE PROCEDURE sp_Forums_GetTopicDetails
                @TopicID int
AS

SELECT * FROM v_Forums_Topics WHERE TopicID = @TopicID
GO
```

The only procedure that really has something new is sp_Forums_GetTopicsByPage, which returns only a virtual page of topics, not all of them.

The sp_Forums_GetTopicsByPage Procedure

This procedure is quite long, but it's well worth showing it split up in pieces, explaining a few lines of code at time. We first create a temporary table, with the fields we want to retrieve from v_Forums_Topics, plus a new ID column that we declare as IDENTITY, so that its value is automatically set with an auto-increment number for each record we add:

```
CREATE PROCEDURE sp_Forums_GetTopicsByPage
                @ForumID  int,
                @PageNumber int,
                @PageSize int
AS

-- create a temporary table with the columns we are interested in
CREATE TABLE #TempTopics
(
  ID      int IDENTITY PRIMARY KEY,
  TopicID      int,
  Subject      varchar(100),
  AddedDate      datetime,
  TopicReplies    int,
  TopicLastReplyDate  datetime,
  TopicLastPostDate datetime,
  MemberID      int,
  MemberName      varchar(15),
  Email      varchar(50),
  ShowEmail    bit
)
```

Then we copy all the records of v_Forums_Topics to this #TempTopics table:

```
INSERT INTO #TempTopics
(
  TopicID,
  Subject,
  AddedDate,
  TopicReplies,
  TopicLastReplyDate,
  TopicLastPostDate,
  MemberID,
  MemberName,
  Email,
  ShowEmail
)
SELECT
  TopicID,
  Subject,
  AddedDate,
  TopicReplies,
  TopicLastReplyDate,
  TopicLastPostDate,
  MemberID,
  MemberName,
  Email,
  ShowEmail
FROM
  v_Forums_Topics WHERE ForumID = @ForumID ORDER BY TopicLastPostDate Desc
```

Now we have to calculate the ID of the first and last record to retrieve, and return that range of records from the temporary table. The `#TempTopics` table with the `IDENTITY` ID column is necessary because we need a column whose IDs ascend from one to the total number of records, without holes in the middle. We can't use the `TopicID` column to do this, because we could have deleted records. Here is the code:

```
-- declare two variables to calculate the range of records to extract for
-- the specified page
DECLARE @FromID int
DECLARE @ToID int
-- calculate the first and last ID of the range of topics we need
SET @FromID = ((@PageNumber - 1) * @PageSize) + 1
SET @ToID = @PageNumber * @PageSize

-- select the page of records
SELECT TopicID, Subject, AddedDate, TopicReplies, TopicLastReplyDate,
       TopicLastPostDate, MemberID, MemberName, Email, ShowEmail
   FROM #TempTopics WHERE ID >= @FromID AND ID <= @ToID
GO
```

The first and last ID in the range are calculated according to the current page and the page's size parameter, and the returned records as sorted by `TopicLastPostDate` in descending order, as we saw for the `sp_Forums_GetTopics` procedure.

Later, in the client code, we'll need to know the number of pages in order to build the links that allow the user to navigate through all the topics. This information could be returned as an output parameter by this stored procedure, but we decided that this was not needed. Instead, the number of pages is calculated on the client, in the presentation layer. If you look back at the `v_Forums_Forums` view, you'll see that we return the total number of topics of any forum, and that value is exposed by a property of the `Forum` class. Therefore, from the client we can get that number, and also the number of topics per page, retrieved from the settings, so it's really straightforward to get the number of pages.

Implementing the Data Layer

As we mentioned above, the data layer is made up of classes whose members exactly map all the stored procedures listed in the design section. For this reason, it's not worth showing the code here – the only difference from previous chapters is the name of the stored procedures and the respective parameters.

The data layer consists of a new project, called `Forums.Data`, which is included in the `ThePhile` Visual Studio .NET solution. The assembly and the namespace are called `Wrox.WebModules.Forums.Data`, and it needs a reference to the `Core` assembly since it inherits from `DbObject`. The full implementation is in the code download.

Implementing the Configuration Layer

As for the data layer, the implementation of the configuration assembly (`Wrox.WebModules.Forums.Configuration`) is similar to the respective components already developed for other modules. What changes here is the file name in the `GetSettingsFile` private function, the name of the cache entry to which the settings are stored to be retrieved quicker, and of course the properties of the `ModuleSettings` class. However, these are all simple changes and are not really worth another complete discussion here. You can refer back to see the implementation of the main methods `GetSettings` and `SaveSettings`.

Here is a sample settings file, to see how it is structured and to use as a test:

```xml
<?xml version="1.0"?>
<ModuleSettings xmlns:xsd="http://www.w3.org/2001/XMLSchema"
                xmlns:xsi="http://www.w3.org/2001/XMLSchema-instance">
  <ConnectionString>
    server=(local);database=ThePhile;uid=sa;pwd=;
  </ConnectionString>
  <SmiliesFolder>./Images/Smilies</SmiliesFolder>
  <TopicsPerPage>5</TopicsPerPage>
  <RepliesPerPage>5</RepliesPerPage>
  <HtmlEnabled>false</HtmlEnabled>
  <SpecialTagsEnabled>true</SpecialTagsEnabled>
</ModuleSettings>
```

Of course, we also need to add a custom key in the web.config file, with the path of the settings file:

```xml
...
<appSettings>
  <add key="NewsManager_SettingsFile" value="~/Config/NewsManager.Config" />
  <add key="Forums_SettingsFile" value="~/Config/Forums.Config" />
  ...
</appSettings>
...
```

Implementing the Business Layer

The structure of the classes is not new in this component, either. However, since the business assembly is the core of the module, we'll show at least one of the typical classes, Forum, as an example. We'll also look at the Helper class as it has business logic that is really specific to this module. First of all, we create the new Class Library project, and name it Wrox.WebModules.Forums.Business. Then we edit the AssemblyInfo.cs file to set some attributes and specify the key file, and add references to the Data, Configuration, and Core projects.

The Forum Class

At this point, we can start coding the Forum class (in Forum.vb). First, we declare the namespace and class:

```vb
Imports System
Imports System.Data
Imports System.Data.SqlClient

Namespace WebModules.Forums.Business

  Public NotInheritable Class Forum
    Inherits Wrox.WebModules.Business.BizObject
```

The class is defined as NotInheritable – since we know we won't need to create derived classes.

Next, we declare private variables and the public properties that read, and sometimes write, to them. There's no point in looking at all of these here – let's move straight on to the constructors and methods.

The Constructors

We have three constructors for each class. The first simply sets member variables to their default state, ready to create a new forum. The second loads the specified forum, and populates the class's members appropriately. The final one initializes the variables by loading the record identified by an existing Forum object. Here's the code:

```
Public Sub New()
   mySettings = Configuration.ModuleConfig.GetSettings()
   ResetProperties()
End Sub


Public Sub New(ByVal existingForumId As Integer)
   mySettings = Configuration.ModuleConfig.GetSettings()
   myForumId = existingForumId
   LoadFromId()
End Sub


Public Sub New(ByVal existingForum As Forum)
   mySettings = Configuration.ModuleConfig.GetSettings()
   myForumId = existingForum.Id
   LoadFromId()
End Sub
```

Each constructor creates and saves to a private variable an instance of `ModuleSettings`, with the current module's settings. This way any other methods can access the settings from the private variable without retrieving them every time.

Resetting and Initializing the Variables

Each constructor calls a private method to populate the variables. If we are loading an existing forum record then we set this object's `ForumID` variable, and call `LoadFromID`:

```
Private Overloads Sub LoadFromId()
   Dim forums As New Data.Forums(mySettings.ConnectionString)
   Dim details As Data.ForumDetails = forums.GetDetails(myForumId)

   myForumId = details.ForumId
   myCategoryId = details.CategoryId
   myName = details.Name
   myDescription = details.Description
   myPosition = details.Position
   myTopics = details.Topics
   myPosts = details.Posts
   myLastPostDate = details.LastPostDate
End Sub
```

If we are creating a blank forum, we just want to set our variables to appropriate starting values:

```
      Private Sub ResetProperties()
        myForumId = -1
        myCategoryId = -1
        myName = ""
        myDescription = ""
        myPosition = 0
        myTopics = 0
        myPosts = 0
        myLastPostDate = New DateTime()
      End Sub
```

We also have a public overload of LoadFromID, which takes a forum ID and populates the object based on that ID. In reality it just stores the ID and calls the private LoadFromID, as does the constructor:

```
      Public Overloads Function LoadFromId( _
        ByVal existingForumId As Integer) _
        As Integer

        myForumId = existingForumId
        LoadFromId()
        Return myForumId
      End Function
```

This last method is useful when you have an existing Forum instance that already represents a record. If you no longer need that object but need to manipulate another record, instead of creating a new object or destroying and recreating the one you have, just load another record to the existing object by calling this method.

Adding, Updating, or Deleting Forums

To create, update, and delete a record we use the respective methods of the Data.Forums class. Here's the business layer's Forums.Create method:

```
      Public Function Create( _
        ByVal forumCategoryId As Integer, _
        ByVal forumName As String, _
        ByVal forumDescription As String, _
        ByVal forumPosition As Integer) _
        As Integer

        Dim forums As New Data.Forums(mySettings.ConnectionString)

        myForumId = forums.Add( _
          forumCategoryId, forumName, forumDescription, forumPosition)
        LoadFromId()
        Return myForumId
      End Function
```

This creates a new record. The method takes every value as a parameter – the Forum object's properties prior to calling Create are ignored and lost.

The Update method saves the current state of the Forum object back to the database. The way we have designed the business layer means that some properties cannot be changed once the forum is first created – for example, we cannot move a forum to a new category once it has been created. Only fields exposed as read-write properties are editable:

```
Public Function Update() As Boolean
    Dim forums As New Data.Forums(mySettings.ConnectionString)
    Return forums.Update(myForumId, myName, myDescription, myPosition)
End Function
```

If a user calls this method on a *new* Forum object, nothing will happen. The ID property would be -1, so the stored procedure would find no record to update and the method would return False.

The Delete method is also very similar, except that after deleting the row we must reset all the properties, since the record that was described by the object no longer exists:

```
Public Function Delete() As Boolean
    Dim forums As New Data.Forums(mySettings.ConnectionString)
    Dim ret As Boolean = forums.Delete(myForumId)

    ResetProperties()
    Return ret
End Function
```

Returning and Adding Child Topics

GetTopics uses methods in the Data.Forums class to obtain the topics in the current forum:

```
Public Overloads Function GetTopics() As DataSet
    Dim topics As New Data.Topics(mySettings.ConnectionString)
    Return topics.GetTopics(myForumId)
End Function
```

The same applies to the overloaded version that returns the specified page of topics. However, the page size is not passed as a parameter (as it is for the method in the data layer), but is retrieved internally through the ModuleSettings instance saved in a private variable by the constructors:

```
Public Overloads Function GetTopics(ByVal pageNumber As Integer) _
    As DataSet
    Dim topics As New Data.Topics(mySettings.ConnectionString)
    Return topics.GetTopics( _
        myForumId, pageNumber, mySettings.TopicsPerPage)
End Function
```

The AddTopic method adds a child topic and returns a Business.Topic object describing the new record. It does not directly map to the Data.Topic.Add method – instead it calls the Create method of the Business.Topic class, which is similar to the Create method we created above for the Forum class:

```
    Public Function AddTopic( _
      ByVal topicKey As String, _
      ByVal subject As String, _
      ByVal message As String, _
      ByVal memberId As Integer) _
      As Topic

      Dim topic As New Business.Topic()

      topic.Create(myForumId, topicKey, subject, message, memberId)
      Return topic
    End Function
```

Remember that `topicKey` is a unique name for the topic, which we can use to provide links to a given topic from other parts of the site.

The Helper Class

This class has one static method to process text into HTML format. This includes replacing the special tags (such as `[b]`) with HTML, replacing smilies with images, and replacing carriage returns with `<br>` tags. Here is the code. Note that we are using `System.Text.RegularExpressions`:

```
Imports System
Imports System.Data
Imports System.Web
Imports System.Text.RegularExpressions

Namespace WebModules.Forums.Business

  Public Class Helper
    Inherits Wrox.WebModules.Business.BizObject


    Public Shared Function ProcessSpecialTags(ByVal text As String) _
      As String

      Dim settings As Configuration.ModuleSettings = _
        Configuration.ModuleConfig.GetSettings()
```

If we are not allowing HTML tags, and in most cases we are not, this will ensure that HTML code is *displayed* rather than *processed*. (For example, it will convert `<p>` to `&lt;p&gt;`, which browsers will display as `<p>` rather than creating a new paragraph):

```
      If Not settings.HtmlEnabled Then
        text = HttpUtility.HtmlEncode(text)
      End If
```

If the special tags are enabled, they are processed:

```
If settings.SpecialTagsEnabled Then
    Dim smiliesFolder As String = settings.SmiliesFolder

    If Not smiliesFolder.EndsWith("/") Then
      smiliesFolder &= "/"
    End If

    ' Replace the bold special tags
    text = Regex.Replace( _
      text, _
      "\[B\](?<boldText>.*)\[/B\]", _
      "<b>${boldText}</b>", _
      RegexOptions.IgnoreCase)
```

Other tags are handled in a similar way. We also need to replace smilies tags with <img> tags. Here's how we do this (remember we've already assigned our smiliesFolder variable):

```
text = text.Replace("[:)]", _
  "<img src=""" + smiliesFolder + "Smile.gif"" border=""0""/>")
text = text.Replace("[:D]", _
  "<img src=""" + smiliesFolder + "LargeSmile.gif"" border=""0""/>")
```

The process is the same for other smilies. Next the URLs:

```
    ' Replace the URL tag
    text = Regex.Replace( _
      text, _
      "\[URL\](?<url>.*)\[/URL\]", _
      "<a href=""${url}"" target=""_blank"">${url}</a>", _
      RegexOptions.IgnoreCase)

    ' Replace the EMAIL tag
    text = Regex.Replace( _
      text, _
      "\[EMAIL\](?<email>.*)\[/EMAIL\]", _
      "<a href=""mailto:${email}"">${email}</a>", _
      RegexOptions.IgnoreCase)
End If
```

Outside of the if block, we replace the quote tags. Quoting is enabled even if the special tags are not:

```
text = Regex.Replace( _
    text, _
    "\[QUOTE\]", _
    "<font size=""1""><blockquote>quote:<hr height=""1"" noshade>", _
    RegexOptions.IgnoreCase)
text = Regex.Replace( _
    text, _
    "\[/QUOTE\]", _
    "<hr height=""1"" noshade></blockquote></font>", _
    RegexOptions.IgnoreCase)
```

469

Finally, we need to replace the new line and carriage return characters. HTML will ignore carriage returns, so we need to use <br>:

```
        text = text.Replace(ControlChars.Lf, "<br/>")
        text = text.Replace(ControlChars.Cr, "")
        Return text
    End Function
End Class
```

We use .NET's **regular expression** support to help with replacing the text (refer back to Chapter 9 for an introduction to the basic regular expressions syntax rules). Using the String object's Replace method would be insufficient because it does not handle case-insensitive situations very well.

The System.Text.RegularExpressions namespace contains classes for working with regular expressions, and Regex is a principal one. This class has several methods for searching substrings, splitting a string into an array, and replacing strings. We use the Replace method to execute a case-insensitive search, by passing RegexOptions.IgnoreCase as the last parameter. Look again at this piece of code:

```
        text = Regex.Replace( _
            text, _
            "\[QUOTE\]", _
            "<font size=""1""><blockquote>quote:<hr height=""1"" noshade>", _
            RegexOptions.IgnoreCase)
```

Note that [is a special character, so we escape it using \. Replacing a substring is straightforward, but for the [URL] and [EMAIL] tags we need something more complex. Say that we have the text:

```
[URL]http://www.thephile.com[/URL]
```

We want to transform it to:

```
<a href="http://www.thephile.com" target="_blank"> http://www.thephile.com</a>
```

We have to extract the URL and place it inside the <a> tag for the href attribute, leaving it between the opening and closing tags. Using the regular expressions engine we can do everything in a single line, covering the whole text. Look at the code that does the magic:

```
        text = Regex.Replace( _
            text, _
            "\[URL\](?<url>.*)\[/URL\]", _
            "<a href=""${url}"" target=""_blank"">${url}</a>", _
            RegexOptions.IgnoreCase)
```

The pattern string specifies that we want to find all the block [URL]sometext[/URL], capture the sometext substring, and assign it the name url. In the replacement string, the captured url substring is recalled through $(url), and placed as the value for the href attribute as well as the link text between <a> and </a>.

Regular expressions can do much more than this, and are often used for string validation. We've actually shown a couple of examples when validating ZIP codes in Chapter 5, or e-mail addresses in Chapter 9. For more information on regular expressions, see a book such as *Teach Yourself Regular Expressions in 24 Hours* (SAMS Press, ISBN 0-672-31936-5).

The Presentation Layer

We can finally start to write the presentation layer, and see the results of our hard work. We've already decided that we won't have a separate administration section – we will display different options on the pages depending on the user's permissions.

To give an idea of the final pages, here is the Forums homepage in 'standard' mode:

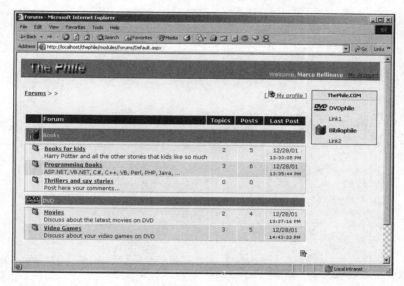

We can see how this page uses our business layer objects – we have our two categories, and our topics with their message counts and last dates calculated. Let's look at how we built this page.

The Categories and Forums Page

The page shown above is `Default.aspx`. Its structure is quite complex, because it has to modify itself for the current user, and because it has two 'levels' – the categories and their child forums.

The early part of the ASPX file is concerned mainly with administration features, hidden from most users – so we will start by looking at them.

Administration Features

The code is quite long, so we'll pick out highlights. To make the system more user friendly, and reduce the chance of accidental edits, we will use JavaScript alerts to confirm forum and category deletions:

```
<script language="javascript">
  function DeleteForum(id)
  {
    if (confirm('Are you sure that you want to delete this forum and all
                                          its discussions?'))

    {
      document.forms['Forums'].elements['paramID'].value = id;
      __doPostBack('DeleteForum', '');
    }
  }

  function DeleteCategory(id)
  {
    if (confirm('Are you sure that you want to delete this category and
                                          all its sub-forums?'))

    {
      document.forms['Forums'].elements['paramID'].value = id;
      __doPostBack('DeleteCategory', '');
    }
  }
</script>
```

We used the built-in `__doPostBack` method to fake the user clicking on a button called `DeleteForum` or `DeleteCategory`. For this to work we need to have buttons that would expose the click event – then we can add event handlers in the code-behind. We define the buttons, hidden, first thing in the page:

```
</HEAD>
<body>
  <form ID="Forums" method="post" runat="server">
    <Forums:Header Runat="server" ID="Header" />
    <!-- hidden server controls for handling the events on the server -->
    <input type="hidden" ID="paramID" runat="server">
    <asp:LinkButton ID="DeleteCategory" runat="server"
                    OnClick="DeleteCategory_Click" Visible="False" />
    <asp:LinkButton ID="DeleteForum" runat="server"
                    OnClick="DeleteForum_Click" Visible="False" />
```

We used the same technique in Chapter 4, for deleting directories and files – refer back for further details about ASP.NET server event handling.

The next section defines a hidden form for editing or creating forums, and another for editing or creating categories. There is nothing complex about the code, so we won't list it here. Here is the page with the forum editor displayed:

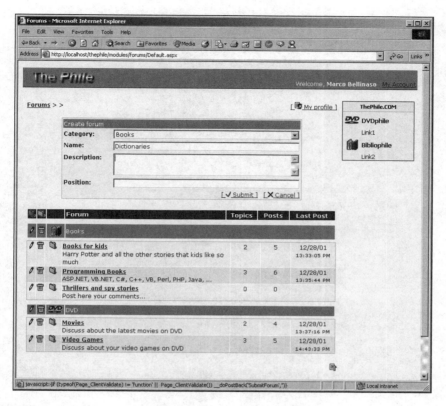

The Forum Menu

Now we get to the main attraction – a table listing the categories with their child forums. We need a way to handle the two 'levels' of data. Here's a brief outline of what we will do:

❑   Have a main `DataList` where each item (record) occupies two rows. The first row contains the header for a given category (in the image above we have Books and DVD). The second row contains the topics `DataGrid`.

❑   The topics `DataGrid` contains a row for each topic under that category – so in the Books category above, the second row of the category grid contains a `DataGrid` for 'Books for Kids', 'Programming Books', and 'Thrillers and spy stories'.

Now let's look at the code. This section defines the overall header for the `DataList`, which simply contains column headings:

```
<asp:DataList ID="CategoriesList" runat="server"
              DataKeyField="CategoryID"
              OnEditCommand="CategoriesList_Edit"
              Width="100%">
  <HeaderTemplate>
    <table width="100%">
```

```
            <tr>
              <td>
                <table width="100%">
                  <tr class="Forums_Header2">
                    <td width="16px" runat="server"
                        Visible='<%# CanAdministerCategories %>'>
                      <asp:LinkButton ID="NewCategory" runat="server"
                                      OnClick="NewCategory_Click"
                                      CausesValidation="False">
                        <img border="0" src="./Images/FolderNew.gif"
                                        Alt="Create a new category">
                      </asp:LinkButton>
                    </td>
                    <td width="16px" runat="server"
                        Visible='<%# CanAdministerCategories %>'>
                      <asp:LinkButton ID="NewForum" runat="server"
                                      OnClick="NewForum_Click"
                                      CausesValidation="False">
                        <img border="0" src="./Images/Folder.gif"
                             Alt="Create a new forum">
                      </asp:LinkButton>
                    </td>
                    <td class="Forums_Header2" width="32px"> </td>
                    <td class="Forums_Header2">Forum</td>
                    <td class="Forums_Header2" width="60px"
                                              align="center">Topics</td>
                    <td class="Forums_Header2" width="60px"
                                              align="center">Posts</td>
                    <td class="Forums_Header2" width="90px"
                                              align="center">Last Post</td>
                  </tr>
                </table>
              </td>
            </tr>
          </table>
        </HeaderTemplate>
```

The NewCategory and NewForum buttons are declared within two table cells declared with the runat="server" attribute, and whose Visible attribute is bound to the value returned by CanAdministerCategories, a public property declared in the code-behind. We'll see the implementation of the property in the code-behind section; for now you just need to know that the property checks the permissions of the current user and returns True if they have the AdministerCategories permission.

After HeaderTemplate, we have the ItemTemplate, whose code is repeated for each record in the datasource:

```
        <ItemTemplate>
          <table width="100%">
            <tr>
              <td>
                <table width="100%">
```

```
<tr class="Forums_Header">
  <td width="15px" runat="server"
      Visible='<%# CanAdministerCategories %>'>
    <asp:LinkButton CommandName="Edit"
               runat="server" CausesValidation="False">
      <img border="0" Alt="Edit this category"
                      src="./Images/Edit.gif">
    </asp:LinkButton>
  </td>
  <td width="15px" runat="server"
      Visible='<%# CanAdministerCategories %>'>
    <a href='<%#
           string.Format("javascript:DeleteCategory({0});",
           DataBinder.Eval(Container.DataItem,
                                  "CategoryID")) %>'>
      <img border="0" Alt="Delete this category"
                      src="./Images/Delete.gif" />
    </a>
  </td>
  <td width="35px" align="center">
    <asp:Image Runat="server" BorderWidth="0"
           ImageUrl='<%# DataBinder.Eval(Container.DataItem,
           "CategoryImageUrl") %>'
           Visible='<%# DataBinder.Eval(Container.DataItem,
           "CategoryImageUrl").ToString().Length > 0 %>'
    />
  </td>
  <td>
    <%# DataBinder.Eval(Container.DataItem,
                                  "CategoryName") %>
  </td>
</tr>
</table>
</td>
</tr>
```

The code above creates a table and defines the first row, with the following cells:

❑   A LinkButton shows the CategoryBox in editing mode when clicked. The cell is visible according to the CanAdministerCategories property.

❑   A link that calls the DeleteCategory JavaScript, passing the current category's ID as a parameter. The cell is visible according to the CanAdministerCategories property.

❑   The category's image. The Image server control is only visible if the length of the image URL is longer than zero (that is, there is an image to display).

❑   The category's name.

The DataList's ItemTemplate continues with a second row – this time with a single cell. The content is a DataGrid control for this category's child forums. The DataGrid has columns for the forum's name and description, number of topics, number of posts, and the date of the most recent post. The forum's name is a hyperlink, which points to the Forum.aspx page – with the ForumID value as a parameter on the URL. There are also buttons to edit or delete the forum. The deletion requires a confirmation, through the JavaScript function as seen above. The code is quite verbose, because there is so much HTML, so we will just pull out some highlights.

475

First, let's look at the definition of the `DataGrid`:

```
<asp:DataGrid runat="server"
              AutoGenerateColumns="False"
              CssClass="Forums_General"
              ItemStyle-CssClass="Forums_Item"
              AlternatingItemStyle-CssClass="Forums_AlternatingItem"
              DataKeyField="ForumID"
              DataSource='<%# GetForumsSource(int.Parse(DataBinder.Eval
                         (Container.DataItem, "CategoryID").ToString())) %>'
              OnEditCommand="ForumsGrid_Edit"
              ShowHeader="False"
              Width="100%">
```

Here we set the `DataGrid`'s `DataSource` to the `DataView` returned by `GetForumsSource` in the code-behind. The function takes a category ID as a parameter, and returns the child forums. We do this because we can't set the `DataGrid.DataSource` property from the code-behind – `DataGrid`s are built dynamically and have no reference to them in the code-behind. Most of the columns are not new, and only show the data without further processing, but there are a few that it is important to show:

```
<Columns>
  <asp:TemplateColumn ItemStyle-Wrap="True"
                      ItemStyle-Width="1px">
    <ItemTemplate>
      <asp:ImageButton Runat="server" CommandName="Edit"
          Visible='<%# CanAdministerCategories %>'
          ImageUrl="./Images/Edit.gif"
          AlternateText="Edit this forum" BorderWidth="0"/>
    </ItemTemplate>
  </asp:TemplateColumn>
  <asp:TemplateColumn ItemStyle-Wrap="True"
                      ItemStyle-Width="1px">
    <ItemTemplate>
      <asp:HyperLink Runat="server" NavigateUrl='<%#
              "javascript:DeleteForum(" + DataBinder.Eval(
              Container.DataItem, "ForumID") + ")" %>'
              Visible='<%# CanAdministerCategories %>'
              Text="<img border=0 Alt='Delete this forum'
              src=./Images/Delete.gif" />
    </ItemTemplate>
  </asp:TemplateColumn>
```

The second `TemplateColumn` defined in the code above declares a `HyperLink` that points to the JavaScript `DeleteForum` routine explained earlier, with the forum's ID as an input parameter. The routine will ask for confirmation, and if the user presses OK it will pass this ID to the server, indicating which forum has to be deleted.

Going ahead, we find the column with the forum's name and description. The name is rendered as a link that points to `Forum.aspx`, with the `ForumID` value passed as a parameter in the URL:

```
<asp:TemplateColumn>
  <ItemTemplate>
    <asp:HyperLink runat="server" Font-Bold="True"
```

```
                        Text='<%# DataBinder.Eval(
                        Container.DataItem, "ForumName") %>'
                        NavigateUrl='<%# "Forum.aspx?ForumID=" +
                        DataBinder.Eval(Container.DataItem, "ForumID") %>'
                        />
                        <br>
                        <asp:Label runat="server" Text='<%#
                                DataBinder.Eval(Container.DataItem,
                                "ForumDescription") %>' />
                </ItemTemplate>
            </asp:TemplateColumn>

            ...declaration of the columns Topics, Posts,
            and Last Post goes here...

            </Columns>
        </asp:DataGrid>
```

The page ends with the closing tags of the category `DataList`'s `ItemTemplate` and the `DataList`:

```
            </td>
        </tr>
      </table>
    </ItemTemplate>
  </asp:DataList>
  <br>
  <Forums:Footer Runat="server" ID="Footer" />
</form>
</body>
</HTML>
```

The Code-behind for Default.aspx

We start the code-behind with the basics – declaring the namespace and class, and implementing basic methods such as `Page_Load`. Here is the `Page_Load` event:

```
Private Sub Page_Load(ByVal sender As Object, ByVal e As EventArgs)
    ' Do not allow to manage categories if the user is not authenticated
    ' or does not have the proper permission
    myCanAdministerCategories = Context.User.Identity.IsAuthenticated _
        AndAlso CType(Context.User, SitePrincipal).HasPermission( _
          CInt(ForumsPermissions.AdministerCategories))
    If Not IsPostBack Then
        BindList()
    End If
End Sub
```

This sets the `canAdministerCategories` variable appropriately, using the `Accounts` system we created in Chapter 5. `canAdministerCategories` is a private variable, accessed through the `CanAdministerCategories` property. Note how easy it is to get the `SitePrincipal` object from `Context.User` – we really benefit from integrating our security system with .NET's built-in authentication.

477

Next, we call the `BindList` method, provided we are not processing a postback. `BindList` binds the appropriate `DataView` to our `DataList` (the list of categories, which contains the `DataGrid` for child topics). Here is the code for `BindList`:

```
Private Sub BindList()
   ' Bind a DataView with all the categories to the DataList
   CategoriesList.DataSource = _
      Business.Category.GetCategories().Tables(0).DefaultView
   CategoriesList.DataBind()
End Sub
```

Because there are multiple `DataGrid` instances, generated dynamically, we cannot access it as an object. So we will expose a method that our main page can call, to return a `DataView` listing topics in a given category:

```
Public Function GetForumsSource(ByVal categoryId As Integer) As DataView
   ' Get the DataView with the forums for the specified category
   Return New _
      Business.Category(categoryId).GetForums().Tables(0).DefaultView
End Function
```

Adding and Editing a Category

When we want to edit an existing category, we show the box, but set the textboxes with the current properties of the clicked category. The properties are exposed by an instance of `Business.Category`, as you see below:

```
Protected Sub CategoriesList_Edit( _
   ByVal sender As Object, _
   ByVal e As DataListCommandEventArgs)

   ' If the user cannot administer categories/forums redirect
   ' to the login page
   If Not myCanAdministerCategories Then

      Response.Redirect( _
         "/ThePhileVB/WebModules/Accounts/Login.aspx?ShowError=true", True)
   End If
   ' Get the Id of the clicked category
   Dim categoryId As Integer = CInt( _
      CategoriesList.DataKeys(e.Item.ItemIndex))

   ' Get the category's details
   Dim category As New Business.Category(categoryId)

   ' Set the controls for editing the record
   CategoryName.Text = category.Name
   CategoryImageUrl.Text = category.ImageUrl
   CategoryPosition.Text = category.Position.ToString()
   CategoryIdCurr.Text = category.Id.ToString()
   CategoryBoxHeader.Text = "Edit category"
```

```
            ' Hide the forum box, if visible
            ForumBox.Visible = False

            ' Show the category box
            CategoryBox.Visible = True
    End Sub
```

Before doing anything else we must check if the current user has the permission to edit a category. If not, they are redirected to the login page. It's true that the permissions are checked in Page_Load, and that if the ForumsPermissions.AdministerCategories permission is not present the controls for editing and deleting records are not shown, but an expert user could still hack the page by manually calling the __doPostBack function with the parameters to call this server event. It's quite difficult, but not impossible, to guess the required parameters, because they are dynamically generated according to the index and name of the inner columns and links.

It's also worth noting that we set the CategoryIDCurr textbox (that is hidden) to the category's ID. Later, when the box is submitted, this will tell us the ID of the category to update, or, if empty, will tell us that we're adding a new category.

When the administrator clicks the image button to add a new category, the page calls NewCategory_Click. This is similar to EditCategory_Click, except that all of the textboxes are blank (except CategoryBoxHeader, of course).

These methods display the edit box, but the real addition or update of a category is done when the box is submitted. Look at the following code:

```
    Protected Sub SubmitCategory_Click( _
        ByVal sender As Object, _
        ByVal e As EventArgs)

        ' If the user cannot administer categories/forums redirect
        ' to the login page
        If Not myCanAdministerCategories Then

            Response.Redirect( _
                "/ThePhileVB/WebModules/Accounts/Login.aspx?ShowError=true", True)
        End If

        Dim categoryPos As Integer = _
            IIf(CategoryPosition.Text.Length > 0, _
                Integer.Parse(CategoryPosition.Text), 0)
        ' If the hidden textbox is empty, it means that we're adding a category
        If CategoryIdCurr.Text.Length = 0 Then

            ' Add a new category
            Dim category As New Business.Category()
            category.Create( _
                CategoryName.Text, _
                CategoryImageUrl.Text, _
                categoryPos)
        Else
            ' Edit a category
```

```
        Dim category As New Business.Category( _
          Integer.Parse(CategoryIdCurr.Text))
        category.Name = CategoryName.Text
        category.ImageUrl = CategoryImageUrl.Text
        category.Position = categoryPos
        category.Update()
      End If
      ' Hide the category box
      CategoryBox.Visible = False
      ' Refresh
      BindList()
    End Sub
```

As mentioned above, if the `CategoryIDCurr` textbox is empty it means that we're adding a category, otherwise we retrieve the ID and update that category with the new values. At the end of the procedure we hide the box and call `BindList` to refresh the data bound to the `DataList` control.

If the user presses the **Cancel** link instead of submitting the form, the box is simply hidden:

```
    Protected Sub CancelCategory_Click( _
      ByVal sender As Object, _
      ByVal e As EventArgs)
      CategoryBox.Visible = False
    End Sub
```

Deleting a Category

To delete a category we create an instance of `Business.Category` for that category, whose ID is retrieved from the HTML hidden control set by the `DeleteCategory` JavaScript function, and call its `Delete` method:

```
    Protected Sub DeleteCategory_Click( _
      ByVal sender As Object, _
      ByVal e As EventArgs)
      ' If the user cannot administer categories/forums...
      If Not myCanAdministerCategories Then

        ' Redirect to the Login page; this is required because a hacker
        ' could manually call the DeleteCategory javascript
        Response.Redirect( _
          "/ThePhileVB/WebModules/Accounts/Login.aspx?ShowError=true", True)
      End If
      ' Extract the Id of the category to delete
      Dim categoryId As Integer = Integer.Parse(paramId.Value.ToString())

      ' Delete the category
      Dim category As New Business.Category(categoryId)
      category.Delete()

      ' Re-bind the list to show the updated records
      BindList()
    End Sub
```

Note that here it is really crucial to check if the user has permission to delete a category. In fact, hacking the parameters for __doPostBack to edit a forum or category is quite complex, but hacking the page to delete a category would be a breeze: it would be sufficient to call the DeleteCategory JavaScript trying to pass some IDs! Therefore, before doing anything else we check the permissions, and redirect to the login page if the user is not supposed to be able to delete records.

Working with Forums

The operations to add, update, or delete a forum are very similar to the respective category methods, so we won't go through everything again – for the full code, see the code download.

The Header Control

We declared the header and footer controls (the files Header.ascx and Footer.ascx, located in the same folder together with the ASP.NET pages) at the top of Default.aspx, but we haven't developed them yet. The footer control has a link to jump to the top of the page, and some closing tags of the table we open in the header to create the layout with two columns (the real content on the left, and the menu in the right side column). This control is the same as the one we developed in earlier chapters (Chapters 6, 8, and 9), so we won't show it again here.

The header control, in addition to opening the layout table and adding the site-wide header and the menu box, also adds the following parts:

- ❑ Up to three links to navigate forum sub-levels, giving links to the Forums homepage, the page listing the topics for the selected forum, and the page with the topic and its replies. This means that we can move up to higher levels in the forum's hierarchy. The link to the topic is shown when the user is reading the topic itself, and can be used to go to the first page of replies if there is more than one, but it is also shown when the user is editing a topic/reply (if the user is the administrator) and wants to go back to the topic page before submitting the changes.

- ❑ A link to the module's settings page, visible to users with the EditSettings permission only.

- ❑ A link to the MyProfile.aspx page, allowing users to edit their current profile if it already exists, or create a new one.

There's nothing new, or particularly interesting, about the ASCX file so we will move on to the code-behind. But to understand the code-behind, we need to know that the ASCX file declares four ASP.NET HyperLink objects – LinkToCategories, LinkToForum, LinkToTopic, and LinkToSettings. It also exposes a Label object called LinkToProfileText – we use a label here because the link's target and visibility will always be the same (MyProfile.aspx, and True), only the text will change. These links map to the links described above.

With that said, let's look at the code-behind.

The Code-behind for Header.ascx

We'll look at the code-behind class in two parts. First we will look at the Page_Load event, which shows the Settings link only if the user is authenticated and has the EditSettings permission. It also sets the text of the MyProfile.aspx link to Register if the user is not authenticated or does not have a forums profile, or to My Profile otherwise. We'll leave out the namespace and class definitions, to keep things brief:

```
Private Sub Page_Load(ByVal sender As Object, ByVal e As EventArgs) _
   Handles MyBase.Load

  If Context.User.Identity.IsAuthenticated Then
     ' Check if the current user is allowed to change the settings
     Dim currentPrincipal As SitePrincipal = _
       CType(Context.User, SitePrincipal)

     ' If not, hide the link
     If Not currentPrincipal.HasPermission( _
       CInt(ForumsPermissions.EditSettings)) Then
       LinkToSettings.Visible = False
     End If
     ' Change the title of the link to the MyProfile page whether the
     ' current user is registered for the forum or not
     Dim currUser As SiteIdentity = _
       CType(Context.User.Identity, SiteIdentity)
     Dim member As New Business.Member()

     member.LoadFromUser(currUser.UserId)
     LinkToProfileText.Text = IIf(member.Id = -1, _
       "Register", "My profile")
  Else
     LinkToProfileText.Text = "Register"
     LinkToSettings.Visible = False
  End If
End Sub
```

To check if the currently logged in user has a profile for the forums, we create a new instance of
Business.Member, and try to load the member profile 'attached' to the user's ID specified with the
LoadFromUser method. If the member is not found, the object's ID property is set to -1, and we set
the link's text to Register.

Now let's look at the public properties that allow the host page to specify the ID of the current topic or
forum shown on the page. According to the ID specified, the code shows the complete path of links
from the Forums homepage through to our topic:

```
Public Property ForumId() As Integer
   Get
      Return myForumId
   End Get
   Set(ByVal Value As Integer)

      myForumId = Value
      myTopicId = -1

      Dim forum As New Business.Forum(myForumId)

      LinkToCategories.Text = forum.Category.Name
      LinkToForum.Text = forum.Name
      LinkToForum.NavigateUrl = "Forum.aspx?ForumId=" + forum.Id.ToString()
```

```
      End Set
  End Property

  Public Property TopicId() As Integer
    Get
      Return myTopicId
    End Get
    Set(ByVal Value As Integer)

      myForumId = -1
      myTopicId = Value

      Dim topic As New Business.Topic(myTopicId)

      LinkToCategories.Text = topic.Forum.Category.Name
      LinkToForum.Text = topic.Forum.Name
      LinkToForum.NavigateUrl = "Forum.aspx?ForumId=" + _
                                topic.Forum.Id.ToString()
      LinkToTopic.Text = topic.Subject
      LinkToTopic.NavigateUrl = "Topic.aspx?TopicId=" + topic.Id.ToString()

    End Set
  End Property
```

The `ForumID` property is used by the `Forums.aspx` page, while `TopicID` is used by `Topic.aspx`. The `PostMessage.aspx` page uses either one or the other, according to whether it's being used to create or edit a topic. If it's creating a new topic the page will use the `ForumID` property to point to the parent forum, since there is no topic to point to. Otherwise, if the page is used to edit an existing topic, we'll use the `TopicID` property to show the link to that topic. We'll see the implementation of these three pages in the following sections.

The Forum.aspx Page

This page is loaded when the user selects a forum from the list on `Default.aspx`. It allows users to browse the selected forum's topics – represented by the `ForumID` parameter in the URL.

It lists topics in a `DataGrid` that employs the custom pagination described earlier, and shows other information such as the name of the topic's author, the number of replies, and the date of the last reply. With an administrator signed in, it looks like this:

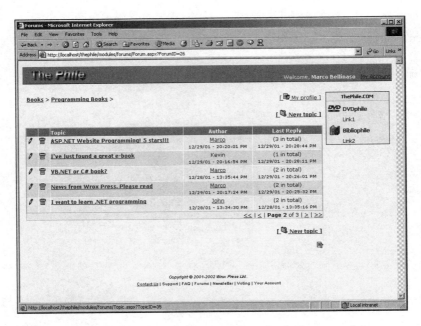

We'll show only the most interesting part of the page here: the declaration of the DataGrid and the controls for custom pagination. Let's explain the code in small pieces:

```
<table class="Forums_General" width="100%" cellpadding="0" cellspacing="0"
                                                           border="0">

   <tr>
     <td>
       <asp:DataGrid runat="server" ID="TopicsGrid"
                AllowCustomPaging="True" AutoGenerateColumns="False"
                CssClass="Forums_General" ItemStyle-CssClass="Forums_Item"
                AlternatingItemStyle-CssClass="Forums_AlternatingItem"
                HeaderStyle-CssClass="Forums_Header" DataKeyField="TopicID"
                OnDeleteCommand="TopicsGrid_Delete" Width="100%">
```

Here the grid is declared, and we say that we want to implement our own pagination by setting AllowCustomPaging to True. Here's the declaration of the grid's columns:

```
<Columns>
   <asp:HyperLinkColumn ItemStyle-Width="25px"
            DataNavigateUrlField="TopicID" DataNavigateUrlFormatString=
            "PostMessage.aspx?Action=EditTopic&TopicID={0}"
            DataTextFormatString=
            "<img border=0 Alt='Edit this topic' src=./Images/Edit.gif>"
            DataTextField="TopicID"
   />
```

This column has a link to jump to the `PostMessage.aspx` page, with parameters that indicate that we want to edit the clicked topic (later we'll see the meaning of the parameters in detail, but you should be able to guess it). Next we have a column with a link to delete the topic:

```
<asp:ButtonColumn CommandName="delete" ItemStyle-Width="25px"
                  Text="<img border=0 Alt='Delete this topic'
                  src=./Images/Delete.gif>"
/>
```

Both these two first columns will be made invisible at runtime if the user does not have the `ModerateForums` permission. Here we can easily reference the grid from the code-behind, so there is no need to bind to a `CanModerateForums` public property, as we've done with the `CanAdministerCategories` property for the `Default.aspx` page. Instead, we can do everything from the code-behind.

Next, we add the templated columns that show the topic's subject (that is a hyperlink that points to `Topic.aspx` with the topic's ID as a parameter), the name and e-mail address of the topic's author, the date when the topic was posted, the number of replies, and the date of the last one. We don't show the code here, since the structure of these columns is something we've already explained many times, but of course you can find the complete code in the download package.

At the bottom of the `DataGrid`, we add controls to move to the previous and next pages of the grid, and to view the index of the current page. The current index and the total number of pages are displayed by two separate labels, and we have four linkbuttons (first, previous, next, and last) to navigate between the pages:

```
<tr>
  <td align="right">
    <asp:LinkButton runat="server" ID="FirstPage" Text="<<"
          OnCommand="TopicsGrid_PageChanged" CommandName="FirstPage" />
    |
    <asp:LinkButton runat="server" ID="PreviousPage" Text="<"
          OnCommand="TopicsGrid_PageChanged" CommandName="PreviousPage" />
    | <b>Page
      <asp:Label runat="server" ID="PageNumber" Text="1" /></b> of
    <asp:Label runat="server" ID="TotalPages" Text="10" />
    |
    <asp:LinkButton runat="server" ID="NextPage" Text=">"
          OnCommand="TopicsGrid_PageChanged" CommandName="NextPage" />
    |
    <asp:LinkButton runat="server" ID="LastPage" Text=">>"
          OnCommand="TopicsGrid_PageChanged" CommandName="LastPage" />
  </td>
</tr>
</table>
```

It's worth noting that all the linkbuttons declare the same event handler for `OnCommand`, but they have different values for the `CommandName` property, to specify which link posted the form back, and to increment or decrement the index of the current page accordingly.

To conclude, at the top and bottom of the grid there are also two links that point to `PostMessage.aspx`, with parameters to indicate that we want to add a topic to the current forum:

```
<asp:HyperLink runat="server" ID="NewTopic2"
               NavigateUrl="PostMessage.aspx?Action=NewTopic&amp;ForumID=">
  [ <img src="./Images/Folder.gif" Alt="New topic" border="0"> New topic ]
</asp:HyperLink>
```

Note that the ID of the current forum is not specified, as it will be added to the `NavigateUrl` value from the code-behind.

The Forum.aspx Code-behind

The code-behind starts with the usual `Page_Load` procedure. It first checks the permissions of the current user, and hides the first two columns of the grid (those for editing or deleting a record) if they don't have the `ModerateForums` permission. It also extracts the `ForumID` parameter from the `QueryString`, and sets the `ForumID` property of the `Header` control:

```
Private Sub Page_Load(ByVal sender As Object, ByVal e As EventArgs)
    ' Check if the user has the permission to moderate the forums
    myCanModerateForums = Context.User.Identity.IsAuthenticated _
      AndAlso CType(Context.User, SitePrincipal).HasPermission( _
        CInt(ForumsPermissions.ModerateForums))

    ' Get the ForumId from the QueryString
    Dim forumId As String = Request.Params("ForumId")

    If Not Page.IsPostBack Then
        ' Set the hyperlinks to jump to the parent category
        NewTopic1.NavigateUrl &= forumId
        NewTopic2.NavigateUrl = NewTopic1.NavigateUrl
        Header.ForumId = Integer.Parse(forumId)

        ' Bind the data to the grid
        TopicsGrid.Attributes("ForumId") = forumId
        BindGrid()

        ' Hides the first 2 columns for editing/deleting a record, if the
        ' current user does not have the permission to do that
        TopicsGrid.Columns(0).Visible = myCanModerateForums
        TopicsGrid.Columns(1).Visible = myCanModerateForums
    End If
End Sub
```

Binding the Records and Handling the Custom Pagination

Before looking at the `BindGrid` procedure that retrieves and binds the data to the grid, let's look at how the custom pagination works. When one of the page-navigator links is clicked, we calculate the new index of the page to show, and call `BindGrid` to refresh the grid. To identify the clicked link, we check the `CommandName` property of the `CommandEventArgs` object passed as a parameter to the event handler, and update the current index accordingly. Here's the code:

```
Protected Sub TopicsGrid_PageChanged( _
    ByVal sender As Object, _
    ByVal e As CommandEventArgs)
```

```
    If PageNumber.Text.Trim().Length = 0 Then
      Return
    End If

    Select Case e.CommandName
      Case "FirstPage"
        PageNumber.Text = "1"
      Case "PreviousPage"
        PageNumber.Text = (Integer.Parse(PageNumber.Text) - 1).ToString()
      Case "NextPage"
        PageNumber.Text = (Integer.Parse(PageNumber.Text) + 1).ToString()
      Case "LastPage"
        PageNumber.Text = TotalPages.Text
    End Select

    ' Show the new page
    BindGrid()
  End Sub
```

Note that when the user clicks the link to move to the last page, the index is calculated by taking the value displayed by the TotalPages label. The value of that label is set by BindGrid, which occurs before the user can change the page – so we can be sure that the label is displaying a value.

The BindGrid method retrieves the records of the current page (the index is retrieved from the other label) by calling the GetTopics method of a Business.Forum object for the current forum. It also updates the TotalPages label, and enables or disables the links to navigate through the grid's pages according to the current index. (For example, if we're on the last page, the links to the last page and the next page are disabled.) Here it is:

```
Protected Sub BindGrid()
  ' Get the ForumId value from the Grid's attributes.
  ' if null, redirect to the Default.aspx page
  If TopicsGrid.Attributes("ForumId") Is Nothing Then
    Response.Redirect("Default.aspx", True)
  End If

  ' Get the current forum's Id
  Dim forumId As Integer = _
    Integer.Parse(TopicsGrid.Attributes("ForumId"))

  ' Get the number of topics per page
  Dim pageSize As Integer = _
    Configuration.ModuleConfig.GetSettings().TopicsPerPage

  ' Get the current forum page
  Dim pageNum As Integer = IIf( _
    PageNumber.Text = "0", _
    1, Integer.Parse(PageNumber.Text))

  ' Retrieve and bind the records to the grid
  Dim forum As New Business.Forum(forumId)
  Dim topics As DataSet = forum.GetTopics(pageNum)
```

```
TopicsGrid.DataSource = topics.Tables(0).DefaultView
TopicsGrid.DataBind()

' Show the total number of pages
Dim numPages As Integer = CInt(Math.Ceiling( _
  (System.Convert.ToDouble(forum.Topics) / pageSize)))

If numPages = 0 Then
  numPages = 1
End If
TotalPages.Text = numPages.ToString()

' Enable/disable the links to navigate through the pages
FirstPage.Enabled = pageNum <> 1
PreviousPage.Enabled = pageNum <> 1
NextPage.Enabled = pageNum <> numPages
LastPage.Enabled = pageNum <> numPages
End Sub
```

The last method used to show the records is `GetAuthorText`, which returns the HTML link pointing to the e-mail of the topic's author if their `ShowEmail` property is `True`, or simply displays their name:

```
Public Function GetAuthorText( _
  ByVal memberName As Object, _
  ByVal eMail As Object, _
  ByVal showEmail As Object) _
  As String

  ' Return the member Name only or a link to its e-mail address,
  ' according to the ShowEmail value
  If Not Convert.ToBoolean(showEmail) Then
    Return memberName.ToString()
  Else
    Return String.Format( _
      "<a href=""mailto:{0}"">{1}</a>", _
      eMail.ToString(), _
      memberName.ToString())
  End If
End Function
```

Deleting a Topic

Deleting a topic is a simple task, and it is something that we've already shown in previous chapters for other `DataGrids`. We first check if the current user is allowed to moderate the forum, and if so we retrieve the ID of the record from the grid's `DataKeys` collection, create a `Business.Topic` object for that topic, and call its `Delete` method:

```
Protected Sub TopicsGrid_Delete( _
  ByVal sender As Object, _
  ByVal e As DataGridCommandEventArgs)

  ' If the user cannot moderate forums redirect to the login page
  If Not myCanModerateForums Then
```

```
        Response.Redirect( _
          "/ThePhileVB/WebModules/Accounts/Login.aspx?ShowError=true", True)
      End If


      ' Delete this topic
      Dim topic As New Business.Topic( _
        CInt(TopicsGrid.DataKeys(e.Item.ItemIndex)))
      topic.Delete()

      BindGrid()
    End Sub
```

The Topic.aspx Page

Topic.aspx shows the selected topic (identified by the TopicID parameter in the URL), and all its replies. The list is divided into pages in a similar way to the Forum.aspx page we just looked at. We use a DataGrid to list the replies, and a set of server controls aligned through a table with a single row for the topic.

Here is a screenshot of the finished page as a moderator sees it, with some replies to the topic. The third reply quotes the previous one, and the messages have some HTML formatting. Although the first message looks similar to the others, it is taken from the topics table, and implemented in a different way from the replies. It is shown only on the first page of the discussion; in the following pages the users will only see the replies. They will still see the topic's subject in the navigation link at the top of the page:

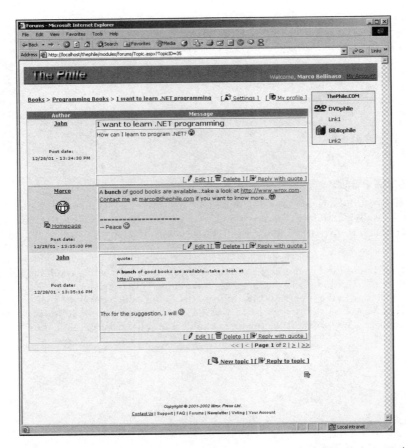

Below you see a partial declaration of this table and the controls to display all the topic's parts (subject, body, author name, homepage, e-mail address, date, etc.):

```
<table Runat="server" id="TopicTable" class="Forums_General" width="100%"
                        cellpadding="0" cellspacing="0" border="0">
  <tr>
    <td class="Forums_Item" align="middle" width="160">
      ...in this column show the author's name, e-mail, web site
      and the date of the post...
    </td>
    <td class="Forums_Item">
      <table width="100%" height="160" cellpadding="1" border="1">
        <tr height="20">
          ...show here the message and the author's signature...
        </tr>
        <tr height="20">
          <td align="right">
            <asp:HyperLink Runat="server" ID="EditTopic">
              [ <img border=0 Alt='Edit this topic'
```

```
                                                    src=./Images/Edit.gif> Edit ]
                </asp:HyperLink>
                <asp:LinkButton Runat="server" ID="DeleteTopic"
                                                OnClick="DeleteTopic_Click">
                  [ <img border="0" Alt="Delete this topic"
                                        src="./Images/Delete.gif"> Delete ]
                </asp:LinkButton>
                <a href="<%= "PostMessage.aspx?Action=NewReply&TopicID=" +
                            Request.QueryString["TopicID"] + "&QuoteTopicID=" +
                            Request.QueryString["TopicID"] %>">[
                      <img src="./Images/Reply.gif" Alt='Reply with quote'
                                                border="0"> Reply with quote ]
                </a>
              </td>
            </tr>
          </table>
        </td>
      </tr>
    </table>
```

No control is bound to a `DataSource`. We'll set the controls' content from the code-behind, control by control, since we have references to them.

The structure of the `DataGrid` follows the pattern of the table above – it has two `TemplateColumn` objects that extract from the data to display from the `DataSource`. Here it is:

```
<asp:DataGrid Runat="server" ID="RepliesGrid" AllowCustomPaging="True"
      AutoGenerateColumns="False" CssClass="Forums_General"
      HeaderStyle-CssClass="Forums_Header" DataKeyField="ReplyID"
      OnDeleteCommand="RepliesGrid_Delete" ShowHeader="False" Width="100%">
  <Columns>
    ...add here a templated column that shows the author's name, e-mail,
    website, and the date of the post...
    <asp:TemplateColumn>
      <ItemTemplate>
        <table width="100%" height="160px" cellpadding="1" border="1">
          <tr>
            ...show here the message and the author's signature...
          </tr>
          <tr height="20px">
            <td align="right">
              <asp:HyperLink Runat="server"
                        NavigateUrl='<%#
                        PostMessage.aspx?Action=EditReply&ReplyID=" +
                        DataBinder.Eval(Container.DataItem, "ReplyID") %>'
                        Visible='<%# CanModerateForums %>'>
                        [ <img border=0 Alt='Edit this reply'
                        src=./Images/Edit.gif> Edit ]
              </asp:HyperLink>
              <asp:LinkButton CommandName="delete" Runat="server"
                              Visible='<%# CanModerateForums %>'>
                              [ <img border="0" Alt="Delete this reply"
                              src="./Images/Delete.gif"> Delete ]
```

```
                     </asp:LinkButton>
                     <asp:HyperLink runat="server"
                             NavigateUrl='<%#
                             "PostMessage.aspx?Action=NewReply&TopicID=" +
                             Request.QueryString["TopicID"] + "&QuoteReplyID=" +
                             DataBinder.Eval(Container.DataItem, "ReplyID") %>'>
                             [ <img src="./Images/Reply.gif" Alt='Reply with quote'
                             border="0"> Reply with quote ]
                     </asp:HyperLink>
                 </td>
             </tr>
         </table>
       </ItemTemplate>
     </asp:TemplateColumn>
   </Columns>
 </asp:DataGrid>
```

We declare a HyperLink to jump to PostMessage.aspx and edit the reply, and a LinkButton to delete the reply, but these are visible according to the CanModerateForums property, defined in the code-behind. There is also another link to PostMessage.aspx, used for replying to a comment and quoting from the original message. The difference between the links that point to PostMessage.aspx is the list of parameters attached to the URL: the Action parameter is EditReply or NewReply, and in the latter case the optional QuoteReplyID parameter indicates whether we want to post a simple reply or we want to quote an existing one. We'll say more about these and the others parameters when we talk about the PostMessage.aspx page.

One last thing before moving ahead to the code-behind: we don't directly display the Message and Signature values as they are retrieved from the database, but pass them through ProcessTags – the method we created to encode the HTML.

The page ends with links to navigate between the DataGrid pages, and one more link to reply without quoting any message. The pagination controls are the same as those in the Forum.aspx page, so there is no need to show them again here.

The Code-behind for Topic.aspx

The code-behind of this page has to take care of binding the data to the replies grid and topic controls, and handling the custom pagination. We'll start looking at the code from Page_Load, as usual. The method begins by checking if the current user has the right to modify forums:

```
    Private Sub Page_Load(ByVal sender As Object, ByVal e As EventArgs)
       myCanModerateForums = Context.User.Identity.IsAuthenticated _
          AndAlso CType(Context.User, SitePrincipal).HasPermission( _
          CInt(ForumsPermissions.ModerateForums))

       Dim topicId As String = "-1"
```

Next, we obtain the ForumID from Request.QueryString, which contains the URL parameters. Then we set properties on the EditTopic link, depending on the user's permissions and the selected topic:

```
If Not (Request.QueryString("TopicId") Is Nothing) Then
  topicId = Request.Params("TopicId")
End If

EditTopic.NavigateUrl = "PostMessage.aspx?Action=EditTopic&TopicId=" _
  & topicId.ToString()
EditTopic.Visible = myCanModerateForums
DeleteTopic.Visible = myCanModerateForums
```

Remember, we want to be able to link to topics from other parts of the site. To do this we allow a topic to have a `TopicKey` – a string that we can use to identify a topic. If a user follows a link based on `TopicKey`, we want to obtain the `TopicID` and redirect the user. Redirecting to the same page but with the `TopicID` parameter is not a big waste of time, because everything happens on the server and there are no round trips, and it makes it easier to load the topic when the page is loaded or posted back. In fact, if we just used the key to obtain the ID, and assigned the ID to a local variable, we would need to do this every time the users go to another page of replies, since the URL would still have the key as its parameter and not the ID. In reality we could persist the obtained ID between postbacks in the `StateBag` hashtable, accessible through the `ViewState` property, but at this point it's easier and faster to just redirect to the same page with the ID as the parameter. Here is the code:

```
If Not Page.IsPostBack Then
  Dim topic As Business.Topic
  ' If the TopicKey value is not null, find the topic with that
  ' key and redirect to it
  If Not (Request.QueryString("TopicKey") Is Nothing) Then
    topic = New Business.Topic( _
      Request.QueryString("TopicKey").ToString())
    ' If found, redirect to it, otherwise redirect to Default.aspx
    If topic.Id <> -1 Then
      Response.Redirect( _
        "Topic.aspx?TopicId=" & topic.Id.ToString(), True)
    Else
      Response.Redirect("Default.aspx", True)
    End If
```

Otherwise, we set properties on the `HyperLink` objects and page position appropriately and bind the data to the `DataGrid`:

```
  Else
    ' Set the links for posting a new topic/reply
    topic = New Business.Topic(Integer.Parse(topicId))
    NewTopic.NavigateUrl &= topic.Forum.Id.ToString()
    NewReply.NavigateUrl &= topic.Id.ToString()

    ' Set the navigation bar TopicId
    Header.TopicId = Integer.Parse(topicId)

    ' If there is the paramter idicating to show the last page, set
    ' the(number) in the label. This will be read in the BindGrid
    ' procedure
```

```
        If Not (Request.QueryString("Display") Is Nothing) _
          AndAlso Request.QueryString("Display").ToString().ToLower() _
            = "lastpage" Then

          Dim pageSize As Integer = _
            Configuration.ModuleConfig.GetSettings().RepliesPerPage
          Dim totalPages As Integer = CInt(Math.Ceiling(( _
            System.Convert.ToDouble(topic.Replies) / pageSize)))
          PageNumber.Text = totalPages.ToString()
        End If

        ' Bind the data to the grid
        RepliesGrid.Attributes("TopicId") = topicId
        BindGrid()
      End If
    End If
End Sub
```

Now we can go on with the `BindGrid` procedure, in which the custom pagination management is similar to the respective procedure in `Forum.aspx`. However, here we must also show or hide the table containing the `Topic` record – we only want it to display on the front page. Let's look at the code:

```
Protected Sub BindGrid()
    ' Get the ForumId value from the Grid's attributes.
    ' if null, redirect to the Default.aspx page
    If RepliesGrid.Attributes("TopicId") Is Nothing Then
      Response.Redirect("Default.aspx", True)
    End If

    ' Get the current forum's Id
    Dim topicId As Integer = _
      Integer.Parse(RepliesGrid.Attributes("TopicId"))

    ' Get the number of topics per page
    Dim pageSize As Integer = _
      Configuration.ModuleConfig.GetSettings().RepliesPerPage

    ' Get the current replies page
    Dim pageNum As Integer = _
      IIf(PageNumber.Text.Trim().Length = 0, _
        1, Integer.Parse(PageNumber.Text))

    ' Retrieve and bind the records to the grid
    Dim topic As New Business.Topic(topicId)
    Dim replies As DataSet = topic.GetReplies(pageNum)
    RepliesGrid.DataSource = replies.Tables(0).DefaultView
    RepliesGrid.DataBind()

    ' Show the total number of pages
    Dim numPages As Integer = CInt(Math.Ceiling( _
      (System.Convert.ToDouble(topic.Replies) / pageSize)))
```

```
      If numPages = 0 Then
        numPages = 1
      End If
      TotalPages.Text = numPages.ToString()

      ' Enable/disable the links to navigate through the pages
      FirstPage.Enabled = pageNum <> 1
      PreviousPage.Enabled = pageNum <> 1
      NextPage.Enabled = pageNum <> numPages
      LastPage.Enabled = pageNum <> numPages

      ' Show also the topic, if this is the first page
      If pageNum = 1 Then
        BindTopicControls(topicId)
        TopicTable.Visible = True
        ' If this is the first page, also swap the styles for the Item
        ' and AlternatingItem of the DataGrid, because the Topic has
        ' the Item style
        RepliesGrid.ItemStyle.CssClass = GridAlternatingItemStyle.Text
        RepliesGrid.AlternatingItemStyle.CssClass = GridItemStyle.Text

      Else
        TopicTable.Visible = False
        RepliesGrid.ItemStyle.CssClass = GridItemStyle.Text
        RepliesGrid.AlternatingItemStyle.CssClass = _
          GridAlternatingItemStyle.Text
      End If
    End Sub
```

If the page to show is the first one, the `TopicTable` is shown (otherwise the topic is hidden), and we also call `BindTopicControls` with the ID of the current topic. This retrieves the required data and sets the labels, links, and other controls. Here's the code for this method:

```
    Private Sub BindTopicControls(ByVal topicId As Integer)
      ' Retrieve all the topic's info
      Dim topic As New Business.Topic(topicId)
      Dim author As Business.Member = topic.Member

      ' Show the data
      TopicAuthor.Text = GetAuthorText( _
        author.Name, _
        author.Email, _
        author.ShowEmail)
      TopicAuthorAvatar.ImageUrl = author.AvatarUrl
      TopicAuthorAvatar.Visible = author.AvatarUrl.Length > 0
      TopicAuthorHomepage.NavigateUrl = author.Homepage
      TopicAuthorHomepage.Visible = author.Homepage.Length > 0
      TopicDate.Text = String.Format("{0:MM/dd/yy}", topic.AddedDate)
      TopicTime.Text = String.Format("{0:HH:mm:ss tt}", topic.AddedDate)
      TopicSubject.Text = topic.Subject
      TopicMessage.Text = Business.Helper.ProcessSpecialTags(topic.Message)
      TopicAuthorSignature.Text = _
        Business.Helper.ProcessSpecialTags(author.Signature)
    End Sub
```

Before concluding the discussion for this page, here's the code for `ProcessTags`, which simply wraps a call to the `ProcessSpecialTags` static method of the `Business.Helper` class:

```
Public Function ProcessTags(ByVal rawText As Object) As String
  Return Business.Helper.ProcessSpecialTags(rawText.ToString())
End Function
```

The code for deleting a `DataGrid`'s reply or the topic itself has nothing new or particularly interesting, so we won't show the code for that part – for full details see the code download.

The PostMessage.aspx Page

This page is used to edit an existing message, or to post a new topic or reply. It has a simple table with some textboxes, some of which are made visible or invisible according to the action we're taking. For example, we cannot specify subjects for replies, so if we're replying we should not see the `Subject` textbox. And the textbox for the topic's key should be visible only when the moderator is adding a new topic, and invisible to normal users. We will handle this in the code-behind. Here is the code for the ASP.NET page:

```
<%@ Page language="vb" Codebehind="PostMessage.aspx.vb"
        AutoEventWireup="false"
        Inherits="Wrox.WebModules.Forums.Web.PostMessage" %>
<%@ Register TagPrefix="Forums" TagName="Header" src="Header.ascx" %>
<%@ Register TagPrefix="Forums" TagName="Footer" src="Footer.ascx" %>
<!DOCTYPE HTML PUBLIC "-//W3C//DTD HTML 4.0 Transitional//EN" >
<HTML>
  <HEAD>
    <title>Forums</title>
    <meta name="CODE_LANGUAGE" Content="VB">
    <link href="/ThePhile/Styles/ThePhile.css" rel="stylesheet" />
    <link href="/ThePhile/Styles/Navigator.css" rel="stylesheet" />
    <script language="javascript">
      function InsertTag(tagcode)
      {
        document.PostMessage.Message.value += tagcode;
      }
    </script>
  </HEAD>
  <body>
    <form ID="PostMessage" method="post" Runat="server">
      <Forums:Header Runat="server" ID="Header" />
      <br>
      <asp:Table Runat="server" ID="MessageBox" Width="500px"
              HorizontalAlign="Center" CssClass="Forums_General">
        <asp:TableRow CssClass="Forums_Header">
          <asp:TableCell Runat="server" ID="MessageBoxHeader"
                        HorizontalAlign="Center" Font-Bold="True" />
        </asp:TableRow>
        <asp:TableRow Runat="server" ID="SubjectRow">
          <asp:TableCell>
            <b>Subject:</b>
            <asp:TextBox ID="Subject" Runat="server" MaxLength="100"
                        Width="100%" CssClass="TextBox" />
```

```
        <asp:RequiredFieldValidator Runat="server"
                         ControlToValidate="Subject" Display="Dynamic">
          * This field is required
        </asp:RequiredFieldValidator>
      </asp:TableCell>
    </asp:TableRow>
    <asp:TableRow Runat="server" ID="KeyRow">
      <asp:TableCell>
        <b>Key:</b>
        <asp:TextBox ID="Key" Runat="server" MaxLength="15"
                  Width="100%" CssClass="TextBox" />
      </asp:TableCell>
    </asp:TableRow>
    <asp:TableRow Runat="server" ID="SpecialTagsRow">
      <asp:TableCell>
        <a href="javascript:InsertTag('[B] [/B]')">
          <img src="./Images/EditorBold.gif" alt="Bold">
        </a>
```

There are similar JavaScript calls for all the supported tags. Let's just jump to the end of the toolbar:

```
      </asp:TableCell>
    </asp:TableRow>
    <asp:TableRow>
      <asp:TableCell>
        <b>Message:</b>
        <asp:TextBox ID="Message" Runat="server" MaxLength="100"
                  TextMode="MultiLine" Rows="15" Width="100%"
                  CssClass="TextBox" />
        <asp:RequiredFieldValidator Runat="server"
                         ControlToValidate="Message" Display="Dynamic">
          * This field is required
        </asp:RequiredFieldValidator>
      </asp:TableCell>
    </asp:TableRow>
    <asp:TableRow>
      <asp:TableCell HorizontalAlign="Right">
        <asp:LinkButton ID="SubmitMessage"
                     OnClick="SubmitMessage_Click" Runat="server">
          [ <img border="0" src="./Images/OK.gif" Alt="submit"> Submit ]
        </asp:LinkButton>
         
        <asp:LinkButton ID="CancelMessage" OnClick="CancelMessage_Click"
                     CausesValidation="False" Runat="server">
          [ <img border="0" src="./Images/Cancel.gif"> Cancel ]
        </asp:LinkButton>
      </asp:TableCell>
    </asp:TableRow>
  </asp:Table>
  <br>
  <Forums:Footer Runat="server" ID="Footer" />
  </form>
  </body>
</HTML>
```

In addition to the textboxes we also have a row with images that, when clicked, call the custom `InsertTag` JavaScript function that adds the specified text tags to the message textbox, to help users who don't know or don't remember them. This toolbar is only visible when special tags are allowed by the module's settings. However, we don't care about the visibility of the controls in this page, everything will be done from the code-behind.

The Code-behind for PostMessage.aspx

This code-behind can seem complex, because we have to handle different actions according to the `Action` parameter passed along with the URL, as well as the usual `ForumID`, `TopicID`, `ReplyID`, `QuoteTopicID`, and `QuoteReplyID` parameters that we've used in the previous pages. To recap, here's a list of the possible values for the `Action` parameter, their respective meanings, and the companion parameters:

❑ `NewTopic`: posts a new topic to the forum identified by the `ForumID` parameter.

❑ `EditTopic`: edits the topic identified by the `TopicID` parameter.

❑ `NewReply`: posts a new reply to the topic identified by the `TopicID` parameter. Checks if the `QuoteTopicID` or `QuoteReplyID` parameter is specified, and if so quotes the respective message.

❑ `EditReply`: edits the topic identified by the `ReplyID` parameter.

The textboxes for the subject and message text are set to empty, or populated with the values of the topic or reply accordingly to the parameters above. However, before doing this, the page checks whether the current user is authenticated: if not, they are redirected to the login page, to log in or create a new account. Otherwise in `Page_Load` we also check if the current user is registered for the forums system: if not they are redirected to the `MyProfile.aspx` page to create a new profile. All this translates to the following code:

```
Private Sub Page_Load(ByVal sender As Object, ByVal e As EventArgs)

  ' If the user is not authenticated, redirect to the login page
  If Not Context.User.Identity.IsAuthenticated Then
    Response.Redirect("/ThePhileVB/WebModules/Accounts/Login.aspx", True)
  End If

  ' Retrieve the current user/member
  myCurrUser = CType(Context.User.Identity, SiteIdentity)
  myCurrMember = New Business.Member()
  myCurrMember.LoadFromUser(myCurrUser.UserId)

  ' If the user is not registered for the forum, redirect to
  ' the profile page
  If myCurrMember.Id = -1 Then
    Response.Redirect("MyProfile.aspx", True)
  End If

  ' Check if the user has the permission to moderate the forums
  Dim currentPrincipal As SitePrincipal = _
    CType(Context.User, SitePrincipal)
  myCanModerateForums = currentPrincipal.HasPermission( _
```

```
        CInt(ForumsPermissions.ModerateForums))

    ' If the user wants to edit a topic or reply, but does not
    ' have the permission to do so, redirect to the login page
    If Request.QueryString( _
        "Action").ToString().ToLower().StartsWith("edit") _
        AndAlso Not myCanModerateForums Then

        Response.Redirect( _
            "/ThePhileVB/WebModules/Accounts/Login.aspx?ShowError=true", True)

    End If


    ' Extract the ForumId, if specified
    If Request.QueryString("ForumId") Is Nothing Then
        myForumId = -1
    Else
        myForumId = Integer.Parse(Request.QueryString("ForumId"))
    End If


    ' Extract the TopicId, if specified
    If Request.QueryString("TopicId") Is Nothing Then
        myTopicId = -1
    Else
        myTopicId = Integer.Parse(Request.QueryString("TopicId"))
    End If


    ' Extract the ReplyId, if specified
    If Request.QueryString("ReplyId") Is Nothing Then
        myReplyId = -1
    Else
        myReplyId = Integer.Parse(Request.QueryString("ReplyId"))
    End If


    If Not Page.IsPostBack Then

        ' Show/hide the icons for the special tags, according
        ' to the settings
        SpecialTagsRow.Visible = _
            Configuration.ModuleConfig.GetSettings().SpecialTagsEnabled
```

After adding or updating a message, we redirect back to the page that originally called `PostMessage.aspx`. The URL can't be retrieved through the `Request.UrlReferrer` property, because when the button is clicked and the form posted back, the referrer becomes the `PostMessage.aspx` page itself. To solve this simple problem, we save the original referrer's URL into the `ViewState` collection. We will retrieve it in `Submit_Click`, and redirect to that page:

```
    ViewState("ReferrerUrl") = Request.UrlReferrer.ToString()

    Dim forum As New Business.Forum(myForumId)
    Dim topic As New Business.Topic(myTopicId)
    Dim reply As New Business.Reply(myReplyId)
```

```vbnet
' Show the fields and the navigation path, according to the
' action to complete, and the forum/topic/reply Id
Select Case Request.QueryString("Action").ToString().ToLower()
  Case "newtopic"
    SubjectRow.Visible = True
    KeyRow.Visible = myCanModerateForums
    MessageBoxHeader.Text = "New topic"
    Header.ForumId = myForumId
  Case "edittopic"
    SubjectRow.Visible = True
    KeyRow.Visible = myCanModerateForums
    MessageBoxHeader.Text = "Edit topic"
    Subject.Text = topic.Subject
    Key.Text = topic.Key
    Message.Text = topic.Message
    Header.TopicId = myTopicId
  Case "newreply"
    SubjectRow.Visible = False
    KeyRow.Visible = False
    MessageBoxHeader.Text = "New reply"
    Header.TopicId = myTopicId

    ' A topic or another reply can being quoted by this new
    ' reply, check it it is the case
    Dim quoteTopicId As Integer
    Dim quoteReplyId As Integer

    ' Extract the QuoteTopicId, if specified
    If Request.QueryString("QuoteTopicId") Is Nothing Then
      quoteTopicId = -1
    Else
      quoteTopicId = Integer.Parse( _
        Request.QueryString("QuoteTopicId"))
    End If

    ' Extract the QuoteReplyId, if specified
    If Request.QueryString("QuoteReplyId") Is Nothing Then
      quoteReplyId = -1
    Else
      quoteReplyId = Integer.Parse( _
        Request.QueryString("QuoteReplyId"))
    End If

    ' If a topic is being quoted, add it to the MessageBox
    If quoteTopicId <> -1 Then
      Dim existentTopic As New Business.Topic(quoteTopicId)
      Message.Text &= String.Format( _
        "[QUOTE]{0}[/QUOTE]", existentTopic.Message)
    End If

    ' If a reply is being quoted, add it to the MessageBox
    If quoteReplyId <> -1 Then
      Dim existentReply As New Business.Reply(quoteReplyId)
      Message.Text &= String.Format( _
```

```
                        "[QUOTE]{0}[/QUOTE]", existentReply.Message)
                End If

            Case "editreply"
                SubjectRow.Visible = False
                KeyRow.Visible = False
                Message.Text = reply.Message
                MessageBoxHeader.Text = "Edit reply"
                Header.TopicId = reply.Topic.Id
        End Select
    End If
End Sub
```

When the form is submitted we again check the `Action` parameter and create or edit a record, as follows:

```
Protected Sub SubmitMessage_Click( _
    ByVal sender As Object, _
    ByVal e As EventArgs)

    Dim forum As New Business.Forum(myForumId)
    Dim topic As New Business.Topic(myTopicId)
    Dim reply As New Business.Reply(myReplyId)

    Select Case Request.QueryString("Action").ToString().ToLower()
        Case "newtopic"    ' Create a new topic
            Dim newId As Integer = forum.AddTopic( _
                Key.Text, _
                Subject.Text, _
                Message.Text, _
                myCurrMember.Id).Id
            Response.Redirect("Topic.aspx?TopicId=" + newId.ToString(), True)
        Case "edittopic"    ' Edit an existent topic
            topic.Key = Key.Text
            topic.Subject = Subject.Text
            topic.Message = Message.Text
            topic.Update()
        Case "newreply"    ' Add a new reply
            topic.AddReply(Message.Text, myCurrMember.Id)

            ' add the parameter to the Referrer Url to jump to the last
            ' page of the topic
            If Not ViewState("ReferrerUrl").ToString().ToLower().EndsWith( _
                "&display=lastpage") Then
                ViewState("ReferrerUrl") &= "&Display=LastPage"
            End If
        Case "editreply"    ' Edit an existent reply
            reply.Message = Message.Text
            reply.Update()
    End Select
    ' Redirect to the referrer page
    Response.Redirect(ViewState("ReferrerUrl").ToString())
End Sub
```

> Note that in this procedure there is no need to check if the user is trying to edit a record and has the right permissions to do that. This is already checked in **Page_Load**, which is called before this event, even if the page is posted back, as in this case. Therefore, if the user is not allowed to edit a record but tries to do it, this will be recognized when the page loads, and the execution will not get to **SubmitMessage_Click**. The browser will instead be redirected to the login page.

If we're adding a reply, we redirect to the referring page, but add a `Display=LastPage` parameter at the end of the URL, so that the `Topic.aspx` page (the only page with links to post a reply), shows the last page of replies – which will include the message just posted.

The `CancelMessage_Click` procedure, executed when the user presses the Cancel button, simply makes the browser jump back to the referrer page:

```
Protected Sub CancelMessage_Click( _
  ByVal sender As Object, _
  ByVal e As EventArgs)
  ' Go back to the referrer page
  Response.Redirect(ViewState("ReferrerUrl").ToString())
End Sub
```

Here is a screenshot of the complete page, when a moderator is adding a new topic (only moderators can set the topic's key):

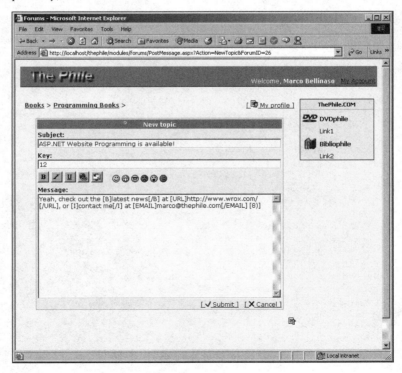

The MyProfile.aspx Page

This page allows a registered member to change their profile, namely the signature, the avatar URL, the homepage URL, and the flag indicating whether the e-mail address can be publicly shown. The member name is shown in a disabled textbox, since it can't be changed – if the user wants a different name, they must first create a new account for the site and then create a new profile for the forum. The code for the ASPX page is simple – there is just the declaration of a table and the textboxes, as you see from the following screenshot:

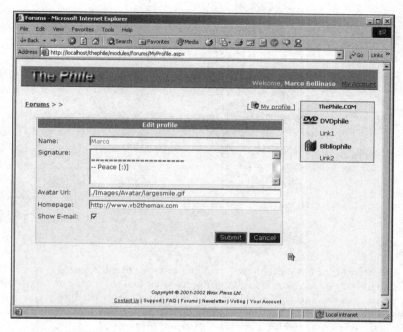

The Code-behind for MyProfile.aspx

When the page loads, it first checks if the current user is logged in. If not, it can mean that they are a registered user but currently not logged in, or they have not registered at all. In both cases, a user can't create or edit a forums profile if they don't own a site account first, or if they aren't logged in. Thus, the browser is redirected to the site's Login.aspx page, to log in or create a new account. If the current user has been authenticated, the page is rendered to create or edit a profile, depending on whether they have one already. Here's the code:

```
Private Sub Page_Load(ByVal sender As Object, ByVal e As EventArgs)
    ' If the user is not authenticated, redirect to the login page
    If Not Context.User.Identity.IsAuthenticated Then
        Response.Redirect("/ThePhileVB/Modules/Users/Login.aspx", True)
    End If
    ' Retrieve the current user/member
    myCurrUser = CType(Context.User.Identity, SiteIdentity)
    myCurrMember = New Business.Member()
    myCurrMember.LoadFromUser(myCurrUser.UserId)
```

```
        If Not IsPostBack Then
          ' Save the referrer Url
          ViewState("ReferrerUrl") = Request.UrlReferrer.ToString()

          ' If the member's ID is not -1, we have to edit the current
          ' profile so load the current properties and disable the textbox
          ' with the member name
          If myCurrMember.Id <> -1 Then
            ' load the profile of the current member
            ProfileBoxTitle.Text = "Edit profile"
            Name.Text = myCurrMember.Name
            Name.Enabled = False
            Signature.Text = myCurrMember.Signature
            AvatarUrl.Text = myCurrMember.AvatarUrl
            Homepage.Text = myCurrMember.Homepage
            ShowEmail.Checked = myCurrMember.ShowEmail
          Else
            Name.Text = myCurrUser.FirstName + " " + myCurrUser.LastName
            ' Ensure that the member name is no longer that 15 chars

            If Name.Text.Length > 15 Then
              Name.Text = Name.Text.Substring(0, 15)
            End If

            ProfileBoxTitle.Text = "Register"
          End If
        End If
      End Sub
```

To check if the current user has a profile we create an instance of Business.Member, and try to load the profile through LoadFromUser. If the ID property is set to –1 it means that a profile has not been created yet, so the textboxes are all enabled and we set the username textbox to the first 15 letters of the user's first name plus last name. If a profile already exists, the textbox for the member name is disabled, and the other textboxes are set with the member's current properties.

When the user clicks the Submit button, the code in the Click event handler creates or updates a profile, depending on whether the textbox for the member name is enabled or not:

```
      Protected Sub Submit_Click(ByVal sender As Object, ByVal e As EventArgs)
        ' If the textbox with the name is disable, it means that we're
        ' editing an exisiting member, otherwise create a new one
        If Not Name.Enabled Then
          ' update the profile of the current member
          myCurrMember.Signature = Signature.Text
          myCurrMember.AvatarUrl = AvatarUrl.Text
          myCurrMember.Homepage = Homepage.Text
          myCurrMember.ShowEmail = ShowEmail.Checked
          myCurrMember.Update(
        Else
          ' Create a new member
          Dim member As New Business.Member()
          If member.Create( _
            myCurrUser.UserId, _
```

```
        Name.Text, _
        ShowEmail.Checked, _
        Signature.Text, _
        AvatarUrl.Text, _
        Homepage.Text) = -1 Then

        ' If a member with this name is already present,
        ' show the error message
        ErrorMessageRow.Visible = True
        Return
    End If
End If

    ' Redirect to the referrer page
    Response.Redirect(ViewState("ReferrerUrl").ToString())
End Sub
```

When the profile has been created or updated, the browser is redirected to the page that originally redirected to `Profile.aspx`, in the same way as `PostTopic.aspx`.

Summary

In this chapter we've built a forums system from scratch. We've seen how to integrate other modules such as the `Core` and the `Accounts` modules, as well as ASP.NET's built-in authentication. Our `Forums` module supports multiple categories and sub-forums, displays topics and replies through custom pagination, enforces the user currently registered to the site to also create a forums profile with their username, signature, avatar, and homepage, and supports or prevents the use of HTML code and other special tags.

We've written quite a lot of code to fuel the discussion board system below; we just list the most important techniques that this chapter should have taught you:

❑ Creating nested data-bound controls: in the `Default.aspx` page we showed how to create a `DataGrid` inside a `DataList` to represent a parent-child relationship.

❑ Custom implementation of the `Delete` command for the `DataList` and `DataGrid` in `Default.aspx`, namely the JavaScript popup box that asks for a confirmation and calls `__doPostBack` to generate an event on the server.

❑ How to implement the `DataGrid`'s custom pagination, by using a stored procedure that returns the specified page of records, the `DataGrid`'s `AllowCustomPaging` property, and custom controls to navigate through the pages.

❑ Using regular expressions and the `RegEx` class to extract and replace string patterns.

However, we've really only scratched the surface of the features we could implement for a professional forum. Below we list some of the features they offer, in case you want to enhance our module with some more advanced functionality:

❑ E-mail notification of forum activity, or even e-mail message digests – eventually we could integrate the web forum with an e-mail discussion list.

- ❑ Add some kind of preview or revision system for users to edit their own messages.

- ❑ Banning certain words, and using regular expressions to replace them with acceptable alternatives.

- ❑ An administration console, that allows administrators to browse members, edit their profiles, or ban them from the forum.

- ❑ A feature that allows moderators to move a topic to another forum.

- ❑ Threaded discussions, where it is possible to follow a particular thread within a topic, rather than seeing all messages arranged by date.

- ❑ Allow all users to submit topics for approval.

- ❑ Allow users to see what forums contain the current hot topics, where a hot topic is one that has been posted to most frequently in a given time period. This generates cross-forum interest.

- ❑ Private forums, where only restricted members can read and post messages.

We've now implemented all of the modules for our website, and in the next chapter will look at how we can deploy it as a live site.

11

Deploying the Site

Now that we have developed our website, we need to **deploy** it – prepare and distribute the site so that users can access it.

The release of ASP.NET forces us to reconsider many pre-conceptions about the deployment of websites. For example, we need to get used the possibility of running multiple copies of the same site on a single server, sharing different versions of identically named DLLs. Another thing that developers might find incredible is XCopy deployment, which allows a developer to deploy an application by simply copying files to the target location. There's no need to use the Registry or any complex COM registration.

In the past, deploying a large-scale web application could become a nightmare. Most enterprise web sites comprised dozens (or more) COM and COM+/MTS components. Maintaining the information on all of those components in the Registry and making sure that the information was updated properly when upgrading to a new version was an incredibly difficult task. ASP.NET allows entire websites to be configured with simple XML text files, and components to automatically register themselves in COM+. There's no need to look to the registry for anything in deployment of ASP.NET, completely alleviating one of the biggest ASP deployment headaches.

This chapter will discuss the general issues surrounding the deployment of ASP.NET websites and the various approaches we can take. We will describe the deployment techniques we used for ThePhile.com.

The Problem

Our problem for this chapter is deploying our fully functional website to our production server.

It is a common practice to develop a site on a *development* server, then deploy to a *staging* server, and finally after a successful test on the staging server, deploy to the *production* server. We want a solution that will allow us to deploy the entire functioning site to a production server. However, we also want to be able to easily deploy the code to multiple machines so that we can test it in various scenarios. In our solution, our production server is hosted by Wrox, but it could just as easily be a segment of disk space allocated to us by a website hosting company.

So, in this chapter we want to explore the various ways we can deploy ASP.NET websites and then choose the one that best suits our needs. The chapter will provide some useful information about ASP.NET deployment that will help decide which method is most appropriate for different organizations.

The Design

There are two parts to deploying the website: the database and the application. First of all, we will discuss how to deploy the database. Then we will move on to look at the web application itself.

Deploying the Data Store

A data store for a website can be anything from a set of XML files or simple Access database, to a complex SQL Server or Oracle database. Each of the website deployment options has a different set of limitations and advantages for database deployment. However, since database deployment is an important topic all on its own, we'll discuss it here rather than split up the discussion among the different installation scenarios.

Deploying a database is easiest when we own the machine to which it needs to be deployed. We can use whatever deployment scenario is most convenient for copying our particular data store. For SQL Server or Oracle there are several options, including:

❑ Making a backup of the development database and restoring from that backup on another machine.

❑ Transferring data structures and data between linked servers in some fashion, perhaps using script files.

We often don't fully control the database server. Web hosting companies often set up a single database with a certain quota of disk space, for example. In situations like this, our options are more limited. We probably can't restore from a backup, because we won't have access to Enterprise Manager against the host's database servers. Even if we do have access to Enterprise Manager, we might not have the right permissions to perform a database restore. In these cases, we are limited to using text queries to create the data structures and load the data.

For an Access database, the file just needs to be copied to a certain directory and the file is deployed. It doesn't matter what server access we have. This does pose a serious danger: if an unwanted intruder happens to find out that your Access database is available in a public internet directory, they'll be able to download it. You'll want to keep the MDB file somewhere non-obvious and preferably in a private location, so that only code from our application can access the file.

Consult your SQL Server, Oracle, or Access manual for the various options available for transferring your database from your development PC to a deployed production environment.

For automated deployment, where we create an installation program for our website, we have another option. We can take the scripts that re-create the data structures required for the application, and can have our installer execute them at installation-time, guaranteeing that the data structures will be available before the application is run for the first time.

Preparing the Site for Deployment

There are three main scenarios that we will consider for deploying our ASP.NET website:

❑ XCopy deployment

❑ A specialized type of XCopy deployment for deploying a website to a hosted server that we have little control over

❑ Using Visual Studio .NET to create an installation program that will perform the installation and deployment process automatically

While there are a great number of variations in the ways to deploy an ASP.NET website, all of them will derive from a combination of the above three. We will discuss each of these methods in detail and explain the benefits and drawbacks of each, and then apply that information to our situation in terms of deploying ThePhile.com.

The following diagram shows a sample website directory structure. It includes a list of some DLLs that the sample application might be using. The directory structure contains everything that is required to run the application, except the database. There are no Registry entries to be made:

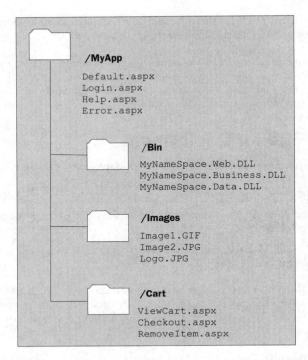

During development, the folder structure will not be this neat. In fact, things can get downright messy. In ThePhile's development folder, we have many copies of the same DLL and source code for all classes, even supposedly secret business and data-layer classes. Deploying all this would waste our disk space and pose a security risk. We should only deploy the files required to execute the application – one copy of each DLL, and only source code for classes that compile on the fly.

Visual Studio .NET enables us to copy a web project to a new location. While at first it might not appear all that beneficial to copy a web project, there is a subtle feature that comes in extremely handy. On the Copy Project dialog box, accessible from the Project menu, there is a radio button that allows us to exclude source code files from the destination copy of the application. Choosing "Only files needed to run this application" when copying the project creates a copy of the entire solution, without the source code files. This includes all supporting assemblies (which will be copied to the \bin directory), all .aspx pages, all .ascx controls, and all .asmx files, as well as all images and other non-code items associated with the project. This copy can then be used as the source for all of the deployment options that we will discuss in this chapter.

If we are copying to a location that has not been set up as a web folder, Visual Studio .NET will do everything it can to create the new site. If the site already exists, make sure that its FrontPage extensions are configured properly to allow Visual Studio .NET to make whatever changes are necessary.

Once we have created a 'clean' copy the website, we can carry out one of the available deployment options.

In fact, using this method we can create a clean copy on our host's machine in one go – we just need to ensure that the host is running FrontPage Extensions.

Manual (XCopy) Deployment

XCopy deployment is a painless way to install .NET software. It gets its name from a DOS command for copying a whole folder, including its subfolders, to a different location. In DOS this was often all you needed to do to install software in new locations – create an exact copy of the folder structure. Because of COM component registration, and other OS complications, this often doesn't work in Windows. .NET brings the facility back.

In the case of ASP.NET, when a code-behind class or an ASP.NET page makes a request involving an external assembly, that request is directed to the web application's \bin directory.

When using Visual Studio .NET to build a web application, compiled code-behinds will be placed in a file called Web.dll, which will be placed in the \bin directory. Therefore when ASP.NET handles a request for a page with a code-behind class, that class is obtained from the Web.dll file.

With XCopy, we only need to copy all of the files from the 'clean' application directory and all related sub-directories to the deployment location and the application is deployed.

The benefit of the XCopy approach is that it is incredibly simple, quick, and relatively painless. The downside is that it is manual. We end up deploying websites by manually dragging and dropping folders and files. If you are in control of both your clean application and the machine you are deploying to, this approach is fine. If you plan on bundling your site for distribution to a wider audience, this approach might not be suitable and you may instead have to build a deployment project in Visual Studio .NET. This latter approach is the one we took when deploying ThePhile.com, and is described in *The Solution* section.

When using XCopy there is one extra thing that must be done. XCopy only copies the files. In order for the newly deployed web application to work properly, we need to make sure that IIS has been configured properly.

Configuring IIS for your Application

Although we've hyped XCopy deployment, in ASP.NET it is not an entirely hands-free process. We can't simply copy our files to a directory and expect the directory to magically become a web application. We still need to configure IIS to replicate our local configuration. In some cases you won't have direct access to IIS and will need to communicate your needs to the host's IT staff. If this is the case, knowing the IIS issues will make it far easier to explain what you need.

To get a web application working properly, we need an IIS application to be running and serving HTTP requests for the application's virtual directory. The **IIS Virtual Directory Creation Wizard** can help do this.

Here we will set up a folder in IIS that will allow us to deploy by XCopy. First, open up the Internet Services Manager console. Expand the node for your computer, select the **Web Sites** node, and choose **New | Virtual Directory** to start this wizard.

From there, you will be prompted for an alias name (for example, ThePhile or MyApp) for the virtual directory. Then you will be asked for the physical directory to which the virtual directory should point. This will be where you manually copied your directory structure, or an empty directory if you are going to copy the files in later. Select the folder to which you copied your 'clean' website and proceed to the next step. Here you specify what permissions you would like to create for the application. Leave the checkboxes set at their default values: only read and script (ASP) execution should be allowed. These permissions are sufficient to run an ASP.NET website.

If you already have a web application created for this website, and you want to deploy to the existing IIS application, the procedure varies slightly. First, you still need to make sure that you have a clean deployment source, with no legible source code in it. Secondly, you should delete any existing files in the web application. If you created a virtual directory with IIS, or if you created a web application using VS .NET, there will be some default 'clutter' in the directories that you can get rid of before copying your files into the directory. From there, your `web.config` file will take care of the rest of the administrative tasks for your web application. With ASP.NET you no longer have to worry about other kinds of configuration methods, because all required settings are controlled by `web.config`.

Deploying to a Hosting Service

We do not all work for large corporations that can provide Internet connectivity, bandwidth, databases, and servers capable of hosting the .NET Framework and storing web pages. In these cases a hosting service comes in handy.

The Visual Studio .NET start page contains a link to a current list of participating .NET web-hosting services. There are standard and premier services listed here. The standard services usually provide a web application, some limited storage space, and possibly some data-access method. Premier services often offer e-commerce initiatives, larger disk space allowances, dedicated servers, and other services more useful to businesses than individual programmers. Premier services also tend to give us more control over the web and database server configurations.

Providers will vary in the services they provide, the fees they charge, and the methods they support for updating the website. It's a good idea to prepare for the least amount of supported functionality in order to make your deployment plan flexible, just in case you have to suddenly change providers (a surprisingly common event).

The first thing we need is a 'clean' version of the website to be deployed. As discussed earlier, this means either manually removing sensitive source code from the web directories, or using the project copy feature in Visual Studio .NET to do this for us.

Typically, the hosting services will provide a single web application to do with as we please. For example, we might end up with a web application running at www.hostingcompany.com/myapp. If the web hosting company also provides DNS resolution, we might be able to get that particular application to be the destination for an address, for example www.myapplication.com.

To deploy an application to a hosting service, we follow the typical XCopy model, except that the destination machine is not our own, and is often an FTP site provided by the web hosting company. This works fine, allowing us to copy our files as we please. The two main differences between standard XCopy deployment and deploying to a web hosting company are:

❑ With XCopy deployment, we control our own IIS configuration manually. By deploying to a web host, the web host is in control of the IIS configuration and any changes to our application's IIS configuration often go through their technical support department.

❑ When using traditional XCopy deployment, we can use Visual Studio .NET to develop directly against the web application. However, with a web-hosting company, FrontPage extensions may not be available, so we have to use VS .NET to develop the solution in an offline fashion and then FTP the files to the server later.

Before deciding on a particular web-hosting company, read as much technical information about the process by which pages get uploaded to the site, their technical support policy, and any uptime guarantees they may have. Do not put a critical application on a web-hosting site unless they guarantee a reasonable level of uptime.

Because the technical support department controls our site's configuration, *always* check it before agreeing to anything. Check references, and if possible get information from other people currently running applications on their site. When looking for a hosting service, you should check out what kind of access you would have to your database (for example, if they allow Enterprise Manager), and what kind of application control you would have (for example, will they allow you to have more than one application or must you run everything from the same root application?).

Another thing to consider are the resources that your application will use. If you're designing your application with deployment to a third-party server in mind, there are some design and architecture decisions that you might want to consider. Resources are generally limited or entirely restricted in availability on hosting servers. For example, most applications will typically not have access to the Event Log. Even if the application has access to it, you won't, so you would be unable to see the results of your application's log. In cases like this, you'll want to design your code to require the least amount of environment-specific resources so that you can be prepared for deployment to a variety of environments.

Automated Deployment (Building Installers)

Automated deployment is obviously the preferred solution, but it isn't always available. If you have built a website to sell to clients, those clients need to easily install the site on their own servers. For example, if you have developed a support call center application using ASP.NET and are selling that application, you will need some robust, easy-to-use way for the clients to install and set up that application.

In the past, this was accomplished by using a tool such as InstallShield or WISE Installmaster. These tools would allow you to create scripts that dictated which files were copied during the installation. They also registered COM components and handled creation of COM+ applications. These tools are complex and take some time to fully master their use.

Visual Studio .NET provides a built-in method for creating installation programs. Visual Studio .NET allows us to create CAB files, self-installing executable files, and even MSI files for use with the Microsoft Windows Installer package. While using these installers is a good solution and helpful, it only works if you actually have access to the console of the server on which you're installing the application. This pretty much rules out this method for building deployment scenarios to web hosting companies, but is still an excellent idea for providing shrink-wrapped software to clients or departments within a company.

The Solution

Wrox Press will host the final version of ThePhile.com, so we do not need to enlist the services of a web-hosting company. This makes a deployment project in Visual Studio .NET an appropriate choice. We will create two – one with the source code and one without.

In this section we'll cover in depth the steps involved in creating a deployment project for ThePhile.com, which will result in a Windows Installer file to distribute for deploying ThePhile.

First, we open up Visual Studio .NET and choose the option to create a new project. Then we highlight the **Setup and Deployment Projects** option in the left pane, and the right pane shows the following options:

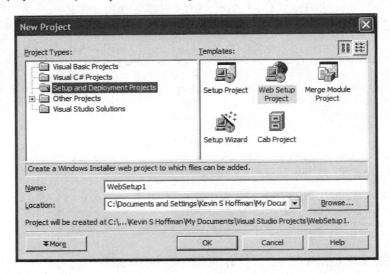

The following are the different types of setup and deployment projects available:

❏ **Setup Project** – this will create a blank installation project. It will be up to us to choose all of the various activities and files for the installer. This is typically recommended for those programmers who know ahead of time what activities need to be performed and which files need to be copied.

❏ **Web Setup Project** – this is similar to the blank Setup Project, except it comes with a few settings and directories already created to guide us in the right direction for installing a website.

❏ **Merge Module Project** – this is a slightly more advanced project for creating merge modules for use with the latest versions of the Windows Installer. Merge Modules are an advanced technique that we won't discuss here.

❏ **Setup Wizard** – this is basically a front-end to all of the other project types. We will choose this one – it's easy and it guides us step by step through creating the appropriate type of setup project.

❏ **Cab Project** – this project builds a Windows installation cabinet file. This is another advanced technique. Find out more on Cabinet files in the .NET Framework SDK and Windows documentation.

For our purposes, we're going to create a new project called `ThePhileSetup`, using the **Setup Wizard** option. We enter our new project's filename and click **OK**. Once we've done this, we're presented with a dialog that looks like this:

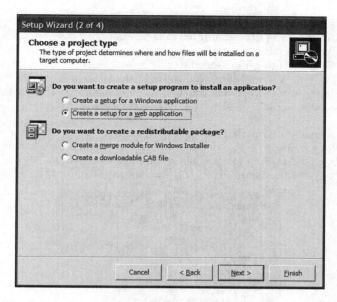

The Setup Wizard guides us through creating a new setup project. It asks a couple user-friendly questions, and then creates a variety of blank template projects that we can expand as needed. The above dialog asks whether the setup is for a Windows application, a web application, a merge module, or a downloadable CAB file. These options should look familiar from the New Project panel. We'll choose web application and click Next. After Visual Studio .NET does some initial setting up, we're presented with a Project view:

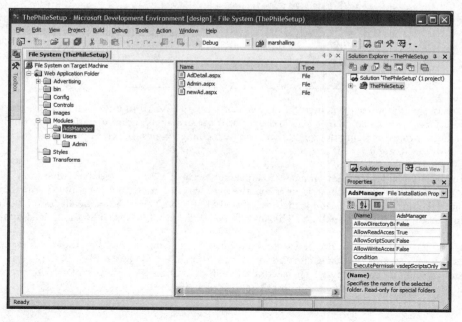

This is the **File System** view of the deployment project. It is actually quite intuitive – it shows the state of the file system we would like to exist *after* the installation. In our case, once the installation is over we want to place the above directory structure under a web application created in the **Web Application Folder**. The main benefit of using Visual Studio .NET's deployment projects, beyond the ease of use, is that we don't have to leave Visual Studio .NET to create the setup projects. The beauty of this model is that we only need to create an image of our final destination in the **File System** tab. To do this, we drag and drop directories and files into the file system tree and its ready to go.

The setup project designer is far more powerful than it might first appear. If you right-click the project itself and choose **View**, you will be able to modify all kinds of details about the deployment project. This includes the user interface, registry settings, and much more. For example, the following screenshot shows the top left corner of a window for editing the user interface tree of a deployment project:

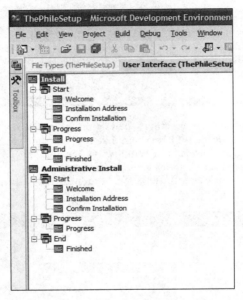

As you can see, the interface is incredibly easy and straightforward to understand. There are two sets of user interfaces, one for standard users and one for those users with administrative rights on the machine to which the project is being deployed. You can also change views, program prompts, and embed commands in the deployment project.

In short, creating a deployment project is so amazingly easy in Visual Studio .NET that there is no reason not to use this feature to its fullest. Unless you already own, and are extremely proficient in, another third-party installation tool, this method is the best. Visual Studio .NET can automatically 'build' your project, resulting in an MSI file or a CAB file. This used to be a black art, but Visual Studio .NET illuminates it.

When we've created our two projects (one with source, one without), building them will result in two files: `ThePhileSetup.msi` and `ThePhileSourceSetup.msi`. The first file will deploy the entire website without any source code. The second file will deploy the website complete with source code, plus a Visual Studio .NET client solution file and project file.

To launch the installation program we just created, double-click the `msi` files. This assumes that you have the latest version of the Windows Installer on your machine. If you are deploying to a location that might not have the latest installer, there is an option to package the installer itself with your `msi` files when you build the installation projects.

Summary

We have seen how to deploy and install ASP.NET websites. We've discussed some of the issues that tend to arise during deployment and the various options available for installation. After having read this chapter, you should be familiar with the following types of deployment and their associated issues and concerns:

❑ XCopy deployment

❑ Deployment to a hosted environment

❑ Automated deployment using VS .NET deployment projects

12

The End

This is the end of the book but it is not the end of the road. By now you should have played with the site, both by browsing the code in Visual Studio .NET, and playing with the site on your local machine.

You should also have seen how and why we built the site the way we did, and how to use those techniques on your own website.

Get Building

The next step is to start building your site. This book will have given you a framework, and some modules to use or modify. Now you will want to tailor our modules and pages to fit the needs of your site.

We also hope that you will build your own modules in our framework. A lot of our design went in to making it easy to add new modules – we don't want it to go to waste! You will be able to link your modules to our central accounts system, modify our header and footer controls, and so on. This book will provide a reference for building your own modules employing similar techniques.

Join Our Community

We don't want you to develop alone. This book will have its own forum at p2p.wrox.com where you can discuss it with us and other readers. This is a great place to get help with problems, share ideas, and find out if other people have written the module you need. Or you can just show off the sites you've developed! This service is free to all readers.

Through P2P, we hope to build up a list of the best websites built with the help of this book. If you do anything really impressive, we might even ask you to write a book about it!

Read More

This book has touched on a large number of subjects: web services, server controls, security, ADO.NET, and more. If you want to find more about any of these subjects, there are several Wrox books that will help.

Web Services

This book has presented a couple of very simple web services. Professional ASP.NET Web Services contains lots of detailed information on web services and how to develop them. It looks at a variety of issues, including how XML is used to transmit the data, how to send complex data types, and how to ensure web services support thousands of users.

Security

Our site uses the extensibility of the ASP.NET security framework to give us a flexible accounts system. Professional ASP.NET Security delves deeper into these topics, showing how we can build our own custom security frameworks. It also contains many tips on ensuring code is secure.

ADO.NET

Data access and manipulation have played a major part in developing our website. Efficient use of databases is one of the best things we can do to ensure performance and scalability. Professional ADO.NET covers a wide range of data-handling techniques, while Professional SQL Server 2000 gives information on setting up and using SQL Server in the most effective way.

Server Controls

Our site uses server controls in a number of places. Building good controls puts us in an excellent position to reuse functionality and save development effort. Professional ASP.NET Server Controls looks at how to build solid, reusable and flexible controls for your ASP.NET projects.

We hope that you have enjoyed this book, and that it will prove useful as you develop ASP.NET websites.

Index

A Guide to the Index

The index is arranged hierarchically, in alphabetical order, with symbols preceding the letter A. Most second-level entries and many third-level entries also occur as first-level entries. This is to ensure that users will find the information they require however they choose to search for it.

Symbols

.NET Framework
security, 150
identity object, 150
principal object, 150
user authentication, 149
XCopy deployment, 513
@Register directive
see Register directive.
__doPostBack function
categories and forums page, 472
directories, creating, 106
including in generated HTML, requirements, 107
text files, creating, 109
3-layer design of website
business services tier, 11
data services tier, 11
user interface, 11

A

Access database
database deployment, 510
accounts
see user accounts.
AccountsTool class
business services tier, 182
data services tier, 170
Add method
Attachments collection, 420
Cookies collection, 350
News class, 230
Add Web Reference option
news ticker web service client, 280
Poll web service client, 386
AddNews method
Category class, 239
address, validating
CustomValidator control, 428
problems with, 428
regular expressions, 426
RegularExpressionValidator control, 426
AddTopic method
Forum class, 467

AdMaster class
business services tier, 303
data services tier, 297
DbObject base class, 297
AdminFooter control
categories manager page, 249
news management, 243
online polls, 352
question manager page, 357
user controls, 241
AdminHeader control
categories manager page, 246
news management, 242
online polls, 352
question manager page, 353
user controls, 241
administration, 13
advert details page, 312
advertising admin page, 309
advertising on the web, 293, 309
categories and forums page, 471
mailing lists, 410, 425
Form Wizard, 410, 434
settings, modifying, 433
settings, storing and retrieving, 433
new advert page, 314
news management, 240
settings, modifying, 265
online polls, 351
settings, modifying, 364
option manager page, 361
question manager page, 352
user accounts, 153, 191
role editor, 191
AdRotator control
advertising on the web, 289
limitations, 289
SiteFooter control, 308
user interface, 293
using, 289
XML files, 289
synchronizing entries between database and XML file, 300
updating XML file, 302
advert details page
administration, 312
DropDownList control, 313
pre-populated web form, 312

Advertisement class
  business services tier, 304
  data services tier, 298
  information aggregation, 298
  synchronizing entries between database and XML file, 300
    updating XML file, 302
advertisement spots
  newsletter, 394
advertising
  Header control, 53
advertising admin page, 309
  DataGrid control, 309, 310
advertising on the web, 12, 14, 287
  administration, 293, 309
    advert details page, 312
    advertising admin page, 309
    new advert page, 314
  AdRotator control, 289
  business services tier, 293, 303
    AdMaster class, 303
    Advertisement class, 304
  data services tier, 292, 297
    AdMaster class, 297
    Advertisement class, 298
    problems with two data stores, 292
  database design, 290
    AdsManager_Advertisements table, 294
    AdsManager_Clicks table, 295
    AdsManager_Companies table, 294
    AdsManager_Impressions table, 295
    stored procedures, 292, 295
    warehousing data, 291
  designing advertising modules, 289
  hits, 288
  impressions, 287
  module configuration, 293, 315
  problems and solutions, 287, 294
  requirements, 288
  ThePhile.com, 307
  user interface, 293, 307
    AdRotator control, 293
    pass-through page, 293, 307
    SiteFooter control, modifying for advertising, 308
aliases for table names
  stored procedures, 155
AllowCustomPaging property
  DataGrid control, 484
AllowPaging property
  DataGrid control, 311
AllowVote property
  Question class, 348
anonymous users
  user identity, 140
AppException base class, 39
  deriving from ApplicationException class, 39
  exception handling, 39, 54
  LogEvent method, 40
ApplicationException class
  deriving AppException base class from, 39
  System namespace, 39
<appSettings> element
  Web.Config file, 152
architectural requirements, website, 18
Array class
  IndexOf method, 90
arrays
  compared to XML files, 116

ASP.NET
  AdRotator control, 289
  deploying website, 509
  dynamic output caching, 268
    problems with, 373
ASP.NET websites
  see websites.
Assembly attribute
  Register directive, 68
associate table
  see linking table.
atomicity
  transactions, 225
Attachments collection
  Add method, 420
  MailMessage class, 420
Attributes property
  DirectoryInfo class, 92, 122
  FileInfo class, 92, 122
attributes, displaying
  FileManager web application, 87
    displaying item attributes, 91
    displaying item creation & modification dates, 96
    displaying item icon, 88
    displaying item size, 93
attributes, modifying
  client-side JavaScript, 122
  FileManager web application, 122
AuthenticateRequest event
  HttpApplication class, 188
  retrieving authentication cookie in subsequent requests, 188
authentication, 77
  Forms-based authentication, 77, 141
  Passport authentication, 77
  PhilePage class, modifying, 188
  SiteHeader control, 64
    modifying to support authentication, 185
  user identity, 139
    .NET Framework, 149
    extending .NET Framework, 150
    UML case diagram, 140
  user interface
    Login page, 186
    modifying to support authentication, 185
    user profile page, 189
  Windows authentication, 77
authentication cookie, 187
  retrieving authentication cookie in subsequent requests, 187
<authentication> element
  Web.Config file, 188
automated deployment
  Cab project, 516
  database deployment, 511
  deploying website, 511, 515
  installers, 515
  Merge Module project, 516
  Setup project, 516
  Setup Wizard, 516
  Visual Studio .NET, 511, 515
  Web Setup project, 516
AutoPostBack property
  DropDownList control, 256, 362
  RadioButton web control, 256
availability
  data services tier, 29

B

backup system, database design, 28
base class for tier
  business services tier, 30, 38
  data services tier, 30, 34
BinaryReader class
  System.IO namespace, 78
BinaryWriter class
  System.IO namespace, 78
BindGrid method
  categories manager page, 250
  Forum page, 487
  news manager page, 260
  question manager page, 358
  Topic page, 494
BindList method
  categories and forums page, 478
BindTopicControls method
  Topic page, 495
BizObject base class, 38
BoundColumn
  DataGrid control, 249, 357
branding
  Header control, 53
BrowseFiles web form, FileManager web application, 81
  CopyDirectory procedure, 131
  FillFoldersAndFilesTable procedure
    deleting files, 126
    displaying additional attributes, 87
    downloading files, 100
    editing text files, 115
    listing folder contents, 84
    modifying attributes, 123
    renaming files and directories, 118
  FormatSize procedure, 94
  GetAttributesDescription procedure, 92
  GetDirectorySize procedure, 93
  Rename procedure, 121
BuildIntCommand procedure
  DbObject base class, 35
BuildQueryCommand procedure
  DbObject base class, 36
business services tier, 30
  3-layer design of website, 11
  advantages, 30
  advertising on the web, 293, 303
    AdMaster class, 303
    Advertisement class, 304
  base class for tier, 30, 38
  building, 30
  forums, 455
    Forum class, 455, 464
    Helper class, 456, 468
  mailing lists, 405, 415
    Helper class, 409, 423
    List class, 405
    Newsletter class, 408, 419
    separation, 405
    Subscription class, 407, 415
  maintainability, 30
  modifying settings, 409
  news management, 211, 235
    Category class, 211, 239
    News class, 214, 235
    UML diagram, 211
  online polls, 331, 346
    Option class, 333
    Question class, 331, 346

separation, 31
  user accounts, 147, 171
    AccountsTool class, 182
    Role class, 148, 179
    SiteIdentity class, 174
    SitePrincipal class, 171
    User class, 147, 176
Button web control
  CausesValidation property, 112, 254
  modifying settings online, 364
  news ticker web service client, 280
  Poll web service client, 386
ButtonColumn
  CommandName property, 259
  DataGrid control, 248, 259, 311, 355, 485

C

Cab project
  automated deployment, 516
Cache class
  Insert method, 375
  Remove method, 376
caching
  dynamic output caching, 268
    problems with, 373
  using with Poll user control, 373
camel casing convention, 21
cascading stylesheets
  see CSS.
categories and forums page
  adding categories, 478
  administration, 471
  BindList method, 478
  code-behind page, 477
  DataGrid control, 473, 475
  DataList control, 473
  deleting categories, 480
  editing categories, 478
  Footer control, 481
  Forum menu, 473
  GetForumsSource method, 478
  hacking, preventing, 479, 481
  Header control, 481
    code-behind page, 481
    HyperLink control, 481
    Label control, 481
  JavaScript functions, 471
    __doPostBack function, 472
  user interface, 471
  working with forums, 481
Categories class
  data services tier, 209
categories manager page
  AdminFooter control, 249
  AdminHeader control, 246
  BindGrid method, 250
  code-behind file, 250
  creating category, 253
  DataGrid control, 247
  deleting category, 253
  editing categories, 251
  GetImage method, 251
  RequiredFieldValidator control, 247
  sorting categories, 251
  updating categories, 252
  user interface, 244, 245

Category class
AddNews method, 239
business services tier, 211, 239
GetCategories method, 239
GetHeadlines method, 240
GetNews method, 239
CategoryDetails class
data services tier, 209
CausesValidation property
Button web control, 112, 254
LinkButton web control, 361
CDO
using with SmtpMail class, 419
character classes
regular expressions, 427
character escapes
regular expressions, 426
CheckBox control
Checked property, 357
modifying settings online, 364
question manager page, 353
TemplateColumn, 258, 357
Checked property
CheckBox control, 357
RadioButton web control, 357
child options, managing
Question class, 346
choose project type dialog
Setup Wizard, 516
client properties, web services
Timeout property, 388
Url property, 388
client-side code
compared to server-side code, 196
client-side JavaScript
attributes, modifying, 122
directories, creating, 105
files, copying or moving, 129
files, deleting, 125
renaming files and directories, 117
text files, creating, 109
code reviews, naming and coding conventions, 21
coding conventions
see naming and coding conventions.
Collaboration Data Objects
see CDO.
Command object
see SqlCommand class.
CommandEventArgs object
CommandName property, 486
CommandName property
ButtonColumn, 259
CommandEventArgs object, 486
DataGridCommandEventArgs class, 311
LinkButton web control, 485
communities
see online communities.
community building for website, 11, 14, 139
see also online communities.
user identity, 139
authentication, 139
user accounts, 139
user-friendliness, 140
CompareValidator control
ControlToValidate property, 265
modifying settings online, 365

news management administration
settings, modifying, 265
Type property, 265
content
mailing lists, 393
news management, 201
designing news management tool, 202
problems and solutions, 201, 218
targeted content, 394
spam, avoiding, 394
websites, 9, 12, 13
Control class
Render method, 61
Server controls inherit from, 61
System.Web.UI namespace, 61
controls, website design, 11
ControlToValidate property
CompareValidator control, 265
RequiredFieldValidator control, 247
Convert class
ToBoolean method, 259, 357
cookies
authentication cookie, 187
retrieving authentication cookie in subsequent
requests, 187
Forms-based authentication, 141
preventing or allowing multiple voting, 322
user identity, 140
Cookies collection
Add method, 350
HttpRequest class, 350
Copy method
File class, 131
CopyDirectory procedure
BrowseFiles web form, FileManager web application, 131
Create method
Forum class, 466
News class, 238
Create Retrieve Update Delete functionality
see CRUD functionality.
creation date of item, displaying
FileManager web application, 96
CreationTime property
DirectoryInfo class, 96
FileInfo class, 96
cross-browser compatibility
role editor, 196
server-side code, 196
cross-site scripting
forums, 446
problems with, 446
CRUD functionality
User class, data services tier, 156
CSS (cascading stylesheets)
code listing, 55
compared to XSLT, 50
display classes, 49, 54
home page, user interface, 68
navigation control, 53, 57
user interface, designing, 48, 55
Current property
HttpContext class, 349
CurrentPageIndex property
DataGrid control, 262
CustomValidator control
e-mail address, validating, 428

D

data binding
  role editor, 193
  user profile page, 190
data services tier, 29
  3-layer design of website, 11
  advantages, 29
  advertising on the web, 292, 297
    AdMaster class, 297
    Advertisement class, 298
    problems with two data stores, 292
  availability, 29
  base class for tier, 30, 34
  building, 29
  forums, 454, 463
  information aggregation, 298
  mailing lists, 402, 415
    ListDetails class, 402
    Lists class, 402
    NewsletterDetails class, 403
    Newsletters class, 403
    SubscriptionDetails class, 403
    Subscriptions class, 403
  maintainability, 30
  news management, 208, 226
    Categories class, 209
    CategoryDetails class, 209
    News class, 210, 226
    NewsDetails class, 210
    UML diagram, 208
  online polls, 328, 344
    OptionDetails class, 329
    Options class, 329
    QuestionDetails class, 328
    Questions class, 329
    VoteDetails class, 330
    Votes class, 330
  performance, 30
  scalability, 29
  storing and retrieving settings, 215, 330, 394, 404
  synchronizing entries between database and XML file, 300
    updating XML file, 302
  user accounts, 145, 155
    AccountsTool class, 170
    Permission class, 166
    PermissionCategory class, 169
    Role class, 163
    User class, 156
      CRUD functionality, 156
data warehousing
  see warehousing data.
database deployment
  automated deployment, 511
  deploying website, 510
database design
  advertising on the web, 290
    AdsManager_Advertisements table, 294
    AdsManager_Clicks table, 295
    AdsManager_Companies table, 294
    AdsManager_Impressions table, 295
    stored procedures, 292, 295
  backup system, 28
  forums, 446, 458
    Forums_Categories table, 448
    Forums_Forums table, 448
    Forums_Members table, 451
    Forums_Replies table, 450
    Forums_Topics table, 449
    stored procedures, 452, 461

  hardware, 28
  linking table, 324
  mailing lists, 396, 411
    MLists_History table, 399
    MLists_Lists table, 396
    MLists_Subscriptions table, 398
    MLists_Users table, 397
    optional information, 398
    separating from user accounts database, 397
    stored procedures, 399, 411
  network topology, 28
  news management, 203, 218
    News_Categories table, 204
    News_News table, 205
    stored procedures, 206, 221
  online polls, 324, 337
    Polls_Options table, 325
    Polls_Questions table, 324
    Polls_Votes table, 325
    stored procedures, 326, 339
  permissions, 142
  relationships between database tables, 218, 338
  roles, 142
  scalability, 28
  security, 29
  Server Explorer, 337
  ThePhile.com, 29
  triggers, 221, 411, 414, 458
  user accounts, 142, 154
    separating from mailing list database, 397
    stored procedures, 144, 155
  users, 142
  views, 451, 458
  warehousing data, 291
  website design fundamentals, 28
database management, website, 75
  Enterprise Manager, 75
  T-SQL statements, 75
database views
  see views.
DataBind method
  DataGrid control, 250, 312
  DataList control, 192
  DropDownList control, 190, 194, 313, 314, 363
  Headlines control, 274
  Page class, 372
  Poll user control, 372
  Repeater control, 382
DataBinder class
  Eval method, 249
DataGrid control
  advertising admin page, 309, 310
  AllowCustomPaging property, 484
  AllowPaging property, 311
  BoundColumn, 249, 357
  ButtonColumn, 248, 259, 311, 355, 485
  categories and forums page, 473, 475
  categories manager page, 247
  compared to DataList control, 368
  CurrentPageIndex property, 262
  DataBind method, 250, 312
  DataKeyField property, 247
  DataKeys property, 253, 488
  DataSource property, 250, 312, 358, 476
  EditCommandColumn, 248, 355
  EditItemIndex property, 252, 253, 359
  Forum page, 483
  Headlines control, 273
  HyperLink control, 486

DataGrid control (continued)
HyperlinkColumn, 249, 357, 485
ItemCommand event, 311
LinkButton web control, 485
managing newsletters archive, 433
news manager page, 256
news ticker web service client, 280
option manager page, 363
PageIndexChanged event, 311
PagerStyle, 311
Poll web service client, 386
question manager page, 355
showing abstracts page, 269
TemplateColumn, 249, 257, 357, 476, 485, 491
    CheckBox control, using, 258
Topic page, 491
DataGridComandEventArgs
CommandName property, 311
DataGridItem class
FindControl method, 252
DataKeyField property
DataGrid control, 247
DataKeys property
DataGrid control, 253, 488
DataList control
categories and forums page, 473
compared to DataGrid control, 368
DataBind method, 192
DataSource property, 192
HeaderTemplate, 474
ItemTemplate, 268, 368, 474, 477
Poll user control, 368, 372
RepeatColumns property, 368
showing categories page, 267
templates supported by, 368
DataSet class
Relations collection, 38
DataSource property
DataGrid control, 250, 312, 358, 476
DataList control, 192
DropDownList control, 260
Repeater control, 382
DataTextField property
RadioButtonList web control, 368
DataValueField property
RadioButtonList web control, 368
DataView class
RowFilter property, 261
Sort property, 358
DbObject base class, 34
AdMaster class, 297
BuildIntCommand procedure, 35
BuildQueryCommand procedure, 36
News class, 226
Role class, 163
RunProcedure procedure, 36
    overloading RunProcedure, 37
User class, 156
Delete method
Forum class, 467
News class, 232, 238
deploying website, 14, 509
automated deployment, 511, 515
configuring IIS, 513
copying web project without source code, 512
database deployment, 510
designing deployment, 510

problems and solutions, 510, 515
shared hosting for website, 511, 514
XCopy deployment, 509, 511, 513
deployment requirements, website, 18, 20, 32
architectural requirements, 18
logical requirements, 18
physical requirements, 18
de-serialization
XML files, 151
development requirements, website, 18
Direction property
SqlParameter class, 230
directories, creating
client-side JavaScript, 105
FileManager web application, 105
directories, renaming
client-side JavaScript, 117
FileManager web application, 117
Directory class
does not have Copy method, 131
Move method, 131
System.IO namespace, 78
directory structure
see folder structure.
DirectoryInfo class
Attributes property, 92, 122
CreationTime property, 96
does not have Length property, 93
LastWriteTime property, 96
System.IO namespace, 78
discussion boards
see forums.
display classes
advantages of using, 55
CSS (cascading stylesheets), 49, 54
Display property
RequiredFieldValidator control, 247
<div> element
expanding or collapsing, 382
downloading files
see files, downloading.
DropDownList control
advert details page, 313
AutoPostBack property, 256, 362
DataBind method, 190, 194, 313, 314, 363
DataSource property, 260
new advert page, 314
news manager page, 255
news ticker web service client, 280
option manager page, 361, 362
SelectedIndexChanged event, 364
Duration parameter
OutputCache directive, 268, 382
dynamic output caching, ASP.NET, 268
problems with, 373

E

EditCommandColumn
DataGrid control, 248, 355
EditFile web form
code-behind for, 112
FileManager web application text file editor, 111
RequiredFieldValidator control, 112
EditItemIndex property
DataGrid control, 252, 253, 359

e-mail address, validating
 CustomValidator control, 428
 problems with, 428
 regular expressions, 426
 RegularExpressionValidator control, 426
e-mail newsletter
 see newsletter.
Enterprise Manager
 website database management, 75
Error event
 Page class, 65
error handling
 see exception handling.
escape characters
 see character escapes.
Eval method
 DataBinder class, 249
event handlers
 PhilePage class, 65
 testing, 67
exception handling
 AppException base class, 39, 54
 problems with, 39
 testing, 67
 user interface, designing, 54, 65
 website design fundamentals, 32
ExecuteNonQuery method
 SqlCommand class, 36
ExecuteReader method
 SqlCommand class, 35
extending website, 11, 13
Extensible Stylesheet Language Transformations
 see XSLT.

F

fault tolerance
 website design fundamentals, 32
File class
 Copy method, 131
 Move method, 131
 SetAttributes method, 125
file management, website, 74
 FTP, 74
 online file manager, 75
  designing, 75
  FileManager web application
   Integrated Windows Security, 133
File System view
 Setup Wizard, 518
FileInfo class
 Attributes property, 92, 122
 CreationTime property, 96
 LastWriteTime property, 96
 Length property, 93
 System.IO namespace, 78
FileManager web application
 directories, creating, 105
  client-side JavaScript, 105
 directories, renaming, 117
  client-side JavaScript, 117
 files, copying or moving, 129
  client-side JavaScript, 129
 files, deleting, 125
  client-side JavaScript, 125
 files, downloading, 99
 files, renaming, 117

 client-side JavaScript, 117
 files, uploading, 102
 Footer control, 79
 Header control, 79
 Integrated Windows Security, 133, 135
 Main Page, 80
  displaying additional attributes, 87
  listing folder contents, 82
  modifying attributes, 122
 text file editor, 111
 text files, creating, 109
  client-side JavaScript, 109
 text files, editing, 115
files, copying or moving
 client-side JavaScript, 129
 FileManager web application, 129
files, deleting
 client-side JavaScript, 125
 FileManager web application, 125
files, downloading
 FileManager web application, 99
 streams, using, 100
files, renaming
 client-side JavaScript, 117
 FileManager web application, 117
files, uploading
 FileManager web application, 102
FileStream class
 System.IO namespace, 78
FileSystemWatcher class
 System.IO namespace, 78
FillFoldersAndFilesTable procedure
 BrowseFiles web form, FileManager web application
  deleting files, 126
  displaying additional attributes, 87
  downloading files, 100
  editing text files, 115
  listing folder contents, 84
  modifying attributes, 123
  renaming files and directories, 118
FindControl method
 DataGridItem class, 252
flexibility, website design, 20
 user interface, 46
folder contents, listing
 FileManager web application, 82
folder structure
 namespace hierarchy and, 27
 website design fundamentals, 27
folders
 compared to namespaces, 23
Footer control
 AdminFooter control, 241, 352
 categories and forums page, 481
 compared to Header control, 53
 FileManager web application, 79
 SiteFooter control, 65
 user interface, designing, 53
foreign keys
 primary keys and, 219
 triggers, 221
Form Wizard
 creating subscription form, 434
 mailing list administration, 410, 434
FormatSize procedure
 BrowseFiles web form, FileManager web application, 94
<forms> element
 Web.Config file, 188

FormsAuthentication class
SetAuthCookie method, 187
Forms-based authentication, 77
configuring, 188
cookies, 141
description, 142
reasons for using, 141
user identity, 141
Forum class
AddTopic method, 467
business services tier, 455, 464
constructors, 465
Create method, 466
Delete method, 467
GetTopics method, 467
handling child topics, 467
handling variables, 465
LoadFromID method, 465
modifying forum records, 466
ResetProperties method, 465
Update method, 467
Forum menu
categories and forums page, 473
Forum page
BindGrid method, 487
code-behind page, 486
custom pagination, 486
DataGrid control, 483
deleting topics, 488
GetAuthorText method, 488
user interface, 483
forums, 11, 14, 445
business services tier, 455
Forum class, 455, 464
Helper class, 456, 468
compared to online polls, 445
cross-site scripting, 446
data services tier, 454, 463
database design, 446, 458
Forums_Categories table, 448
Forums_Forums table, 448
Forums_Members table, 451
Forums_Replies table, 450
Forums_Topics table, 449
stored procedures, 452, 461
triggers, 458
views, 451, 458
designing, 446
handling child topics, 467
modifying forum records, 466
module configuration, 454, 463
ModuleConfig class, 454
ModuleSettings class, 454
settings file, 464
permissions, 456, 471
posting to, 446
user profiles, 446
problems and solutions, 445, 457
security, 479, 481
ThePhile.com, 445
threaded discussions, 450
user interface, 456, 471
categories and forums page, 471
Header control, 481
Forum page, 483
MyProfile page, 503
PostMessage page, 496
Topic page, 489

forums and categories page
see categories and forums page.
front-end
see user interface.
FTP
compared to online file manager, 75
website file management, 74

G

GetAttributesDescription procedure
BrowseFiles web form, FileManager web application, 92
GetAuthorText method
Forum page, 488
GetCategories method
Category class, 239
GetCurrent method
Question class, 347
GetDetails method
News class, 228
GetDetailsRow method
News class, 229
GetDirectorySize procedure
BrowseFiles web form, FileManager web application, 93
GetForumsSource method
categories and forums page, 478
GetHeadlines method
Category class, 240
News class, 227
GetImage method
categories manager page, 251
GetNews method
Category class, 239
News class, 227
GetOptions method
Question class, 346
GetTopics method
Forum class, 467

H

hacking, preventing
categories and forums page, 479, 481
checking permissions, 479, 481
hardware, database design, 28
Header control
AdminHeader control, 241, 352
advertising, 53
branding, 53
categories and forums page, 481
code-behind page, 481
HyperLink control, 481
Label control, 481
compared to Footer control, 53
FileManager web application, 79
SiteHeader control, 63
user interface, designing, 53
HeaderTemplate
DataList control, 474
HTML controls, using in ASP.NET
runat="server" attribute, 474
Headlines control
DataBind method, 274
DataGrid control, 273

Headlines control (continued)
news management, 216, 272
plug-in headlines, 216
testing, 274
Headlines web service
news management, 216, 277
news ticker web service client, 280
testing, 278
WebService class, 278
Helper class
business services tier, 409, 423, 456, 468
processing text into HTML format, 468
ProcessSpecialTags method, 456, 496
hits
advertising on the web, 288
definition, 288
economics of, 288
home page, user interface, 68
CSS (cascading stylesheets), 68
navigation control, 69
Register directive, 68
SiteHeader control, 69
HTML controls, using in ASP.NET
runat="server" attribute, 102, 474
HttpApplication class
AuthenticateRequest event, 188
HttpContext class
Current property, 349
Request property, 349
System.Web namespace, 150, 349
User property, 150, 185, 188-190, 264, 276, 442
HttpRequest class
Cookies collection, 350
QueryString property, 492
System.Web namespace, 349
UrlReferrer property, 499
UserHostAddress property, 349
<httpRuntime> element
maxRequestLength attribute, 104
Web.Config file, 104
Hungarian notation, avoiding, 23
HyperLink control
DataGrid control, 486
Header control
categories and forums page, 481
NavigateUrl property, 259
TemplateColumn, 476, 492
Text property, 259
HyperlinkColumn
DataGrid control, 249, 357, 485

I

icon for item, displaying
FileManager web application, 88
identifying users
see user identity.
identity object
.NET Framework security, 150
Identity property
IPrincipal interface, 150, 171
SitePrincipal class, 150
IgnoreCase value
RegexOptions enumeration, 470

IIdentity interface
IsAuthenticated property, 175
SiteIdentity class, 150, 174
System.Security.Principal namespace, 150, 174
IIS
configuring for website deployment, 513
Integrated Windows Security, 134
Virtual Directory Creation Wizard, 513
Image web control
ImageUrl property, 88
ItemTemplate, 475
ImageUrl property
Image web control, 88
<img> tag
src attribute, 59, 89
implementation
online file manager, design issues, 76
impressions
advertising on the web, 287
definition, 287
economics of, 288
include files
see server-side include files.
IndexOf method
Array class, 90
information aggregation, 298
Advertisement class, 298
information hiding
see information aggregation.
Insert method
Cache class, 375
installers
automated deployment, 515
Integrated Windows Security
see also Windows authentication.
FileManager web application, 133, 135
IIS, 134
Internet Explorer, 135
Web.Config file, 136
Internet Explorer
Integrated Windows Security, 135
Internet Information Server
see IIS.
intranet websites, 18
IP locking
preventing or allowing multiple voting, 323
IPrincipal interface
Identity property, 150, 171
SitePrincipal class, 150, 171, 442
System.Security.Principal namespace, 150, 171
IsAuthenticated property
IIdentity interface, 175
IsPostBack property
Page class, 250, 362
item attributes, displaying
FileManager web application, 91
ItemCommand event
DataGrid control, 311
ItemTemplate
DataList control, 268, 368, 474, 477
Image web control, 475
LinkButton web control, 475
Repeater control, 382

J

JavaScript functions
__doPostBack function, 106, 109, 472
categories and forums page, 471
expanding or collapsing <div> element, 382
PostMessage page, 497
prompt function, 105, 109

L

Label control
Header control
categories and forums page, 481
Poll web service client, 386
subscription form, 440
Text property, 198, 254, 437
LastWriteTime property
DirectoryInfo class, 96
FileInfo class, 96
Length property
FileInfo class, 93
LinkButton web control
CausesValidation property, 361
CommandName property, 485
DataGrid control, 485
ItemTemplate, 475
question manager page, 361
linking table
advantages and disadvantages, 324
List class
business services tier, 405
ListBox control
SelectedIndexChanged event, 196
ListDetails class
data services tier, 402
Lists class
data services tier, 402
LoadFromID method
Forum class, 465
News class, 237
location attribute
<soap:address> element, 389
LogEvent method
AppException base class, 40
logical requirements, website, 18
Login page
Page_Load event, 186
user interface, 186

M

mailing lists, 393
administration, 410, 425
Form Wizard, 410, 434
settings, modifying, 433
settings, storing and retrieving, 433
advertisement spots, 394
business services tier, 405, 415
Helper class, 409, 423
List class, 405
modifying settings, 409
Newsletter class, 408, 419
separation, 405
Subscription class, 407, 415

content issues, 393
targeted content, 394
data services tier, 402, 415
ListDetails class, 402
Lists class, 402
NewsletterDetails class, 403
Newsletters class, 403
storing and retrieving settings, 404
SubscriptionDetails class, 403
Subscriptions class, 403
database design, 396, 411
MLists_History table, 399
MLists_Lists table, 396
MLists_Subscriptions table, 398
MLists_Users table, 397
optional information, 398
separating from user accounts database, 397
stored procedures, 399, 411
triggers, 411, 414
designing mailing list system, 396
module configuration, 415
newsletter and, 393
personalizing messages, 394
problems and solutions, 393, 395, 411
security, 411, 441
subscribing to mailing list, 438
confirmation of subscription, 439
ThePhile.com, 394
user interface, 410, 425
managing newsletters archive, 432
sending newsletters to subscribers, 429
MailMessage class
Attachments collection, 420
System.Web.Mail namespace, 420
Main Page, FileManager web application, 80
BrowseFiles web form, 81
displaying additional attributes, 87
displaying item attributes, 91
displaying item creation & modification dates, 96
displaying item icon, 88
displaying item size, 93
listing folder contents, 82
modifying attributes, 122
client-side JavaScript, 122
maintainability
business services tier, 30
data services tier, 30
user interface, 46
maintaining website, 11, 13, 73
database management, 75
file management, 74
FTP, 74
online file manager, 75
designing, 75
security, 133
problems and solutions, 74, 77
using shared hosting, 74
MapPath method
Server object, 61
maxRequestLength attribute
<httpRuntime> element, 104
MemoryStream class
System.IO namespace, 78
Merge Module project
automated deployment, 516
messages, personalizing
newsletter, 394
Microsoft Solutions Framework
user interface, designing, 47

modification date of item, displaying
FileManager web application, 96
modifying settings online
Button web control, 364
CheckBox control, 364
code-behind page, 366
CompareValidator control, 365
online poll administration, 364
TextBox control, 364
modular design of websites, 9, 11, 13
module configuration for advertising, 293, 315
module configuration for forums, 463
ModuleConfig class, 454
ModuleSettings class, 454
settings file, 464
module configuration for mailing lists, 415
module configuration for news management, 232
ModuleConfig class, 233
ModuleSettings class, 232
settings file, 235
module configuration for online polls, 344
ModuleConfig class, 345
ModuleSettings class, 344
settings file, 345
module configuration for user identity, 151
ModuleConfig class, 152, 183
ModuleSettings class, 152, 183
Web.Config file, 151
ModuleConfig class
implementing ModuleConfig, 183
module configuration for forums, 454
module configuration for news system, 233
module configuration for online polls, 345
module configuration for user identity, 152
ModuleSettings class
implementing ModuleSettings, 183
module configuration for forums, 454
module configuration for news system, 232
module configuration for online polls, 344
module configuration for user identity, 152
Move method
Directory class, 131
File class, 131
MSF
see Microsoft Solutions Framework.
multiple voting
preventing or allowing, 320
AllowVote property, Question class, 348
cookies, 322
IP locking, 323
MyProfile page
code-behind page, 503
TextBox control, 503
user interface, 503
user profiles, 503

N

namespace attribute
Register directive, 68
namespace hierarchy
designing, 23
advantages of good design, 26
folder structure and, 27
ThePhile.com, 24

namespaces
compared to folders, 23
naming and coding conventions, 21
camel casing, 21
code reviews, 21
Hungarian notation, avoiding, 23
Pascal casing, 21
underscore character, avoiding, 22
NavigateUrl property
HyperLink control, 259
navigation control
creating, 58
CSS (cascading stylesheets), 53, 57
home page, user interface, 69
re-usability, 51
user interface, designing, 51, 58
XML files, 52, 58
converting XML into HTML, 59
XSLT, 59, 69
NET Framework
see .NET Framework.
network topology, database design, 28
new advert page
administration, 314
DropDownList control, 314
News class
Add method, 230
business services tier, 214, 235
constructors, 236
Create method, 238
data services tier, 210, 226
DbObject base class, 226
Delete method, 232, 238
GetDetails method, 228
GetDetailsRow method, 229
GetHeadlines method, 227
GetNews method, 227
LoadFromID method, 237
ResetProperties method, 237
SetApproved method, 231
Update method, 230, 238
using System.Data namespace, 226
using System.Data.SqlClient namespace, 226
news management, 13, 201
AdminFooter control, 243
AdminHeader control, 242
administration, 240
settings, modifying, 265
business services tier, 211, 235
Category class, 211, 239
News class, 214, 235
UML diagram, 211
data services tier, 208, 226
Categories class, 209
CategoryDetails class, 209
News class, 210, 226
NewsDetails class, 210
storing and retrieving settings, 215
UML diagram, 208
database design, 203, 218
News_Categories table, 204
News_News table, 205
relationships between database tables, 218
stored procedures, 206, 221
triggers, 221
designing news management tool, 202
required features, 203

news management, (continued)
  module configuration, 232
    ModuleConfig class, 233
    ModuleSettings class, 232
    settings file, 235
  news submitted by users, 271
  permissions, 217, 276
  problems and solutions, 201, 218
  security, 217, 275
  showing news to users, 267
  ThePhile.com, 202
  user interface, 216, 240
    categories manager page, 244, 245
    Headlines control, 216, 272
    Headlines web service, 216, 277
    news manager page, 254, 255
    showing abstracts page, 269
    showing categories page, 267
    showing news item page, 270
news manager page
  adding news items, 263
  BindGrid method, 260
  code-behind file, 259
  DataGrid control, 256
  DropDownList control, 255
  RadioButton web control, 260
  user interface, 254, 255
news ticker web service client
  Add Web Reference option, 280
  Button web control, 280
  DataGrid control, 280
  DropDownList control, 280
  Headlines web service, 280
  Timer control, 280
  Windows Forms applications, 280
NewsDetails class
  data services tier, 210
newsletter, 13, 14
  advertisement spots, 394
  mailing list and, 393
  managing newsletters archive, 432
    DataGrid control, 433
  personalizing messages, 394
  sending newsletters to subscribers, 429
    using dedicated mailing server, 431
  spam, avoiding, 394
  targeted content, 394
Newsletter class
  business services tier, 408, 419
  Send method, 420
  using System.Web.Mail namespace, 419
NewsletterDetails class
  data services tier, 403
Newsletters class
  data services tier, 403

O

OnInit method
  Page class, 58
    overriding in PhilePage class, 58, 65
online administration
  modifying settings online, 364
online communities
  see also community building for website.
  forums, 11, 445
  online polls, 11

online file manager
  compared to FTP, 75
  designing, 75
    implementation design, 76
    security design, 77
  FileManager web application
    Integrated Windows Security, 133
  website file management, 75
online news management
  see news management.
online polls, 11, 14, 319
  AdminFooter control, 352
  AdminHeader control, 352
  administration, 351
    option manager page, 361
    question manager page, 352
    settings, modifying, 364
  business services tier, 331, 346
    Option class, 333
    Question class, 331, 346
  compared to forums, 445
  data services tier, 328, 344
    OptionDetails class, 329
    Options class, 329
    QuestionDetails class, 328
    Questions class, 329
    settings, storing and retrieving, 330
    VoteDetails class, 330
    Votes class, 330
  database design, 324, 337
    linking table, 324
    Polls_Options table, 325
    Polls_Questions table, 324
    Polls_Votes table, 325
    relationships between database tables, 338
    stored procedures, 326, 339
  designing, 321
  module configuration, 344
    ModuleConfig class, 345
    ModuleSettings class, 344
    settings file, 345
  problems and solutions, 319, 337
  requirements, 321
  security, 337, 384
  ThePhile.com, 320
  user interface, 334, 351
    Poll user control, 334, 367
    Poll web service, 336, 385
    show archived polls page, 381
  voting, 320
    preventing or allowing multiple voting, 320, 322
Option class
  business services tier, 333
option manager page
  administration, 361
  code-behind page, 363
  DataGrid control, 363
  DropDownList control, 361, 362
  options for questions, 361
OptionDetails class
  data services tier, 329
Options class
  data services tier, 329
options for questions, 325, 329
  child options, managing, 346
  option manager page, 361
Oracle
  database deployment, 510

Output value
ParameterDirection enumeration, 230
OutputCache directive
Duration parameter, 268, 382
VaryByParam parameter, 268, 269

P

page base class
see PhilePage class.
Page class
DataBind method, 372
deriving PhilePage class from, 51
Error event, 65
IsPostBack property, 250, 362
OnInit method, 58
System.Web.UI namespace, 51
PageIndexChanged event
DataGrid control, 311
PagerStyle
DataGrid control, 311
Parameter object
see SqlParameter class.
ParameterDirection enumeration
Output value, 230
System.Data namespace, 230
Pascal casing convention, 21
Passport authentication, 77
pass-through page
advertising on the web, 293, 307
Path class
System.IO namespace, 78
performance
data services tier, 30
news management stored procedures, 207
user interface, 46
Permission class
data services tier, 166
PermissionCategory class
data services tier, 169
permissions
checking
preventing hacking, 479, 481
database design, 142
forums, 456, 471
news management, 217, 276
personalizing messages
see messages, personalizing.
PhilePage class
creating, 57
Visual Studio .NET, 57
deriving from System.Web.UI.Page, 51
event handlers, 65
modifying to support authentication, 188
OnInit method, 58, 65
user interface, 51, 57
physical requirements, website, 18
plug-in headlines
Headlines control, 216
Poll user control
caching, 373
code-behind page, 369
DataBind method, 372
DataList control, 368, 372
design options, 334
handling Postback event, 372

online polls, 334, 367
optimizing control, 373
question manager page and, 377
RadioButtonList web control, 334, 368, 372
hiding radio buttons, 334
style properties, 370
TableCell class, 368
testing, 377
Poll web service
online polls, 336, 385
Poll web service client, 386
SOAP protocol and, 385
testing, 385
WebMethod attribute, 385
Poll web service client
Add Web Reference option, 386
Button web control, 386
DataGrid control, 386
Label control, 386
Poll web service, 386
Timer control, 386
web service client properties, 388
Windows Forms applications, 386
polls
see online polls.
PostMessage page
code-behind page, 498
JavaScript functions, 497
TextBox control, 498
user interface, 496
pre-populated web form
advert details page, 312
presentation tier
see user interface.
primary keys
foreign keys and, 219
principal object
.NET Framework security, 150
Process class
System.Diagnostics namespace, 282
ProcessSpecialTags method
Helper class, 456, 496
ProcessTags method
Topic page, 496
programming language selection, 27
porting from C# to Visual Basic .NET, 27
using several .NET languages, 27
prompt function
directories, creating, 105
text files, creating, 109
public key
SNK file, 33

Q

quantifiers
regular expressions, 427
QueryString property
HttpRequest class, 492
Question class
AllowVote property, 348
business services tier, 331, 346
child options, managing, 346
GetCurrent method, 347
GetOptions method, 346
Vote method, 350

question manager page
adding question, 360
AdminFooter control, 357
AdminHeader control, 353
administration, 352
BindGrid method, 358
CheckBox control, 353
code-behind page, 357
DataGrid control, 355
deleting question, 360
editing questions, 359
LinkButton web control, 361
Poll user control and, 377
RadioButton web control, 353
sorting questions, 358
TextBox control, 353
updating questions, 359
QuestionDetails class
data services tier, 328
Questions class
data services tier, 329

R

RadioButton web control
AutoPostBack property, 256
Checked property, 357
news manager page, 260
question manager page, 353
TemplateColumn, 357
RadioButtonList web control
DataTextField property, 368
DataValueField property, 368
Poll user control, 334, 368, 372
hiding radio buttons, 334
Regex class
Replace method, 470
System.Text.RegularExpressions namespace, 470
RegexOptions enumeration
IgnoreCase value, 470
System.Text.RegularExpressions namespace, 470
Register directive
Assembly attribute, 68
home page, user interface, 68
namespace attribute, 68
src attribute, 68
TagName attribute, 68
TagPrefix attribute, 68
regular expressions
character classes, 427
character escapes, 426
description, 426
e-mail address, validating, 426
processing text into HTML format, 470
quantifiers, 427
string validation, 471
syntax, 426
System.Text.RegularExpressions namespace, 468
RegularExpressionValidator control
e-mail address, validating, 426
Relations collection
DataSet class, 38
relationships between database tables
news management, 218

online polls, 338
Remove method
Cache class, 376
Rename procedure
BrowseFiles web form, FileManager web application, 121
renaming files and directories
client-side JavaScript, 117
FileManager web application, 117
Render method
Control class, 61
RepeatColumns property
DataList control, 368
Repeater control
DataBind method, 382
DataSource property, 382
ItemTemplate, 382
nested Repeateer controls, 382
show archived polls page, 382
Replace method
Regex class, 470
String class, 470
Request object
see HttpRequest class.
Request property
HttpContext class, 349
RequiredFieldValidator control
categories manager page, 247
ControlToValidate property, 247
Display property, 247
EditFile web form, 112
requirements list, website design, 20
deployment, 20
flexibility, 20
re-usability, 20
scalability, 20
separation, 20
testing, 20
ResetProperties method
Forum class, 465
News class, 237
re-usability, website design, 20
navigation control, 51
Role class
business services tier, 148, 179
data services tier, 163
DbObject base class, 163
role editor
cross-browser compatibility, 196
data binding, 193
membership of roles, 197
Page_Load event, 192, 194
server-side code, 196
user account administration, 191
roles
advantages of using, 148
database design, 142
definition, 148
membership of roles, 197
RowFilter property
DataView class, 261
runat="server" attribute
HTML controls, using in ASP.NET, 102, 474
RunProcedure procedure
DbObject base class, 36
overloading RunProcedure, 37

S

sample mockup of website
  user interface, deigning, 47
scalability
  data services tier, 29
  database design, 28
  website design, 20
ScriptTimeout property
  Server object, 431
security
  .NET Framework, 150
    identity object, 150
    principal object, 150
  authentication, 77
    Forms-based authentication, 77
    Passport authentication, 77
    Windows authentication, 77
  database design, 29
  FileManager web application, 133
  forums, 479, 481
  mailing lists, 411, 441
  news management, 217, 275
  online file manager, design issues, 77
  online polls, 337, 384
select attribute
  <xsl:value-of> element, 59
SelectedIndexChanged event
  DropDownList control, 364
  ListBox control, 196
Send method
  Newsletter class, 420
  SmtpMail class, 419
separation
  business services tier, 31
    mailing lists, 405
  website design, 20
serialization
  XML files, 151
server controls
  inherit from Control class, 61
  navigation control, 58
Server Explorer
  database design, 337
  Visual Studio .NET, 337
Server object
  MapPath method, 61
  ScriptTimeout property, 431
server-side code
  compared to client-side code, 196
  cross-browser compatibility, 196
  role editor, 196
server-side include files
  problems with, 51
SetApproved method
  News class, 231
SetAttributes method
  File class, 125
SetAuthCookie method
  FormsAuthentication class, 187
settings file
  module configuration for forums, 464
  module configuration for news system, 235
  module configuration for online polls, 345
settings, modifying
  business services tier
    mailing lists, 409
  mailing list administration, 433

  news management administration, 265
    code-behind file, 266
    CompareValidator control, 265
  online poll administration, 364
    modifying settings online, 364
settings, storing and retrieving
  data services tier
    mailing lists, 404
    news management, 215
    online polls, 330
  mailing list administration, 433
Setup project
  automated deployment, 516
Setup Wizard
  automated deployment, 516
  choose project type dialog, 516
  File System view, 518
  modifying deployment project, 518
shared hosting for website, 74
  choosing hosting company, 515
  deploying website, 511, 514
  XCopy deployment, 511, 514
show archived polls page
  code-behing page, 383
  Repeater control, 382
  user interface, 381
showing abstracts page
  DataGrid control, 269
  user interface, 269
showing categories page
  DataList control, 267
  user interface, 267
showing news item page
  user interface, 270
site
  see website.
SiteFooter control
  AdRotator control, 308
  modifying for advertising, 308
  user interface, 65
SiteHeader control
  authentication, 64
  building, 63
  code-behind class, 64
  home page, user interface, 69
  modifying to support authentication, 185
  user interface, 63
SiteIdentity class
  business services tier, 174
  IIdentity interface, 150, 174
  table of members, 150
SitePrincipal class
  business services tier, 171
  Identity property, 150
  IPrincipal interface, 150, 171, 442
  table of members, 150
size of item, displaying
  FileManager web application, 93
SmtpMail class
  Send method, 419
  SmtpServer property, 419
  System.Web.Mail namespace, 419
  using with CDO, 419
SmtpServer property
  SmtpMail class, 419
SNK file
  public key, 33
  strong-naming, 33

SOAP protocol
  Poll web service and, 385
<soap:address> element
  location attribute, 389
Sort property
  DataView class, 358
spam, avoiding
  mailing lists, 394
SQL Server
  database deployment, 510
SqlCommand class
  ExecuteNonQuery method, 36
  ExecuteReader method, 35
SqlParameter class
  Direction property, 230
  System.Data.SqlClient namespace, 227
src attribute
  <img> tag, 59, 89
  Register directive, 68
stored procedures
  advertising on the web, 292, 295
    creating advertisements, 295
    obtaining advert list, 295
    obtaining campaign reports, 296
  aliases for table names, 155
  forums, 452, 461
    GetTopicsByPage procedure, 461
    managing categories, 452
    managing forums, 452
    managing members, 453
    managing replies, 453
    managing topics, 452
  mailing lists, 399, 411
    deleting subscriptions, 414
    inserting subscriptions, 413
    retrieving subscriptions, 411
    retrieving subscriptions by ID, 412
  news management, 206, 221
    adding news, 223
    approving news, 225
    deleting news, 225
    performance issues, 207
    returning headlines, 223
    returning news details, 222
    returning news items, 221
    updating news, 224
  online polls, 326, 339
    adding new question, 341
    assigning current question, 341
    returning current question, 340
    returning options for question, 343
    returning questions, 340
    updating question, 342
  transactions, 224
  user accounts, 144, 155
  views and, 461
Stream class
  System.IO namespace, 78
StreamReader class
  System.IO namespace, 78
streams, using
  files, downloading, 100
StreamWriter class
  System.IO namespace, 78
String class
  Replace method, 470
string validation
  regular expressions, 471

strong-naming
  SNK file, 33
style properties
  Poll user control, 370
stylesheets
  CSS (cascading stylesheets), 48
    display classes, 49, 54
    navigation control, 53, 57
  XSLT, 50
Subscribe method
  Subscription class, 416
Subscription class
  business services tier, 407, 415
  Subscribe method, 416
  Unsubscribe method, 417
  using System.Web.Mail namespace, 416
subscription form
  code-behind page, 440
  creating subscription form, 434
  Label control, 440
  subscribing to mailing list, 438
    confirmation of subscription, 439
SubscriptionDetails class
  data services tier, 403
Subscriptions class
  data services tier, 403
System namespace
  ApplicationException class, 39
System.Data namespace
  ParameterDirection enumeration, 230
  using in News class, 226
System.Data.SqlClient namespace
  SqlParameter class, 227
  using in News class, 226
System.Diagnostics namespace
  Process class, 282
System.IO namespace, 78
  BinaryReader class, 78
  BinaryWriter class, 78
  Directory class, 78
  DirectoryInfo class, 78
  FileInfo class, 78
  FileStream class, 78
  FileSystemWatcher class, 78
  MemoryStream class, 78
  Path class, 78
  Stream class, 78
  StreamReader class, 78
  StreamWriter class, 78
  TextReader class, 78
  TextWriter class, 78
System.Security.Principal namespace
  IIdentity interface, 150, 174
  IPrincipal interface, 150, 171
System.Text.RegularExpressions namespace, 468
  Regex class, 470
  RegexOptions enumeration, 470
System.Web namespace
  HttpContext class, 150, 349
  HttpRequest class, 349
System.Web.Mail namespace
  MailMessage class, 420
  SmtpMail class, 419
  using in Newsletter class, 419
  using in Subscription class, 416
System.Web.Services namespace
  WebService class, 278

System.Web.UI namespace
Control class, 61
Page class, 51
System.Xml.Xpath namespace
XPathDocument class, 61
System.Xml.Xsl namespace
XslTransform class, 62

T

TableCell class
Poll user control, 368
Text property, 368
TagName attribute
Register directive, 68
TagPrefix attribute
Register directive, 68
targeted content
mailing lists, 394
spam, avoiding, 394
TemplateColumn
CheckBox control, 258, 357
DataGrid control, 249, 257, 357, 476, 485, 491
HyperLink control, 476, 492
RadioButton web control, 357
testing, website design, 20
text file editor, FileManager web application, 111
EditFile web form, 111
text files, creating
client-side JavaScript, 109
FileManager web application, 109
text files, editing
FileManager web application, 115
Text property
HyperLink control, 259
Label control, 198, 254, 437
TableCell class, 368
TextBox control, 190, 252, 265, 437
TextBox control
modifying settings online, 364
MyProfile page, 503
PostMessage page, 498
question manager page, 353
Text property, 190, 252, 265, 437
TextReader class
System.IO namespace, 78
TextWriter class
System.IO namespace, 78
ThePhile.com
advertising on the web, 307
database design, 29
deploying website, 509, 515
forums, 445
introduction, 10
mailing lists, 394
namespace hierarchy, 24
news management, 202
online polls, 320
user identity, 139
user interface, 54
threaded discussions
advantages and disadvantages, 450
Timeout property
web service client properties, 388
Timer control
news ticker web service client, 280
Poll web service client, 386

ToBoolean method
Convert class, 259, 357
Topic page
BindGrid method, 494
BindTopicControls method, 495
code-behind page, 492
DataGrid control, 491
ProcessTags method, 496
user interface, 489
transactions
atomicity, 225
stored procedures, 224
Transform method
XslTransform class, 62
triggers
database design
forums, 458
mailing lists, 411, 414
news management, 221
foreign keys, 221
T-SQL statements
website database management, 75
Type property
CompareValidator control, 265

U

UML case diagram
authentication of users, 140
news management business layer, 211
news management data layer, 208
underscore character, avoiding, 22
Unified Process
user interface, designing, 47
Unubscribe method
Subscription class, 417
Update method
Forum class, 467
News class, 230, 238
uploading files
see files, uploading, 102
Url property
modifying, 389
web service client properties, 388
UrlReferrer property
HttpRequest class, 499
user accounts
administration, 153, 191
role editor, 191
business services tier, 147, 171
AccountsTool class, 182
Role class, 148, 179
SiteIdentity class, 174
SitePrincipal class, 171
User class, 147, 176
community building for website, 139
data services tier, 145, 155
AccountsTool class, 170
Permission class, 166
PermissionCategory class, 169
Role class, 163
User class, 156
database design, 142, 154
permissions, 142
roles, 142
separating from mailing list database, 397
stored procedures, 144, 155
users, 142

User class
  business services tier, 147, 176
  data services tier, 156
    CRUD functionality, 156
  DbObject base class, 156
user controls
  Footer control, 79
    AdminFooter control, 241, 352
    categories and forums page, 481
    SiteFooter control, 65
  Header control, 79
    AdminHeader control, 241, 352
    categories and forums page, 481
    SiteHeader control, 63
  Headlines control, 216, 272
  Poll user control, 334, 367
user identity
  anonymous users, 140
  authentication, 139
    .NET Framework, 149
    extending .NET Framework, 150
    Forms-based authentication, 141
    UML case diagram, 140
    user interface, modifying, 185
  community building for website, 139
  cookies, 140
  membership of roles, 197
  module configuration, 151
    ModuleConfig class, 152, 183
    ModuleSettings class, 152, 183
  problems and solutions, 139, 153
  ThePhile.com, 139
  user accounts, 139
    administration, 153, 191
    business services tier, 147, 171
    data services tier, 145, 155
    database design, 142, 154
user interface, 31, 45
  3-layer design of website, 11
  AdRotator control, 293
  advertising on the web, 293, 307
  categories and forums page, 471
    Header control, 481
  categories manager page, 244, 245
  designing, 47
    CSS, 48, 55
    exception handling, 54, 65
    Footer control, 53
    Header control, 53
    Microsoft Solutions Framework, 47
    navigation control, 51, 58
    sample mockup of website, 47
    Unified Process, 47
    XSLT, 50
  flexibility, 46
  Forum page, 483
  forums, 456, 471
  Headlines control, 216, 272
  Headlines web service, 216, 277
  home page, 68
  Login page, 186
  mailing lists, 410, 425
  maintainability, 46
  managing newsletters archive, 432
    DataGrid control, 433
  modifying to support authentication, 185
  MyProfile page, 503
  news management, 216, 240
  news manager page, 254, 255
  online polls, 334, 351

  pass-through page, 293, 307
  performance, 46
  PhilePage class, 51, 57
    modifying to support authentication, 188
  Poll user control, 334, 367
  Poll web service, 336, 385
  PostMessage page, 496
  problems and solutions, 46, 54
  sending newsletters to subscribers, 429
    using dedicated mailing server, 431
  show archived polls page, 381
  showing abstracts page, 269
  showing categories page, 267
  showing news item page, 270
  SiteFooter control, 65
    modifying for advertising, 308
  SiteHeader control, 63
    modifying to support authentication, 185
  ThePhile.com, 54
  Topic page, 489
  user profile page, 189
  website design fundamentals, 13, 19, 33
user profile page
  data binding, 190
  Page_Load event, 190
  user interface, 189
user profiles
  forums, posting to, 446
  MyProfile page, 503
User property
  HttpContext class, 150, 185-190, 264, 276, 442
user-friendliness
  community building for website, 140
UserHostAddress property
  HttpRequest class, 349
users
  categories and forums page, 473
  database design, 142
  deleting all record of, 458
  frequent visits, 12, 14
  news submitted by users, 271
  posting messages to forums, 496
  showing news to users, 267
  subscribing to mailing list, 438
    confirmation of subscription, 439
using keyword, 226

V

VaryByParam parameter
  OutputCache directive, 268, 269
views
  forums, 451, 458
    v_Forums_Forums view, 458
    v_Forums_Members view, 459
    v_Forums_Replies view, 460
    v_Forums_Topics view, 460
  stored procedures and, 461
Virtual Directory Creation Wizard, IIS, 513
vision statement
  website design fundamentals, 19
Visual Studio .NET
  automated deployment, 511, 515
  copying web project without source code, 512
  deploying website, 14
  PhilePage class, creating, 57
  Server Explorer, 337
  web services, 217

Vote method
Question class, 350
VoteDetails class
data services tier, 330
Votes class
data services tier, 330
voting
online polls, 320
options for questions, 325, 329
child options, managing, 346
option manager page, 361
preventing or allowing multiple voting, 320
cookies, 322
IP locking, 323
question manager page, 352

W

warehousing data
advertising on the web, 291
Web Service Description Language file
see WSDL file.
web services
client properties, 388
Timeout property, 388
Url property, 388
Headlines web service, 216, 277
Poll web service, 336, 385
WSDL file, 389
Web Setup project
automated deployment, 516
Web.Config file
<appSettings> element, 152
<authentication> element, 188
<forms> element, 188
<httpRuntime> element, 104
Integrated Windows Security, 136
module configuration for user identity, 151
WebMethod attribute
Poll web service, 385
WebService class
Headlines web service, 278
System.Web.Services namespace, 278
website design fundamentals, 17
business services tier, 30
controls, 11
data services tier, 29
database design, 28
deployment requirements, 18, 32
design process, 20
development requirements, 18
exception handling, 32
folder structure, 27
modules, 11, 13
namespace hierarchy, 23
naming and coding conventions, 21
problems and solutions, 18, 33
programming language selection, 27
requirements list, 20
user interface, 13, 19, 31, 33
vision statement, 19
websites
3-layer design, 11
business services tier, 11
data services tier, 11
user interface, 11

administration, 13
advertising, 12, 14, 287
community building, 11, 14, 139
user identity, 139
content, 9, 12, 13, 201, 393
news management, 201
deploying website, 14, 509
design fundamentals, 17
designing, 10
extending website, 11, 13
forums, 11, 14, 445
further information, 521
intranet websites, 18
introduction, 9
mailing lists, 393
maintaining website, 11, 13, 73
modular design, 9, 11, 13
news management, 13
newsletter, 13, 14, 393
online communities, 11, 445
online polls, 11, 14, 319
problems and solutions, 9, 13
ThePhile.com, 10
user interface, 13, 45
using shared hosting, 74
well-formed XML
produced by XSLT, 60
whitespace
XSLT and, 63
Windows authentication, 77
see also Integrated Windows Security.
Windows Forms applications
news ticker web service client, 280
Poll web service client, 386
Windows security
see Integrated Windows Security.
WSDL file
web services, 389

X

XCopy deployment
advantages, 513
configuring IIS, 513
deploying website, 509, 511, 513
limitations, 513
shared hosting for website, 511, 514
XML files
AdRotator control, 289
synchronizing entries between database and XML file, 300
updating XML file, 302
compared to arrays, 116
converting XML into HTML, 52, 59
de-serialization, 151
navigation control, 52, 58
serialization, 151
well-formed XML, 60
XPath
updating XML file, 302
using with XSLT, 59
XPathDocument class
System.Xml.Xpath namespace, 61
<xsl:attribute> element, 59
<xsl:for-each> element, 59
<xsl:value-of> element, 59
select attribute, 59

XSLT
compared to CSS, 50
converting XML into HTML, 59
elements, 59
navigation control, 59, 69
produces well-formed XML, 60
user interface, designing, 50
using with XPath, 59

whitespace and, 63
<xsl:attribute> element, 59
<xsl:for-each> element, 59
<xsl:value-of> element, 59
XslTransform class
converting XML into HTML, 52
System.Xml.Xsl namespace, 62
Transform method, 62

Become an ASP.NET expert

If you want to know more about ASP.NET, read Marco Bellinaso's contributions on VB-2-The-Max (www.vb2themax.com), the popular web site dedicated to VB, VB.NET, and ASP.NET programming.

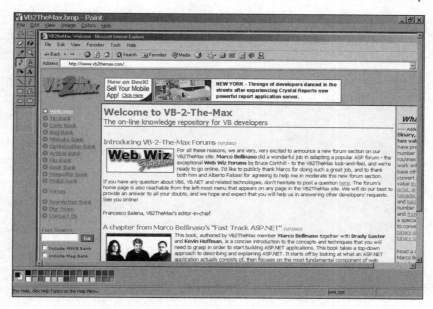

These are some of the things that VB-2-The-Max offers you:

- ❏ More than 1000 tips and ready-to-use optimized routines
- ❏ Articles of basic, intermediate and advanced level about COM, .NET and all the related technologies
- ❏ Free add-ins and utilities
- ❏ An always up-to-date index of articles that have been published on the most important programming magazines
- ❏ Sample chapters for many Wrox books

Marco is one of the administrators of the VB-2-The-Max's discussion forums (www.vb2themax.com/forum), where you can leave your questions and get answers from the site's team members and from the other member of our community. He also writes for the News-2-The-Max newsletter, sent out on a weekly basis with the latest .NET news and with code and tips that you can't find on the site.

VB-2-The-Max is powered by **Code Architects Srl** (www.codearchitects.com), an Italian company specialized in .NET training, consulting and development. Both VB-2-The-Max and Code Architects gather together internationally known authors and developers such as Francesco Balena, Dino Esposito and Giuseppe Dimauro.

Notes

Notes

ASPToday - Your free daily ASP Resource . . .

A discount off your ASPToday subscription with this voucher!!! see below for more details.

Expand your knowledge of ASP.NET with ASPToday.com - Wrox's code source for ASP and .NET applications, with free daily articles!

Every working day, we publish free Wrox content on the web:

- Free daily article
- Free daily tips
- Case studies and reference materials
- Index and full text search
- Downloadable code samples
- 11 Categories
- Written by programmers for programmers

And for just-in-time, practical solutions to real-world problems, subscribe to our Living Book - our 600+ strong archive of code-heavy, useable articles.

Find it all and more at http://www.asptoday.com

This voucher entitles you to a discount off your annual ASPToday subscription; to claim your reduced rate please visit:

http://www.asptoday.com/special-offers/

If you have any questions please contact customersupport@wrox.com

ASP Today

The daily knowledge site for professional ASP programmers

ASPToday brings the essence of the Wrox Programmer to Programmer philosophy to you through the Web. Every working day, www.asptoday.com delivers a new, original article by ASP programmers for ASP programmers.

Want to know about Classic ASP, ASP.NET, Performance, Data Access, Site Design, SQL Server, and more? Then visit us. You can make sure that you don't miss a thing by subscribing to our free daily e-mail updates featuring ASPToday highlights and tips.

By bringing you daily articles written by real programmers, ASPToday is an indispensable resource for quickly finding out exactly what you need. ASPToday is THE daily knowledge site for professional ASP programmers.

In addition to our free weekly and monthly articles, ASPToday also includes a premier subscription service. You can now join the growing number of ASPToday subscribers who benefit from access to:

- Daily in-depth articles
- Code-heavy demonstrations of real applications
- Access to the ASPToday Living Book, our collection of past articles
- ASP reference material
- Fully searchable index and advanced search engine
- Tips and tricks for professionals

Visit ASPToday at: www.asptoday.com

p2p.wrox.com
The programmer's resource centre

A unique free service from Wrox Press
With the aim of helping programmers to help each other

Wrox Press aims to provide timely and practical information to today's programmer. P2P is a list server offering a host of targeted mailing lists where you can share knowledge with your fellow programmers and find solutions to your problems. Whatever the level of your programming knowledge, and whatever technology you use, P2P can provide you with the information you need.

ASP
Support for beginners and professionals, including a resource page with hundreds of links, and a popular ASP.NET mailing list.

DATABASES
For database programmers, offering support on SQL Server, mySQL, and Oracle.

MOBILE
Software development for the mobile market is growing rapidly. We provide lists for the several current standards, including WAP, Windows CE, and Symbian.

JAVA
A complete set of Java lists, covering beginners, professionals, and server-side programmers (including JSP, servlets, and EJBs)

.NET
Microsoft's new OS platform, covering topics such as ASP.NET, C#, and general .NET discussion.

VISUAL BASIC
Covers all aspects of VB programming, from programming Office macros to creating components for the .NET platform.

WEB DESIGN
As web page requirements become more complex, programmer's are taking a more important role in creating web sites. For these programmers, we offer lists covering technologies such as Flash, Coldfusion, and JavaScript.

XML
Covering all aspects of XML, including XSLT and schemas.

OPEN SOURCE
Many Open Source topics covered including PHP, Apache, Perl, Linux, Python, and more.

FOREIGN LANGUAGE
Several lists dedicated to Spanish and German speaking programmers; categories include: NET, Java, XML, PHP, and XML.

How to subscribe:
Simply visit the P2P site, at http://p2p.wrox.com/

Wrox Press
Web Services

A selection of related titles from our Web Services Series

Professional Java Web Services
ISBN:1-86100-375-7
Professional Java Web Services concisely explains the important technologies and specifications behind web services. The book outlines the architecture of web services, and the latest information on implementing web services.

Professional C# Web Services: Building Web Services with .NET Remoting and ASP.NET
ISBN: 1-86100-439-7
This book covers building web services and web service clients with both ASP.NET and .NET Remoting. We also look at the generic protocols used by web services: SOAP and WSDL.

Professional XML Web Services
ISBN: 1-86100-509-1
The technologies presented in this book provide the foundations of web services computing, which is set to revolutionize distributed computing, as we know it.

Professional ASP.NET Web Services
ISBN: 1-86100-545-8
This book will show you how to create high-quality web services using ASP.NET.

Early Adopter Hailstorm
ISBN: 1-86100-608-X
Hailstorm Preview of Version 1.0 - Using SOAP and XPath to talk to Hailstorm - Hailstorm Data Manipulation Language (HSDL) - Practical Case Studies.

Professional Java SOAP
ISBN: 1-86100-610-1
Organized in three parts: Distributed Application Protocols, Sample Application, and Web Service, this book is for all Java developers and system archictects.

 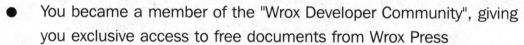

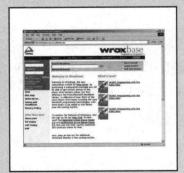

Programmer to Programmer™

Registration Code: 816329V25YI0C001

Wrox writes books for you. Any suggestions, or ideas about how you want
information given in your ideal book will be studied by our team.
Your comments are always valued at Wrox.

Free phone in USA 800-USE-WROX
Fax (312) 893 8001

UK Tel.: (0121) 687 4100   Fax: (0121) 687 4101

ASP.NET Website Programming – Registration Card

Name _____

Address _____

_____

_____

City _____ State/Region _____

Country _____ Postcode/Zip _____

E-Mail _____

Occupation _____

How did you hear about this book?

❑ Book review (name) _____

❑ Advertisement (name) _____

❑ Recommendation _____

❑ Catalog _____

❑ Other _____

Where did you buy this book?

❑ Bookstore (name) _____ City _____

❑ Computer store (name) _____

❑ Mail order _____

❑ Other _____

What influenced you in the purchase of this book?

❑ Cover Design ❑ Contents ❑ Other (please specify):

_____

How did you rate the overall content of this book?

❑ Excellent ❑ Good ❑ Average ❑ Poor

What did you find most useful about this book? _____

_____

What did you find least useful about this book? _____

_____

Please add any additional comments. _____

_____

What other subjects will you buy a computer book on soon?

_____

What is the best computer book you have used this year?

_____

Note: This information will only be used to keep you updated
about new Wrox Press titles and will not be used for
any other purpose or passed to any other third party.

wrox

Programmer to Programmer™

Note: If you post the bounce back card below in the UK, please send it to:

Wrox Press Limited, Arden House, 1102 Warwick Road,
Acocks Green, Birmingham B27 6HB. UK.

Computer Book Publishers